Sound Structure in Language

Jørgen Rischel 1934–2007

This book is dedicated
to
Anna-Grethe Rischel
Jørgen Rischel's widow

SOUND STRUCTURE IN LANGUAGE

Jørgen Rischel

edited and with an introduction by
Nina Grønnum, Frans Gregersen,
and Hans Basbøll

OXFORD
UNIVERSITY PRESS

OXFORD
UNIVERSITY PRESS

Great Clarendon Street, Oxford, OX2 6DP,
United Kingdom

Oxford University Press is a department of the University of Oxford.
It furthers the University's objective of excellence in research, scholarship,
and education by publishing worldwide. Oxford is a registered trade mark of
Oxford University Press in the UK and in certain other countries

First Edition published in 2009

Published in the United States of America by Oxford University Press
198 Madison Avenue, New York, NY 10016, United States of America

British Library Cataloguing in Publication Data
Data available

Library of Congress Cataloging in Publication Data
Data available

ISBN 978-0-19-954434-9

CONTENTS

Introduction   vii

Acknowledgements   xxi

PART I.   PREREQUISITES AND ANALYSIS

1. Formal Linguistics and Real Speech   3

2. Consonant Gradation: A Problem in Danish
   Phonology and Morphology   26

3. On Functional Load in Phonemics   44

4. Derivation as a Syntactic Process in Greenlandic   54

5. Consonant Reduction in Faroese
   Noncompound Wordforms   64

PART II.   PROSODY

6. Stress, Juncture, and Syllabification in
   Phonemic Description   85

7. Is There Just One Hierarchy of Prosodic Categories?   96

8. Compound Stress in Danish without a Cycle   103

9. On Unit Accentuation in Danish—and the Distinction
   Between Deep and Surface Phonology   116

10. Morphemic Tone and Word Tone in Eastern Norwegian   167

11. Asymmetric Vowel Harmony in Greenlandic
    Fringe Dialects   175

12. Structural and Functional Aspects of Tone Split in Thai   211

PART III.   SPEECH SOUNDS IN HISTORY AND CULTURE

13. A Note on Diachronic Data, Universals, and
     Research Strategies   245

14. Phoneme, Grapheme, and the 'Importance' of Distinctions.
     Functional Aspects of the Scandinavian Runic Reform   254

15. A Unified Theory of Nordic *i*-umlaut, Syncope, and Stød   272

16. Diphthongization in Faroese   312

17. Devoicing or Strengthening of Long Obstruents
     in Greenlandic   343

18. The Role of a 'Mixed' Language in Linguistic
     Reconstruction   356

19. Typology and Reconstruction of Numeral Systems:
     The Case of Austroasiatic   369

20. The Mlabri Enigma: Is Mlabri a Primary Hunter-Gatherer
     Language or the Result of an Ethnically and Socially
     Complex Founder Event?   408

Jørgen Rischel's Bibliography   441

References   457

Author Index   475

Subject Index   479

INTRODUCTION

This book contains twenty papers, selected among nearly 200 publications, written during Jørgen Rischel's long and varied career in the linguistic sciences.[1] As such it is intended as a testimony to his efforts to understand all matters linguistic. The results are assembled here for the first time and the insights they offer readers are to our minds inestimable. This bringing together of a lifetime's work enables us to appreciate the unity of purpose which guided Rischel throughout: to understand what he—in the first chapter of Part I, Prerequisites and Analysis—calls 'formal linguistics and real speech'.

This calls for an explanation. Jørgen Rischel was brought up in the great European structuralist tradition, the primary research strategy of which was idealization and abstract analysis. Rischel himself contributed substantially to this paradigm in major papers many of which are reprinted here (e.g. Chapters 6, 8, and 10). Gradually, however, he became dissatisfied with the constraints implied in relying solely on this strategy: in line with a general naturalistic trend in research within the humanities in the period from the 1970s and onwards, Rischel sought to integrate into his thinking about language and linguistics the vast knowledge which he and others had gathered of language use in everyday settings and embedded in its cultural context. We are referring here to his field work in the 1970s on West Greenlandic and his extensive field work during nearly a quarter of a century in South East Asia. In a sense Rischel turned the development, so exemplary in the case of early American structuralist linguistics, on its head, thus completely reversing the Chomskyan revolution.

Early American structuralists like the twin giants Leonard Bloomfield and Edward Sapir faced the immense task of having to describe a plethora of American Indian languages so vastly different from one another as well as from the intensively studied Indo-European core languages. By necessity they had to study these languages in close collaboration with the people who actually spoke them, and thus they often also contributed greatly to our knowledge of

---

[1] See Jørgen Rischel's complete bibliography pp. 441–56.

the varied patterns of interaction between culture and language. The Sapirian tradition in particular firmly held that the two were inseparable. But this paradigm began in the 1930s to lose ground to the Bloomfieldian ever more strict separation of language from culture; in line with the then dominant behaviourist thinking, Bloomfieldians further insisted on an isolation of language (study) from the mind. In this manner, the Bloomfieldians hoped to be able to keep the lid firmly on the Pandora's box of semantics.

From these endeavours emerged what became the dominant topic of 'discovery procedures': how does the analyst linguist proceed from the unordered chaos of utterances to the underlying 'system', be it phonological, morphological, or syntactical?

The whig interpretation of the history of American linguistics in the twentieth century goes like this: the entire American inductivist-behaviourist trend of the first half of the twentieth century was gleefully overturned by the Chomskyan revolution. The self-styled revolutionaries stressed a deductive and mentalist approach to linguistics which placed linguistics as a sub-discipline of psychology. That also came at a price, however, in the separation of language from usage and culture and the concomitant isolation of linguistics from the cultural sciences and sociology.

Rischel chose a different approach: while he was still deeply respectful of the insights which both European and American structuralism brought to linguistics and phonology, his experience from field work told him that both schools severely underestimated the role which language users and their culture play in shaping their language. Hence the crucial question: what is the relationship between language users' speech and the linguist's analysis of it? Or in other words: what status does the analysis have, what is it a representation of, if anything? In posing the questions in this manner, he also dissociates himself completely from the generative paradigm.

Rischel prefaces his analysis of Minor Mlabri as follows:

> When one deals with a virtually unknown language spoken in a little-known culture, one faces a gamut of phenomena all calling for analysis and explanation. These phenomena range from topics which normally form the core of descriptive and comparative linguistics to topics which are interdisciplinary or belong to cultural and social anthropology in a wide sense. The study of such a language is an all-encompassing enterprise which requires the integration of all kinds of available information (although it is possible

afterwards to abstract certain structural phenomena of the language and look at these from a typological or comparative perspective). At the same time, thorough understanding of the language is a prerequisite to in-depth study of the culture of such a tribal group. This is not just a matter of understanding oral traditions (cf. my mention of the myths above); the indigenous language underlies the establishment of cultural patterns and social institutions of all kinds and on all levels.

(Rischel 1995: 12f; italics in the original)

Rischel's answer to his own questions about linguistic description resulted in an original attempt to integrate (European) structuralism and the cultural sciences, or rather in an attempted adaptation of structuralism that would remain faithful to that which is of lasting value in it, primarily the concept of structure itself. Structure does not, however, imply autonomy and Rischel, in fact, rejected autonomy as the watchword for both the initial field work and the resultant linguistic analysis. Rischel's vision was a linguistics which would produce results that allowed constant interaction with other sciences, notably anthropology, the study of religion, archaeology, and genetics.

In the next section of this introduction we shall trace the history of this generous and independent spirit in a brief biographical sketch. In the last section, we outline the structure of the book and thus give the reader something to go by in enjoying it.

JØRGEN RISCHEL'S VITA

Jørgen Rischel was born on 10 August 1934 in the small town of Kullerup on the island of Funen, Denmark. He died in Birkerød north of Copenhagen on 10 May 2007. While his maternal grandfather was a church historian well known in his day for his versatile and engaging writings, his paternal grandfather was a highly skilled guitar player. Jørgen Rischel thus had a rich inheritance and he had an extraordinary number of rare talents. He could have become anything he wished and he would have excelled in it. Fortunately, he was drawn, more than anything else, towards language. As a very young boy he displayed an interest in the local Funen dialect. An excursion with his school to Norway inspired an enthusiasm for Norwegian. And while still at school he read Bernhard Karlgren's introductory Chinese textbook and a grammar of Old Norse, and he also studied Danish runic inscriptions. Inspired by a Faroese girl in his high school class he became interested in Faroese and thus mastered nearly all the Nordic languages. In his autobiography, written in 1994 for the Royal Chapter of Orders upon receiving from Her Majesty Queen Margrethe the Second the Order of the Knight of Dannebrog in 1991, Rischel states as his belief and guiding principle: 'It has been my main principle (a principle which would not be endorsed by all linguists!) that I would rather not analyze linguistically material which I did not have a first hand knowledge of. [...] In general, I prefer only to speak about languages which I speak myself.' (Autobiography ms: 12)

Jørgen Rischel commenced his university studies in 1952, choosing Danish as his major and French as his minor subject. He later abandoned French in order to concentrate on Nordic Philology, with a specialization in West Nordic. He obtained a Government scholarship to study in Reykjavík in 1956–57, and in 1958–59 in Oslo. In Reykjavík he met the famous Norwegian scholar Einar Haugen who became an important mediator between Europe and the United States as a professor of linguistics at Harvard, and whose ideas about linguistics greatly influenced him. In Oslo Rischel studied with Knut Bergsland who was kind enough to teach Eskimo languages to him as the only student for a whole year. Knut Bergsland was later to become first faculty opponent at Rischel's (German style) doctoral dissertation (equivalent to the *Habilitationsschrift*) on West Greenlandic.

Rischel also took classes in Danish dialectology with Poul Andersen and in phonetics with Eli Fischer-Jørgensen. During his student years he completed an analysis of Lepcha, although he later regretted that he had never learnt to speak it. In 1958 he was awarded Copenhagen University's Gold Medal for a treatise about morphophonemics; and in 1960 he obtained the Danish *magisterkonferens* in Nordic Philology. The following academic year he spent in Bergen as lecturer in Danish language and literature; and in 1961 he left for Wisconsin where he was to be assistant editor on Einar Haugen's Norwegian–English dictionary project. Rischel had married Anna-Grethe Rischel, *née* Andersen, before leaving for the States, and they finished the stay by touring the country in search of emigrants speaking the old Danish dialects. This was the first in a long series of joint (ad)ventures. The resulting tapes were, alas, stolen from them in New York upon leaving America.

Jørgen Rischel gave his first international paper at The Ninth International Congress of Linguists in Boston in 1962 (Chapter 6 in this volume). This paper was to become of lasting significance to his readers but unfortunately they were, at the time, very few. In a long interview with Nina Grønnum which was intended to throw light upon Rischel's own perception of his lifetime work, he told the story about this paper: Haugen had originally suggested to him to submit a proposal for a paper to this conference. To Rischel's amazement it was accepted as a section paper. This of course was a gratifying début but the final reception was only lukewarm, although Eugene A. Nida, for one, said that he liked the paper. What happened then was that it simply drowned in the great flood of the Chomskyan revolution; only now has it risen to its rightful place in the history of stress studies. Sad to say, this is a recurrent theme in the history of Rischel's career and one which actually sometimes marred Rischel's own perception of his true importance. First, his papers were too often overlooked at the time of their publication. Secondly, a number of his significant contributions appeared in rather obscure publications which would be hard to find even for the enthusiast.

In 1963 Rischel obtained a three-year research scholarship with Paul Diderichsen, the famous professor of Danish language. However, Diderichsen felt that Rischel belonged in phonetics and after a year he was reallocated to the grand lady of Danish phonetics Eli Fischer-Jørgensen. At this point an opportunity arose for a tenured position as assistant professor in phonetics. Rischel consequently gave up the scholarship for the security of the permanent post (advancing to associate professor in 1968), not least because of his obligations to provide his family, now consisting also of three daughters, with a secure and steady income.

In Denmark the mid-1960s marked the end of the glorious era of glossematics, the Danish structuralist school founded by Louis Hjemslev. Hjelmslev died in 1965 and this necessitated a complete restructuring of the linguistic milieu at the University of Copenhagen. In 1966 a new chair in phonetics was inaugurated for Eli Fischer-Jørgensen who then created her own Institute of Phonetics, separate from the original Institute of Linguistics. The new Institute of Phonetics was eminently successful in the years to come and very modern in its collective spirit and enthusiasm. But the milieu had become discouraged with too much theory and too little empirical work and did not care much for further endless discussions about the proper relationship between phonetics and phonology. So, the top priority on the agenda became experimental phonetics. That was probably a good thing in and of itself, but it actually created a schism for Rischel, because from that point on he always felt torn between linguistics and phonetics.

Jørgen Rischel taught mainly phonetics in the mid-1960s, but his research activities were primarily within linguistics, with one major exception: Rischel's interest in technology and his previous studies with Gunnar Fant at the Royal Institute of Technology (KTH) in Stockholm led him in the late 1960s to embark upon what was to be a very significant project, the construction of a terminal analog speech synthesizer. Again it was a successful endeavour in so far as the synthesizer produced speech of high quality, but only two seconds at a time, which was a distinct limitation. The synthesizer has, however, been used in a number of research projects in speech perception. In more recent years, of course, it has been superseded by digital speech synthesis.

In 1975 the entire Rischel family set sail for Greenland in order to do field work in a small hamlet close to Kap Farvel. The field work was the continuation of the important 1974 doctoral dissertation, *Topics in West Greenlandic Phonology*. During the next years the upcoming Ninth International Congress of Phonetics, scheduled for August 1979, was the overshadowing concern at the Institute, and loyalty towards this huge collective effort led by the indefatigable Eli Fischer-Jørgensen prevented Jørgen Rischel from accepting offers to become visiting lecturer abroad or from taking up a permanent international position. In 1978 he finally became Hjelmslev's successor as professor of linguistics and accordingly left the Institute of Phonetics for the neighbouring Institute of Linguistics. That was a deeply troubled department at the time, marred by personal conflicts, and Rischel never felt at ease there. He therefore agreed, only three years later, to let himself be called to the chair in phonetics, vacant after Eli Fischer-Jørgensen's retirement in February 1981. The chair in linguistics which he vacated remained vacant, much to his chagrin, until, in 1998, he took early retirement in order to be able to concentrate on his research.

Jørgen Rischel had worked on Faroese based on his own field work from 1954, and he had studied West Greenlandic *in situ*, but in 1982 he was to embark on the journey which brought him back to a childhood fascination of his, the scrutiny of the language and culture of the Mlabri of Thailand and Laos. The journey started with Søren Egerod, the well known sinologist and a close associate of Rischel's, as the instigator, but soon Rischel was to continue on his own. In his autobiography he states that true to his own principle, 'I am now in the fortunate position to be able to speak with this small group[2] in their own language which gives me the very best of conditions for a more detailed study. It has been difficult to grasp the Mlabri language and to understand their world view. At the present time I see it as the most pressing problem to gather the mythological and cosmological narratives of this culture . . . " (Autobiography: 15).

It bears witness to his long range planning and to his unstinting efforts that he actually managed during the following twelve years to complete exactly that project. His manuscript for a Mlabri book was published post mortem in 2007 by the Royal Danish Academy of Sciences and Letters, of which Jørgen Rischel became a member in 1978. In a supplement to the autobiography which Rischel composed for us with a view towards this anthology, he laconically states: 'In 2002 I was diagnosed with cancer which resulted in no less than four operations during 2003–06. In the fall of 2006 I was given to understand that they had not stopped the cancer and that it was now actually terminal. I immediately flew out to Thailand and stayed there for $2\frac{1}{2}$ months until the Christmas of 2006, in particular in order to complete my material on the Tin language[3]; after that time I have had to cease all travelling.'

Jørgen Rischel was a traditionalist in all matters but his own vision of linguistics. He did indeed write on the great figures from the Danish past—Rasmus Rask, Otto Jespersen, Louis Hjelmslev—often giving original and insightful comments on their œuvre. And he himself revered tradition wherever he found it, in the Royal Danish Academy, in the Linguistic Circle of Copenhagen, in the Society for the Publication of Faroese Sources and in all the other connections where his contribution was needed, and often indispensable. For him, tradition was a way to keep in contact with real values of the past, and in some ways we see it as the backdrop to his boldness in analysis. But tradition was also living within him in the guise of a vast and continued reading of the linguistic literature. With his unusually broad background and his profound knowledge, he would always be listened to with reverence once his listeners had appreciated who was talking.

In the interview with Nina Grønnum a recurrent theme is a certain insecurity which marred his youth and early career, and which in a

---

[2] Editors' note: A language related to Mlabri, cf. Chapter 20.
[3] Editors' note: There are three groups of Mlabri speakers, cf. Chapter 20, including a very small group comprising only thirteen speakers at the time.

sense he never completely conquered. When he was celebrated—on the occasion of his sixtieth birthday—with a huge Festschrift bearing testimony to his unique position on the Danish and international scene,[4] he was genuinely amazed to discover that he was universally admired.

Although he was ever the most self-conscious and self-effacing of men this is not to say that he did not actually know that he was special. He was simply captured by the magnitude of the project he had established for himself and thus had a clear sense of what he had accomplished and what he had not. As with all great men, we believe that he measured himself only by his own yardstick.

Jørgen Rischel was well known by linguists from many subspecialties and uniformly respected for his wisdom, his detailed, yet incredibly broad, knowledge, his independence and his honesty. He was the perfect judge of applications, theses and dissertations and consequently spent far too much of his time reading other people's work and giving detailed and precise comments on it, instead of writing his own stuff.

The *Leitmotifs* of Jørgen Rischel's work are perhaps easily discerned but difficult to grasp completely. They are three, roughly corresponding to the three parts in this volume. The first is his insistence that linguistic and phonological theory should be explicit and firmly grounded in empirical research. See, for example, Chapter 1, 'Formal Linguistics and Real Speech'. The second is Rischel's concern with the integration of sound systems with morphology and syntax (documented already in his early prize essay on morphophonemics)— witness for example the deeply original paper on consonant gradation in Chapter 2. He was particularly intrigued by the prosodic phenomena of stress and tone: as in Norwegian and Thai (Chapter 10 and 12) and in the Mon Khmer and Austronesian languages in general. The leading principle here is that the early American insistence on strict separation of descriptive levels in the linguistic analysis simply cannot do justice to the complexity of stress assignment and that morphology and syntax cannot be divorced without losing important generalizations. The third guideline is Rischel's attempt to integrate contributions from linguistic, cultural, and, lately also, biological research. In this book Chapter 20 about the Mlabri hunter-gatherers is a prime example; but all of Rischel's work is informed by the knowledge that

[4] Jens Elmegaard Rasmussen *et al.* (eds), *Linguistic Studies in Honour of Jørgen Rischel, Acta Linguistica Hafniensia* volume 27, parts one and two, C.A. Reitzel, Copenhagen 1994.

language is part of culture and history and thus partly a key to them, partly determined by them. Here, again, the complexity of the relationship did not escape him.

In looking back upon his œuvre, we cannot fail to notice that it was both a late flower of the blooming structuralism of his formative years and a personal reaction to it. He integrated variation—historical, dialectal, and sociolectal—within his view of structure and thus abandoned the strict notion of autonomy without abandoning relative autonomy in the guise of structured relationships between layers or strata of language. In this, he fulfilled the promise of an empirically based complex structuralism which may well point to future investigations rather than end an era.

Jørgen Rischel's vita would not be complete if we did not briefly touch upon the inestimable role his wife of forty-six years, Anna-Grethe, has played—not only in his private life, of course, but also in his work. She has been an astoundingly acute observer, an unbelievable aide-memoire, and lately an eminently loyal companion on some of his travels to Northern Thailand. Thus it was Anna-Grethe Rischel who, when he was no longer able to fly, travelled to his field station in Thailand and brought back home all his invaluable field work material. It is only fitting that we should dedicate this book to her.

A NOTE ABOUT THE STRUCTURE OF THIS BOOK

The collection has three parts. The provenance of each paper is stated in a footnote to its title and repeated in Rischel's bibliography on pp. 441–56.

Part I, entitled 'Prerequisites and Analysis', contains five chapters which are comparatively short and easy to read. Together they introduce the reader to topics which are recurrent in Jørgen Rischel's publications and thus turn up again in chapters in the next sections as well.

The first paper, 'Formal linguistics and real speech', is far-reaching in its implications since it treats a central topic: the relationship between natural speech as it is found outside the laboratory and the models we build in the guise of descriptions. Particular emphasis is put on distinctness and tempo and their interaction in, for example, sociolinguistically and stylistically significant processes.

Chapter 2, 'Consonant gradation: a problem in Danish phonology and morphology', is a classic. Within the framework of generative phonology, Rischel turns his attention to the very real morphophone-mic processes that permeate the structure of the Danish lexicon. Inter-estingly, as with Chomsky and Halle's analysis of English, the rela-tionship between historical processes, in this case lenition processes, and synchronic alternations turns out to be crucial, a point that does not escape Rischel's attention.

In Chapter 3, 'On functional load in phonemics', Rischel opposes the tendency within mathematical linguistics to calculate the likeli-hood of occurrence of phonological segments on a purely stochastic basis (the paper was published in the modest mouthpiece for this branch of linguistics: *SMIL, Statistical Methods in Linguistics*). In contrast, Rischel notes that structure partly determines the likelihood of occurrence.

In Chapter 4, 'Derivation as a syntactic process in Greenlandic', Rischel argues that a morphological process, in casu derivation, interacts with (deep level) syntax. This is challenging because Green-landic is a polysynthetic and agglutinating language which forms long words with an internal sentence-like structure. The insistence upon integration of different levels in the linguistic description recurs in Chapters 8 and 9.

Chapter 5, 'Consonant reduction in Faroese noncompound word-forms', ought, according to Rischel himself in the interview with Nina Grønnum, to be entitled 'Cluster simplification ...' since this is what it is all about. It presents fascinating data from Faroese demonstrating the centrality of this process and, as Rischel puts it (ibid.), 'what strange things may happen when a language is left to itself.'

In Part II we have assembled the papers which deal with Rischel' s favourite topic of *prosody*. The languages treated range from Danish and Norwegian to Greenlandic and Thai, but throughout the focus is on the relationship between stress and the higher strata of morphology and syntax.

Above we have told the story of Chapter 6, 'Stress, juncture, and syllabification in phonemic description', alias the lecture given as a section paper at the Ninth International Congress of Linguists in Boston 1962. It is, in other words, quite early in Rischel's production but essential to any understanding of his work on stress and also his dissatisfaction with later treatments of it. The contrast between strong and weak stress and the fundamental independent feature of syllable weight are themes that turn up again in Chapters 8 and 15.

Chapter 7, 'Is there just one hierarchy of prosodic categories?', is a much later paper but belongs with Chapter 6 in its insistence that syllable weight and prosodic prominence are not synonymous. It demonstrates convincingly that prosody should be conceived as a layered structure open to influence from both morphology and syntax. The role of stressed syllables is emphasized.

Chapter 8, 'Compound stress in Danish without a cycle', takes the argument one step further by demonstrating how in the case of Danish a central morphological process like compounding is manifested in the stress pattern. Rischel refutes the infinite gradation of stress which was a central feature of the cyclical processes of generative phonology. For Rischel the bifurcation of strong and weak stress was psychologically as well as linguistically a much more satisfactory model.

Chapter 9, 'On unit accentuation in Danish—and the distinction between deep and surface phonology', deals with a fascinating construction prevalent in Danish and several other Nordic languages: the use of stress (reduction) to create a unit consisting of a verb and its complement. Phonetically, the process is simple enough to account for: the verb loses its main stress. But the conditions for this intriguing process are a matter for discussion. Rischel demonstrates completely convincingly, however, that stress and syntax, hard core syntax at that, have to be related, if we are to account succinctly for unit accentuation in Danish.

In Chapter 10, 'Morphemic tone and word tone in Eastern Norwegian,' the theme of the relationship between suprasegmental processes and morphology is played out with Norwegian word tones as the chosen field of demonstration. Published in *Phonetica* and referred to by Haugen in his classic 1967 paper on Norwegian word tones,[5] this is probably the one among Rischel's many papers which reached the largest proportion of its intended audience.

Chapter 11, 'Asymmetric vowel harmony in Greenlandic fringe dialects', takes us to another type of fascinating data straight from Jørgen Rischel's treasure trove: Greenlandic vowel harmony. And Chapter 12, 'Structural and functional aspects of tone split in Thai', closes this part with a comprehensive paper on a tone language. Rischel explores the interrelations between syllable structure and tones and shows how the main Thai dialects fall into three groups. The

---

[5] Einar Haugen, 'On the Rules of Norwegian Tonality', *Language* 43/1 (1967): 185–202.

characteristic tonal systems can be interpreted in evolutionary terms as 'individual and functionally optimal solutions to the preservation of contrasts between syllable types' at a time when the dialects had already split, rather than as different simplifications of a reconstructed, extremely complex, proto-system.

Part III, entitled 'Speech Sounds in History and Culture', presents eight papers which together take the reader on a straight path from sounds viewed as structured systems to the much heavier traditional theme of language in history and culture. In this way, they more or less represent Rischel's own development.

Chapter 13, 'A note on diachronic data, universals, and research strategies', is a brief paper written as a lecture at the fourth international *Phonologie-Tagung* in Vienna in 1980. It gives compelling reasons for being extremely wary of conventional wisdom when it comes to the possibility of using alleged universal tendencies to discard or corroborate claims about a specific reconstructed language development. Two examples are analysed in depth. The first is the weakening of Danish stops (cf. Chapter 2 above). Rischel shows that the alleged skewed process leaving the **b**-sound unaffected by the lenition process should probably rather be interpreted as a restitution process under the influence of a conservative orthography. The second case is the devoicing of long obstruents in Greenlandic. On the basis of philological evidence, Rischel reconstructs earlier forms which actually reflect Kleinschmidt's 'historical' writing system positing an original /dl/ as the basis for the later voiceless long [ɬ:] (/ll/).

In Chapter 14, 'Phoneme, grapheme, and the "importance" of distinctions. Functional aspects of the Scandinavian runic reform', the issue is whether the reform of the runic writing system, reducing a twenty-four letter system into a sixteen letter one, was a reflection of a phonological development or simply an orthographical reform—or both. The paper is original in its convincing argumentation that the simplification was indeed a consequence of a development in the sound system towards fewer phonological contrasts in certain positions.

Chapter 15, 'A unified theory of Nordic *i*-umlaut, syncope, and stød', together with Chapter 20 on the Mlabri enigma were the last two papers Jørgen Rischel wrote. They were finished shortly before his death but they both had long pre-histories, Chapter 15 originating in Rischel's lecture for his finals for the *magisterkonferens* in 1960. The paper is as complex as it is rewarding. First the theory prepares the ground and then Rischel posits three major stages in the history of the

Northern Germanic languages in a completely new all-encompassing thought involving a new interpretation of syncope, umlaut, and an explanation in terms of a complete reversal of stress assignment. The analysis raises the further intriguing question of how this reversal was carried out and why it began. Whether one agrees or not, the paper will be a self-evident starting point for a renewed discussion of the traditionally central themes of Nordic philology, that is to say the intriguing relationship between stress, syncope, umlaut, word tones, and the Danish' stød'.

In Chapter 16, 'Diphthongization in Faroese', which corresponds in its subject matter (but not the treatment of it) to Chapter 5, Rischel gives a history of the Faroese vowel system based on his own data from dialect field work as well as all the known sources, both the textual evidence and dialect data. Two systems are posited that differ fundamentally. Some of the old long vowels diphthongized and entered into a new system with the old diphthongs, some of them passed through a stage as monophthongs which were related to the old short vowels. Throughout, the concept of a system is seen as one but not the sole determinant of this development. Rather what we have are complex interactions between natural phonetic processes (strengthening, shortening, lengthening) and the need for a clear system.

Chapter 17, 'Devoicing or strengthening of long obstruents in Greenlandic', returns to Greenlandic to make a point which was alluded to in Chapter 13, but is treated here more fully in Rischel's contribution to the Bergsland-Festschrift. The long unvoiced consonants which result from gemination of /v ɣ ʁ l/ are the result not of spontaneous devoicing but of a so-called segmentalization. The first consonant of the geminate dissimilates to become an unvoiced stop; subsequently the second consonant is devoiced, and finally the (first) stop assimilates completely to the second member of the original geminate.

The three final papers of this collection form a small subsection where various general themes are taken up on the basis of Jørgen Rischel's long life in and with the Mlabri language, its speakers and neighbouring languages. First in line, in Chapter 18, entitled 'The role of a "mixed" language in linguistic reconstruction', are the problems for reconstruction, arguably the oldest linguistic scientific endeavour, of having to do with a so-called mixed language like Mlabri. The intricate relationship between Mlabri and its neighbouring languages Kammu and Tin is revealed with the word for 'tooth' as the

illuminating example. In the next Chapter 19, 'Typology and reconstruction of numeral systems: the case of Austroasiatic', Rischel is
concerned with semantic reconstruction and its message for typological work, while finally Chapter 20, 'The Mlabri enigma: is Mlabri a
primary hunter-gatherer language or the result of an ethnically and
socially complex founder event?' is a *tour de force* demonstrating how
far profound knowledge of the languages in a region can be brought
to bear on the reconstruction of the cultural pre-history of the people
who speak them. In this case, the possibility of a cultural reversal creating a hunter-gatherer tribe from an agricultural culture is a complete
novelty and an important lesson for all of us about the implications of
a linguistic analysis. The point is that Jørgen Rischel carefully avoids
the vicious circle by first isolating the linguistic analysis *per se* to fill
in only later the great picture of pre-history by placing the linguistic
development firmly in its context. By definition, the answer to the
question in the title cannot be given until the linguistic analysis has
been finalized according to its own rules.

Finally, the book contains a full bibliography of Jørgen Rischel's
papers as well as the integrated set of references for all the papers in
the volume.

ACKNOWLEDGEMENTS

The following publishers graciously gave permission to reprint material included in this book: Elsevier (*Speech Communication*), Mouton de Gruyter (*Studies for Einar Haugen; Proceedings of the IXth Internatinal Congress of Linguists 1962; Linguistic Reconstruction and Typology; Folia Linguistica*), Cambridge University Press (*Phonologica 1984*), S. Karger (*Phonetica*), The Linguistic Circle of Copenhagen (*Acta Linguistica Hafniensia*), Sprachwissenschafliches Institut der Universität Innsbruck (*Phonologica 1980*), Novus (*Riepmočála: Essays in Honor of Knut Bergsland*), and Syddansk Universitetsforlag (*NOWELE*).

We are grateful to Michael Lerche Nielsen for his invaluable assistance with the runic script in Chapter 14. We express our gratitude for Lisbet Bruzelius Larsen's immensely competent help with Jørgen Rischel's bibliography and references; and we thank Naja Kühn Riegels for careful and competent proof-reading of the first print of the manuscript. We also owe a debt of gratitude to John Ohala for the lovely early (1979) portrait of Jørgen Rischel.

Finally, we are indebted to John Davey at Oxford University Press for his enthusiastic endorsement of the idea of publishing a selection of Jørgen Rischel's papers and his unfailing support during the ensuing process. We gratefully acknowledge the support of the Royal Danish Academy of Sciences and Letters through a grant from the Aksel Tovborg Jensen trust.

Nina Grønnum, Frans Gregersen,
and Hans Basbøll

Copenhagen
December 2007

Part I

Prerequisites and Analysis

1

Formal Linguistics and Real Speech[1]

1.1. INTRODUCTION

Contemporary linguistics has a higher level of ambition than ever before in history. For many linguists the ambition is not just to account for the design of language as a system. Some are most interested in relating that system to a more or less innate language faculty of human beings; others (possibly the same persons) are interested in universal constraints on the production and perception of language, and the relevance of such putative universals for the patterns found in languages and the tendencies observed in linguistic change. And then some are interested in the variational aspect of linguistic data, or in setting up socio-pragmatic parameters to account for the ways in which language is put to use in different situations. This spectrum of interests and fundamental assumptions creates an incomparably more complex situation than in the earlier history of linguistics.

So far the vast majority of the research on speech with the application of rigid instrumental and quantitative methods has been based on laboratory recordings made under controlled conditions, the task of the informant(s) being to read aloud a set of more or less meaningful linguistic samples, or to make judgements about such samples in listening tests, and the research objective being to reveal something about the basic mechanisms underlying speech production and speech perception. Seen in this perspective, the study of natural speech, as it is used meaningfully by communicating human beings, is at best a very distant goal. This has something to do with choice of research strategies, but it has also something to do with the formidable methodological and practical problems involved in the study of natural speech.

---

[1] Reprinted from *Speech Communication* 11 (1992): 379–92.

Still, the limitations of our descriptive techniques and the apparent unfeasibility of the task should not deter us from setting up as a major research objective the phonetic analysis of real speech and eventually even of spontaneous speech. After all, spontaneous speech, with its annoying multidimensional complexity, is the most basic type of communicative use of language. If we see as a descriptive goal of linguistics and phonetics to describe what goes on in language, it seems highly unsatisfactory to refrain from studying the most important use of language.

Maybe the greatest obstacle to an exhaustive study of spontaneous speech is the lack of insight into the structure of meaning. At the ESCA Workshop 1991, Olle Engstrand rightly observed that we do not have the pragmatic grammar for the specification of spontaneous speech. Still, it is possible to tackle this problem to some extent. Fretheim (1991) is one of those who try to integrate studies of the information structure of utterances with studies of their prosody.

In Copenhagen we have had a project on the prosody of natural speech running for a couple of years. At one point, two of my younger colleagues, Ole Nedergaard Thomsen and Birgitte Jacobsen, worked out a system for manual (and of course interpretation-dependent) pragmatic labelling of speech data, and they subjected a transcript of natural speech data (samples of interviews made for a sociolinguistic study, see Gregersen *et al.* 1991) to such labelling. At the same time the transcript was provided with stress marks. Another young colleague, Jann Scheuer, used this annotated corpus of connected speech as raw material and made very interesting observations on phrasal stress in Danish[2]. The findings are still awaiting publication, but a pattern is clearly emerging. Several years ago, cf. Rischel (1983*a*), I tried to formulate provisional rules referring to syntactic categories to account for the mechanism of phrasal stress ('unit accent') in Danish on the basis of introspective data. Since some of the conditioning factors in these rules can be identified by automatic parsing, an algorithm of this kind is being applied to text-to-speech synthesis by my colleague Peter Molbæk Hansen, cf. Molbæk Hansen (1991). However, in the more recent work on natural speech my aforementioned colleagues have disclosed a complex of localized and contextually-determined pragmatic factors which contribute to trigger or block phrasal stress. Personally I do not think of this situation as a conflict between two

---

[2] Editor's note: published as Scheuer (1995)

modes of description. Rather, I view the text-pragmatic factors as superimposed on a set of syntactic default regularities. This is a case of true interlocking of linguistic levels in the speech output.

The study of spontaneous speech would not only open new vistas by forcing us to look more at dimensions of speech variation which are otherwise more or less neutralized, but also throw new light on very basic issues concerning the mechanisms of speech production and speech perception.

It is a wise, in fact indispensable, research strategy to study simplified (in particular variationally restricted) data first and make assumptions and formulate hypotheses on that basis. It is a wise research strategy to start with word phonology before studying reduction in allegro speech, and to study prosodic mechanisms under simplified conditions before entering the study of pragmatically more complex data. But eventually all hypotheses made on a simplistic basis must be confronted with more variegated, genuine speech data. This, in turn, may lead to refutation of the previous hypotheses, or perhaps to a happy confirmation of these in conjunction with certain supplementary hypotheses necessitated by the new data.

The latter has turned out to be the case, for instance, with data on Danish intonation. My colleague N.-J. Dyhr, in an unpublished study of intonation in connected speech (made within the Copenhagen project on prosody mentioned above, and using some of the same speech data),[3] has quite recently found that such data largely corroborate the validity of Nina Grønnum's model of Danish sentence intonation[4], although that model was first developed on the basis of a study of highly schematized types of utterances recorded under typical 'lab speech' conditions. Dyhr found deviations mainly in long utterances, which he suggests may have to do with performance factors concerning the preplanning of intonation in natural speech. Bruce and Touati, in their ESCA Workshop paper (1992), make largely the same observation for Swedish. Thus, the intonation of natural, even spontaneous speech may not be basically but only superficially different from the intonation used when reading aloud.

On the basis of such reflections as those sketched above, one may ask to what extent current phonological and phonetic theory can provide the format for dealing with the multidimensionality of variation in natural speech. Are we able to handle the essential categories

---

[3] Editors' note: published as Dyhr (1995).   [4] Editors' note: see Grønnum (1992).

involved? It must be acknowledged that there are both 'low-level' phonetic mechanisms and linguistic as well as paralinguistic factors involved in the realization of an utterance with more or less predictable prosody, and with greater or lesser reduction in different speaking styles. How does formal linguistics, and in particular formal phonology, contribute to the totality of such a description? This is a problem both at the 'high-level' end and at the 'low-level' end. To what extent should variational phenomena be built into the phonological model, and how? Should multidimensional phonological representations be closely interlocked with parametric descriptions of the dynamics of vocal tract configurations, as many phonologists seem to believe, or is the relationship more indirect, as many of us (including myself) believe? John Ohala, in his plenary lecture to the ESCA Workshop (Ohala 1992), has made the very important point that the phoneme may be a psychological entity, but that it may not be input to the speech motor system. I emphatically agree; I believe in phonemes, I think phonemes play a role in speakers' organization of their lexica and grammars, but we must distinguish carefully between abstract linguistic patterning and speech (also cf. Rischel 1991: 235–6).

I prefer this concept of a more indirect relationship between language and speech to Abbs' suggestion that 'phonological units are abstract *intentions* which are implemented by generating perceptually acceptable acoustic waveforms' (Abbs 1986: 202); also cf. Linell's very important discussion of this issue (Linell 1982). We are left, however, with very fundamental questions such as that of *speech rate*. To what extent should speech rate-conditioned variation be handled in a speech production model as something outside phonology proper?

The *invariance–variation* dichotomy is a strange problem in language study. Obviously, the original point of distinguishing phonology from phonetics was to define a level of phonic invariance by reference to the diacritic (semiotic) function of speech sounds. But in phonetics proper many attempts have been made to find levels of invariance. Björn Lindblom, in his plenary lecture to the ESCA Workshop (Lindblom *et al.* 1992) has referred to some of these efforts and proposals in phonology and phonetics, including his own early work on vowel reduction, which presupposes that there is an underlying target for speech sounds and thus invariance in that particular sense.

If we totally skip the notion of invariance in phonetics proper, we shall have difficulties distinguishing between, on the one hand, modifications caused by properties of the speech apparatus and, on the other hand, modifications caused by the speaker's choice of style and tempo, and we shall miss the chance of observing the effect of articulatory constraints under deliberate variations of tempo and style. But the question remains how to specify an invariant representation if we want to make the claim that it has some kind of cognitive status. Phonology has so far been based on very exaggerated *idealizations* of speech and exaggerated expectations about the power of *rule machinery* as the format in which to take care of variation. But once we admit that a phonetic surface form may have multiple underlying representations in the speaker's internal lexicon, phonology is in a flux. What we have to search for, then, is not just semiotically defined invariance for the linguistic code as a whole, but such invariance specified for each of several possible speech norms. The question then is: can we define a limited set of discrete *style and tempo bound norms* all mastered by the same speaker?

In the following I comment on some of the issues raised above. It must be emphasized that this is not a state-of-the-art report but just a personal appraisal of selected aspects of the langue–parole dichotomy with special reference to natural speech. (I consider highly specialized meetings like the ESCA Workshop to be the proper place for a rather informal exchange of viewpoints, and I had chosen to define my task in that particular context as being to provoke such scholarly debate rather than to give a broad overview of the accumulated research done in the field.)

1.2. REFLECTED VERSUS UNREFLECTED SPEECH AND FORMAL LINGUISTICS

In the title of this paper I have used the somewhat odd term 'real speech'. A more felicitous synonym is 'natural speech', but I would like to take that term in a somewhat more restricted sense. In using the awkward term 'real speech' my point is to distinguish a vocal activity (and the data resulting from such activity) where language is put to one of its normal, meaningful uses from speech production provoked, without communicative function, in an experimental situation. Among normal, meaningful uses are all kinds of play with the language: imitation of others, speaking with an artificial accent to create a particular effect, twisting the language for fun, and testing one's own speech by making meaningful noises during linguistic introspection or during more or less sophisticated discussions with others about correct or incorrect language. The linguist or phonetician using speech data must of course distinguish carefully between such different uses of speech, but they may all provide relevant raw data.

One particularly tricky distinction is that between speech with and without accompanying linguistic introspection; that is what I mean by linguistically reflected and linguistically unreflected speech (in the following, for short, just reflected and unreflected speech). In discussions of reading and spelling strategies, for example, concepts such as 'phonemic awareness' turn up all the time. It is important to make entirely clear what is meant by awareness. A person may have more or less easy access to a metalinguistic level permitting him to look at structural features of linguistic forms by introspection, and this may be done consciously or subconsciously. Then again the more or less systematic relationship between spoken and written wordforms may have been drilled in classrooms, so that the structural awareness is an acquired skill.

When linguists elicit linguistic data, for example in a field work setting, or when the experimental phonetician instructs an informant to produce noises or listen to noises with a particular task in mind, we are certainly not dealing with unreflected language use, since informants can hardly be unaware of the fact that the purpose is to furnish data for a metalinguistic discussion of some topic, be it grammar or speech production or perception, although the precise nature of the topic may be unknown to them.

By far the greatest part of our knowledge about spoken language is based on information stemming from reflected uses of language: the person producing or perceiving the speech samples was doing so not for the purpose of meaningful communication but to demonstrate the functioning of the linguistic code. As said already, this kind of data is highly relevant and useful, but it is outside what I have called *real speech*, and I think it is high time for speech studies to put more emphasis on data produced in genuine communicative situations. This certainly does not mean that it should all be spontaneous speech: the most rigid and formal interview, or a reading of a prose text, or an oral reproducton of a narrative in a fixed form, all may represent what I here mean by unreflected speech, even though the speaker may be highly conscious of aspects of his performance other than possible violations of the linguistic code.

1.3.   ELICITED VERSUS SPONTANEOUS SPEECH AND FORMAL LINGUISTICS

In an earlier paper (Rischel 1983*b*: 128–34) I have discussed the empirical status of the linguistic or phonetic raw data that emerge from the application of various conventional elicitation techniques. Elicitation techniques as such did not in themselves fall within the theme for the ESCA workshop, although their application is crucial to the nature of the speech data, and I shall be rather brief on this issue.

Descriptive linguistics/phonetics typically deals with language data that are more orderly than truly genuine specimens of human communication by means of language. In actual practice not only armchair linguists but also field workers (including this speaker) lean heavily on the elicitation of data. Much of this elicitation is done by introspection if, as is most often the case nowadays, the linguist works on his own language. In other cases, an informant is approached and more or less strongly guided as to what kinds of responses are relevant for the linguist, and what kinds of responses are irrelevant, no matter how pertinent they may seem to the informant himself. In still other cases, the data may be furnished by forms or constructions which the linguist happens to hear during conversations. This may seem to ensure the best quality of data, but then there is the grave problem of selection and representativity: there is an inherent danger that the linguist may selectively memorize 'interesting' data at the expense of apparently trivial data and thus end up distorting the overall picture.

Similar things may happen in phonetics, and paradoxically (considering that phonetics is generally construed as more 'real speech' oriented than other aspects of linguistics), the problem of getting to grips with natural, real language seems greater in phonetics than in morphosyntax, for example. In looking for grammatical phenomena the linguist can in actual practice (except for limitations to the labour to be invested) manage to use texts of all kinds, including specimens of highly spontaneous conversation. One might expect the same to obtain in phonetic research, but that is not the case. Reduction phenomena and foregrounding/backgrounding effects may cause so much variation that a stretch of very lively speech may be extremely difficult even to transcribe properly, and may seem practically inaccessible to instrumental analysis of prosodic parameters (although the ESCA Workshop on Phonetics and Phonology of Speaking Styles in 1991 demonstrated that some speech scientists fare quite well in such an adventure, as long as the scope of the investigation is reasonably narrow).

In contradiction to this, it often takes massive phonetic reduction in fast or casual speech before substantial parts of the morphosyntactical expression also really begin to be affected and, if grammatical information seems to be lost in indistinct speech, this is probably typically a function of phonetic reduction (e.g. deletion of unstressed inflectional endings) rather than a grammatical modification triggered by speech tempo or casualness. Strange as it seems, systematic phonetic research thus, on the whole, seems to require more well-behaved and more simplified data than grammatical research (although in actual fact syntactic analyses very often fail to exploit the possibility of dealing with truly empirical speech data).

Therefore, in spite of the programmatically empirical nature of phonetic research it is normal research strategy for all of us to use as our data not genuine, unmonitored speech, but on the contrary 'lab speech' specimens that are explicitly devoid of any linguistic function for the speaker. We make our informants record maybe five or six randomly ordered repetitions of a set of context-free and hence pragmatically meaningless utterances (nonsense words in a carrier phrase being the extreme case). Certain phenomena can be very insightfully illuminated in this way since they are highly 'mechanical' aspects of speech articulation; but even with very innocent-looking types of data such as formant frequencies one should not forget the socio-pragmatic perspective: the informant's performance may be highly dependent on the addressee.

It would be naive to assume that read sentences represent speech production in a vacuum: genuinely context-free samples. If there is no overt addressee, the speaker may construe the phonetician who arranges the recording to be the addressee (in which case the speaker may wish to comply with the expectations of that person), although the speaker might also visualize someone else (i.e. an imaginary conversational partner).

Moreover, read sentences often have more than one possible reading depending on the context in which they are used, and different readings may be realized phonetically with crucially different prosody. In the context-free situation we cannot be sure what reading the reader chooses; there is not always an obvious default reading, and even if there is, we cannot be sure that the reader will behave as expected and will not put the sentence into a more or less far-fetched imaginary situational context. And finally, of course, consecutive sentences on a test page may be construed to form a fragment of a meaningful though perhaps very far-fetched monologue or even dialogue, so that the reader pretends to be communicating something rather than just performing phonically.

All this entails that, for example, phonetic signals for anaphoric reference and other cross-sentence relationships may come into play. This means that the borderline between the recording of test sentences and the recording of read prose texts, as studied by Fant and Kruckenberg (1989, and later) may become somewhat fuzzy.

Prosodic phenomena in particular are known to be highly sensitive to semantic and pragmatic factors related to the situation and the addressee, so we run the risk of getting only partial and perhaps even misleading information from such recordings. The crucial thing, then, is to understand exactly the possibilities and the limitations of the 'lab speech' approach.

Some of us feel a strong desire to revolt against the paradoxical situation sketched above. Although it is hard to see how to overcome the obstacles, we may still entertain an almost naive ambition: that descriptive phonetics—including both narrow transcription and instrumental processing—should eventually be prepared to deal with 'natural speech' raw data: genuine specimens of oral communication which are not idealized for the purpose of documenting abstract regularities but are tackled in all of their complex and intriguing variation.

Many linguists would argue that this is not the goal of linguistics proper. Others would argue, and certainly with reason, that we are very far from possessing descriptive techniques that enable us to cope with the phonetics of spontaneous speech, but that some genuine progress can be made by studying read, meaningful though not spontaneous production of connected speech, such as recordings of read prose or poetry or oral performances of narrative texts. This is of course true. Such studies represent a very important transitional step between the study of arranged 'lab speech' and the study of spontaneous speech.

1.4.   STYLE AND 'TEMPO' CONDITIONED VARIATION AND FORMAL LINGUISTICS

I shall turn now to *variations in speed* which have to do with style, tempo, and related parameters. This is a very essential component of the study of spoken language, and for several reasons. First, the variations from slow, distinct, formal speech to fast, slurred, casual speech constitute an important empirical research object for phonetics. Secondly, this is one of the areas in which phonetic evidence consti- tutes a major challenge to phonological theory. Thirdly, the ways in which people have attempted to approach variation related to tempo, formality, and/or distinctness illustrate the search, within our science, for a fruitful research paradigm. Both phonology and phonetics suffer from the lack of a convincing, unified research paradigm. The modest progress that has been made so far in the study of speech variation is ample evidence of this unsatisfactory situation.

As far as I am aware, the first serious discussion of how to deal with tempo-conditioned variation in a rigid format was Hans Karlgren's seminal paper at the 4th International Congress of Phonetic Sciences (1962). The paper carried a title that was very typical of its time: 'Speech rate and information theory'. At that time many linguists entertained the belief that the mathematical theory of communication had something very interesting to offer to linguistics and even to phonetics. Karlgren's view was that 'the seemingly careless pronuncia- tion is ... in terms of information theory an efficient coding to fit the channel, a recoding of the phonematic message under consideration of conditional probabilities', or—in terms which were less coloured by the then-fashionable information theory—that the variation 'is not random nor merely individual or haphazard but contains an element of rational adaptation of the signal to the need of the situation' (Karlgren 1962: 674).

As one corollary of this claim, Karlgren expected a difference in speech rate between what he called 'short' and 'long' languages—by way of illustration I suppose German might serve as a relatively 'long' language, and English as a relatively 'short' language, since German has more syllables per wordform and a lot of inflectional redundancy compared to English. Karlgren of course expected 'short' languages to be spoken relatively carelessly and fast, but his statistical studies failed to yield clear evidence of such an overall difference. Karlgren had to conclude that the expected compensation for the 'long-windedness' of some languages is of a small magnitude and is drowned by variation due to 'temperament, style, attitude, and so on'. He looked instead at the size of short-term tempo variations within different languages and found some connection with the structural properties of these languages, the contention being that the structure of some languages favours a relatively even speech rate, whereas that of others favours more temporal fluctuation (Karlgren mentioned Finnish and Swedish as being markedly different in this respect). Such cross-language studies of tempo and style are important from a phonetic as well as a formal linguistic point of view as they contribute to defining a kind of *overall profile* of each language.

Today we should no longer expect linguistics and phonetics to benefit from the application of mathematical models of communication as such. Our key word is no longer information theory but *function*. What, then, is the current research paradigm in which we can approach tempo- and style-conditioned variation? We have not yet acquired sufficient insight into the nature of speech as a vehicle used in communication, and therefore we must attempt to proceed by using a combination of all possible and reasonable approaches. For one thing, we study communication in a *functional* and a *pragmatic* framework, and here one of Karlgren's basic observations is entirely to the point today: namely that there occurs 'adaptation . . . to the need of the situation' (Karlgren 1962: 674). But we also approach variation as a *sociolinguistic* phenomenon, as something to do with properties of language as a social pattern of behaviour. And we may try to capture variation as a feature of optionality in a phonological rule machinery. What is typical today is that researchers tend to *integrate* several or all of these approaches, as in a the (1991) paper by Dressler and Moosmüller.

After admitting that we do not have the ideal paradigm for the study of variation in natural speech, let us now turn to the question how, under these circumstances, we can handle such variation descriptively. From the phonological point of view it has become customary to distinguish between speech tempo settings such as 'lento speech' and 'allegro speech' (Dressler 1975). This is a significant advance over earlier phonological descriptions since probably all languages would turn out to permit some phonological simplification or reorganization triggered by a higher 'tempo' (taken in this particular sense). Several scholars, among whom I shall here mention in particular W.U. Dressler and Kohler (the former within the framework of natural phonology, the latter within a more phonetically based framework), have engaged in discussion of the nature and organization of such reduction rules.

There is, in my view, a host of major issues with which phonological theory must cope if it is to include this single parameter of speaking style variation. It may suffice here to pick ten items which seem to me to belong among the salient issues.

1 What is the functional relationship of 'tempo'-conditioned phonological rules to speech production strategies?
2 What is the functional relationship of such rules to speech perception strategies?
3 What is 'speech tempo', and how is the 'tempo' parameter to be specified?
4 How does the triggering effect of the 'tempo' factor interfere with the effect of other factors varying over different speaking styles?
5 Do 'tempo'-dependent reduction rules appear to be strictly ordered, to judge from the way such rules interact?
6 Do such sequences of ordered rules reflect a well-defined rank-ordering of levels of reduction? And if so, to what extent is such ordering intrinsically conditioned by the nature of each individual rule or package of rules?
7 Can a particular set of ordered reduction rules for a certain speaker be generalized for all of his or her performance?
8 Can an ordered set of reduction rules be generalized for a whole (sociolinguistically defined) speech community?
9 Is the basic nature of phonological representations of phrases preserved throughout such a derivation in terms of 'tempo'-conditioned reduction rules?
10 How are cases of idiosyncratic, although 'tempo'-dependent, allomorphy to be distinguished from genuinely process-like reduction phenomena?

I shall comment briefly on some of these issues, and somewhat more on others (it must be emphasized that like the chapter as a whole this is a personal appraisal of the issues rather than an overview of the scholarship in the field).

1.4.1. What is the functional relationship of 'tempo'-conditioned phonological rules to speech production strategies?

It is a priori a trivial point that increased tempo means increased coarticulation and simplification. This seems explicable as a natural consequence of constraints on human speech production in conjunction with an assumed tendency to economize the expenditure of effort. Accordingly, the effect of 'tempo' on articulatory programming is fertile ground for phonological and phonetic research. However, it is an interesting question to what extent it is just the economy of articulatory effort that is optimized, or to what extent communicative needs enter the picture. This leads to the next issue.

1.4.2. What is the functional relationship of such rules to speech perception strategies?

It is well known that the temporal 'smear' caused by coarticulation is not, or at least is not necessarily, adversarial to speech perception; on the contrary, categorical perception may crucially depend on the expectation that phonological properties of a given segment (or prosodic element) are coded into neighbouring parts of the speech signal. To this must be added that the proper operation of 'tempo'-conditioned reduction and readjustment phenomena contributes significantly to the acceptability of speech, as has been experienced by anybody working seriously on speech synthesis.

However, at high speech rates the articulatory reduction phenomena may cause a significant loss of information content in the natural speech signal. Understanding then benefits less than before from local phonetic information and becomes more crucially dependent on an overall interpretation of the message based on all kinds of top-down and bottom-up strategies, including higher information derived from the linguistic and situational context. This is painfully felt in situations where one suddenly has to rely on the local speech signal itself: for example, when words occur about which the addressee may have little or no qualified expectation (names, unknown words, etc.). It is also felt if a researcher extraneous to a communicative situation wants to 'decipher' and interpret a recording of unknown content from the situation in question. If so, the linguist may struggle hard–use more or less fancy playback methods with slow speed, etc.–but this is of small help if there is too little information in the speech signal.

Although reduction phenomena in natural speech are a natural corollary of fast speech, this relationship need not be considered an entirely automatic property of communication by language. I referred above to the impression that tempo-adjusted synthetic speech may sound more acceptable than highly articulate speech which is speeded up. In the application of speech synthesis to facilities for the blind, however, the question of fast speech is of a somewhat different nature. Here, it is a matter of the efficient transfer of information by means of a medium which is not expected to have exactly the same properties as the human voice, and the users are motivated to go through the necessary training to learn to understand the specific type of rendering. At least for some tasks, blind persons listening to synthetic speech may value a high-speed rendering of speech that is synthesized with the properties of slow speech more highly than less articulate but more natural sounding rapid speech.

1.4.3. What is 'speech tempo' and how is the 'tempo' parameter to be specified?

The reason why 'tempo' is put in quotation marks all through this section is, of course, that it is a highly controversial notion (also cf. discussion of the concepts of 'allegro' and 'lento' in Rischel 1990: 408–9). In discussions of variation over more or less reduced forms due to overall changes in speaking style, or due to more local backgrounding, the notion of 'casual speech' often (and rightly so) turns up instead of 'fast speech', but it is not always made clear what the relation is between the two notions.

It is possible to set up an absolute parameter of speech rate and to define speech rate by the number of units that are coded into the speech signal and thus delivered per second. This could be done in several ways; a priori one might think of defining some kind of acoustic minimal event and counting the number of such acoustic events per second, but obviously this does not create a workable frame of reference because of the reduction phenomena accompanying a higher rate. It is necessary to have a more abstract linguistic reference. One may, in principle, refer to meaningful units such as phrases or words, or to elements of the expression code such as feet (stress units), syllables, or phonemes. A measure in terms of feet introduces analytical decisions depending crucially on stress assessment; moreover, the concatenation of syllables into feet may undergo more or less tempo-dependent reorganization, so that the number of feet per second does not increase as expected with increased speech rate. Syllables have the disadvantage that the number of syllables is affected by sandhi and certain reduction phenomena and is not such a stable property of a lexical form as the number of phonemes; moreover, the syllable as a unit of timing has a very different status depending on stress versus absence of stress. The phoneme number per second is in itself a measure of limited validity as it ignores the hierarchical make-up of spoken strings; on the other hand it is a very robust measure in the sense that the number of phonemes in a read text string is essentially given a priori. The last-mentioned measure was used, with extensive discussion of the relation between phoneme duration, foot duration, and accentuation, by Fant and Kruckenberg (1989: 35–41).

It is a commonplace in phonetics that the durational ratio between different types of segments (and pauses) changes with speech rate, so speech rate is rather a complex notion anyhow.

How, then, does 'tempo', as viewed from the phonological end, relate to speech rate in the more physical sense? It is clear that the phenomena that phonologists study under headings such as 'allegro rules', are not just a matter of speech rate (although Anne Lacheret-Dujour has found that 'speech rate is a good predictor for speech varia-tions' (Lacheret-Dujour 1991)), but relate just as much to a parameter of speaking style, that is the degree of distinctness versus sloppiness (or possibly degree of casualness); many such rules are better labelled 'sloppiness rules' than 'tempo rules'. It adds to the complexity that reduction rules may both apply globally in an utterance, which is thus characterized as being 'allegro speech', or whatever, or they may apply more locally: for example, a phrase may be signalled as backgrounded by using rapid and more indistinct speech because it is a peripheral comment, or words in the vicinity of a strongly emphasized word may be backgrounded in a more or less similar manner in order to enhance the emphasis.

Overall speech rate is rather age-dependent: in Denmark, for exam-ple, rather slow and (within the capabilities of the person) highly artic-ulate speech can be heard from young children and from old people, whereas fast and sloppy speech can be heard typically from adoles-cents and young adults. Both overall speech rate and overall degree of distinctness are, however, also highly individual (although, of course, in part ultimately socially determined): some persons speak relatively slowly but indistinctly, for example with relatively little lip articulation and with overall nasalization, not as a defect but as a speech habit, whereas others of the same age may speak very rapidly but with very distinct articulation. I may here also refer to Anne Lacheret-Dujour's pertinent observation that the slow rate of one speaker can be the rapid rate of another (Lacheret-Dujour 1991). Thus, speech rate may be better viewed as a relative rather than an absolute measure.

It is obvious that this complex of speech rate and distinctness level, globally and locally, must be disentangled in order for the 'allegro rules' to be seen in their proper perspective.

1.4.4. How does the triggering effect of the 'tempo' factor interfere with the effect of others varying over different speaking styles?

As I have stated already, we face a complex of parameters. Let us look first at the distinctness–sloppiness parameter. It is very possible, as has been argued, that this parameter should be separated into two: one defining a range from distinct rendering of lexical items to sloppy rendering (this might be called the sloppiness parameter), and another ranging from normal distinct rendering to over-distinct dictation style (this might be called the over-distinctness parameter). This complex of parameters relates directly to the communicative need for distinctness in the speech signal.

The parameters of distinctness are closely related to, but (I think) not identical with, the style parameters defining the range from high formality to casualness. These are not a function of the higher or lower demand on communicative efficiency but much rather socially determined. However, in the case of an adolescent who as part of his or her personality normally speaks very fast, indistinctly, and casually, it may occasionally happen that he or she chooses to speak in a very much more articulate manner, for example to an elderly family member, or in a highly formal style in imitating a teacher's performance or stage speech. One may argue that this falls outside our proper concern, but it certainly gives evidence that the person masters (not only passively but also actively) a larger repertory of styles than one's prejudices would predict, and ultimately it bears on the question what phonological frame of reference should be chosen in studying 'allegro speech' data from the person in question.

I have attempted to distinguish between *distinctness* and *formality*, the former being supposed to serve the purpose of *adapting the phonetic signal to communicative needs*, and the latter being supposed to serve a different purpose: to serve the purpose of defining the participants' roles in communicative interaction both socially and situationally. Both of these parameters seem to be involved in Lindblom's Hyper- & Hypo-Model. Maybe we should rather say however that the distinction between two such parameters belongs to a higher level of linguistic specification than the hyper–hypo-parameter. The relationship is complicated further by the fact that *speech rate* understood as a pure tempo parameter also enters the picture. Distinctness, formality, and speech rate are not orthogonal parameters, but they are not reducible to a smaller number of properties either.

Altogether, it is a very complex issue to decide which parameters are required in the description of speaking styles. First of all, there is the distinction between what Joan Argente has referred to as *situational* versus *intergroupal* variation (Argente 1992). When studying reduction phenomena in natural speech we tend to focus only on situational factors, but in fact we cannot neglect intergroupal variation patterns, since a speaker may be informal in different ways depending on the addressee's and his or her own group memberships. Informal or casual speech may or may not contain *colloquialisms* belonging to a particular sociolect, and since a speaker's linguistic performance may to a certain extent vary over sociolects the notion of *casual speech* becomes a very complex notion indeed.

A further complication in describing speaking styles is that speech has many functions in addition to that of *delivering an intellectual message understandably* and that of *signalling the social relationship between speaker and listener*. One such additional function is what we often (following Roman Jakobson) refer to as *phatic* communication, that is, talking in order to *keep contact and have an open line* between participants in a social interaction. In that case it is often less important what is said or how it is said as long as *something* is said. A closely related function is exemplified by *baby talk* or *motherese*. As pointed out in Lindblom's paper to the ESCA workshop (Lindblom *et al.* 1992), this style of speaking is characterized inter alia by high-pitched intonation having an affective function; here we enter what would be the *emotive* component of speech communication according to Roman Jakobson (e.g. 1960). At the same time the performance of the mother obviously serves the phatic function of maintaining contact. These are probably the most relevant components in early baby talk; there is not necessarily any expectation about effective transmission of more complex information in spite of the use of articulate and coherent speech on the part of the mother, which puts the choice of speaking style in a special perspective. The same may be true, to a considerable extent, of the exchange of affectionate remarks and other smalltalk in which a couple of lovers may engage; here is another potential topic within the study of speaking styles.

1.4.5. **Do 'tempo'-dependent reduction rules appear to be strictly ordered?**

Although the case for elaborate rule machinery is considered weak in contemporary phonological theory, it would seem that the realm of phonological–phonetic processes triggered by speaking style variations must be one area in which the concepts of rule and of rule ordering have more genuine descriptive potential than elsewhere. Traditional orthodox generative phonology operates with relationships among rules in terms of their application and effects such as 'feeding' versus 'bleeding' and 'conjunctive' versus 'disjunctive'. Is it so that the regularities of more and more extensive assimilation and a reduction in faster and more sloppy speech invite a treatment in terms of strictly ordered rules? Do the rules then perform as single rules or as packages of rules? The answer to such questions requires extremely extensive empirical study of several speakers' performance over a range of styles. Personally, I rather doubt that we would arrive at a well-defined algorithm in this manner (also cf. Rischel 1991: 260).

I totally agree with those who find that *variation phonology* is genuine generative phonology (unlike much of earlier generative phonology which concerned itself with far-fetched reformulations of morphophonemic regularities observed over morphologically related wordforms). However, I wish to sound a very general note of reserve as regards the very notion of rule in this context; this note will appear in Section 1.4.10 below.

1.4.6. **Do such sequences of ordered rules reflect a well-defined rank-ordering of levels of reduction? And if so, to what extent is such ordering intrinsically conditioned by the nature of each individual rule or package or rules?**

The first question might be formulated like this: is it possible to set up well-defined, rank-ordered categories of rules such that the rules of the different ranks are triggered by successively higher 'tempo' parameter settings? The second question might be formulated like this: is the place of a rule within such a total set of rules more or less uniquely determined by its domain of application, its output effect, and/or the nature of the process which the rule expresses, or must one allow for more or less arbitrary extrinsic ordering?

I shall not go into these issues at all but just emphasize that it is both empirically and theoretically highly important to determine whether reduction rules in a particular linguistic usage form an implicational hierarchy, to determine to what extent such a hierarchy is universal, and—to the extent that there is sufficient evidence—to try to determine why. The answers to such questions are crucial for the epistemological status of the whole application of phonology to the description of natural speech in terms of models that depict reduction in fast/sloppy speech as stages of phonological modification. And, since we are talking about a formalization of phonetic relationships, these issues also bear crucially on the phonetic mapping of slow/distinct onto fast/sloppy speech in terms of more or less modular models of articulatory programming.

1.4.7. Can a particular set of ordered reduction rules of a certain speaker be generalized for all of his or her performance?

If one takes the concept of ordered reduction rules—but not necessarily universal ordering principles—for granted, one may further ask: is the individual language user consistent in his or her ordered application of such rules, irrespective of context?

The input to the discovery of implicational hierarchies of reduction rules may be from a variety of sources such as: (a) anecdotal evidence as well as information from pronouncing dictionaries and other textbooks, (b) introspection, (c) more or less systematic (or casual) observation of one or more speakers' performance, or (d) controlled experiments. Disregarding evidence of type (a), it is also proper to state that this area is hardly the most suitable one for introspective studies (even if the researcher is a native speaker). Approach (c) is, of course, in principle perfectly possible within a sociolinguistic framework, and such studies certainly form the basis of much of the current knowledge about this aspect of linguistic variation; however, anybody who has been working with natural speech data realizes how formidable a task it is to gather data that can be controlled for all the relevant parameters. Personally, I am rather sceptical about the possibility of totally sorting out the various parameters of speed, distinctness, formality, etc. (cf. the discussion in Sections 1.4.3 and 1.4.4 above) in a data set of this kind, but that is certainly no argument against engaging in such highly interesting endeavours. Then, finally, there is the possibility of lab-speech experiments, which of course have advantages and also severe limitations, but that is rather outside my present topic.

Considering the complexity of the task, and the difficulty of controlling parameters of variation in natural speech, there is a heavy burden of proof involved in showing that there is a unique rule ordering for increased speech 'tempo'. This, of course, does not exclude the that there is some degree of indispensable implicational ordering. A priori it seems particularly plausible that such strict and maybe even universally determined ordering may obtain between different sub-parts of a rule–for example an assimilatory rule with some segments assimilating more easily than others; whereas ordering among totally different reduction rules might be expected to be more idiosyncratic, also because of the possible interference between different speaking styles in a speaker's internalized phonology. If so, the speaker may sometimes have a choice between more than one path of derivation and hence between more than one output form on a certain level of rendering. His choice may then be determined by socio-pragmatic factors other than 'tempo'.

1.4.8. Can an ordered set of reduction rules be generalized for a whole (sociolinguistically defined) speech community?

Do different speakers in a speech community share a particular set of reduction rules in the sense that such a rule set is representative of all performance within a particular linguistic usage? This question is closely related to the preceding one. To the extent that the complications envisaged above obtain for one speaker, the complexity is of course many times higher for a linguistic community.

There is, under these circumstances, every reason to welcome the impressive and fruitful efforts made in recent years to come to grips with 'tempo'-determined variation; I am thinking in particular about the work done on Viennese German by Dressler and others (e.g. Dressler (1975)).

1.4.9. Is the basic nature of phonological representations of phrases preserved throughout such a derivation in terms of 'tempo'-conditioned reduction rules?

Are representations in terms of features, segments, and so on equally adequate at all stages in such a derivation, or is segmentality more or less lost with the successive coarticulations and reductions happening in fast/sloppy speech?

This question implies another, more basic question about the nature of phonological and phonetic representations, which I cannot address here (see Rischel 1990 for some general reflections on this issue). I shall just assume, for the sake of the present discussion, that it makes sense to posit phonological representations which make reference to segments and features as the input to reduction rules (by which I do not mean motor commands but linguistic rules underlying motor commands). The question then is to what extent the output of assimilation, coarticulation, and fusion processes is still of a segmental nature, and to what extent it can still be specified by means of the same repertory of segments. Obviously, this question bears on the nature of surface phonology as well as the nature of phonetic segmentation (impressionistic or automatic). It is, however, very unclear to me how to relate one level of specification to the other, given the current analytical practice in phonology.

In my type of Danish, for example, the words *det ved jeg* (in a phrase such as *Det ved jeg ikke* meaning 'I don't know') can be contracted in very casual speech into various reduced complexes which I might perhaps choose to represent as an alveolar stop followed by a long, slightly labialized alveolar or labiovelar approximant (with or without final laryngealization) followed by an open unrounded vowel. Such examples are legion in numerous languages. The question then is what the status of a transcription is in terms of IPA segments. In the particular example the initial and the final segments are direct reflexions of segments also occurring in the most distinct rendering, which suggests that the segmental structure has not broken down, whereas the intermediate stretch corresponds to five consecutive segments in the distinct rendering. What really remains is the speaker's and (normally also) the addressee's internalized knowledge of the linguistic identity of this reduced string with the sequence of three words which appears as three consecutive syllables in the same speaker's more distinct speech. The addressee can use this knowledge if there are cues enough to cause him/her to access it. In short, invariance is a linguistic property, and although the difficulty with phonological–phonetic mapping between full and reduced forms is real enough both as a problem for descriptive phonology and as an issue in the modelling of speech production, presentation of it as an IPA transcription problem is obviously an artefact of the conventions we cling to (and, I think, have to cling to) in practical phonetics.

As for transcription of more or less natural connected speech, many years of experience in classroom and particularly field work situations has convinced me that the outcome of such an activity is highly dependent on access to higher-level linguistic information (in other words: understanding of the text via textual and situational context and via implicit morphosyntactic analysis of the string). One may attempt to devise transcription systems (e.g. modified IPA systems) for the transcription of highly reduced or deviating speech, but this does not do away with the problem.

1.4.10. How are cases of idiosyncratic, although 'tempo'-dependent allomorphy to be distinguished from genuinely process-like reduction phenomena?

Several languages have instances of allomorphic, that is phonemically distinct, doublets–for example a sequence of two separable morphs versus one portmanteau morph resulting from contraction. Examples are legion; from Danish I can mention *det er* ('it is'), in my usage /deə/ or /deː/ (with *er* assimilating as if it were schwa!). Is it possible to keep such instances of variation over more or less contracted forms distinct from general, rule-governed processes such as schwa-assimilations in post-tonic syllables of words? That depends on how easy it is to distinguish between, on the one hand, idiosyncratic variation and, on the other hand, variation types that are both of high generality and phonologically 'natural'; maybe in some cases the phenomena are triggered differently so that a distinction between factors such as distinctness, formality, and speech rate might also be relevant.

However, I think the issue is more complex than that. If the description is construed to reflect a hypothesis about the speaker's internalized command of his or her native phonology, the question immediately arises as to what extent variant forms are really related, in internalized phonology, via process rules. To the extent that we are speaking about phenomena that occur 'mechanically' as a function of speech rate differences (phenomena which hence may be easily reproducible in experimental situations) there is a very strong case for the process view, but what about variation that also involves the speaker's deliberate or unreflected choice of speaking style? In other words, if a speaker speaks sloppily, does he or she then do all the extensive coarticulation, assimilation, fusion, and whatever, by applying processes to a relatively distinct representation, or does a mental lexical entry store information about alternative morphs which can be picked and used for different distinctness levels, even though the behaviour of the morphs could be stated and predicted in a general rule format? How do we know? As pointed out at the ESCA workshop by Solé and Ohala (1991) we cannot even assume that the strategies for storing and/or processing are the same for all kinds of linguistic material.

1.5.   CONCLUDING REMARKS

It is essential to change the research strategies within both linguistics and phonetics in the direction of more emphasis on the empirical analysis of natural speech. It is a particularly crucial issue whether we can move in the direction of developing methods to cope with some aspects of more or less spontaneous speech, although that is undeniably a formidable task. This should of course be done without at all discarding the indispensable analytical approaches used in the study of the basic structure of language: controlled elicitation and introspection, experiments with lab speech, and so on.

The need for studies of natural speech may be claimed to be most urgent within speech technology, that is in synthesis and automatic speech recognition (ultimately also understanding?). It is important in these fields to appreciate that the complex nature of natural speech is a linguistic problem rather than an engineering problem (a challenge for signal processing). However, the real issue is how to integrate such studies with formal linguistics. As it is now, linguistics leaves much of its natural field to other disciplines or just leaves it uncultivated. In order for general linguists and phoneticians to be able to claim that linguistic and phonetic sciences taken together cover the subject of Language, we must take up the obligation to apply rigid research methods also to language in communication, and to approach that topic, not just as a challenge to speech technology but as one of the most important aspects of the general study of language.

2

Consonant Gradation: A Problem in Danish Phonology and Morphology[1]

2.1. INTRODUCTION

It is a well-known characteristic of Danish that the patterns of OBSTRUENTS (stops and fricatives) in word-initial and word-final position are phonetically very different but can be made to match each other fairly well if some of the stops and fricatives be considered allophones of the same series of phonemes. It is also well known that the diphthongs found in Danish are related to the class of fricatives, since the second component of the diphthongs (here termed a SEMIVOWEL) can be considered to be in allophonic variation with fricatives. (See the distributional survey below.)

The present paper is concerned with another aspect of the relationships between these sounds, namely, the formulation of rules governing the morphological alternations between them, as in such instances as [kɔ:ɣə] 'cook', pret. [kɒgdə], [sdi:'v], or [sdiu̯'] 'stiff', neut. [sdift].[2]

The existence of these alternations is also well known from the literature on Danish phonology and morphology, but to this author's knowledge they have not been subject to a systematic analysis by modern linguistic methods. Alternations of the kind exemplified above are used quite extensively as evidence for phonemic identity, above all in Hjelmslev's paper on the expression system of Danish (Hjelmslev 1951), but here they compete with criteria of a quite different kind,

[1] Reprinted from Proceedings of the International Conference of Nordic and General Linguistics, University of Iceland, Reykjavik, 6–11 July 1969 ed. H. Benediktsson, Reykjavik: Vísindafélag Íslendinga (1970): 460–80.

[2] Phonetic forms are given in a rather broad transcription. [b, d, g] are voiceless unless the opposite is explicitly stated. Vowels with stød are given as long vowels although they are (normally) shorter than long vowels not accompanied by the stød. Word-final [t] means [d] (voiceless) or [t], indiscriminately.

and it is not altogether clear how crucial it is to reduce all instances of such alternations to phonetic (bound) variation. In most other contributions to Standard Danish phonology they play a less central role.

In an unpublished paper read before the Linguistic Circle of Copenhagen in 1967 Eric Hamp sketched a generative phonology of Danish. Hamp's paper, which presented feature matrices for vowels and consonants as well as a number of rules relating the classificatory matrices to phonetic realizations, is of course quite crucial to the present study. He was not, however, specifically concerned with the problems considered here (except for a few rules on diphthongs), and since his paper is available only in the form of a handout from the session it is somewhat difficult to enter into a detailed discussion of his analysis, however informative it has been.

In accordance with the rather specific scope of this paper—and for considerations of space—I have considered it justifiable to treat the subject matter with only occasional references to the literature on Danish phonology, although an appraisal of the various analyses from the point of view of simplicity of morphological (morphophonemic) rules would be highly interesting. Bibliographical references to papers and monographs on Danish phonology, some of which are pertinent to the present study, have been given elsewhere (Basbøll 1969; Rischel 1969).

The present analysis is chiefly based on forms occurring in my own usage, but these largely agree with those given in standard works on Modern Danish grammar and phonetics (see, e.g., Andersen 1954: 319, 344, 347; Diderichsen 1957: 53–4, 60–1; Hansen 1956: 50–1, 59, 64–72, 88–9, 105; 1967: 1.302, 2.365–368, 3.18–19, 118; Spore 1965: 138).

The complicated problems associated with /r/, which are in some respects related to those treated here, are disregarded.

2.2. DISTRIBUTIONAL SURVEY

Before proceeding to the discussion of alternations it may be advantageous to take stock of the stops, fricatives, and semivowels occurring in different positions (only facts relevant to the present study will be mentioned here).

It is useful to distinguish between two types of position: STRONG and WEAK POSITION (cf. Jakobson *et al.* 1961: 5). These will here be taken as essentially synonymous with (syllable-)initial and (syllable-)final position, but they cannot be directly characterized in these terms without a discussion of the concept of syllable, which is outside the scope of this paper. Instead, the following working definition referring to morphophonemic environments may suffice: A consonant is in strong position if it fulfils the following two requirements: (1) it is preceded by juncture (morpheme border) or by a segment that is (phonemically) voiced; (2) it is followed by a full vowel (i.e. not schwa) with or without an intervening voiced consonant but without an intervening juncture. Examples are: [g] in [gliːðə] 'glide', [b, g] in [lomˈbæːgo] 'lumbago'. Otherwise a consonant is in weak position. Examples are: [ɣ, ð] in [tɔːɣəðə] 'foggy' (plur.), [ð, ɣ] in [jøːðisg] 'Jewish' (the latter word has a morpheme border between [ð] and [i]), and [ð] in [feðmə] 'fatness'.

In strong position there are maximally ten contrasting obstruents (disregarding [h], which is not considered an obstruent here): aspirated [p, t, k], unaspirated (and voiceless) [b, d, g], voiceless [f, s, (ʃ)] (ʃ can be considered as *s* + *j*), and voiced [v, j]. It has been suggested (most recently by Hamp) that [p, t, k, f, s] should be defined as tense (this feature may be redundant in [s] according to Hamp), the others as lax. Aspiration and voice are then phonetic features introduced by manifestation rules. In the present paper it is assumed that there is a classificatory distinction of [–VOICED] in the segments underlying [p, t, k, f, s] vs. [+VOICED] in those underlying the rest, and that aspiration and voicelessness in the stops (and in fricatives following aspirated stops) is introduced by rules. This may be little more than a question of terminology.

In weak position there is only one stop series, mostly without aspiration and thus phonetically best rendered as [b, d, g]. In word-final position the stops may be aspirated (and the coronal stop may exhibit the affrication typical of Danish [t]). In this paper final -*t* is given as [t] for convenience, although [d] is probably heard more often.[3]

---

[3] Hansen (1956: 50) and Diderichsen (1957: 47) rightly consider the optional aspiration of word-final stops as being related to a general tendency toward word-final aspiration (before pause) in Danish. From this point of view it is more meaningful to transcribe [-b, -d, -g] than [-p, -t, -k], the optional aspiration being a junctural phenomenon. One might, on the other hand, question whether it is phonetically reasonable to transcribe the coronal

The sparseness of stops in weak position is compensated for by the occurrence of two additional fricatives, [ð, ɣ], and of two semivowels, [i̯ u̯]; the sound [i̯] is, of course, phonetically closely akin to the [j] of the strong positions.

According to the interpretation in terms of tenseness the classificatory feature distinguishing [b, d, g, f, s] must be [+TENSE] or strong; the other segments are [–TENSE] or weak. In the terminology used here the segments underlying at least some occurrences of [b, d, g, f] and underlying [s] are [–VOICED], those underlying the rest (and underlying some occurrences of [b, (d), g, f]) are [+VOICED]. (This is in clear agreement with the phonetic manifestation, although [b, d, g] may become voiced in intervocalic position in rapid speech.)

2.3.   MATCHING OF INITIAL AND FINAL CONSONANTS

The matching of initial [p, t, k, b, d, g] with final [b, d, g, ð, ɣ] is a classic problem in Danish phonology. The matching [p- -b, t- -d/t, k- -g, d- -ð, g- -ɣ] suggested by the feature definitions above reveals a skewness in the pattern, since there is no counterpart of [b-].

As stated above the consonants should be studied in their occurrence in various types of strong and weak positions rather than just initially and finally, at least if this be understood as absolutely word-initial and word-final position. An inspection of the behaviour of the entities in other environments reveals a very complex pattern.

Contrasts like [p] versus [f] make it plausible that there is a classificatory distinction between segments that are [–CONTINUANT] or [+INTERRUPTED] and segments that are [+CONTINUANT] or [–INTERRUPTED], according to one's terminology. One may now ask quite generally whether [d, g] of the strong positions and [ð, ɣ] of the weak positions have the same phonemic status, that is the same definition in terms of distinctive features.

A proof of the relatedness of the two series is furnished by alternations in foreign words with and without stressed suffixes, cf. [filolo'giː'], [meto'dig], with [g, d] in strong position, versus [filo'loː'ɣ, filoloː'ɣisg],

---

stop as [d] in cases where it is clearly affricated. (Admittedly, this phenomenon may also be confined to the position before a pause.)

[me'toːðə, me'toː'ðisg], with [ɣ, ð] in weak position.[4] (Note that there is no trace of juncture before the last vowel of *filologi, metodik*.) This does not, however, prove that all occurrences of voiced fricatives must be derived from underlying stops.

In order to round off the picture of the relationships between initial and final or, more generally, strong and weak, positions one must consider also the semivowels [i̯, u̯]. In an autonomous phonemic analysis the former must obviously be paired with the [j] found in strong positions (phonetically it is not very easy to distinguish [j] and [i̯] in Danish at all), but a study of morphological alternation (variation) immediately shows that it is related by alternation to [ɣ, g]; [u̯] can be identified phonemically with [v] in an autonomous analysis, but it is also related by alternation to [ɣ, g] and also to [b].

A survey will now be given of the more commonly found types of alternation.

2.4. FRICATIVE ALTERNATING WITH STOP BEFORE SUFFIX -t(e)

Cases like [koːɣə]—[kɒgdə] (past part. [kɒgt]) exhibit both an alternation [ɣ] ~ [g] and an alternation long vowel ~ short vowel. The two phenomena are apparently related: in the adjective forms [klɔː'ɣ] 'wise'—neut. [klɔː'ɣt], plur. [klɔːɣə], we find neither quantity shift nor consonant alternation.

Alternations as exemplified by the verb *koge* seem to occur in all verbs (taking the suffixes in question) which end in [ɣ] when no suffix is added to the stem (cf. *bage, bruge, koge, læge, sige, sluge, smage, spøge, søge, øge*). Moreover, they are observed if one compares certain verbs or adjectives with related nouns derived by means of a suffix -*t* or with verbs derived by a similar suffix (*jage* ~ *jagt, klog* ~ *kløgt, svige(fuld)* ~ *svigte, våge* ~ *vagt*).

The invariance exemplified by the adj. *klog* is found with most adjectives ending in [ɣ] (cf. *klog, klæg, læg, myg, spag, svag, træg, vag, veg*). Possible exceptions are some adjectives with a narrow vowel–*lig, rig, slig, syg*–but some of these can also be (and probably mostly are) pronounced without modification: [syː'(ɣ)t] rather than [sygt], etc.

---

[4] Pronunciations with the stop alternants generalized to weak position also occur (Andersen 1954: 344).

If we turn now to verbs and adjectives whose stems end in [ð] (phonetically), the picture is different.

The verbs with a long vowel in forms without the suffix -*t*(*e*) may or may not exhibit a short vowel before the suffixes, cf. [ɛːðə] 'eat'– past part. [ɛt] (similarly *bide, bryde, byde, flyde, forlade, fortryde, græde, gyde, lide, lyde, møde, nyde, skide, skyde, slide, smide, stride, svede, træde*; some of these verbs have ablaut shift) versus [klɛːðə] 'dress' – [klɛːˀt] (similarly *bede, brede, føde, lede, nøde, rede, sprede, stede*).

Some of the verbs listed above may be heard with a different quantity in the past participle than the one indicated. In such forms as [bløt] from [bløːðə] 'bleed' and [usgat] 'unhurt' (cf. [sgæːðə] 'hurt') both pronunciations with a long and a short vowel seem quite normal.

Vowel shortening can also be observed by a comparison of some verbs with derived nouns or verbs, cf. *ride ~ ridt, skride ~ skridt, svide ~svitse* (cf. also *bide ~ bidsel, føde ~ fødsel, øde ~ ødsel* with a short vowel and loss of [ð] in the derived nouns and adjectives).

If we turn now to adjectives in (alternatively) long vowel plus [ð], three different types of behaviour with added -*t* can be seen:

1 Some adjectives have no modification, cf. [leːˀð] 'repulsive' – [leːˀðt] (or [leðˀt] according to an optional modification common to all combinations of phonetically long vowel plus voiced fricative). It is difficult to exemplify these, since there is a tendency to avoid inflection of such adjectives (a word like *ked (af)* 'sorry' is probably never used with -*t*); possible examples are *fad, lad* (pejorative words like *led*), *kåd*, and foreign words, *gravid, invalid, perfid, stupid*.
2 A few adjectives are often or generally pronounced with a long vowel but loss of [ð] in the neuter: [sbrøːˀð] 'crisp' – [sbrøːˀt] (like *sprød*, possibly, also *spæd, vid*).
3 Most of the common adjectives have both a short vowel and loss of [ð] in the neuter: [brɛːˀð] 'broad' [brɛt] (similarly *blid, blød, død, fed, flad, god, hvid, rød, solid, strid, sød, vred, våd*).

2.5. VOICED FRICATIVE ALTERNATING WITH VOICELESS FRICATIVE

There are a few instances of alternation [v] ~ [f] in verbs and adjectives, the latter alternant occurring in connection with the suffix -*t*; these forms have a short vowel: [sdiːˀv] (or [sdiu̯ˀ], see below) 'stiff' – neut.

[sdift] (similarly, though with a short vowel throughout: [grɒw'] 'rough'
– neut. [grɒft]), [hæ:və] (or more frequently [hæ:']) 'have' – past part.
[haft].

Further examples of this alternation can be found in word derivation, cf. *drive ~ drift, grave ~ grøft, kløve ~ kløft*, but on the whole it
seems to be infrequent.

In most cases no modification takes place, cf. [læ:'v], [læ:'u̯] 'low'
neut. [læ:'vt læ:'u̯t] (similarly *brav, døv, gæv, skæv, sløv*).

Put in rule form the alternation of [v] and [f] would obviously be
formulated as a replacement of the former by the latter under specific
conditions. In spite of the sporadic occurrence it is worth noting the
existence of the process

$$[+\text{VOICED}] \rightarrow [-\text{VOICED}]\_\_t$$

found in *stiv ~ stift*, etc., since it is only with the labiodentals that this
process can be isolated.

2.6.   VOICED FRICATIVE ALTERNATING WITH SEMIVOWEL

We have to do here with two categories of alternations: (i) differences
between different grammatical forms, (ii) vacillations within the same
grammatical forms. These two categories of phenomena must be kept
carefully apart.

(i) There are numerous cases of alternation between monosyllabic
forms with a short vowel and bisyllabic forms with a long vowel. This
pattern is particularly frequent in noun inflection. In these cases [v]
after a long vowel alternates with [u̯] after a short vowel, for example [hau̯] 'sea'—plur. [hæ:və]. (The same alternation may be found,
although less regularly, in connection with derivation and compounding, cf. [gæ:və] 'gift' vs. [gau̯mil'] 'generous'.) In some cases double
forms occur, cf. [lɒu̯] 'law'—plur. [lɔ:və] or [lɒ:u̯ə].

In connection with alternations between long and short vowels one
can also observe alternations between [ɣ] on the one hand and [i̯]
or [u̯] on the other, [i̯] occurring after the short vowel if this is an
(underlying) front vowel, and [u̯] occurring if the vowel is an (underlying) back vowel. However, these alternations are not regulated in
the same way as those with [v] ~ [u̯]. In the first place, the vowel

quantity is normally generalized in such a way that the vowel is either long or short throughout, or so that double forms occur, cf. [sbøːˀɣ] or (definitely more frequently) [sbɒi̯ˀ] 'joke', [sbøːɣəlsə] or [sbɒi̯əlsə] 'ghost' (*spøge* means both 'joke' and 'haunt'); cf. also [ai̯ən] 'own' versus [eːɣən]- or [ai̯ən]- as the first member of compounds. In the second place, the alternant [u̯] for [ɣ] is used only in some types of Standard Danish. To many speakers of this language it is a slightly (or definitely) substandard alternative, whereas others do not seem to discriminate sharply between [ɣ] and [u̯] after a short back vowel, that is in forms like *sagn* [sɑɣnˀ] or [sɑu̯nˀ] 'legend' (as against *savn* [sɑu̯nˀ] 'need, want', which has only [u̯], that is underlying /v/).

A good example of these unstable tendencies is the word *slag* 'stroke, hit', definite form *slaget*. With the vowel quantity alternation operating one would expect [slaɣ]—[slæːˀɣð̩], and with the fricative ~ semivowel alternation also in operation one would expect [slau̯] – [slæːˀɣð̩]. The pronunciations familiar to (and probably all used by) this writer are, in fact, many more: [slæːˀɣ, slaɣ, slau̯] – [slæːˀɣð̩, slæːˀi̯ð̩ slau̯ˀð̩]. The last-mentioned pronunciation (and similarly [tau̯ˀð̩] for [tæːˀɣð̩] 'the grip') is used only with special connotations and perhaps only in fixed phrases. (Note that [tæːˀɣð̩] 'the roof' cannot be pronounced [tau̯ˀð̩] in Standard Danish.)

It may be added that vowel shortness (and thus obligatory or optional replacement of fricative by semivowel) is a regular feature of combinations of vowel plus voiced fricative plus liquid or nasal. However, many such forms ([sɑu̯nˀ], for example) do not enter into obvious alternations with forms with a phonetically-manifested fricative, so it is only by generalization that many of these forms may be said to reflect an underlying fricative (if this interpretation is at all valid in all cases).

(ii) After a (phonetically) long vowel many people have more or less free variation between [v] and [u̯], between [ɣ] and [i̯] after front vowels, and between [ɣ] and [u̯] after back vowels. In the speech of the younger generation in Copenhagen [ɣ] is apparently entirely replaced by [i̯, u̯] (cf. Basbøll 1969).

After nonobstruent continuants the fricatives may be optionally replaced by semivowels or by zero: [v] is replaced by zero after /l/, cf. [halˀv] → [halˀ] 'half', but by [u̯] after /r/ (→ [ɒ̯]), cf. [væu̯ˀv] → [væɒ̯ˀu̯] 'task'; [ɣ] is replaced by [i/j] after /l/, cf. [bølɣə] → [bøljə] 'wave', but by [u̯] (occasionally by zero) after /r/ (→ [ɒ̯]), cf. [bjæɒ̯ˀɣ] → [bjæɒ̯ˀu̯] 'mountain'. In ordinary usage [ð] is not found in these positions at all, but there is an alternation between [d] and zero in such forms as [søndi] 'sinful' – [søn'] 'sin', [joṇdisg] 'earthly' – [joːˀṇ] 'earth', [hɛldi] 'lucky' – [hɛl'] 'luck', provided that the suffixes be assumed to contain no initial [d] (cf. [køːli] 'cool' (adj.) – [køːlə] 'cool, chill' (verb)). In agreement with the glossematic analysis of Danish (see Hjelmslev 1951) the stems in question may be assumed to contain a final coronal obstruent, which is subject to obligatory deletion in positions where the manifestation *[ð] might be expected.

If an underlying coronal obstruent in stem-final position is posited for the last-mentioned forms, an extra rule must be set up in order to explain why it appears as a stop before suffixes like -ig, -isk (in contrast to such cases as [dyːði] 'virtuous' – [dyð'] 'virtue', [jøːðisg] 'Jewish' – [jøːðə] 'Jew', with apparently the same suffixes). The formulation of this rule will not be considered here.

[i̭, ṷ] plus a following schwa frequently fuse into more or less homogeneous, syllabic sounds, yielding forms like [løːu] (∼ [løːvə]) 'lion', [kɔːu] (∼ [kɔːɣə]) 'cook'.

A similar variation with semivowel, although more sporadic, is found with the stop [b]. Pronunciations with [ṷ] for [b] are strictly colloquial and in many cases distinctly substandard or dialectal. In my speech they are normally accompanied by shortness of the preceding vowel, which is not necessarily true of forms with [ṷ] alternating with [v] (or [ɣ]), cf. [kniuː] (∼ [kniːbə]) 'be difficult for somebody' versus [kniːu] (∼ [kniːvə]) 'knives'.

(iii) It is expedient to add here (although it has nothing directly to do with the consonant alternations) that there is a strong tendency in Modern Danish toward shortening of the vowel in monosyllables before voiced nonnasal, nonlateral segments. In some cases the quality of the vowel shows that it is a shortened long vowel, and that the shortening is accomplished by a very late rule, cf. [blæð'] (∼ [blæːˀð]) imper. of [blæːðə] 'turn over the leaves' versus [blað] 'leaf'.

2.7.   VOICED FRICATIVE ALTERNATING WITH ZERO AFTER NARROW VOWEL

The fricative [ɣ] is optional (unless modified into a stop) after narrow vowels, cf. [sluːɣə] ∼ [sluːə] 'swallow' – past part. [slugt]. If we assume a semivowel [i̭, ṷ] in this position (by assimilation to the vowel), the further reduction of [iːi̭, yːi̭, uːṷ] to [iː, yː, uː] can be stated in extremely simple terms and does not entail any complications of the general pattern.

2.8.   ORDERED RULES AND UNDERLYING FORMS

In order to get a system out of the many consonant alternations one may choose to formulate these as unidirectional replacement rules, and to establish an order of application among the rules. The following remarks give some suggestions concerning a generative description of this kind. I keep rather close to the methodological framework of transformational phonology, although no attempt is made to give feature matrices (this would require a lengthy discussion) or rigid formulations of rules.

If we start from the surface it is immediately clear that certain phenomena are generated by very late rules not affecting the rest of the system. These include the reduction of fricatives to semivowels and the optional vowel shortening before these semivowels (in monosyllables)– see Sections 2.6–2.7 above. This part of the rule system will be disregarded in what follows. This means, very roughly speaking, that the rules discussed below do not go any further than the maximally distinct (and conservative) phonetic forms.

The problems to be considered are thus centred around the alternation stop ~ fricative and the alternation long vowel ~ short vowel occurring in connection with the suffixion of -t(e).

As for the alternation stop ~ fricative, it is immediately clear that one of these must be generated from the other in the sense that the segment in question is marked as stop ([–CONTINUANT]) or as fricative ([+CONTINUANT]) in the underlying form. It is, however, not evident which of these alternatives is preferable, that is which direction the process should be assumed to take. Is the inf. [kɔːɣə] derived from a form with /g/ by means of a stop weakening rule, or is the past part. [kɒgt] derived from a form with /ɣ/ by an assimilation rule?

The alternation as such is not automatic since not all instances of voiced fricative (or semivowel) are matched by a stop before -t, and conversely, not all instances of stop before -t are matched by a voiced fricative (semivowel) elsewhere (cf. [ræɡə] 'to hand' – past part. [rɑɡt], [sgɛːˀg] 'funny' neut. [sgɛːˀgt]; cf. also the special problems associated with [b]). Historically, this has, of course, something to do with the overlap between old forms with stem-final fricative and with stem-final stop, and with the shortening of old long stops (geminates). It is quite tempting to formulate a set of synchronic rules which more or less directly reflect this multiple origin of the sounds without, of course, necessarily leading to a one-to-one correspondence between synchronically underlying forms and historical forms.

If the stems in question are considered to differ in that some contain an underlying fricative (e.g. [klɔːˈɣ]), others an underlying single stop (e.g. [kɔːɣə]), and still others an underlying double or long stop (e.g. [ræɡə], [sɡɛːˈɡ]), it is possible to formulate rules according to which postvocalic single stops in stem-final position are weakened to fricatives (and possibly further to semivowels) if no -t follows, whereas fricatives and long stops are not modified.

According to this analysis we have /ɡ/ → [ɣ] in [kɔːɣə], that is:

$$\begin{bmatrix} -\text{CONTINUANT} \\ -\text{LONG} \end{bmatrix} \rightarrow [+\text{CONTINUANT}]^5 \text{ in weak position unless} \\ \text{followed by a stop}$$

but underlying /ɣ/ in [klɔːˈɣ] since underlying /ɡ/ would give neut. *[klɒɡt] instead of [klɔːˈɣt].

This analysis implies that such forms as [sɡɛːˈɡ] have a succession of two segments with underlying length (except in a western variety of Danish which has [sɡɛːˈɣ]). One may claim that this analysis is not quite reasonable. A possible alternative is to replace the alleged distinction [+LONG] : [−LONG] in stops in weak position by a distinction [+TENSE] : [−TENSE] (Jakobson *et al.* 1961: 5–6, 38) or [−VOICED] : [+VOICED]. Such a distinction must be used anyway to take care of [p, t, k, f] versus [b, d, g, v] in strong position.

If the feature is called voicedness,[6] a number of rules must be set up in order to introduce (a) aspiration of voiceless stops in strong position, (b) (partial or complete) devoicing of stops in strong position and before voiceless stops, and (c) weakening of voiced stops to

[5] Rule algebra and feature terminology largely follow the practice exemplified in Chomsky and Halle (1968), except that I use a feature [+OBSTRUENT] to define the common class of stops and fricatives.

[6] Since the two series do differ in voicedness in some positions, whereas tenseness in a phonetic sense does not seem to play any role in Danish stops (unless the term be taken as synonymous with aspiration), the choice of voicedness seems preferable. See, however, Ejskjær (1954: 51–2) for an interesting interpretation of the obstruent system of a Danish dialect in terms of tenseness.

fricatives elsewhere. If the abbreviations [SP] and [WP] are used to denote strong and weak position, respectively (see 2.2 above), the rules can be sketched like this:

(a) $\begin{bmatrix} -\text{CONTINUANT} \\ -\text{VOICED} \end{bmatrix} \rightarrow [+\text{ASPIRATED}]/\begin{bmatrix} \text{SP} \\ \underline{} \end{bmatrix}$

(b) $\begin{bmatrix} +\text{OBSTRUENT} \\ -\text{CONTINUANT} \end{bmatrix} \rightarrow [-\text{VOICED}]/\begin{Bmatrix} \begin{bmatrix} \text{SP} \\ \underline{} \end{bmatrix} \\ \underline{} + [-\text{CONTINUANT}] \end{Bmatrix}$

(c) $[+\text{VOICED}] \rightarrow [+\text{CONTINUANT}]$

(The formulations presuppose that the rules be ordered as indicated.)

In addition there must be a separate rule taking care of the special behaviour of the labial series (possibly a rule reversing the weakening rule unless a further weakening to the semivowel has taken place; as stated above the further reduction rules are left out of consideration here). There must also be a rule simplifying [dt] into a single stop, in order that forms like [feː'ð] – [fet] may be in agreement with the rules (underlying /d/ being assumed here).

The variations of vowel quantity pose specific problems, cf. [møːðə] – [møt] versus [føːðə] – [føː't], [brɛː'ð] – [brɛt], versus [brɛːðə] – [brɛː't], [kɔːɣə] – [kɒgt] versus [klɔː'ɣ] – [klɔː'ɣt]. The last-mentioned pair suggests that a generalization can be made according to which the vowel is shortened before an underlying stop plus stop but not before an underlying voiced fricative plus stop. Accordingly, we assume underlying /d/ in *møde, bred*, but /ð/ in *føde, brede*, and an additional rule must be introduced according to which /ð + t/ is simplified to a single stop (like /d + t/) except in a few adjectives of a special type (*fad*, etc.).

It is interesting that this analysis agrees with historical facts in cases like *møde* versus *føde*. However, it is a serious shortcoming that it assigns different underlying forms to the stems of *bred* (adj.) and *brede* (verb), which are obviously very closely related.

If the phonetic difference between neut. and past part. *bredt* is not due to the underlying stem-final consonant, it may likewise be assumed that the difference between neut. *klogt* (with a long vowel and stem-final voiced fricative) and past part. *kogt* (with a short vowel and stem-final voiceless stop) is not due to a difference in the underlying stem-final consonant but has some other explanation.

Under this assumption the sets */t, d, ð/ and */k, g, ɣ/ reduce to sets of two phonemes. These will be denoted by /t, D/ and /k, G/ in what follows: the symbols /D, G/ are understood as neutral to the eventual specification of these units as either stops or continuants (i.e. as /d, g/ or /ð, ɣ/). It is assumed, however, that there is an underlying difference of voicedness between /t, k/ and /D, G/. According to this interpretation the stems of *føde, møde, brede, bred* all end in /D/, and those of *klog, koge* both end in /G/.

It seems immediately reasonable to assume that the forms with stem final /D/ all have an underlying long vowel.[7] If this is true the difference of vowel length between (neut.) *bredt* and *mødt* on the one hand and (past part.) *bredt* and *født* on the other must apparently be conditioned by the suffixes. The neuter suffix is /t/; there is no question about that. But the verb suffixes may have either /t/ or /D/, as may be seen from the inflexion of verbs with no stem-final consonant: [sgeːʼ] 'happen' – [sgeːdə] – [sgeːʼt] versus [døːʼ] 'die' – [døːðə] – [døːʼð] ([døðʼ]). The suffix consonant of the former verb reflects /t/ (unless the suffix is added to a stem augmented with /D/, in which case the forms *skete, sket* correspond to *bredte, bredt, fødte, født*). The suffix consonant of the latter verb unquestionably reflects /D/.

If verbs like *møde* are supposed to take suffixes in /t/, and verbs like *føde, brede* are supposed to take suffixes in /D/ (this happens also to agree with historical evidence), we get the following combinations among members of the set /t, D/:

Underlying   /t/ + /t/, cf. past part. [sat] from [sɛdə] 'put',
"   /D/+ /t/, cf. [møt], [brɛt],
"   /D/+ /D/, cf. [føːʼt], [brɛːʼt]; also [brɛːʼdə] 'width'.

It can be seen that combinations among members of this set all reduce to one segment, which is identical with the surface representation of single /t/, that is [d] or [t]. Exceptions are some peripheral neuter forms with /D/ + /t/ manifested as [ð] plus stop (e.g. *perfid-t, led-t*; see Section 2.4).

If the manifestation of /D/ as continuant or stop is considered to depend on whether the underlying feature [+VOICED] is retained or changed by a rule into [–VOICED], three processes may be assumed in order to account for the reductions:

[7] This would immediately seem most natural since the vowel is long in monosyllabic forms (without a stop suffix).

1 devoicing before /t/,
2 devoicing of /D/ + /D/, and
3 shortening of geminates.

The relationship between these processes and vowel quantity is a straightforward one, since VOWEL SHORTNESS IS ASSOCIATED WITH DEVOICING BEFORE /t/ (but not with devoicing of /D/ + /D/, which probably must be stated as a 'late' rule), cf. [sat], [møt], [brɛt] (neut.) with process (1) and shortness versus [føː't], [brɛː't] (past part.), [leː'ðt] ([leð't]) with no (obligatory) shortness of the vowel.

If we turn now to the velar and labial series, there is the same association between vowel shortness and devoicing before /t/, cf. [kɒgt], [kløgt][8] versus [klɔː'ɣt], all with underlying /G/, [købt] with underlying /B/, and [sdift], [drɛft], [hɑft] versus [sgɛː'ut] (or [sgɛu't]), [læː'ut] (or [læu't]) all with underlying /v/.

The fact that underlying /v/ is represented as /f/ before /t/ in forms with obligatory vowel shortness but otherwise remains voiced corroborates the assumption that the process associated with vowel shortness is a matter of VOICEDNESS, the alternation between stops and continuants being a secondary phenomenon. It thus seems legitimate to formulate a vowel shortening rule and a devoicing rule, and to let one of these depend on the other: that is, either

$$[+\text{OBSTRUENT}] \to [-\text{VOICED}] \text{ (conditions to be specified)}$$

$$[\text{V}] \to [-\text{LONG}]/\_\_ \begin{bmatrix} -\text{VOICED} \\ -\text{SIBILANT} \end{bmatrix} [-\text{VOICED}]$$

or

$$[\text{V}] \to [-\text{LONG}] \text{ (conditions to be specified)}$$

$$[+\text{OBSTRUENT}] \to [-\text{VOICED}]/\_\_ \begin{bmatrix} \text{V} \\ -\text{LONG} \end{bmatrix} \begin{bmatrix} -\text{VOICED} \\ -\text{SIBILANT} \end{bmatrix}$$

(Note that the rules normally do not apply to combinations with /s/; the problem of whether /s/ is defined as a sibilant in the classificatory matrix is not at issue here.)

---

[8] I disregard here the fact that there are a few words with a long vowel before these groups, e.g. *sagte* 'low, soft (of sound)', *lægd* 'recruiting area'; these are quite obviously exceptions to the general pattern.

The former ordering may seem preferable because it is immediately plausible that vowels should be shortened before voiceless clusters.[9] (This is supported by the sporadic occurrence of shortening also before /s/ plus stop, cf. the adj. neut. [lyst] 'light' and the noun [blɛst] 'wind' as against the past part. [lyː'st] 'lit', [blɛː'st] 'blown'.)

However, apart from the obligatory shortening dealt with here there is in Danish a strong tendency (obviously to be stated as a much later, more or less optional, rule) toward vowel shortening before a voiced fricative or before a voiced semivowel generated from a voiced fricative (see Section 2.6, item (iii) above). Thus it would not be against the general phonetic tendencies of the language to posit vowel shortening before clusters beginning with a voiced fricative; that is, the devoicing rule need not precede the shortening rule. The second ordering of the rules is consequently possible, too.

A third possibility is not to postulate any ordering between the processes. They can be collapsed into one complex rule. Within the framework of this chapter, this solution is preferable, as nothing is gained by the ordering.

No matter how the two processes are ordered, the conditions under which the complex of rules comes to apply must be stated.

If the neuter forms of adjectives are disregarded, the conditions are quite simple: vowel shortening and devoicing occur in forms with a nonsibilant obstruent before /t/. In adjectives, however, the two processes are practically limited to forms with a cluster of homorganic obstruents: /D, t/ + /t/. This important difference between adjectives and other word classes can be marked in the phonological notation by using a special juncture symbol before the neuter suffix, but of course this is just another way of stating that the rules are conditioned by higher-level information.

It has been assumed above that all the words under consideration have an underlying long vowel. In fact this is not at all certain. Some alternations between phonetically long and short vowels are quite certainly to be explained as due to lengthening, rather than shortening, rules. However, a consideration of verbs and adjectives from this angle gives a very complex picture, and it would lead too far to go into this here. The presentation given above has been preferred for the present discussion because of the relative ease with which the rules can be stated (see below).

---

[9] I am indebted to Dr Sven Öhman for a discussion of this point.

It remains to be considered whether /(B), D, G/ are stops or fricatives in the classificatory matrix. If these consonants are defined as FRICA-TIVES there must be a special rule changing /B/ into a stop in most environments (although with some alternation with [u̯], cf. Section 2.6 above).[10] Taken as a whole, the series /B, D, G/ must be changed into a series of stops whenever these consonants are devoiced. (I disregard here the possibility of [xt] beside [gt].)

It is a difficulty that the rule changing devoiced /B, D, G/ into stops must not apply to the fricatives /f, v, s/. According to modern distinctive feature terminology (Chomsky and Halle 1968: 176–7, 329) these latter may be defined as STRIDENT (although Danish voiced [v] is hardly strident in a phonetic sense), and I have here chosen to define /B, D, G/ as nonstrident in contradistinction to them.

It is possible to collapse the voicing and closing rules into one complex rule (provided that the behaviour of /B/ in environments other than before /t/ is taken care of by another rule). If vowel shortening is included as well, the whole complex of rules can be given in this somewhat informal way:

$$[\text{V}] \begin{bmatrix} +\text{OBSTRUENT} \\ <-\text{STRIDENT}> \end{bmatrix} \rightarrow [-\text{LONG}] \begin{bmatrix} -\text{VOICED} \\ <-\text{CONTINUANT}> \end{bmatrix} / \underline{\quad} \begin{bmatrix} -\text{CONTINUANT} \\ -\text{VOICED} \end{bmatrix}$$

(with the grammatical constraints indicated above).

If, alternatively, /B, D, G/ in weak position are STOPS in the classificatory (phonemic) matrix, the rule above is simplified by the deletion of <-STRIDENT> and <-CONTINUANT>. In return, there must be a rule weakening voiced stops to fricatives in weak position:

$$[+\text{VOICED}] \rightarrow [+\text{CONTINUANT}] / \begin{bmatrix} \text{WP} \\ \underline{\quad} \end{bmatrix}$$

This rule does not apply if devoicing takes place according to the rule above: that is there is an order between these two rules, the former applying before the latter.

---

[10] The specific problems associated with /B/ have not been properly considered in this chapter. It should be noted that the numerous words with postvocalic labial fricative or semivowel pose a great problem since some or several of them should perhaps be generated from underlying /B/ rather than /v/. Hjelmslev (1951) explains some differences of stød (cf. skov 'wood' with stød vs. tov 'rope' without stød) in terms of a difference /b/:/u/. A consideration of problems associated with the stød cannot, however, be contained within the framework of this chapter.

The voiced fricatives generated one way or the other are further opened to semivowels or dropped under certain conditions. These later rules will not be formalized here (see, however, Sections 2.6 and 2.7 above and Rischel 1969: 191–3).

It is apparently possible to make a reasonable description no matter whether /D, G/ of weak positions are assumed to be fricatives /ð, ɣ/ or voiced stops /d, g/, phonemically. (/B/ requires special rules, which will not be formulated here, no matter which analysis is chosen.) The former solution may be preferable since it postulates no modification of /D, G/, that is /ð, ɣ/ in the most general environments (the fricative manifestations being found not only in intervocalic and final positions but also, for example, before /s/ and even before /t/ in forms like [klɔː'ɣt]). However, the latter solution (i.e. phonemic stops) has two advantages. First, it assigns the same features to /b, d, g/ in strong position and /B, D, G/ in weak position, whereas these are phonemically different if the latter are fricatives in the underlying matrix. (Note, however, that the total number of distinctive features is not affected since /f, v/ must be distinguished as fricatives from /p, b/ anyway.) Secondly, the latter solution makes the alternations between [d, g] in strong position and [ð, ɣ] in weak position found in some foreign words (*filologi* versus *filolog*, etc.; see Section 2.3 above) fit into the general framework without requiring any additional rule. According to the former solution (i.e. /D, G/ = /ð, ɣ/) an additional weakening rule must be set up in order to take care of these alternations. A rule common to both native and foreign words can be obtained only if [b, d, g] in strong positions are supposed to be generated from underlying fricatives. One may then set up a general CLOSING rule:

$$
\begin{bmatrix} +\text{OBSTRUENT} \\ +\text{VOICED} \\ -\text{LABIAL} \end{bmatrix} \rightarrow \begin{bmatrix} -\text{CONTINUANT} \\ (-\text{VOICED}) \end{bmatrix} \Big/ \begin{bmatrix} \text{SP} \\ \underline{} \end{bmatrix}
$$

This rule is however intuitively wrong, as it turns the whole thing upside down.

From a general point of view it is apparently profitable to generate [ð, ɣ] from /d, g/ rather than generating [d, g] from /ð, ɣ/. However, this may be true only as long as both strong and weak positions are taken into consideration. If only weak positions are considered, that is the positions in which the morphological and derivational processes of native words occur, it may be simpler to have the rules work the opposite way, from /ð, ɣ/ to [d, g]. It may not be quite meaningless to compare this analytical ambiguity with the double origin of the sounds in question: from old stops and from old fricatives.

The relationship between stops and fricatives is a classic problem in Danish phonology. This paper does not solve it but is an attempt to show that the problem is basically a morphological (morphophonemic) one. It is not just a question of arranging a phoneme system in the most economical way.

3

On Functional Load in Phonemics[1]

If a linguistic text is looked upon as a unilinear sequence of phonemes, it is a rather simple procedure to measure the relative frequency of each phoneme. One sets up an overall inventory of phonemes and postulates that it is meaningful to characterize the use of the different phonemes as 'drawn from a hat'. The overall frequencies are computed, and the probability of occurrence of each phoneme is expressed by its relative overall frequency. One can also focus on 'items in context' and compute the probabilities of the different phonemes occuring in a specific context or in a specific class of contexts. And finally, one can look upon the text as a 'linear Markoff-process' and interpret the probability of a specific sequence as the product of the subsequent *transition probabilities*.[2] This in itself is a quite trivial procedure.

Let us say that we are faced with a code with the inventory *a, b, c, d*, and that we want to describe the probability of the sequence *abcd* in terms of transition probabilities. We choose at random a series of sequences from our text material (for the sake of simplicity we can say that the sequences are all 'whole utterances' of the same length). The sample may, e.g. comprise ten sequences: *babc, abcd, adba, abbd, bacd, dbca, acba, abdc, abca, abbd* (the material must of course be much larger in practice). The sequences (of which two appear to be identical occurrences) can then be arranged as follows:

abbd
abbd
abca
abcd (NB)
abdc

---

[1] Reprinted from *SMIL: Statistical Methods in Linguistics* 1 (1962): 13–23.

[2] Transition probability is a fundamental concept in *information theory*: high transition probability means low information value.

acba
adba
babc
bacd
dbca

The transition probabilities for $a + b + c + d$ can now easily be computed. In the first state a stands for 7/10, i.e. the probability of a occuring is .7; in the second state b after a stands for 5/7 (five of the observed transitions from a result in b), i.e. the probability of b occuring after a is .7143; in the third state c after ab stands for 2/5, i.e. the probability of c occuring after ab is .4; in the fourth state d after abc stands for 1/2, i.e. the probability of d occuring after abc is .5. The probability of *abcd* occuring is thus .7 $\times$ .7143 $\times$ .4 $\times$ .5 = .1, which is evidently right according to our material, since 1/10 of all the sequences we have observed is constituted by the occurrence of *abcd*. In the analysis of real languages the situation will of course be enormously more complicated, because linguistic texts do not consist of such independent sequences.[3]

However fruitful the purely sequential analysis may be, it raises serious problems in phonemics just as it does in syntax. A *graphic* notation (writing system) may be purely unilinear, so that every occurrence of an element is defined as *after* and *before* the remaining parts of the sequence: in the sequence *abcd* in our code above, *c* comes after *ab* but before *d*. But in the interpretation of *phonetic* sequences the assumption of unilinearity causes difficulties of three kinds.

(1) If phonetic sequences are to be rendered as phonemically unilinear, there are two alternatives: (i) all that is generally looked upon as 'suprasegmental' phonemes: stresses, tones, and the like, must be restated as parts of the unilinear sequence, for example as *features* of the vowels (in Mandarin Chinese, a syllable *san* with high tone might thus be analysed as /sa^{1}n/, and a syllable *san* with rising tone as /sa^{2}n/, (/a^1/ and /a^2/ being different members of the vowel inventory). (ii) The 'suprasegmentals' must by some restatement be interpreted as *segmental phonemes*. The former solution (i) is chosen in Jakobson and Halle's (1956) phoneme theory which on the whole seems to

---

[3] The various approaches based on a sequential aspect of language are illustrated in such works as Herdan (1956) and Guiraud (1960). For a numerical application to a specific language, see Roberts (1961).

represent the sequential view in its purest and most consequent form.[4]

(2) Another difficulty is the well-known fact that certain contrasts between phonemes are 'neutralized' under specific conditions, cf. the neutralization of the opposition aspirated stop : unaspirated stop in final position in Danish: [pas] : [bas] but [lap] = [lab].[5] If one does not want to speak of neutralization, one is sometimes forced to make an arbitrary choice between equally reasonable interpretations (Danish [-p, -b] = /p/ or = /b/?) This arbitrariness reduces the validity of computations of overall phoneme frequencies (the rank order of Danish /p/ and /b/ according to frequency of occurrence will depend on the way [-p, -b] is interpreted).

The 'existence' of neutralizations makes it essential to work with more than a single set of variables. The overall probability of occurrence of a phoneme, e.g. of /b/ in Danish, has no real sense if it is admitted that /b/ is sometimes neutralized with /p/, for this means that under certain circumstances the phoneme occurrences are 'drawn from a hat' containing /p/-slips *and* /b/-slips, while under other circumstances the phoneme occurrences are 'drawn from a hat' in which /p/ and /b/ *are not* distinguished on the slips. We must therefore compute the relative frequency of those *places* where /p/ and /b/ *are* distinguished, and the relative frequency of those *places* where /p/ and /b/ *are not* distinguished; only within the former class can we compute the relative frequency of the phoneme /b/ (as against /p/, etc.). As far as overall frequencies are concerned, it is strictly speaking only meaningful to compute the relative frequency of the common denominator for /p/ and /b/, i.e. the frequency of the 'labial stop'. The invalidation of the concept 'overall frequency of a phoneme' may perhaps be a reason to focus the interest on distinctive features (or 'linear phonemes' and 'additive components'[6]) rather than phonemes in the ordinary sense.

It may, however, be possible to introduce a concept of 'neutralization' in the purely sequential aspect of language as a Markoff-process. This would involve that surely not only the probabilities but the code inventory itself varies throughout sequences: *after certain sequences the difference between two elements is neutralized.* In Danish /p/ has

---

[4] For an example of the other solution cf. Rischel (1960).
[5] It is true that one *can* argue in favour of the solution [-p, -b] = /p/.
[6] Cf. Voegelin (1956).

one probability of occurrence and /b/ another, but this is only true under certain conditions; after /a/, for example, we cannot compute the probability of /p/ or of /b/ but only the probability of the common matching unit: p/b. This solution presupposes that all the neutralizations we want to register are defined in terms of '*after*' (not 'before').

In all contributions to linguistic methodology which build on the basic notions of information theory, it seems to be implied that linguistic sequences are built up of members from one inventory. The probabilities of the different elements occuring vary from stage to stage, but in principle the possibilities of choice are the same throughout the text. One may register restrictions against specific combinations (e.g. against geminate clusters in English), but this does not alter the viewpoint: there is one fixed inventory of phonemes, and all combinations among these phonemes are looked upon as latent possibilities (the mere formulation of a restriction against geminate clusters presupposes that it is meaningful to speak of geminate clusters in the investigation of English, namely as a theoretical possibility). This assumption concerning the overall-nature of the phonemic inventory is hardly tenable, and at any rate it is quite unnecessary: as outlined above the concept of *neutralization* may be introduced without causing any problem at all.

(3) Although some of the difficulties in making an adequate linear transcription are eliminated by such *restatements* as mentioned under (1) and (2) above, there are still some fundamental weaknesses in the sequential description of phonemic structures, weaknesses which can probably only be eliminated by a hierarchical analysis.

Just as the constituents of the grammatic phrase combine in different steps in constituents belonging to different steps in a hierarchy (*or in a transformation procedure*), so the phonemes '*cluster*' in syllables, and these syllables 'cluster' in larger units, which in turn 'cluster' in still larger units, and so on. This clustering is not a thing which can be adequately described in terms of the mere distribution of the linear phonemes (as is generally maintained by the 'distributionalists'); it is a formal arrangement by means of *phonemic features of arrangement* (analogous to the grammatic features of arrangement).

The 'prosodic' features are probably the most problematic items in phonemic analysis: as a matter of fact they are seldom accounted for in a really adequate way. The phenomena need a *hierarchical* interpretation: juncture differences and stress differences reflect differences of hierarchical arrangement (this is the obvious reason why one is instinctively reluctant to set juncture phonemes on a par with other phonemes and to interpret stresses as features of vowels).

In the *hierarchical analysis* one must of course proceed step by step *down the 'ladder'*. On some step one arrives at the syllables, and one can then treat the material of syllables statistically by computing the frequencies of different syllable types. One can then proceed one step and compute the frequencies of the different syllable positions, and within each position finally the frequencies of the different phonemes. The procedure will be described in somewhat more detail in the next section in connection with the measurement of the functional load of phonemic contrasts.

3.1.   FUNCTIONAL LOAD OF PHONEMIC CONTRASTS

As pointed out by Martin Kloster Jensen in his report to the Scandinavian Symposium on Statistical Linguistics (1960)[7] the functional load (the degree of utilization) of the different *oppositions* among phonemes is an important thing to measure, and it is essential *not* to confine oneself to measurements of the frequencies of occurrence of the single phonemes.[8] Hockett (1955: 216–17) has outlined a method to compute the functional load of a contrast (opposition) on the basis of the Markoff-process aspect of linguistic messages, but he regretfully admits that 'the amount of counting and computation necessary is formidable'. The keyword of the approach is *entropy*, that is 'the uncertainty for each state, as to what the next state will be'. (Hockett 1955: 9). In the terminology of information theory, 'the functional load carried by a given contrast is the ratio of the entropy of the unchanged system' (*ibid.*).

A more feasible procedure is obtained if one chooses some unit as the frame of reference. The *word* may (in some languages) be a suitable unit. Within the word one can measure the direct differential power of each contrast on the basis of the number of minimal pairs in which it is operative (for example, /b/ : /m/ in *bad : mad, bake : make*, etc.). It will of course be a huge task to compute the differential power of the

---

[7] Editors' note: The meeting was organized by Hans Karlgren and held at Sundbyholm in Sweden in 1960. However, we are unable to validate the reference.

[8] On the various concepts of 'functional load', cf. Kloster Jensen (1961: 34–6).

contrasts, even if one limits oneself to the *differential power within the word*, but it is perfectly possible to measure it both within the lexicon and in words in *running text*. These two sets of data must probably be obtained independently, although the correlation between them may be fairly close. Herdan (1958: 9) has shown that in English the frequency of occurrence of the consonants in text can be derived from the functional load in the lexicon by a computation of chance: 'The mutual relation between phonemes as regards functional burdening determines that of the categories of phonemes in speech output'. However, the correlation may not be quite as close in the case of *contrasts*, for the differential power of a contrast in the text will to a large extent depend on the existence of minimal pairs among the most frequent words.

Let us say that we have registered a contrast /p/ : /t/ in some language, and that the lexicon shows five minimal pairs: /po/ : /to/, /pana/ : /tana/, /ipo/ : /ito/, /nipa/ : /nita/, and /poi/ : /toi/. Now, if the words /po/, /pana/, /to/, /tana/ are extremely frequent in the language, the contrast /p/ : /t/ will have *a high functional load in the text*. If, however, /po/, /pana/, /ito/, /nita/ are extremely frequent, but the other words with /p/, or /t/ rather infrequent, then the contrast /p/ : /t/ has *a low functional load in the text*, although the number of minimal pairs in the lexicon is the same, and *although the frequency of occurrence of /p/ and of /t/ may be the same as in the other situation*. The functional load of a contrast in the text depends on the existence of minimal pairs of words that are *both* frequent. It can be computed in the following way: for each minimal pair in the lexicon one lists the two words under different headings: in our example above we must set up a list with two columns for /p/ : /t/ and list /po/, /pana/, etc., in one column and /to/, /tana/, etc., in the other. (If a word /para/ is found, /pana/ will of course also figure on the list for /n/ : /r/). We then count the frequency of occurrence of each single item on this list and similarly for the other lists (representing the minimal pairs of other contrasts). After this has been done we take each minimal pair and multiply the frequency of occurrence of the one member with the frequency of occurrence of the other member. These products are then added (for each list separately), and the sum is a measure of the functional load of the contrasts in question (in running text).

Martin Kloster Jensen (1961: 36) states that 'the study of the degree of utilization of the contrasts has no proper method'. This especially applies to tonemic contrasts of the Norwegian type. As far as 'segmental' phoneme contrasts are concerned, it was pointed out above that the functional load of a contrast in the lexicon does not directly reflect the degree of utilization of the contrast in speech. The method for estimation of the functional load within the word in running text obviously gives a better approximation, but still the situation is very much simplified. Even if both members of a minimal pair are frequent, this does not mean that the minimal contrast between them is necessarily used very often in speech communication. The two words may be bound to completely different types of context, so that it is only in very rare cases that they directly 'commute'. Such pairs as *bad* : *mad, bake* : *make* may be commutable in a good many phrase contexts (*a bad boy* : *a mad boy*), but such a pair as *bean* : *mean* can hardly occur in identical contexts (they can only be commuted in one-word utterances).

In order to get an optimal approximation to the real degree of utilization of a phonemic contrast, one must therefore apply the method outlined above to phoneme contrasts in words, word contrasts in phrases, phrase contrasts in sentences, etc., i.e. one must use a hierarchical procedure. In this optimal form of the procedure, the amount of counting and computation necessary will probably be just as formidable as it will be in the sequential procedure outlined by Hockett (see the beginning of this section). It is, however, obvious that in practice one must stop somewhere on the hierarchical ladder—i.e. one must choose a suitable *highest unit* for reference; if one does not do so, one will finally observe that everything is in complementary distribution with everything else (the context of each phoneme occurrence being the whole text material). So the computations will not be endless anyhow.

It is essential to know about the degree of utilization of a contrast, because it will show how much the coalescence of the two phonemes involved will impair correct identification of speech. This factor must of course be taken into consideration in sound history, although there does not seem to be any simple correlation between low functional load and tendency towards coalescence (cf. the non-coalescence of English /ʒ/ : /z/ in spite of the obviously very low functional load of the contrast).

However, the distinction of minimal pairs may not be the only important or not even the most important factor in speech identification. A contrast may be very important for the fluent identification of utterances and words, although there are few and infrequent minimal pairs.

If phonetic sequences are interpreted as unilinear phoneme sequences (i.e. without a phonemically distinctive hierarchical arrangement) we must assume that in principle all differences between phonemes are relevant in the identification of the sequences. In the sequence /grey/, /g/ is then identified as non-/k/, non-/b/, etc., in fact as nothing except /g/. And if the structures /grey/ and /haws/ are identified as different, it may theoretically be explained in the following way: /g/ is identified as different from /h/, /r/ as different from /a/, /e/ as different from /w/, and /y/ as different from /s/. There is obviously no restriction against oppositions between vowel and consonant: every phoneme is distinctively different from every other phoneme. It is only a *secondary* process that /ey/ of /grey/ is found to correspond positionally to /aw/ of /haws/, so that proper matching of the two structures is /g/ : /Ø/; /r/ : /h/, /e/ : /a/, /y/ : /w/, /Ø/ : /s/. The 'proper matching' presupposes that one has first identified the peaks of /grey/ and /haws/ by confronting the (already identified) sequential units within each structure: in /grey/, the constituent parts are confronted with each other and the peak is found to be constituted by /e/ + /y/; similarly for /haws/. Also the identification of the inner organization of /grey/ and of /haws/ thus involves a confrontation of vowels and consonants. From the sequential point of view, the distinction between positions and between positionally-defined categories such as vowels and consonants, is obviously a secondary thing: the result of a phonetic-distributional classification. The primary contrasts are between all the elements of the code.[9] It will be an almost impossible task to measure the functional load of each contrast within the framework of this theory, which also gives a wrong picture of the process of identification. As stated by Mol and Uhlenbeck (1959), the identification of speech must involve not only an identification of phonemes on the basis of the distinctive differences between their phonic manifestations, but also an identification on the basis of place and position and context. In the terminology adopted here: the process of identification must involve hierarchical processes as well as sequential matching processes.

From the hierarchical point of view the process may be assumed to be as follows. First, through a whole series of steps, /grey/ is identified as one of the few words possible in the context in question, and afterwards it is identified completely through an analysis of its shape. We can rather easily make statistical computations on this basis

---

[9] Cf. Roman Jakobson's theory of distinctive features!

by starting with the wordforms, i.e. by assuming that the words are deprived of context (this means that our description will be nothing but an approximation). A description in which all steps are taken into account is hardly practicable. The essential thing is to *know* that we are making an oversimplification.

The hierarchical analysis of /grey/ may perhaps run as follows: the form is first identified as having two constituent parts: 'initial margin' /gr/ and 'centre' /ey/, while /haws/ is identified as having three constituent parts: 'initial margin' /h/, 'centre' /aw/, and 'final margin' /s/. Secondly, both constituents of /grey/ and the central constituent of /haws/ are identified as consisting of two phonemes each, while the marginal parts of /haws/ are found to consist of one phoneme only. Only after these steps in the identification procedure do we arrive at the step where each phoneme is identified not by an elimination of *all* other phonemes but by an elimination of those other phonemes which can occur in the same position within the syllable: /g/ of /grey/ is identified as non-/k/, non-/b/, etc., but not as non-/h/ or non-/e/, for these phonemes do not belong to the set.

We thus see that from the sequential point of view all differences among phonemes are relevant, but from the hierarchical point of view only the differences among phonemes in the same syllable position are relevant. It may be discussed how perception actually works in the human nervous system: do we identify the syllable structure first and the single phonemes afterwards, or the other way round? I see no reason why the perception should not involve both sorts of processes simultaneously. At any rate, it must be of interest to measure the functional load of phoneme differences from both points of view. It will now be outlined briefly how this can be done from the hierarchical point of view.

Let us say that we have a language with three syllable types: CV, CVC, and VC, i.e. with two consonantal positions: precentral and postcentral, and let us say that we have registered four consonants /b c d f/ in the precentral position with the following probabilities of occurrence in this position: /b/: .4, /c/: .3, /d/: .2, /f/: .1. We get a relative measure of the functional load of each difference between two phonemes by multiplying the probabilities of the phonemes: probability of /b/ × probability of /c/ = .12 for /b/: /c/, etc.

This gives for /b/ : /c/ .12, for /b/ : /d/ .08, for /b/ : /f/ .04, for /c/ : /d/ .06, for /c/ : /f/ .03, and for /d/ : /f/ .02. We now divide each of these numbers by the sum of the numbers, result: for /b/ : /c/ .12 divided by

.35 = .3428, i.e. 3.4, for /b/ : /d/ .23, for /b/ : /f/ .11, for /c/ : /d/ .17, for /c/ : /f/ .09, and for /d/ : /f/ .06. These numbers show the functional load of each phoneme difference in the precentral position. Similar computations must be made for the postcentral position. Here we may find quite different results, for example only .15 for /b/ : /c/.

Now, let us say that the three syllable-types are not equally frequent: the percentages are 60% for CV, 30% for CVC, and 10% for VC. If we want to know the overall load of the difference /b/ : /c/ within the consonant positions we must weight the results according to the different frequencies of the different positions. The percentages of the different syllable types show that for every ten syllables there will be, on average, 6 + 3 = 9 precentral and 3 + 1 = 4 postcentral positions, together with 13 consonant positions. The average functional load of /b/ : /c/ among the consonant differences is thus:

$$\frac{.34 \times 9}{13} + \frac{.15 \times 4}{13} = .28$$

The whole procedure outlined here works well as long as one keeps within one position or within the positions in which both phonemes have the same status. But here the problem of *neutralization* comes in again. If we want to measure the functional load of /p/ : /s/ in Danish, we will encounter difficulties because postvocalic /p/ = /b/, i.e. we cannot keep /p/ : /s/ distinct from /b/ : /s/.[10] This means that if we do not keep our analysis within positions where the phonemes have the same status, we will have to go a step down the hierarchical ladder and take the distinctive features (components), rather than the phonemes, as the terms of the contrasts to be investigated, i.e. the units referred to will no longer be /p/ : /s/ and the like but 'stop': 'continuant', 'labial': 'nonlabial', and the like. The hierarchical approach attaches a primary importance to the ultimate constituents of linguistic structures.[11]

[10] One may, however, choose a solution suggested by Mr Tom Broch: the occurrences of the postvocalic labial stop are divided into /p/s and /b/s in accordance with the relative frequencies of these two phonemes in other positions.

[11] The present paper has in previous drafts been read to Språkvitenskapelig Forening i Bergen, The Scandinavian Symposium on Statistical Linguistics (1960) and Norsk Forening for Sprogvitenskap. The author is especially indebted to Professor Bjarne Ulvestad for valuable critical remarks.

4

Derivation as a Syntactic Process in Greenlandic[1]

4.1. INTRODUCTION

A major issue in modern linguistic theory has been how to account for derivational morphology. Chomsky (1970) argued that there are some types of nominalization which cannot be adequately described as transforms of sentence-like structures, and which accordingly must be present as constituents in underlying representations. This 'lexicalist' attitude towards derivational morphology is taken more generally by Kiefer (1972). It is argued that derived words function essentially like non-derived words, that derivations are often lexicalized, that most types of derivation are only quasi-productive, and that derivational elements are more closely associated with the stem than flexional elements, all of this supporting a distinction between inflexion and derivation, as well as a non-transformational approach to the latter.

In the present paper[2] I demonstrate that the complex wordforms of a polysynthetic language like Greenlandic Eskimo do not altogether agree with this view of derivational morphology. Affixation is generally a productive process, also with affixes which cannot in any reasonable sense be called flexional. Moreover, affixation in this language seems to involve transformational processes since it may apply to complex noun phrases and even to inflected wordforms. Hence the question arises whether affixation in polysynthetic languages like West Greenlandic

[1] Reprinted from *Derivational processes: proceedings of the KVAL Sea-borne Spring Seminar, held on board M/S Bore, 9–10 April, 1972, Stockholm–Turku*, F. Kiefer (ed.). Stockholm: Research Group for Quantitative Linguistics (1972): 60–73.

[2] In this somewhat revised version I have left out a section on causative verbs, which seems to me unnecessary for the main argument of the paper.

Eskimo requires a more powerful theory of derivation than assumed, e.g. by Kiefer, or whether the crucial examples can be dismissed as irrelevant to the issue. The latter solution is possible, of course, if it is meaningful to describe the constructions in question as sequences of words rather than as single words. I shall present some evidence bearing on this question.

4.2. AFFIXATION TO NOUN PHRASES

Noun phrases in Eskimo may contain possessive constructions or appositional constructions, or both. In the following I shall deal only with possessive constructions. These constructions (whose syntactic derivation is not at issue here; for discussion see Mey 1969 and Rischel 1971*b*) may consist of a noun denoting the possessor plus a noun denoting the possessed item. The former, whose presence is structurally optional, is (under certain morphological conditions) marked by a case affix (*-p* in the examples below), whereas the latter carries an affix or a cluster of affixes that indicate the grammatical number of the possessed item as well as that of the possessor (*-a* in the examples below). There are also possessive constructions with a marking for grammatical person, but such examples (involving 1st or 2nd person or reflexive) are disregarded here for simplicity.

The surface structure of possessive constructions with two nouns is illustrated by the following examples:

(1) *niqï* 'meat', with affixes: *niqi-* or *niqa-*

(2) *niqaa* 'flesh, singular item of singular possessor', i.e. 'his/her/its flesh'

(3) *tuttu* 'reindeer'

(4) *tuttup niqaa* 'of reindeer its flesh', 'reindeer meat'

(5) (*niqï* + *utï* → *niqaati-* or *niqaata-* (with *aa* by normal assimilation of *a* + *u*) 'meat being possessed'

(6) *niqaataa* 'his/her meat owned'

(7) *piniartuq* 'hunter'

(8) *piniartup niqaataa* 'of hunter his meat owned', i.e. 'the hunter's meat supply'.

The stem meaning 'possessed meat' in (5), (6), (8) is derived from the stem meaning 'meat' by means of an affix *-uti-*, *-uta-*, which occurs in numerous other forms of the language.[3]

Constructions like (4) have, at least in principle, two readings. They may refer to a particular individual with the attribute referred to, or they may be semantic entities on a par with mass nouns like *niqi*. On the latter reading (4) is equivalent to a nominal compound in languages having this type of construction (cf. Danish *rensdyrkød*).

What now happens if the Greenlander wants to say 'the hunter's (supply of) reindeer meat'? According to (8) we should have a construction of the form *piniartup* X-*utaa*, but since X should be identical in meaning to (4), X and (4) should be transforms of the same underlying representation.

One might expect derivation with the affix *-uti-/-uta-* to require that the noun phrase be replaced by a single surface word. However, what we actually find is (9):

(9)   *piniartup tuttup niqaataa*

Faced with such constructions one might claim that *tuttup niqï-* (*tuttup niqa-*) is hereby proven to be one compound word, which is expanded by derivation. However, this leaves the morphological parallelism between such compounds and 'normal' possessive constructions (compare (4) with (8)) unexplained. The interesting thing about *tuttup niqaataa* is that it is formally ambiguous: it can be interpreted either as

[*tuttu* + *p niqï*] + *utï* + *a* 'his supply of reindeer meat'

or as

tuttu + *p*[*niqï* + *utï*] + *a* 'Reindeer's (supply of) meat'

and correspondingly, (9) has two readings. In addition to 'the hunter's reindeer meat' it may also mean 'the hunter Reindeer's meat'. The existence of this ambiguity[4] shows that the apparent 'compound'

---

[3] Cf. *amia* 'his skin' versus *amiutaa* 'the fur he possesses'. The distinction is not exactly one of non-alienable versus alienable properties, unless the former are taken to include all items forming an integral part of the outfit for Eskimo life, cf. *illua* 'his house' versus *illuutaa* 'the house which he possesses (and which may be rented by somebody else)', also cf. *qimmia* 'his dog', not **qimmiutaa*.

[4] The latter reading is perhaps rather far-fetched. According to mag.art. Robert Petersen (Copenhagen, Institute of Eskimology) it is conceivable in referring to a situation where there are two persons both called *tuttu* 'Reindeer', and where one of these is distinguished from the other by being a hunter.

does not necessarily differ in surface representation from a succession of two wordforms. It seems to me immediately more reasonable to conclude that (9) on the first-mentioned reading does in fact exhibit affixation to a noun phrase.[5] The syntactic derivation of this structure involves certain transformations which attach the affix to the head of the construction and blocks the appearance of preceding flexional affixes in the same word. There are several affixes which behave in the same way, cf.:

(10) *siffap naalagaa* 'of shore its surveyor'

(11) *siffap naalagaqarput* 'they have a chief of the shore'

(12) *niqiturpuq* 'he eats meat'

(13) *tuttup niqiturpuq* 'he eats reindeer meat.'[6]

Again, the sequence *tuttup niqi-* is semantically equivalent to (4) and forms a constituent at the point in the syntactic derivation where the more complex structure is formed.

It has been demonstrated above that affixes may be attached to the last constituent of possessive constructions (for further examples of acceptable, or at least conceivable, constructions of this kind see Rischel 1971*b*: 234–6 with footnotes). In the types exemplified the affixation implies absence of the inflection that otherwise characterizes the constituent of a corresponding possessive construction (see e.g. (9) versus (4)).

It is different, however, with certain affixes which involve a notion of directionality towards something. This is illustrated by the examples below (also see Rischel 1971*b*: 233):

---

[5] There are of course a number of intricate questions associated with the generation of phrases like *tuttup niqaa*. One can imagine two readings of (4): 'reindeer meat' and 'the meat from the reindeer' (or 'Reindeer's flesh'). I assume that the embedding of the phrase in another noun phrase, as in (8), is possible only on the former reading, i.e. *piniartup* and *tuttup* cannot both have specific referents (unless they refer to the same person). If, for brevity, we refer to the two readings of *tuttup niqaa* as respectively a 'semantic compound' and a 'semantic phrase', there must be some rule complex in syntax which makes the semantic compound appear as a noun phrase (cf. the idea of 'idiom generator' sketched very tentatively in Rischel 1971*a*).

[6] Example (13) cannot mean 'the reindeer eats meat' or 'Reindeer eats meat'. The latter meaning would be expressed as *tuttu niqiturpuq* (without case affix *-p*, because the construction is intransitive). However, the final *p* of *tuttup* is dropped by an external sandhi rule in casual speech so that the two sentences may overlap phonetically.

(14) *upirnawik* 'Upernavik' (place-name)

(15) *upirnawiliaq* 'traveller going to Up'.

(16) *nuna* 'country'

(17) *kalaallit nunaat* 'of Greenlanders their country' i.e. 'Greenland'

(18) *kalaallit nunaaliaq* 'traveller going to Greenland'

As shown by (15) the affix involved here is *-liaq*. Hence, instead of (18) we should expect **kalaallit nunaliaq* in accordance with the examples presented earlier. The form *nunaaliaq* can be explained only as derived from the form *nunaat*. The deletion of *t* is explicable by a phonological rule of truncation which applies regularly to consonants before this affix (cf. the deletion of *k* in (15)), i.e. affixes like *-liaq* are attached to inflected forms *without affecting their overt inflection*, although the wordform as such is affected by phonological rules which must be stated anyway.

4.3. AFFIXATION OR ENCLISIS?

Swadesh (1946) speaks of *enclisis* as a relatively unimportant phenomenon in Eskimo. By enclisis he refers to the occurrence of such elements as *-lu* 'and', *-guuq/-ŋuuq* 'somebody says that -', cf. (20), (22), (24):

(19) *qimussirarluni nannunniarpuq* 'while he was out on a sledge trip (cf. *qimussit* 'sledge (in function)') he hunted bears' (cf. *nannunniaq* 'bear-hunter')

(20) *qimussirarlunilu nannunniarpuq* 'he was out on a sledge trip and he hunted bears'

(21) *aap* 'yes'

(22) *aaŋŋuuq* 'yes, somebody (or: he, she) said (or: is supposed to say)'

(23) *iqaluffuarniariartuqquʃaagaluaqaagut* 'we have actually got a strict order to go out fishing sharks'

(24) *iqialuffuarniariartuqquʃaagaluaqaaguŋŋuuq* 'it is said that we have actually got *ditto*'.

((22) and (24) exemplify that a final consonant is retained before *-ŋuuq* but assimilated to ŋ by a phonological rule applying to all clusters).

When looking at forms like (23) and (24), which are perfectly acceptable constructions in this language,[7] one may perhaps question the whole terminology used so far. *Why* are such stretches to be treated differently from multi-word sentences in other languages? Consider the following two examples:

(25)   *niqiturpuq* (cf. (1) *niqi*) '(he) meat-eats' i.e. 'he eats (some) meat'

(26)   *niqi niriwaa* 'meat he eats it' i.e. 'he eats the meat'

The forms written as typographical wholes in these and other examples above share a number of characteristics. (i) Each form is unified and delimited by a prosodic contour (whose shape depends on the syllable and mora composition of the form); there is no possibility of dividing a stretch like (23) into several parts each characterized by a separate contour, and it is absolutely impossible to make a pause within such a stretch. (ii) There is a set of internal sandhi processes which apply obligatorily within such a stretch, and another set of external sandhi processes which apply optionally across boundaries from one stretch to another. (iii) The morphemes occurring initially in such stretches form a set which is (almost) entirely different from the set of morphemes that occur non-initially. In terms of morpheme structure rules the two sets differ in that the first segment of non-initial morphemes may be any vowel or consonant of the language, whereas initial morphemes exhibit essential restrictions in this respect.

Without committing oneself with regard to the syntactic status of 'stretches' like (24) one may safely argue that they are phonologically similar to wordforms in other languages.[8] One might speak of phrases, but it is necessary anyway to recognize the existence of an entity which is intermediate between the 'stretch' and the sentence. This intermediate entity, which is characterized by the unifying effect of external sandhi processes (including tonal contour modification) among its constituents, may be aptly termed a 'phonological phrase', and hence I prefer to speak of such stretches as (24) as 'phonological words'.

---

[7] Example (23) occurs—as an illustration of the complexity of Eskimo wordforms—in an essay by the late Schultz-Lorentzen.

[8] An exposition of phonological data relevant to this problem cannot be contained within the framework of this paper. A good deal of information on the segmental processes can be found in Bergsland (1955); as for the prosodic pattern, work by Hideo Mase and by the present author is in progress [editors' note: published as Mase and Rischel (1971)].

Within this framework it may be meaningful to speak of enclisis, as Swadesh does. But what exactly does that imply? Elements like -*lu* or -*guuq*/-*ŋuuq* are not variants of morphemes occurring as 'free forms'. As for the former, there is a near equivalent (semantically speaking), viz. *aamma*, but it hardly makes sense to speak of these as allomorphs of one morpheme. It is worth noting that -*lu* may combine with *aamma*; the resulting form *aammalu* means something like 'also' (apparently, *aamma* in itself means 'as well (as)' or 'in addition' rather than just 'and'[9]). As for -*guuq*/-*ŋuuq* this element differs sharply from forms like *uqarpuq* 'he said' in that it is indeclinable and moreover neutral with respect to person and number. Hence, if we speak of elements like -*lu* and -*guuq*/-*ŋuuq* as enclitic words it must be stated that they are *obligatorily* enclitic. This holds true of all elements of this category.

Exactly the same difficulty meets us if we define the affixation of -*liaq* 'traveller', and the like, as a kind of enclisis. There is no free form corresponding to any such affix. It is perfectly possible to say that -*liaq* is a word, but then we must recognize yet another category of words that occur only enclitically. Thus it seems that enclisis must, from a *phonological* point of view, be synonymous with suffixation.

So far I have argued that morphemes which form a phonological word together with a preceding inflected form are bound forms constituting separate lexical items, i.e. there is no lexical or phonological motivation for calling them anything but affixes. This applies equally to morphemes which block the occurrence of inflection of the preceding part of the phonological word, e.g. -*uti*-/-*uta*- in (9), or -*turpuq* in (13). The lexicon clearly consists of a set of items that occur initially in phonological words, and another set of items that occur as 'affixes'. There are nearly synonymous pairs from the two sets in certain cases, but in principle they are unrelated.[10]

The phonological word in Eskimo thus presents a genuine problem for linguistic theory. One possibility is to describe the phonological word as a syntactic constituent which is not transformationally derived, and to leave it to derivational morphology to account for the internal organization of such constituents. However, this seriously burdens morphological theory with the task of explaining the grammatical relationship of surface constituents to parts of other constituents

---

[9] The standard dictionary of West Greenlandic does not give the translation 'and' for *aamma* at all.

[10] I disregard here the unique verb *ippuq* 'is in a certain state, is situated', which may occur in true enclisis, but only in a highly restricted set of environments.

in constructions like (9) and of explaining the occurrence of internal inflection in constructions like (18).[11]

Another possibility is to consider the evidence for phonological words given above as irrelevant to syntax. In the syntactical component, it may be argued, forms like (24) consist of a string of words,[12] the formation of phonological words being due to some kind of adjustment rules. However, by this approach one may easily obscure the fundamental role played in Eskimo syntax by the constituents that are reflected by phonological words. The occurrence or absence of concord, and the distinction between transitive and non-transitive morphology, are phenomena which are directly influenced by the formation of such constituents. As for verb morphology this is exemplified by (25), (26) (-*pug*/-*wuq* intransitive ending, -*paal*-*waa* transitive ending). As for noun concord, examples (27) to (31) may suffice to illustrate the pattern (for clarity morpheme-by-morpheme translations are given):

(27)   *ugaluwwiſſuaq* 'church-big' i.e. 'a big church'

(28)   *ugaluwwik aqisuuq* 'church big' i.e. 'a big church'[13]

(29)   *uqaluwwiſſuit* 'church-big-pl' i.e. 'big churches'

(30)   *ugaluwwiit aŋisuut* 'churches big-pl' i.e. 'big churches'

(31)   *uqaluwwiſſuaqarpuq* 'church-big-has' i.e. 'there is a church' or 'there are big churches'

(32)   *aŋsuumik uqaluwwiqarpug* 'big-one-by church-has' 'there is a big church'

(33)   *aŋisuunik uqaluwwiqarpuq* 'big-ones-by church-has' 'there are big churches'.

Note that there is concord with regard to number in noun phrases like (28), (30). Number inflection of the head noun is blocked by affixation of -*qarpuq* 'has' (just as the inflection of the head of a possessive construction was blocked by affixation in (9), (11), (13)). If the meaning 'big' is expressed by a constituent reflected by a phonological word, this constituent expresses the number, but if it is represented as an

[11] Schultz-Lorentzen (1945: 15) calls the type of construction found in (18) something that happens 'as an anomaly, but very often'.

[12] This position is taken by Collis (1971: 24ff and elsewhere).

[13] Note that here, as elsewhere, forms which may seem to qualify as bound and free allomorphs (-*(r)ſuaq, aŋisuuq*) are lexically unrelated.

affix, the grammatical number is indefinite. This kind of phenomenon must be accounted for, either by positing a noun phrase like (28) as underlying (32), or in some other way. The formation of phonological words clearly belongs in syntax, and it has essential consequences for late processes in the syntactic component.

At this point it is appropriate to mention that there is a conspicuous tendency for otherwise productive affixes to form lexicalized items in the case that there is an option consisting of free forms, cf.

(34)   *illu aŋisuuq* 'house big', 'big house'

(35)   *illuʃuaq* 'house-big' i.e. 'store-house (or the like)'.

It may be added furthermore that the affixes cover a rather restricted set of meaning spheres.

In these respects the affixes of Eskimo are clearly akin to derivational affixes in other languages. Apparently, it is not easy to define the difference between 'word' and 'affix' universally on the basis of the shape and behaviour of lexical items, if the definition is to be appropriate for languages like Greenlandic Eskimo.

4.4.   CONCLUDING REMARKS

As far as I can see, the examples given above strongly suggest that there are syntactic constituents in Eskimo which occur only as affixes but which nevertheless behave in some respects as self-contained constituents.[14] It may be suggested that affixation in such cases arises through syntactic transformations, for example (1–9) exhibits a complex structure involving two possessive constructions:

[[the hunter's][[reindeer's meat] + possessed]]

and is strongly suggestive of a cyclic derivation, affixation blocking preceding inflection.

If we turn to (18), the situation is syntactically different. There is a striking parallelism between such constructions and constructions involving the allative case affix, cf.

---

[14] In the present paper I have not included a consideration of Capell (1967), who speaks of 'fused units' in referring to the stretches which I have called phonological words above.

(36) *kalaallit nunaaliarpuq* 'he travels to Greenland'

(37) *kalaallit nunaanukarpuq* ditto

(38) *kalaallit nunaanut aallarpuq* ditto

In (37) we have a complex affix verb -*nukar*-, which directly contains the allative case affix. But a similar semantic component may be posited for -*liar*- of (36). It may be suggested that sentences like (36) and (38) are rather similar in their underlying structure, and that the presence of an affixal or non-affixal verb is a surface phenomenon, the conjunction of *nunaaliarpuq* into one constituent being due to a very late rule. If it makes sense to assume that the structure *prior to* that transformation has a major break between a constituent meaning 'to Greenland' and another constituent meaning 'travel' (rather than between 'Greenland' and 'travel-to'), the existence of surface forms like *nunaaliarpuq* may be said to present a case for the generative semantic conception of syntax. Lexical insertion of the affix verb seems, under this analysis, to occur very late. The form *nunaaliarpuq* can be described as the result of two processes: (i) adding the allative element to the second member of the NP *kalaallit nunaat* and (ii) adding a semantic configuration 'travel' to the resulting complex. It is only after a readjustment of the whole structure has taken place that the verb can be inserted as a lexical item covering both the underlying case and the underlying verb. However, it is not particularly evident that this is the most appropriate derivation.

It may be suggested quite generally that the transitive and intransitive constructions in Eskimo are formed in detail before lexical insertion, so that the choice of an affixal or non-affixal lexical item simply depends on the position within a syntactic constituent. However, this spells trouble since numerous semantic configurations (e.g. verb meanings) lack an affixal representation in the lexicon. Hence it may be necessary to assume that verbs are somehow marked for 'affix' or 'non-affix' in underlying representations, and that this marking plays a role in triggering various transformations. This leaves the matter undecided as to how late the insertion of lexical material actually occurs.

5

Consonant Reduction in Faroese Noncompound Wordforms[1]

5.1.   INTRODUCTION

In recent years Faroese phonology has attracted the attention of several linguists. A series of analyses has appeared which, interestingly enough, display a wide range of assumptions about the goals and methods of linguistic description. It may be expedient to mention some of the more complete analyses. Werner has given an AUTONOMOUS PHONEMIC description of the consonant system (1963) and more recently of the vowel system (1968). The former part of his analysis is remarkable for its insistence on phonetic sequentiality among the entities that are assigned a phonemic status. By applying the linearity principle very rigorously, Werner arrives at a phoneme system that is widely different from others that have been proposed (see below). Also within an essentially autonomous phonemic framework, Hagström (1967) has set up the phoneme system more in agreement with the type of analysis demonstrated for Icelandic by Einar Haugen (1958). O'Neil (1964b), McCawley (1968), and Anderson (1968)[2] have approached the sound pattern, especially the vowels, in terms of GENERATIVE PHONOLOGICAL theory. Particularly the last-mentioned contribution seems to me to lead to significant new insights into the matter. The present paper is based on some of the same assumptions concerning the nature of the rules that operate in Faroese phonology.

---

[1] Reprinted from E.S. Firchow *et al. Studies for Einar Haugen, presented by friends and colleagues*, The Hague: Mouton, (1972): 482–97. (=Janua linguarum, Series maior, 59)

[2] Unfortunately, Anderson's unpublished dissertation (West Scandinavian Vowel Systems and the Ordering of Rules, 1969) was not available to me when this paper was written.

In spite of the work referred to above (which is far from being a total list) the most comprehensive presentation of the consonant pattern is still that of Marie Bjerrum (1962). Her paper gives a GLOSSEMATIC analysis of the 'expression system' of Faroese. In the context of the current research on Faroese phonology it is important to realize that the glossematic analytical practice, by its emphasis on the formal invariance of linguistic signs (morphemes, in non-glossematic terminology), leads to results that are clearly related to those obtained by a generative phonological approach. The abstract forms posited in Bjerrum's paper share essential properties with the underlying forms of generative phonology,[3] and in particular the evidence given in favour of the analysis is crucial evidence also from a generative phonological point of view. Bjerrum's findings are, therefore, highly relevant to current research, at least as regards the consonant pattern (her treatment of the vowels must, I think, be considered definitely superseded by later work, although her data are, of course, valid).

It is a trivial observation that there is a wide discrepancy between the highly archaic orthography and the pronunciation of Faroese. When reading linguistic literature on the subject, on the other hand, one is struck by the similarity between orthography and the abstract forms posited in glossematic and generative phonological analyses. This implies that several of the (in part highly specific) rules that have operated on Faroese to remove it phonetically from Old Norse can be postulated as contemporary phonological rules of grammar. Just to what extent this contention makes sense must be considered an open question as yet. I shall not attempt to survey the problem in general in this paper, but a few controversial issues will be considered below.

However, it is not the main purpose of this paper to challenge the repertory of underlying segments posited in previous literature. Rather, I wish to consider a section of the processes that affect consonant clusters in Faroese in order to see which generalizations can be made concerning these phonetically interesting phenomena. I do not claim that the data given here are new; they consist for the most part of forms given in standard handbooks.[4] I have deliberately tried to avoid issues

---

[3] As long as the formal elements, taxemes, of the glossematic analysis are compared to the underlying segments of the generative phonological analysis. The ultimate dimensions by means of which taxemes are further reduced have nothing to do with the classificatory features of generative phonology.

[4] A short survey of some cluster-simplifying rules was given in Rischel (1961: XXXII ff.).

depending crucially on dialect differences; the phonetic transcriptions are supposed to represent the pronunciation of the central area.[5]

5.2.   UNDERLYING SEGMENTS

The problems associated with the vowel pattern of Faroese are, for the most part, rather immaterial to the present study. A workable frame of reference has been suggested by Anderson (1968), who simply sets up an inventory of symbols that agree with those of the orthography, except that the homophonous letters *i* and *ý* are collapsed into *í*, and likewise *i* and *y* into *i*, and *æ* and *a* into *a*[6] (note that orthographical *ý, y, æ* often reflect segments derived from underlying back vowels by umlaut). This gives the underlying vowels /i e ø u o a í ú ó á/ plus three underlying diphthongs /ei̯ oi̯ ai̯/. In the following I shall use this system of notation. However, I assume that ablaut and umlaut processes operate prior to the consonant modifications to be dealt with in this paper, and hence the input representations are given everywhere with the post-ablaut and post-umlaut qualities.—Phonetic 'surface' forms are given with a minimum of phonetic detail; in particular it should be noted that the late rules which specify the absolute tongue-height and duration of each segment are disregarded (phonetic information can be found, e.g., in Rischel 1962, 1964*a*). The neutralized reflex of /ø/ and /ó/ is transcribed [ø], and the neutralized reflex of /o/ and /á/ is transcribed [o]. Thus the phonetic transcriptions are not terminal representations but rather a simple type of autonomous phonemic representations.

As for the consonants there is far-reaching agreement between the glossematic and generative phonological analyses (disregarding the reduction of /p t k f/ to /hb hd hg vh/ suggested in Bjerrum 1962: 58–60[7]). I tentatively posit 14 distinct consonant segments in the input to the phonological rules; in traditional terminology the categories are:

---

[5] A survey of the geographical distribution of the cluster-simplifying processes dealt with in this paper would give a highly variegated pattern as regards what are called 'sporadic' processes below. However, it is my impression that the general rules stated in Section 5.4 work in an essentially similar fashion all over the area.

[6] Similar simplifications of the standard orthography have been suggested more than half a century ago.

[7] The placement of /h/ before or after the obstruents is determined entirely by distributional criteria (it has no phonetic sense at all).

stops /p t k b d g/, nasals /m n ŋ/, fricatives /f v s j/, liquids /1 r/, and /h/. Occurrences of [ŋ] are derived from /n/ or (before a stop in the same lexical item) from an unspecified nasal. However, the latter is fully specified in the input to the phonological rules proper, and therefore included here. As for /j/, which I tentatively posit as a palatal FRICATIVE, its relationship to the semivowel occurring as the second member of diphthongs is controversial.

An important problem is posed by the distinctions between /p t k/ and /b d g/ and between /f/ and /v/. Word-initially we have the general Scandinavian pattern: /p t k s f/ are voiceless, and (especially) the stops are clearly postaspirated; /b d g v/ are nonaspirated, and /v/ is phonetically fully voiced, whereas there may or may not be vocal chord vibration in /b d g/. In postvocalic clusters we find similar differences between the two sets /p t k s f/ and /b d g v/, but here aspiration works backwards: the clusters of stops are realized with preaspiration (as in Icelandic and some West Norwegian dialects) in such forms as /søt + t/ 'sweet, neut.', /søk + t/ 'sought'. As an obviously related phenomenon we find complete devoicing of consonants preceding /p t k s/ in postvocalic clusters, i.e. in such forms as /pen + t/ 'nice, neut.', /mál + s/ 'of language'.

It is reasonable to assume that there is a common classificatory feature distinguishing /p t k f s/ and /b d g v/. It is not evident whether the difference should be defined phonetically in terms of articulatory force[8] or of voicing. It should be kept in mind that a classificatory distinction [+voice] : [–voice] does not mean 'presence of vocal fold vibration' versus 'absence of *ditto*', since the degree and extent of such vibrations are symptoms of concurrence of a number of articulatory features rather than an independent variable. It is more meaningful to 'restrict the term "nonvoiced" or "voiceless" to sounds produced with a glottal opening that is so wide that it prevents vocal vibration if air flows through the opening' (Chomsky and Halle 1968: 327). I hence take the classificatory feature [±voice] to mean: presence (versus absence) of vocal fold adduction to a degree that permits vibration under favourable supra- and sub-glottal conditions. Under this definition /b d g/ may be classified together with /v/ and the sonorants as

[8] Haugen (1958: 72) defines the Icelandic distinction /p t k/ : /b d g/ as a fortis–lenis distinction. The phonetic facts are much the same as for Faroese, except that vocal fold vibration seems more consistently absent in Icelandic /b d g/ than in the corresponding Faroese consonants.

[+voice];[9] /p t k s f/ are [–voice]. This does not imply that there is no distinction of force of articulation (the priority of one of these features over the other in lexical representations is not at issue here), but I wish to argue that the representations forming the input to the phonological rules proper may be considered as specifying all obstruents as either [+voice] or [–voice].

Aspiration, as well as partial or complete devoicing of adjacent segments, can be explained as an extension of the glottal gesture associated with /p t k f s/. In sequences of obstruents the sounds undergo a process that makes them more uniform, creating important neutralizations: the final cluster is pronounced alike in /vak + t/ 'waked, supine', /brúk + d/ 'used, p.p. fem.', and /høg + t/ 'high, neut.', as against /søg + d/ 'said, p.p. fem.'. I shall not go into the nature of these processes here. For simplicity I shall disregard all 'partial devoicing' phenomena, including aspiration affecting the initial or final portion of vocalic segments. As for the remaining 'complete devoicing' phenomena, it seems convenient to split the rule into two parts (the relationship between these is not entirely clear to me):

(1)   (a) $\begin{bmatrix} -contin \\ -nasal \end{bmatrix} \rightarrow$ [–voice] / [–voice] __

(b) C → [–voice] /__ [–voice]

The first rule says that a stop becomes voiceless if preceded by a voiceless segment; the second says that a consonant becomes voiceless before a voiceless segment. Of course these rules do not tell the whole story about the manifestation of voicedness or voicelessness in obstruent sequences. They say that the final consonant of /brúk + d/ becomes similar to that of /vak + t/, but they do not state that nevertheless the essential auditory difference between /brúk + d/ and /søg + d/ seems to reside in the segments preceding the final consonant. The latter type of observation is crucial for Werner's autonomous analysis, according to which the final cluster of such forms as /vak + t/, /brúk + d/, /høg + t/ is /hgd/, whereas that of /søg + d/ is /gd/, but it is not clear to what extent it should be accounted for in a generative phonology.[10] The important thing about the rules is the feature values they specify; it

[9] A clear difference in the position of the vocal folds can be observed in Danish /p t k/ versus /b d g/ (see Frøkjær-Jensen et al. 1971), although vocal fold vibration is absent in both sets in initial position. There are no glottographic observations available for Faroese.

[10] For one thing, the configuration of more or less important acoustic cues does not coincide with the configuration of articulatory gestures. It is not clear to me how either of these is related to the 'systematic phonetic' level of generative phonological theory.

is not interesting (within this framework) to discuss whether a given
segment in a given form after the application of the rules is, say, 'a *k*'
or 'a *g*'.

In order to reflect the neutralizations mentioned above I write the
'output' forms with [kt] ([vakt], [brykt], [høkt]) versus [gd] ([søgd]),
and similarly for other obstruent clusters (/v/ with devoicing is likewise
rendered as [f]), but for notational simplicity I have left the devoicing
unmarked in other consonant segments (it should thus be kept in mind
that a consonant before a voiceless consonant, e.g. /l/ in /følk/ 'folk',
is voiceless). I do not think that this inconsistency does any serious
harm.

A major problem in Faroese phonology is constituted by alternations between [g] (or by rule (1b): [k]), [d] (or by rule (1b): [t]) and
zero.[11] The glossematic and generative papers referred to above have
provided overwhelming evidence of a rule that deletes underlying /g/
in postvocalic position when it is not part of a consonant cluster, i.e.
in forms like /dag/ 'day, acc.', phonetically [dea] (cf. genitive [daks] and
the derivation [daglija]). The evidence for underlying /d/ → Ø is more
limited. There are instances where zero alternates with [d] before affixes
beginning in a dental consonant (cf. [sti:ja] 'support, inf.' – pret. [stud:i]
[studniŋur] 'support (noun)').[12] But with the vast majority of stems
that might seem possible candidates as regards underlying final /d/, no
such alternation occurs, or it is questionable whether forms with and
without [d] are directly related from a synchronic point of view.

In the framework of current phonological theory it must probably
be stated that there are two underlying segments /g/ and /d/ which,

---

[11] Under certain, well-defined circumstances adjacent vowels belonging to different
syllables are separated by the insertion of a glide, which after non-high vowels go further
towards fricative [j] and [v]. I also speak of a 'zero' representation of intervocalic /g/ or /d/
in such cases, e.g. høg + ur 'high, masc.'. høur → hø:vur.

[12] In my opinion the best examples are the contrasting nouns given by Bjerrum
(1962: 50): [ri:jil] 'row' pl. [ridlar] (or [ri:lar], according to the *Føroysk-donsk orðabók*),
versus [sni:jil] 'snail' pl. [sniglar] *versus* [bi:jil] 'suitor' pl. [bi:lar]. It seems entirely reasonable to state that the underlying forms are /ridil/, /snigil/, and /biil/. The numerous verb forms with [d:] and [t:] in the preterite and past participle forms cannot
be taken as safe evidence of stem-final /d/, since there are clear instances of 'intru-
sive' dental stops in affixes, cf. [trigv] 'faithful, fem.' neut. [tryt:], which in agreement with the analysis of 'Verschärfung' by Anderson (1968) can be interpreted as
/trú/—/trú + tt/, but not possibly as */trúd/—*/trúd + t/. O'Neil (1964*b*: 370) derives the
preterite form [gled:i] 'pleased' from *gle + d:i*, and this analysis could be extended to
a multitude of other verbs (irrespective of whether they are continuations of verbs
with ON *ð* like *ráða* 'rule' or of verbs without a stem-final consonant like *fáa*
'get').

under certain conditions, are deleted by a phonological rule. However, with many stems these conditions are always or nearly always met, and hence many stems are more or less indeterminate with respect to their final segment, the degree of indeterminacy being inversely proportional to one's ability to find 'related' wordforms that decide the issue. In the case of Faroese postvocalic /g/ and /d/ I think that this type of argumentation often tends to become somewhat far-fetched, and it is worthy of serious consideration whether a good many alternations between [g] or [d] and zero should not be treated as idiosyncracies of lexical items rather than products of a phonological rule.

If there is a set of underlying, postvocalic segments which are deleted if no consonant follows, it seems to me quite reasonable to identify these (in terms of classificatory features) with the stops /g/ and /d/ that must be posited anyway in postvocalic clusters. Anderson (1968: 238) expresses a different opinion. By comparing alternations like [haijin] 'heathen' – acc. [haidnan]; [soːjin] 'cooked, p.p.' – acc. [sodnan]; and [veːvur] 'weather' – dat. [vegri] he arrives at the conclusion that there is a common underlying segment which before a consonant is represented as [d] in some cases but as [g] in others, and he further assumes 'that it is a spirant corresponding to g (ɣ), and that there is a rule of the grammar that deletes this segment in most cases'. The reason for claiming that it is a velar is that 'there are rules which assimilate a velar to a dental in any event', e.g. in [nuija] 'to sink down' – p.p. acc. (masc. sg.) [nidnan] (all phonetic transcriptions mine), where, according to Anderson, we have /g/, not /ɣ/. This analysis seems to me highly ad hoc, and I do not understand how Anderson is able to decide that we have /g/ in [nuija] but (if I understand correctly) /ɣ/ in [haijin]. According to Anderson /ɣ/ differs from /g/ in assimilating more to dental stops, but I do not see how any clear pattern can be made out of this. It seems definitely more reasonable to me to mark some of the forms he cites as morphologically idiosyncratic, rather than positing an entirely arbitrary segment. [13]

As for the relationship between stops and other consonant segments it is essential to note that Faroese shares in the widespread

---

[13] There are unfortunately some erroneous forms in Anderson's paper. Thus dat. sg. *traðri* is given as [treagri] (the word has EITHER diphthong OR [gr] in inflected forms), and he gives the spurious forms [sujgdi] 'lowered (sg.)' and [sagdi] 'said (sg.)' of which the former is known to me only as a strong form [sai] (or [sei]), whereas the latter must be [seiji] if it is meant to be a finite form. Incidentally, these details do not affect his arguments, which could easily be supported by other forms.

differentiation of sonorant clusters: ON *rn* → [dn], (*nn* → [dn]); *rl*, *ll* → [dl]. Anderson (1968: 234) considers this a phonological rule in modern Faroese on the basis of examples such as [sainur] 'late, masc.' – comp. [saidni], and [morgun] 'morning' – dat. [modni] (transcriptions mine). I should rather suggest that these processes are historical events only, and that [dn], [dl] are derived from underlying /dn/, /dl/ in modern Faroese,[14] inflections like those cited above being morphologically exceptional. As for *rn, rl* occurring in inflected forms (because of the syncope of an intervening vowel) the normal treatment is to preserve [r], cf. [boːrin] 'carried, p.p.' – pl. [bornir]; also compare derived forms like [skuirn] 'baptizing' (from [skuira] 'baptize') and [tirla] 'bristle' (related to [tiːril] (a kind of whisk)). Many other examples of this kind could be adduced to show that the change of *r* to [d] is blocked on condition of morphological analysability, which strongly suggests that it is not a phonological rule of modern Faroese but a past event in the language. If we are to derive [dn] and [dl] in general from /rn/ or /nn/ and from /rl/ or /ll/, it will indeed be most difficult to state the conditions under which the process takes place, cf. minimal pairs like [tadna] 'become loose in structure' vs. [tarna] 'delay' (see further Hagström 1970: 351 note 10).

The three places of articulation exemplified by /p/, /t/, and /k/ can be defined in terms of the features [±anterior], [±coronal], and [±back] in accordance with current practice. There is an additional set of palatal affricates [č ǰ], but these can be derived from underlying sequences of velar and dental segments plus /j/, or from velar segments before /i, e/; cf. [loːk] 'lid', definite form [loːči] from /lok + i/ (see further Section 5.4.3 below).

The segments *j* and *w* play a special role in Anderson's explanation of the 'Verschärfung' in forms like [doǰːa] 'to die' and [bigva] 'to live, dwell'. He derives these from /doi + a/ and /bú + a/ by a rule of glide insertion followed by a rule complex converting front vowel plus *j* into [ǰː], and back vowel plus *w* into [gv]. (Intermediate stages: /doi + ja/, /doj + ja/; /biu + wa/, /biw + wa/.) Monosyllables like [brigv] 'bridge' are assumed to have final /w/ in their lexical form: /brúw/. The crucial problem with this analysis is that one is forced to explain why there is no 'Verschärfung' in forms like [suija] 'side', although the phonetic

---

[14] This is not contradicted by such alternations as [adlur] 'all, masc.' – neut. [alt], or [badn] 'child' – [banslijur] 'childish', since the shorter stem forms are accounted for by a complex of rules that must be in the phonology in any case: see Section 5.4.

conditions (diphthong plus glide insertion) are present. The problem is easily solved by positing underlying intervocalic /d/, i.e. /sída/, but a less abstract solution would be preferable. I shall, however, leave this problem aside here.

5.3.   SOME SPORADIC CONSONANT MODIFICATION RULES

Before considering the core of regular processes affecting consonants in postvocalic clusters, it may be expedient to sort out some processes that do not stand out as clear-cut phonological rules of contemporary Faroese. It is true of all of these that they reflect historical processes which often make the shape of Faroese wordforms differ dramatically from those of other Scandinavian languages. It is, therefore, easiest to point them out by referring to Old Norse forms, and to check afterwards whether there is any basis for formulating corresponding synchronic rules.

A number of these minor processes affect the place of articulation. One of the processes seems perfectly regular under certain morphological conditions, namely the change of velar to dental in inflected past participle forms like ON *hnignan*, Far. [nidnan]. It is, however, a question whether a verb stem like that of [nidnan] (inf. [nuija], cf. above) has underlying velar from the point of view of modern Faroese. The process has not affected *k* before *n*, i.e. it only operates in cases where a stem final consonant is dropped in other cases, so that the stem becomes phonologically ambiguous (unless evidence can be found in other related words). There are more sporadic cases of assimilation of labials and velars to a following dental stop—cf. ON *hǫfðu* 'had, pl.', *sǫgðu* 'said, pl.', – Far. [hødːu], [sødːu]. Synchronically, an underlying labial and an underlying velar may be posited in these forms by comparison with, e.g., the supine forms [haft], [sakt], but the assimilated forms are quite clearly morphological exceptions. In some cases, on the other hand, historical comparison shows that dentals have become velars before *n, r, s*, and there are even sporadic occurrences of a change of labial to velar articulation before *n*. As for the change of dental to velar before dental, alternations like [iːtri] 'outer' – superl. [ikst] (or [ist]) may seem to suggest that it is a synchronically relevant process. However, forms like [ikst] occur very irregularly in the grammar.

I do not wish to deny that there are rudiments of the above-mentioned processes in modern Faroese grammar, but these must in any case be stated as highly restricted, non-productive rules. In most lexical items a phonological restatement has taken place so that the place of articulation prior to the processes is not synchronically recoverable.

Another conspicuous sound-law of Faroese states that (with a limited number of exceptions) ON *vl* and *vr* have become *lv* and *rv*: for example, ON *gafl*, Far. [galvur] 'gable'. (This metathesis may be sporadically represented in combinations of *m* and liquid as well, cf. that a wordform like [ørčimla] 'disturb' is given in the *Føroysk-donsk orðabók* with a variant form with *lm*.) If forms like [ui̯ erva] 'high up' and [trilva(st)] 'fumble' are associated with respectively [i:vir] 'over' and [trui̯va] 'seize', they may be said to provide evidence of metathesis as a contemporary process, but the morphological evidence is meagre, to say the least. I think it can be stated generally that the *vl, vr* metathesis has caused a restructuring of (practically) all lexical items that previously contained these combinations.

In an important contribution to Faroese diachronic and synchronic phonemics Werner (1970) shows that both *v* and *m* reduce to a semivowel before certain dentals under conditions that are considerably more general than hitherto noticed. In an historical perspective the transition of *v* to [u̯] is interesting because it works together with the metathesis of *vl, vr* and with the rules changing *vn* into [m] before dental stops (see Section 5.4), the combined effect of these rules being that [v] is largely avoided as the first member of postvocalic clusters.

Alternations like [leamin] 'lame' – plur. [lavnir], [lau̯nir] may be explained in terms of a rule that changes a nasal into continuant obstruent, i.e. a fricative, followed by an (apparently optional) rule that changes this fricative into [u̯], cf. that the latter rule is shared by *v* before *n*: [so:va] 'sleep' – [sou̯na] 'fall asleep'.

The cases of direct alternation between labial fricative and semivowel are not too numerous. As for words like *navn* 'name', it may be argued that a restructuring has taken place in dialects which always pronounce a diphthong here, but I am not too sure that the lexical marking of the sequence would be different in any case.

In the analysis of consonant clusters below I only take consonantal segments into account. The second component of diphthongs, be it from an underlying semivowel or from underlying /v/, is not considered as part of a following cluster.

The (more or less sporadically occurring) processes mentioned above are all taken to be prior to those stated below. An exception is the devoicing rule (1a), (1b) which should probably be considered as applying within persistent consonant clusters (i.e. after vacuous application of weakening rules that change consonants into semivowels) whenever its structural descriptions are met.

5.4.   CLUSTER SIMPLIFICATION

The following survey comprises the major processes that take place in postvocalic consonant clusters of inflected and derived wordforms. The study is limited to non-compound wordforms. More correctly stated: it disregards clusters that involve a boundary before a syntactically marked word. I do not deny that the behaviour of clusters in the latter type of environment is particularly interesting in Faroese, but it would lead much too far to go into the intricate and highly unpredictable processes that characterize fixed compounds in this language.[15]

5.4.1. sk -*metathesis*

Examples like [feskur] 'fresh, masc.' – neut. [fekst], [danskur] 'Danish, masc.' – neut. [daŋ(k)st], [inskja] (→ [inšča]) 'wish, inf.' – pret. [iŋ(k)sti], and several others, show that there is a rule of metathesis of $sk \Rightarrow ks$, which, unlike the v-metathesis, has not lead to restructuring but is an important rule of contemporary phonology:[16]

(2)   SD: $\begin{bmatrix} +\text{syllabic} \\ +\text{stress} \end{bmatrix} \left(\begin{bmatrix} +\text{nasal} \\ +\text{coronal} \end{bmatrix} \right) [+\text{sibilant}] \begin{bmatrix} -\text{contin} \\ +\text{back} \end{bmatrix} \begin{bmatrix} -\text{contin} \\ +\text{coronal} \end{bmatrix}$

   SC: 1 <2> 3 4 5 ⇒ 1 <2> 4 3 5

(the feature 'sibilant' posited here will be discussed in Section 5.4.4).

   The sk-metathesis rule does not apply to sk preceded by r or in unstressed syllables. In these environments the velar stop is deleted

[15] As regards consonant assimilation in compounds, we are badly in need of a systematic study of the rich material found in Svabo's dictionary as well as an investigation of the distribution of more and less assimilated forms in the different modern dialects.

[16] Note that if the sequence [eŋ] in northern and central Faroese is to be derived from /aŋ/ (in forms like [geŋga] 'go, inf.', cf. the imperative [gak:]), then the rule accounting for this vowel shift must precede the metathesis rule, since the output of the latter preserves [a] in this type of environment.

instead by rule (7) below (in examples like /norsk + t/ 'Norwegian, neut.', /imisk + t/ 'of various kinds, neut.' – the latter form acquires initial stress by the general accentual rules of the language).

5.4.2. Deletion of *r* before dental continuants

There is deletion of *r* before *s* in a long series of wordforms. In most cases where ON *rs* reduces to plain *s* the underlying *r* is not synchronically recoverable (e.g. [toskur] 'cod'), but there are alternations like [størːi] 'bigger' – [støstur] 'biggest, masc.', i.e. /r + st/ → [st]. Similarly, *r* may be deleted before *n* plus stop, cf. [spirna] 'kick, inf.' – pret. [spinti]. There are, however, counter-examples. Thus /vern + d/ 'protection' (a literary word) is pronounced with [rnd], and in /bor + s/ 'of table' (in compounds) or /skur + sl/ 'abrasion' there is not deletion but fusion of [rs] into a retroflex sibilant by a late rule (which is disregarded in this paper[17]). It may be that regular application of the deletion rule requires *t* as the third member of the cluster, that is:

(3)
$$\begin{bmatrix} +\text{sonorant} \\ +\text{coronal} \\ -\text{nasal} \\ -\text{lateral} \end{bmatrix} \rightarrow \varnothing\ /\ \_\_\ \begin{bmatrix} +\text{contin} \\ +\text{coronal} \end{bmatrix} \begin{bmatrix} -\text{contin} \\ -\text{voice} \\ +\text{coronal} \end{bmatrix}$$

5.4.3. Dorsal assimilation

In Faroese, as in numerous other languages, the fact that nasals before stops share the place of articulation of the following stop appears both as a lexical convention and as a rule relating different wordforms to each other. The latter rule produces alternations between dental and velar nasals, cf. [minːi] 'less'—[miŋka] 'diminish'.[18] The interesting thing is that in Faroese the rule is not confined to nasal segments but applies to stops as well, cf. [svaiti] 'sweat'—[svaikːast] 'become moist with perspiration' (from /svait + k + a + st/, derived with the same affix

---

[17] In all cases where *r* is retained before dentals the consonant cluster is subject to optional or obligatory rules concerning supradental articulation (see the detailed account in Hagström 1970).

[18] In compound words assimilation of underlying /n/ to a following labial segment also occurs, although irregularly. Svabo's dictionary contains such forms as [bamburur] (meaning 'the time when a woman can give birth to a child'), composed of the words [badn] 'child' and [burur] 'carrying' (the *Føroysk-donsk orðabók* has [ban-] not [bam-] in such compounds).

as /min + k + a/). If it is agreed that a stem like [braḭ-] 'wide' has under-lying final /d/ the process applies to this segment as well, cf. [braḭk:a] 'widen'. These phenomena seem quite regular in the language.[19]

Before deciding how the assimilation rule should be formulated, it is useful to consider the behaviour of velars before palatal segments. In Faroese /k g ŋ/ become palatal before /j/ and before /i e/ in word initial as well as medial clusters. If stated like this, the rule must be relatively early since it fails to apply to the outputs from a number of vowel modification rules. Thus it fails to apply in initial position before [i e] arising by the rules associated with 'Verschärfung', cf. [kigv] 'cow', [skegvur] 'shoe' (both with underlying back vowel), and also before [e] followed by the velar nasal, which may be derived from /ang/, e.g. [geŋga] 'go, inf'. In intervocalic position (intervocalic clusters) it fails to apply before the secondary [i] which in some dialects replaces [u] (both as a continuation of ON *u* and as a svarabhakti vowel), e.g. [taskir] 'bags' (as against [raščir] 'brave, pl.'). Finally, there are some lexical exceptions like [ki:s] (for [kvi:s]) 'the slightest sound' (part of an idiom).

There are NO exceptions to the palatal manifestation of /kj gj/. I should like to suggest that the shift of /k g/ is in fact a modification of intermediate [kj gj] in all cases, and that there is a separate rule that inserts [j] between a dorsal consonant and a front vowel under certain conditions. I do not quite know what these conditions are, but to a first approximation the rule may be given in this form:

$$
(4)\quad(a)\qquad \varnothing \rightarrow \begin{bmatrix} -\text{sonorant} \\ +\text{high} \\ -\text{back} \\ \alpha\text{voice} \end{bmatrix} \Big/ \begin{bmatrix} -\text{syll} \\ +\text{high} \\ \alpha\text{voice} \end{bmatrix} - \begin{bmatrix} +\text{syll} \\ -\text{back} \\ -\text{round} \\ -\text{low} \end{bmatrix}
$$

The clusters [kj gj] produced by this rule, as well as underlying /kj gj/, now fuse into palatal affricates [č ǰ]. Similarly, the cluster /sj/ fuses into [š]. I do not know to what extent these phenomena should be considered as effects of the same rule, nor how this rule is best formalized, so I just note the existence of a rule:

(4) (b) 'palatal fusion'.

---

[19] Historically the process has even applied to labial before velar, cf. [čøg:a] 'accuse of theft', derived from the continuation of ON *þjóf-*. (Synchronically, however, the underlying structure of this stem is controversial. It is interesting to note that the derivation [čøskur] 'thievish, masc.' has neuter [čøkst] with metathesis according to rule (2).)

Finally, there must be some accessory (probably 'late') rules that make all consonantal segments palatal before a palatal consonant in the same cluster. I disregard these here (though, somewhat inconsistently, I write [š] rather than [s] before [č]).

In accordance with the rules above, a form like /svaı̯t + k + i + st/ (1st person sg.) ends up with intervocalic [č:]. As stated earlier, /t/ assimilates to a following /k/, but rather than deriving the palatal affricate in the just-mentioned form via a rule that explicitly introduces the feature [+back] in the first consonant, one may state the assimilation in terms of dorsality. It is then implied that the intermediate stage of backness, if it is at all postulated for this derivation, is a matter of conventions. The basic assimilation rule, then, says

(5) $\begin{bmatrix} -\text{contin} \\ +\text{coronal} \end{bmatrix} \rightarrow [+\text{high}] \Big/ \_\_ \begin{bmatrix} -\text{contin} \\ +\text{high} \end{bmatrix}$

5.4.4. Sonorization and reduction rules

A crucial problem is posed by alternations like (a) [jaṷnur] (from /javn + ur/) 'even, masc.' neut. [jamt]; [badn] 'child' – [bans] 'of child'; [rigna] 'rain, inf.' – pret. [rin̯di];[20] (b) [fidla] 'fill' – pret. [filti]; [sigla] 'sail' – pret. [sildi]. In some cases it makes sense to say that the first consonant is dropped, but this leaves the place of articulation of the nasals unaccounted for.

Let us consider another set of alternants: (a′) [rembast] 'stretch oneself' – pret. [remdist]; [senda] 'send' – pret. [sendi] (from /send + di/); [rin̯gur] 'bad, masc.' – neut. [rin̯t]; (b′) [holvur] 'half, masc.' – neut. [holt]; [yldur] 'high (of meat), masc.' – neut. [ylt], [filʲa] (from /filg + j + a/) 'follow, inf.' – pret. [fildi]. The fact that the consonant combinations that are simplified in (a′) and (b′) are mirror images of those in (a) and (b) (except for certain restrictions on possible sequences) suggests that there is one rule that applies appropriately regardless of the order of the segments.

One way to account for this would be in terms of a mirror image rule that deletes an obstruent regardless of whether it is first or second. However, this would require an earlier rule changing underlying /javn + t/, /rign + t/ into something like /javm + t/, /rign̯ + t/ before the output forms [jamt], [rin̯t] are produced by deletion of the obstruent. Such a derivation does not look very plausible.

---

[20] Also cf. [gan̯samlijur] 'useful' from /gagn/ + /sam . . . /.

One might assume instead that there is a metathesis rule which interchanges obstruent plus sonorant before obstruent. Types (a) and (b) are thereby changed into (a′) and (b′). If we assume intermediate (*/janv + t/, */ring + t/ → */jamb + t/, */riŋg + t/, the remaining work can be done by a rule that always deletes the consonant before the last one in clusters of more than two segments. However, in general linguistic theory metathesis rules must be considered 'costly' rules, no matter how one's simplicity metric is. It would take very strong evidence to burden Faroese phonology with yet another metathesis rule.

A third, in my opinion more appealing, solution is to have a rule that modifies the initial segment of certain consonant clusters before the deletion rule applies. The rule may be assumed to sonorize obstruents before obstruent plus consonant:

$$(6) \quad [-\text{sonorant}] \rightarrow \begin{bmatrix} +\text{sonorant} \\ \alpha\,\text{nasal} \\ \beta\,\text{lateral} \end{bmatrix} \Big/ \; V \underline{\quad} \begin{bmatrix} +\text{sonorant} \\ \alpha\,\text{nasal} \\ \beta\,\text{lateral} \end{bmatrix} C$$

This rule changes obstruents to nasals before nasal plus consonant, and it changes obstruents to laterals before lateral plus consonant, certain conventions being required to give [m] as the nasal output for /v/, and [l] as the lateral output for /g/, in /javn+ t/ → /jamn + t/, /sigl + di/ → /sill + di/ (note that these adjustments follow universal phonetic tendencies of preferred articulations).

After the application of rule (6) we have sequences of the types sonorant–sonorant–obstruent (for (a), (b)) and sonorant–obstruent–obstruent (for (a′), (b′)). There are, however, also (at this stage in the derivations) sequences of three obstruents: consider /føri + sk + t/ 'Faroese, neut'. In sequences that contain a succession of two like segments the desired output forms are obtained by reducing these to one segment. In the remaining cases the desired output forms are obtained by deleting the segment before the last one. Obviously, deletion of the 'last segment but one' takes care of the simplification of sequences of like segments as well, so the rule can be stated quite generally in this way. By referring to the last consonant but one, rather than the medial consonant, we are able to account for the deletion also in clusters of four segments, e.g. /falsk + t/ → [falst].

There is one important exception to the deletion rule: /s/ is not deleted. If we want to define the rule in such a way that it excludes sibilants, that is consonants that are, in current terminology

$$\begin{bmatrix} +\text{contin} \\ +\text{coronal} \\ +\text{strident} \end{bmatrix}$$

then this cannot be conveniently done by negating the feature matrix above. One may instead add an exception to the rule saying that it does not apply to segments of the just-mentioned feature specification. However, it is very often the case in languages that sibilants behave differently from other consonants, and I feel inclined to reckon with the existence of a feature 'sibilant' defining this important natural class (phonetically the definition does not pose particularly great difficulties). Hence the rule can be stated thus:

(7) $\begin{bmatrix} C \\ -\text{sibilant} \end{bmatrix}^{21} \rightarrow \emptyset \,/\, V(C)C \_\_ [-\text{sonorant}]$

Unfortunately, it is not correct as it stands, since it would erroneously predict a deletion of /m/ in /arm + t/ 'poor, neut.', /herm + di/ 'imitated, pret'. Apparently an exception must be made for sequences in which two sonorous segments before the last one differ in the feature 'nasality'. This could be built into the rule by stating its last part as

$/\, V(C) \begin{bmatrix} C \\ < \alpha \text{ nasal} > \end{bmatrix} \left[\left\langle \overline{\begin{matrix} +\text{sonorant} \\ \alpha\text{nasal} \end{matrix}} \right\rangle \right] [-\text{sonorant}]$

but I am not sure that this brings us much closer to a real insight into the process.

5.4.5. Assimilation of *t* to *s*

There is a rule, which somehow is related to the rules above, that deletes dental stops before *s* plus consonant in such forms as /it + st/ 'outermost (fem.)' → [ist] (if not pronounced [ikst]), and also in cases where there are two underlying stops in succession (or, alternatively analysed, a long stop segment): /stitt + st/ 'shortest, fem.' → [stist]. This is probably best explained as assimilation plus simplification of the resulting sequence of two like segments, i.e. (iteratively):

(8) (a) $\begin{bmatrix} -\text{sonorant} \\ +\text{coronal} \end{bmatrix} \rightarrow \begin{bmatrix} +\text{contin} \\ +\text{sibilant} \end{bmatrix} \,/\, \_\_ [+\text{sibilant}]\, C$

    (b) SD: $C_a C_a C_b$
       SC:1 1 2 ⇒1 2

Note that (8b) applies in some of the same cases as (7).

[21] It may be that the initial segment in rule (6) should likewise be defined as nonsibilant.

5.5. THE UNIFIED EFFECT OF THE PROCESSES

Many of the rules that I have sketchily stated above are substantially identical to (or at least closely related to) rules that
apply elsewhere within the West Scandinavian area. Probably the
most conspicuous feature of Faroese consonantism (except for the
'Verschärfung') is the importance of METATHESIS, both the historical
metathesis of *v* plus liquid and the synchronically relevant metathesis
of *sk*. Another strange area of partly unproductive, partly fully regular
processes is CHANGES IN PLACE OF ARTICULATION (some of the
diachronically most interesting phenomena of this type have been
disregarded in the present paper because they have led to a change
of the underlying form of lexical items, cf. ON *vápn* → [vokn] 'spear
for killing whales' with [vopn] 'weapon'). It is, moreover, interesting
to observe that the ASSIMILATION AND REDUCTION rules do not
work quite the same way as in Icelandic, cf. the simplification of
/barn+ s.../ to [bans-] according to the rules above, as against Icelandic. [bars-, bas-] with immediate deletion of /n/. Finally, it is worthy
of note that Faroese lacks the synchronic differentiation of sequences
of stop plus stop, which in Icelandic become sequences of spirant plus
stop, cf. Icelandic. [köγpa] 'buy' – pret. [kjefti] and Faroese. [čeị̯pa],
[čepti]. The prevailing tendency in Faroese is in the direction of a more
unified articulation of consonant sequences.

As a result of the processes dealt with in this paper there is a
solid mass of consonant neutralization in Faroese phonology. This is
witnessed by the examples of sonorant plus *t* and velar plus *st* below,
where each column of forms is characterized by identity of the final
consonant clusters in the phonetic representations (needless to say, the
series of forms are not intended to be exhaustive):[22]

final [lt]:	final [rt]:	final [mt]:	final [nt]:	final [ŋt]:	final [kst]:	final [ŋst]:
sel + t	ber + t	dám + t	lin + t	toŋk + t	lag + st + t	iŋg + st
fidl + t	turr + t	skamm + t	menn + t	riŋg + t	løg(g) + d + st	insk + t
úld + t	ert + t	remb + t	send + t	rign + t	tók + st	
velt + t	sirg + t	javn + t	sint + t		fekk + st	
holv + t	sterk + t		spirn + t		fesk + t	
figl + t	gjarv + t		fodn + t			
filg + t						
velk + t						

---

[22] In standard orthography the wordforms are: *selt, fylt, últ, velt, hálvt, fyglt, fylgt, velkt; bert, turt, ert, syrgt, sterkt, djarvt; dámt, skamt, rembt, javnt; lint, ment, sent, sint, spirnt, fornt; tonkt, ringt, rignt; lægst, løgst, tókst, fekkst, feskt; yngst, ynskt.*

It is obvious that the various rules work together to produce a simple pattern of syllable structures. A consideration of this 'output' pattern from the point of view of constraints on permissible sequences and constraints on the utilization of contrast (which I understand as autonomous phonemics) is essential for a real understanding of the FUNCTIONAL UNITY of the rules. The emphasis on this aspect in recent phonological work (Kisseberth 1970) is highly promising.

Part II
Prosody

6

Stress, Juncture, and Syllabification in Phonemic Description[1]

6.1. PROSODIC UNITS IN LANGUAGE DESIGN

In spite of numerous theoretical divergences, phonemic descriptions are, on the whole, considerably uniform in the basic framework. This is especially true of the large-scale activity in the USA in the last decades, which has had considerable influence elsewhere. The bulk of phonemic work reflects a tradition which has largely favoured the study of *segmental* units: vowels and consonants. The highly refined techniques of contrasting sounds by means of paradigmatic substitution and of classifying sounds on the basis of distribution and phonetic similarity have been evolved primarily for the purpose of setting up segmental phoneme inventories and transcribing texts in terms of these. Toneme systems have proved a fruitful field for the application of similar techniques, but certain phenomena—stress, pause, and the like—do not fit well into the framework.

Bloomfield observed that stress in English is not a phoneme like /p/, for example, although the *placement* of stress is phonemically distinctive,[2] and more recently a number of specific properties of '*prosodic*' or '*suprasegmental*' units have been noted by various scholars (partly in accordance with earlier 'prephonemic' concepts). Bloomfield also pointed out that stress differences in English function on several levels.[3] The natural conclusion to be drawn from this is that stress cannot be functionally accounted for in terms of substitution classes

[1] Reprinted from H. G. Lunt *Proceedings of the IXth Internatinal Congress of Linguists 1962*, The Hague: Mouton (1964: 85–93).

[2] For an elaboration of the idea, see Haugen (1949).

[3] Bloomfield (1914: 43 ff.) distinguishes syllable-stress, group-stress, and sentence-stress. Similar levels of stress have been set up by several scholars.

on one level. In spite of such difficulties, there has been a rather dominating tendency to apply the phonemic principle of *commutation* or contrastive substitution and partly also the principle of *unilinearity* throughout the analysis.

The principle of commutation has been widely accepted as valid throughout the domain of phonology. The analyst is thereby forced into a desperate search for a definite number of stress or juncture units, a search which is impeded by the failure of stresses or junctures to commute properly. (A typical example is the current disagreement about the number of stress phonemes in English.) In spite of the obvious difficulties in applying the method it has not been generally realized that the principle in question may not be universally applicable at all. It is the merit of Firth (1948) to have emphasized this.

As to the principle of unilinearity, it is often an obvious advantage to interpret ambiguous arrangements as sequential rather than simultaneous. However, it is structurally disputable to base the phonological description on a rigid 'vertical' segmentation of the sound sequences, whereby the prosodic or suprasegmental units are reduced to distinctive features of segmental phonemes. One example is the suggestion of Roman Jakobson and his collaborators that stress accents may be considered features of vowel phonemes; another example is their interpretation of the distinction between syllable peaks and margins in terms of inherent features of vocality and consonantality.[4]

It is not sufficient to state that the prosodic and segmental (inherent) features behave differently with respect to phonotactic rules. The difference is not a difference of behaviour but a difference of kind. Prosodic and segmental features have no direct relationship to each other; they constitute different parts of the structural model of language. And even though the structural model may be looked upon in different ways, it is obvious that there is a fundamental difference with respect to information conveyed by different kinds of units in minimal and nonminimal contexts: distinctions like voiceless–voiced are normally of maximal importance in minimal utterances, whereas stress, juncture, and syllabicity phenomena are only distinctive in nonminimal utterances. The syllable-initial *j* has a high functional load in the utterance *Joe!* (vs. e.g. *Go!*), but a lower functional load in *My name is Joe*. Contrary to this we convey essential information by stating that

---

[4] See e.g. Jakobson and Halle (1956).

aim has strong stress and is preceded by open juncture in the utterance *an aim*, whereas this statement is at best redundant if applied to the utterance *aim*.

It is hardly to be doubted that linguistic descriptions gain in lucidity and consistency by emphasizing the heterogenous character of the expression categories and utilizing the advantages of a multidimensional model of the expression form of language, as has been done by Hjelmslev, who defines, e.g., the syllable by the interplay between prosodic and nonprosodic categories (prosodemes and constituents), cf. Hjemslev 1939.[5] However, the diversity of the criteria chosen by different scholars[6] to distinguish prosodic and nonprosodic units is suggestive of a situation more complex than a mere dichotomy.

6.2.   DEFINING CATEGORIES

The definition of the various prosodic and nonprosodic categories, and even the motivation of the choice of categories, raises serious problems.

It is sometimes stated that the reason for separating prosodic or suprasegmental units from other units in the description is that they belong to separate morphemes, i.e. the distinction is *grammatically* motivated (a recent American exponent of this view is Archibald Hill, cf. Hill 1961: 468). This, no doubt, is true to a great extent, but it seems that some features which we should like to call prosodic do belong grammatically with the segmental phonemes; this is true of lexical stress in English and other languages and of the quantity oppositions within stress-syllables in Scandinavian languages, cf. Haugen's analysis of stress and length in Icelandic (1958: 63 ff.).

Now, on the other hand, it has been suggested that suprasegmentals exhibit specific *phonetic* parameters, namely such as are connected with laryngeal or sublaryngeal activity, cf. Twaddell (1953). However, it is not very satisfactory to define a formal category of invariants by means of a phonetic criterion of this kind. As to the distinction of mutually contrastive units within one category, it is of course true that every phonological opposition must somehow or other be reflected in

---

[5] As to 'exponents' vs. 'constituents' see also Hjelmslev (1938: 155).

[6] Surveys in Wells (1945: 27–30) and in Pike (1967, vol. III: 53).

the phonetic substance, and it is by virtue of this phonetic evidence that the opposition can be registered. But this criterion fails to apply to categories that are not in contrast. If we distinguish prosodic and nonprosodic or suprasegmental and segmental categories in the structural model, these categories differ only by their different placement in the model; their existence cannot, in the final analysis, be either motivated or rejected on the basis of phonetic discreteness or lack of phonetic discreteness. There is not a priori any reason to assume that it is fruitful to make a universal division of the phonetic parameters into two groups of which one is reserved for segmental systems and the other for suprasegmental systems. For example, it may well be that vowel harmony in some languages is most conveniently handled in terms of a suprasegmental system with distinctions which would generally be considered typically 'segmental', like front–back or unrounded–rounded. Thus, a gain in structural simplicity is the ultimate motivation of the separation of categories like segmentals and suprasegmentals, or of suprasegmental categories such as stress, tone, and intonation in the phonemic description. Since these categories do not function as terms of oppositions, we may expect any degree of overlap between their phonetic parameters. We may be fully justified in setting up a category of syllable stress without knowing how to distinguish a parameter of stress from other parameters on, e.g., the acoustic level,[7] and it does not in itself affect the structural status of a stress system very much, whether it can be characterized phonetically as pitch accent or as dynamic accent, or perhaps as accent of duration. There may be structural reasons for separating categories of intonations and tonemes in some languages, although we cannot easily distinguish two phonetic parameters.

6.3.   FOUR CATEGORIES OF PHONEMIC UNITS

How many main categories of expression units are we to distinguish on purely structural grounds?

One fundamental distinction is between units or features that are primarily *paradigmatic* in function, and units or features that are primarily *syntagmatic* in function.[8] The former group comprises all units

[7] For a good survey of research on the phonetic nature of stress, see Wang (1962).

[8] The distinction between paradigmatic and syntagmatic contrast was emphasized simultaneously by Martinet (1954) and Prieto (1954).

that commute regularly (in an 'either/or' contrast) with other members of the same category—vowels, consonants, tonemes, intonation phonemes in some analyses of English intonation. The pitch accents postulated for English by Bolinger (1958) must belong to this category, and so do some kinds of emphasis (constituting a paradigmatic series of gradual contrast), whereas non-emphatic stress typically belongs to the latter group. The units of the latter group contrast syntagmatically with preceding and following members of the same category (in a 'both–and' contrast of prominence: Trubetzkoy's (1939: 180) 'kulminative [gipfelbildende] Hervorhebung') and/or have a distinctive placement relative to other units (cf. Haugen's (1949) criterion of 'timing'; the latter type is perhaps exemplified by length in those Scandinavian languages which have either V:C or VC: in all closed stress syllables), but these units do not enter into regular commutation series.

In this paper I shall call units of the former kind *phonemes*, and those of the latter kind *prosodemes*.

The difference between prosodemes and phonemes thus defined is not always clear-cut. The lexical stress-contrast in Russian ('*muka* vs. *mu'ka*) is, in my opinion, prosodic, since both members of the contrast must be present (only their arrangement may be reversed), but it would be theoretically possible to set up two contrasting word-long components of stress: one falling (in '*muka*), and one rising (in *mu'ka*); in this case the category would be phonemic (but suprasegmental, see below). Tonemic systems of the type found, e.g., in Chinese are clearly phonemic (with paradigmatically contrasting tones), but register differences nevertheless have the prosodic property of demanding a tonal context to be well perceived.

Another important distinction is the (American) distinction between segmental and suprasegmental units. However, to serve the purpose here, this distinction must be formulated in strictly formal terms, as follows:

A text is assumed to contain at least one unilinear sequence of phonemic units; it is usually advantageous to describe it in terms of more. We may call the chain of vowels and consonants the segmental or *basic* sequence (probably to be defined as the chain which contains the maximal number of successive units). All members of a basic sequence are *basic*; all members of other (phonemically simultaneous) sequences are *supra*-units. The hierarchic organization of the text into stress-groups, syllables, etc., is established through the interaction between these sequences, which are most fruitfully looked upon as a series of *levels*: the basic sequence constitutes the lowest level (since vowels and consonants participate directly in the establishment of small-size constructions only), while the uppermost level is probably constituted by a sequence of intonation terminals (participating in the establishment of whole utterances).

The two distinctions made here provide us with a fourfold grouping of phonemic units into *basic phonemes* (vowels and consonants), *basic prosodemes* (possibly /:/ in some Scandinavian languages), *supra-phonemes* (tonemes, etc.), and *supra-prosodemes* (certain stress systems, etc.). A rather different fourfold grouping has been suggested by Hill (1961) on morphological grounds.

6.4.   CULMINATIVE CONTRASTS

In the case of culminative contrasts it may be advantageous to set up a single opposition operating on several levels rather than distinguishing a number of categories. This is not only a simplification but even a necessity in cases where there is no fixed number of levels recurring from one utterance to the other. We may thus postulate a prosodic feature of *culmination* or peak formation, which is found on various levels in the form of stress and syllabicity. Culmination is an abstract feature of widely different manifestations; but its allo-members all share the property of being of a culminative kind.

It has been suggested by several scholars that the stress contrast in Germanic languages is dichotomous. Complex stress patterns are accounted for by Chomsky *et al.* (1956) in terms of junctures, whereas Weinreich (1954), among others, distinguishes levels of stress. The latter viewpoint, on which the present paper is based, has been stated very explicitly by Eli Fischer-Jørgensen (1961: 88): 'stress in the Germanic languages [is] an opposition between two members in different functional layers ... and not ... a category of 3 or 4 members.'

The stress contrast obviously does not operate on a fixed number of levels. In, e.g., German or English, the number of levels may vary within wide limits, depending on the complexity of the sequence. The sequence within which we can describe the hierarchic arrangement of stress, is Hockett's (1958: 38) macrosegment: 'the stretch of material spoken with a single intonation', i.e. a sequence delimited by a terminal contour. Every macrosegment has its separate number of levels. A monosyllabic macrosegment has no supra-prosodeme of stress (there is no possibility of syntagmatic stress contrast), but with more syllables we get one or several levels of stress contrast, namely maximally *n–1* levels for a macrosegment with *n* syllables. Thus, if we render the two terms of the stress opposition as contours with plus and minus, we may present various patterns such as:

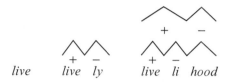

The relative phonetic stress (in a strictly impressionistic sense) of each syllable or syllable group within the macrosegment can be read from such a notation, since (i) a syllable or syllable group 'A' has weaker stress than another syllable or syllable group 'B' if 'A' has a minus-contour, and 'B' a plus-contour on the same level (*-li-* has weaker stress than *live-* in *livelihood*); and (ii) 'A' has weaker stress than 'B' if 'A' exhibits a minus-contour on a lower level than 'B' does (*-li-* has weaker stress than *-hood* in *livelihood*). The latter difference does not reflect a contrast (*-li-* and *-hood* do not contrast except through the higher-level contrast between *liveli-* and *-hood*), but it is a cue to the differentiation of levels of stress contrast.

The dichotomous model leaves no room for considerations of 'absolute degree of stress'. The morpheme *live* has three different stress patterns superposed in the three words above, although it is current phonemic practice to consider the accentuation of *live* identical in all three cases (on the assumption that utterances having only one vowel are said with a loudness equal to the greatest loudness found in larger utterances, cf. Trager and Smith (1951: 35).

One reason for choosing a representation of this kind is that it corresponds in many ways to the grammatical structure. In the English example above the distribution of plus- and minus-contours clearly reflects the word structure. In German this correlation between the grammatical and phonological hierarchies is very tight, but in English rythmical factors may change the picture rather a lot. The hierarchic model of stress patterns is thus not to be considered a part of grammar, although there is a very close *affinity* between phonology and grammar on these levels.

6.5.   JUNCTURE

The phonemic status of junctural phenomena is a much debated problem. In a recent acoustic-phonetic study Lehiste (1960)[9] rejects the interpretation of internal open juncture in English as a phoneme; she reduces it to a marker of higher-level boundaries. On this basis Fowler (1960) has reintroduced Bloomfield's old interpretation of open juncture as the placement of an onset of stress.

If stress is accounted for by contours, the difference between close and open juncture must be a difference in the way one contour ends and the next contour begins. We may assume that such contours may or may not *overlap* relative to the basic sequence, and that syllables with separate contours are phonetically (at least potentially) more separate than syllables with overlapping contours;[10] in the Germanic languages overlapping contours are typically found when a stress syllable is followed by an unstressed syllable belonging to the same stress group (i.e. not separated from it by a higher level contour):

The border between two contours is phonemically predictable in some cases but distinctive in other, as in

We may define *minus-juncture* as an overlap between adjacent stress contours; a basic phoneme on which two contours overlap is by definition ambisyllabic—consider *m* in coming.

---

[9]   With an extensive survey and bibliography on juncture in English.
[10] Cf. Pike (1967, vol. II: 51) for a similar presentation of minus-juncture.

Non-overlap between adjacent stress contours defines a *syllable border*, as in *an aim*. Phonetic open juncture is just one variety of non-overlap: a pattern resulting in open juncture before a vowel may give no audible break before a consonant:

A syllable border is the potential place of an open juncture. The supra-prosodemic configurations must be presented in such a way as to take care of the varying degrees of open juncture at various places in the sequence. If there are several syllable borders in a macrosegment, rules of this kind will apply to juncture in, e.g., English: (i) syllables that have separate contours on higher levels are phonetically more separate than syllables which share contours on higher levels; (ii) there is generally a wider spacing between adjacent syllables of which neither has a minus-contour than between syllables of which either or both have minus-contours; (iii) some combinations of syllable-final and syllable-initial phonemes (to be specified) favour the occurrence of a break, as compared to other combinations.

In some cases we find contours which have a constructional function without exhibiting culminative contrasts. Such neutral contours (level stress contours) account for the syllable borders and the closeness or separation of syllable centres (disjuncture, cf. Bolinger and Gerstman 1957), and may probably in some cases account for apparently paradigmatic contrasts between 'secondary' and 'weak' stress. Stress-neutral contours may also be postulated to account for the delimitation of stress groups of equal prominence (in cases where there is a distinct segmentation before or after, e.g., a weakly stressed syllable). In other cases such contours are redundant (cf. *-hood* of *livelihood* above).—In the original version of this paper, such contours were tentatively rendered as plus-contours.

6.6. SYLLABICITY

It may sometimes be advantageous to recognize a level of culminative contrast below the stress levels in order to account for the distinction between syllable centre and margin(s). It is perfectly possible to abstract a feature of syllabicity and to treat it as a supra-feature rather than a segmental feature, because the feature belongs to units of larger extension than the single basic phonemes. While the contours on the lowest level of stress-contrast establish syllables, the contours on this syllabicity level establish parts of syllables.

In English, and probably many other languages, the main division within the syllable is between initial margin and remainder.[11] We may, therefore, set up a culminative contrast between a minus-contour, which establishes the initial margin, and a peak-forming plus-contour, which establishes the remainder:

$$\begin{array}{cc} - & + \\ b\ l\ \textit{æ}\ k \end{array}$$

The plus-contour indicates that the peak is situated in the part of the syllable which it covers, but it does not indicate which phoneme is syllabic. The exact specification of this appears to be structurally irrelevant in English (one may set up a purely phonetic rule saying that the peak is formed by the first phoneme of the plus-contour part of the syllable). It is essential for the simplicity of the structural statements that the prosodic contours are set up in such a way that they do not convey redundant information.

The syllabicity feature is a typical example of a syntagmatic feature; it does not work well to set up segmental features of 'vocalic' and 'consonantal' within a hierarchic model, because vowels and consonants do not enter into commutation with each other under typical conditions.[12]

In the case of English, the prosodic interpretation of syllabicity enables the analyst to identify /u/–/w/, /i/–/j/, and perhaps /ə/–/h/, so that, e.g., a transcription /wuwl/ *wool* (following the Trager–Smith notation) might be rewritten as

$$\begin{array}{cc} - & + \\ u\ u\ u\ l \end{array}$$

[11] A division of the syllable into initial margin and remainder was suggested by Kuryło-wicz (1948) and even earlier by de Saussure (1960 [English translation]: 49 ff. and 57–8). Hockett (1955: 150) chooses this solution for English.

[12] Cf. Borgstrøm's (1954: 551) criticism of *Preliminaries* on this point.

6.7. FINAL REMARKS

It is not the aim of the present paper to suggest any change of the principles followed in phonemic transcriptions. For notational purposes linear interpretations of sound sequences are greatly to be preferred to any attempt at a hierarchic display, but, at the same time, such transcriptions may not be structurally adequate. The failure of linear transcriptions to place the various features on their proper levels introduces a considerable amount of redundancy in the transcription—a redundancy which does not reflect the structure of the language but the shortcomings of the transcription system.

There is no reason to attempt to identify the structural model and the transcription system, but the two kinds of representation should supplement each other. The present paper offers an attempt at an interpretation of the stress and juncture marks and the distinction between vowels and consonants in phonemic transcriptions.

7

Is There Just One Hierarchy of Prosodic Categories?[1]

This paper is a reaction to some claims made in recent metrical theory. I limit myself here to certain ideas about language stratification and prosodic categories which are expressed by Elisabeth Selkirk in papers such as 'The Role of Prosodic Categories in English Word Stress' (1980) and above all 'On Prosodic Structure and Its Relation to Syntactic Structure' (1978, 1980).

My selection of topic does not imply that the issues I discuss are necessarily the ones on which I disagree most with current work in the metrical trend, but I think the topic of my paper can be discussed in rather general terms without going into much technical detail.

By way of introduction I wish to state that it was a significant event when—in the late 1970s—it suddenly became legitimate, and very soon almost compulsory, to handle certain phonological phenomena in terms of *non-linear structures*. For many years the basically sequential representation of phonological strings forced the strict adherents of transformational-generative phonology to handle prosodic phenomena (in the widest sense) as components of a strictly linear representation, even though this led to obviously unsatisfactory and counterintuitive solutions.

Today, metrical phonology seems to play much the same role as classical transformational-generative phonology used to do, in challenging and stimulating linguists worldwide to look for phenomena in their own languages which are amenable to such description and which are crucial in this framework either because they support current claims or because they provide evidence that certain revisions *must* be made,

[1] Reprinted from *Phonologica 1984*: Proceedings of the Fifth International Phonology Meeting, Eisenstadt, 25–8 June 1984, ed. W. U. Dressler. London: Cambridge University Press (1987): 253–9. (=Innsbrucker Beiträge zur Sprachwissenschaft 36).

if this can be done without violating the most basic assumptions of the theory.

The question, in such a case, is whether the change of theory just meant leaving one Procrustean bed in order to enter another. I shall return to this issue at the end of this paper.

To make my position clear from the start, I must express complete loyalty towards the idea that relative prominence relations in phonology are hierarchically arranged, at least to some extent. But I am anything but sure that this should be construed to mean that *all* prosodic phenomena should be described with reference to *one* prosodic hierarchy of great complexity. In an early paper (1964c) I suggested that stress patterns and syllabicity should be handled in terms of a prominence feature operating within different kinds of units in such a hierarchy (the resulting complex tree being supposed to take care of both juncture and syllable parsing). However, I would consider it an open issue today how prosodic structures should be represented. For one thing, there seem to be good arguments in favour of treating phonological structures with more than one category of prosodic features as multi-dimensional (cf. the multi-'tier' approach of autosegmental phonology), although such a representation is inadequate if it does not express the difference of hierarchical rank between such categories as intonation, stress accent, and syllabicity.

In the present paper I wish to take up another issue having to do with the limitations of a unitarian representation of, say, stress patterns in terms of tree structures with labelled branches. The question is: does a single, hierarchical representation insightfully reflect all mechanisms having to do with relative stress assignment, or is it necessary to operate with two or more strata (differing in 'abstractness', according to well-established terminology)? Note that this is not a question of cyclic stress assignment (and of the operation of such devices as 'deforestation' and 'arborization'); rather it is a question of the *coexistence of non-isomorphous stress hierarchies*.

(1) (a) Foregrounding of information:
          (local) focus or emphasis vs. neutral (flat) rendering

     (b) Prosodic hierarchy and rhythm:
          syntax-dependent vs. 'autonomous' organization

     (c) Rendering of single words/syllables:
          distinct vs. reduced (slurred)

     (d) Style of speech:
          formal vs. casual

In (1) I have listed (rather at random) some parameters which any serious theory of prosodic organization must deal with. I shall not refer here to item (1a), that is, focus or emphasis, but just mention that there are languages such as Danish which permit speakers to have main stresses of equal weight throughout an utterance, without a focal stress on any particular word. This, of course, invites a separation of focal and emphatic stress from the remaining machinery of relative prominence assignment, which is what I am going to discuss under (1b) in a short while.

If we jump for the moment to (1c) and (1d), these parameters should *not* be equated with a parameter going from 'more underlying' to more 'surfacy' in the transformational-generative sense. The possibility of speaking at different distinctness levels or in different styles obviously complicates the matter enormously, especially since it is perfectly possible—and normal—within one utterance to switch back and forth between different distinctness levels in order to foreground or background parts of the message. This in itself puts a question mark on homogeneous representations in the form of enormous prosodic trees. We have to allow for heterogeneity in such representations.

One may wonder why I have not put *tempo* here. I think tempo is in part a derived parameter, which is a function of the desired level of distinctness, of the person's individual speech habits, and of the time allotted to the paper he is giving. For this reason I do not much believe in milliseconds as part of the conditioning input to phonological rules (although the *temporal organization* of speech is in itself a major issue, also for phonology).

Leaving aside the variables in (1a, 1c, and 1d), we are left with a certain definable pattern of relative syllable prominence for many languages. The danger of analyses in terms of prominence trees—and I say this although I hope it is clear that I adhere to such representations myself—is that too-rich structures are posited. One thing that should be factored out, of course, is the impression of relative syllable prominence which is a direct function of syllable structure, as against extrinsically—specified prominence.—If a long syllable sounds more prominent than a short one, or one with a full vowel sounds more prominent than one with a reduced vowel, it is to my mind confusing to build this into the stress hierarchy in the form of a redundant strong–weak assignment, unless a very good case can be made for arguing that such differences in inherent syllable weight play the same role in phonological rules as do differences in relative prominence which are *not* predictable from syllable structure.

So much for unwarranted hierarchical structure. I want to switch to the central issue, namely *stratification*.

In various papers Selkirk has made the point that there is a prosodic hierarchy which is *not* isomorphic to syntactic structure, and she makes a case for positing a definite set of prosodic categories including an intonational phrase, a phonological phrase, a prosodic word, and two types of foot, all belonging to successive steps from utterance down to syllable (I disregard here the further analysis of the syllable).

In Fig. 7.1, I have tried to reproduce one of Selkirk's examples which serves to demonstrate the non-conformity between syntax and prosodic structure. Although I fully agree that there are non-conforming and indeed non-isomorphous structures involved in the

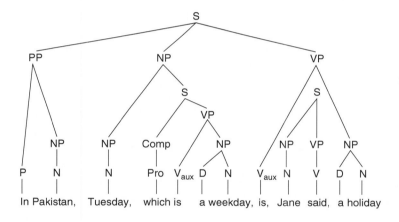

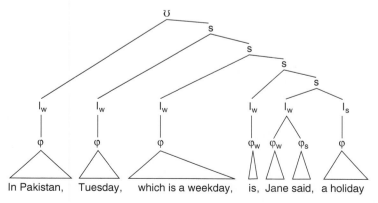

Figure 7.1

syntax-prosody area, I fail to see that Selkirk's example is well-suited to show this. You will see that her intonational phrases (marked by capital I) and her phonological phrases (marked by Greek φ) are all in some sense syntactical constituents, and that the interesting difference is in the arrangement of branches. But on reading the paper on Prosodic Structure one learns that 'the question to be asked is whether the φ's ... are joined in a binary branching tree labelled s/w or whether the structure is flatter, with, possibly, no s/w prominence relations being defined.' Then the author opts for the solution with binary branching, her only explicit motivation being that this is 'consistent with the overall Liberman and Prince-type approach we have been taking to prosodic structure.' And this leads the author to a principle governing intonational phrases which says, concerning constituency, that 'The I is composed of φ joined in a right-branching structure', and concerning prominence: 'In I, the nodes ... are in the relation w/s.'

I fail to see how a decision to adhere to a Liberman and Prince-type approach provides proof that there is a *real* lack of isomorphy at play between syntax and prosody.

In Fig. 7.2 I have given what I consider a *genuine* case for nonconformity. In Danish a verb phrase such as *går i 'skole* 'goes to school' takes what I have called unit accentuation with downgrading of the first constituent of the Prepositional Phrase *i 'skole*, and similarly downgrading of the constituent of the whole Verb Phrase *går i 'skole*. We have in this example a Bresnan type of stress modification across an intervening surface constituent, namely the sentence adverb *ikke*. This is the mechanism of *phrasal accentuation*, and it clearly operates on a level associated with the syntactical representation. May I just add that such a syntax-dependency has been shown for other languages as well (thus, Paul Verluyten[2] has expressed somewhat related ideas in dealing with French).

But then we have in normal rendering a realignment of the words and syllables according to a kind of Abercrombian feet—what I call *Maximal Intonational Foot Formation* in Fig. 7.2. As shown by Nina Thorsen[3] for Danish, every fully stressed syllable is the line-up point for a new intonational contour, and in casual speech this realignment ignores word boundaries and phrase boundaries, so that we get

[2] Editors' note: see Verluyten, S.P.M. 1982, Investigations on French prosodics and metrics. Ph.D. dissertation, Univ. Instelling, Antwerpen (Belgium). Ann Arbor, Michigan: University. Microfilms International.

[3] Editors' note: now Nina Grønnum.

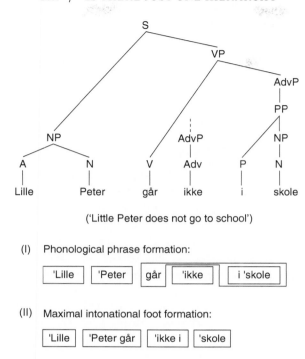

('Little Peter does not go to school')

(I)   Phonological phrase formation:

| 'Lille | 'Peter | går | 'ikke | i 'skole |

(II) Maximal intonational foot formation:

| 'Lille | 'Peter går | 'ikke i | 'skole |

Figure 7.2

intonational feet such as *'Peter går*, and *'ikke i*, which totally cut across the boundaries of the phrasal constituents that were responsible for unit accentuation in the first place.

The intonational structure, in turn, is subject to greater or lesser flattening according to the effect of the parameters exemplified in (1) above. Or, as I like to put it with regard to parameter (1b), the outcome is the result of *interference* between two principles of prosodic organization. The speaker may or may not choose to signal the bounding of phrases or words, and it is probably only in very casual, high-tempo speech or in downgraded parts of utterances that the intonational foot in its maximum extension takes over *completely*, so that we get a very flat structure.

(2)   *Some possible entities in abstract (morphosyntactically and lexically determined) representations*:
      Sentence (etc.)
      Phonological Phrase
      Phonological Compound

Phonological Simplex Word
Phoneme viewed as a 'Figura'
Some possible entities in 'surfacy' (rhythmically organized) representations:
Utterance (etc.)
Intonational Foot
?Foot of lesser complexity
Surface Syllable
Phoneme as Syllable Constituent

In the list in (2) I have attempted to set up some possible candidates for inclusion in a more abstract and a more 'surfacy' stratum of phonological representation. But I consider it ill-conceived to squeeze *all* apparent differences of more abstract versus more concrete categories into such a two-strata model. Phonological phrases versus intonational feet is one thing; abstract syllables versus surface syllables—provided that such a distinction is fruitful—may be quite another thing.

It is at best a very indirect way to advance our science if one starts out by propagating yet another taxonomy in the hope that it will end up being adhered to by confession. What I am insisting is only that there *are* interfering principles of prosodic organization, and that there is such a thing as global or local shrinkage or flattening of structures. It seems to me that these phenomena cause certain problems for the current metrical conceptions of language design.

What is most important now is to study prosodic phenomena in the languages we happen to speak, in all their richness of typological variation, and to approach them with an open mind also to things that do not fit current descriptive formats nicely; even if this means that we can handle linguistic phenomena only piecemeal, at the expense of overall homogeneity and elegance.

8

Compound Stress in Danish without a Cycle[1]

8.1. INTRODUCTION

The existence or non-existence of cyclic rules in phonology is an important issue in the current debate. Among the processes which are widely assumed to be cyclic, the graded reduction of stresses in compound words probably holds a particularly high rank. The mechanism involved was stated in such terms by Chomsky *et al.* (1956), and the more recent formulation of it in Chomsky and Halle (1968) largely dominates descriptive approaches at the present time.

I wish to point to the fact that compound stress in Danish can be described without reference to cyclic rule application (at least in the sense in which 'cyclic' is generally taken), and that this approach enables us to abandon the parameter of 'degree of stress', which (unlike the abstract dichotomy [±stress]) seems to me fictitious in a description of Danish. Although I do not generalize the results to other languages, the very possibility of describing compound stress in a Germanic language in this way seems to me of interest to phonological theory in general.

The model for generating complex stress patterns, which I use below, was actually outlined ten years ago in a paper using English for illustration (Rischel 1964c, also cf. the much earlier outline of the hierarchical concept in Fischer-Jørgensen 1961). However, the said paper was highly sketchy and moreover contained a number of contentions which are not directly relevant to the present issue. I shall, therefore,

[1] Reprinted from *Annual Report of the Institute of Phonetics, University of Copenhagen* 6 (1972): 211–28.

confine myself to mentioning the paper rather than referring to it in more detail.

8.2.   THE HIERARCHICAL MODEL

We assume a basic difference between stressed and unstressed syllables, the distribution of [+stress] and [–stress] being either lexical or introduced by rule.[2] There must then be a device that converts [+stress] into degrees of stress (and a device that converts [–stress] into degrees of stress under certain conditions) if, for the moment, we assume that 'degree of stress' is a linguistic parameter (this will be questioned later in the present paper). As shown by Chomsky *et al.* (1956) the grading of [+stress] is closely dependent upon the constituent structure of the syntactic surface representation (although obviously with some adjustments). If degrees of stress that are intermediate between the strongest and the weakest are considered as *reduced* occurrences of [+stress], the amount of reduction in each instance has something to do with the relation of the constituent involved to other constituents of the complex structure. In compounds the general rule is that stress reduction is triggered by the occurrence of a stressed constituent to the left of the constituent under consideration, and—at least to a first approximation—the effect of stress reduction is stronger the closer the

---

[2] In Rischel (1970) it was shown that the stress placement in Danish formatives (morphemes) is largely predictable from their segmental structure, and that the stress placement in Danish noncompound words is (normally) found by deleting all but the last formative stress. The rules for this simple mechanism of stress assignment were presented without a sufficiently clear statement of the theoretical framework in which they are to be understood (the attempt on pp. 140 ff to harmonize the approach with that of Chomsky and Halle must be considered a failure). The stress assignment rules for formatives are most naturally understood as redundancy rules, whereas the word-stress rule is a process rule, belonging to phonology proper. It must be conceded that not all formative stresses in Danish are predictable, i.e. some formatives are lexically marked for idiosyncratic stress placement, whereas the majority are unmarked (i.e. stressed according to redundancy rules). In a reasonably realistic phonological representation stress may have to be marked more often than suggested in the said paper, but a solution cannot be found until other types of evidence in favour of more or less abstract representations have been investigated, in particular the stød (cf. Basbøll 1972). As for word stress assignment, I wish to point to the fact that the rule involved requires only a distinction of [+stress] and [–stress], which agrees with the starting point of the present paper. (The short section on compounds (p. 138) was kept in quite traditional terms and may be disregarded.)

connection is between the two constituents. This can be taken care of by a cyclic approach, and indeed invites such an approach. However, the concept of cyclicality may be unnecessary here, and hence should be abandoned if it is not required for independent reasons. If stress grading depends on the syntactic 'tree-structure', it may be directly deducible from this representation.

In the following I confine myself strictly to compounds with initial 'main stress'. The exceptions to this general pattern are few (subregularities for these will not be stated here).

Consider compounds like *fædrelandssang* 'patriotic song' (literally: 'father-land's-song') and *perlehalsbånd* 'pearl necklace'. The internal constituent structures of these compounds (which can be posited no matter whether the compounds are considered to be entirely or partially lexicalized), are obviously different. In the former the primary break is between *fædrelands* and *sang* (with a secondary break between *fædre* and *lands*), in the latter the primary break is between *perle* and *halsbånd* (with a secondary break between *hals* and *bånd*). However, both compounds consist of a sequence of three noun stems: a bisyllabic one followed by two monosyllabic ones. Assuming that each of these gets initial stress by rule (cf. Rischel 1970: 119ff), we arrive at structures which can be roughly represented like this:[3]

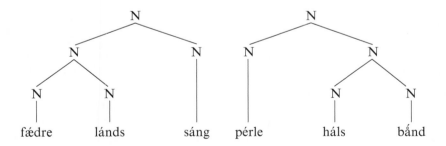

A compound stress rule with associated conventions for stress adjustment may be considered to have the effect of reducing stresses. Under a cyclic application stress reduction would apply twice to *lánds* in the former compound, and to *bånd* in the latter, but only once to *sáng* in the former and *háls* in the latter. This seems plausible enough, since

---

[3] I assume some readjustment by which, for example, the formative *s* in *fædrelandssang* is incorporated into the second noun.

it would not be too difficult to make phoneticians agree that the two forms are stressed like this:[4]

'fædre‚lands,,sang
'perle,,hals,bånd

where [,,] indicates a less reduced stress, and [,] a more reduced stress. However, this very accentuation can be read off the tree structure representation, provided that we have a rule saying that left branches are given relatively more prominence than right branches in compounds. If this difference of prominence is indicated by plus versus minus we get the following representations (with omission of the N labels for simplicity):

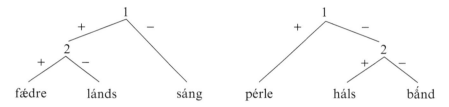

The degree of stress reduction cannot, of course, be determined solely by counting minuses. The convention involved must refer to the position of the minuses in the hierarchy, e.g. by assigning each minus the number of the node above it. The phonetic stress reduction would then be a function of such numbers. Since this function is unknown[5] I shall represent a nominal amount of stress reduction by simply indicating the hierarchical number, '2' meaning a stronger reduction than '1', etc.

Now one might imagine different ad hoc conventions for stress reduction. The coefficients might add up, for example. Under a convention of this kind *sáng* and *háls* above would get a reduction of the order of '1', and *lánds* would get a reduction of the order of '2', whereas *bånd* would get a reduction of the order of '1 + 2' (i.e. have a stronger reduction than *lánds*).

Another possibility would be that the degree of reduction directly reflects the depth of compounding, i.e. that the convention applies to

---

[4] Alternatively, [,] might be used instead of [,,], if the syllables here marked with [,,] are assumed to be reduced to 'weak stress'. A reduction of stresses all the way to 'weak stress' might entail a process [+stress] → [−stress]. I have not considered the occurrence of such a rule in compounds in the present paper.

[5] A priori it need not be a linear function at all. Since I shall abandon the use of stress coefficients later in this paper, the problem is of no real interest here.

the lowest minus in each case. Under this convention *fædrelandssang* gets stress reductions according to the pattern '0–2–1', and *perlehals-bånd* according to the pattern '0–1–2'.

This is an empirical issue. It is a difficulty that the phonetic correlates to concepts like 'primary stress' and 'secondary stress' are so poorly defined. As for my own subjective judgement, however, I find no support for the former assumption, i.e. that stress reduction operates on a summation basis. If there is at all a difference between the reduction of stress on *lands* and *bånd* in the examples above, it is rather such that the former is more reduced than the latter.[6] This can be taken care of by a rhythmic convention applying optionally (Section 8.3 below) if we assume that the basic degree of reduction is the same in both cases.

In compounds like *forbundsdomstol* 'Federal Tribunal' we have a more complex constituent structure which can be represented like this (with some adjustment[7]):

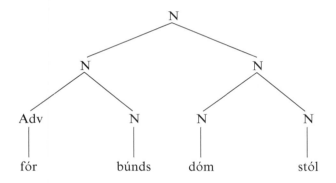

Here we get the strongest stress on *fór*, and the next strongest on *dóm*, under any reasonable convention. However, the weaker stresses on *búnds* and *stól* would differ crucially depending on the functioning of stress reduction. If it is additive (in some way), we should get less stress on *stól* than on *búnds*. Again, this is at variance with my subjective judgement; there is rather a tendency in the opposite direction, which can be taken care of as suggested above.

I would suggest, therefore, that the convention for Danish *reduces each stress of a compound (in relation to the leftmost stress) solely according to the order of (the number assigned to) the lowest node*

---

[6] This is a highly subjective evaluation. I do not really know how to arrive at a valid criterion for this decision.

[7] Cf. note 3.

that dominates the constituent in question, and from which it hangs in a branch that is labelled 'minus'.

This convention is thus sensitive to depth of compounding and to occurrence in non-initial position under the lowest dominating node.

If we now return to the possibility of cyclic rule application, it is interesting that a simple mechanism for compound stress can be devised within the Chomsky and Halle framework which gives exactly the stress reductions posited above. Hence the presentation above does not invalidate the cyclic principle; it only argues that cyclicality is unnecessary.

8.3.   STRUCTURE SIMPLIFICATION

Both approaches referred to above, cyclic and non-cyclic, can be made to work ad infinitum, although it goes without saying that there is a limit to the degrees of stress that are distinguished in actual communication.[8] In Danish it is possible to construct very complex compounds, and if these are entirely right-branching or left-branching the depth of compounding may be considerable. A fancy compound like *storestrømsbrosekspropriationskommissionsbetænkningen* 'the report of the commission for the expropriation for the Storestrøm Bridge (lit.: the bridge of the Great Current)' sounds funny, of course, but is in no way unacceptable from a linguistic point of view. Assume a tree structure like the following:

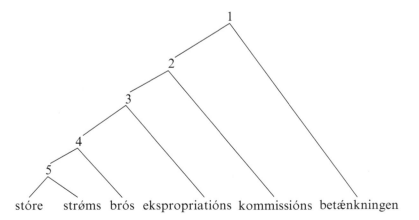

stóre   strøms brós ekspropriatións kommissións betænkningen

[8] Cf. Householder's remark to Rischel in Rischel (1964*c*: 93), with which I entirely agree.

According to the alleged convention we should get increasing stress reduction from *betænkningen* (1st order) through *strøms* (5th order). Or put differently: *strøms, brós*, etc. through *betænkningen* should have increasing stress in the order in which they are spoken. I doubt if anybody could make a convincing performance of this theoretical stress pattern. There will necessarily be some kind of adjustment reducing the depth.

One possible type of adjustment may be described with reference to a *threshold*, depending to some extent on tempo and style of speech,[9] below which hierarchical differences vanish. Assuming, for instance, that nodes cannot be of more than second order in casual speech, the structure above would simplify into:

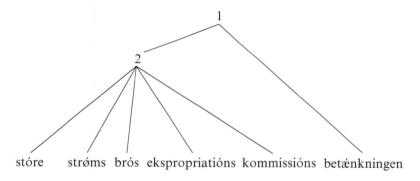

which gives 1st order reduction on *betænkningen*, and 2nd order reduction on the other, non-initial constituents; that is, in conventional stress notation,

'store+‚strøms+‚bros+ekspropria‚tions+kommis‚sions+be‚‚tænkningen.

To what extent (under what conditions) such node-collapsing actually occurs, could be studied by observing the neutralizations among different hierarchical structures that occur in a given type of speech. With the threshold referred to above we should get a neutralization of the structures in A and B below, whereas A/B would remain distinct from C:[10]

---

[9] For a device related to this idea of 'threshold', cf. Bierwisch (1966: 166 ff.)

[10] The words mean 'submarine chaser', 'member of a subcommittee', 'private agreement'.

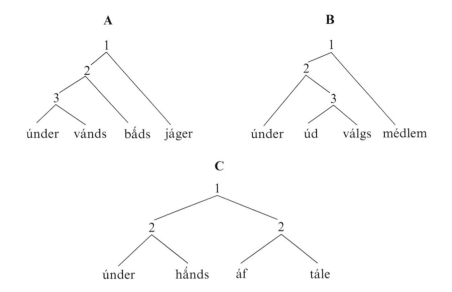

In rapid speech the reduction (and neutralization) may well go even further. Data throwing light on this would deserve close study.

The pattern is complicated by a tendency, in some constructions, to perturb the relative stresses of constituents. This occurs very clearly in a form like *edsaflæggelse* 'taking the oath', which has the structure:

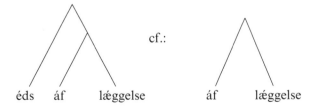

so that we should expect the stress on *áf* to be less reduced than that on *lǽggelse*. However, the form *edsaflǽggelse* can be pronounced with more stress on the ultimate than on the penultimate constituent.

Synchronically, there are several possible explanations of this. First, it may be suggested that we have an optional simplification of the structure to a one-node structure:

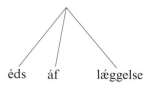

éds   áf   lǽggelse

This should give full stress on *éds*, and evenly reduced stresses on *áf* and *lǽggelse*, according to the convention given earlier. Now it may be assumed that there is a phonetic tendency to replace similar stresses on successive constituents by an alternation of relatively stronger and relatively weaker stresses; such a tendency toward contrast would reduce *áf*, and enhance *lǽggelse*, as required.

This explanation fails, however, to account for the fact that the tendency to perturbation is not equally strong in all forms, for example *perlehalsbånd* (see above) could hardly occur with stress perturbation. In this respect we are better off if we connect the deviating accentuation with the fact that *aflæggelse* contains a succession of *adverb plus verb*, since constructions involving adverb plus verb or verb plus adverb have special prosodic properties anyway. Compounds containing adverb plus verb sometimes have non-initial stress (regularly with +lig, e.g. *aftagelig* 'detachable') and thus break the most basic rule of initial compound stress. I shall not go further into this here.

There are other cases, however, where it seems to me possible (in my own idiolect, at least) to have stress perturbation although the structure involves no adverb plus verb. Take a technical term like *vandluftpumpe*. This means 'water jet air pump', i.e. according to meaning criteria the structure should be:

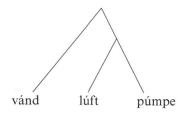

vánd   lúft   púmpe

However, even if I have looked up the meaning of the word, I am inclined to pronounce it with more reduction on *lúft* than on *púmpe*. This is hardly a matter of simplifying the structure to a one-node structure, since the technicality of the term does not invite casual pronunciation, but rather a straightforward readjustment to:

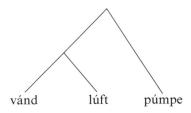

I suggest that there exists a tendency to reinterpret awkward compounds of the former structure as compounds of the latter structure.

Note that the effect of this restatement is that we get an alternation of degrees of stress, rather than a monotonous decrease of stresses. This tendency to avoid stress monotony may also seem to operate in cases where the constituent structure is genuinely ambiguous, e.g. if we take the compound *landbrugsstøtteordning* which can be read as [*landbrugsstøtte*][*ordning*] ([arrangement of] [financial support of agriculture]) or as [*landbrugs*][*støtteordning*] ([arrangement of financial support][for agriculture]), it seems 'easier' to pronounce the latter option, viz. the right-hand structure below.

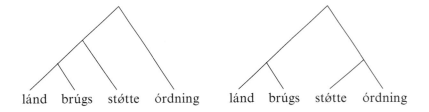

Again, the preferred alternative provides rhythmic alternation, and in this case it moreover reduces the depth of compounding.

It is interesting to note that the preferred analysis posited for these forms has the same effect as structure simplification combined with a phonetic tendency toward rhythmic alternation of the stresses on successive constituents (cf. above). It also has the same effect as destressing of adverbs internally in compounds (cf. *edsaflæggelse*). Thus, until considerably more is known about the ways in which different compound structures are distinguished or fail to be distinguished phonetically, we cannot decide what is really going on in the forms with superficial stress 'perturbation'.

8.4.   ABOLITION OF 'DEGREE OF STRESS' AS A LINGUISTIC PARAMETER

Throughout this paper I have referred to 'degrees of stress' (disregarding unstressed syllables, i.e. syllables which are not assigned a [+stress]), but I have deliberately avoided any discussion of the meaning of the phonetic label 'degree of stress'. Thanks to our phonetic tradition, it is not difficult to communicate by means of such terms, and I have therefore found it practical to use the terms without any definition whatsoever.

The question of the parameters of stress is crucial the moment we want to give the convention stated in Section 8.2 in an exact form. It may be possible to find a reasonable correlate to stress at the level of speech production, but the signalling of constituent structure is known to be highly complex, at least in English (see Scholes 1971 and references), where it includes both intensity and pitch changes as well as separation in time (i.e. 'disjuncture'). On the basis of the limited data available[11] it may be assumed that pitch jump is an important correlate of stress in Danish, and 'disjuncture' is undoubtedly an essential marker of constituent structure also in this language.

Now the question is: do we want our stress rules to give an output in which each syllable is assigned a 'degree of stress' represented by a coefficient? Since these coefficients must undergo a highly complex transformation into different parameters before we arrive at anything that can be measured phonetically, the assignment of stress coefficients seems to me warranted only if there is a solid basis for assuming that these coefficients represent a significant level of linguistic specification. As far as Danish is concerned, at least, it does not seem to me intuitively meaningful to specify coefficients of stress the way this is done in Chomsky and Halle (1968) and elsewhere, or for that matter, to specify stress degrees by symbols like ['], [ˌ] and [ˌ], although, as said above, such representations have a communicative value among linguists who know what they refer to.

In my opinion indications of graded stresses are linguistically significant only indirectly, namely by defining types of constructions. Hence it seems to me superfluous to introduce such representations

[11]   Eli Fischer-Jørgensen has done some instrumental research on the prosodic characteristics of Danish compounds. Her results indicate that shift of pitch is an essential correlate to 'stress' (personal communication).

if the constructions themselves contain sufficient information without being transformed into representations with graded stresses. In order to specify the parameters that signal the structure of compounds, it would seem appropriate to have recourse to two types of linguistic information, viz. *the location of the syllables marked as* [+*stress*] and *the location and order of the constituent boundaries*. But this is indeed what the adjusted phrase-marker presents after application of the stress redundancy rules.

I should prefer, therefore, to replace the convention outlined in Section 8.2 above by a convention which specifies more useful phonetic parameters. This means that the expression 'reduction of *n*th order' should be replaced, e.g. by information referring to pitch jumps and temporal relations. The pitch change and temporal distance between the stress points of consecutive constituents would be assumed a priori to be less the higher the order of the node involved, e.g. in *fædrelandssang* (see Section 8.2) the first two constituents should be specified as spoken on almost an even pitch and closely adjacent to each other, whereas in *perlehalsbånd* this would apply to the last two constituents. In so far as a valid set of conventions could be set up, this type of phonetic characterization would seem to me immensely more satisfactory for Danish than an appeal to fictitious concepts such as 'stronger' or 'weaker' reduced stresses.—The 'main' stress of a (normal) compound is simply the leftmost occurrence of the category [+stress]. A 'secondary' stress of a (normal) compound is secondary by virtue of *not* being the leftmost occurrence of [+stress]. The vocal effort or intensity contour of the word may exhibit a peak associated with the first occurrence of [+stress], or a more complex pattern depending on the constituent structure, but this is not inherently the most interesting feature of accentuation although it should be built into the convention, of course, like other parameters. The interesting question is not how to specify degrees of stress as a parameter, but how to choose the phonetic parameters (= instructions to the speech-organs, auditory parameters, or what?) which should be specified by the 'stress' convention.

The direct consequence of the contentions stated above is that the output of the phonological component must take the form of a hierarchical representation (i.e. a tree structure or its equivalent: a bracketed representation). The phonetic conventions, whatever they are, operate on this hierarchical representation. The tree structure is not necessarily congruent with a syntactic surface representation, since various readjustments take place, but surface syntax and lexicon together make it deducible by rule.

It has been argued quite recently by Pyle (1972) that there are no phonological rules (conventions) that replace formative boundaries by boundary markers, i.e. that boundary markers do not exist as phonological units. Pyle argues that the jobs which boundary markers (junctures) do in current formulations should actually be assigned to the formative boundaries. I agree, since the introduction of boundary markers would be entirely redundant once the adjusted constituent structure (which defines the location of such boundary markers) is present for rules to refer to. There is, however, a problem with lexical items, since 'formative' boundaries are marked (i.e. have a phonological effect) in some cases but not in others. If one does not insert boundary markers to indicate the marked boundaries, it is necessary to have rules (triggered, at least in part, by lexical idiosyncrasies) which delete boundaries that have no phonological effect. The consequences of such an approach must be investigated.

One is, quite generally, faced with the serious question: what kinds of readjustment of boundaries do we have to assume? I think the answer to this question depends on how the lexicon is assumed to be organized and how lexical insertion is assumed to take place. Without a theory of the lexicon there is no point in discussing whether the constituent structure that is relevant to phonology on different levels has a more or less direct relation to surface syntax.

9

On Unit Accentuation in Danish—and the Distinction Between Deep and Surface Phonology[1]

9.1. STRESS AND THE HIERARCHICAL APPROACH

It is no coincidence that the first part of the title of this paper is strongly reminiscent of that of a paper read by L. Hjelmslev before the Linguistic Circle of Copenhagen twenty-five years ago (Hjelmslev 1957). In spite of obvious affinities to 'metrical phonology' the present paper is not directly coupled to the work of the MIT school (some recent advances in 'lexical phonology', which are crucially relevant to issues raised in this paper, could not be considered before completion of the manuscript). Rather, I am trying to summarize and follow up my previous work on the hierarchical nature of Danish stress, with special emphasis on certain issues which have vexed me since I was exposed to Hjelmslev's and Eli Fischer-Jørgensen's views on prosodic patterning in the late 1950s (also cf. Fischer-Jørgensen 1961). At the same time, of course, I am drawing heavily on theoretical advances within generative phonology. In fact, the general setting within which I am dealing with stress is generative, but I have preferred to stick to fairly loose formulations and a minimum of formal apparatus in agreement with my earlier work. I hope that the presentation is sufficiently explicit to make my points clear, though.

Probably the most important concession to be made is that my paper does not link to any particular, fully explicit theory of syntax and semantics. The descriptive approach used here involves the generative notion of surface syntax versus (some kind of) more abstract syntax (and it furthermore implies that lexical material is specified at a level on

[1] Reprinted from *Folia Linguistica* XVII (1983): 51–97.

which the order of syntactic constituents may be somewhat different from that appearing 'on the surface'), but it is anything but clear to me what would be the most appropriate model (among those currently available) to link one's phonology to. (It may deserve mention in particular that I have stuck to traditional labellings such as NP for noun phrase rather than using the X-Bar convention, and that I do not comment on the relevance of Trace Theory for the analysis of the interplay between syntax and phonology.)

Some of the topics dealt with in this paper are treated in more detail in earlier papers to which I refer for further information (Rischel 1964c, 1970, 1972, 1975, 1980, 1981). In the present paper one major omission is made in order not to make the presentation unduly complex, viz. that a variety of *discourse phenomena* are disregarded (some phenomena belonging within this sphere are dealt with, under the common heading 'emphasis', in Rischel 1981). Thus, the types of data referred to here are supposed to represent a neutral, colourless rendering of phrases and utterances, or, to quote Liberman and Prince (1977: 251), 'the null-hypothesis patterns that emerge when there is no good reason to take some other option.'

On the other hand, this paper differs from my earlier reports on Danish stress in that it attempts to deal more specifically with *the relationship between underlying and surface prosodic patterns* (see the last sections of this paper), which is a really challenging issue.

I hope that I shall succeed in demonstrating that Danish stress is interesting both typologically (among other things, because of the dissimilarity between English and Danish stress) and from the point of view of general phonological theory.

In approaching the analysis of stress patterns and stress mechanisms it may be advantageous to start with a consideration of surface patterns and move from there towards more abstract analyses.

9.1.1. The theoretical groundwork

It was one of the major advances in American phonological (at that time phonemic) theory when N. Chomsky, M. Halle, and F. Lukoff (1956) introduced the derivation of degrees of stress from underlying representations with only a binary stress contrast plus a marking of ranked boundaries. Although not so often referred to today, this paper forms an important link between Bloomfieldian phonemics and generative phonology and helps to put into relief the close connection between the two trends. What is interesting in this context is that the paper offered a more fruitful alternative to a theory that posits several degrees of contrastive stress as members of one phonemic category (which had been an obstacle to an adequate handling of the functions of stress).

Within the Copenhagen school of structural linguistics it was recognized quite early that the inventory of Danish stress prosodemes comprises just two members: /'/ (manifested typically as strong stress) and /₀/ (manifested typically as weak stress), cf. the contrasting patterns in ['bi₀lisd] 'cheapest' and [₀bil'isd] 'automobile driver', and observe that the various degrees of stress that one may attempt to distinguish in phonetic transcriptions are contextually determined variants ('varieties'). However, it was never shown in any detail what the rules of stress manifestation really look like. It was made quite explicit, though, that in defining the relevant context it is necessary to have recourse to what would be termed 'higher level information' in the American tradition.

One of the important points in this approach is the emphasis on prosodic relations establishing units of different size (or, more precisely, different hierarchical rank). The relation between /₀/ and /'/ establishes a stress-group or 'expression junction' (comprising one stress-syllable flanked by zero, one, or several zero stress-syllables on either side). In addition to the relation between /'/ and /₀/ proper, there is also a relation involving *reduction* of /'/ in constructions containing another /'/. Such stress reduction was recognized as a signal of an intimate union of consecutive constituents.

Hjelmslev, in dealing with the secondary stresses of compounds (such as Danish ['beːn‚knɑb] 'bone button') claimed that secondary stress here reflects a replacement of ' by ₀ under the dominance of the other ', i.e. on a higher level of abstraction there is a succession of two /'/ in such a compound. Likewise, according to Hjelmslev, the weak stress of the first constituent in expression junctions such as [han 'kʌm'ʌ] 'he is coming' reflects a replacement of ' by ₀ under the dominance of the other ' in the string (see, for example, Hjelmslev 1957: 203; 1973: 253, 260–1). —It was not made very explicit how one can predict from the formal representation that it is the second of two consecutive ' that is replaced by ₀ in compounds, but the first of the two in expression junctions; but it is important that the concept of stress reduction as a signal of close union was somehow built into the analysis. This point was made in a congress paper by Fischer-Jørgensen as early as 1948 (although the Proceedings of the congress did not become available until 1961).

Fischer-Jørgensen's paper makes another important point, viz. that degrees of stress, as they occur in compounds, should be handled in terms of a hierarchical model. I shall quote one of the relevant passages of her brief paper:

> Especially in German very complicated examples of reduction may be found, e.g. ((('Kurz‚waren)‚‚händler)ver‚‚‚ein), where it is possible to distinguish several degrees of reduction. But this can only be done for each group of this kind separately. It is not possible to identify the different degrees of stress from one group to the other, e.g. to decide if the stress of -macher [as part of another compound, viz. 'Hand‚‚schuh‚macher or 'Hand‚schuh‚‚macher] is the same as that of -händler or as that of -verein. And it is completely arbitrary to maintain that a language has 3 or 4 degrees of reduced stress. It is only a way of stating the syntactical possibilities of the language. The important thing is always a comparison between two members and two members only, but this may take place on different levels.

My own paper of twenty years ago (Rischel 1964c) was an attempt to outline a fully hierarchical approach to prosodic structure (comprising at least stress and syllabicity) in a structuralist format.

So much for the pre-generativist basis of the approach to Danish stress which I shall outline here. The remainder of this paper will contain an exposition of certain components of an all-round description of Danish stress but with particular emphasis on the mechanism of stress reduction.

In generating stress patterns from underlying forms in Danish, I have not found it very promising to use the approach of Standard Generative Phonology, as explicated in the sections on English word stress and the transformational cycle in SPE (Chomsky and Halle 1968). The complex rules involved do not make it very transparent what is the basic relationship between stress patterns and the remainder of the phonology on the one hand, and between stress patterns and syntax on the other.

The principle I apply is to start strictly from the bottom up in terms of grammatical structure, the components of such an approach being the following: (i) stress placement in individual morphemes; (ii) downgrading in simplex wordforms; (iii) downgrading in compounds; and (iv) downgrading in phrases. The stress pattern of a complex string is supposed to be derivable from these components taken together, although—as I shall show later—the relationship between the components is somewhat intriguing.

A note on terminology and transcription: throughout this paper I use terms such as 'stress pattern' and 'accentuation' rather indiscriminately (I would prefer to use *Accent* for the more abstract category, and *Stress* for the phonetic category, or rather the subjective experience of extrinsically-determined syllable prominence, but this would presuppose a clarification of the distinction between abstraction levels which I do not think has been achieved so far). As for the notation of degrees of stress, I have earlier (Rischel 1972) expressed my scepticism about the phonetic meaning of these elements, at least for Danish, and in this paper I prefer to avoid the notation of degrees of secondary stress. In transcriptions I have simply indicated the placement of stresses that have *not* undergone reduction: in the (few) cases where phonetic transcription is used, these stresses are indicated by ['] before the syllable in question, but otherwise they are indicated by an acute accent over the vowel. The same mark (acute accent) is also used to mark lexical stresses in strings of morphemes in those cases where the prosodic structure is specified in terms of a tree structure with labelled branches; I hope that these two (mutually exclusive) uses of the accent mark do not cause confusion.

The term *Prominence*, as it is used in this paper, is an impressionistic term referring to a subjective assessment of how much a syllable stands out in relation to other syllables. Unfortunately, as is generally the case with the use of this term in phonology, it remains rather obscure what the relation is between this alleged parameter of prominence and, say, (i) the inherent syllable weight as determined by segmental structure, length, and presence or absence of *stød*; (ii) the extrinsic pitch which the syllable gets by virtue of its placement in an utterance with a specific intonation and a specific distribution of full stresses; and finally (iii) linguistic stress (lexical and emphatic) on this particular syllable. I do *not* here take 'prominence' to be an independent parameter, however.

Finally, there is the question of terminology referring to degrees of stress. There is a proliferation of terms referring either to stresses as such or to syllables, or both, and in part referring to the function of stress as a signal of subordinating constructions, cf. such pairs as 'strong'–'weak', 'heavy'–'light', 'main stress'–'secondary stress'. I have not striven to be strictly consistent in this paper, but whenever it is important to make clear that I take stress gradation (outside of emphasis) to be a matter of reduction or downgrading, I refer to the unreduced stress as *full stress* and to all occurrences of an underlying stress that undergoes reduction, as *reduced stress*. Syllables whose stress is reduced to such an extent that they might just as well be underlyingly unstressed are said to have (reduction to) *weak stress.* The term *zero stress* is used in some cases to refer to lexical absence of stress, which comes out phonetically as weak stress, of course. In many cases, however, I have found it more convenient to speak of *stressed* versus *unstressed.*

9.1.2. Morpheme stress

If one looks at individual morphemes (disregarding for the moment all stress gradings that are conditioned by the larger context), there are two basic questions to be asked about accentuation: (i) is the morpheme in question inherently stressed? and (ii) if so, where is the inherent stress placed?

9.1.2.1. *Inherent stress*

As for the question of inherent stress, it is possible to start with the formulation of a phonological condition: a morpheme cannot be inherently stressed unless it contains at least one full vowel. This takes care of inflectional endings, which contain only consonants and schwa. There are also a couple of derivational suffixes, viz. *-(l)ig* and *-(n)ing*, which are unstressed (at least if they are not followed by one or more inflectional syllables) and which may be claimed to have schwa underlyingly although they surface with a full vowel ([i] and [e], respectively); under this analysis (which, by the way, has been current in Danish structural dialectology) the absence of stress is straightforward. It is less simple, however, with other derivational affixes.

As for prefixes, I wish to contend that these are, as a rule, inherently stressed but undergo the process of Intra-Word Unit Accentuation dealt with in the next section. The inventory of items that count as prefixes in this sense includes a variety of roots and prefixes of Latin and Greek origin, a few (but highly frequent) prefixes of Low German origin, and at least one prefix of Danish origin, viz. *u-* 'non-'. Some of these items have a complex morphosyntactic and phonological behaviour in that they behave like root morphemes (forming compounds or quasi-compounds) in some cases but like prefixes (undergoing Intra-Word UA) in other cases; this very complex issue has to be left totally aside in the present paper. There are some other items, however, such as the Low German ones (e.g. *be-*) or Greek *filo-, antropo-, theo-* etc., which do not normally occur under stress and which might thus be defined as inherently unstressed. If, however, such items are put in relief for the sake of contrast with other prefixal material, the stress invariably falls on one specific syllable (unless it is some other syllable, rather than the whole item, that is put in relief): *jeg sagde "antroposof, ikke "theosof* 'I said a., not th.' (without such relief, both words have a main stress on the last syllable). Thus it is relevant to know where to put the emphatic stress in such cases, in casu on the first syllable of the item in question.

This raises the question whether the specification to be made here— viz. for inherent stress placement—presupposes inherent stress or not. It depends, of course, on the definition of these concepts, and I am not sure what is the best solution. At present I am assuming, however, that the concept of *inherent stress* should be extended to cover not only morphemes that actually surface with a stress degree above 'zero stress', but in fact all morphemes with a full vowel. 'Inherent stress', then, does not imply that the morpheme in question typically occurs with a main stress but rather that *there is a unique syllable within this morpheme serving as the carrier of potential stress*, and that *the morpheme appears with a main stress unless it enters a construction conditioning some other accentuation*. Some morphemes, then, rarely or never occur under conditions where a normal main stress can occur, but they may still have inherent stress in this weaker sense.

Suffixes containing a full-vowel syllable are inherently stressed, and as with prefixes, there are some idiosyncrasies of word formation associated with individual suffixes. No attempt will be made here to account for these idiosyncrasies. It can be mentioned, however, that there are just a couple of suffixes that behave phonologically like root morphemes, i.e. which form quasi-compounds (this set includes *-dom, -hed, -skab,* cf. German *-tum, -heit, -schaft*), and that these suffixes consistently do so. Otherwise, the vast majority of suffixes enter into a proper simplex word construction with the preceding material so that the rule for simplex word accentuation (Intra-Word UA) applies. I refer to an earlier paper (Rischel 1970) for a more detailed discussion (including the special pattern of accentuation exhibited by lexical cognates such as *mekaník, mekánisk, mekániker*).

As for root morphemes, it would be perfectly possible to claim that some function words are inherently unstressed. This would not be true of all the 'small' words that are normally unstressed, however. If we take a pronoun such as *mig* 'me', it certainly is the case that this item mostly occurs with a weak stress, cf.:

   han besøgte mig   'he visited me'

but it should be noted that the pronoun is stressed as part of a complex noun phrase even if there is no additional emphasis:

han besōgte Péter og míg   'he visited Peter and me'.

However, it is true of certain conjunctions and of certain modal particles (such as *skam* 'certainly') that they occur with weak stress under all normal syntactical conditions (conjunctions may be emphasized, however), so that their situation resembles that of prefixes like *be-* or *filo-* (to the extent that these are synchronically morphemes at all).

Generalizing the notion of inherent stress to comprise all morphemes with a full vowel might seem to create a descriptive problem, viz. that of accounting for the difference between those morphemes that actually do emerge with a main stress in phonetic strings, and those that do not (under normal conditions). However, this problem turns up anyhow: if certain lexical items are inherently unstressed, we have to try to account for that fact; if they are considered inherently stressed, the fact that they normally occur with a weak stress will largely follow from a description of the types of constructions into which they enter, which must be supplied in any complete grammar. Still, I wish to leave it open whether one should exploit the possibility of distinguishing between morphemes with, and morphemes without, inherent stress in formulating stress rules.

9.1.2.2. *Where is inherent stress placed?*

Now, for morphemes with more than one syllable with a full vowel, the next question is to what extent the placement of stress on a particular syllable is predictable. The morphemes in question are almost all borrowings such as *violin, diamant* ('diamond'), *alabaster, petroleum, jeremiade*, but there are also a few fossilized compounds of Old Danish origin such as *vindu(e)* ('window,' from *vind* 'wind' and *ōghæ* 'eye'). Moreover, there are numerous items which more or less transparently consist of a prefixal part and a remainder. Among those that are historically formed with a Low German prefix there are many which are readily analysable, although they are lexicalized with a more or less unpredictable shade of meaning, e.g. *beholde* 'keep' (cf. *holde* 'hold'); whereas others contain no meaningful stem after the prefix (e.g. *begynde* 'begin': there is no **gynde*). It is obviously true of many of these borrowings from Low German (or in some cases from High

German) that they form a transitional area between straightforward derivations and monomorphemic stems. The same is true of complex formations containing Greek or Latin material such as the above-mentioned examples *antroposof, filosof, teosof*. Technically, there is evidence enough for a synchronic analysis into constituents, e.g. *-sof* contrasts with *-log* in *antropolog, filolog, teolog*; but again, such items are typically lexicalized with specialized meanings, and there is no sharp limit between synchronically complex and monomorphemic items of this kind.

This is well known from other languages as well. The important thing is that the stress rules must be designed in such a way that the words come out right even if they are taken to be monomorphemic; it must simply be allowed for that some speakers lexicalize them as complexes, and others as monomorphemic items.

As shown in detail elsewhere (although in a very provisional format: Rischel 1970: 119–30) stress placement is to a considerable extent predictable from surface segmental structure.[2] The strongest generalization is that *if one syllable has a long vowel, the stress falls on this syllable*. Otherwise there is a rank-ordering so that (with the exception of certain loans from French) *a closed syllable takes precedence over an open syllable* in attracting the stress. If an intervocalic consonant is supposed to go with the following syllable from the point of view of stress assignment (which, by the way, may be in conflict with the role of syllabification in segmental phonology), the second principle takes care of the final stress in forms such as *parýk* 'wig', *stakít* 'railing', *parasól* 'parasol', but there is a more general prevalence of *final stress if the last syllable is closed*, cf. *komplót* 'plot', *bandít* 'rascal' (this is certainly not without numerous exceptions, however). If the final syllable is open (and the vowel short), the stress is non-final: *fóto, gálla* (with a short *l*), with the exception of French loans such as lain *coupé* ([kuˈpe] as a designation of a shape of a car, but *kupé* [kuˈpeː] in the sense of 'compartment').

---

[2] For convenience, the Danish forms are mostly given in normal orthography, which should not cause trouble if it is remembered that double consonants are pronounced short, and *ld, nd, rd* mostly as short *l, n, r*. Word final *e, en, er* are in most cases schwa-syllables. For clarity, vowel length and the presence of *stød* in a syllable are indicated in these orthographical renderings by : and ' respectively (this is only done in Section 9.1, however, since it is not crucial in the later discussions). By doing so I do not imply anything about the role of the *stød* in the phonology of Danish, an issue which I have preferred to keep entirely out of consideration in this paper (see Basbøll 1972, and elsewhere, for an analysis of this aspect of Danish phonology).

The accentuation of a variety of structure types is thus predictable; cf. the following examples (note that *-er* of *alabaster* and *-e* of *jeremiade* are schwa-syllables, spelled—as is regularly done—with *e*):

violí':n, diamán't, alabáster, petró':leum, jeremiá:de, víndu (etc.).

> It is interesting that there is a tendency in low-standard Danish toward initial stress in root morphemes; this tendency manifests itself only sporadically but typically in cases where it is in direct conflict with the very strongest generalization concerning syllable structure and stress placement, viz. that a long vowel has stress. One such example is *remoulade,* in standard pronunciation with stress on the penultimate syllable, which contains a long vowel: *remulá:de,* but in a low-standard usage it has initial stress: *rémula:de.* It is conceivabe that one should speak here of a restructuring into the prosodic structure of compounds; anyway, this tendency (possibly toward quasi-compounding) does not invalidate the stress placement rules as such, since it hits only sporadically.

The accentuation of wordforms that surface with more than one long vowel is not defined by such criteria as those above; the generalization here is that the wordform behaves like a compound (see Section 9.1.5), and this happens also with some wordforms which do not syntactically qualify as compounds (quasi-compounding). Another problem is raised by stems with alternating placement of vowel length and hence of stress, for example *mó:tor*, pl. *motó:rer* (cf. Rischel 1970: 134–6).

Now, simple principles like those outlined above (or the more elaborate set given in Rischel (1970) without reference to syllable boundaries) predict a good proportion of the word stresses, but they are contradicted by several forms such as (*abrúpt* versus) *mástiks* 'mastic', *dámask, Cán'ada, basíl'ikum*. It is possible to exploit the differential placement of syllable boundaries in clusters (thus refining the concept of 'light' versus 'heavy' syllables), but there will be a residue anyway, the most stubborn cases being those with non-expected stress on a non-final syllable (cf. *mástiks, dámask, Cán'ada* above). It should be noted in this context that Danish differs sharply from the other Scandinavian languages in having short stressed syllables (there is no 'reverse length correlation' of V:C versus VC:); the final consonant of a stressed syllable is always short (irrespective of its historical origin). This means that we do not have consonant length at our disposal as a criterion in placing stress (incidentally, this typological aberration from the 'Scandinavian' type also means that vowel length in Danish cannot possibly be predicted on the basis of information about surface properties of the consonantal parts of the syllables).

It is possible, however, to argue for the existence of underlying long consonants or clusters surfacing as single, short consonants. Such an analysis is motivated by the distribution of the *stød* (cf. the discussion in Basbøll 1972: 8–12), and if it is adopted, the same device can be used in a number of cases to define syllables as underlyingly heavy, so that they count as preferred stress placements. In itself, this is just a notational device, but it becomes more interesting because of the mutual support of the *stød* and stress evidence in a number of cases (e.g. *Cán'ada*). If one sets up underlying long consonants, it turns out that this feature can be assumed to take precedence over the presence of clusters consisting of two different consonants, i.e. in determining the placement of stress, one has to pass through a set of ordered rules (which are disjunctive in the sense that if one gives a positive result, the rest are skipped), the first such rule referring to the presence of a long vowel, the second referring to the presence of a long consonant, and the remaining ones referring to syllable boundaries and consonant clusters. The very last rule, then, assigns final stress if nothing else has applied. Such a set of rules can be made to assign stress correctly with few exceptions. I shall not go into more detail with this here, however (the reader is referred to Rischel 1970: 127–9 rules A–E for a provisional formulation; the formulation on pp. 142–3 of the same paper is, however, quite invalid).

From the point of view of surface phonology, stress placement must be considered contrastive in Danish, but it is hard to find monomorphemic relevant pairs. The two pairs that are normally cited are:

['plasdig] *plastic* versus [pla'sdig] *plastik* (gymnastics)

and

['bilisd] *billigst* 'cheapest' versus [bi'lisd] *bilist* 'car driver'

but in both of these cases the final stress of the second member is explicable by the nature of the suffixation involved (-*ik* and -*ist* are inherently stressed suffixes).

Thus, from the point of view of the lexicon, the utilization of stress placement as a distinctive feature is extremely low.

9.1.3. The hierarchical model

As will appear from the generalizations about morpheme stress above, a monomorphemic lexical item may contain both pretonic and post-tonic zero-stress syllables. Is there in this case a simple concatenation of syllables in a linear arrangement, or do they enter a hierarchical arrangement? It is dubious whether there is any evidence for such a hierarchy as far as stress is concerned. If some syllables among the unstressed ones are felt to be more prominent than others, this is probably ascribable to two factors, viz. (i) that each syllable has an inherent degree of prominence, which is a function of its phonological make-up (closed syllables having more prominence than open syllables, and syllables with a full vowel having more prominence than syllables with schwa), and (ii) that the pitch contour associated with a full stress (Thorsen 1980) supplies each syllable with a tone level (F_0 level) which contributes to the impression of more prominence or less prominence. I have not considered it useful to build such considerations into the assignment of hierarchical structure to a clustering of zero-stress syllables around a full-stress syllable (and my model therefore comes to look somewhat different from those posited for English in recent work such as Liberman and Prince 1977 and Selkirk 1980). However, there seems to be more of a break between *the pretonic part and the remainder* than between the post-tonic part and the syllables preceding it; this can be seen from the fact that it is possible to hesitate between the (last) pretonic syllable and the stress-syllable rather than elsewhere, and that there may be an extremely sharp intonational break here. I therefore venture to suggest a hierarchical arrangement as follows, where each branch that has the stress-syllable as one of its ultimate constituents is supplied with the label 'plus', and all other branches are supplied with the label 'minus' (corresponding, respectively, to the labels s = 'strong' and w = 'weak' of the nomenclature used in metrical phonology):

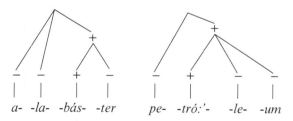

It appears from these examples that there is a redundancy built into such a hierarchical representation, since the plus-labelling is associated with the presence of lexical stress /'/. It has been argued recently by

Selkirk (1980) that the feature of stress, as something distinct from the labelling of the hierarchical trees, can and should be eliminated from phonological theory. This approach obviously eliminates both the redundancy and certain well-formedness conditions such as the following: 'only a stressed syllable may be the strong element of a metrical foot' (Liberman and Prince 1977: 265, see also 279–80).

However, I prefer to preserve the distinction between inherent stress (in the sense in which it has been defined above) and the labelling of prosodic trees, since the properties are essentially different. Inherent stress has to do with the fact that there is a syllable which can occur with a full stress, and whose presence is a condition on the well-formedness of a hierarchical structure of a certain type. In turn, there are well-formedness conditions on syllables with inherent stress saying, for example, that such a syllable must have a full vowel. It is possible to collapse these findings into one complex set of conditions on the well-formedness of hierarchical structures, but it should be noted that lexical (inherent) stress is not fully predictable, so that some syllables must be underlyingly marked for stress anyway. Thus, it seems to me that it is more meaningful to say that the hierarchical organization refers to inherent stresses in all cases, and that there are redundancy conditions predicting where these stresses are located in a great many cases.

9.1.4. **Intra-Word Unit Accentuation**

Examples such as *plastik, bilist* illustrate the basic mechanism of Unit Accentuation (UA), as it operates on sequences of stressed morphemes to produce simplex wordforms with one single full stress.

> In accordance with tradition (including O. Jespersen's insightful contributions to the understanding of how Danish stress functions) I use the term *Unit Accentuation* (UA) about stress reduction as a function of hierarchical patterning (in contradistinction to, say, the lower prominence associated with backgrounding under certain discourse conditions, or stress enhancement due to emphasis for contrast). It is traditionally used in Danish phonetics about phrasal stress, but I use it also about the stress mechanism in simplex words consisting of several, inherently stressed, morphemes (whereas I use the term 'compound stress' for the pattern of compounds, although this is also a matter of unit accentuation, albeit of a different kind). The term UA is more directly suggestive of the actual function of this stress mechanism (as I see it) than other terms which are

more current in the phonological literature ('nuclear stress' focuses on some alleged enhancement of a stressed syllable, not on stress gradation as a signal of the union *per se*, and the term 'phrasal stress' is obviously more restrictive than the term I have adopted here).

Like the nuclear stress rule of Chomsky and Halle (1968) this rule of word-internal stress reduction simply downgrades all non-final stresses. However, provided that the impression of syllable prominence as a function of pitch contours and inherent sonority is taken care of separately, there seems to be no need for a grading of stresses beyond the distinction between full stress and weak stress (= zero stress): all non-final syllables simply appear as pretonic ones. Thus it is perfectly possible to formulate the rule of *Intra-Word UA* like this: delete all inherent morpheme stresses except for the last one within the wordform. Example:

violí':n 'violin'
violín + íst → violiníst 'violinist'
violí':n + íst + índe → violinistínde 'female violinist'

This approach has the attractive property that the output of the rule looks exactly like a monomorphemic lexical item. Thus the theory does not force the analyst to generate the accentuation of such derivatives by rule: they come out the same way if they are taken to be lexicalized as monomorphemic items (although the inherent stress on the last syllable with a full vowel is then only in part structurally predictable).

It is also possible, however, to handle the operation of this UA rule in terms of stress trees. The trees for individual morphemes are then taken to be united by the application of UA (i.e. UA is a structure transformation), the right-most inherent stress being the determinant for the selection of the resultant highest 'plus' branch:

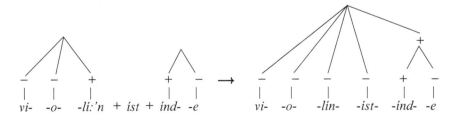

This somewhat more complex way of handling the process has the advantage that the output fits directly into the prosodic tree that will be needed anyway; it just requires a convention to the effect that pretonic occurrences of inherent stress, i.e. /'/ occurring under left branches labelled 'minus', are neglected in the phonetic interpretation of the surface representation (as are the boundaries between the constituent morphemes).

> In this paper I do not go into the question of whether boundary symbols have a status in phonological representations except insofar as they mark the boundaries of a unit of a certain rank in the prosodic hierarchy (cf. Selkirk 1980: 580 for arguments against the separate relevance of grammatical boundaries in phonological representations). It is obvious, however, that grammatical structure is relevant to prosodic structuring, although there is non-conformity between the two. In the representations below I indicate morpheme boundaries and certain other boundaries, whenever it seems useful to make the type of construction clear.

9.1.5. Compound stress

The next step is the generation of compound stress. I demonstrated in an earlier paper (Rischel 1972) what a hierarchical model of compound stress may look like for Danish. I shall just summarize the main points here without going into much detail (especially since the model I am using is quite similar to that of recent metrical phonology, and since the basic mechanism of compound stress is the same as in English). For an alternative treatment which generates a three degree system of stress, see Basbøll (1978*b*).

A tree structure being defined in accordance with the syntactic constituent structure of the compound (with or without certain adjustments), the resulting syntactic tree is matched by a prosodic tree in which the left-most constituent on each level hangs under a branch labelled 'plus', whereas all other branches are assigned the label 'minus' (cf. *hundehalsbånd* 'dog's collar' and *undervandsbåd* 'submarine'—literally: 'under-water boat'):

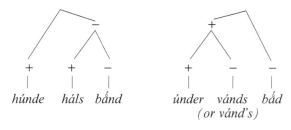

The relative degree of stress is, then, a function of this structure, there being an interpretive convention looking at the ranks of nodes and saying something to the effect that (i) a minus branch implies weaker stress than a plus branch under the same node, and (ii) a minus branch under a node of rank X implies weaker stress than a minus branch under a node of rank X–1. (It is open to much debate how one should formulate such an interpretive convention; first of all, it depends on what 'degree of stress' really means, but I shall not go into that here). Accordingly, in the first example *bånd* has weaker stress than *hals*, and both of these items have weaker stress than *hunde*; in the second example *vands* has weaker stress than *under* and *båd*, and *båd* in turn has weaker stress than *under*. Thus in transcription with stronger and weaker secondary stresses we have: ['hunə͵͵hals͵bʌn'] ['ɔnʌ͵vans͵͵bɔːˀð].

It is typologically relevant to mention that this scheme generalizes to the vast majority of Danish compounds. It was mentioned above that, basically, the prosodic mechanism of compounding is similar to that of English, but it differs in having a very much stronger preference for plus–minus (= strong–weak) rather than weak–strong marking on sister branches (the opposite, i.e. stronger stress on the rightmost constituent, occurs only in a small set of compounds typically belonging to specialized spheres of usage).

There has been some discussion as to whether such a model of accentuation makes it possible to assign stress without the use of a phonological cycle. This is an extremely important theoretical issue since the alleged cyclicality of (English) stress assignment has been used as a main argument for the very existence of such a thing as a phonological cycle. I do not wish to challenge the view that hierarchical structure assignment involves a cyclical application of rules (cf. Kiparsky 1979); Liberman and Prince (1977) show the existence of 'translexical' regularities in English which invite a treatment in terms of cyclicality. But in the present context the essential thing is that the specification of phonetic stress on the basis of a hierarchical representation is accomplished in one complex operation (Rischel 1972; also cf. Liberman and Prince 1977: 258 on the direct encoding of relative prominence as a local feature of constituent structure). That is, there is no compelling reason to assume that other phonological operations intervene between successive applications of some rule translating properties of the hierarchical structure into phonetic stress. A more crucially important question is how rules (prosodic, segmental) *interact* in connection with, e.g., emphatic stress and shrinkage of hierarchical structure above the word level; this complex of problems is not really dealt with in the present paper.

Returning now to the hierarchical model as such, it goes without saying that it is too simplistic to posit a one-to-one correspondence between syntactic and prosodic trees. For one thing, it is often anything but evident what the internal syntactic structure of a compound *is*. In actual practice the stress pattern is often—implicitly or explicitly—taken into consideration in the syntactic analysis. This is perfectly legitimate (stress is as respectable a cue to syntactic constituent structure as is constituent order), but of course such an approach means that no additional insight is gained by explaining the prosodic hierarchy in terms of syntax. Another thing is that the accentuation of Danish compounds often reflects a tree structure that is in conflict with an intuitively reasonable IC analysis. It must, then, be the case that certain structure transformations (STs) are involved in defining the relationship between syntactic and prosodic trees, unless the compound in question is lexicalized with an idiosyncratically aberrant syntactic structure (or no such structure at all). —As for compounds exhibiting no structural idiosyncracies, there are several ways in which these may be handled in a linguistic description, since (i) the syntactic constituent structure may be lexically stored or generated by rule, and (ii) the prosodic structure may likewise be part of the lexical representation or derived by rule. Under the assumption that we are dealing with productive patterns I prefer to assume that the relevant structural generalizations and mapping rules all exist in duplicate form: as rules for productive compound formation and as redundancy conditions on lexicalized items.

The most important ST is *loss of ranking differences* or, put differently, *shrinkage of structure* (the hierarchy ultimately collapsing into a simple concatenation). There is in Danish an overwhelmingly strong tendency to lower all but the two highest degrees of stress (as predicted from the hierarchical representation) to the lowest level, and there is even a strong tendency to lower the next highest degree of stress ('secondary' stress) in right-branching structures. What remains, then, is a sequence of weakly stressed syllables, whose relative prominence is a function of properties of the string which are not included in the labelled tree as such. If these are disregarded, the structure of *hundehalsbånd* above looks as follows if shrunk (for clarity, the branching within each lexical constituent is indicated here as well, in contradistinction to the simplified representation above):

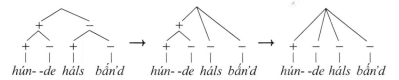

The same applies to more complex compounds such as *patent-hunde-halsbånd* 'patented dog's collar' (possibly not in current use, but a perfectly well-formed compound):

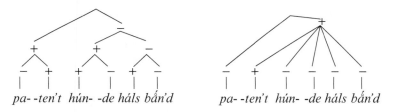

(the pretonic syllable here being assumed to attach to the reduced structure as an immediate constituent, which may not be an adequate analysis).

Left-branching structures such as that of *undervandsbåd*, on the other hand, are less likely to shrink to structures of minimum complexity, but may do so in allegro speech.

In some instances it is difficult to decide whether we really have a shrinkage of structure or a change in the assignment of branches to nodes. There may be a tendency to swing a branch that branches off to the left under a right branch and to attach it so that it branches off to the right under a left branch:

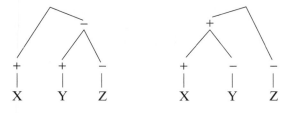

Maybe the ST involved—if this occurs—is rather to be construed as affecting the right-most constituent (Z in the structure above), moving this constituent from under the lower node and Chomsky-adjoining it to the remainder of the structure in terms of a new, higher node (the lower node vanishing by convention). The basic question, however, is whether there is empirical evidence for the general occurrence of this mechanism (as something distinct from shrinkage of structure). In any case, it may be the source of lexical restructuring in several compounds with the adverbial *for* such as *stationsforstander* 'station master'. This compound is formed on *forstander* 'master' (literally 'fore-stander') with full stress on *for-* and accordingly one would expect the right-branching prosodic structure of *hundehalsbånd*, but what actually occurs is a stress pattern with more prominence on the third constituent than on the second (unless all reduced stresses are downgraded to weak stress). It is possible to argue that this is an instance of the ST outlined above; however, the end result is rather lexical restructuring to a compound with only two word-level constituents, the latter containing prefixal *for-* (I disregard the fine structure of the hierarchy here):

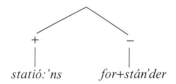

Restructuring is not surprising in this type, since adverbial (and inherently stressed) *for* is easily confused with prefixal *for-* (from Low German); in the particular example under consideration it may even have been supported by the spurious similarity with formations such as *forstán'd* (meaning 'wit' and being semantically quite unrelated to the noun *forstander*).

Otherwise there may not be very much restructuring of this kind and, on the whole, the accentuation of Danish compounds does not seem to require much machinery for its specification. So far I have found no compelling evidence for operating with rhythmic perturbations which are determined by the word structure itself, but then the phonetic details of Danish stress await closer investigation.

9.1.6. **Phrasal unit accentuation**

The last component to be dealt with in this package of stress assignment mechanisms is Phrasal UA (Unit Accentuation). This operates according to the same principle as Intra-Word UA, i.e. all but the rightmost constituent hang under minus branches, and the expected hierarchical structure typically shrinks to a one-node structure, cf.

gå: i:' sén'g → gå i sén'g

or, in the tree structure model:

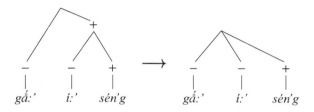

Except for a high level of distinctness, the difference between inherent /'/ and zero stress seems to be ignored in such constructions, but it is an open question whether there is a structure-independent impression of differences in prominence between syllables with a full vowel and syllables with schwa (whatever its surface reflex), e.g. between the underlying full-vowel syllable *gå* and the underlying schwa-syllable *-ger* ([gɔ] versus [gʌ]) in

> *hun vil gå i seng* [hun ve gɔ i 'sɛŋ'] 'she intends to go to bed'
> *hun ligger i sengen* [hun legʌ i 'sɛŋ'n̩] 'she is in bed (as a patient)'

This whole area awaits further phonetic study.

I shall state the conditions for Phrasal UA in considerable detail later in this paper. For the moment the above remarks may suffice.

At this point I wish to comment on another issue, viz. the necessity for operating with a 'metrical grid' as posited in Liberman and Prince (1977). One of the interesting mechanisms handled in terms of a metrical grid is 'iambic reversal' (p. 319). We do find a phenomenon of this kind in Danish but, interestingly enough, it does not seem to be crucially dependent on whether the constituent in question is inherently stressed, so one may question whether the conditions set up for 'iambic reversal' are really met in Danish, cf. that the prefix syllable *be-* (which never occurs with a full stress) may perhaps be experienced as more prominent than the root syllable *gå* in phrases such as *begå selvmord* (with stress on *selvmord*) 'commit suicide', although the wordform *begå* in itself invariably has stress on the root syllable. Maybe we have here a more general tendency toward a gradual downstepping in a series of pretonic syllables, which should perhaps be kept apart from the specification of the hierarchical structure proper.

9.1.7. **How are the components of stress assignment ranked?**

We have seen that UA operates both within simplex words and within phrases, and that there is a compound stress mechanism (with the reversed marking of sister branches in terms of 'plus' and 'minus') operating on compounds in the widest sense. Now, each part of a compound may be a derivative undergoing Intra-Word UA (cf. *violinist* derived from *violín+ist* as occurring in compounds such as *hofviolinist* 'court violinist' and *violinistkonkurrence* 'v. competition'), and since compounds may also occur as constituents of phrases undergoing phrasal UA (e.g. the compound *indføre* '(to) import' with stress reduction in the phrase *indføre våben* '(to) import weapons'), there seems to be no way to avoid having UA apply twice: once at the word level and once at the phrase level. It is possible, however, to claim that the results of both types of UA are collapsed into one structure, and that this is true even if the last constituent of the phrase in question is a compound, as in *hun vil til violinistkonkurrence* 'she intends to go to a violinists' competition'. This implies that the highest-ranked branching in such a construction is between all material up to the boundary between the two (immediate) constituents of the compound on the one hand, and the second (immediate) constituent of the compound on the other, i.e. that the compound boundary has a higher rank than other phrase-internal boundaries (this point has been made in Basbøll 1978*a*).

There may well be a level of phonological specification for which this yields the most adequate representation. However, in surface phonology a basic rearrangement seems to take place, the syllables grouping now in clusters defined by an initial full stress. Nina Thorsen, who has demonstrated the relevance of this segmentation in connection with the specification of intonation contours, refers to such clusters as 'stress groups'. I shall venture to speak here of a *foot*, although this certainly does not fall in with the use of this term in, say, Selkirk's work (1980). It will be shown toward the end of this paper how this concept of foot structure in Danish surface phonology can be reconciled with the model(s) outlined so far. As I shall argue later, this is in part a matter of more abstract versus more 'surfacy' levels of specification. The status of Phrasal UA is crucial for the understanding of such differences in level of abstraction. I shall, therefore, consider the conditions for the application of this mechanism in some detail before returning to the theoretical discussion of models of phonological description in Section 9.4. (Section 9.2 takes stock of the phrase types in which UA occurs in Danish and hopefully demonstrates that the distribution of Phrasal UA in this language is very different from that of the other Germanic languages that have been within the sphere of interest in recent discussion. Section 9.3 deals with the accentual pattern of phrases which have become disrupted by movement transformations.)

9.2.   SYNTACTIC AND SEMANTIC CONDITIONS FOR DANISH PHRASAL UNIT ACCENTUATION

Looking at phrases devoid of emphatic stress (in the widest sense), what are the basic generalizations to be made about UA?[3] We shall consider first certain modifiers with idiosyncratic behaviour, then noun phrases with a noun as head of the construction, then phrases with an adjective or adverb as head, then prepositional phrases, then auxiliary plus main verb, then verb phrases with an object, a 'subject-object' (Diderichsen's term), or a subject or object predicate. Needless to say, this survey has to be very brief, and numerous problems must be totally left aside. One major omission is made for the sake of space and clarity of exposition: fixed idiomatic phrases which exhibit unit accentuation, but do so without conforming to the general pattern, are ignored here for the most part, the point being to describe the productive pattern of accentuation of ordinary grammatical constructions, not to give an exhaustive account of the whimsies of lexicalized phrases.

---

[3] This account is extremely sketchy. A detailed description of the conditions under which words appear with a full stress in Danish will soon be available in a forthcoming monograph by Erik Hansen and Jørn Lund. Unfortunately, their manuscript became available to me too late to be utilized in the text of this paper, except for this and the following footnotes. [The reference is to Hansen and Lund (1983)—editors' note.]

9.2.1. A survey of phrase types with Unit Accentuation

9.2.1.1. *Minor categories of words which normally undergo stress reduction*

In order not to complicate later parts of this survey, it is necessary to start by mentioning the existence of certain restricted sets of words which normally occur with weak stress (when not emphasized), and whose lack of a full stress may be ascribed to a more generalized application of UA than the types listed below. The words in question fall into two main groups.

One group consists of certain words ranging in syntactic function and semantic content from an article-like status over a more general quantifier status to clearly adverbial, numeral, or pronominal status. It comprises, for example, such items as *en* 'a, one' (neuter *et*), *lidt* 'a little', *nogen* 'some' (neuter *noget*, plural *nogen/nogle*), and personal pronouns: *jeg* 'I' (cf. Section 9.1.2 above), etc. The generalization is that these items have stress reduction to weak stress if they occur as the leftmost immediate constituent of a syntactic construction of which they are not the head (that is, the item in question must either be a modifier, or an IC of an exocentric construction). Examples: *en mánd* 'a man,' *lidt mére* 'a little more', *lidt sént* 'a little late', *noget óst* 'some cheese'. This occurs only if the item is semantically reduced to an indefinite article or article-like quantifier or is used anaphorically (not deictically). Accordingly, there is a difference between *en mánd* 'a man' and *én mánd* 'one man (numeral)' and between *nogen (nogle) ménnesker* 'a few persons' and *nógen (nógle) ménnesker* 'certain people' or 'quite a few people'.

There are obviously three ways of accounting for such contrastive pairs. One is to say that *en* and *én* are simply distinct lexical items (and similarly for the other pairs), and that some such items are inherently unstressed, others stressed. Another possibility is to take them as distinct lexical items but to claim that all these items take stress underlyingly, although one subset (definable on semantic grounds) normally appears with weak stress due to UA. Finally, one may use the same explanation in terms of stress reduction due to UA, but attempt to group the forms with and without susceptibility of UA as pairwise variants of one lexical item each. The question of how to handle such phenomena lexically is of course outside the scope of this paper; I shall just point to the possibility of speaking of UA even in these cases.

With the personal pronouns there are additional generalizations to be made, however, since weakly-stressed forms also occur finally in constructions: *han sér mig* 'he sees me', *han gik éfter hende* 'he followed her' (literally: 'went after her'), i.e. stress reduction occurs as a general feature of these items unless a syntactic or semantic condition blocks stress reduction. One syntactic feature blocking it is its occurrence in construction with a sister constituent, cf. *han sér míg og Péter* 'he sees me and Peter', and one semantic feature blocking it is a distinctly deictic function.

The other main group comprises certain conjunctions such as *og* 'and', *at* 'that'. I shall confine myself to stating that these are normally weakly stressed, as are certain modal particles such as *skam* 'certainly' (which are probably inherently unstressed, cf. Section 9.1.2 above).

9.2.1.2. *Noun phrases*

Although most types of NPs do *not* exhibit UA, there are some that do (in addition to those containing the items mentioned above). This is true of constructions indicating a unit of measure + species: *en sum pénge* 'a sum of money', etc. Quantifiers not belonging to the category mentioned in 9.2.1.1 are *not* included in the domain of UA, however, cf. *tré* in *tré liter mælk* 'three litres of milk'; *dénne* 'this' in *dénne liter mælk*. —The measure nouns are stressed outside such constructions, i.e. phrase-finally: *en (stór) súm, en (hálv) líter*, or if the following constituent is not of NP status: *et kílo af dét dér* 'a kilo of that'.

Other such noun phrases likewise take UA. Various subgroups may be distinguished, depending on whether the constituent parts are proper names or not, and depending on the type of reference involved (unique reference or other), cf. such subsets as: (i) *Anker Jórgensen*,[4] (ii) *Dronning Margréthe* 'Queen Margrethe', (iii) *Margrethe den Ánden* 'Margrethe the Second', (iv) *linje tólv* '(bus) no. 12', *hjerter dáme* 'queen of hearts', (v) *pastor eméritus* 'retired clergyman'.

A considerably more complex situation is found with clearly hypotactical *proper names*, viz. those *consisting of modifier plus head*. If the second constituent is in itself a compound, the general rhythmical tendencies favour UA: *Kongens Nýtorv* ('the King's New Square',

---

[4] UA does not always occur in the rendering of personal names (see further Hansen and Lund 1983), but it is definitely an option.

a place name in Copenhagen), *Østre Lándsret* 'the High Court of East Denmark' (*østre* means 'eastern'). We can also recognize UA in several proper names consisting of an N in the genitive plus a (not otherwise determined) simplex N. Such names are normally written as single words, although they fit perfectly into the pattern of two-word phrases and in spite of their being in conflict with the regular accentuation of *compounds*; an example is *Christiansbórg* (literally: 'Christian's Castle'), as against the regular compound type *Christians-kirken* 'Christian's Church', *Fólketinget* 'The Parliament' (note the definite article on these compounds). —Note that proper names whose second constituent is a simplex common N do *not* normally exhibit UA but rather occur with compound accentuation like *Christianskirken* (with or without this phonological compounding being reflected in the spelling).

Complex noun phrases other than the types mentioned above but consisting of separate nouns and/or adjectives (i.e. *not* compounds) fail to exhibit UA. If there is no emphasis, there simply is no stress grada-tion. Unlike the alleged pattern of English, for example, the adjective and the noun have equal stresses in phrases such as *en gámmel mánd* 'an old man'.

The most general statement about noun phrases, then, is that UA does *not* apply except in certain rather well-defined types of construc-tions.

9.2.1.3. *Phrases with an A or Adv as head*

Modifiers of the type discussed in Section 9.2.1.1 left aside, such con-structions do *not* normally exhibit UA. (There is a marginal exception, viz. the type *derhénne* 'over there', *herínde* 'in here' with a largely anaphoric function, as against the overtly deictic *dérhènne* 'over there', *hérìnde* 'in here'.)

9.2.1.4. *Prepositional phrases*

The statements below only refer to the accentual relationship between preposition and remainder, the latter constituent being in itself an NP (which follows the rules of accentuation as outlined in 9.2.1.3, if the head is a noun).

The 'remainder', i.e. the constituent part governed by the prepo-sition, is in itself fully accented. As for the preposition, it is true of most of the frequent, monosyllabic prepositions that these *trigger the application of UA in prepositional phrases*, provided that the preposition is immediately followed by the material it governs. Prepositions seem to have a very different susceptibility to stress reduction, however. This is in part a matter of their phonological 'heaviness', inherently short syllables being more strongly affected than long syllables, and monosyllables more so than bisyllables (this scale may be exemplified by *ved, bag* [bæ:'i̭], *bagved*: *ved åen* 'at the river', *båg/bag húset, bågved húset* 'behind the house'. Semantic factors are also involved, although their role is still poorly understood (cf. that there may be a discernible difference in meaning between *han sprang over åen* and *han sprang óver åen*, both literally meaning 'he jumped across the river', but with the possible difference that the former focuses on the route, and the latter rather on the accomplishment of crossing the river).

The generalization above about UA is contradicted by the occurrence of two types of construction in which the preposition does not undergo stress reduction. One of these types is defined by the occurrence of only a 'light' pronoun in the NP slot of the PrepP. Light pronouns include personal pronouns and the (closely related) anaphoric *den* 'it', neuter *det*, plural *de* 'they' (also in suppletion with the 3rd person personal pronouns). Such pronominal forms as NPs are weakly stressed in anaphorical function and acquire stress only under emphasis. A PrepP consisting of a preposition and such a pronoun accordingly preserves the inherent word stress of the preposition: *på mig* 'on me', *méd ham* 'with him,' *fóran hende* 'in front of her', etc. (note that these phrases agree with phrases with normal UA by having only one main stress). If there is additional, heavier material in the NP slot, however, UA applies instantly: *på mig sélv* 'on myself', *på os bégge* 'on both of us', and if the function is not strictly anaphoric (but more or less clearly deictic), the pronoun takes word stress, and UA applies as expected: *med hám* 'with him (over there)'; also cf. *med hám vi besógte* 'with the one we visited'.

The other type is defined by the occurrence of an infinitival or sentential construction after the preposition, and with no pronominal constituent intervening. In this case there are, as pointed out by Hansen (1977: 161), two options: the preposition may lose its main stress by UA, or the stress may be retained:

> *tænker Óle på/på at réjse?* 'is Ole thinking of leaving?'
> *tror dú på/på at han har gjórt det?* 'do you think he did it?'

Now, why is this? Hansen suggests that diachronically speaking, the construction is moving from an earlier type in which the infinitival or sentential constituent is in extraposition, towards a modern type in which that constituent is incorporated in the preceding sentence (viz. as the material governed by the preposition). The occurrence of UA with stress reduction on the preposition, then, represents the latter type, while the stressed preposition reflects the former type, being stressed by virtue of its standing alone as an adverbial phrase.

Old Danish had a construction with the preposition governing pronominal *det* 'it' followed by the remainder in extraposition. This would be literally reflected in Modern Danish as something like

> *tænker Ole på det at rejse?* (stresses ignored)
> *tror du på det at han har gjort det?*

According to Hansen's explanation, the option with a stressed (adverbial) preposition before *at* reflects an intermediate step between this old construction and the expected construction with UA uniting the preposition and all of the remainder.

It seems to me that this is plausible enough, and in synchronic grammar it seems indeed warranted to seek a description along these lines.

9.2.1.5. *Auxiliary plus main verb*

The normal pattern with sequences of auxiliary verb(s) plus one main verb (not carrying emphasis) is to have UA involving all verb forms (disregarding the infinitive particle *at* 'to'):

> *(hvád ér det vi) skál?*   '(what are we) supposed to do?'
> *(hvád ér det vi) skal háve?*   '(what are we) supposed to get?'
> *(hvád ér det vi) skal have at spíse?*   '(what are we) supposed to have
>   to eat?'

also cf.

> *(du) skal lade være*   'don't do it' (literally: 'you shall let be')
> *(jeg) fik skrévet (artíklen)*   '(I) managed to write (the paper)'

and even comprising stretches such as:

> *(det) skulle kunne have været gjórt*   'it should have been possible to
>   do (it)'

There is, on the other hand, no phrase formation with UA comprising the sequences of verb forms in examples such as

vi pléjer at spíse hér 'we usually eat here'
hun élsker at sýnge 'she loves to sing'

The difference is obviously that UA occurs with auxiliary plus main verb but not with main verb plus main verb. (This generalization requires, of course, that the distinction between auxiliary and main verb is well defined, and that we have independent evidence for claiming that such verbs as *lade* 'let', *få* 'get' are auxiliaries in some constructions.)

9.2.1.6. *Verb phrases with adverbial complements*

This is probably the most difficult pattern to account for. There are specific problems associated with the verb 'to be', which will be left aside here. But even so, generalizations are difficult to make, especially because there is such an enormous number of fixed phrases with UA that it is difficult to test such generalizations empirically without running into the question of what can be labelled a fixed phrase.

UA, as in *gå hjém*, 'go home', occurs in an extremely large number of instances. The most conspicuous (and well-known) regularity is that *constructions indicating translocation of an object (be it the sentence subject or the sentence object) exhibit UA*, whereas related constructions which do not involve such a change of location, fail to take UA. Examples:

(han) svømmer dérhén '(he) is swimming towards that place over there'
(han) svómmer dérhénne '(he) is swimming (about) over there'

In such cases the difference in meaning is reflected not only by the accentuation but also by the quasi-inflection of the adverb. There is a small class of place adverbs which are monosyllabic when they have an allative meaning, but take an argument *-e* (phonologically /-ə/) when they have a locative meaning, and *hen–henne* is one of these adverbs.[5]

---

[5] As pointed out to me by Erik Hansen, it requires a more explicit syntactic analysis of the relation between the verb and other sentence members than the one I have employed here, to account for the accentuation of the verb cf. how *er* 'is' is stressed differently in the following two sentences:

den ér óppe på lóftet 'it is (to be found) up there in the attic'
han er óppe på lóftet 'he is (temporarily) up in the attic'.

(Note, however, that even in this pair a movement is implied in the case with weak stress). Unfortunately, I cannot incorporate the necessary elaborations and corrections in the present paper.

Needless to say, the adverbial complement may instead be one that takes no such 'inflection', be it an adverb proper or a PrepP. It then occurs that the only difference is one of accentuation (there being no difference in the orthography), cf.

> *(han) faldt i vándet*   '(he) fell into the water'
> *(han) fáldt i vándet*   '(he) fell (while walking) in the water'

or

> *(det var dé pénge han) smed i vándet*   '(that is the money he) threw into the water'
> *(det var dé pénge han) sméd i vándet*   '(that is the money he) chucked away while (he was) in the water'

9.2.1.7. *Verb phrases with an object, 'subject-object', or subject predicate*

Constructions involving a verb plus a 'naked' object noun take UA in Danish: køb hús 'buy a house' *in contradistinction to constructions with an article accompanying the object noun: køb et hús* 'buy a house' (note that in this case the meaning is so alike that it is not self-evident how to reflect it when translating); or *køb húset* 'buy the house'.

Examples are legion. It is interesting to observe how the indefinite and the definite article function alike in blocking UA, independently of the status of the article as a separate wordform preceding the noun or as an enclitic form:

> *kan du rede séng?*   'do you know how to make a bed (arrange the sheets, etc.)?'
> *kan du réde en séng?*   (same meaning but perhaps indicating a slight scepticism on the part of the speaker as against the neutral question above)
> *kan du réde séngen?*   'do you know how to make the bed?' (this construction is also possible as a command).

The construction also occurs with mass nouns. Here there is no contrasting alternative with an indefinite article unless the mass noun is used in the sense of a species:

han købte óst	'he bought some cheese'
han købte en óst med húller	'he bought a cheese with holes in it'
jeg pléjer at købe vín fra Bordéaux-distriktet	'I usually buy wine from the Bordeaux district'
jeg pléjer at kóbe en vín fra Bordéaux-distriktet	'I usually buy a wine from the Bordeaux district'

or unless the sense of a standardized quantity (a bottle, a package, or the like) is understood:

han bestilte ól	'he ordered some beer'
han bestílte en ól	'he ordered a beer'

However, there is a certain semantic equivalence between the indefinite *en, et* and the form *noget* 'some', the latter occurring before mass nouns:

han kóbte noget óst	'he bought some cheese'[6]

In the plural another form of the same word, *nogle* (or *nogen*) performs the function of the indefinite article. We thus get contrasts such as:

han solgte húse	'he was selling some houses' (or 'he was a house-seller')
han sólgte nogle húse	'he sold some houses'
han sólgte húsene	'he sold the houses'.

It is a difficulty in the analysis of such data that the difference in meaning between constructions with and without the indefinite article (including the suppletive *noget, nogen/nogle*) is often extremely subtle (and virtually untranslatable into English). To the extent that there is a clear difference of meaning, the construction *without* the article is used when a more or less *standardized type of action* is referred to, and when it is the action or the result, rather than the object, of this action, that is talked about.

Viewed from a slightly different angle, the constructions with an article (or *noget*, etc.) involve some kind of *reference*, unless the object is to be understood as generic. Thus, in the examples above, not only the definite object nouns but also *en séng, en ól, noget óst, nogle húse* may be said to have reference, albeit of a totally indefinite kind, since

---

[6] As pointed out by Hansen and Lund (forthcoming [i.e. 1983—editors' note]) this also applies to constructions with *lidt* 'a little', and even if this word occurs adverbially as in *han fik lidt bédre tíd* 'he became somewhat less pressed for time' versus *han fik bédre tíd* 'he got less pressed', which is really intriguing.

the existence of some *particular* specimen(s) or quantity somewhere in the world is implied in these cases.

Syntactically speaking, however, the overt difference is that UA occurs if there is no article, but is blocked if there is an article in the wide sense in which this term is used above.

As shown in Rischel (1980), this finding can be generalized to a syntactically much more interesting statement, viz. that UA occurs *whenever the object NP is devoid of a determiner*. That is, UA is not blocked by the occurrence of modifiers before the object noun (cf. *købe nýt hús* 'buy a new house', *købe flére húse* 'buy additional houses'); it is so *only* if such a modifier has the function of a determiner.

This statement hinges on the independently motivated contention that proper nouns are inherently [+Det], cf. that UA fails to apply in *(han) héntede Péter* '(he) fetched Peter' versus *(han) hentede øl* '(he) fetched some beer'. It also hinges on the contention that some quantifiers have determiner status, others not, and that still others have determiner status in some cases and not in other cases, cf.

> *(de) købte forskélligt tøj*   '(they) bought various clothes'
> *(de) købte forskélligt tøj*   '(they) bought different clothes',

with *forskelligt* having a syntactico-semantic feature [+Det] in the first but not in the second case. (For further examples and discussions, see Rischel 1980.)

The same generalization applies to the type of construction exemplified by the following two examples:

> *(der) bor ménnesker (i húlerne)*   '(the caves) are inhabited by
>   human beings'
> *(der) bór nogle ménnesker (i húlerne)*   '(there) are some persons that
>   live (in the caves)'

(again with a rather subtle difference of meaning). Diderichsen (1946) called such a constituent of sentential subject function but occurring in object position a 'subject-object' (not to be confused with a normal subject occurring after the verb because of inversion).[7]

---

[7] The difference between 'subject-object' and a true subject appears overtly in that an adverbial constituent such as *ikke* 'not' always appears before the subject-object: *der bor ikke ménnesker i húlerne* 'the caves are not inhabited by human beings'; or *hvórfor bor der ikke ménnesker i húlerne?* 'why aren't the caves inhabited by human beings?'.

There are exceptions to this rule about UA occurring if the object NP (or subject-object) contains no Det. Quite a few of these seem explicable if we assume that *generic meaning* blocks UA, cf. *(han) élsker óst* '(he) loves cheese' (i.e. cheese as such, not just some particular cheese); *(det) lígner múg* '(it) looks like mould'. Incidentally, this statement may help to explain why a sequence of verb plus (ordinary) subject NP without a Det fails to exhibit UA: the point is that in Danish a subject NP without an (explicit or implicit) Det is (almost invariably) generic: *régnorme léver af bláde* 'earthworms live on leaves' and with inversion: *sådan léver régnorme* 'that is how earthworms live'; or *óst frémstilles af mǽlk* 'cheese is made from milk', and with inversion: *sådan frémstilles óst* 'that is how cheese is made'. It is, however, not all that obvious that there is a difference in genericity between the subject of the just-mentioned sentence and the object of the following: *det er sådan man frémstiller/fremstiller óst* (same, active construction). Maybe it is rather a difference of degree, the subject NP without a Det being distinctively [+Generic], whereas the 'naked' object NP is rather neutral with respect to genericity. There is an obvious problem here, which has not been properly solved, and whose solution may lie elsewhere.

Finally, we shall briefly consider what happens in constructions with a subject or object predicate. The generalization here is that, unlike verb phrases with an object, those involving a subject or object predicate have UA (removing the full stress from the verb) obligatorily, irrespective of the status of these constituents in terms of [±Det] or [±Generic]. Examples are:

han blev lǽge	'he became a doctor'
han bliver en dýgtig lǽge	'he will become a competent doctor'
han fandt kátten dód på gúlvet	'he found the cat dead on the floor'
de kaldte pígen Ída	'they called the girl Ida'
han kaldte dréngen et fjóls	'he called the boy a fool'
han gjorde hende rásk	'he cured her' (literally: made her well)

whereas it comes after the true subject in the case of inverted word order: *ménnesker kan íkke léve af grǽs* 'humans cannot live on grass (as a nourishment)'; *hvórfor kan ménnesker íkke léve af grǽs* 'why cannot humans live on grass?'; *hvórfor léver ménnesker íkke af grǽs?*; 'why don't humans live on grass?'. (Incidentally, the verb *leve(r)* may not be fully stressed in these constructions, which is immaterial in the present context, however).

9.2.2. **Generalizations about Phrasal UA**

Looking at the data presented above and the rough generalizations made, is it now possible to arrive at a generalized statement about *all* occurrences of UA in Danish?

It was pointed out by Jespersen (1934: §13.6.3) that constructions with stress on their final constituents always denote 'a single concept', and he substantiated this by showing that nominalizations (involving compounding) occur as possible transforms of verb + object constructions with UA, cf.

> *læse románer*   '(to) read novels'
> *románlæsning*   'reading of novels'

or

> *købe hús*   '(to) buy a house'
> *húskøb*   'purchase of a house'.

(Similarly, participial compounds occur, such as *románlæsende* 'reading novels', although these are mostly confined to strictly literary language).

Such nominalizations are *not* possible in the case of constructions without UA: there is no way of forming a nominal compound indicating the type of specificness and definiteness implied by constructions such as *købe et hús* 'buy a house', *kóbe húset* 'buy the house'. I do not want to challenge Jespersen's insightful characterization of phrases consisting of verb plus object with UA: it is clearly true that such a construction forms a close-knit semantic unit in the instances with UA. This basic notion of semantic unity may also be extended to phrases consisting of verb plus adverbial complement and to noun phrases with UA such as *en sum pénge, linie tólv, Kongens Nýtory* (cf. Section 9.2.1.2 above). It is a question of whether it suffices to characterize all and only the phrases with UA (see below), but it is worth pointing out that it agrees beautifully with the occurrence of UA in a wide variety of *fixed phrases*, including such as are in conflict with the statement that determiners block UA in constructions of verb plus object (see Section 9.2.1.7 above). In such cases UA often occurs as an option, with considerable variation in usage among Danish speakers. The following examples are in agreement with my own usage (which may be more in favour of UA with violation of the [+Det]-constraint than that of most younger speakers of Danish), and it should be kept in mind that the notation of UA in these instances refers to the *possibility* of UA rather than *obligatory* UA.

One of Jespersen's examples is:

har du hørt mågen 'have you ever heard such a thing?'

Jespersen uses the co-occurrence of UA with the definite article in constructions of the type exemplified here as evidence *against* the generalization pointed out in Section 9.2.1.7 above, viz. that the *occurrence or absence of a determiner* is crucial in the case of verb + object constructions. However, although I agree that phrases such as *hørt mågen* point to a connection between semantically close-knit construction and phonological UA, I cannot agree that they constitute evidence against the generalization involving the feature [+Det]. It is important to note that there are counter-examples, but the most interesting ones are such that have to do with standardized actions, cf. *tage tóget* 'take the train'. Similarly with phrases referring to the (experience of) performances of plays or compositions, and the like (inherently [+Det]): *vi skal se Élverhøj* 'we are going to see (the play) Elverhøj' versus *vi skal sé Élverhøj* 'we are going to see (the locality) Elverhøj'.

Most of the examples given by Jespersen are obvious *idioms*, however. If UA is a signal of semantic tightness or unity, this is indeed a type in which one may expect UA, so it is reasonable enough to include idioms from that point of view. However, it must be taken into consideration that the determiner has lost its separate semantic content in such cases. This is true of *hørt mågen* above. Now, since *magen* is morphologically a definite form consisting of *mage* 'mate' (formerly also: 'something matching') and the enclitic article *-(e)n*, it is also possible to conceive of a different reading of the typographical stretch *har du hørt magen*. This may seem far-fetched, but it is not entirely unlikely that somebody might utter this very stretch in a context in which the singing of some bird is at issue. In this case it is *impossible* to have UA:

har du hórt mágen? 'have you heard its mate?'

(The full stress on *hørt* vanishes only if the verb forms a phrase with UA together with some later constituent, such as the verb *synge* in *har du hørt mágen sýnge?* 'have you heard its mate singing?'; such discontinuous phrases with UA are dealt with elsewhere in this paper.)

Thus, on the literal reading of *magen* its determiner effectively blocks UA, which shows that this blocking effect is not a matter of morphology but rather of the *function* of the morphological material.

Moreover, UA does not occur in *all* idiomatic expressions containing verb + object. For example, UA is absent in some of those referring to dying (like the English 'kick the bucket'), cf. *stille træskoene* ('take off the clogs') or *tåge billetten* ('take the ticket'). These expressions are certainly no less close-knit semantically than *hørt mågen* and the like, on their metaphorical reading. Thus UA is a possible but hardly a *necessary* accompaniment of semantic unity.

The idiom status of examples like these is evident from the impossibility of moving the object NP out of the VP: cleft sentences splitting up the VP make sense only on their literal reading. However, there is no similar indivisibility in the case of certain other verb–object constructions with UA:

købe øl	'(to) buy some beer'
du skal også købe øl	'you must buy some beer, too'
øl skal du også købe	(the same with explicit focus on 'beer')
han købte ikke øl	'he did not buy beer'
øl købte han ikke	(the same with explicit focus on 'beer')

There is a similar mobility in the case of a 'subject-object':

der står mælk i køleskabet	'there is some milk in the refrigerator'
mælk står der også (i køleskabet)	'there is some milk, too (in the refrigerator)'

Syntactically, then, it is not very obvious that UA accompanies a specific type of construction, since the criterion of divisibility distinguishes between idioms and free constructions rather than between constructions susceptible to UA and others. What then about semantic or syntactico-semantic properties such as selectional restrictions?

In the case of a 'naked' object, one may claim that the object NP must denote something that can go with the verb in question, but that still leaves us with an open set of verb + object constructions which can—and indeed do—take UA if no determiner is present, i.e. a totally productive type of construction. It cannot be the semantic relation between the basic meaning of the verb and that of the object that is decisive; the alleged semantic unity must be a function of the construction as such, not of the constellation of individual word meanings. In the case of a verb + 'subject-object', the number of verbs possible is very limited unless they are passive in form: they are otherwise motoric or situative verbs. On the other hand, anything that can be situated somewhere may occur as 'subject-object', so that the productivity is again in principle unlimited. It is hard to see what would be implied by claiming that the construction signals some particularly close-knit unit of meaning, any more than constructions involving subject and verb do quite generally.

If we look at the total array of constructions with UA (noun phrases, prepositional phrases, and various kinds of verb phrases, to mention the main categories), there is something intuitively very attractive in Jespersen's statement about UA constructions denoting a 'single concept', at least for constructions with verb + object or complement. But as I have tried to demonstrate, this criterion is not *generally* valid unless it is formulated in such vague terms that it can hardly be considered an operational criterion.

It should be noted, nevertheless, that there are various rather solid generalizations to be made about the individual types of phrases taking UA, as shown in Sections 9.2.1.2–9.2.1.7 above. Thus, since UA goes with the absence of an object determiner in verb phrases, we have at our disposal not only a quasi-explanation of why there is UA but—what is perhaps more interesting—*a criterion which can be used in syntactico-semantic analysis*; that is, in the analysis of quantifiers. Similar kinds of criteria may be established for other types of constructions with UA.

From the point of view of phonology, it is essential to determine to what extent phrase formation with UA reflects syntactic phrase formation of a specific and well-defined kind. Is there any difference in syntactic gross structure between sentences such as, on the one hand:

han købte hús	'he bought a house'
han faldt i vándet	'he fell into the water'

and on the other hand:

han kóbte et hús	'he bought a house'
han kóbte húset	'he bought the house'
han fáldt i vándet	'he fell (while he was) in the water'

and, if so, on what level of abstraction? I would like to suggest that such phenomena be accounted for in terms of syntactic structure, since otherwise it is hard to see how reasonably generalized phonological rules can be worked out. This means that there must be *a rather 'surfacy' syntactic process of phrase adjustment establishing close-knit phrases under a number of semantico-syntactic conditions* (absence of [+Det] in sequences like *købte hús* being just one among several such

conditions). This solution may seem like pushing a phonological problem into some other compartment of grammar in order to obtain a
spurious simplicity, but I hope to demonstrate below that the problems
do belong in syntax, and, as shown already, there are really quite a
few solid statements to be made even at the present state of research.
I assume that what really needs to be done is for syntacticians to
make full use of the important evidence furnished by UA as a reflex
of syntactic structure.

9.3.   UNIT ACCENTUATION AND DISCONTINUOUS CONSTITUENTS

The next question is: why should UA be analysed as a reflex of syntactic structure rather than as a property of an autonomous phonological
hierarchy?

If we look at the examples given earlier in this paper, it will be
apparent that the phrases with UA are in some cases broken up by syntactically extraneous material. This is in fact quite normal, although
it may render it somewhat obscure what the phrase limits really are.
Among Jespersen's examples adduced to demonstrate that UA may
apply in spite of the presence of a definite article is *ta hatten 'av* 'take off
your hat' (in my system of notation: *tag hátten áf*, since there are two
essentially equal main stresses if there is no special emphasis). Here it
is *not* a matter of idiom formation, cf.

> *tag frákken på*   'put on your coat!'
> *læg bógen væk*   'put the book aside!'

and so on. The type is perfectly productive, but still it does not contradict the rule about [+Det] blocking UA. The reason for UA is
obviously that *verb and adverb form a phrase* on a more abstract level,
cf. that these occur adjacently in examples like

> *hvád skal jeg tage på*   'what shall I put on?'

Danish has simply generalized a word order according to which the
object NP must intervene between verb and adverb if it is not placed
frontally in the sentence.

More generally, it holds true that *a string exhibiting UA may be
broken up by extraneous material without the accentual pattern being
disturbed* (except insofar as certain rhythmical adjustments may apply

if, for example, the resulting sequence contains an awkward sequence of unstressed items). Let us start with another example of the same type as those above:

dén skal du tage méd 'take that one with you'
det er dén bóg du skal tage méd 'that is the book you are supposed to take with you.'

These examples show the unbroken phrase *tage méd* (literally: 'take with'), which can then be made discontinuous by, say, an intervening object NP:

du skal tage bógen méd 'take the book with you'

or, with more material intervening:

du skal tage dén bóg der står 'take the book (standing) over there
 dérhénne méd with you'

The lack of stress on *tage* is still directly dependent on the construction *tage med*, cf. that UA fails to apply the moment there is no such adverb in the construction:

du skal táge dén bóg der står 'take the book (standing) over there'
 dérhénne

since now we have a simple verb + object construction with an object NP containing [+Det] and hence blocking UA.

 Now let us look at another type:

du skal táge med dén hånd 'you are supposed to use that hand
 (when putting sth. on your plate)'

Here we have UA in a PrepP introduced by *med*. In this case a still more drastic rupture of the unity of the phrase is possible, since the NP governed by the preposition may be moved out of the phrase (as in English):

det er dén hånd du skal táge med 'that is the hand you are supposed to use'

The effect of such movement transformations on accentuation has been discussed for English by Bresnan (1972) and others. Thus there is nothing novel in pointing to the fact that accentual patterns may survive such moving around of constituents, but it is important to emphasize that such observations must somehow be integrated into a general model of accentuation. Obviously, if we say that UA is dependent on a surface-syntactic phrase adjustment, this statement must be modified so that it refers to a level of abstraction beyond that of movement transformations ('root transformations') of the type exemplified by the last mentioned example. Maybe that is the level that is sometimes referred to as 'shallow surface syntax'.

Finally, let us look at a construction involving phrase formation with UA on two levels. A verb indicating transposition followed by an adverbial phrase undergoes stress reduction by UA, as shown in Section 9.2.1.6 above. As for the adverbial phrase, this may be implemented as a PrepP with UA within its own bounds. Similarly, there may be a sequence of auxiliary and main verbs exhibiting UA. We see the operation of three such applications of UA (V + V́, Prep + Ń, V + PrépP) in the following examples:

> *du skal tage med bússen*   'you must go by bus'
> *du skal tage med dén bús*   'you must take that bus'

Again, as above, the phrase (or phrases) may be made discontinuous by movement transformations:

> *det er dén bús du skal tage med*   'that is the bus you are supposed to
> take'

Now it may be useful to confront the phonological results to be expected from these three kinds of phrase manipulation, viz.

> *det er dén bóg du skal tage méd*
> *det er dén hånd du skal táge med*
> *det er dén bús du skal tage med*

These are the accentuations that would be predicted from a simple application of UA (as long as we stick to just marking main stresses), and indeed, it is perfectly possible to make an accentual difference along these lines. On the syntactic surface the sequences look suspiciously alike as long as we disregard phonology, since they are perfectly analogous in terms of lexical material. From the point of view of phonology, in turn, there is no way of accounting for the accentual differences unless we have recourse to a more abstract level of syntax. I think the inevitable conclusion must be that the relevant phrasal structurings originate somewhere at a level more abstract than surface syntax, that they are reflected as partly discontinuous phrasal constituents of a special type in surface syntax (although such constituency has been more or less neglected in syntax based on written language), and finally that they trigger the occurrence of UA.

So much for accentuation as directly dependent on syntax or syntactico-semantic features and structurings. It should be added that the last Example sentence above will tend to be uttered with some degree of stress on *med* which makes this word more prominent than *tage*, there being a range of possible prominence all the way from a weak stress to a main stress as in *méd* of the first sentence. That is, the first and last sentence may optionally sound alike, due to the range of variation possible in the last sentence. Another option is to have less stress reduction on *tage*, with the result that the last sentence becomes more similar in accentuation to the second rather than the first one.

We see here that the application of UA, combined with movement transformations, may cause a string of weakly-stressed wordforms to occur in succession without any main stress following, and that in such cases there is a tendency to remedy the situation by restoring the main stress to a greater or lesser extent on one of the wordforms. What is at stake here is probably some *rhythmical* constraint, which of course deserves closer scrutiny in a comprehensive analysis of Danish accentuation.

9.4. DEEP AND SURFACE PHONOLOGY: PHRASE STRUCTURE AND FOOT STRUCTURE

9.4.1. Movement transformations and phrase contingency

Let us now take stock of the types of structurings that emerge at various levels of abstraction.

1 At some syntactic level the constructions which eventually exhibit UA must be established as a specifically marked type of phrase. Furthermore, the last constituent that has a lexical stress (predictable by rule or not) is marked as such.
2 At some level UA operates in accordance with the information about underlying phrase structure.
3 At a quite 'surfacy' syntactic level there may be a perturbation of word order, but information about the more abstract phrase structure is preserved.

Now the next important question is whether these more or less pertured phrases provide the basis for surface-phonological rhythmicization, or whether there is a separate, purely phonological mechanism of foot formation, or the like, in Danish. I think there is, and I think that this is the very unit which Thorsen (1983) has found useful as a unit of reference in describing Danish intonation. The stress-correlated pitch contour in Danish starts with a stressed syllable and comprises all material up to the next stressed syllable, unless there are major syntactic breaks (e.g. clause boundaries) signalled as such. This provides us with a further relevant level:

4 At a rather 'surfacy' phonological level, the phonological material is divided up into consecutive feet, each comprising a syllable with main stress plus some number (from zero upwards) of syllables with lower stress.

This foot, of course, divides up the sequence of syllables in a way which may be totally at variance with the phrase structuring responsible for UA:

Phrase marking:	*Péter* | *fáldt í vándet*
UA:	*Péter* | *faldt i vándet*
Foot marking:	*Péter faldt i* | *vándet*
	'Peter fell into the water'

or with a moved constituent:

Phrase marking:	*Jóan* | *kán fólges* | *méd hám*
UA:	*Jóan* | *kan fólges* | *med hám* (emphasis on ham)
Perturbation:	*Hám* | *kan* | *Jóan* | *fólges* | *méd*
Foot marking:	*Hám kan* | *Jóan* | *fólges med*
	'Joan can accompany him'

In the last example the two underlying phrases *kan fólges* and *med ham* have been split up so that no phrase is left quite intact except for the one-word phrase *Jóan*. One may speculate whether there is a way of dividing the surface sequence of words into linear stretches such that each corresponds to a phonological phrase; this is possible only if we take the last word to form an unstressed tail, which is at variance with the generalization about phrase-final stress:

Hám \| *kan Jóan* \| *fólges med*

I doubt that it is useful to posit a phonological level of description at which there are such intermediate phrases. Anyway, the surface structure emerging is the one that is organized in terms of stress-initial feet, as shown above.

In the exposition above, the operation of UA is inserted between a more abstract and a less abstract level of syntactic specification. This is certainly a possibility (cf. the argumentation in Bresnan 1972), but it should be noted that this really amounts to assuming that UA requires for its operation that the constituents of the phrase in question occur in a linear sequence without discontinuities (cf. the phrases *kan følges* and *med ham* above). That may be a meaningful assumption, but in fact the fulfilment of this requirement is possible only if one permits linear orderings of constituents on a non-'surfacy' level which are quite remote from the orderings that can actually surface in the language. Let us see what happens in sentences containing sentential *ikke* 'not'

> *Péter købte íkke hús*   'Peter did not buy a house'

Here, the phrase taking UA is obviously *købte hús*, not **købte íkke*, cf.

> *Péter købte hús*   'Peter bought a house'
> *Péter kóbte íkke*   'Peter did not buy',

but there is no way to place the two words of this phrase *købte... hús* adjacent to each other unless one is willing to claim that UA operates at an extremely abstract and remote level at which *ikke* stands outside the remainder of the sentence (as an immediate constituent of the whole sentence).

To me it seems more attractive to start from the observation that *købte hus* is a discontinuous phrase and to assume that its constituents are nevertheless *syntactically marked as belonging together in one phrase*. UA, then, operates on such phrases, regardless of whether they are discontinuous or not, and each phrase affected by UA thus acquires *final stress*. Further, if UA applies *after 'surfacy' movement transformations*, we can only uphold this principle of phrase-final stress if the constituent that is underlyingly phrase-final preserves some positional marker in spite of the moving around of constituents. This amounts to saying (cf. Bresnan 1972) that the diacritic marking of tree structures for UA is a part of *syntax*, although the actual implementation of stresses is of course a matter of phonology.

9.4.2. The total scenario of prosodic structuring in deep and surface phonology

Let us return now to the question of how the various mechanisms of (non-emphatic) accentuation in Danish cooperate or interact to form an accentual output. The mechanisms involved are: (i) Morpheme Stress by Rule, (ii) Intra-Word UA, (iii) Compound Stress by Rule, and (iv) Phrasal UA (see Sections 9.1.2–9.1.6 above).

It is necessary to consider first to what extent these mechanisms belong to an abstract level in the sense that they are associated with syntactic tree structures occurring at not quite 'surfacy' levels. This was shown above to be the case for Phrasal UA. What about the other mechanisms?

Although the inherent accentuation of morphemes (i.e. whether a morpheme is accented or not) has a connection with syntactic categorization, Morpheme Stress by Rule obviously presupposes a specification of the phonological structure of the morpheme in terms of syllable number and syllable structure. Intra-Word UA, in turn, operates on morpheme stresses in the string it applies to. This just tells us that both of these mechanisms presuppose the occurrence of specific lexical material in syntactic slots; they might for that matter be quite 'surfacy' processes. On the other hand, these two mechanisms are closely associated with the lexical component in the sense that there is a structural and functional equivalence between stress redundancy conditions and these stress insertion mechanisms. If a given lexical item has irregular stress placement, this must of course be part of the underlying phonological representation in the lexicon of Danish, but if the stress placement is regular, there are obviously two ways in which this accentuation can be implemented: (i) it may be part of the underlying lexical representation, although its presence is predictable, or (ii) it may be inserted by rule. I think it is important to emphasize this dual access to intra-word accentuation as an important aspect of language: the language is designed in such a way that the lexicalization of intra-word accentual patterns is possible, but alternatively, it is possible to arrive at the same result by rule. Obviously, in studying the way language is actually mastered, and the ways in which lexical material is actually retrieved in language use, one must operate with both of these options, and one must reckon with the possibility that a given word is handled differently by different speakers of the language, or differently at different stages in one speaker's linguistic development.

This suggests to me that the accentual mechanisms in question are part of an abstract sub-component of phonology which is associated with the very level in syntax at which specific lexical material appears in definite syntactic slots.

As for Compound Stress by Rule, the same line of reasoning is valid. In this case it is further supported by the occurrence of modifications such as shrinking of accentual tree structure and rhythmic perturbations (cf. the *stationsforstander* case in Section 9.1.4 above), suggesting that the full hierarchy of binary accentual contrasts which can be predicted from the syntactic structure of the compound belongs to a relatively abstract level of phonology.

Finally, Phrasal UA operates on word stresses in the string it applies to (cf. the relationship between Morpheme Stress and Intraword UA, as mentioned above). Since it seems clear that Phrasal UA belongs to a level more abstract than surface syntax, we may conclude that the specification of word stress belongs to such an abstract level as well. Thus, all the evidence points in one direction: *there is an abstract component of phonology which is presupposed by surface syntax, and to which both the specification of (morpheme and) word stress and phrasal UA belong.*

It may be necessary to forestall a possible objection to the line of reasoning pursued above, viz. that it is not strictly compelling with regard to the specification of intra-word accentual patterns by rule. It would be possible, in principle, to argue that the properties of the strings which allow us to insert stresses by rule also allow us to predict on what structures UA can operate, i.e. that it is possible in principle to formulate UA in such a way that it blocks stress insertion in certain morphemes or words rather than performing a stress reduction. Stress insertion would, then, operate afterwards, inserting stresses according to rule except in cases where the UA has added a diacritic mark blocking stress insertion. However, apart from the fact that this is a rather roundabout way to account for accentuation, it has one major drawback: it fails to account for the fact that there are some (in fact several) stresses which must by necessity be present underlyingly as part of lexical representations, since they are unpredictable. As for these, they must be processed anyway in connection with the application of Intra-Word or Phrasal UA, and thus it is a most undesirable complication to handle the stresses inserted by rule in a different format. I take it that this is strong enough evidence in favour of the contention that UA implies a full stress specification of each of the constituents in the string it applies to (be it Intra-Word or Phrasal UA).

We have seen that there is an implicational relationship between stress insertion rules and UA rules. Is it possible to set up a full chain of implications among the four mechanisms listed above? The key element in this context is Compound Stress.

Compound stress is generated in terms of various separate structures and mechanisms: (i) a hierarchical structure furnished by syntax and/or the lexical representation of the compound, (ii) a phonological marking of right branches as + (or 'strong') and left branches as − (or 'weak'), (iii) phonologically − conditioned modifications of the hierarchical structure (to the extent that aberrations from the underlying hierarchical structure are not lexically represented), and finally (iv) interpretive rules (and conventions) for translating the surface representation into a phonetic representation. Of these components, the first (i) and second (ii) do not seem to presuppose the other mechanisms generating stress, but they presuppose diacritic markings showing which lexical items are capable of carrying stress, and which lexical items are able to qualify as separate constituents of such a structure.[8]

I do not think that there is any unique answer to the question whether the basic hierarchical structure of compounds is generated 'before' or 'after' the specification of morpheme stresses and the application of Intra-Word UA. *As for components (iii) and (iv) of Compound Stress by Rule, however, these evidently presuppose morpheme stress assignment and UA at the word level.* Further modifications occur as a result of UA at the phrase level, as a result of syntactic movement transformations, and finally as a result of foot assignment. (The prosodic behaviour of compounds as a consequence of such conditioning has not been studied in any detail, however.) Thus, the mechanism of compound stress generation is a complex ranging from the most abstract level to the most concrete level of phonology.

Phrasal UA is, in a sense, equally all-embracing if all components of stress adjustment are included under this heading. As noted earlier, this type of UA does not necessarily convert full stresses into 'zero stress', although this is very often the case in Danish. Syllables with

---

[8] The existence of 'quasi-compounds' which are syntactically and semantically derivatives has been touched upon above. One suffix behaving (regularly) in this way is *-hed* '-ness'; cf. that it patterns just like the adjective *hed* 'hot' in examples such as:

['døgdi‚he:'ð] dygtighed 'cleverness'
['fe:'bʌ‚he:'ð] feberhed 'burning with fever'

an underlying main stress may remain more prominent than true zero-stress syllables, but this is to a large extent a matter of inherent differences in segmental structure. It is important to note, however, that syllables whose stress is reduced as a consequence of Phrasal UA may retain their stød (except if it is a matter of a word-final open syllable, since vowel shortening occurs regularly in such cases). See Basbøll (1972) for details.

The most important readjustments are those having to do with *foot structure*. As said earlier, the Danish foot starts with a fully stressed syllable and comprises the following syllables up to the next fully stressed syllable. A 'minus branch' of a phrase that has undergone UA may finally come to stand in such a foot because of movement transformations, cf. such examples as those cited above, and in that case there is optionally the possibility of giving the syllable in question added prominence. This clearly shows that the status of the word in question as underlyingly stressed is not lost at this stage.

It is different if the placement of such a syllable in the tail of a foot is not a matter of movement transformations but of readjustment of the phonological hierarchy as such, cf. *gik* in *Jóhn gik hjém* 'John went home'; in phrase structure:

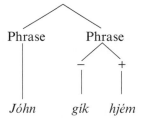

but in foot structure the sequence is reorganized into the following (lexical stresses are here omitted under minus-branches):

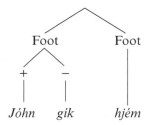

In this case the tendency for such syllables that have been reassigned to a different structural unit is to behave like syllables that are underlyingly devoid of stress. The same is true of the reduced stress-syllable of the second part of a compound, although the distinction between secondary and weak stress, and especially that between syllables undergoing compound UA and those undergoing phrasal UA, may be quite resistant to such rearrangements (this issue is considered in a forthcoming paper by Eli Fischer–Jørgensen).[9] Thus, in

> *ólflasken gik i stýkker*   'the beer bottle broke'

the typical rendering in casual speech is probably with a tail of weakly stressed syllables forming a foot together with the first syllable, i.e. the structure ends up as something like

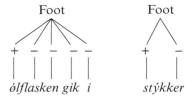

Let us see how a more complex sentence involving both compounding and Intra-Word and Phrasal UA undergoes a stepwise metamorphosis from the syntax-based phrase-structure to a foot-based surface structure. The example is

> *sólohornisten går til spíl*   'the solo horn-player takes music lessons'

Here we have first a compound whose second constituent *hornisten* is in itself an example of Intra-Word UA, the main stress being on the second syllable according to the UA rule:

> *hórn+íst+en* → *hornísten*

(This stress may or may not be audible in the surface rendering of the string above.)

---

[9] Fischer-Jørgensen (1984)—editors' note.

The sentence further contains a Prepositional Phrase with UA: *til spíl*, and a verb phrase (which comprises the PrepP as one constituent) likewise with UA: *går til spíl*. The abstract structure is something like this:

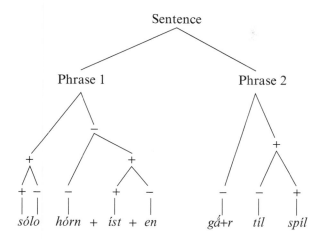

If this were transformed into a sequence of two hierarchies in which the 'pretonic' syllables of Phrase 2 are attached to Phrase 1 with preservation of their mutual ranking by a plus–minus labelling, we would get the following:

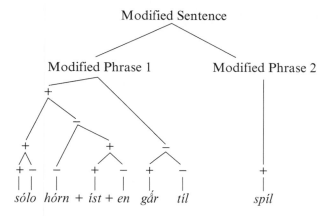

In actual rendering, this structure is shrunk, however, and this may possibly be done to the extent that all syllables between the first and

the last are unstressed (taking into account the inherent differences
of prominence associated with segmental structure). Thus, with the
strongest reduction that is conceivable, the underlying sentence with
its phrase constituency may appear as an utterance with the foot
constituency illustrated below:

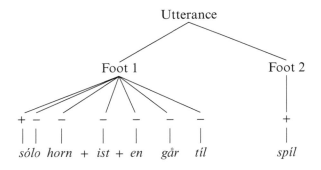

Let us see, finally, what happens if we introduce a sentential adverb
such as *ikke* 'not'. At all the syntactic levels of abstraction with
which we are here concerned, such a constituent turns out to
stand in an awkward position, pushing itself in between the two
parts of the verb phrase *går til spíl*, which is thus a discontinuous
phrase:

> *sólohornisten går íkke til spíl*   'the s.h.pl. does not take music lessons'.

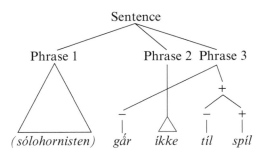

When transformed into an utterance with foot structure, however, the whole hierarchy regains well-formedness in terms of non-
crossing branches. It is rendered here with the ultimate shrinkage of
structure:

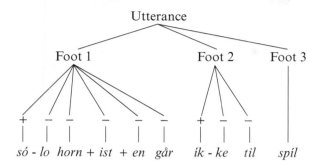

9.5.   CONCLUDING REMARKS

One may dispute the proper formalization of the mechanism of accentuation in Danish. I hope, however, that the exposition given in this paper suffices to show that irrespective of formalization there are some basic points to be made which are typologically and theoretically important.

Typologically it is interesting that Phrasal UA in Danish is largely confined to certain types of phrases, so that, for instance, most noun phrases do not take UA. This has the effect that Danish is characterized by a sometimes very close succession of heavy stresses, an effect that is further enhanced because Danish, as pointed out by Thorsen (1983), has no 'sentence accent'. It is perfectly possible to have quite long utterances without any single focal point signalled by prosodic means.

The other typologically interesting feature is that the foot in Danish goes from a stressed syllable up to the next syllable, and that the preferred internal structure is the prosodically most reduced one, i.e. with just an initial stress-syllable followed by unstressed syllables.

Since there is a glaring non-conformity between the underlying phrase-based hierarchy and the surface hierarchy, quite heavy readjustments are necessary to get from one representation to the other. The nature of the transformations involved is so far somewhat obscure, but it seems obvious that the gap between these two representations speaks in favour of a distinction between a level of deep phonology and a level of surface phonology, at least with regard to prosody. Alternatively, and—I think—more insightfully, one may posit not a machinery of one-way *transformational* relations between two such levels (as suggested by the presentation in this paper) but rather a more intricate *interference* between coexisting principles of prosodic organization, the outcome of this interference depending (inter alia) on the level of distinctness aimed at by the speaker. —Anyway, the evidence of Danish stress suggests not only that one should recognize a self-contained prosodic hierarchy, but that there are different hierarchical organizations involved, and that one of these is closely associated with syntax.

10

Morphemic Tone and Word Tone in Eastern Norwegian[1]

10.1. THE ASSOCIATION OF TONES WITH WORDS

The tonal accents of Norwegian (generally referred to as tone 1 and tone 2) are traditionally described as word tones, i.e. tonemes associated with words. It seems to be implied by the label 'word tone' that there is a basic one-to-one relationship, every word containing one tonal accent, no matter how the word is structured.

It is easily observed that the tonal accents are associated with words if isolated words are taken as the point of issue. It makes sense to state that any Norwegian word occurring in isolation has a tonal contour, and in some words the tonal contour is immediately found to be lexically distinctive (c.f. the plural forms [1]*bønder* 'peasants' and [2]*bønner* 'beans'). The association of tones with words may be confirmed by the observation that there is in some words a close connection between tonal status and segmental structure or stress pattern (the tone 1 of *guano* is predictable on this basis). Nevertheless, it is well known that the validity of the term 'word tone' is limited in important respects. First, the tonal accents are not always associated with lexical words: in numerous cases they go with inflected forms of a word but not with the word as a lexical unit, cf. [2]*sitte* and [1]*sitter*, infinitive and present tense of the verb 'to sit' (also compare that the tonal contrast [1]*bønder* : [2]*bønner* is confined to the plural). Secondly, it has been thoroughly demonstrated that tonal accents occurring in connected speech are frequently associated with syntactic constructions (including compounds) which comprise several words.[2] The single words thus lose

[1] Reprinted from *Phonetica* 10 (1963): 154–64.
[2] See, for instance, Broch (1935: 80 ff.) and Haugen and Joos (1954).

their tonal characteristics, and the tonal contour of the construction may not represent the isolated tonal status of any of its constituents (²*ta på* 'put on', ²*avgang* 'departure', although the isolated words *ta, på, av, gang* have no tone 2).

The tonal accents are thus associated with units on different levels, although they are most easily observed on the word level. In this paper I shall consider some aspects of the relation between tone and word structure in noncompound words spoken in isolation.[3] (The paper continues and revises the argumentation of Rischel 1969.) The aspects of toneme distribution with which this paper is concerned are difficult to handle structurally, but the whole problem definitely deserves consideration, even though it may not be possible to arrive at a very neat system. The syntactic processes affecting the tonal status of word forms in connected speech are left out of consideration here.

10.2. THE ASSOCIATION OF TONES WITH MORPHS AND SYLLABLES

To predict the tone of a Norwegian word form from its segmental structure, it is neither sufficient to identify the root or the stem nor necessary to identify all the morphs of the word form. In the majority of cases the word tone is predictable from the morph which occupies the first syllable after the stress syllable, here referred to as the *post-stress syllable* (exceptions will be mentioned later). If the stem is monosyllabic it may suffice to consider the suffix, cf. the tonal contrast ¹*tanken* 'the tank' vs. ²*tanker* 'tanks'; if the stem comprises the post-stress syllable it suffices to consider the stem, cf. the invariant tone 2 of inflected forms of ²*tanke* 'thought' (²*tanken*, ²*tanker*). This may be accounted for if we assume that the various morphs have inherent tones: in monosyllables the stem is tonally neutral, and the tonal accent of inflected forms belongs morphologically to a suffix, whereas in word forms with a bisyllabic stem it is located in the stem. In a recent paper Einar Haugen criticizes this analysis.[4] He states that it is simpler to locate the contrast between *tank-en* and *tanke-n* in the stems, and to consider the article toneless. This is

---

[3] The norm discussed here is the educated Oslo pronunciation of *bokmål*, as found in Alnæs (1910).

[4] Haugen (1963).

definitely true, but the main problem is not the difference between *tank-en* and *tanke-n*; the crucial point is that *tank* has tone 1 in some inflected forms but 2 in others.

As far as I can see, the plural form ²*tanker* clearly shows that monosyllabic stems are neutral with respect to word tone: the difference in tone between *tank-en* and *tank-er* must be ascribed to the suffixes (unless the whole word tone problem is handled in terms of junctures).

A similar situation is found on the phonemic level: the contrast between the two tonal accents demands the occurrence of a post-stress syllable—there is no contrast in monosyllables.[5] I have previously tried to interpret tone 1 and tone 2 phonemically on the basis of this evidence. I do not want to insist on the details of that attempt, except for the suggestion that there is a specific, functional connection between the tonal distinction and the post-stress syllable. The basic idea is that the tonal contour represents a prosodic unit belonging to the stress syllable *plus* a prosodic unit belonging to the post-stress syllable, and that the functional evidence is in favour of a solution which places the tonally distinctive prosodeme in the post-stress syllable. The problem is mainly in the phonemic doctrine. It has been emphasized that there is a clear phonetic difference *within* the stress syllable, and that the two tones may (in Oslo speech) be distinguished on the basis of the stress syllable alone (in my previous paper—Rischel 1960—I certainly over-emphasized the *phonetic* role of the post-stress syllable). In this case we face a phonemic problem of a very general nature: can a feature be associated phonemically with one segment (syllable) if it is phonetically more prominent in another, adjacent segment (syllable)? The problem is not crucial for the present paper, since the relation between morphemic tone and word tone can be accounted for without any reference to phonemic notation. However, it should be mentioned in this context that Haugen (1963: note 8) has ventured the possibility of ascribing the tonal contrast to the presence *versus* absence of a tone 2-element (possibly in the post-stress syllable), the phonetic tone 1-contour occurring if the element is not present. This implies that tone 1 is 'zeroed out' completely. The elimination of the tone 1-unit is attractive also from a morphological point of view, and I have chosen to adopt it here.

[5] The literature on Scandinavian tonemes shows disagreement as to the structural status of monosyllables, that is whether they have tone 1 or no phonemic tone.

10.3.   THE MECHANISM OF 'MORPHOTONEMICS'

In the following a morph is said to have an *inherent tone* if the occurrence of the morph in a word may condition the occurrence of a tone 2-contour. In some cases inherent tones are obviously predictable from the (remaining) structure of the morphs (we may predict that *²tanke* has tone 2 and that *guano* has no tone 2 on the basis of the stress patterns and the segmental structure of the forms), but in other cases it is not predictable, cf. the minimal contrast in tone between *²bruke* 'to use' and *bruket* 'the factory'; which shows that the morphs representing infinitive and definite neuter differ only with respect to inherent tone.

The difference in predictability is important, especially from the point of view of a 'generative' grammar. The unpredictable tone forms part of the structure of a basic morph, whereas the predictable tone is introduced by simple morphotonemic processes. To distinguish the two types I shall speak of *primary* tone (as in infinitive *²-e*) and *secondary* tone (possibly in *²tanke*). From a descriptional point of view it must be advantageous to reduce as many instances of inherent tone as possible to a secondary status.

The tonal status of a word form may be deduced from the basic morphs which make up the form according to two sets of rules: (i) a set of rules generating a secondary inherent tone in certain morph types, and (ii) a set of rules determining under which circumstances a morphemic tone survives as a word tone. Logically, the processes must come in this order, but for the present discussion it is more convenient to set up the latter set of rules first in a postulative form and to discuss the former set of rules afterwards within the framework given.

As said earlier in this chapter, the tonality of a word depends on the morph occupying the post-stress syllable. If this morph has an inherent tone 2, the word form gets tone 2, otherwise the word gets zero (tone 1). All other inherent tones disappear by an automatic alternation.

10.4.   RULES CONCERNING WORD TONE

Some of the distributional features of the tonal accent are related to the stem as a whole; others are related to single morphs.

The rules can be formulated in a very simple way if we assume that the morphs have inherent tones: (i) if the stem has a 'iambic' stress pattern, the word form has zero; (ii) if the morph occupying the post-stress syllable has zero, the word form has zero; (iii) if the morph occupying the post-stress syllable has an inherent tone 2, the word form has tone 2. Needless to say, a word form has zero if it ends in a stressed syllable.

Rule (i) actually says that in a word form whose stem exhibits an initial unstressed syllable and a final stressed syllable, all inherent tones are neutralized, i.e. the word form has zero (*general*, pl. *generaler*); this applies also to derivations from such stems (*besett-e*, *besett-else*), and it also applies if the stress is moved during the process of affixation (either moved to the stem-final position: *rektórer*, pl. of *réktor*, or sometimes from the final position: *mágisk*, derived from *magí*). This rule is independent of the morph structure of the stem: it applies equally to monomorphic and multimorphic stems. There are other rules which may be formulated with reference to the stem, but most of these actually belong on the morph level as rules concerning the occurrence or non-occurrence of secondary inherent tone.

As far as the single morphs are concerned, the rule is that all inherent tones except the one going with the syllable after the stress syllable are neutralized (in *grekere* 'Greeks' the zero tone of *-er* is decisive, and the inherent tone of the following plural morpheme ^{2}-*e* can exert no influence; in ^{2}*malere* 'painters' the tone 2 of ^{2}-*er* is decisive). It is essential to emphasize that this rule applies before morphophonemic rules about fusion of morphs: the definite form ^{2}*kona* 'the woman' has tone 2 because it consists of ^{2}*kone* + -*a*; it is only a secondary process that this -*a* replaces the final vowel of the stem and thus comes to occupy the syllable after the stress syllable. The definite plural of nouns may profitably be viewed in this light. Forms like *dyr-ene* 'the animals' indicate that the definite plural -*ene* has zero (or, more correctly, consists of zero -*en* plus plural ^{2}-*e* whose tone 2 vanishes because of the position after the post-stress syllable). A form like ^{2}*hestene* 'the horses' must, therefore, be explained as *hest* plus plural ^{2}-*e* (*r*) plus the definite ending. In this word form the whole ending is ultimately a fusion of ^{2}-*e* (*r*) + -*en* + ^{2}-*e*, and the first of these affixes dominates the tonality of the word because it occupies the post-stress syllable until the morphophonemic fusion has taken place.

10.5. TONALITY OF ROOT MORPHS

The vast majority of root morphs have no primary tone. Roots with final stress—including monosyllables—have no inherent tone at all (although those with one or more pretonic syllables neutralize the tones of suffixes). Roots with nonfinal stress mostly have an inherent tone 2. The tonal status of these roots is, however, to a large extent predictable, i.e. the tone is in most cases secondary.

The tonality of roots will not be discussed in detail here. The suggested morphophonemic approach does not shed any new light on the relationship between root structure and tone. It suffices to mention that there are rules but also exceptions to these rules. For example, zero is typical of roots in unstressed -a, -i, -o (*svada, pari, solo*), and, on the other hand, roots in unstressed -e almost invariably have tone 2 (²*kone,* ²*kutyme*), but exceptions like *ordre, orgie* make it questionable whether the tone *is* predictable in the numerous tone 2-roots in -e, unless we restrict the material to 'genuine' Norwegian words.

The vast majority of roots in -el, -en, -er have zero tone (*hjemmel, laken, hinder*), but there are exceptions with tone 2 (²*himmel,* ²*aften,* ²*sommer,* and some others). A specific problem is constituted by those roots which drop the e in certain word forms. As mentioned before, the tonality of a word form depends on the morph to which the syllable after the stress syllable belongs *before* morphophonemic reductions have taken place. We therefore expect zero in *mangler,* pl. of *mangel* 'lack' as against the tone 2 of ²*djevler,* pl. of ²*djevel* 'devil' (also cf. the minimal pair *aksel* 'shoulder': ²*aksel* 'axle' with the corresponding plurals *aksler* : ²*aksler*). There are, however, a few zero nouns which fall outside this pattern: *aker, finger, sei(e)r, skulder, seter, vinter,* and possibly others have tone 2 plurals (²*akrer,* etc.). Moreover, tone 2 is generally found in inflected forms of zero adjectives in -el, -en, -er, cf. *ekkel* 'disgusting', pl. ²*ekle*.

As the problem is presented here, it is taken for granted that roots in -el, -en, -er are bisyllabic roots, and that the monosyllabic forms without e are reduced forms. However, it is an equally valid assumption that the roots are monosyllables, which develop a connective e under certain circumstances. Both processes are simple from the morphophonemic point of view. I venture the opinion that some roots are basically bisyllabic, others basically monosyllabic, since a structural difference of this kind might account for the tonal contrasts. Roots like *hinder,* ²*himmel* are consequently considered basically bisyllabic in contradistinction to *vinter, ekkel*, which are basically *vintr, ekkl*. Segmentally, the two types of roots have the same phonemic appearances because the bisyllabic ones drop the *e* in those contexts where the monosyllables remain monosyllabic, while the monosyllables develop an *e* in those contexts where the bisyllabic roots remain bisyllabic. Tonally, however, *vintr* + ²-*er* is distinguished from *mangel* + ²-*er* in accordance with the rules formulated earlier.

10.6. TONALITY OF SUFFIXES

Suffixes consisting of two or more syllables mostly have tone 2 (²*hendelse* 'event', ²*løv-inne* 'lioness'), but there are exceptions like -*asje* (*apanasje*), so the tone must be considered primary. The tone of monosyllabic suffixes is altogether unpredictable (in terms of general rules); there are several minimal contrasts of, e.g., infinitive forms versus definite neuter forms.[6] We must conclude that syllabic suffixes have a primary tone 2 or zero.

The main problem in connection with suffix tone is the alternating tonality of three homonymous suffixes: the nomen agentis -*er* (²*maler* 'painter', *skipper* 'shipper'), the plural -*er* (²*hester* 'horses', *bøker* 'books'), and the present tense -*er* (²*kaster* 'throws', *sitter* 'sits'). We must perhaps confine ourselves to observing that these suffixes have basic morphs with and without tone 2 (as far as the plural formative suffix is concerned, the tone 2 morph is certainly more widespread than the toneless morph; we may confine the latter to a small group of 'irregular' nouns). It would be possible to explain the zero tone forms of the plural and present tense suffixes as non-syllabic -*r* developing a svarabhakti *e*; such nonsyllabic allomorphs are otherwise found (namely after a good many roots consisting of an open syllable: *sko-r* 'shoes', *dø-r* 'dies'), so the solution would reduce the number of basic morphs.[7] Possibly, a similar interpretation may also solve the problem of the nomen agentis forms.

Another problem is the tonal difference between indefinite and definite superlative forms like *høyest* 'highest', ²*høyeste* 'the highest'. This phenomenon is structurally isolated. Strangely enough, the word tone

[6] The material has been collected by Kloster Jensen (1958).
[7] By a basic morph I understand a morph which is not derived morphophonemically from other morphs, cf. Bloomfield (1935: 212).

seems in this case to depend on the morph occupying the second syllable after the stress syllable. I have found no satisfactory interpretation.[8]

10.7.   CONCLUSION

I have tried to show that the so-called word tones of Norwegian simplex words are morph components. Moreover, it appears that in many
cases the tones (of which tone 1 may be 'zeroed out') are predictable
from the segmental structure and stress placement of the morphs, so
that the tones may be said to signal certain (basic) morph structures. In
addition, however, there is a contrast of tone in many types of morph.
The tones have no independent morphemic status, nor do they signal
the occurrence of specific *grammatical* types.

With respect to these properties, the tone of noncompound words
differs sharply from the tone of higher-level entities. Compound
words as well as phrases exhibit tonal contours which have a distinct grammatical function, as for example to signal the difference
between nominal and verbal compounds whose first part is an adverb:
²*uttale* 'pronunciation' versus *uttale* 'pronounce' (and the derivation
uttalelse 'statement'). Under the influence of such higher-level contours the single morphs and words lose their tonal individuality (*uttale*
in spite of ²*tale*).

This double role—as grammatically arbitrary components of lower-
level units and as grammatically motivated components of higher-level
units—is similar to the different roles of stress placement. An analogy to contrastive morphemic tone is furnished by examples like the
Danish lexical contrast *plástic* : *plastík*; an analogy to the noun : verb
contrast is found in English: *óverthrow* (noun) vs. *overthrów* (verb).

---

[8] Miss Ingeborg Hoff has kindly informed me that some of the irregularities pointed
out here are due to the mixed character of the Oslo norm. The surrounding 'pure' dialects
probably exhibit a much higher degree of tonal invariance in connection with some of the
suffixes.

11

Asymmetric Vowel Harmony in Greenlandic Fringe Dialects[1]

11.1. INTRODUCTORY REMARKS ON VOWEL HARMONY

To a very first approximation, *vowel harmony* (henceforth: VH) may be defined as some kind of *principled agreement, with regard to phonetic quality, among the vowels of consecutive syllables.* In languages with VH it may be the case that consecutive syllables agree more or less (under conditions to be specified) with regard to the labial articulation and/or frontness–backness and/or degree of openness of their vowels (under this provisional definition 'umlaut' is included in the category of VH, of course).

There are other, more or less related regularities which refer to consecutive syllables but affect features other than the above-mentioned ones; unlike VH these other regularities often imply that consecutive syllables should be *dissimilar rather than similar.* Examples are: sequential alternation of long and short vowels or syllables; sequential alternation of stressed and unstressed syllables. (There may even be a specific conditioning among different features in consecutive syllables, i.e. the phenomenon referred to in Nordic philology as 'vowel balance', i.e. an interrelation between the quantity of a stressed syllable and the vowel quality of a following, unstressed syllable.)

VH has received considerable attention in the phonological literature, because the descriptive problems posed by this phenomenon are crucial for virtually all major aspects of phonological theory. There are numerous important contributions representing both structural

[1] Reprinted from *Annual Report of the Institute of Phonetics, University of Copenhagen* 9 (1975): 1–48.

linguistic schools and the transformational–generative trend. The emphasis on the different aspects varies, of course.

It should be realized from the beginning that VH may be approached from different angles. It is a commonplace that one should not confuse diachronic and synchronic statements (although the terminology, in the case of 'assimilatory' phenomena, may invite such a confusion), but even from a strictly synchronic angle there are different kinds of statements to be made about VH in a language.

On the one hand, one may perhaps observe that there are some formatives (morphemes) whose phonetic shapes alternate in terms of VH, i.e. depending upon the vowels of adjacent formatives. Turkish is generally quoted as a case in point (cf. the alternating shapes of the plural formative in *adam-lar* 'men', *türkler* 'Turks'). It is then an immediate task to search for, and state, a generalization about these alternations, and more specifically, to make statements according to which the choice of alternants in all possible types of environments can be predicted. I shall refer to a generalization of this kind as a GENERATIVE statement. (Note that the term, as used here, does *not* refer specifically to the transformational trend in linguistics: statements about automatic alternation in the morphophonemic component of a structural linguistic grammar may be equally 'generative'.) The essential property of such a regularity, if stated in rule form, is that it is *assimilatory*, e.g. it is of the type: 'a suffix vowel assumes the same frontness–backness specification as the vowel of the immediately preceding syllable'. In addition to this specification of the assimilatory mechanism, the rule must, of course, be supplied with a definition of *its domain* (i.e. the kind of stretch within which the rule exerts its power, be it a non-compound wordform, a wordform regardless of its complexity, or possibly even more complex stretches). And finally, it should be clearly defined *how the rule applies* to a form, e.g. whether it applies iteratively so that a suffix vowel undergoing VH can, in turn, condition the quality of a following suffix vowel. Needless to say, there is a certain trading relationship between the formulation of the rule itself and the formulation of its conditions for application (if the rule referred to above is found to apply iteratively, one must consider an alternative, viz. the possibility of modifying the rule so that it assimilates *all* non-initial vowels 'simultaneously' to the initial vowel).

On the other hand, one may observe that wordforms in a given language obey a phonetic constraint of VH type, e.g. a constraint which may be formulated like this: 'within a wordform all vowels must agree with respect to frontness–backness'. Note that this is *not* necessarily a statement supported by observed cases of vowel alternation; the statement simply implies that there are no wordforms in the language which are at variance with the VH constraint: there may be forms such as *ili, olu,* but **ilu, *oli* are not well-formed since they violate the constraint. I shall refer to a generalization providing this kind of information as a STRUCTURAL GENERALIZATION. (Note again that the terminology is not intended to refer to particular 'schools'; no sensible approach to linguistic description can do without structural generalizations of some kind, and indeed, well-formedness conditions are fully recognized in recent transformational–generative work, although there has been some uncertainty as to how such statements should be fitted into the total phonological description.)

It is important to note that generative VH rules, and structural generalizations about VH, may or may not coexist with the same domain of applicability in a given language. Like other assimilatory phenomena, vowel alternation conditioned by VH may well occur in connection with the affixation of one formative to another, even if there are formatives whose internal structure violates a strict VH constraint. This situation may be found in VH languages with a stratum of loanwords. Obviously, it may be that the internal structure of some loanwords violates an otherwise existing VH constraint (Turkish may be quoted again: cf. *otobüs* 'bus' without internal VH, but plural *otobüsler* with VH between base and suffix). However, it is also possible for loanwords to be accommodated in terms of a mechanism of VH which is not otherwise found in the language. I shall illustrate this from West Greenlandic.

As mentioned briefly in Rischel (1974: 459), Dano-Norwegian loanwords which are of some age in West Greenlandic have been modified so that they are (more or less) congruent with the well-formedness conditions of the 'genuine' vocabulary. In this process of accommodation, VH comes in under three different kinds of conditions. First, since the language has only three vowel phonemes, /i, a, u/, each vowel shade in a foreign word must be allocated to one of these (and replaced by an appropriate allophone), but this leaves the neutral, unstressed vowel (schwa) unaccounted for. With some exceptions the indeterminacy has been solved by choosing a vowel exhibiting VH with a neighbouring syllable: for example *Jørgen* → /juulut/ or /juurut/ (*ø* is replaced by its nearest equivalent, viz. the long rounded back vowel /uu/, and the value of the final vowel is chosen accordingly). Secondly, initial consonants in foreign words which do not occur in Greenlandic words are often made non-initial by adding a vowel in accordance with a VH rule: for example *Jørgen* → /ujuulut/ (old variant form from southernmost West Greenlandic). And thirdly, if impermissible consonant clusters are eliminated by the insertion of vowels, the quality of each epenthetic vowel is determined by VH. Examples are legion: *blæk* (*blekk*) → /pilikki/ 'ink' (the final /i/ is not interesting in this context; it will appear from the following examples that loanwords ending in a consonant are often augmented with a final /i/); *trumf* /turuffi/ 'trump'; *Knud* (*Knut*) /kunuut/; *æble* → /iipili/ 'apple'. There is also a component of VH in the treatment of loanwords such as *rør* → /ruujuri/ 'tube'; *wire* → /vaajari/.

It is probably clear from these few examples that VH plays a prominent role in the accommodation of loanwords in Greenlandic Eskimo. At the same time, there is no well-formedness constraint according to which consecutive vowels *must* exhibit VH: existing full vowels in loanwords are replaced by the nearest equivalent regardless of VH; hence *kartoffel* → /katurfili/ 'potato'; *Efraim* → /iikaliimi/ (southernmost West Greenlandic[2]), where there is no vowel insertion since the desired accommodation is obtained by metathesis. This does not mean that it is satisfactory to characterize the application of VH as 'sporadic'. Rather, it must be stated that VH in this context is *a mechanism providing underspecified vowels with a full specification*, or, in a different format of description, *a mechanism that determines a unique representation for a variable*. It is *not* a mechanism that changes one possible type of vowel into another possible type of vowel. Vowels that already have a fully determinate—and possible—representation, remain unaffected. But the mechanism of VH is no less regular for that reason.

It might be claimed that this kind of regularity is of peripheral importance for the phonology of a language: it is not part of the functional phonology *per se* but only an accommodation device that comes into force in the process of borrowing. In support of this claim one might mention that *vowel epenthesis without VH* seems to exist as a rule of the language, cf. the variant shapes of the relative case ending in /nuna+p/ versus /aqq+up/ and of the plural ending in /nuna+t/ versus

---

[2] This dialect has /k/ or /q/ (depending on the environments) as the counterpart to general West Greenlandic /f/.

/aqq+it/ (/nuna/ 'country'; /a¢iq/ ~ /aqq/ 'name'). If one chooses to speak of epenthesis here (see extensive data and discussion in Rischel 1974, Part II, §2), the quality of the epenthetic vowel is determined by the following consonant, not by any vowel in an adjacent syllable. These two sets of findings need not be in descriptive conflict, however; one may claim that the VH mechanism taking care of loanwords is a kind of 'morpheme structure rule': it has the single formative as its domain, and hence the suffix vowels of /Vp/, /Vt/ cannot be affected by it. However, it is different if the vowel–zero alternation in the base of /a¢iq/ ~ /aqq/ (previously /atəq/ ~ /atq/) is accounted for in terms of epenthesis. In complex forms this base (and other bases of analogous structure) occurs with or without its second vowel, depending on the structure of the suffixes or suffix clusters; when occurring alone it is obligatorily bisyllabic in accordance with a well-formedness constraint prohibiting word-final consonant clusters. If this second vowel is epenthetic, the existence of a VH rule would require that it came out as /a/, i.e. */ataq/ rather than /a¢iq/ (/t/ and /¢/ regularly alternate according to the quality of the following vowel). However, the vocalic reflex of this alternating set is invariably /i/ (similarly /tupiq/ 'tent', relative case /tuqqup/, plural /tuqqit/, does not occur in the shape */tupuq/).

Under these circumstances I should certainly *not* like to dismiss the loanword data as being of peripheral importance. On the contrary, these forms, if anything, provide us with hard facts about mechanisms employed at the time of borrowing. It is, on the other hand, a matter of descriptive principles, and of more or less intimate knowledge of the pertinent data, whether one chooses to describe the vowel–zero alternation in /a¢iq/~ /aqq/ in terms of epenthesis, syncope, or straightforward alternation between two representatives of a category defined underlyingly by alternation. I have found, on quite independent grounds, that the synchronic data are *not* in favour of an epenthesis solution for /a¢iq/ ~ /aqq/, /tupiq/ ~ /tuqq/ (see Rischel 1974, Part II, §2), but I am at variance on this point with some phonologists writing about West Greenlandic. Anyway, I think the attested existence of a VH 'blank-filling' rule for loanwords should cast grave doubts upon the validity of an epenthesis solution for the other bi- or polysyllabic bases.

I have stated that generative rules of VH may, or may not, be matched by well-formedness constraints, and vice versa. In fact, situations in which there is some kind of 'mismatch' are more interesting than situations in which there is perfect coincidence: the former provide more information as to the internal structure of the languages in question.

There is a different angle to the question of how much information one can deduce from a set of generalizations about VH: 'asymmetric' systems (see further below) give more information about the phonological make-up of the language than do 'symmetric' systems.

If one faces a suffixational language in which every non-initial vowel exhibits strict VH with the preceding vowel (with regard to the features involved in the mechanism of VH for this particular language), there may be no more to be done about this than just stating the pattern of vowel alternation, e.g. 'front vowel after front vowel, back vowel after back vowel', or 'rounded vowel after rounded vowel, unrounded vowel after unrounded vowel', or whatever simple or complex statement may be true for this particular language. There are, of course, different formats of description that may be employed. One may say that (i) only word-initial vowels are specified underlyingly for the features involved in VH, whereas all non-initial vowels are underlying incompletely specified ('archi-vowels' or 'Pro-vowels') and only receive their full specification by a VH rule, or one may say that (ii) each non-initial vowel is a variable ranging over a variety of vowel qualities, the choice of one specific alternant (i.e. the exclusion of other alternants) in a particular type of environment being predictable from a well-formedness constraint (strict VH). Given the VH data alone, it does not seem permissible to build more pattern into the description. Several phonologists prefer to elevate one of the alternants to the status of unique underlying representation and thereby introduce a directionality in the rule schema (e.g. one may postulate that suffix vowels are underlyingly all back but become front after front vowels). From the point of view of immanent description (description of patterning that is *in* the language) this solution distorts the picture, however (a solution working with underlying front vowels and a rule according to which vowels are retracted after back vowels might serve the purpose equally well, and hence the directionality is spurious).

There may be external criteria for making such a choice, e.g. the analyst may believe in some theory about universal markedness according to which one or the other alternant is more natural and 'hence' the more basic one, but this is something different from statements about regularities inherent in the language under study. No matter how one approaches linguistics, it seems to me legitimate to require that the two kinds of criteria be kept distinct from one another.

Now, what is an asymmetric system, and why does it provide more phonological when information compared to a symmetric system? The phonological literature contains reports about languages in which most vowels participate in a system of VH although some vowels (possibly just one) behave differently. It may be that these latter vowels are totally excepted from undergoing VH, or totally excepted from conditioning VH in adjacent syllables, or it may be that they participate (one way or another) in VH when occurring in some formatives but not when occurring in other formatives. Such a situation is interesting, both for the theory of VH rules and for the theory of underlying representations. There are well-known instances of *umlaut* that are just like this. For example, u-umlaut before a surfacing *u* (modern [ʏ]) in Icelandic has regular exceptions, cf. the stem *dag-* 'day' in nominative singular *dagur*, versus dative plural *døgum*. It is a well-known argument that the reason why some occurrences of *u* fail to produce umlaut is that these are epenthetic (*dagur* from *dag-r* as against *søgur*, plural of *saga* 'story', whose *u* is not epenthetic). The connection between epenthesis and failure to produce umlaut can, in turn, be accounted for in terms of rule ordering: umlaut precedes epenthesis, or at least umlaut precedes the mechanism by which the epenthetic vowel gets a specification identical with that of umlauting *u* (this may be read as a diachronic interpretation or, if one believes in synchronically ordered rules, as a synchronic description).

By asymmetry I refer to a particularly conspicuous type of skewness, viz. the situation in which it is true that X → Y next to a syllable whose vowel shares the differential features with Y, but *not* that Y → X next to a syllable whose vowel shares the differential features with X. Icelandic u-umlaut may again serve as an illustration: *a* goes to *ö* before *u*, but it is probably generally assumed that it is inadequate to posit a rule with the opposite polarity, i.e. switching *ö* to *a* before non-*u*. If this contention is beyond discussion, it is tantamount to stating that there is an interesting determinacy in the underlying representation; instances of alternation between *a* and *ö* should all be derived from underlying *a* (not from underlying *ö* or from something in between). It is definitely of interest to distinguish such an (alleged) asymmetric mechanism from the kind of symmetry observable in Turkish VH, rather than concealing the difference by introducing a spurious directionality in the description of the latter. A careful distinction between the two kinds of pattern is useful also from a diachronic perspective: it may be that a pattern which is now perfectly symmetric originated as an asymmetric one (e.g. that suffix vowels whose underlying status is now indeterminate, used to behave asymmetrically so that one might speak of a unique underlying representation at an earlier stage). It should be possible, within the format of the description chosen, to state the transition from one situation to the other.

To be honest, I do not consider it all that evident that the *a–ö* alternation in Icelandic is synchronically a matter of a unidirectional rule. Under that analysis, forms in which the alternant *ö* occurs in a word-final syllable must be accounted for by positing underlying *w* or *u* which vanishes (is deleted by some rule) after producing umlaut, but how can it be proved that this is always the appropriate solution? What prevents us from positing underlying *ö* in some instances and making the rule work both ways, so that *ö* is switched to *a* before a vowel that is not *u*—e.g. in *röð* 'row', genitive *raðar*? The argument runs, of course, that there are (always?) related wordforms whose vocalism is best accounted for in terms of underlying *a*, but what is meant by 'related' in this context? Forms that are related historically may not have the same underlying vowel from the point of view of synchronic analysis, and what about paradigms such as *gata* 'street'—(oblique case) *götu*, for which related forms provide no cue (as far as I can see)? The very question whether *a* goes to *ö*, or *ö* goes to *a* here may be an artefact of the descriptive approach. (As for possible appeals to 'psychological reality', I see no reason whatsoever to assume that either of the two proposals is true in that sense—maybe speakers simply master the paradigm as an alternation set; if so, an analysis claiming to reflect something psychologically real can, at most, define the vocalic entity in question as a category of alternants, not as underlying *a* or *ö*).

It is no real complication of the description to make the umlaut rule work both ways; on the contrary, it becomes a more generalized type of assimilatory mechanism. The important thing is to find unmistakable evidence for or against a symmetric conception of the pattern. Again, it is interesting to trace the diachronic development, which obviously supports the asymmetric solution (underlying *a*), but the process by which u-umlaut came into existence should not be apriorically assumed to continue its existence as such. The synchronic data may not be unanimously in favour of such a description.

I think it is typologically worthwhile to search for VH patterns which provide unmistakable descriptive evidence (not necessarily psychological evidence)[3] for an asymmetric solution. The vowel harmony pattern of Greenlandic fringe dialects which is called 'i-dialect' (see Section 11.2.2) is a typical case, and that is one reason why I shall give a brief description of it below. Another reason is that the nature of this paper, and in fact the very existence of a strict pattern, has not been stated in the literature on Greenlandic, the phenomenon being generally taken to be a matter of unconditional sound substitution (with inexplicable exceptions). There is thus a straightforward task of linguistic documentation to be taken care of.

11.2. THE CONCEPT OF 'i-DIALECT'

11.2.1. Dialects of Greenland

Before entering into a discussion of 'i-dialect' it may be expedient to give a brief survey of the major dialect divisions in Greenland.

The most obvious grouping of dialects is indicated by roman numerals in Fig. 11.1 (for details on dialect differences, see Petersen 1970). There are seven major groups of dialects, some of which are more homogeneous than others. I is Polar Eskimo, which is totally outside the scope of this paper. II is the Upernavik dialect, which exhibits the peculiarity referred to as 'i-dialect'. III is the group of dialects (differing but little from one another) spoken in the Uummannaq district and all along the Disko Bay. IV is the group of dialects spoken from Sisimiut (Holsteinsborg) in the North through Maniitsoq (Sukkertoppen) and Nuuk (Godthåb) and with several isoglosses North and South of Paamiut (Frederikshåb) providing a fuzzy boundary toward the next dialect group. 'Standard' West Greenlandic is based on the dialects of group IV, which I shall refer to as Central West Greenlandic (CWG). V is southern West Greenlandic, as spoken in different varieties from Paamiut (Frederikshåb) and southwards to Nanortalik (as mentioned above, Paamiut belongs to the former group in some respects). VI is the Kap Farvel (Cape Farewell) dialect, as spoken at the southernmost settlements (my material is from Narsaq kujalleq = Frederiksdal).

---

[3] The term 'descriptive' as used in this paper simply means 'stating generalizations emerging from a study of the data'. I must emphasize that it is not intended to mean 'allegedly internalized'.

Figure 11.1

Finally, VII is East Greenlandic spoken in and around the towns Ammassalik and Scoresbysund. Dialects II, V, VI, and VII all share the peculiarity referred to as 'i-dialect'. Thus, 'i-dialect' is encountered in the northernmost (Upernavik) and southernmost parts of West Greenland as well as East Greenland, i.e. viewed from the geographical centre in West Greenland, 'i-dialect' is a characteristic of the fringe dialects (with the exception of Polar Eskimo, which entirely breaks off the dialect geographical continuity of the rest of Greenland).

11.2.2. **What is currently meant by 'i-dialect'?**

In Schultz-Lorentzen's Greenlandic dictionary (1927) the entry 'ersangavoq' is translated by 'speaks dialect; speaks with the Southland accent; speaks the i-dialect'.

This word, which is derived from *ersappoq* 'shows his teeth', refers to a characteristic of the southern dialects of West Greenland, viz. that some forms are pronounced with /i/ as against /u/ in the dialects of the central region of West Greenland, example: /inik/ 'human being', plural /ini^{v}it/ as against Central West Greenlandic /inuk/, plural /inu^{w}it/.

Thalbitzer (1921: 124–5) finds that this use of *i* instead of *u* occurs throughout East Greenland and assumes that it has spread from there to southern West Greenland: 'This tendency has gone round Cape Farewell and has reached all the way up to the southern neighbourhood of Godthåb (64° N. lat.).' Later, it was emphasized by Lynge (1955: 7) that *i* instead of *u* is also dominant in the Upernavik district of northern West Greenland (and also among some speakers in the vicinity of the capital Godthåb).

According to these findings, which are entirely supported by linguistic data, there is not just one 'i-dialect', but a number of dialects sharing the phenomenon in question. Petersen (1970: 331) nevertheless speaks of 'the so-called "i-dialect"' in referring to *all* of the dialects involved, and although this terminology is slightly confusing, I find it convenient to continue the terminological tradition. Hence, the term 'i-dialect' (in quotation marks) as used below does not refer to a dialect but rather to a phonological characteristic common to a number of dialects.

The comparative and diachronic aspects are immediately interesting. As for the question whether /u/ has changed into /i/ (in 'i-dialect'), or /i/ has changed into /u/ (outside 'i-dialect'), comparative evidence is entirely in favour of the former assumption, since Eskimo dialects outside Greenland (as well as Polar Eskimo) have /u/ not /i/ in these instances. Moreover, 'i-dialect' entails a phonological merger of /u/ and /i/ (to the extent that /i/ is used instead of /u/), 'i-dialect' /inik/ 'human being', /sinik/ 'sleep' versus non-'i-dialect' /inuk/, /sinik/. Thalbitzer (1921: 124–5) also takes this position without any hesitation: '*i* ... has superseded *u* in a great many words and suffixes. ... The change is limited to certain words while others have retained their *u* unmolested.' Nonetheless, Lynge (1955: 7) contends that 'the genuine Greenlandic *i*, which had been replaced by *u* in the further development of the language at other settlements, is still dominant up here [i.e. in the Upernavik district]' (translation mine). Although this view of the matter seems untenable in a comparative framework, there is some truth in it as far as the recent development is concerned, since non-'i-dialect' is now gaining ground, i.e. /u/ is being increasingly used in areas which are traditionally 'i-dialect' areas (this process, which is promoted by the use of non-'i-dialect' in broadcasting and at school, is quite a slow one, however).

It is not the purpose of this paper to discuss the possible reasons why the phenomenon of 'i-dialect' is shared by areas that are widely separated geographically, viz. Upernavik (II), East Greenland (VII), and southern West Greenland (VI, V, sporadically even IV). At all events, the dialect-geographical evidence strongly suggests that. 'i-dialect' must be of considerable age, but it cannot be decided easily whether inhabitants of different parts of Greenland successively took over the feature of 'i-dialect' from their neighbours, or whether settlers at different places brought this linguistic feature with them in the first place (the former proposal is Thalbitzer's, as far as I understand him; the latter seems to be in agreement with Lynge). The present lack of a geographical continuity between the 'i-dialect' areas may seem to suggest that these are relic areas, or offspring from a common source which one might call 'Proto-Fringe-Greenlandic'. However, there used to be Eskimo settlements in both northern East Greenland and (more recently) the southernmost part of East Greenland, so there may have been more linguistic continuity all the way round from Upernavik via East Greenland to southern West Greenland at an earlier time. A priori, this makes the 'Wellentheorie' equally plausible. I shall leave the question at that here.

Now, to return to a characterization of the phenomenon of 'i-dialect', it may not be exactly correct to say that /u/ just changes into /i/. An /i/ that stems from /u/ is sometimes accompanied by labialization of a following consonant, and if it is followed by /i/ or /a/, the vowel sequence is invariably reflected as /i/ plus a labial glide plus the second vowel (/ini^{v}it/ for /inu^{w}it/, etc.). The long (homosyllabic) vowel /uu/ changes into /ii/ (i.e. *not* /i^{v}i/, or the like) with or without a following labial component as in the case of single /i/ from /u/. I have suggested (Rischel 1974: 113–14) that /u/ did not change directly into /i/ but rather into a diphthong /iṷ/ whose second member is sometimes reflected as a labial component, and sometimes lost. This is entirely hypothetical; the hard fact is that the labialization or labial glide sometimes betrays the origin of /i/ as a reflex of /u/ (another such criterion is the different pronunciation of /t/ before original and secondary /i/ in the Upernavik dialect—see Petersen 1970: 332).

The 'embarassing' thing about 'i-dialect' is that the sound shift in question has seemed so entirely unsystematic in character. Petersen (1970: 331–2), who just speaks of a tendency and who does not seem to assume that the sound shift is contextually conditioned, adds: 'The "i-dialect's" tendency to change /u/ to /i/ is far from consistent or sustained. There are still a great many words which preserve the /u/. A comprehensive explanation of these omissions is lacking. One can ... point out a few causes which work independently of one another. The first is the danger of syncretism with frequently occurring words in analogous contexts. The second is apparent consideration for practical articulation in that /u/ is often preserved as a back vowel with back consonants /k/ and /q/'.

11.3.   MY OWN INVESTIGATION

11.3.1. Material

During a stay in southern West Greenland in the winter of 1974–5 I worked intensely on 'i-dialect', my first purpose being to gather as much material as possible for later comparison with material to be gathered in the Upernavik district. Since the chances of defining conditions for the sound shift seemed poor, I had chosen to attack the problem from the point of view of 'lexical diffusion'. It seemed to me that if it were known whether or not the sound shift occurs in largely the same lexical items in different dialects, this might provide a clue as to the connection between these various representatives of 'i-dialect'.

Most of the time I worked with the Kap Farvel dialect (VI) in the village of Narsaq kujalleq (Frederiksdal); this was later supplemented by material from the Alluitsoq (Lichtenau) fjord, which is within the general southern dialect area (V). My recordings (mostly tapes; to a lesser extent direct phonetic transcriptions) consist partly of free narrative prose, and partly (mostly) of responses to questionnaires which I worked out during my stay. The present paper is based exclusively on the latter type of material (the free prose still awaits processing). This means that I am making statements about the forms that dialect speakers prefer to use when they are conscious about their own dialect. There is no doubt that this gives a more regular pattern than analyses of fluent speech might give. It is conspicuous that 'i-dialect' speakers often fluctuate between /i/ and /u/, and I have the impression that the bias is in favour of /i/ in such cases as far as my questionnaire material is concerned.

During my work I gradually realized that the phenomenon of 'i-dialect' is explicable in terms of phonological rules, and fortunately it was possible to design new, supplementary questionnaires every time a new generalization emerged from the data. Thus, there was ample opportunity to re-check the validity of my observations and of my provisional generalizations.

The following is a quite preliminary report which focuses on the patterns that are firmly established after a cursory inspection of my data. Several problems are left out of consideration here, since they must await not only a closer study of the present data but also a gathering of comparative material from other 'i-dialect' areas. As far as these other areas are concerned, the very limited experience I have with phonetic material from the Upernavik district and from East Greenland seems to me clearly to indicate that the basic pattern—as outlined in the present report—is the same everywhere, but the validity of this contention remains to be proven.

In view of the sketchy character of this report I do not feel that it would be reasonable to give anything like a catalogue of my data here. Recorded forms are cited 'anonymously'. They are taken from Kap Farvel (VI) material, unless otherwise stated. As for the phonetic presentation I have chosen a broad phonetic (semi-phonemic) transcription of the type used in my monograph (Rischel 1974). The only innovation is that I use an exponent letter /ᵛ/ to indicate the rather faintly articulated labial glide in forms such as /iniᵛit/ 'human beings'.

11.3.2. **Comparative generalizations to be made about 'i-dialect' forms**

Before attempting to establish phonological conditions for 'i-dialect' forms it is reasonable to test one specific hypothesis: that mutually related forms tend to have the same vowel (i.e. either /u/ throughout a set of related forms, or /i/ throughout). A tendency or regularity of this kind might seriously confuse the pattern. Interestingly enough, a glance at the data immediately reveals that levelling of this kind plays no discernible role in the Kap Farvel dialect (on this point I dare not make any statements about other dialects). The verb for 'being shy' (CWG /ittuuʳppuq/) is /it¢ iʳpuq/ (previously undoubtedly /ittiiʳppuq/), but the participle (meaning 'shy') is /ittuuʳtuq/ (CWG /ittuuʳttuq/), i.e. there is no avoidance of a vowel alternation in the second syllable of the base. Similarly, although the counterpart to CWG/ inuuniq/ 'life' is /iniiniq/, the greeting /inuuʟʟuʷaʳnna/ 'goodbye' (literally 'live well!') is reflected as /inuuḍuʷaʳnna/.[4] The counterpart to CWG /iʟʟu/ 'house' is /iḍḍiq/, but the word for cottage ('wretched house') is /iḍḍurujuk/. These examples give further evidence of vowel alternation in the second syllable of a base.

An abundance of data of this kind entirely disproves the hypothesis that there might be a significant tendency toward invariance within sets of etymologically related forms. At the same time they testify to a phonological regularity in the Kap Farvel dialect: that /u/ is (normally) preserved if followed by a non-labial consonant (cluster) plus /u/. I shall return to this regularity below.

As mentioned above, Petersen (1970) suggests that neighbouring /k/ and /q/ may help to preserve /u/. It is easy to prove that this is at least not a strict constraint: cf. /inik/ for /inuk/ 'human being', /maanakkit/ for /maan(n)akkut/ 'now', /sikiq/ for /siku(q)/ 'ice', /¢ikiqqirippuq/ for /¢ikiqqurippuq/ 'is at right angles'. I do not see how one can formulate a constraint that permits all these forms.

It may prove useful to search for other constraints, however; i.e. to search for environments in which /u/ *never* changes to /i/. No matter how sporadic and irregular the sound shift may be, it would not be expected to violate constraints, and thus the formulation of constraints (rather than positive conditions for the sound shift) is a way of detecting whether there is at all anything like phonological regularities involved. It is not a priori clear what would be the appropriate *domain* of such constraints, but I decided tentatively to use a stretch corresponding to the typographical word (i.e. anything written without internal interspace) as a frame of reference. As it turned out, this domain, which can be redefined phonologically as a 'phonological word' on the basis of prosodic characteristics (Rischel 1974: 11 and 79), turned out to be a highly appropriate choice.—The most conspicuous constraints detected in this way will be listed (in random order) below. I shall stick to structural generalizations in this section,

---

[4] /ḍ/ is the regular counterpart to /ʟ/ of other West Greenlandic dialects (/ḍ/ is a retroflex affricate, as far as I have been able to ascertain; Petersen (1970) writes /dʒ/ but does not consider this symbol quite appropriate).

but in Section 11.3.4 I shall demonstrate how a study of phonological alternation adds significantly to an understanding of the nature of the constraints in question, with regard to both diachrony and synchrony.

1 There is never /i/ against CWG /u/ in a word initial[5] syllable: KF- = CWG /su̱li/ 'still', /u̱uma/ 'of that one', /nu̱taaq/ 'new', etc.
2 There is never /i/ against CWG /u/ if the vowel is immediately preceded by a consonant or consonant cluster with labial articulation: KF = CWG /apu̱t/ 'snow', /immu̱k/ 'milk'.
3 There is never /i/ against CWG /u/ after a syllable with /u/. The preceding syllable may have /u/ because of constraint (1): KF = CWG /u̱ku^wa/ 'those', /u̱nnuk/ 'evening', or because of constraint (2): KF = CWG /immu̱ssu̱^waq/ 'cheese' (traditional CWG: /immu̱ṣṣu̱^waq/). But it may also be because of constraint (4) below, which considerably complicates the pattern.
4 As mentioned earlier, there is a strong tendency to preserve /u/ if the following vowel is /u/ and there is no intervening labial consonant: KF = CWG /i^rnnisu̱ttuq/ 'giving birth' (but with an intervening labial: KF /i^rnnisippuq/ 'gives birth' against CWG /i^rnnisuppuq/; further examples at the beginning of this section). This is at first sight a rather crazy constraint: why should /u/ be protected before /u/ only if there is *no* intervening labial? One might suggest that there is an umlaut mechanism involved: /u/ has gone at least part of the way to /i/, but /u/ is restated due to influence from the vowel of the following syllable; however, the distant assimilation in terms of lip rounding cannot work if the chain is broken by a labial segment.

Another explanation has been offered to me by Eli Fischer-Jørgensen (personal communication): in forms such as /i^rnnisuttuq/ the consonantal stretch /tt/ was probably influenced by preceding and following /u/ and hence spoken with liprounding; it therefore *protected the preceding vowel from going to /i/*. The labial /pp/, on the other hand, would not show any clear difference between rounded and unrounded varieties, and hence did not give similar information regarding the preceding vowel. Therefore, /u/ was not protected before labial plus /u/. This is a very interesting possibility; I entirely agree that there must have been labialization of consonants in some environments (see below), and that this feature was probably masked in labial consonants. However, there is a seeming conflict in that—as far as the evidence at my disposal goes—such secondary articulation in consonants is preserved more in the dialects that make the least use of constraint (4). As long as there is insufficient information especially with regard to the Upernavik dialect, I dare not argue about this, however.

[5] Editors' note: KF signifies Kap Farvel.

I think it is plausible enough to suggest that there used to be
a shift of /u/ (either all the way to /i/ or to something that would
eventually end up as /i/) also in these environments. This is in fact
attested by other representatives of 'i-dialect': I have noted forms such
as /sikik̲k̲ut/, e.g. from the Upernavik district, against CWG and KF
/sikukkut/ 'via the ice'. But the reestablishment (or preservation) of /u/
in the southernmost dialects may be a *protective* measure. If the first of
two consecutive syllables with /u/ changes its vowel into /i/, one of two
things may happen: the vowel shift may reapply and shift /u/ of the next
syllable since it is no longer preceded by /u/ (in an alternative analysis:
the vowel shift may apply simultaneous to both syllables); or the vowel
shift may not be allowed to reapply. Apparently the Upernavik and
East Greenland dialects are characterized by *prohibiting a reapplica-
tion*, whereas the southernmost dialects favour a uniform treatment of
both syllables.

In the case of two consecutive syllables with /u/ there is a very
obvious prevalence of *preservation of both vowels as* /u/. I have nevertheless noted some instances where *both vowels are shifted*. Thus, one of
my KF informants insisted that one would say /kaagiʳt¢iʳd̲d̲ita/ corresponding to CWG /kaaɢituʳʟʟuta/ (/kaagiʳttuʟʟuta/) 'we, eating cake',
but I suppose that other persons might say /kaagiʳttuʳd̲d̲uta/. As for
the Alluitsoq dialect (within area V of Fig. 11.1), a young informant
of mine used such forms as /maʳʟʟiʟʟiiniit piŋasiʟʟiiniit/ 'either two
or three' (CWG /maʳʟʟuʟʟuunniit piŋasuʟʟuunniit/), although he had
a general prevalence of preserved /u/ in two consecutive syllables with
etymological /u/. Now, this shifting of both vowels would lead to forms
such as /sikik̲k̲it/ (which I have encountered as a variant of /sikuk̲k̲ut/),
and similarly */iʳnnisit¢ iq/ instead of /irnnisuttuq/ (which I have heard
only with /u...u/). Forms such as /iʳnnisuppuq/, on the other hand,
could never get any further than /iʳnnisippuq/ since the following /u/
is protected anyway by the labial consonant (constraint (2)). Hence,
if for some reason there was a reaction against such a drastic change
as /iʳnnisuttuq/ to */iʳnnisittiq/, modern /iʳnnisit¢iq/, it would only be
necessary to restate /u/ in cases where there was *no intervening labial*,
since this is the only case in which two consecutive syllables can both
undergo the vowel-shift.

For the sake of completeness I shall add that /u/ may be preserved
by constraint (4) in more than two consecutive syllables. Thus the KF
form corresponding to CWG /niiqquluttuq/ 'creaking' is /niiq̲u̲l̲u̲ttuq/,
as expected.

It is interesting to note that paradigmatic levelling plays *no* role in the treatment of /u/ before /C_1u/; on the contrary, the occurrence of /u/ here often creates an alternation, because the vowel is shifted in other forms. This fact might perhaps speak in favour of the umlaut interpretation since umlaut is known from other languages to produce alternation, whereas one might perhaps expect a protective mechanism to preserve, rather than break down, a conspicuous relatedness among wordforms. That is hardly conclusive, however.

Constraints (1) to (4), if properly applied (see below) appear to account for the vast majority of forms that are consistently spoken with /u/, not /i/. There is, nevertheless, a residue of bases, suffixes, and complex stems which defy any explanation in terms of a phonological generalization. One may attempt to define certain *tendencies* to preserve /u/ under specific circumstances, and indeed, some of the forms with unexpected /u/ agree with Petersen's suggestions (1970: 332), which I cited above. The allative ending /nut/, for instance, has /u/ in southern WG, and it is natural to assume that this is due to the need of avoiding a merger of allative /nut/ and ablative /nit/. (East Greenlandic permits the vowel shift in allative *-nun, -nin*, according to Thalbitzer 1921: 133; note that the ablative forms have been replaced by instrumental forms in this dialect.)

As for Petersen's contention that /u/ is often preserved in the context of back consonants, there are quite a few exceptions to the shift of /u/ to /i/ which may have this explanation, viz. forms with a uvular plus /u/, e.g. the suffix /qu/ 'command' (KF /qaaqu^{w}aa/ 'invites him'), and the suffix alternant /ru/ 'future time' (KF /aasaru/ 'next summer') as against /ŋi/ (from /gu/) 'id'. '(KF /aqaŋi/ 'tomorrow').

But as mentioned earlier, these are not real constraints since it is easy to find counter-evidence. Moreover, there is a residue of unexpected occurrences of /u/ anyway, often such that a formative may occur in some lexicalized forms with /u/ and in other forms with /i/ although there is (according to my statements) no relevant difference in the phonological environments, cf. /piluk/ 'bad' in KF /naasupilu̱ᵂit/ 'weeds', versus /uqalipilippuq/ 'scolds'. A study of Thalbitzer's (1921) texts from East Greenland even shows a certain amount of *free variation* between /u/ and /i/, e.g. in forms containing the stems /taku/ ∼ /taki/ 'see', /isuma/ ∼ /isima/ 'thought; think' before invariant suffix configurations. I have no explanation for this. In the Kap Farvel dialect the norm of elderly and middle-aged persons did

not seem to waver very much, whereas there was a discernible difference between the norms of different generations, as one might expect.

I have tried to show that the general picture is not just fuzzy, not
even in East Greenlandic. It is significant that the exceptions to the
generalizations are *forms in which /u/ is unexpectedly retained* rather
than forms in which /u/ is unexpectedly shifted to /i/. In the following
I shall neglect the exceptions, since there is such a massive bulk of
evidence in favour of the linguistic significance of the regularities.

Constraints (1)–(4) above are not well-formedness conditions on
phonetic forms. It is perfectly possible to have /i/ in all of the environments in question if only this /i/ does not reflect /u/ diachronically,
cf. the underlined vowels of /imiq/ 'water', /usii/ 'its cargo', /ilumut/
'certainly'. The constraints only define the conditions under which /u/
cannot go to /i/.

Now, it is interesting both from the point of view of diachrony
(relative chronology of sound-shifts) and from the point of view of
synchronic analysis to know whether these constraints are properly
stated in terms of *surface structure*, i.e. whether the segments entering
the prohibiting contexts are always surfacing. There is no doubt that
this was the case at the time when the pattern came into existence, but
is it correct to formulate these constraints with reference to the surface
structure of modern Greenlandic? It is possible to throw light upon
this question by studying forms in which the relevant segments in the
context of /u/ have undergone assimilation.

In most dialects of Greenland the diphthongs /ai/ and /au/ have been
entirely assimilated to /aa/ word-internally (Rischel 1974: 73 ff). Now,
what is the fate of /auC$_1$u/ in 'i-dialect': is it reflected as /aaC$_1$u/ or
/aaC$_1$i/? My material suggests that there is a good deal of vacillation
here. At any rate, there are examples enough of preserved /u/ to make
it entirely implausible that these are random exceptions to the general
pattern: /nausut/ 'flowers' is reflected as KF /naasut/; /auk+luunniit/
'or blood' is reflected as KF /aaquuniit/; etc.

As for /u/ preceded by a labial consonant or consonant cluster,
it is worthwhile examining what happens if the cluster consists of
a labial plus another consonant since there is regressive assimilation here (Rischel 1974: 34 ff). In this case there is overwhelming
evidence in favour of a constraint to the effect that /u/ is preserved
after a labial even if the labial is eventually assimilated: /aaŋuuq/
'yes, it is said' (obviously containing /aap/ or /aam/ 'yes') is reflected

as KF /aaŋŋuuq/; ?/ani+wluni/ (CWG /aniʟʟuni/) 'going out' as KF /aniḍḍuni/; etc.

11.3.3. **The vowel shift as distant assimilation**

In the preceding section I have attempted to demonstrate that 'i-dialect' is not a matter of 'sporadic' replacement of /u/ by /i/. If the sound shift is assumed to occur without any language-internal, phonological conditioning, it is nevertheless subject to systemic limitations. It is natural now to ask: do these limitations make sense? Is it 'natural' that /u/ is preserved in such and such environments? If a sound-shift is subject to phonological conditioning (positive or negative), it is hopefully so that the conditions are either all explicable in terms of general phonetic mechanisms or all deducible from one general principle.

Constraints (2), (3), and (4) may be referred to one common principle if rounded vowels and labial consonants are supposed to share a cover feature of labiality. The generalization, then, runs as follows: /u/ is protected if it is part of a segment sequence exhibiting labial harmony, viz. a sequence of the structure [+labial]C_o[+labial]. This is true, in *all* dialects, of a vowel that is non-initial in such a sequence (i.e. which occupies the position *after* /uC_o/ or after a labial consonant). If, however, /u/ is absolutely initial in the sequence (i.e. is followed but not preceded by a labial segment) the principle applies regularly only in the southern dialects, and only if the closest following labial segment is a vowel (see discussion of constraint (4) in Section 11.3.2).

The fact that /u/ is not protected *before* a labial consonant (cluster) plus /u/ (/iᵣnnisippuq/ in spite of /iᵣnnisuttuq/) disturbs the otherwise neat principle of labial harmony. It makes diachronic sense, however, if the vowel-shift was initiated as a diphthongization, i.e. a delabialization of the initial part of /u/: under that interpretation it is not surprising that preceding and following labial consonants have had different effects.

Constraint (1) has no connection whatsoever with the other constraints. It is not very obvious why the position in an initial syllable should prohibit a change of vowel quality which occurs spontaneously in other syllables, unless the change in question were some kind of laxing (reduction), which clearly is not the case.

It must be concluded that the constraints formulated in Section 11.3.2 are observationally adequate but fail to provide a simple

and natural characterization of the phenomenon of 'i-dialect' in terms
of general phonetic theory. The logical move, then, is to turn the whole
thing around and work on the assumption that we do not have a
spontaneous sound-shift which is subject to a number of constraints
but rather a *conditioned* sound-shift. Can it be true that the change of
/u/ to /i/ occurs only in one particular type of environment, and is in
fact due to the influence of that type of environment?

If we look at the repertory of forms with /i/ for /u/, it is a true
generalization that this vowel segment is preceded by a syllable with an
unrounded vowel, and that there are no intervening labial consonants.
Hence the sound-shift may be described as *assimilation to a preceding
non-labial sequence of segments*. The vowel /u/ (perhaps first the initial
part of the segment) is delabialized by assimilation to a preceding
vowel /i/ or /a/ unless there is an intervening labial. From the phonetic
point of view this is an entirely natural type of mechanism.

This description absorbs constraints (1), (2), and (3) into one rule of
assimilation but sets off constraint (4) from the rest. That is interesting
since it is exactly constraint (4) that has a more limited distribution
than the others. I think the assimilation hypothesis lends support to the
assumption that constraint (4) is in fact a protective measure found in
cases where /i/ from /u/ might serve as a new context for delabialization
of a following /u/, i.e. where the assimilation might apply iteratively.
Now, why would the southern dialects admit such iterative application,
rather than the Upernavik and East Greenlandic dialects? I think there
is an answer to this. In the Upernavik area there is evidence (according to Lynge 1955 as well as my personal experience) of a sporadic
retention of a labialization component in consonants that follow after
a /u/ that has been shifted to /i/, e.g. something like /naakkaŋii^{w}q^w/
as the counterpart of CWG /naaxxaguuq/ 'no, it is said'; and this
phenomenon is also attested in Thalbitzer's (1921) East Greenlandic
material. Now, as long as such labialization is present it prohibits a
following /u/ from shifting to /i/: if /sikukkut/ goes to /siki^{w}kk^{w}ut/ it is
entirely regular for the last /u/ to be preserved since it is still preceded
by a sequence containing labiality, and it is no wonder that such a form
may be continued as /sikikkut/ with an eventual loss of labiality but no
extension of the assimilation rule so that it would apply iteratively or
across the board. In the southern dialects, on the other hand, there
is no trace of such labialization: it may have vanished so early that
the assimilation had not yet been stabilized as a mechanism operating
just across one syllable boundary but no more. Hence the situation

was stabilized by restoring /u/ according to the sequential constraint (4) so that the ultimate output was /sikukkut/ (or possibly /sikikkit/ if the assimilation was given a free run) rather than /sikikkut/. (Incidentally, the existence of a mechanism of restoration is corroborated by a number of forms in the southernmost dialects, in which etymological /i/ or /ï/ is shifted to /u/, e.g. /uᵂaŋuttunni/ 'in us', as against CWG /uᵂat¢inni/. There are some quite specific generalizations to be made about these 'hypercorrect' forms, but they fall outside the scope of the present paper.)

11.3.4. Alternations created by the vowel-shift

I have mentioned several times that the KF dialect has numerous, and in fact regular, alternations between indicative and participle forms, the last syllable of the stem alternating between /u/ and /i/ if the conditions for delabialization are present: a model example is /iʳnnisippuq/, /iʳnisuttuq/ as against /tuquppuq/ 'kills', – /tuquttuq/ with invariant /u/ (the preceding syllable has /u/) and /¢ikippuq/ 'arrives', – /¢ikit¢iq/ with invariant /i/ (the vowel was /i/, not /u/, in the first place). There are innumerable other instances of alternation due to constraint (4), cf. /inik/ 'human being' (from /inuk/) but /inurujuk/ 'giant' (suffix /rujuk/); also cf. the example /sikiq/ – /sikukkut/ mentioned earlier. Transparent suffixes may exhibit the same alternation due to the influence of a following suffix: /paamiʲit/ (from /paamiʲut/ 'inhabitants /-miut/ of the mouth of the fjord /paa/') 'Frederikshåb' but /paamiʲunukarppuq/ 'travels to Frederikshåb'.

Suffixes also exhibit extensive alternation depending on the structure of the *preceding* stem, cf. the participle suffix /tuq/ ~ /¢iq/ in /tuŋujuʳttuq/ 'blue', versus /qiʳnniʳt¢iq/ 'black', /suŋaaʳ¢iq/ 'yellow', or the suffix /suuq/ ~ /siiq/ 'who has the quality (or: does so) to a high degree' in /puʳttusuuq/ 'high', versus /puᵂalasiiq/ 'fat'. This is *not* just a matter of lexicalized forms with one or the other vowel, since the same alternation occurs in suffixes that can occur after practically every conceivable wordform, cf. KF /ŋuuq/ ~ /ŋiiq/ 'it is said (that)' in /nuŋuppuŋŋuuq/ 'they have been used up, it is said', /aaniʲaruŋŋuuq/ (or /aaŋŋuuq/) 'fetch it!, it is said', versus /tassaŋiiq/ 'that's enough!, it is said', /ikiʲiʳssinnaavaa¢iŋŋiiq/ 'he can help you, it is said'.

As a final example I shall quote the suffix /luunniit/ 'or', which occurs in the KF dialect in a variety of forms with /uu/ or /ii/, and with /l/ or /q̣/ (depending on the preceding formative). If occurring in two consecutive forms (with the meaning 'either/or'), it may or may not alternate depending on the last syllables of the forms to which the suffix is added, e.g. /ataasiʳq̣q̣iiniit maʳq̣q̣uq̣q̣uuniit/ 'either one or two' (cf. the deviant forms in the Alluitsoq dialect cited in Section 11.3.2 above); /puuʳluluuniit kaagiʳq̣q̣iiniit/ 'either a ball or a cake'.

This shows that there is no general tendency to achieve an invariant manifestation of formatives as far as /i/ for /u/ is concerned. Examples like the last-mentioned ones are clearly reminiscent of the appearance of forms in languages with a functional system of vowel harmony (Thalbitzer 1921: 124 did in fact notice a tendency toward VH in East Greenlandic, but he speaks of it as a quite sporadic phenomenon found with some suffixes).

11.4.   PROBLEMS IN A SYNCHRONIC, GENERATIVE DESCRIPTION OF 'i-DIALECT'

In the preceding sections I have shown that (i) the sound-shift initiating the phenomenon known as 'i-dialect' was rule governed, and (ii) this sound-shift has implemented a rather regular pattern of vowel alternation. The question, now, is how to deal synchronically with the behaviour of vowels in dialects of this type. For simplicity I shall start with the question of a synchronic rule, and approach the question of *underlying representation* afterwards.

11.4.1. **Is there a synchronic rule?**

Generative phonologists have always taken much interest in alternations because these were taken as evidence for phonological rules. There has been a tendency to go very far in the claim that alternations reflect synchronic rules, but recently there has been an increasing degree of scepticism toward an indiscriminate use of rule schemata in linguistic description. This scepticism is the offspring of a desire to make the description reflect something *real* in particular: some kind of *psychological* reality. Unfortunately, the meaning of this term in modern linguistic literature is quite vague, and there has not been too much progress so far toward a real understanding of the nature of the problem.

Even a description that does not claim to be psychologically 'real' may be subject to evaluation in terms of plausibility. We do not know what goes on in individual speaker-listeners' heads, nor do we know what mental patterns are common to users of a particular language, and one may argue that linguists have no obligation to describe precisely that. But it must certainly be worthwhile trying to distinguish *regularities which may be relevant to the way in which users of the language master it* from other possible generalizations, which are likely to be irrelevant from that point of view. One should, of course, be gravely suspicious of rigid (and generally quite aprioric) 'psychological' interpretations to the effect that a certain regularity *is* a rule in the generative sense, but it seems fruitful to attempt to provide evidence for (or against) the contention that speaker-listeners are likely to internalize a mechanism that is functionally equivalent to such a rule. To provide, or evaluate, such evidence is no straightforward task, however.

In the case of a pattern of alternation, it is an oversimplification of the problem just to ask: is the regularity likely to be mastered by rule? There are at least three meaningful proposals: (i) all the forms involved may be individually stored (lexicalized in a strict sense); (ii) there is an awareness of mutual relatedness among partially similar forms, and the recurrent patterns of alternation within paradigms are mastered so that they can be used productively; (iii) there is some kind of analysis of wordforms building-blocks (more or less co-extensive with the linguist's formatives), each of which is stored mentally together with information about its own pattern of alternation as well as its conditioning effect on alternations in adjacent items. In all likelihood there is normally a good deal of redundancy in the mental representation; there is no reason why a speaker-listener should not store several inflected or derived forms containing the same base (solution (i)) although some of them may be deducible from the others according to patterns mastered by him/her (solution (ii) or (iii)). We do not know, in principle, *what* is stored mentally, although studies on productivity (as suggested by Ohala[6]) may provide some information.

The formulation and testing of such proposals (and of other, more or less similar, proposals that one might find worth formulating) has not got much to do with the current, transformation–generative paradigm of linguistic description (although it is a merit of recent work

---

[6] Editors' note: a specific reference here would be to Ohala (1974).

to have emphasized the importance of the question of internalized representation of linguistic patterns). I do not think that one should start by asking: 'is there, or isn't there, an internalized equivalent to the schema $X \rightarrow Y/W\_\_ Z$' (meaning: representation X is *replaced* by representation Y in environment W__Z); it must be determined first to what extent an alternation is at all mastered in terms of generalized mechanisms. That, in itself, is certainly a difficult issue.

With regard to 'i-dialect', the null-hypothesis, i.e. that all wordforms exhibiting some reflex of etymological /u/ are completely lexicalized (stored in their entirety in the brain), can be dismissed without serious testing. Eskimo is a 'polysynthetic' language, which in principle allows for an unlimited number of different wordforms to be construed by suffixation to one common base. The unlimited character of suffixation is proved by the fact that a suffix may even recur in such a stretch, each time restoring the same conditions for further suffixation, e.g. a noun stem may be converted into a verb stem by suffixation of /u/ ('to be'), and the resultant verb stem (with more or less elaboration by other suffixes) may in turn be converted into a noun stem by suffixation of /ṣu(q)/ ('one who -s'), so that the conditions for forming a verb by suffixation of /u/ ('to be') once again are met. (Maybe such repeated use of a suffix occurs chiefly if part of the sequence is lexicalized with a specific meaning, e.g. /iga+ṣuq/ 'one who cooks' has a lexicalized counterpart /igaṣuq/ 'cook' from which one may form /igaṣu+u+ṣuq/ 'one who is a cook'. However, it is worth noting that the relatedness of /igaṣuq/ to /iga/ and /ṣuq/ is transparent enough.) Given the considerable number of different suffixes, and the enormous number of consecutive suffixes that one may often identify in Greenlandic wordforms, it is a priori clear that speakers and listeners cannot do with a stored inventory of wordforms (this is not in the first place a matter of assumptions about limited storage capacity in the brain; the core of the problem is that it cannot possibly be true that every fluent speaker-listener has previously encountered all grammatically possible wordforms). Anyway, the general lexicalization hypothesis can be easily disproved by the fact that one can take international (Danish) terms and add Greenlandic suffixes to them (often with little or no accommodation of the stem to Greenlandic phonotactics). Stems such as *trillebøri* 'wheelbarrow', or *præsidenti* 'president' are entering the language all the time, and such a base may be elaborated by suffixation at one's discretion. In oral or written communication such hybrid forms will normally be immediately understood. The interesting thing is that the principles according to which suffixes are added after each other in such forms are entirely Greenlandic. It is only the base that constitutes a chunk of foreign matter.

In principle, the inventory of forms is *an open inventory whose size can not be defined*. This is true both of entire *wordforms* and of invariant *stems* (understood as the part of a wordform—however elaborate—that is invariant in an inflectional paradigm).

There is a different proposal, however, that might be more worthy of serious consideration, viz. that *dyads of formatives* are stored lexically. If, for a moment, we disregard loanwords and other foreignisms and consider the inventory of bases as a closed inventory, it is certainly possible to set up a model according to which every conceivable sequence of two formatives (or of formative clusters in some instances)[7] is lexicalized. The number of such dyads will be very large, of course, but not unlimited, and hence it cannot be disproved a priori that wordforms containing bases which are already well-established in the language are mastered with reference to such dyads.

Under such a hypothesis the conversion of content into expression—in generative–semantic terms: the lexical insertion—would be a complex matter. Each constituent of a wordform must be looked up in the internalized lexicon twice: it must be checked whether it has an entry together with the preceding constituent, and whether it has an entry together with the following constituent (unless, of course, the constituent in question is word-initial or word-final, in which case there is only one dyad involved). Hence, if the KF form /muluḍḍuni/ 'as he stayed away longer than expected' (/mulu/ 'stay away etc.', /ḍḍu/ 'contemporative mood', /ni/ 'he himself') does not happen to be stored in its entirety, it must be looked up as /muluḍḍu/ and /ḍḍuni/. There must then be some strategy according to which such consecutive dyads are amalgamated. This strategy is simple if it is just a matter of shrinking material of the type XY, YZ into XYZ (as in /muluḍḍuni/), but what if there is an alternation in the shared part? The dyad consisting of 'contemporative' plus 'himself' must have a variant /ḍḍini/ since 'as he slept' is /siniḍḍini/, composed of /siniḍḍi/ and /ḍḍini/. Apparently there must be a *rule* saying: 'choose the alternant, in each

---

[7] The concept of 'formative dyad' raises the same question as to psychological reality (e.g. of grammatical boundaries) as the concept of 'formative' itself (in addition to the implausibility caused by the syntactically dubious status of the dyad).

case, that gives no conflict between the phonological representations of two dyads to be amalgamated'. This solution is probably sufficient for dialects that adhere strictly to constraint (4) of Section 11.3.2: assume that 'because I ate meat' is /niqiȼirama/; 'if I eat meat' is /niqituruma/; 'because I entered' is /isirama/; and 'if I enter' is /isirima/. We can, then, posit the following dyads: /niqiȼir/ ∼ /niqitur/ 'eat meat'; /ȼira/ 'because of eating'; /turu/ 'if eating'; /isira/ 'because of entering'; /isiri/ 'if entering'; /rama/ 'because I'; /ruma/ ∼ /rima/ 'if I'. There will be only one possible output in each case on account of the principle of no conflict (whereas there would be two possible outputs for 'if I eat meat': /niqituruma/ and /niqiȼirima/, if there were a variant /ȼiri/ along with /turu/ 'if eating').

Dialects without constraint (4) pose no specific problems. The difference can be handled in terms of lexical representation of dyads: 'eat meat' is stored as /niqiȼir/, 'if eating' is stored as /ȼiru/ (/tiru/) ∼ /turu/. The principle of no conflict between dyads uniquely determines the output for 'if I eat meat' as /niqiȼiruma/ (/niqitiruma/).

Etymological /u/ is sometimes reflected 'idiosyncratically' as /u/. Now, if the conditional mood formative does not ever occur as /ri/ (i.e. if we find /ru/ in environments where the general principles of 'i-dialect' would suggest /ri/), the dyads containing this formative are simply not stored in a variant with /i/: we have /ruma/ 'if I' but no /rima/, /isiru/ 'if entering' but no /isiri/ for such a dialect, and hence the form meaning 'if I enter' comes out automatically as /isiruma/.

To a first approximation, then, phenomena such as the /u/ – /i/ alternation can be handled in terms of the storage of dyad variants plus an entirely general principle of selection. Are there any principled arguments about such an approach to linguistic description?

If one believes that there is a level of linguistic description at which lexical items (or lexical entries) are grammatical constituents, a description in terms of formative dyads is not immediately attractive. Let us consider /niqituruma/ 'if I eat meat' from the point of view of internal structure. The first formative dyad, /niqitur/ 'to eat meat' is (according to my definition) a stem, and hence it makes perfect sense to speak of it as a grammatical constituent at a non-abstract level of syntactical description. The final dyad, /ruma/ 'if I do', may be looked upon as a cluster of inflectional material modifying the stem, and hence it also makes sense to speak of that as a constituent. But what about the middle one: /turu/ 'if eating'? It cannot be a constituent at the same time as the others. However, in semantically-based syntax the formation of stems such as /niqitur/ may be interpreted as a kind of incorporation, the abstract constituents being 'meat' and 'eat'. In the framework of such an analysis there is nothing strange in claiming that the verb component 'eat' goes together with the modal modifier to form a surface constituent. We are thus faced with the possibility of conflicting analyses. There may be other types of forms in which it is much more difficult to find a reasonable correlation between formative dyads and possible grammatical constituents, but at least it should be realized that the whole issue is controversial. One cannot a priori dismiss the dyad approach on these premises (as long as it has not been proved that the internalized lexicon is accessible at only one level of syntactico-semantic abstraction).

Another possible argument against the dyad approach is that it is 'clumsy'. It entails a storage of numerous dyads in two or more variants instead of a phonological rule. In the framework of transformation–generative phonology one might also claim that it is not 'insightful' because it fails to reveal the phonological mechanism involved. The latter argument is valid in the context of a strictly descriptive linguistic approach; but the descriptive appropriateness of phonological generalizations does not, of course, imply that such generalizations are components of the mental representation of language. We do not know what is elegance and insightfulness in the latter context. It is highly interesting if generalized phonological mechanisms can be demonstrated to have a mental counterpart, but one does not ever achieve that goal by just showing that rules 'work'. It seems to me more useful to examine whether there is perhaps something else that works. It is only in cases where one *cannot* envisage other, equally or more plausible, models accounting for speakers' use of their language that it is likely to be really rewarding to make comprehensive research into the possible 'psychological reality' of phonological mechanisms.

From this point of view I find it worthwhile taking a phonological phenomenon such as vowel harmony (or other assimilatory mechanism) which really presents a strong case for the adequacy of phonological generalizations, and to see if the relevant data can be handled entirely without specific phonological machinery,[8] i.e. by putting more

---

[8] By 'specific' I here mean: specific to the statement of this particular regularity; as against general mechanisms such as the arrangement of items in a sequential order manifested as temporal order.

stuff into the 'lexicon'. I think the dyad approach is, in principle, an interesting alternative to formulaic phonologies because it does not make any reference whatsoever to the specific phonological structure of the constituents that make up wordforms, but only to the quite general criterion of greater or lesser partial similarity between dyads. Notions such as 'segment', 'feature', '(segmental) environment', 'alternation' (or 'X becomes Y') have no place in this model; it is in fact *aphonological*. That is its interesting property. (Other aphonological models might serve the purpose of the argument equally well.)

Accordingly, the question is not whether the dyad approach looks more or less silly from the point of view of current phonological theories but whether or not this kind of model fails (totally and irreparably) on some capital point.

At the beginning of this lengthy discussion of formative dyads I mentioned that loanwords and other foreignisms would be disregarded for a moment. Now they must be taken into consideration. It is of crucial importance whether there is evidence for a *productive*, creative use of some phonological mechanism in establishing new formative dyads, or new variants of formative dyads. A study of lexical borrowing is one approach to the solution of that question (along with studies of language acquisition and language change).

As I see it, examples such as KF /kaagiʳdḍiiniit puuʳluluuniit/ 'either a cake or a ball' are clearly indicative of the use of a generalization referring to configurations of segments. At the time when the Danish words *kage* and *bolle* came into the dialect, the pattern of 'i-dialect' was already there (there is indisputable evidence for 'i-dialect' in southernmost Greenland in the earliest phase of colonization). The possibility of extending this pattern to newly-acquired lexical items proves the existence—at the time of borrowing, at least—of a synchronic regularity that is sensitive to the specific vowel qualities of successive syllables.

This, then, is the core of the matter: phonological generalizations emerging from a corpus of wordforms do not constitute evidence for the (synchronic) mental reality (in any sense of this term) of the regularities in question, even though the finding that the generalizations hold for any size of corpus that the linguist chooses to work with may be strongly suggestive of productivity. On the other hand, the dynamics of language, as it appears in the process of borrowing (inter alia), may give irrefutable proof. If sequences containing borrowed items are operated upon in accordance with a well-established phonological generalization, this must be substantial evidence for the relevance of that generalization to the speakers' command of their language (I here make use of Paul Kiparsky's classical notion of 'substantial evidence' in linguistics, which is hardly a controversial issue today, although it has not quite had the practical effect on linguistic work in the more recent years that one might expect).

It must be emphasized, at this point, that the processing of borrowed lexical items only testifies to the existence of *some kind of phonological mechanism* (as against the lexical storage exemplified by the dyad model). It does not necessarily give us any hint as to *the nature of that mechanism*. In the case of 'i-dialect' the evidence just tells us that the conditioned alternation of /u/ and /i/ is, or rather was at some time, a psychological reality. Whether it is appropriate to describe that regularity in terms of a rule replacing /u/ by /i/, or in terms of alternation in the strictly static sense, is not at issue as yet. We have, however, solid evidence for *the psychological reality of phonological conditioning*: /kaagiq/ has come to condition the suffix alternant with /ii/ just because it contains a front vowel, and for no other conceivable reason. This is all I wish to argue here, as far as mental representation is concerned.

Even such a modest claim as this should be taken with all appropriate reservations. First, it should be understood that the loanword evidence only proves the *possibility* of a phonological regularity to be employed; it does not directly tell us anything about the way in which wordforms in general are handled by 'i-dialect' speakers. If a descriptive model makes psychological claims, it is wise to consider these as claims about phonological regularities which the speaker(-listener) *may* make use of rather than claims about his actual strategy. It must be understood once and for all that there is a practically infinite capacity of lexical storage at his disposal.

Secondly, it must be stressed again that the loanword evidence is temporally limited. 'i-dialect' speakers today, who use suffixal /i/ for /u/ after /kaagiq/ 'cake', may not have access to any phonological conditioning pattern. If they use suffixal /i/ (not /u/) quite regularly after /kaagiq/, it may be because they master the fact that this lexical item 'takes' suffixes in /i/ rather than /u/; if this is true, they still master a phonological regularity since the alternation between /u/ and /i/ is involved, but the conditioning is no longer phonological. However, it is also possible that neither the phonological conditioning nor the phonological alternation is mastered as such any longer: this means either generalization of one alternant or complete lexicalization of formative clusters, and this is the point where the phenomenon ceases to have any phonological content.

From the point of view of phonological typology, one may be content with the finding that there *has been* some kind of psychological reality associated with the phonologically-conditioned alternation between /u/ and /i/, and I shall leave it at that here. Nevertheless, it may be of separate interest to trace the fate of this pattern in some particular dialect (for contemporary speakers this may be done by 'experimental phonological' methods, as suggested by John Ohala 1974). It would be interesting to know exactly under which circumstances, and at which rate, a phonological regularity is likely to decay.[9]

If, now, we consider the pattern of 'i-dialect' as a fully operative phonological regularity, the question is how to state it. What does such a mechanism do, and what kinds of representations does it operate upon? I shall touch upon these questions in the next section. To avoid being misunderstood, I shall emphasize again that the following discussion in terms of rule formulation, etc., is strictly descriptive: it entails absolutely no claims about the nature of internalized phonology, except for the very claim that it is possible for the 'i-dialect' pattern to be mastered (somehow) as a phonological regularity.

11.4.2. **Directionality and underlying representations**[10]

As shown in Section 11.3.2, etymological /u/ in a non-initial syllable may be continued as /u/ or /i/. If none of the constraints (1), (2), and (4) apply, the vowel reflex will be dependent upon the vowel of the preceding syllable. In Section 11.3.2 it was suggested that we get

[9] 'Assibilation' in Greenlandic is a typical example of a decaying rule, cf. Rischel (1974: 260–75). Again, a study of loanwords turns out to be rewarding. For example, it may be observed that the participial suffix /tuq/ becomes /suq/ by assibilation after syllables with /i/ in loanwords of a certain age. Hence one says /hiisɛiˣssuq/ (not /hiisɛiˣttuq/) 'one who rides a horse; rider' (from /hiisɛi/, Danish *hest* 'horse'), whereas there seems to be vacillation in /sikkiliˣssuq/ or /sikkiliˣttuq/ 'one who rides a bicycle' (/sikkili/, Danish *cykel*) and no assibilation at all in /piiliˣttuq/ 'one who drives a car' (/piili/, Danish *bil*). Note that the treatment of the loanword stems is essentially the same in all instances: addition of final /i/; but this added syllable does not have the same conditioning effect with regard to assibilation in recent loans as it used to have.

[10] The term 'directionality' is used here in accordance with Eliasson (1974) and Rischel (1974).

/i/ unless constraint (3) applies; in Section 11.3.3 it was suggested that we get /i/ only if the conditions for distant assimilation (delabialization harmony) with the preceding syllable are met. In terms of underlying representation, these statements may be considered equivalent: we have underlying /u/ which sometimes shifts into /i/. But is there *synchronic* evidence for anything but an alternation set /u/ ~ /i/: is it possible to argue in favour of underlying /u/ on a synchronic basis?

Word initial syllables have /u/, not /i/, as a continuation of /u/. It makes absolutely no sense to speak of anything but underlying = surfacing /u/ in this position, e.g. in /u¢iʳppuq/ 'returns' versus /i¢iʳppuq/ 'awakes'. It is interesting what happens if the alternating vowel of a suffix comes to stand in a word-initial syllable, or if the invariant vowel in the first syllable of a base comes to stand in a non-initial position. Unfortunately, it is hard to find evidence of this kind, since the categories of word-initial and non-initial formatives are largely complementary. However, there is at least one interesting formative, viz. /una/ 'that one' (or: 'it is'). If occurring as a separate word, it invariably has /u/: /una/, but it may be attached 'encliti-cally' to another form, and in that case it follows the rules of /u/ – /i/ alternation: KF /iḍḍinina/ 'is that one yours?', Alluitsoq /iʟʟiina/ (id.), versus /uʳssuruna/ 'that is blubber (/uʳssuq/)'. Since /u/ and /i/ are equally possible, from a surface phonotactical point of view, in word-initial syllables, the behaviour of this formative is evidence that /u/ is the neutral reflex of the alternating set. It is the alternant which occurs when no conditions are specified. I think it is useful to interpret the concept of 'underlying representation' as meaning just that.

I assume, therefore, that insofar as there is a synchronic rule, it is statable as a rule that specifies conditions under which /i/ occurs instead of the neutral representation /u/, rather than a rule that specifies conditions under which /u/ occurs instead of /i/.

This solution is supported by a *simplicity* criterion: a rule to the effect that /u/ goes to /i/ under specific conditions is found to apply rather regularly (although some formatives, or formative clusters, must be marked as exceptions). If, on the other hand, the rule were made to state that /i/ goes to /u/ under specific conditions, it must be marked for every formative with /i/ whether this vowel can or cannot undergo the rule. That is, the degree of predictability is incomparably much higher under the former analysis than under the latter.

By the convergence of these two criteria, the alternation seems clearly characterized as an *asymmetric* one. It thereby differs from the regularity observable in languages with a strict pattern of vowel harmony, and—as I argued in Section 11.1 above—that difference is typologically interesting.

As for phonological formalization, the implications of this conclusion are as follows: it is legitimate to represent the alternation set as /u/ on an abstract level of description (it is not an ambivalent segment in the sense of Rischel 1974: 346 ff), and to set up a unidirectional rule of distant assimilation. The rule in question must produce a delabialization (unrounding) of /u/ after a syllable with an unrounded vowel, but there are two sets of restrictions associated with it. First, the applicability of the rule is constrained by conditions on the structural description: /u/ does not undergo the rule if immediately preceded by a consonant or consonant cluster containing a feature of labial articulation (constraint (2) of Section 11.3.2); and in some dialects it does not normally undergo the rule if the following syllable has a rounded vowel (constraint (4)). Secondly, most dialects prohibit the rule from reapplying to a form (i.e. /u/ cannot be assimilated to /i/ of a preceding syllable if that vowel, in turn, represents underlying /u/). I do not think it is very interesting (in the present, rather floating state of linguistic formalization) to go into details about rule algebra; the remarks above will probably suffice to characterize what the rule does, and does not do.

The rule works without any difficulties in most types of forms. But what about KF /aaᵭᵭuuniit/ 'or blood', /aniᵭᵭuni/ 'going out', etc. without the expected change of /u/ (/uu/) into /i/ (/ii/)? Diachronically, these exceptions are due to constraints (3) and (2), respectively (see Section 11.3.2, end), but synchronically it is most reasonable to speak of lexicalization: /aak/ is lexicalized as a base which fails to *trigger* the rule; /ᵭᵭu/ is lexicalized as a suffix which fails to *undergo* the rule unless it follows after a consonant stem (as in /siniᵭᵭini/ 'sleeping', cf. /sinik/ 'sleep'). In certain instances, however, the conditioning segment is synchronically transparent—consider /aaŋŋuuq/ 'yes, it is said' from /aap/ 'yes'; but it may also be more reasonable to posit lexicalization here than to operate with 'bleeding' order between the rule of distant vowel assimilation and the rule of consonant assimilation. In the framework of the dyad approach outlined in Section 11.4.1, lexicalization would imply that dyads consisting of /aa(k)/ plus something else, and dyads consisting of a vowel stem plus /(ᵭ)ᵭu/, etc., are lexicalized only in variants with /u/ (in the appropriate position) as a continuation of etymological /u/.

The final question is: to what extent is etymological /u/, reflected as /i/, synchronically recoverable? Is it still transparent, in the majority of cases, that we have an alternation set which can be reduced to underlying /u/, or is it the use that the majority of forms containing /i/ as a reflex of /u/ have undergone restructuring (so that one must now speak of invariant, underlying = surfacing /i/)? I shall briefly review the conditions in various positions.

1 Etymological /u/ in a word-initial syllable is always preserved.
2 Etymological /u/ in the initial syllable of a suffix may behave in three ways: (a) The vowel is preserved if the suffix itself is 'irregular' or meets the structural description of some constraint on the vowel shift (examples in the KF dialect: /pu(q)/ 'indicative mood'; /kuluuq/ 'big').—(b) The vowel alternates if the suffix is subject to no constraint (numerous examples above).—(c) It is theoretically possible that the vowel may occur only as /i/ if the suffix occurs only after stems whose last syllable has /a/ or /i/, but I can think of no such examples.
3 Etymological /u/ in the final syllable of a bisyllabic or polysyllabic formative may behave in three ways: (a) The vowel may be preserved 'irregularly' or by a constraint ((2a) above with the example /kuluuq/).—(b) The vowel alternates as conditioned by the following formative (if the dialect has constraint (4) of Section 11.3.2: /it¢iir+puq/, /ittuur+tuq/).—(c) If a dialect does not at all make use of constraint (4) of Section 11.3.2, formative final /u/ may be reflected consistently by /i/ (provided that none of the constraints (1), (2), (3) of Section 11.3.2 apply within the formative).
4 Etymological /u/ in an internal syllable of a polysyllabic formative may behave in two ways: (a) The vowel may be preserved 'irregularly' or by a constraint (examples: the second syllable of /puugutaq/ 'plate', /qipuqqaq/ 'humpback whale').—(b) If there is no constraint on the shift of /u/ to /i/, the vowel occurs only as /i/ (example: /ikusik/ reflected as /ikisik/ 'elbow').

According to this taxonomy, there are three sets of conditions under which etymological /u/ may be reflected consistently as /i/, viz. (2c), (3c), and (4b). The first of these is entirely theoretical and will be disregarded here. The second may be exemplified by formatives such as /inuk/ 'human being' in a dialect which does not at all know constraint (4) (if such a dialect exists), i.e. a dialect in which /inuk/ has become /inik/, /inuttu^{r}ttuq/ 'who eats human flesh' is /initti^{r}ttiq/ or /init¢i^{r}t¢iq/, etc. I have at present no data for such a dialect; the Upernavik and East Greenland material that I have seen is suggestive of a sporadic use of the constraint in question, and I cannot decide whether there is any formative which never partakes in it. Moreover, even if there is such a formative, /i/ from /u/ will differ from etymological /i/ in that there occurs a labial glide between this vowel and the initial vowel of a following formative (unless that vowel is /u/ → /i/): even if the second syllable of /inik/ is always /i/, the possessive form /iniᵛa/ 'its occupant' and the plural /iniᵛit/ 'human beings' betray the specific status of /i/ (as against /panik/ 'daughter', /paniʲa/ 'his daughter', /paniit/ 'daughters'). In that case one may claim that a formative with etymological /u/ is restructured with /i/ plus a labial glide, e.g. that /inuk/ is restructured as underlying /iniᵛk/, whose labial appears on the surface *if* the final consonant is deleted before a suffix vowel. However, this solution introduces an underlying representation which never surfaces in the southern dialects of modern WG. Since the surface forms would be just as predictable from underlying /inuk/, I see no compelling reason to speak of restructuring. (There is a further criterion in West Greenlandic dialects showing that /i/ from /u/ remains functionally different from etymological /i/: if the former occurs before a suffix initial /u/, and the two together are shifted, we get a long vowel /ii/, cf. /qiṣuk+uṣaq/ 'resembling wood' reflected as /qiṣiiṣaq/, whereas etymological /i/ plus suffix initial /u/ are reflected in many cases as bisyllabic /iʲi/ or /i . . . i/, cf. /malissaviʲuk/ 'are you going to follow him', KF /malissaviʲik/.) It must be repeated that this situation is hypothetical, given the data that I have examined.

There remains just one genuine possibility for the restructuring of etymological /u/ to /i/, viz. if the vowel occurs in a *formative internal* syllable (condition (4b)). In the southernmost dialects of West Greenland forms such as /ikisik/ 'elbow', /asikijaq/ (from /asukiʲaq/) 'I do not know' may have entire restructuring. In other dialects, however, the 'history' of /i/ may be betrayed by a more or less optional retention of the labiality feature of etymological /u/ in the form of a labialization of the following consonant or consonant cluster. I think it is extremely likely that such labialization used to occur in the southern dialects as well.

To sum up: it is only in syllables that are neither immediately preceded nor immediately followed by a formative boundary that there is no possible alternation of /i/ (from /u/) with a rounded vowel, or a cluster consisting of a vowel plus a labial glide, to betray the special status of /i/. In most forms the underlying feature of rounding is recoverable. Hence, the phenomenon of 'i-dialect' invites a generative treatment in terms of rules. Since these rules are essentially correspondence rules between the standard language and 'i-dialect', they may be used, e.g. for pedagogical purposes, if there is any need for that.

It is an interesting question to consider to what extent the alternation patterns betraying the origin of the changed vowel are mastered actively by speakers of 'i-dialect'. There is a specific issue which has not been touched upon in this paper: to what extent are these alternations employed in transforming dialect forms into standard WG, e.g. in writing? Investigations of errors in forms with recoverable versus irrecoverable etymological /u/ may throw light upon this question.

12

Structural and Functional Aspects of Tone Split in Thai[1,2]

12.1. INTRODUCTION: PROTO-TONES AND TONE SPLIT

There is overwhelming evidence (from orthography, from earlier sources, from internal reconstruction, and from comparative work) that early Proto-Thai had an inventory of three tones[3] functioning distinctively on a par with vowels and consonants to keep lexical items apart.[4] A minimal set may suffice to demonstrate this: if we symbolize the tones of the proto-language by *A, *B, and *C, there is a three-way contrast between */khaa,A/ 'leg', */khaa,B/ 'galangal (plant species)', and */khaa,C/ 'servant'.

It is crucial to the history of tones in Thai that we are dealing with a tonal language as far back as the language can be safely reconstructed. It is irrelevant in this context whether and how the origin of the proto-tones themselves can ultimately be explained by comparative work.[5]

[1] Reprinted from *Acta Linguistica Hafniensia* 30 (1998): 7–37.

[2] The literature on the history of consonants and tones in Thai is extensive. It should be pointed out that this paper only contains a very small selection of directly relevant references.

[3] To be cautious, one may speak more abstractly of syllable prosodies. These were probably characterized in part by phonation type (cf. Egerod 1971) such as a stød-like laryngealization in syllables with proto-tone *C, but they must be assumed also to have involved pitch, since this is what one finds across Tai languages, including the Southwestern branch to which Thai belongs.

[4] Since words of the Tai lexicon are monosyllabic and (at least synchronically) monomorphemic, there are three units: simplex words, morphemes, and syllables which coincide as the domain of tones (this holds true only as long as one disregards loans from Indic or Mon-Khmer).

[5] The proto-tones already existed in Proto-Tai (cf. Li 1977), and their obscure origin is an issue for comparative Tai-Kadai linguistics and for work on even wider linguistic connections.

The various Modern Thai dialects have tonal systems with from four to seven distinct tones in syllables with a voiced termination (unchecked syllables); these are the syllables in which we find reflexes of the three proto-tones. Roughly speaking, the inventory of tones has doubled from Proto-Thai to the modern dialects. The most well-known tonal system is that of (Bangkok) Central Thai, with five tones: high, mid, low, falling, and rising, although one finds more complex tonal systems both north and south of Bangkok.

The five tones of Central Thai are all mutually contrastive on unchecked syllables: if the string /khaa/ is spoken with each of the five tones in turn, it means respectively 'to trade', 'thatching-grass', 'galan-gal', 'servant' or 'cost', and 'leg'. These words were not all segmentally homophonous in Proto-Thai, however: the initial /kh/ of 'galangal', 'servant', and 'leg' is from Proto-Thai */kh/ but the /kh/ in 'to trade', 'thatching-grass', and 'cost' is from Proto-Thai */g/. This illustrates a basic feature of tonal diachrony in Thai: it involves coalescence (the complete homophony of 'servant' and 'cost' is due to tonal as well as segmental coalescence: the former has proto-tone *C with proto-initial */kh/, the latter has proto-tone *B with proto-initial */g/).

The modern dialects do not directly reveal the salient properties of the proto-tones, and it is not known what these used to be like. They may have been prosodies with both tonal and non-tonal properties. There are certain characteristics of the modern tones which may reflect properties of the old proto-tones but there is so much phonetic variation across dialects that it is difficult to make interesting generalizations. The most conspicuous feature is found with the tones of modern dialects which are continuations of proto-tone *C: these tend to be strongly falling and are often accompanied by syllable-final laryngealization. This, however, is true only of dialects spoken north of the Malaccan peninsula; the tonal phonetics is very different in the dialects of Southern (peninsular) Thailand.

The story behind the multiple tonal distinctions found in unchecked syllables is that each of the proto-tones has split—to a greater or lesser extent—into mutually distinct tones. This process is still poorly understood (notwithstanding frequent claims to the contrary), although the tone splits happened in well-defined syllable environments, and although both the starting point and the end results of the whole process are fairly well documented. As for the alleged distinction between three tones in the old language, this is directly attested by tone marks in the earliest (thirteenth-century) Thai orthography.

In contemporary Thai orthography the convention of marking the proto-tones is preserved: they are represented by superscript symbols (unmarked for *A, superscript 1 for *B, and superscript 2 for *C). The spelling of Thai words is mostly in clear accordance with their etymology. The modern orthography functions well as a common denominator for the whole array of dialects, although the tone symbols do not stand in a straightforward relationship to the tones of any modern dialect. Given the reconstruction of a word in Proto-Thai, or its conservative spelling in Thai orthography, one can perform the necessary transformations and in most cases predict successfully what must be its tone in any given modern dialect. It is, however, not possible to make equally successful deductions the other way, since tonal development in Thai involves both split and coalescence (affecting tones as well as consonants), so that the Proto-Thai wordforms can only be retrieved by comparative work.

In addition to the three tones, Proto-Thai had, and modern Thai still has, a prosodically relevant distinction between checked (so-called 'dead') syllables, i.e. those ending in a non-nasal voiceless (oral or glottal) stop, and unchecked (so-called 'live') syllables, i.e. those ending in a voiced sound (a vowel or a nasal). The phonemic distinction between tones *A, *B, and *C in Proto-Thai was found in unchecked syllables only. Along with the tone splits in such syllables, however, tones developed in checked syllables as well, and the tonal reflexes in these latter syllables show that another contrast—that between long and short vowels—became prosodically relevant in checked syllables.

Thus the tones of modern Thai dialects are the combined result of two different processes. In unchecked syllables we have *tone split*, a process which essentially resulted in the doubling of an already existing tone inventory from three to around six. In checked syllables, however, it makes sense to speak of genuine *tonogenesis 'from scratch'*. In both types of syllables, the new tonal contrasts represent rephonologization: they somehow reflect the loss or reorganization of laryngeal distinctions formerly found in syllable-initial consonants. There are at least three phonetic properties of consonants involved: voicing, aspiration, and glottalization (Egerod 1961 and Brown 1965 give excellent surveys of the complicated array of tonal reflexes of these laryngeal properties in the various dialects). Very briefly stated, what happened was consonant mutation by which certain consonants coalesced, and the distinctive load was taken over by tones.

12.2.   MARVIN BROWN AND THE TONAL DIACHRONY OF THAI

Why did Thai undergo such drastic tonal changes? Why did all dialects end up with tone inventories of rather similar size although the tone systems and the etymological relationships differ very much from one dialect to another? The present paper addresses some of these issues.[6]

There seem to be two assumptions which are shared by almost all researchers in the field (although the first of them is in fact laden with problems, cf. Rischel 1986 and the commentary with regard to assumption (vi) below):

1 tone split is the direct reflex of phonetically-conditioned pitch differences in syllables with different types of onsets (e.g. voiced versus voiceless initials);
2 these so-called pitch perturbations became contrastive because of coalescences among the different types of syllable-initial consonants.

This looks plausible enough, but there are some vexing problems. Although the etymological correspondences as such display highly regular patterns within each dialect, it is a challenge to explain the actual distribution of tones. In discussions of tone split there has been a tendency to focus on the behaviour of stop consonants. Tone split, however, also occurred with other obstruents (i.e. fricatives) and, what is more interesting, with initial sonorants. It is a non-trivial fact that *sonorants have played exactly the same role as obstruents in the tonal scenario*. Originally aspirated/voiceless sonorants condition the same tone as originally aspirated stops; originally voiced sonorants condition the same tone as originally voiced stops. This is true across all dialects.

The immediate conclusion is that any serious attempt at a phonetic explanation of tone split via pitch perturbation must be able to account for sonorants as pitch perturbators (cf. Rischel 1986; Thongkum 1993), not just for stop consonants. But equally importantly, one must take into consideration that the obstruents and sonorants of Thai have very different histories: they do not at all behave alike with respect to segmental coalescences. The coalescences among initial obstruents which are relevant to tone split always involve loss of voicing

---

[6] This paper is part of a more comprehensive study of tone split in Thai. For considerations of space, the subject matter is drastically (and somewhat artificially) delimited in the exposition below.

(e.g. */b/ > /p/, or */b/ > /ph/); the coalescences among initial sonorants, however, always involve the opposite: voiceless or aspirated
sonorants becoming fully voiced (e.g. */hm/ > /m/). Still, sonorants
side perfectly with obstruents in their tonal effects, and these effects
are entirely dependent on their laryngeal features *prior to coalescence*.

All of this makes the tone-split scenario more complex than one
might a priori expect, and it suggests that tone split in Thai cannot be
explained exclusively with reference to phonetic mechanisms such as
automatic pitch perturbation. The speakers' implicit appreciation of
structural categorization must have played a very specific role in the
diachronic scenario. For some reason, it seems, words whose Proto-
Thai initials were produced with a wide open glottis (as must have
been the case with */ph/, */f/, */hm/), formed a category which was
cognitively relevant and remained so all the way through consonant
mutations and tone splits. Similarly with words whose initials were
produced with normal voicing in Proto-Thai (such as */b/, */v/, */m/).
This issue is taken up later in this paper.

Explaining how and why the tonal inventory of Thai increased is
only part of the story, however. Tone split does not suffice to account
for the complex relationship between modern tones and the old syllable types that can be specified in terms of tones, syllable-initial consonant types, and other properties of the proto-language. It is true
of all dialects that at least some of the tones are shared by etyma
which belonged to different syllable classes in Proto-Thai, and there
is evidence of coalescences among tones across these *different* syllable
classes, as when /thii/ 'place' and /thaa/ 'if', both with the same falling
tone in modern Central Thai, go back to */dii,B/ and */thaa,C/, with
different initials as well as different tones in Proto-Thai.

The most widely held view of tone split and tonogenesis in Thai is
probably the one stated and elaborated in the influential monograph
of Brown (1965). The specific claims which seem to be implied by that
hypothesis are presented[7] as (3)–(7) below. In the interspersed comments the present author attempts to point out some of the problems
that must be tackled in order to make each assumption work.

Brown's exposition is consistent with assumptions (1) and (2) above.
In addition, he makes specific claims about the development of the

---

[7] The identification of these themes, and the formulation of them in the present paper,
represent an interpretation of Brown's (1965) text for which the present author is solely
responsible.

phonological inventories of tones from 'Ancient Thai' (a stage of Proto-Thai so named by Brown) to modern dialects. Starting from the basic assumption that the old prosodic system had to do with the termination of the syllable (the 'ending') which gives a total of five Proto-Thai prosodies or, for short, tones, he claims that there was an enormous increase in prosodic distinctions followed by dialect-specific simplifications:

> The initial laryngeal components affected the tones in different ways and increased the number of tones from five to fifteen. The fifteen tones later coalesced in various ways through the dialects. . . . We cannot be sure that there were ever fifteen tones since the coalescence might have started before the separation was complete.   (Brown 1965: 51).

And later:

> The major upheaval in the tonal system of ancient Thai . . . boils down to this: the initials unloaded part of their burden onto the tones. Five tones distinguished only by endings multiplied to fifteen with the help of the three register distinctions. But even with the help of register, the load was too heavy and two things happened: (1) some distinctions were lost, and (2) a new dimension was called on to bear the load. This dimension was contour. (Brown 1965: 57).

Leaving aside for the moment the intricate question of whether the tonal diachrony can be accounted for with reference to three properties of tones ('ending', 'register', and 'contour'), the scenario depicted by Brown can be construed as involving two assumptions to which most scholars seem to subscribe:

3 the tonal scenarios of all Thai dialects are direct reflexes of tone split occurring in late Ancient Thai;
4 the immediate result of tone split in Ancient Thai was a grossly over-complex tonal system which soon underwent simplification, although differently in different dialects.

This may be right, but in fact it is difficult to prove. An alternative assumption, which has also been aired in the literature (e.g. in Li 1977) and which is explored in the present paper, is that each dialect developed only the tonal contrasts needed to preserve structural categories in that particular dialect. Although we observe the same basic set of phenomena in all Thai dialects—coalescences between initial consonants formerly contrasting in terms of laryngeal features, and tone split as a corollary of this—there is no a priori reason why this state of affairs must have occurred before the dialects separated from each other.

Tone split, i.e. tonogenesis via consonant coalescences, has happened as part of a wave that swept across a vast expanse in South East Asia, in some instances hitting mutually related and unrelated languages alike. Tai languages were particularly prone to this typological change from complex manner-of-articulation systems to complex tonal systems. Infectious tonogenesis has happened much more recently in various minority languages, particularly of the Mon-Khmer family, which probably have become tonal by contact with surrounding peer languages, which are all tonal. This means that tone splits in Thai dialects must not necessarily be explained as reflexes of phenomena in the common ancestral language; they may be more recent. If a dialect shows a tone split, it can only be given an *ante quem* dating within the relative chronology of that particular dialect: all we know with certainty is that it must have arisen before the dialect had complete segmental coalescence of the consonant types in question.

Brown's model is maximalistic in the sense that he assumes as much tone split in the ancestral language as seems corroborated by the combined evidence from modern dialects. This leads to a reconstruction of a state of Ancient Thai with three tonal allophones for each of the proto-tones *A, *B, and *C, i.e. the diachronic assumption may be paraphrased as follows:

5 the tone split scenarios of all Thai dialects are direct reflexes of three-way tonal allophony within each of the prosodic categories of the ancestral language.

The idea that tone split in Thai started out globally as a pre-stage, with allophonic trifurcation of each tone depending on the laryngeal properties of the syllable initial, has apparent support from the occurrence of three-way splits in some Thai dialects, especially those that are spoken in Southern Thailand. With proto-tone *A, i.e. the one that is unmarked in Thai orthography, three-way splits are also found sporadically in other parts of the Southwestern Tai area. Otherwise, however, the general pattern is a binary split of each proto-tone.

Although Brown assumes a bifurcating situation for proto-tone *B and in part for proto-tone *C quite early in the proto-dialects which were continued as non-southern dialects (1150 'Chiang Saen', Brown

1965: 76; 1150 'Yunnan', Brown 1965: 87), he still assumes a preceding
trifurcating situation in an older stage of Thai underlying both of
these (950 'Yunnan', Brown 1965: 75). Many scholars (e.g. Wulff 1934;
Haudricourt 1972; Li 1977), however, have assumed that tone split
in Thai is basically bifurcating rather than trifurcating, although a
three-way distinction might arise as the consequence of further binary
splits.

According to the assumption of a basic trifurcation, Ancient Thai
developed a three-way difference in pitch contour depending on
whether the onset of each syllable was (I) voiceless with airflow (e.g.
*/ph/, */hm/), or (II) glottalized (e.g. */ʔb/), or (III) (plain) voiced
(e.g. */b/, */m/). Accordingly, the three proto-tones had at some period
three allotones each, i.e. there was an abundance of allophonic pitch
contours which might become distinctive tones as a consequence of
segmental coalescences among initial consonant types. According to
Brown's reconstruction, there arose 3 × 3 = 9 different pitch contours
in syllables with the three proto-tones.[8] The tonal system of each
dialect is assumed to represent a partial, but only partial, retention
of such pitch differences as tonal contrasts.

In his 1965 monograph, Brown reconstructs a stage of late Ancient
Thai which is consistent with the tone systems of later dialects.
Although it is in itself a complex enough problem to work out a
reconstruction which can account satisfactorily for the *inventories* of
tones and their distribution in the dialects, it is also the aim of the
reconstructive work in Brown's monograph to trace the *pitch characteristics* of the tones all the way from a hypothetical pre-stage to modern
dialects:

6 the actual pitch shapes of the tones in Thai dialects are seen as modifications of pitch shapes postulated for a late stage of Ancient Thai;
7 the diachrony of tone shapes is reconstructed with reference to a hypothesis
about the mechanism of change (Brown's scenario crucially involves three
aspects of tone which he calls 'endings', 'registers', and 'contours').

This part of Brown's impressive edifice has met with surprisingly
little criticism in the literature, considering that it rests on internal

---

[8] For simplicity I here disregard the checked syllables; by including these one reaches
a theoretical total number of 15 pitch contours on monosyllables in Ancient Thai, which
is the number which Brown assumes to be diachronically relevant; cf. the quotes in the
Introduction.

reconstruction without any other substantiation of the reconstructed pitch shapes of tones in earlier stages of Thai.

As for pitch shapes, one faces a crux in Thai tonal history: there is one, and only one, group of contemporary Thai dialects whose tones are easily aligned with the assumed pitch perturbating effects of aspirated, glottalized, and plain voiced stops: namely the dialects that belong to Southern Thai. If we consider the northern dialects (Shan, Northern Thai, Lao: see below), it rather looks as if we have some kind of cross-over of the expected tone contours in these dialects: the initial pitch is lower with an old voiced initial (as in */gaa,A/ 'thatching grass', */mii,A/ 'to have') than with an old voiceless aspirated initial (as in */khaa,A/ 'leg', */hmii,A/ 'bear'). This forces Brown to assume two alternative and potentially competing mechanisms of pitch perturbation. A more trivial hypothesis would be that the opposite relationships between consonant and tone found in different dialects are the fortuitous result of secondary phonetic changes affecting the tones over a span of several centuries. In any case, the phonetic mismatch between the dialects with respect to tonal contours weakens the case for tone split as a monolithic phenomenon dating back to a Common Thai period (cf. above).

Considering that Brown's work stems from the first half of the 1960s, his preoccupation with physiological hypotheses about phonetic mechanisms is impressive (it was only later that tonogenesis became a live issue in linguistics and phonetics). One wonders, however, how it is possible to make such specific claims about the laryngeal phonetics and the shapes of tones in a language spoken a millennium ago.[9]

Brown refers to his own approach as 'control phonology', which is consistent with its emphasis on the monitoring of speech production both in synchronic phonology and as a factor in language change. Claims about such articulatory control mechanisms become overly hypothetical, however, when the alleged immediate effects of the postulated mechanisms in the proto-language are likewise hypothetical.

Another striking thing about the trend of diachronic research set in Brown's monograph is that whereas the whole scenario of tone split is depicted with much emphasis on diachronic correspondences

---

[9] It would appear as highly ambitious if a similar approach to reconstruction were to be applied to the history of tones in Scandinavian languages, for example.

and pitch shapes, there is little emphasis on the *function* of the tonal systems. Why would Thai develop a grotesquely over-crowded tone system, only to undergo subsequent, dialect-specific reductions of the system so that all dialects ended up with manageable inventories? If over-differentiation > instability > simplification is a plausible assumption about the way tonal diachrony works, we would expect there to be evidence, among the living languages of the world, of transitional tonogenetic stages characterized by such grossly over-sized inventories of mutually distinctive tones. What is typically observed in cases of incipient tonogenesis is, on the contrary, the development of binary tonal contrasts.

It is the intention of this paper to challenge the third, fourth, and fifth claims above and to do this with special emphasis on functional considerations. It will be shown that tonal bifurcation is on the whole a well-motivated process of change, considering what has happened to the initial consonants, whereas trifurcation implies some kind of over-compensation for the loss of distinctions in the initials. The other four claims (1), (2), (6), and (7) referred to above are, in fact, no less controversial but will not be addressed in the present paper.

A central issue, then, is whether there was originally a three-way split across all of Thai, or whether most dialects never had more than a two-way split. It will be shown below that if the tones developed in each dialect are considered from the point of view of their category-preserving function, the resulting scenario seems consistent with the latter assumption.

12.3.   THAI LANGUAGES OR DIALECTS REFERRED TO IN THIS PAPER

'Thai' can be understood as referring specifically to Central Thai or as a wide term embracing more or less all dialects of the Southwestern Tai branch of Tai-Kadai languages.[10] When used in the latter sense it comprises Central Thai, Lao, Shan, and some other, closely related, languages or dialects spoken in Mainland South East Asia.

---

[10] The term Southwestern Tai stems from Fang-Kuei Li's taxonomy of Tai languages (1977).

In the sections below, reference is made to five languages or dialect clusters:

- *Shan* is spoken (in a variety of rather different dialects) north of the border between northernmost Thailand and Burma;
- *Northern Thai* includes Kammueang, spoken in much of the former Lanna region of Northern Thailand, i.e. just south of the Burmese Shan area; Khün and Lü are spoken outside Thailand;
- *Lao* comprises a cluster of dialects spoken east and southeast of the Northern Thai area, i.e. in Laos and Eastern Thailand;
- *Central Thai*, spoken south of the Northern Thai area; it includes Bangkok Thai and Standard Thai;
- *Southern Thai* is a set of dialects spoken in peninsular Thailand down to the Malaysian border.

As mentioned already, the various offspring of Proto-Thai show tone systems of comparable complexity. Brown's survey (1965: 113) shows one area with only four different tones in such syllables: this is the Khorat dialect spoken in part of Eastern Thailand, which is transitional between Lao and Central Thai and whose sound pattern may reflect a strong substratum. Otherwise, one typically finds six tones in unchecked syllables in the northernmost dialects (Shan, Northern Thai), five tones in Lao and Central Thai, and six or seven tones in Southern Thai.

In all dialects the tonal system shows direct reflexes of the three proto-tones but the relationships are very different from one dialect area to another. The observation that the northernmost and southernmost dialects agree on six distinct tones, is deceptive: the situations are not at all similar.

The northern dialects have preserved a rigid separation between the proto-tones *A, *B, *C, largely such that two of the six modern tones represent the split of one of the proto-tones, two others represent the split of another proto-tone, and the remaining two represent the split of the third proto-tone. This seems straightforward enough, both phonetically and phonologically, although the tonal contours found nowadays cannot be explained easily by reference to automatic pitch perturbation mechanisms.

Among the southern dialects, however, some dialects have three distinct tones for each proto-tone, and there is a clear tendency for these tones to correlate with voicing in the expected fashion (tones are lowest after old voiced consonants). On the other hand, the old tonal system has broken down in Southern Thai:[11] two of the proto-tones, *A and *B, have coalesced in syllables with HIGH and MID initials. If one includes checked syllables as well, one finds (e.g. by inspection of the charts in Brown 1965: 77–134) that Southern Thai has four different tones with LOW initials versus only three different tones with HIGH initials.[12] This is different from all other dialect areas and is a relevant feature of tonal typology.

The tendency to coalescence between proto-tones in Southern Thai suggests that the tonal trifurcation in these dialects has overloaded the tonal pattern and thus paved the way for massive coalescence, unlike the situation in the northern dialects (it is not at all certain that there is such a direct cause–effect relationship, however). In any case, attempts at a unified account of tone split in Thai should take into consideration that the patterns of tonal development in the northern and southern dialects are not just divergent but are *basically different* with respect to the whole scenario of tonal change. This has not been fully appreciated in the classic literature on Thai tones and their development.

Of the languages or dialects referred to above, Lao and Central Thai have the status of national languages with official orthographies. There are also traditional orthographies for Shan and Northern Thai, although these languages nowadays survive mainly as a spoken minority language and as a spoken 'dialect', respectively. Southern Thai is a cluster of dialects with no orthography; Brown (1985), however, speculates that these may continue a displaced dialect that was spoken in the city of Sukhothai (north of Bangkok) in ancient time when that city was the capital of Thailand. His arguments in favour of the Sukhothai hypothesis are not directly relevant to the present paper.

The earliest written form of Thai is from the Sukhothai Kingdom and dates back to the late thirteenth century. The orthography of present-day Standard Thai being very conservative and thus rather dialect-independent, there are only minor discrepancies between transliterated Sukhothai spelling and Modern Thai spelling. If used with care (i.e. correction of etymological mistakes), the latter works excellently as a frame of reference in diachronic studies of the development of tones and consonants in Thai dialects.

---

[11] With the exception of the strange Chumphon dialect (Brown 1965: 117).

[12] These sweeping observations disregard the Tak Bai dialect on the Malaysian border (Brown 1965: 135), which is quite aberrant anyway by only having a two-way tone split with each of the proto-tones as well as in checked syllables.

12.4. THE GENERAL TONE-SPLIT SCENARIO

As is apparent from the exposition above, a comprehensive study of the tonal development in Thai dialects requires consideration of a considerable number of syllable types. It is a gross simplification to refer, as is often done, specifically to tone split in syllables with tone *A and with initial stops. On the other hand, it is an overly complex enterprise to account for the total pattern of proto-tones and syllable-types.

This paper follows the simplistic line of exposition since it is only intended to illustrate that a certain type of functional consideration may be relevant to the understanding of the tonal scenario with its otherwise bewildering variation across dialects. To show this, it is not necessary to include all tonally-relevant syllable-categories, although the other categories are of course just as relevant to an overall study as the ones included here.[13]

If syllables with tone *A are considered in their diachronic development across the various dialects of Thai, one finds that each dialect exhibits a split into two or, in some dialects, three tones as the consequence of coalescences between initial consonant types. Tone split is, however, not conditioned by the same difference(s) in consonant type in all dialects. In an overall format of description it is necessary to distinguish between four different manners of laryngeal articulation in initial consonants as reconstructed for Proto-Thai. These may be illustrated by the labial series:[14]

   I. Aspirated voiceless: */ph/, */f/, */hm/ ('HIGH')
  II. Unaspirated (laryngealized?) voiceless: */p/ ('MID1')
 III. Glottalized voiced: */ʔb/ ('MID2')
  IV. Plain voiced: */b/, */v/, */m/ ('LOW')

In traditional Thai terminology, initial consonants of class I are called HIGH consonants; those of classes II and III are called MID consonants, and those of class IV are called LOW consonants, a ternary set of labels which is interesting for its (somewhat enigmatic) allusion to pitch characteristics associated with the consonants in old Thai. This terminology will also be used below; the so-called MID

<hr>

[13] Cf. note 6 above.
[14] It is hardly necessary for the purpose of the present paper to give the total consonant inventory; cf. Li (1977) for Proto-Tai and Rischel (1985) for Modern Thai.

consonants are, however, here split up into MID1 (= class II) and MID2 (= class III).

The main factor provoking tone split is that categories I and IV— HIGH and LOW—coalesce as the result of two kinds of processes: (A) the aspirated sonorants of category I become voiced; (B) the obstruents of category IV become voiceless, with or without aspiration. Both of these processes have happened in all Thai dialects (and indeed more widely). The outcome of the latter process is different for different dialect areas and is also dependent on the type of consonant involved.

From the point of view of the consonant inventory, the main change is that the number of categories, as defined by laryngeal manner of articulation, shrinks, voiceless sonorants becoming voiced and voiced obstruents becoming voiceless. In modern Central Thai, the hole created by the latter process (*/b/ > /p/ or > /ph/, etc.) has been partly filled by an independent phonetic change: the glottalized voiced consonants */ʔb/, */ʔd/ of Proto-Thai (class III) now appear as plain voiced stops /b d/, although often pronounced with varying degrees of (nondistinctive) glottalization. There are only two places of articulation, labial and dental, for this series although Thai otherwise has four (as in the series /p t c k/); this preference for anterior articulations clearly reflects the origin of the two voiced stops as formerly distinctively glottalized.

One may ask how consonant mutations, by which plain voiced obstruents become voiceless and voiceless sonorants become voiced, could ever result in more than a binary tonal cleavage. Both within the class of obstruents and within the class of sonorants the number of laryngeally-defined categories has been reduced by only one (in this exposition I disregard the rare glottalized sonorant *ʔj). Part of the answer is that the increase in the phonemic inventory of tones does not just compensate for coalescences among syllables with proto-tone *A; it does so also for the other two proto-tones, and it also serves— more or less efficiently—to preserve distinctions between syllables with different proto-tones but with coalescing initials (the example above of complete phonological coalescence between the syllable types of */dii,B/ 'place' and */thaa,C/ 'if' in modern Central Thai is in fact rather exceptional if we look across all Thai dialects).

Dialects typically end up with inventories of the size of six distinctive tones. Thus, tonal split (and tonogenesis in checked syllables) has resulted in an overall inventory of phonemic tones which is typically three times as large as would be necessary to maintain contrast among syllables with the same prosodic pre-history (i.e. with the same proto-tone). Diachronically, we find dialect-specific rearrangements of the consonant system and hence dialect-specific solutions to the question how to distribute this surplus of tones onto syllable categories. The latter issue is taken up in the present paper (whereas the overall size of the tonal inventory of each dialect, and the motivation for it, falls outside the strictly limited scope of the discussion).

If we look at the tonal cleavage of proto-tone *A, the remarkable thing is that its location within the series I–II–III–IV differs from one dialect to another. It may occur between I and II/III/IV, or between I/II and III/IV, for example. This is, of course, well documented and has also been discussed in the literature on the subject, but the possible causes for such differences have been given remarkably little consideration.

12.5. ARE STRUCTURAL EXPLANATIONS OF TONE SPLIT VALID?

As said above, Brown's approach is greatly ahead of its time in that it does not focus one-sidedly on structure but emphasizes the phonetic nature of sound change, and even attempts to give explanations in terms of specific hypotheses about mechanisms of speech production (Brown 1965) or of speech perception (Brown 1975). Brown's hypotheses antedate various phoneticians' speculations about the phonetic mechanisms underlying tonogenesis or tone split, which makes them interesting in themselves, although they are not based on a well-established phonetic theory and thus stand out as highly speculative.

Historical phonologists of the early 1960s otherwise emphasized the importance of structural factors in sound change, and some tended to over-emphasize the importance of *maintenance of distinctiveness*. It must be admitted that the structural concept of 'functional load' is a much less powerful explanatory factor in sound change than many linguists used to assume. In well-attested language histories, massive phoneme coalescences have occurred without causing disasters and without creating any compelling need for compensation for the loss of contrast; cf. that English and Icelandic have happily survived the loss of the distinction between rounded and unrounded front vowels although it created a considerable amount of surface homonymy.

Category preservation in a more abstract sense is, however, a very important factor in language change. If we stick for a moment to the scenario of medieval West Scandinavian, one can observe that unlike the loss of rounding, there was another change involving potential loss of contrast which affected the whole quantity system and had far-reaching structural consequences. The system of syllable types (which played an essential metrical role in Old Norse poetry, for example) was entirely upset by the lengthening of short vowels in certain syllables and the shortening of long vowels in certain other syllables. The cognitive categories to which words used to belong by virtue of the quantity system were, however, to a large extent preserved by phonologization of qualitative differences between formerly long and short vowels.

It seems plausible that such structure preservation has played an important role also in the history of Thai (and more widely of tone-splitting East and South East Asian languages).

Tone split seems to be a prototypical case of the maintenance of structural categories. As mentioned above, it is a very conspicuous property of tone split in Thai that it operates with reference to categories of initials which were segmentally heterogeneous from the start and which even became more heterogeneous as the result of segmental processes. Both the old category of HIGH and the old category of LOW consonants were phonetically heterogeneous in that they included obstruents as well as sonorants, and when consonants in one of these categories underwent mutation (e.g. devoicing of obstruents, or voicing of sonorants) it was always a phonetic subset, not the whole category, that was affected. The various classes of initials were splintered and their members redistributed on new phonetic classes. For illustration of this redistribution, note that the HIGH initial of */hmii,A/ 'bear' changed to /m/ and thus entered the same phonetic class as the LOW initial of */mii,A/ 'to have' (whereas non-sonorant HIGH consonants remained voiceless aspirates); and that the LOW initial of */gem,A/ 'bitter' changed to /k/ or to /kh/ (depending on the dialect) and thus either entered the same phonetic class as the MID initial of */kin,A/ 'to eat', or the same phonetic class as the HIGH initial of */khem,A/ 'needle, pin' (whereas sonorant LOW consonants remained voiced).

Across the various mutations of the initial consonants, however, words with etymologically HIGH consonants remained united by the shared tone, and likewise words with etymologically LOW consonants, irrespective of the new segmental properties of the subclasses within each category. The cognitive unity of each set of words was preserved by the uniformity of tone split when consonant mutations would otherwise have wiped out the phonological relatedness among the members within each of these sets.

Seen from this angle, tone split is not just an automatic spill-off of pitch perturbation and loss of voicing contrast. This observation may help to make the search for the *phonetic* mechanisms underlying tone split more realistic. It may be that one is not forced to look for a uniform explanation in terms of pitch perturbation which is equally plausible when applied to obstruents and to sonorants. It may well be that tone split started in one subset of words, e.g. words with initial obstruents, and was generalized to another subset of words (with initial sonorants). It may also be that tone splits occurred in different ways in different subsets but underwent a generalization across the whole vocabulary.

In contradistinction to consonant mutations with coalescence, other losses of contrast among consonants in Thai have not had any such effect. The situation is analogous to the Scandinavian one referred to above. In Thai it had little or no effect on what happened to finals, for example, as long as the distinction between checked and unchecked syllables was preserved. For exemplification one may consider syllable-final /-n/ and /-t/ in modern Thai: the former is the reflex of several different sonorants (including */-r/ and */-l/ in loanwords), and the latter is the reflex of a number of dental and palatal obstruents. The complex coalescence underlying /-r/ or /-t/ in Modern Thai has had no tonal consequences; all that happened was that the amount of homonomy was increased (within unchecked and checked syllables, respectively). As for tone split, one can observe that it did prevent a lot of pairwise homonomy between lexical items, but since there is an abundance of such homonomy in Thai anyway, that in itself may not have been the most important driving force in tone split and tonogenesis.

The various dialects all agree on the uniform tonal treatment of *all* HIGH consonants, of *all* MID1 consonants, of *all* MID2 consonants, and of *all* LOW consonants. In other respects, however, the dialects do not at all exhibit uniform tone-split behaviour. That is in fact the most intriguing aspect of the whole scenario. It is the purpose of the remainder of this paper to look into the differential behaviour of Thai dialects with respect to tone split, and to show that there seems to be a simple, system-internal functional explanation: each dialect chooses a tonal categorization, i.e. a placement of the tone split along the aspiration-voicing parameter, which is optimal for that particular dialect, given the overall properties of its sound pattern. In the following, five different dialect clusters will be approached with this objective in mind.

12.6.   ELEMENTS OF THE TYPOLOGY OF TONE SPLIT IN THAI

Theoretically, it might have happened that all Thai dialects split each of the proto-tones into the same number of new tones, be it a bifurcation or a trifurcation of each tone, and preserved this pattern up to the present time. This, however, is not what we observe. The reflexes of the three proto-tones often differ with respect to tone split, and if so, it is always proto-tone *A that shows the maximum degree of split in the dialect in question. Proto-tones *B and *C never split more than *A does. In fact, there are some Lao dialects in which proto-tone *B does not show any split at all, although the very same dialects have a three-way split for proto-tone *A (this is apparent from the charts in Brown 1965: 105–8; also see below). There are also typically fewer tonal distinctions in checked syllables than in syllables with proto-tone *A (the checked syllables are not further considered here).

It makes sense, therefore, to single out words with proto-tone *A as a testing-ground for claims about the relationship between consonant and tone in the dialects continuing Brown's Ancient Thai. Except when otherwise stated, the observations below refer exclusively to words with proto-tone *A.

If one inspects the tonal data as found in Brown's (1965) excellent survey, there is no strong evidence that the northern dialect group comprising Shan and Northern Thai started out with a three-way tone split; they seem to have had from the beginning a two-way split with all proto-tones (contrary to Brown who assumes an original three-way split with proto-tone *A in 1150 'Chiang Saen' 1965: 76). The crucial point is there was no functional reason for HIGH to become tonally distinct from MID1 in these northern languages, since HIGH and MID1 consonants never coalesced (this point is elaborated below). Indeed, we find that in these northern dialect areas there is hardly ever tonal bifurcation between HIGH and MID1, i.e. between I and II, with any of the proto-tones.

In contrast, the other descendants of Ancient Thai, i.e. dialects of Lao, Central Thai, and Southern Thai, typically exhibit more or less redundant tonal bifurcation between HIGH and MID1, i.e. between I and II, with at least one of the proto-tones *A, *B, or *C.

Southern Thai, moreover, differs from all the other dialect areas by being extensively trifurcating in its tonal splits in unchecked syllables across the various proto-tones, and likewise trifurcating with respect to tonogenesis in checked syllables.

It is indeed tempting to claim that the distinction between bifurcating (= northern) and trifurcating (= southern) dialects must represent the original situation at the time of tone split. It is one of the goals of the present paper to check the plausibility of this hypothesis by looking into the functional relationship between consonant coalescences and tonal distinctions in dialects representing five branches of Thai: Shan, Northern Thai, Lao, Central Thai, and Southern Thai.

The present paper does not attempt to make sweeping generalizations by deliberately overlooking details in 'small' dialects. On the contrary, it may be seen at first sight as strengthening the case for Brown's hypothesis (about early tonal tripartition in all of Thai) since it adds crucial data about some sub-dialects of Shan and Central Thai which were not included in Brown's work (1965, 1975), data which can be construed as new evidence for three-way splits also appearing in these dialects.

Still, the present author is sceptical about the assumption of (i) an abundance of early tone splits resulting in tonal overload, as the starting point for (ii) dialect-specific tonal scenarios exhibiting more or less random simplifications of the (allegedly) overly complex system which formed the point of departure. The paper attempts to do without such assumptions and, on the contrary, tests the explanatory power of a different type of assumption: that there were highly specific structural and functional reasons for individual developments in the dialects, which might either increase or decrease the tonal complexity.

The following survey deals with dialects (or rather: clusters of dialects) roughly corresponding to different geographical locations, and the different patterns of tone split found in these. It should be mentioned that a similar approach to systematization in a geographical perspective was outlined in Tienmee (1985); that paper, however, just pointed to dialect-dependent tone splits in various syllable types, with reference to the features glottalization, aspiration, and voice. The essence of the survey below is to show the strict functionality behind the various solutions to the tone split which one can observe all across the Thai-speaking area.

The five main dialects (or rather: dialect groups) will now be presented in a slightly strange order: Northern Thai, Shan, Southern Thai, Lao, and Central Thai. This is because their patterns of development are increasingly difficult to explain, and because it is convenient to discuss the scenarios of some dialects with reference to others.

12.7. TONE IN FIVE AREAS, WITH SPECIAL REFERENCE TO PROTO-TONE *A

12.7.1. Northern Thai

In Northern Thai we find a tonal bifurcation of proto-tone *A, namely between HIGH/MID1 on the one hand and MID2/LOW on the other (this is true both of the so-called Yuan dialects in Northern Thailand and of Khün in Myanmar, although with some difference in tonal contours, cf. the comparative chart in Egerod 1959: 127). This particular two-way split is consistent with the consonant mutations: (i) voicing of voiceless sonorants (*/hm/ > /m/) and devoicing of voiced fricatives (*/z/ > /s/), both entailing a coalescence HIGH/LOW, and (ii) devoicing of plain voiced stops (*/b/ > */p/), entailing a coalescence MID1/LOW. There was no mutation which coalesced MID2 and LOW consonants. Accordingly, a two-way split would serve the role of keeping coalescing categories apart no matter whether it occurred between HIGH/MID1 and MID2/LOW or between HIGH/MID1/MID2 and LOW. From a functional point of view the former placement (separating MID1 and MID2) is the optimal placement of a tonal distinction with proto-tone *A, and indeed, the outcome of all the changes has been a cleavage with a tonal distinction between HIGH/MID1 and MID2/LOW.

With its unique cleavage between MID1 and MID2, Northern Thai happens to furnish evidence on the status of syllables with no initial oral consonant. These syllables are treated in Thai writing, and in phonological analyses of Modern Thai as well, as beginning with a phonemic glottal stop /ʔ/, for example /ʔaan/ 'saddle', /ʔim/ 'satisfied'. One might expect initial */ʔ/ to side with the voiceless oral stops */p t c k/, i.e. MID1 consonants. However, */ʔ/ is found in Northern Thai to side tonally with the MID2 oral initials */ʔb ʔd/. This is consistent with the reconstruction of the MID2 initials as glottalized.

It is interesting that the tonal separation of the two consonant categories MID1 and MID2 is specific to Northern Thai. In this particular dialect group *the tone split for proto-tone *A compensates effectively for the loss of voicing contrast*: the two tones take over the distinction between old voiceless (be it aspirated or unaspirated) and old voiced (be it glottalized or plain) oral consonants.

With proto-tone *A in Northern Thai we thus find the tonal split which we would expect from pitch perturbation theory if MID2 stops were plain voiced like the low ones. As pointed out above, however, they were glottalized, and initial /ʔ/ behaved like them in tonal development. This makes it less straightforward to account for the split in terms of phonetic mechanisms. On the other hand, the pattern of segmental sound changes in this dialect, with its coalescence of MID1 and LOW stops, created a structural situation inviting exactly the tone split we find in Northern Thai: between MID1 and MID2. This was an optimal solution to the placement of the tone split, and it set itself through with proto-tone *A.

It is necessary here to add some remarks about a dialect forming a separate branch in Brown's survey: Phuan (spoken in the Lopburi area well north of Bangkok). In terms of its overall tonal pattern, Phuan looks much like Northern Thai. It has, however, its tonal cleavage between HIGH and MID1/MID2/LOW according to Brown's chart (1965: 83); such a split of proto-tone *A is otherwise found in Central Thai (and in some Lao dialects). Its occurrence in Phuan is thus not surprising, and moreover it seems perfectly consistent with the information about consonant mutations given by Brown himself (in a consonant chart on p. 83): unlike Northern Thai this dialect has aspirated stops as the reflexes of old LOW (voiced) stops, i.e. that LOW and MID1 did *not* merge in Phuan so as to create a need for tonal distinction. A split between HIGH and the rest could apparently serve just as well to preserve structural categories in Phuan.

The remarks above were concerned with proto-tone *A. In the remainder of the pattern, however—with proto-tones *B and *C and in checked syllables—the tone split in Northern Thai occurred between MID2 and LOW, i.e. so as to set off the plain voiced initials from all others. This was likewise an efficient option from the point of view of maintenance of contrast, and indeed, this split is found outside proto-tone *A, not only in Northern Thai but also in Central Thai.

12.7.2. Shan

This language, called Tai Yai by Thai people, is represented by only one dialect in the comparative surveys of Egerod (1957) and Brown (1965) but comprises several dialects spoken in Northern Myanmar and adjacent Yunnan; there are speakers in Northern Thailand as well (cf. Harris 1975; Gedney 1976; Young 1985). Shan is felt by the speakers themselves to divide into two main groups, Southern and Northern Shan.

In Taunggyi and Kengtung Shan of Myanmar, as presented by Egerod (1957, 1961) and Brown (1965), and as observed also by this author, proto-tone *A exhibits a split between words with HIGH/MID initial (these have a rising tone) and words with LOW initial (these have a high tone). The same can be observed in the Northern Shan data of Harris (1975: 203).

It is different with other data on Shan. The Tai Mau glossary in Young (1985) distinguishes three different tones in words with proto-tone *A: a rising tone with HIGH initial, an even mid tone with MID1/2 initial, and a high tone with LOW initial. The same trifurcation appears from the statement about Tai Ya in Ngourungsi (s.a.: 100). The tonal information she gives for words with HIGH initials (her '2nd A1' group), and with MID1 and MID2 initials (her '1st A1' and '3rd A1' groups) agree with those of Young; there is a minor difference in pitch contour with LOW initials (her A2 group), in which she observes a high falling tone (in her notation 53). According to the data in Harris (1976: 114), there is also such a trifurcation, although with deviating tone contours, in the Khamti Shan dialect in Assam and Northwest Burma.

The consonant mutations are very different from those of Southern Thai, for example (see below). The only shared mutation (from the point of view of the end result) is the change of HIGH sonorants to plain voiced sonorants: */hm/ > /m/, which we find in all descendants of Ancient Thai; this entails a coalescence of HIGH/LOW sonorants. As for the mutation of voiced (LOW) stops, the devoicing in Shan caused a segmental coalescence of MID1/LOW stops. Thirdly, Shan has had a unique sonorization of the glottalized voiced stops to continuants: */ʔb/ has become either /m/ or /w/, depending on the dialect, and */ʔd/ has become /l/ or /n/ (the latter in Hkamti Shan according to Haudricourt 1972: 73; in Tai Ya, according to Ngourungsi s.a.: 104, */ʔb/ has become a voiced fricative, and */ʔd/ has become a lateral).

This sonorization entails a coalescence of MID2 stops with LOW sonorants: */w m l n/ (and with the old HIGH sonorants as well, */hw hm hl hn/ having all become voiced).

Shan, in addition, had spirantization of MID1 */c/ and of LOW */j/; */z/ became /s/ as in all other dialects (Li 1977: 161, 164, 168). HIGH */s/, however, changed into a different sound (Li 1977: 152). Hence the genesis of a new sibilant in Shan from different sources did not entail any coalescence between HIGH and MID1, only between MID1 and LOW.

In Shan, most coalescences resulting from consonant mutation have occurred between LOW, i.e. old plain voiced, and something else. The only exception is that the sonorization of MID2 oral stops (*/ʔb/, */ʔd/) and the voicing of HIGH sonorants (*/hm/, etc.) had the joint effect of causing a three-way segmental coalescence HIGH/MID2/LOW producing voiced sonorants (*hm/*ʔb/*m > /m/, *hl/*ʔd/*l > /l/, etc.).

As the combined result of the various events, the tonal distinction between HIGH/MID and LOW had a maximal category-preserving and contrastive function (this is true although Haudricourt 1972 claims that the sonorization of MID2 stops in 'no way affected the tonal system').

We may conclude that in some Shan (i.e. as spoken in Taunggyi and Kengtung), the pattern of consonant coalescence provides an unambiguous explanation of the tonal pattern with its unique two-way split between non-LOW and LOW (as against both the Northern Thai split between MID1 and MID2 and the Central Thai split between HIGH and non-HIGH: see below). The tonal cleavage in Shan simply occurred where it must occur in order to be maximally functional.[15]

The extra split between HIGH and MID in some Shan dialects also has a certain though lesser functional motivation because of the special consonant changes that affected Shan in contradistinction to other Thai dialects: it serves to distinguish between words with initial voiced sonorants as reflexes of HIGH sonorants, e.g. */hlaŋ,A/ 'back', and words with initial voiced sonorants as reflexes

[15] The complete success of tones in keeping old categories apart has been slightly upset by a secondary change of /r/ to /h/. This process in itself just duplicates the existing coalescence HIGH/LOW, but it even affects clusters so that */pr/ and */kr/ tend to become aspirates and to create a new, secondary coalescence HIGH/MID. However, these two clusters occur almost exclusively in Indic and Khmer loans; the original Tai */pr/ is not at all preserved in Thai but has become /t/ (cf. Li 1977: 86, 225).

of MID2 stops, e.g. */ʔdaŋ,A/ 'loud'. These two words have become segmentally homophonous: /laŋ/ but are tonally distinct in, e.g., Tai Mau (as attested by the phonemicized vocabulary in Young 1985).

This coalescence was brought about by two quite separate processes: voicing of one set of initials, and lenition of another set of initials. The initials affected by the two processes used to be distinguished by several features: as voiceless sonorant continuants versus voiced glottalized stops, so the need for a tonal distinction arose in a very indirect way. Moreover, its contrastive load is fairly limited compared to other tonal distinctions, as there were only two consonants in the MID2 set which could engage in segmental coalescence with HIGH sonorants. In short, the need to avoid a merger between HIGH- and MID2-words has hardly had any high cognitive salience.

It is important further to note that the tone split between HIGH and MID2 occurring in some Shan compensated for a (rather marginal) loss of voicing contrast, just like the more important tone split between HIGH and LOW.

All of this may explain why the tonal cleavage between HIGH and MID is not a consistent feature of all Shan. Shan can indeed be classified as having a basic two-way split between HIGH/MID1/MID2 and LOW.

One may finally ask why the extra split in some Shan did not occur between MID1 and MID2, as in Northern Thai. That would also have served the purpose of keeping HIGH and MID2 apart in Shan. There is no obvious reason why the two dialects should differ on the placement of this tonal split, except that Shan (unlike Northern Thai) has another tonal split between MID2 and LOW. In Shan, a split between MID1 and MID2 would thus have resulted in an M2 tone of very restricted distribution (contrastive within the realm of proto-tone *A, only for the initials */ʔb/ and */ʔd/). This line of argumentation may be slightly far-fetched, however. It is the tone split between MID1 and MID2 in Northern Thai which is typologically unique within Thai, and which therefore calls for special motivation, as suggested above.

12.7.3. **Southern Thai**

There is a clear-cut and consistent trifurcation into three tones corresponding to the traditional main categories of old initials: HIGH vs. MID vs. LOW. The tone after HIGH initial contains the tonal property [high] in the sense that allotones of this tone have contours which, in the terminology of Egerod (1971–), 'touch h[igh]' (i.e. touch the ceiling of the tonal space). The tone after LOW initial contains the property [low], i.e. the contours 'touch l[ow]' (the floor of the tonal space). As for the tone after MID initials the contours do not 'touch' either the high or the low level: they are m[id]. There is no tonal distinction between MID1 and MID2. All this is in perfect agreement with traditional terminology, and according to Brown (1985) it should reflect the situation in the old Sukhothai dialect.

In Southern Thai there was total segmental coalescence between HIGH and LOW, that is, between the two sets of laryngeally non-constricted consonants, since HIGH sonorants (*/hm/ etc.) became voiced (unaspirated) and LOW stops (*/b/ etc.) ended up as voiceless aspirated. The segmental coalescence between HIGH and LOW was, as one would expect, compensated for by a consistent tonal distinction.

The MID consonants remained outside the segmental coalescence which affected HIGH and LOW, and they continued to form a separate category consisting of two distinct classes of unaspirated stops: voiceless and voiced.

Words with MID initials might have sided tonally with one of the two other categories. It would not matter which, since the MID consonants were segmentally distinguished in any case. That is, a two-way split would have sufficed to serve the purpose of preserving distinctions in Southern Thai (and likewise in Central Thai and Lao: see below). Nevertheless, Southern Thai developed its ternary split between HIGH, MID, and LOW.

Phonetically it is anything but obvious why voiceless MID1 stops and voiced MID2 stops would condition the same tone. Pitch perturbation theory would rather suggest the same tone for all voiceless oral stops, i.e. HIGH and MID1 stops, and a different tone for all voiced oral stops, i.e. MID2 and LOW stops. This suggests that MID1 and MID2 initials shared a significant phonetic property as against both aspirates and plain voiced consonants, i.e. if we used labials for reference, that */p/ and */ʔb/ formed a phonetic category as against on the one hand */ph/, */hm/, */hw/, and on the other hand */b/, */m/, */w/. This makes sense if the Proto-Thai MID consonants were all in some way *laryngeally constricted*, as against the HIGH consonants which were presumably produced with wide open glottis, and the LOW consonants which were presumably produced with adduced but not strongly compressed vocal folds (i.e. with the vocal folds in the state most favourable for voicing).[16]

It remains somewhat enigmatic why the rather modest differences in pitch perturbation which could be brought about by different laryngeal modes would result in *a redundant three-way tonal split*, when a two-way split would have worked perfectly. It is tempting to assume that the process was not of a purely mechanical nature but was provoked by a high degree of cognitive salience of the distinction between MID initials on the one hand, and all other initials (HIGH, LOW) on the other hand, i.e. that the MID consonants were phonologically *highly marked* in terms of laryngeal properties in early Southern Thai.

The three-way tonal distinction between words with HIGH, MID, and LOW initials in Southern Thai is not found only with proto-tone *A but also with other old prosodic categories. In return, there is extensive mutual overlapping between these old prosodic categories. With non-LOW initials there is complete coalescence between proto-tones *A and *B, although this was phonemically a heavily loaded contrast such that any coalescence *A/*B would lead to homonymy.

To round off, we may repeat that from the point of view of modern Southern Thai, a two-way split would have sufficed for proto-tone *A (and similarly for each of the other proto-tones) as long as one tone reflected old HIGH stops and the other old LOW stops. Words with MID1 and MID2 consonants might have joined one or the other tone category without any loss of contrast but nevertheless took their own course. This structural inconsistency in tone split recurs interestingly in the case of Lao.

12.7.4. Lao

Although the tone contours and levels are quite different from those of Southern Thai, the relationship between consonant coalescences and phonemic tones is essentially the same (in certain Lao dialects). In Lao as elsewhere, there is segmental coalescence HIGH/LOW (*ph/*b,

---

[16] It would be tempting to use terms such as [tense] for the category comprising MID1 and MID2 consonants and [lax] for the category comprising HIGH and LOW consonants. Unfortunately, the term 'tense' is unavailable since it has been used in recent phonology as a cover term for a wide array of consonant types, in some languages including aspirated stops. It may, therefore, be advisable to stick to the terms 'constricted' and 'non-constricted' to avoid confusion, although totally arbitrary labels with no phonetic connotations might be an even better choice.

*hm/*m), and some dialects exhibit a redundant tripartite tonal system just as in Southern Thai: HIGH vs. MID1/MID2 vs. LOW. If this is the old pattern in Lao, an explanation may be sought along the same lines as for Southern Thai, but there are two important differences in the overall system: (i) in Lao, the reflexes of proto-tones *A and *B have remained rigidly distinct (with no tendency to coalesce as in Southern Thai) (ii) some Lao dialects show no tone split at all with proto-tone *B (this is unattested elsewhere; Southern Thai even has a ternary split here).

Not all Lao dialects have a three-way split in words with proto-tone *A; some only exhibit the structurally more adequate two-way distinction. There is significant variation across dialects with respect to the placement of the cleavage: some separate off the HIGH category and have the grouping HIGH versus MID1/MID2/LOW with proto-tone *A, while others separate off the LOW category and have the tonal grouping HIGH/MID1/MID2 versus LOW.

The Phu Thai dialect, which Brown (1965: 67–8) considers a side-branch of Lao, is particularly interesting in that, unlike most Thai dialects, it has an almost perfect tonal bifurcation between HIGH/MID1/MID2 and LOW, and between these only, within all prosodic categories of proto-Thai, including proto-tone *A (the only aberration is in long checked syllables, which have no tonal contrast whatsoever, consider the chart in Brown 1965: 88). Phu Thai thus provides an almost prototypical case of consistent tone split *between plain voiced stops and all other stops*.

The dialect–geographic situation of Lao looks somewhat messy but makes sense from a functional perspective. In Lao, as in Southern Thai but unlike in Shan and Northern Thai, the tonal behaviour of the MID consonants is unimportant since they do not partake in any coalescences whatsoever. Thus they can go with either HIGH or LOW in terms of tone, or they may take their own course, as in Southern Thai, if they form a cognitively salient category. In Lao, we may conclude, the non-uniqueness with respect to tonal categorization can be seen as provoked by the pattern of consonant coalescences; it need not be the reflex of an earlier tripartition.

That Lao, unlike Southern Thai, exhibits geographical variation between basically different tone systems may of course have internal causes which have not been discovered so far, but it may certainly have external causes: by its geographical location, Lao would be rather prone to external influence and to variation caused by language contact. The Khorat dialect of Northeastern Thailand is very obviously the product of language contact between Central Thai and Lao, and there is also a contact area between Northern Thai and Northeastern Thai or Lao. If we look at the placement of the proto-tone *A split, some Lao dialects side with Phu Thai, others with (Eastern) Central Thai (see below), and still others combine the features of both.

12.7.5. Central Thai

Here we find the same segmental results of consonant mutations as in Southern Thai and Lao, i.e. coalescence HIGH/LOW (*ph/*b, *hm/*m). The tonal cleavage with proto-tone *A is in most of Central Thai (including Bangkok) binary and between HIGH and MID1/MID2/LOW. Tingsabadh (1985) has, however, found a difference in tonal pattern between an eastern variety of Central Thai, with the pattern stated above, and a western variety in which there is a tonal cleavage in proto-tone *A between MID2 and LOW. Brown (1965: 85, chart 13) graphically displays a ternary split HIGH versus MID versus LOW in the 'U Thong' dialect of Suphanburi northwest of Bangkok.

It is interesting that as soon as we leave proto-tone *A and look at the other prosodic categories: proto-tones *B and *C as well as long and short checked syllables, Central Thai looks extremely regular, with the same binary tonal cleavage as Phu Thai, i.e. between HIG/MID1/MID2 and LOW.

All of this makes the Central Thai tone scenario resemble that of the genetically and geographically close dialects to the east and northeast, and although Central Thai is more homogeneous than Lao (which may have to do with political history), there are the same problems of phonological development to be tackled.

If we look across the prosodic categories of Proto-Thai, we note one peculiar feature of the tonal pattern of Central Thai viz. that the structural type IV (LOW initials) with proto-tone *B has coalesced with the structural types I/II/III (HIGH/MID1/MID2 initials) with proto-tone *C. This causes extensive homonymy, e.g. in such word pairs as */naa,B/ (a bound stem occurring before verbs) and */hnaa,C/ 'face', which are now pronounced alike with voiced initial /n/ and a falling tone (also cf. the previously quoted example */dii,B/ 'place', */thaa,C/ 'if', which are now phonologically analogous, both having aspirated voiceless initial /th/ and a falling tone).

The Khorat dialect (mentioned under Lao above) which has both Lao and Central Thai features, also has such coalescences between proto-tones *B and *C but not across consonant categories: there is tonal coalescence among *B and *C words with HIGH initials, and similarly among *B and *C words with LOW initials. Homonymy caused by coalescence among proto-tones is otherwise a feature which is typical of Southern Thai; there it occurs between proto-tones *A and *B.

The general impression is that both Central Thai and Lao exhibit more or less strange complications which make them look transitional, with respect to the typology of their tonal development, between the more straightforward northern and southern Thai dialects.

12.8. CONCLUSION

In the bulk of this paper it has been demonstrated that, by and large, the tone splits occurring in the various dialects have very direct and specific relations to the changes which the consonant systems underwent along with the splitting of tones. Dialect-specific consonant coalescences have been crucial for the particular outcome of tone splitting in each particular dialect. Most dialects have accomplished the maintenance of distinctness among categories in terms of a two-way split (bifurcating dialects), others have for various reasons acquired a redundant three-way split (trifurcating dialects), or they vacillate between the two options.

It is interesting that two of the dialect groups are both geographically and typologically extreme. One dialect group is Shan + Northern Thai with a two-way (peripherally a three-way) tone split and good preservation of the phonologically-defined word categories of Proto-Thai. These dialects exhibit a 'reversal' of the tones in relation to the pattern that would be expected if tones were direct reflexes of pitch perturbation, since the tone starts on a relatively low level after */ph/, */hm/, etc. and on a relatively high level after */b/, */m/, etc. The other dialect group comprises only Southern Thai; the general profile here is: three-way tone split, no 'reversal' of the tones, some coalscence between proto-tones.

The dialects in between—Lao + Northeastern Thai and Central Thai—share typological features with both one and the other extreme: the tone contours are more similar to the 'reversed' ones of the north but there are tendencies to a three-way tone split and some coalescence between proto-tones.

This overall scenario could in theory arise both as the reflex of a common ternary tone split in late Proto-Thai followed by dialect-specific simplifications of an over-complex system, or as the reflex of dialect-specific tonal splits.

The question, then, boils down to the following: is it plausible that a redundant and overloaded tone system would arise, only to collapse very soon to a greater or lesser degree? Or is it plausible that each dialect tended to develop a functionally adequate tone system, although redundant solutions (= ternary splits) have popped up repeatedly in various places? The present paper has advocated the latter assumption.

It should be kept in mind that, contrary to the impression one may get from Brown's (1965, 1975) impressive analysis, it is the two-way split, *not* the three-way split, that would be expected if tones compensate for loss of segmental contrasts. The really tricky thing is to explain why any Thai dialect ever acquired ternary tonal splits.

These issues have been approached here without much reference to phonetic properties of the pitch contours found in the modern dialects. It is the inventory of phonological tones and the distribution of these tones on words with the different old initials (HIGH, MID1, MID2, LOW) that form the directly relevant input to structural and functional hypotheses about processes which took place many centuries ago.

The process of tone split was discussed above with special reference to proto-tone *A. It becomes more complex if one also looks at syllables with proto-tones *B and *C, and at stopped ('dead') syllables. There has been a rich variety of developments because the new tonal distinctions were added to an already complex system. Originally, the proto-tones probably differed not only in pitch but also (maybe even primarily) in *phonation type*[17] which may have played a central role in the phonetic development of the later tones resulting from tone split; moreover, the tonal system was affected by other structural properties of syllables as well: quantity, and types of syllable codas.

As for the phonetics of tonal diachrony, it seems that, contrary to Brown (1965), there is no compelling evidence for the assumption that the dialectal variation over different tonal contours reflects allotonic variation occurring already in a common proto-language. The vexing

---

[17] Cf. note 3 above.

variation between the tone systems of different dialects such that some (unexpectedly) have a higher tone after LOW consonants than after HIGH consonants, others not (cf. Brown 1975) may be due to later reshapings and 'reshufflings' of the tones within the different clusters of dialects. The tonal development may have involved such processes as increased or diminished pitch inflection (one might speak of tonal 'diphthongization' and 'monophthongization'), as well as changes in pitch levels due to push-effects within the tone system.[18]

This amounts to saying that the tonal incompatibility between dialects with and without 'reversed' tones reflects two different structural scenarios: the dialect grouping has a long phonological history but the paradoxical apparent reversal of pitch contours may well have a shorter phonetic history. It need not be the result of competing phonetic processes operating in a Big Bang phase of Proto-Thai tone split.

---

[18] The diachrony of pitch contours within the tone systems of Thai dialects is a topic which occupies a rather prominent position in recent literature; it is not approached further in the present paper, however.

Part III

Speech Sounds in History
and Culture

13

A Note on Diachronic Data, Universals, and Research Strategies[1]

In recent years there has been a growing interest in the formulation of universal phonological tendencies or 'laws', and in the application of such universals to synchronic and diachronic research on specific languages. The term 'universal' is used in a variety of senses and often rather loosely. It may have an empirical content or an axiomatic status. It may represent a claim about some absolute condition on language(s), or a claim about what is normal and expected. Strictly speaking, the term 'universal' makes sense in the latter context only if one posits a principled and truly universal *preference* for certain features of structure or processes, not just a high frequency of occurrence. One may further consider it an important task to explain *why* there is such a universal preference.

The establishment and use of universals may be essentially immanent. This does allow interesting claims (e.g. about implicational universals), and interesting applications (e.g. typological considerations in linguistic reconstruction). But to reach a truly explanatory level, and hence a much greater predictive power, one must transcend the boundaries of immanent approaches. Depending on the state of the art this may take place on the theoretical side, as when phonetic theory is adduced to define what is 'natural', or it may take place on the input side, with the combined use of various kinds of substantive evidence.

As for phonological processes, the most promising aspect of linguistics today is the increased interest in direct observation of the *dynamics* of language use in speech communities and individuals: study of

[1] Reprinted from *Phonologica 1980*, Akten der Vierten Internationalen Phonologie-Tagung, Wien, 29 June–2 July 1980, ed. W.U. Dressler, O.E. Pfeiffer, and J.R. Rennison, Innsbruck: Institut für Sprachwissenschaft der Universität Innsbruck, 198: 365–71. (=Innsbrucker Beiträge zur Sprachwissenschaft 36).

ongoing sound change, loanword adaptation, language acquisition, reduction phenomena, etc. Unfortunately, there is so far only a limited body of solid knowledge in these areas, and research on universals will tend to be dominated by the traditional types of evidence, viz. static descriptions of linguistic structures, and reconstructions of events in the history of languages (see, e.g., Ferguson 1978). In such a framework it seems obvious that *change* in the diachronic sense stands out as more direct evidence for types of phonological processes than does synchronic *alternation*, or allophonic variation.

Diachronic findings are, however, not all that easy to use as 'raw data'. First, much of the inherited body of knowledge was established in the framework of nineteenth-century phonetic theory and a specific conception of linguistic change, and there is a danger of both circularity and a lack of real progress if today's theory formation is based on constructs reflecting the typological experiences and assumptions of the nineteenth century. Secondly, many of the data on thoroughly-studied languages appear to be too complex to allow sweeping generalizations. And thirdly, case histories from 'remote' languages are, on the contrary, often over-simplified and, moreover, they are likely to be lacking in area linguistic, sociolinguistic, and cultural historical information which might perhaps have been suggestive of a different analysis of the data under consideration.

One should be perpetually on one's guard against the misconception that, unlike synchronic phonological statements, diachronic ones constitute indisputable substantive evidence by the very virtue of being statements about change. Diachronic data often rely on very strong assumptions about past stages of languages, and the conjectures implied are often so strong that it is a dubious undertaking to base generalizations and hence general assumptions about the nature of phonological processes on such data. In one sense diachronic data are more important for general phonological theory than synchronic descriptive data, namely in the sense that they help to reveal *tendencies* more directly. But on the other hand the burden of proof must be heavier in the case of diachronic data.

There is a gap between making a *typology of sound correspondences* and a *typology of sound change*. It would be highly desirable to have a typology of the latter kind, but what one does get tends to be of the former kind, unless all the data happen to be drawn from languages whose history is recorded in full, minute detail. It goes without saying that this is seldom the case. Apparently straightforward instances of sound change, which seem to support, or be explicable in terms of, certain universal tendencies, may turn out differently on closer inspection of the complex setting. In fact, the most well-documented cases generally turn out to be difficult to deal with. It may be that it is possible to identify too many details and too many factors which are relevant to a true description of the events. Or it may be that the available accounts (even the most authoritative ones) involve too much speculation, perhaps making up for a scarcity of real diachronic information.

A case in point is weakening of stops to fricatives in Danish. It has been repeatedly observed that there tends to be a preference for weakening of back consonants rather than consonants with an anterior articulation (cf. Foley 1977), and one piece of evidence cited is the weakening of Danish *ptk* via *bdg* to something represented in modern Standard Danish as a labial stop [b] and two spirants [ð ɣ]. Now, there seems to be no doubt that there *is* a general preference for weakening of back rather than anterior lenes. Danish, being attested throughout all periods, from before weakening took place to the present time, would then seem excellent evidence in point. However, there is first a general reservation having to do with the relationship between written records and their phonetic interpretation: due to orthographical inertia and so on it is somewhat difficult to know for sure *when* things happened. There is another general problem, and that is the question of scribal practice versus dialect mixture. To what extent can we infer from scribal practices at different times what actually happened? In the case of Danish we are in a sense really well-off, since the sources are rather rich and have been extremely thoroughly investigated precisely for the purpose of determining to what extent one can draw conclusions about the provenance of the manuscripts on the basis of dialect features, and conversely, draw conclusions about the phonetics of the dialects at earlier times from the written records. In fact, two of the leading authorities on early Danish differ enormously in their dating of consonant weakening in Danish. Brøndum-Nielsen (1932, §300) assumes that the weakening chain p > b > w in Zealand Danish (which was a prestige dialect) took place in the time span from approximately 1300 to about 1450, and hence that pronunciations with [β] from /p/ occurred intervocalically around 1400 (*gribæ* etc.). Skautrup (1944, §30), emphasizing the inertia of scribal practice, assumes that the first step of weakenings like p > b > β occurred in the twelfth century, and the last step in the thirteenth century. This is to some extent a matter of how one conceives of the change: as *gradual* or *abrupt* in time, and with respect to diffusion across the lexicon and across dialects. It is also somewhat controversial *in what order* the three consonants were weakened. In any case the philological evidence is extremely complex.

Now, I suppose we are in an immensely worse position in many other instances of interesting sound changes which one wishes to include in the general repertory for the purpose of studies of universals.

To substantiate these general negative remarks about the use of weakening in Danish as evidence for universal preferences, I wish to point to the fact that there is direct evidence that the contemporary Danish skewed series b ð ɣ does not in a very straightforward way reflect a resistance of *b* to weakening. It may reflect a *restitution* of the stop. Medieval Danish manuscripts give indisputable evidence of weakening of *b* to a continuant (and eventually to a glide). This is still a normal feature of Danish dialects, and indeed of colloquial standard pronunciation of some of the words with intervocalic spelled 'b' from early Danish *p*, such as 'æble', colloquially [ɛwlə], or 'købe', colloquially [køwː]. As I see it, it remains an open question *how* the stop [b] came to be dominant in the spoken norm of educated Danish.[2] Several factors are possible. (i) The stop may have been restituted more or less across the lexicon under the influence of an archaic type of orthography. (ii) A genuinely phonetic process of strengthening—if strengthening in weak position is indeed natural at all, which I tend to doubt—may also have applied, that is, first b > β and then β > b again. Finally, (iii) we know that although most dialects had weakening of lenited stops to fricatives, some of the easternmost Danish dialects of what is now southern Sweden did *not* weaken, at least not generally, according to orthographical evidence. Since the easternmost dialects seem to have competed in contributing to the scribal norm, which became significant for the later development of standard Danish, the

---

[2] Haugen (1976: 205) just states that 'in standard Da[nish] the spelling has mostly retained the voiced stops (which are now voiceless lenes) and has even restored the stop pronunciation of *b*.' Hansen (1971) gives a detailed and more complex account, but also speaks of a secondary development of a stop. This is even attested in the case of loanwords from Low German, e.g. LG *streven* to Danish *stræve* and later to Standard Danish *stræbe* (Hansen 1971: 183). Hansen supposes that this is hardly due to High German influence but rather due to a standardization of the norm (the dismissal of the possible influence from High German does not seem compelling, however).

ultimate result may be a conglomerate due to such competition. (If *b* differs from *d* and *g* it *need* not have to do with resistance to weakening, however; to mention a possible systemic cause, it may also reflect an asymmetry in the orthographical system.) It is known that in the late eighteenth century both types of pronunciations—[b] and [w] for etymological -*p*—existed; those with a continuant were typical colloquialisms (Skautrup 1947, §69), and those with the stop were more educated. From about 1800 the orthography is remarkably stable, settling largely on *b* like the prevalent standard pronunciation.

So much for an example of the philologist's appraisal of the diachronic events in a complex sociolinguistic setting which tends to be invisible in studies on universals. Let us turn finally to a seemingly very clear-cut case where there seems to be overwhelming intra-linguistic evidence for positing a particular process. I presume that it is well-known that Greenlandic Eskimo has short voiced fricatives /v ɣ ʁ/ and a lateral or flap /l/, which patterns like the fricatives; and that the language has phonemically long fricatives (still including the lateral), which are phonetically voiceless. Synchronically this is suggestive of an allophonic rule devoicing long obstruents, and diachronically it seems even more convincing that such a process can be posited, since the dialects of Alaska and Canada have long *voiced* rather than voiceless counterparts, and there is every reason to consider the Greenlandic situation *secondary* to that of the dialects to their west. This all seems very obvious and trivial, and hence Greenlandic Eskimo ranges as a nice case for exemplification of a universal tendency to devoice long obstruents. I would not hesitate either to call this a phonetically *natural* tendency. However, the situation I just described is confined to the 'central' area of Greenland, that is, the most densely populated and first colonized part. Peripheral dialects, which have been rather neglected until recently, have long stops instead of voiceless fricatives: the uvulars and velars have straightforward counterparts (/qː kː/ for /χː xː/); the counterpart of the voiceless lateral is a dental or retroflex stop depending on the dialect; and finally the counterpart of the voiceless labial fricative /fː/ is a labial stop /pː/ or, in one dialect, a dorsal stop /kː/ or /qː/ (obviously reflecting former labiovelar articulation).[3]

---

[3] The dialect survey at the end of Petersen (1969/70) shows the distribution of the stop and fricative reflexes.

Since essentially all other Eskimo dialects have voiced continuants in the cases I am talking about, it does seem a strange coincidence that Greenland deviates in two seemingly unrelated ways: (i) by devoicing and (ii) by strengthening. I should very much like to see these as the end results of one starting process. One possible candidate is the type of differentiation known as 'segmentalization' which has taken place widely in western Scandinavian, where in some areas long [l:] has become [dl] and, in a very restricted area of Norway, even became a long stop [d:]. If we assume such an overall differentiation for long fricatives and lateral consonants in *Greenlandic*, the dialect split is reflected in the fact that after differentiation of the long continuants one set of dialects developed stops by progressive assimilation (largely as with l: > dl > d: in West Norwegian), whereas the other (main) dialect area devoiced and regressively assimilated these stop plus continuant sequences. A reasonable account is achieved if we assume that the next step after segmentalization was a desonorization of the syllable final stop, so that the peripheral dialects took the course

$$l: > dl > tl > t:$$

whereas the main dialect area differed in the development following the third step

$$l: > dl > tl > t\ɬ > ɬ:$$

and similarly for other consonants.

This looks like pure speculation, but it does score higher than the explanation in terms of a spontaneous devoicing of long obstruents, which is phonetically rather unconvincing for the lateral /l/ (long /l:/ is clearly a sonorant in other Eskimo dialects); although devoicing would a priori seem plausible enough for the true fricatives. The main point is that the explanation in terms of segmentalization unites all Greenlandic dialects in an appealing fashion, which the assumption of spontaneous devoicing does not.

Now, what does one do with such alternative solutions in research on diachronic language universals? I do not know; I am just wondering how we can be sure to be cautious enough. It is of course crucial to have a convergence of independent evidence.—In the case of Greenlandic there happens to be philological evidence *in favour* of my solution, since the earliest sources write 'l' or 'll' for the now voiceless long lateral;[4] then later on a seemingly clumsy spelling 'dl' turns up, a spelling which persisted until 1973 as a symbol for the voiceless lateral, but which I think originated as a faithful rendering of actual sounds, although it has not generally been seen in this light. To me this suggests that the long lateral was voiced as late as the eighteenth century, then it was differentiated into stop plus continuant, and eventually devoiced and assimilated. For the true fricatives the old spellings are rather suggestive of stop pronunciations, but the spellings are at any rate strongly at variance with the present voiceless pronunciation. To give one example, the present sound [f:] is written 'b' or 'gv' in early sources. Maybe the segmentalization was earlier with the true fricatives than with the lateral (which patterns with the fricatives, but which may have had more sonorous realizations than other members of this set). It is probably impossible, however, to decide whether spellings such as 'ibbiak' or 'igviak' for what is now [if:iaq], [ip:iaq], or [ik:iaq] depending on the dialect, reflect voiced continuants in the earliest sources, or whether an occlusive component had already developed when such spellings were first used.[5] There is no reason why segmentalization in such cases should be reflected in spelling, since the letters involved are already suggestive of stop pronunciation (in Danish orthography 'g' represented both a stop and a continuant, and as mentioned above there was much vacillation between [b] and [w] intervocalically in Danish, so the use of 'b' for something like [β:] cannot be excluded).

Thus it seems that on the basis of internal Greenlandic evidence, paired with the knowledge that the long intervocalic consonants in question were at one time voiced continuants, one can present a reasonably strong case for a unified explanation of the reflexes in all Greenlandic dialects as resulting from segmentalization.

Now, it is interesting that such segmentalization actually occurs in some eastern Canadian dialects. Since these Inuktitut dialects have only been studied to a very limited extent until quite recently, and then mostly with a focus on matters relevant to the preparation of dictionaries and the development of a unified Canadian orthography, there is

---

[4] Eighteenth-century Greenlandic moreover had a contrast between the long /l:/ and a variety of clusters consisting of stop plus lateral. All of these merged into the voiceless lateral of contemporary West Greenlandic.

[5] The spellings 'b(b)' and 'gv' are not on a par, since the latter, reflecting southernmost West Greenlandic, turns up in writings by the scholar Otho Fabricius towards the end of the eighteenth century, whereas the earliest sources reflect Central West Greenlandic. The question concerning the phonetic interpretation is basically the same, however.

little information available so far on the phonetic details of these dialects. However, in the last few years extensive research has been done on the phonology of eastern Inuktitut, and it is likely that the results of this research will eventually force us to see various phenomena in Greenlandic in a new light. One such phenomenon is the behaviour of old long continuants. According to an unpublished dialect survey by L.-J. Dorais (Dorais, ms.)[6] there are dialects which have variant realizations such as [bv] and [vv] (or, in a dialect with glottalization: ['v]) in cases where West Greenlandic has [fː]. The picture is less neat for the other places of articulation, but here, too, we find realizations with either a mixed cluster (containing a stop component) or a long or glottalized stop consonant. It is also important in this context to study the assimilatory phenomena in Polar Eskimo (cf. Holtved 1951, I: 25).

Although the implications of the Canadian and Polar Eskimo material are not entirely straightforward, these data certainly add to the evidence for positing a diachronic process of segmentalization which has affected both West and East Greenlandic.

Altogether, there seem to be good reasons for seriously questioning the existence of a diachronic process of devoicing of long obstruents in Greenlandic, and hence this alleged process should not be adduced as evidence for universal tendencies.

I do not wish to conclude from these observations that one should be in the least deterred from doing research on diachronic universals. It is extremely important to gather extensive information on preferred types of change, but it is imperative that a very careful distinction be made between changes whose course is beyond any reasonable doubt, and cases which allow for different plausible interpretations. It may be tempting to underrate the complexity of the history of less well-documented languages, or to make changes look more transparent or general than they really are. One must assess the validity of reconstructed data as against philologically well-attested data, and one must determine whether data of the latter kind are phonologically unambiguous (which in fact is often difficult to decide). To make successful typologies and successful studies of universals one must, of course, avoid circularity in the sense of forcing data into already established categories and forcing phenomena to comply with already established

---

[6] Editors' note: According to a personal communication with L.-J. Dorais the manuscript appeared as an appendix to his doctoral dissertation 'La structure du vocabulaire moderne de la langue esquimaude du Québec-Labrador', defended in 1972 at Université Paris-III, France.

generalizations, and then afterwards using the same data to support the general claims. But how can that be avoided in the current state of research?

Last but certainly not least, I think it is important that research on language typology and language universals eventually attain such a high degree of reliability that it can become quite generally recognized as important for comparative philology, instead of perhaps nourishing a deep-rooted scepticism on the part of some philologists towards the utility of general linguistics. Maybe the answer to most of these questions lies in emphasizing first and foremost the study of directly observable, ongoing sound change in all, and indeed all, of its complexity.

14

Phoneme, Grapheme, and the 'Importance' of Distinctions. Functional Aspects of the Scandinavian Runic Reform[1]

14.1. THE GENERAL PICTURE OF THE CHANGE IN RUNIC WRITING

The Scandinavian runic inscriptions dating from before 700 AD are nearly all written in a graphic system comprising 21 to 24 runes (originally and when presented as an alphabet or 'futhark' it comprised 24 runes (see Fig. 14.1), but some of these, notably the **p** and the **k**, fell out of use rather early).

Figure 14.1 shows only some typical occurrences of the graphemes. The graphical variation is very great, and especially the **j** and the **ŋ**, may not be sufficiently representative as they stand.

ᚠ	ᚢ	ᚦ	ᚨ	ᚱ	< or ᚲ	ᚷ	ᚹ	ᚺ	ᚾ or ᚺ	ᛁ	ᛇ	ᛃ	ᛈ	ᛉ	ᛊ	ᛏ	ᛒ	ᛖ	ᛗ	ᛚ	ᛜ	ᛗ	ᛟ
f	u	þ	a	r	k	g	w	h	n	i	j	E	p	R	s	t	b	e	m	l	ŋ	d	o

Figure 14.1

The orthographic tradition of that period (roughly 200–700 AD) is remarkably stable. There is a good deal of variation in the shape of each rune; Figure 14.1 only presents some typical shapes, and it must be added to the presentation given here that some of the runes occur in mirror image forms (as shown for the **n**), and some may be turned

---

[1] Reprinted from Interim Report No. 1, Research Group for Quantitative Linguistics, Stockholm, 1966: 1–21.

ᚠ	ᚢ	ᚦ	ᚬ	ᚱ	ᚴ	ᚼ	ᚾ	ᛁ	ᛅ	ᛋ	ᛏ	ᛒ	ᛚ	Y or Ψ	ᛦ
f	u	þ	ą	r	k	h	n	i	a	s	t	b	l	m	R

Figure 14.2

upside down. (It is worth noticing that the shapes of the runes are such that no confusion of units is caused if they are looked at from different angles or read backwards.) The system as such, however, is quite rigid.

Then in the eighth century a rapid change of the system is apparent in a few Norwegian and (shortly afterwards) Danish inscriptions. About 850–900 a new orthography has settled definitely in what seems its ideal form. This new system comprises only sixteen runes; some of the old characters were abandoned, others were kept but associated with new phonic entities, and finally some were modified in shape but otherwise retained as before. Figure 14.2 gives a survey of these sixteen runes in their basic manifestations.

Figure 14.2 shows the so-called 'Danish' runes. A variety of the same system, the 'Swedish(-Norwegian)' runes, was soon developed, and we later find a certain interaction among these and a development of further varieties (not to mention the drastically simplified characters known as 'Hälsinge'-runes). In spite of minor changes in the sound values of the individual runes, we may speak of a general system behind these varieties: the number of runes and the general principles of sound representation are the same.

In the following centuries the 16-character system is gradually elaborated by the addition of diacritics to some of the runes and other modifications, so that in the thirteenth and fourteenth centuries the runic orthography came to surpass the Latin alphabet in sound-distinguishing capability.

What has been presented briefly above (in a very rough summary, of course) is just what can be observed on the runic stones from the different periods. As soon as we get to the formation of theories about what underlies the changes, we find a good deal of controversy among scholars. The classic conception of the change is that it is a gradual development and certainly not a deliberate reform made at a definite time. It is, however, hard to find a satisfactory explanation of a gradual change from the older to the younger runic writing. It has been suggested that there was a cultural decline at the time of transition, and that the runes were at that time mostly used for magic purposes: see von Friesen (1928). These explanations imply that the change is a degeneration or corruption of the writing system.

There are, on the other hand, several features of the change which make it attractive to think of it as at least guided by meaningful principles if not carried out once and for all as a deliberate reform, and we may find some hints in this direction in recent literature on the subject,[2] although an elaborate hypothesis has not been, and can hardly be, set up.

It is immediately apparent from the two 'futharks' given in Figures 14.1 and 14.2 that the younger one avoids characters which do not have one full-size vertical line (the **s** is a special case), probably in order to facilitate writing. The **o** for example, is abandoned, and the **m** is changed by manipulation of its two halves in such a way that one vertical line is established instead of two. This is a very important graphic change, and it is especially important to note that it conditions the exclusion of some runes from the 'futhark' (the **o** and the **g** could hardly be made to conform to the new graphic principle, and the **e** could hardly be manipulated like the **m** without coalescing with some other character).

Still another factor of relevance to the whole process is the change of some of the names of the runes in accordance with the sound-laws. Here again, the **e** is affected (the name changing from initial *e* to initial *j*), and the same is true of the old **j** (the name of which changes from initial *j* to initial *a*, after which it is used to represent the latter sound, whereas the old **a** gets initial nasalized *a* and is used to represent this particular sound quality). It is also assumed that the name of the **w** dropped its initial *w* (in *wun- > *yn-) at that time, but the cause for dropping this rune from the 'futhark' seems less evident than for the others.

And last, but certainly not least, the change may be conditioned directly by sound-changes upsetting the one-to-one correspondence between phonemes and graphemes. Towards the end of the Iron Age

---

[2] The most attractive formulation, in my opinion, is Bæksted's (1943: 47): 'Det ser ud til, at denne nyskabelse er begyndt som en naturlig udvikling, men at en stabilisering saa er fastsat efter et nøje gennemtænkt system. Man maa engang i det ottende aarhundrede paa en eller anden maade ligefrem have besluttet, at fra nu af skulle runerækken være saaledes.'

we find what Sigurd (1961) calls the 'code shift': a phonemicization of umlaut vowels and a reduction and partial dropping of the vowels in unstressed syllables, in addition to a drastic rearrangement of the obstruent system and certain other modifications. Most of these changes must have taken place by the end of the seventh century, if not earlier, and one should not underrate their impact on the orthographic tradition.

At present it is probably not possible to single out one decisive factor leading to the reformation of the runic writing at the end of the Iron Age. There is no reason to deny that it may be due to an interplay between two or several equally important factors. We may safely postulate, however, that the change is not haphazard. There is a good deal of organization in the change, although the inner logic of it may not be immediately apparent. After the transition to the new system was accomplished, this was used with remarkable consistency and stability for a couple of centuries (before the next period of change in which the graphic system was gradually extended by the addition of diacritics).

It is the purpose of this paper to test rather briefly to what extent we can interpret the changes in runic writing as reflections of changes in the sound pattern, and to formulate the findings in structural terms. As this is a report emphasizing the general aspects of the problem, references to the vast literature on runology have been restricted to those that are most directly relevant to structural considerations.

Phonological (phonemic) principles have been applied to this field of study before, notably by Trnka (1938), and Diderichsen (1945), although no comprehensive analysis has been undertaken. Most runologists probably look upon this kind of approach without too much enthusiasm, and it is to be emphasized that the phonological notions of phonemicization, neutralization, etc. only help to illuminate the phenomena from one angle. We are faced with a problem of considerable complexity, and we must not overestimate the explanatory power of structural statements. In applying the analytic techniques of modern linguistics, it is also essential not to define these too narrowly. 'Morphophonemics' is, in my opinion, just as relevant to the problem as 'phonemics' or 'phonology', and considerations of the systemic features of language are of restricted application if not supplemented by data of a statistical kind.

14.2. SURVEY OF PHONEMIC DISTINCTIONS NOT EXPRESSED IN RUNIC WRITING

It is a basic characteristic of both the older and the younger runic systems that *quantity* was not expressed, neither in vowels nor in consonants. Long vowels and consonants were rendered as single elements, and we also find certain clusters (sequences of non-identical phonemes) represented in this way. This is true of the cluster type *nasal plus homorganic obstruent (stop or fricative)*: inscriptions using the younger runes almost invariably represent /mb/ by the **b**, /nd/ by the **t**, etc., and this usage also occurs in older inscriptions. In inscriptions using the older runes *diphthongs* are sometimes represented by the rune for their first member (the **a** for /au/ or /ai/), although this does not seem to be generally recognized as something that was allowed by the norm of the old runic system. On the other hand we often find nondistinctive, connective vowels reflected in writing in inscriptions using the older system (these two contrasting features of under- and over-representation of vowels are illustrated by the attested word form **herAmAlAsAR**,[3] presumably /hermalaus(a)R/).

Prosodic features of all kinds were bypassed in runic writing. Words may or may not be separated in the inscriptions.

Except for these points, the early Proto-Scandinavian inscriptions in the older 'futhark' exhibit a nearly phonemic orthography. This close connection between spoken and written language was broken by the sound-shifts that took place in the sixth and seventh centuries and which completely altered the phonemic structure of the words. The introduction of the younger 'futhark' and the spelling rules associated with it restored the congruity between speech and writing, although so to say on a higher level of abstraction. In the new system each rune stands for a class of phonemes, but the interesting thing is that these classes are *intrinsic* (structurally motivated) categories of the spoken language, and that they are not (or are only sporadically) intersecting. There is a unique one-way relation between speech and writing: given a spoken form of a word one can determine from its sound structure how it must be written, but not the other way round. As compared to the old system, the new one is under-differentiating on three points: (i) syllabic and nonsyllabic functions are not distinguished (/i/ and /j/, /u/ and /w/ are written alike); (ii) the number of graphemes used to

---

[3] Stentoften stone, Blekinge (dating uncertain).

represent vowels amounts to only one-third of the number of vowel phonemes; (iii) no distinction is made between /p/ and /b/, /t/ and /d/, /k/ and /g/.

The non-uniqueness (of writing-into-speech conversion) caused by these graphic coalescences is formidable. To take one example, the **k**, when occurring after a vowel rune, may stand for /k, kk, nk, ɣ (fricative g), gg, ng/, and a following **u** may stand for /w, y, ȳ, ø, ȫ, u, ū, o, ō/. The decipherment of fragmentary inscriptions is certainly no easy task. (From this point of view it is fortunate that most of the runic material preserved to our time is characterized by stereotype phrases, so that runology can profit from extremely high or low probabilities associated with the various interpretations of a rune in a given context.)

In the following we shall consider the graphic coalescences mentioned above under the three separate headings.

14.3. SYLLABIC AND NONSYLLABIC FUNCTION

The graphic coalescence of /i–j/ and /u–w/ in the younger 'futhark' is not surprising. The lack of a graphic distinction between syllabic and nonsyllabic function is well known from Latin, and it may be argued that this is not at all a distinction between phonemes but rather between positions in the syllable. This probably applies to the same extent to the language of the older 'futhark' (referred to as Proto-Scandinavian) and to the language of the younger (hereafter called Old Scandinavian); so we can hardly say that the orthographic reform is in this case provoked by changes in the phonemic pattern. Nevertheless, it may be entirely due to sound shifts. As for /i–j/, the peculiar thing is that word-initial /j/ in Proto-Scandinavian has no genetic relation to word-initial /j/ in Old Scandinavian (there are a few exceptions: words which retained old initial /j/, but these count very little as against the numerous words with secondary /j/): the former was lost, but a new /j/ was developed from vocalic units (e.g. /ja/ from /e/, /jū/ from /iu/), so that the phonemic pattern eventually became the same. The name of the **j** (*jāra*) was affected by the loss of initial /j/, so there would hardly be any motivation left for adopting this runic symbol for the newly developed /j/ (quite naturally, the rune came to be used for /a/ instead).

As for /u–w/ the case is less clear, since word-initial /w/ was retained except before rounded vowels. The adoption of the **u** for /w/ (later /v/) may have been supported by the structural parallelism between

/i–j/ and /u–w/, but one is not surprised to find traces of a vacillation between the **w** and the **u** in the centuries of transition.[4]

14.4.   THE VOWEL SYSTEM

Proto-Scandinavian probably had five vowel phonemes (long and short): /a, e, i, o, u/. In the older 'futhark' there is one rune for each of these. It is reasonable to assume that the vowels exhibited three degrees of opening (tongue-height): 1. /i, u/; 2. /e, o/; 3. /a/; and it is evident that /i, e/ differed from /u, o/ with respect to lip-rounding. Each of the vowels must (at any rate in late Proto-Scandinavian) have had a considerable latitude of (contextually conditioned) variation, to judge from the excessive number of vowel phonemes in Old Scandinavian, which must be explained by 'phonemicization' of bound variants. The phonetic and phonemic processes involved cannot be traced with certainty, but at least these points seem rather clear:

1 /e, i/ split into /e, i/, i.e. unrounded front vowels, and /ø, y/, i.e. a set of vowels which are preserved in the Scandinavian languages as rounded front vowels (phonemically identical with /ø, y/ of item (2) below), although they may in the beginning have had a different articulation (retracted rather than rounded?). The latter /ø, y/ were conditioned by the occurrence of /w/ in the following consonant cluster, and the development /e, i/ → /ø, y/ is thus a phenomenon of rather limited distribution compared to the umlaut-changes listed below.
2 /o, u/ split into /o, u/, i.e. rounded back vowels, and /ø, y/, i.e. rounded front vowels. The latter, /ø, y/, were conditioned by /j/ in the following consonant cluster or /i/ in the following syllable (although the umlaut of /o, u/ to /ø, y/ did not invariably take place before /i/).
3 /a/ split into /a, æ, å/,[5] of which the latter two were probably less open (orally) than /a/; /æ/ and /å/ differed from each other in that /æ/ was a front vowel, while /å/ was not—we cannot say for sure whether there was also from the beginning a difference of lip-rounding. The vowel /æ/ was conditioned by /j/ in the following consonant cluster or /i/ in the following syllable (reservations as above); /å/ was conditioned by /w/ in the following cluster or /u/ in the following syllable; under other conditions we find /a/ as the representative of Proto-Scandinavian /a/.

---

[4] The **w** occurs among younger runes on the Sölvesborg stone, Blekinge. Marstrander (1952: 161) considers this inscription to represent the older 'futhark', although there is an obvious adaption to the orthography of younger inscriptions.

[5] Editors' note: /æ/ corresponds to IPA /ɛ/; /å/ corresponds to IPA /ɔ/.

(This presentation of the development of /a/ into /æ, å/ by umlaut does not reflect the opinion of all scholars. It is widely believed that the distinctive difference between /æ/ and /å/ was rounding rather than place of articulation, and it has also been argued that /æ/ and /a/ differed with respect to place of articulation rather than degree of opening. It is probably safest to say that the Old Norse vowel system can be tabulated in more than one way.)

The following developments are of a somewhat different kind:

4 /i, u/ were in some cases opened to /e, o/; we do not really know what the conditions were.[6] Much earlier, /e, o/ had been closed to /i, u/ before certain consonant clusters, and we thus find in the language of the younger 'futhark' a good deal of contextually conditioned (automatic) alternation between /e/ and /i/, and between /o/ and /u/.

5 /e/ (short vowel) was in most environments diphthongized into /ia, iå/ or the like; in Old Norse and later Scandinavian languages these complexes are generally considered to consist of /j/ plus a vowel (cf. Section 14.3).

It seems that at a certain time after these changes had taken place, there must have been a system of nine vowel phonemes (long or short) occurring in stressed syllables: /a, e, i, o, u, y, æ, ø, å/. (Short /e/ and /æ/ seem to have coalesced quite early.)

In unstressed syllables a vowel reduction took place, operating in the following ways:

1 short vowels were, under certain conditions, dropped;

2 long vowels were shortened, so that /ī/, for example, became identical with short /i/ (if /ī/ be rewritten as /ii/, this may perhaps be taken as a special case of (1), since the rules for syncope would not allow both vowels in a sequence to be dropped).

3 /i, u/ coalesced with /e, o/, so that only three vowels were distinguished in unstressed syllables; we may render these as /a, i, u/ or as /a, e, o/. There may, in some dialects, have been a bound variation between /i, u/ and /e, o/ (vowel harmony or balance).

One would expect these changes to be reflected in runic writing. Since the number of vowels distinguished in stressed syllables was raised to (at least) nine, it would seem the ideal solution to add four vowel symbols to the five already available in the 'futhark'. Instead we find that these are reduced to three: the runes which in Figures 14.1 and 14.2 are labeled **a**, **i**, and **u**.

---

[6] It is commonplace to speak of 'a-umlaut' assuming the opening to be caused by /a/ (preserved or lost) in the following syllable.

If we try to find an explanation for this very strange development of the graphic system, it is immediately clear that it must have been provoked by the desirability to eliminate the **e** and the **o** because of their form (lack of one vertical main axis). There is also, however, a purely linguistic reason why a status quo with five runes could not be preserved. If the nine vowel phonemes were to be distributed on five runes in such a way that these were still used with roughly the same sound values as before, one would be forced to group the vowel phonemes in a way that would violate the pattern of the language. We might imagine, for instance, that the **i** was used for /i/, the **e** for /e, æ/, the **u** for /y, u/, the **o** for /ø, o, å/, and the **a** for /a/ only (incidentally, the younger 'futhark' has separate symbols for /a/ with and without nasalization, a peculiar feature which, however, is not relevant to this problem). Such an attempt to 'broaden the values' of the runes would entail a vehement break with spelling tradition and would be absurd from a morphophonemic point of view. Morphophonemically, the phoneme splits mentioned above are not to be understood as developments of completely dissociated phonemes from one common ancestor. The phonemes /a, æ, å/, for instance, are closely related by morphophonemic alternation, and it is worth noticing that in many cases the sound factor conditioning the presence of /æ/ or /å/ rather than /a/ is preserved, so that /æ/ and /å/ may be said to function as bound variants of /a/. Thus, we can predict the automatic replacement of /a/ by /æ/ before such a suffix as /-il-/, and by /å/ before suffixes containing /u/—cf. Old Norse *ketill* (*e* for assumed earlier /æ/) 'kettle', plur. nom. *katlar*, plur. dat. *kotlum* (the 'original' vowel is seen in the plur. nom.). Similarly, /e/ is morphophonemically associated with /i/—cf. Old Norse *sitja* 'to sit', past part. *setit* with /e–i/ alternation due to /j/ infix (cf. *geta* 'beget, guess', past part. *getit* showing stem vowel identity). Using a common symbol for /e/ and /æ/ would mean a complete disregard of these relationships.[7] We may assume that a wish

---

[7] The Lister and Listerby stones from Blekinge (including Stentoften and Sölvesborg), which are written in the older 'futhark' except for Sölvesborg, and which reflect the language in a state of transition from Proto-Scandinavian to Old Scandinavian, exhibit a good deal of orthographic inconsistency which it is tempting to explain as due to interaction between the older writing system and the younger. We find here a unique example (although occurring twice in immediate succession) of the umlaut vowel /æ/ represented by the old **e**, (Andersen 1956: 9 ff). Important as the phenomenon is, it is entirely anomalous and does not prove that umlaut vowels could be *successfully* represented by the runes available in the old 'futhark'. The Norwegian Eggjum stone, (the dating of which is disputed) also uses runic characters typical of the older 'futhark', but the language is Old Norse, and the

to preserve the word (or sign) identity in writing must have been felt by those who modified the runic writing, just as they may have considered it fortunate to preserve some features of the traditional spelling. The orthography of the younger 'futhark' is typically a *morphophonemic* spelling which preserves certain traditional features whilst at the same time obeying the fundamental laws of the language in its new state.

If we group the phonemes according to their occurrence in automatic alternation (in certain types of umlaut in a broad sense), we arrive at one main group constituted by /i, e, y, ø/, another constituted by /y, ø, u, o/, and a third constituted by /æ, a, å/, i.e. a tripartite grouping corresponding to the three vowel runes of the younger system of writing. Problematic are the phonemes /y, ø/, which both morphophonemically and phonetically have some relation to /i, e/ as well as to /u, o/. They are rendered in runic inscriptions by the **u**, a choice which seems morphophonemically reasonable, since instances of /y, ø/ due to umlaut of /i, e/ are fairly restricted (the only numerous type being verb stems with *short* /ø/).[8]

If we consider the phonemic system without regard to morphophonemics, we also find a basic tripartition. This is typically demonstrated by the presence, in unstressed syllables, of a subsystem of only three vowels, which may be said to form a phonetic triangle:

i   u

a

as against the pentagonal shape of the Proto-Scandinavian system.

A closer inspection of the phonetic structure of the vowel system is best made in terms of distinctive features. Recent analyses of phoneme systems into distinctive features generally appear in the form of branching diagrams, in which the distinctive oppositions among the phonemes, e.g. 'rounded versus unrounded', 'front versus back', form a hierarchy. The idea of hierarchy implies that some items are

orthography has much in common with that of the younger inscriptions: /a/ and /æ/ are not distinguished from each other (although oral /a, æ/ and nasal /a, æ/ are distinguished; /æ/ and /e/, however, are neatly distinguished (/e/ being represented either by the old **e** or by the **i**).

[8] Forms like Old Norse *søkkva* from *sinkwan. As for the representation of /i/ and /e/ by one common rune, and similarly of /u/ and /o/ by one rune, Antonsen (1963: 196) claims that 'neither etymological considerations nor phonetic change can explain this peculiar usage'. The morphophonemic alternations between /i/ and /e/, /u/ and /o/ should, however, not be neglected.

considered prior to, or more basic than, others. One evident criterion for arranging distinctive features in a definite hierarchical order
is that one distinction may be relevant to the whole system but
another to part of the system only. Given, for instance, a vowel system
like

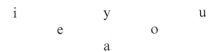

it is obvious that the feature distinguishing /y/ from /i/ or /u/ must be
hierarchically subordinate to the feature distinguishing /i/ from /u/ and
/e/ from /o/, since the latter distinction affects a greater part of the
system than the former. In many cases, however, there is no point in
trying to establish a rank order in this way. Given, for instance, the
system in question here:

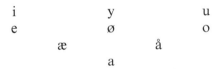

we may consider the feature that distinguishes /i, e, æ/ from /u, o, å/
to constitute a more basic division within the system than the feature
that distinguishes /y, ø/ from either of the series, but we cannot decide
immediately whether the distinction between /i, e, æ/ and /u, o, å/ is one
of 'front vs. back' or one of 'unrounded vs. rounded'. In the former
case /y, ø/ would be branched off from the front series by a second
distinction of 'unrounded /i, e, æ/ vs. rounded /y, ø/'; in the latter case
/y, ø/ would be branched off from the rounded series by a second
distinction of 'front /y, ø/ vs. back /u, o, å/'.

If we really want to examine whether some phonetic distinctions
can be said to be more *basic* to the phoneme system than others,
we must probably consider other types of criteria as well. The criterion just mentioned takes care of the distribution of a distinctive
opposition within the stock of phonemes. We have, however, typically
different subsystems in different positions: in the case under study we
assume that there is in absolutely unstressed syllables a subsystem of
three vowels as against the full system of nine. We may consider the
three unstressed vowels as 'incompletely specified' with respect to
distinctive phonetic features, i.e. we may consider the subsystem of

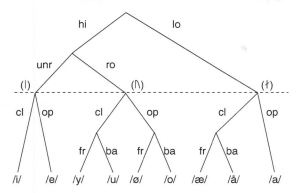

Figure 14.3

three to utilize only some of the distinctions utilized by the entire system. Everything else being equal, these distinctions must be the basic ones.

Figure 14.3 shows a branching diagram of distinctive features made according to these principles. First distinction: 'high–low'; second: 'unrounded–rounded'; third: 'close–open'; fourth: 'front–back'. It is seen that the three runes of the younger 'futhark' represent the classes resulting from the two first divisions, which agrees with the general impression that 'only the crassest oppositions were taken into consideration' (Antonsen 1963: 201).

It requires some explanation that /i, u/ of the basic /i, u, a/ system have been considered to exhibit a distinction of 'unrounded–rounded' rather than 'front–back'. Had the latter been the appropriate distinction, then we would arrive at a fourfold rather than a triangular basic system: a distinction of 'front–back' must apply to both high and low vowels, since /æ/ and /å/ undoubtedly differed in this respect.

(This argumentation may not hold water. It is extremely likely that there was a clear-cut difference of lip-rounding between /æ/ and /å/, and maybe it would be reasonable to say that 'unrounded–rounded' and 'front–back' combined into one distinctive opposition in low vowels. Anyhow, there is still a difference in hierarchical complexity between the high vowel part and the low vowel part of the system: the difference between /i, e/ and /y, u, ø, o/ remains on a higher level than that between /æ/ and /å/ and /a/, so that even with a thorough restatement of the system we may claim that this is basically 'triangular'.)

At the level indicated by the dotted line in the branching diagram it is essential for the adequacy of the model to have a distinction of just three units, and this requirement is fulfilled only by the arrangement presented in Figure 14.3.

The question of the relative *importance* of the various distinctions will be touched upon in Section 14.6 below. At the moment we may just conclude that it is possible to set up a seemingly well-motivated hierarchical model of the phonemic distinctions in such a way that the three vowel runes of the younger 'futhark' are found to reflect only the distinctions of highest rank in the phonic system. This does not suggest that the reformers of the orthography performed a distinctive feature analysis of the spoken language, but it shows that they were able to establish a basic formal agreement between the runic system and the phonic system. From the point of view of 'generative grammar' the keyword to the nature of this formal agreement is *incomplete specification*, not just something like 'rendering of phonetically neighbouring sounds by the same symbol'.[9] This is perhaps even more evident from the runic representation of obstruents, see below.

14.5.   THE OBSTRUENT SYSTEM

In Proto-Scandinavian there was a *fortis–lenis* distinction between, e.g. /x/ (later /h/) and /ɣ/. It is hardly possible to determine the exact phonetic nature of this distinction; for Proto-Germanic it has been suggested that there was a distinction between voiceless fortes [f, þ, x] and voiceless lenes [b̥ d̥ ǥ̊], cf. Baader 1938: 223–32, but in Proto-Scandinavian the distinction is normally assumed to have involved a difference of voice. In the following the terms 'fortis' and 'lenis' may be taken to mean 'voiceless' and 'voiced' without this affecting the argumentation. There was another distinction between *stop* and *fricative*, e.g. /k/ vs. /x/. These two distinctions were carried over into the Old Scandinavian language (Old Norse, etc.), but their hierarchical order was clearly reversed. In this case the purely phonological data are so obvious that it may be most informative to start with these and discuss the morphophonemic relationships later. The *sibilants* are left out of consideration in this exposition.

---

[9] As for the peculiarity of representing vowels with and without umlaut by the same symbol, it may be mentioned *en passant* that this feature occurs in early medieval manuscripts due to influence from English writing (Seip 1954: 12–13). The author of the First Grammatical Treatise explicitly refers to a claim that it is unnecessary to distinguish in writing between *u* and *y* (which he, of course, refutes).

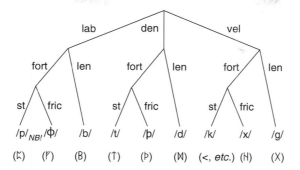

Figure 14.4

For the two distinctions in question, the fortis–lenis distinction seems to have had the higher rank in early Proto-Scandinavian. For the language of that period we may divide the whole field of obstruents (stops and fricatives) into two parts according to the opposition fortis–lenis; thus fortis [þ] and lenis [ð] belonged to two different phonemes, and we may also posit a phonemic difference between fortis [t] and lenis [d] in certain positions, at least after nasals ([n] vs. [nd]). The opposition stop–fricative, on the other hand, seems to have presupposed the presence of the feature *fortis*: we find oppositions between fortis stops and fortis fricatives but not between lenis stops and lenis fricatives. The latter (e.g. [d] and [ð]) were bound variants. We thus arrive at the arrangement presented in Figure 14.4. (The distinction of three points of articulation may probably be reinterpreted in terms of two binary distinctions, but this is irrelevant to the present problem.) As the table shows, each phoneme has its own runic representation (although the **p** was abandoned at an early time for some unknown reason, possibly taboo?).

This system was changed by three kinds of sound shift.

(The survey given here is much simplified. For a thorough treatment of the development, consult Moulton 1954: 1–44.)

1 Lenis stops and spirants occurring in absolutely final position became fortis, so that a bound variation between lenis and fortis articulation was established, cf. late Proto-Scandinavian *bindan 'to bind', past tense *bant, *draɣan 'to draw', past tense *drōx (*drōh). The fortis or voiceless articulation in final position is reflected in runic writing (*gaf* for older *gab* 'gave', etc.)

2 In certain positions (chiefly in absolutely initial positions) lenis fricatives became stops, e.g. [ð] became [d].[10] In initial position there was in early

---

[10]   On this transition cf. Sverdrup (1924: 231).

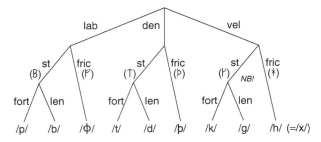

Figure 14.5

Proto-Scandinavian a phonemic opposition between fortis and lenis fricatives as well as between these and fortis stops, but after the change there
was a distinction between fortis and lenis stops as well as between these
and fortis fricatives.
3 As a result of vowel reduction in unstressed syllables, the opposition
between stops and fricatives was extended from the fortis group to the lenis
group: a form like Proto-Scandinavian *waldōn 'to cause' developed into
/walda/ with lenis stop, whereas *walidō, past tense of *walian 'to choose,'
developed into /walða/ with lenis fricative, so that /d/ and /ð/ came to be in
direct opposition.

It thus became necessary to keep the former variants [d] and [ð] apart
as members of different phonemes; on the other hand, [þ] and [ð]
came to be in complementary distribution and came to function as
bound variants of one phoneme. Consequently, we arrive at the system
presented in Figure 14.5.

It will be seen from the figure that the new runic system was moulded
on this new phonemic system but in a peculiar way since it expressed
the higher-ranked distinctions only. Here, as with the vowels, the
younger runic writing is incompletely specifying.

Morphophonemically, the use of a common symbol for /t/ and /d/,
and similarly for /p/ and /b/ and for /k/ and /g/ is motivated—as
in the vowel system—by a close functional connection between the
units sharing a runic representation. It was illustrated above how lenis
consonants are replaced by fortis consonants if they come to stand
in absolutely final position. This is clearly a matter of non-phonemic
variation in fricatives; in stops it is at most 'semi-phonemic', since we
may say that the fortis–lenis distinction is (at the time of transition
from Proto-Scandinavian to Old Scandinavian) neutralized in (short)
consonants occurring in word-final position. The fortis–lenis distinction is also neutralized in some other positions; thus if an obstruent

occurs as a non-initial member of a syllable-initial cluster (/sp-/ = /sb-/) or if it occurs before another obstruent (there is no distinction of, say, /ks/ and /gs/). In some of these positions also the stop–fricative distinction is neutralized (there is no distinction between, say, /pt/ and /ɸt/; we actually find a vacillation between these in the history of a word like Old Norse *eptir* 'after'). But it is quite obvious that the morphophonemic connection is much closer between fortis and lenis than between stop and fricative.

As said above for vowels, we cannot ignore the fact that a wish to abandon certain less suitable runes (those which had no single vertical axis) may have played a considerable role in provoking the change in runic representation. It is interesting, however, that the resulting system is in such close conformity with the basic features of the phonic system.

In early Proto-Scandinavian the phonemes /b, d, g/ had fricatives as their main variants. After the sound shifts they were only manifested as stop consonants, and at the same time they were severely limited in distribution, since all non-initial occurrences of the bilabial and dental lenis fricatives (which were not changed to stops) came to be associated with the phonemes /ɸ, þ/. (The situation is less clear for velars—see below.) From the point of view of spelling tradition, there was thus little left of the original associations, and one would not wonder if the **b**, the **d**, and the **g** surrendered. Nevertheless, the **b** was preserved, but this rune must probably be considered (in late Proto-Scandinavian) as being in practice a **p/b**.

There are thus many factors that point in the same direction, and the redistribution of the phonemes in the classes established by the runic symbols is on the whole not surprising. We must still admit, however, that the whole idea of symbolizing phoneme classes, rather than individual phonemes, is a puzzling phenomenon in the history of alphabetic writing.

The neat system of representation discussed here breaks down in the velars. The **k** has for some reason come to signify the lenis fricative in addition to the fortis and lenis stops. We should expect the **h** to stand for the lenis fricative, this being a variant of the phoneme /h/, but in the oldest inscriptions the lenis fricative [ɣ] is constantly represented by the **k**. It is probable that /h/ (/x/) had lost most of its fricative character so that its place in the obstruent system was less firmly established. Moreover, the stop [g] and the fricative [ɣ] probably did not stand in any opposition at all, so the velar system was ambiguous. There can be no doubt, however, that there was a predisposition in the runic system toward making a thorough distinction between stops and fricatives also in the velar series. In fact we find from the eleventh century and throughout the runic period a considerable number of instances in which the **h** is employed to represent [ɣ]. This usage is quite sporadic in Danish inscriptions[11] but fairly frequent in Norway and Sweden. I have not detected any specific geographical or temporal limitations to this usage, it is, at least in Norway, just frequent. This may suggest that the use of the **h** was latent in the system itself; we need not explain each single occurrence as the result of some local tradition or influence.

Quite early, the need for distinguishing the velar sounds in runic writing was fulfilled in a different way, namely by providing the **k** with a diacritic mark (generally a dot between the 'prongs'). In Norwegian inscriptions we find the lenis fricative represented by the **k**, by the **h**, and by the new diacritically marked rune, in a wonderful mixture. (As we might expect, the latter rune is used also for the stop [g].) Counting the instances of the lenis velar fricative in Norwegian inscriptions (only occurrences where the fricative pronunciation is beyond question were included), I found this sound to be written 55 times with the **h**, 25 times with the diacritically-marked rune, and 22 times with the ordinary **k**. It is quite obvious that although the special rune is used quite often, the **h** plays a more important role, as far as the lenis fricative is concerned.

Just like the **k** for the velar lenis fricative, we also find the **b** used for the labial lenis fricative [β]. This, however, is not a widespread feature, although the usage is encountered in a few quite early inscriptions. It is easily explained as influence from the corrupt velar system. Only the dental system remains intact, probably because it is only in dentals that the opposition between lenis stop and lenis fricative is really significant (*valda* vs. *valða*). (There are a few examples of [ð] written with the **t** in rather late inscriptions, but that probably has to do with the introduction of a diacritically marked rune (in some of the cases there may even have been a dot which is just not visible any longer)). In late inscriptions we may even find the **þ** used for the stop [d], but these queer deviations from normal practice do not alter the general

---

[11] In later Danish inscriptions from 'period 4' (Middle Ages) the use of the **h** becomes customary (Jacobsen and Moltke 1942: column 957).

picture of the dental series as having a very fixed representation in runic writing.[12]

14.6.   FINAL REMARKS: IMPORTANCE OF DISTINCTIONS

I have attempted in this report to show for Old Scandinavian that some phonemic distinctions may be considered more 'basic' to the linguistic system than certain others, and that the strangely defective younger runic alphabet or 'futhark' may be said to reflect just those distinctions which are most basic. Appeal has been made both to the phonetic and distributional characteristics of the sound system and to the morphophonemic relationships among the sound units. We have as yet no well-developed theory about rank ordering of distinctive features; all we can do is to consider the problem from various aspects and to weigh the various criteria as best we can.

The rank ordering which we may try to establish within the linguistic system is not necessarily a true picture of the actual *importance* of the individual features in communication. As for the present problem it would not be without interest to know about the functional load (in a statistical sense) of each of the phonemic distinctions in question, although the possibilities of calculating it may not be the very best.

---

[12] An overall characterization of the orthography of inscriptions employing the older and younger runes has not been attempted in this paper. The orthography of the earliest inscriptions after the change has been analysed in detail by Nielsen (1960). Also see Andersen (1947: 203 ff.).

15

A Unified Theory of Nordic *i*-umlaut, Syncope, and Stød[1]

15.1. INTRODUCTION

This paper comments on the interrelations between three major issues
in early Nordic language history, viz. *i*-umlaut, syncope, and the genesis of stød. The 'unified theory' I propose is deliberately provocative
and meant to invite discussion. It is unified in the sense that I attempt
to explain all three phenomena in terms of a particular model of early
Nordic word prosody. That model is mora-based, i.e. it refers to the
occurrence, within each wordform, of weight units of less-than-syllable
size (in contradistinction to the bulk of Nordic philological literature,
which refers to full syllables in attempting to account for the way
umlaut and syncope worked).

The model posits a diachronic succession of two mechanisms of
rhythmicization in terms of pitch prominence: first the alternation
of prominent and non-prominent morae was determined from the
beginning of the word; at a later stage a new word rhythm took over,
prominence in the unstressed part of the word being now determined
by the distance of morae from the end of the word, that is, the word
prosody was from now on *word-demarcating*. As a result, each word
form now stood out prosodically by beginning in a stressed syllable
(after unstressed prefixes had been lost) and ending with a falling pitch
contour.

i-umlaut, according to my claims, operated throughout both of
the above-mentioned chronological stages, being triggered whenever
the first post-tonic vowel became rhythmically prominent. Syncope

[1] Appeared also in *NOWELE* (North-Western European Language Evolution) 54/55,
October 2008, pp. 191–235.

happened at the end of the second chronological stage. It was followed by automatic readjustments of the prominence pattern but not by new applications of *i*-umlaut. Eventually, the stød developed from a falling pitch contour that resulted from the late prominence pattern, morae being now subordinated under syllables.

The decisive events in this scenario are supposed to belong to the transitional phase between two chronological stages of Nordic. The point of departure is Early Ancient Nordic (early 'urnordisk'), an archaic and seemingly stable language norm looking much like a hypothetical ancestor of Northwest Germanic (cf. Nielsen 2002: 566), which especially in Denmark is attested from around 2000 up to the fifth century AD. The end point of the transition is Old Nordic (= 'fællesnordisk', 'oldnordisk', including Old Norse), a more variable language norm attested (with dialect differences across Scandinavia) from the eighth century onwards. I refer to the transitional phase between these two states as Late Ancient Nordic.

In terms of prominence patterns, the model proposed here is entirely at variance with the traditional view of Ancient Nordic word prosody. That view is due primarily to Axel Kock (e.g. Kock 1901) who was seconded by his congenial pupil Johs. Brøndum-Nielsen for Danish. Kock reconstructed several degrees of expiratory stress, tying these up with syllables. While fully acknowledging that these scholars of the neogrammarian era had an impressive mastery of relevant data from dialects and from early writing (Rischel 2002), I do not feel compelled to believe in the possibility of reconstructing the prosodic pattern of a language spoken more than a millennium ago in terms of scalar and non-distinctive phenomena of a phonetically contro-versial kind, such as three or four degrees of 'expiratory stress' (nor do I find it convincing to explain phonological change in terms of notions such as 'relatively unstressed position', as they sometimes did).

Especially among German and Russian scholars there have been attempts to shed light on early phonological developments within Germanic (not just on the formation of Germanic, cf. Verner's Law) by reference to the old Indo-European accentuation. I leave that field of study entirely out of consideration in the present paper.

My own model takes as its point of departure a minimalistic set of assumptions about alternating rhythm in wordforms, as outlined above. We know for sure that there must have been some kind of alter-nating prominence of the successive morae of wordforms in Ancient

Nordic, since that is directly reflected in syllabification including hiatus phenomena. We also know that a different rhythmicization must have been at play at a later stage, since subsequent segmental and suprasegmental developments would be impossible to account for without that. If readers wish to take issue with my contentions about Ancient Nordic rhythm it will, I hope, be my specific proposals that are questioned rather than the general claim that there was a mora-based rhythmicization in Ancient Nordic, and that that must have changed at some early time, before Ancient Nordic became Old Nordic.

Vis-à-vis Kock, my theory is even more heretical when it comes to the umlaut process itself. There has been speculation as to whether umlaut was a distant assimilation between consecutive vowels or a regressive coarticulary phenomenon, a preceding vowel being coloured by a following vowel via the intermediate segment(s). Traditionally there has been agreement, however, that prosodically-strong vowels were umlauted by prosodically-weak vowels. Axel Kock posited an early round of *i*-umlaut that happened as an accompaniment to vowel syncope, qualitative modification (fronting) of a stressed vowel being a reflex of the loss of a following unstressed *i*-vowel. What predictions such a theory makes depend entirely on whether the concept of syncope is restricted to the loss of single vowels, or whether the shortening of long vowels is considered to be another aspect of the same process. In the former case, an early round of umlaut as an accompaniment of syncope makes the strange prediction that at a certain point in time, long *i*-stem nouns had umlaut in the singular but not in the plural[2] (the situation being remedied only at a later time when the preserved *i*-vowel in the plural caused umlaut); in the latter case the shortening of the long vowel is likewise an umlaut-causing loss of vowel material. The crucial notion in this context is *mora*. The long unstressed vowel consists of two morae, and thus vowel shortening can be viewed as the *syncope of one of its morae.* The theory proposed in the present paper hinges crucially on this extended definition of *syncope*, although it totally dissociates the umlaut process from syncope.

One of the leading Nordic philologists of the pre-war period, Bengt Hesselman, explicitly refuted Kock's whole theory, stating that umlaut was caused by a fully distinct *i*-vowel, and that it antedated and

---

[2] Harry Andersen (1956: 12) deserves credit for having pointed to the absurdity of this scenario.

had occurred independently of syncope (Hesselman 1945: 5). His presentation was already theoretically antiquated at the time it was published but, in spite of that, his general claim about umlaut as a phonetic process stands, unlike Kock's theory.

My own understanding is that the processes of umlaut and syncope were independent of each other and were in fact triggered by mutually exclusive prosodic conditions. Umlaut was *not* a compensation for a vanishing vowel. I prefer the simplest explanation according to general phonetic theory and take it to be straightforward *vowel harmony* (working backwards rather than forwards, as is more often the case), but that implies a process that is expected to spread from strong rather than weak vowels.

Although the main focus of this paper is umlaut and syncope, I consider the establishment of a common basis for such disparate phenomena as umlaut and stød to be the strongest argument in favour of the theory I put forward here.

My model of stød-genesis presupposes word templates with prosodic contours exactly as generated by my umlaut-and-syncope model. Although my theory follows the mainstream literature (in particular Marius Kristensen 1898) in assuming a tonal origin of the stød, I do not see the contrast between stød and non-stød as a special development of the tonal accents, 'tonelag', that still exist in Swedish and Norwegian (nor do I follow Liberman 1982 in reversing that scenario). According to my model, the developments of 'tonelag' and stød were parallel although hardly synchronous developments in the sense that a shared set of Old Nordic word templates with rhythm-conditioned prosodies formed the input to both processes (and to tonogenesis in some Danish dialects). I agree with Riad (1998 and elsewhere) in seeing a high–low (HL) tonal pattern as crucial to the development of the stød as well as Scandinavian word accents, but otherwise our theories are profoundly different.

So far, I have only published the stød-part of the unified theory, and only in the semi-publication of a paper presented to the Linguistic Circle of Copenhagen in 1998 (Rischel 2001), although my preoccupation with Nordic umlaut dates back to the 1960s. The only reflex of my work back then is a paper (Rischel 1966) in which the structural status of umlaut vowels is seen in relation to the runic code shift from the older to the younger futhark.[3] My current views on the origin

---

[3] Editors' note: see chapter 14 in this volume.

of *i*-umlaut and of the stød were presented in provisional form at a workshop headed by Aditi Lahiri in Konstanz in March 2002. The present paper takes an equally comprehensive view in that it attempts to show how three distinct phenomena: *i*-umlaut, syncope, and stød fit into one unified whole.[4]

The literature on early Germanic and Nordic language history is enormous, and so is the accumulated bulk of philological and dialectological data that is relevant to the issues I deal with. The purpose of this paper being to outline a unified theory, I keep the presentation of all aspects of it as brief as possible. Accordingly, I stick to a few well-known exemplars of the various processes (referring to attested forms in Old Norse and Danish, largely ignoring the rich dialect material handled in the Nordic philological literature). My examples include some well-known *apparent* exceptions to *i*-umlaut that are inconvenient for all umlaut theories that I know of, but which I attempt to handle.

References within the text to other literature are likewise kept to an absolute minimum. That is true particularly of recent literature.[5] As for syncope and umlaut, my paper is a critical commentary on traditional Neogrammarian views, which had powerful proponents up to half a century ago and still play an important role in forming the cognitive background for new thinking; it is not a commentary on other attacks on those views. Thus I could not include a discussion of the affinities between my theory and Schulte's (1998) view of the development of unaccented Nordic vowels and umlaut, nor of the relation of my theory to Basbøll's (1982, 1993) thought-provoking contributions to the theory of how *i*-umlaut worked. My model may seem to resemble that of Braroe (1979) in that I posit rhythmical changes over time, but there are few points of real resemblance between our theories, and I think I have a stronger case for my internal reconstructions.

I wish to emphasize, quite generally, that although the theory runs counter to the classic views, many (if not most) of the separate assumptions inherent in the proposed theory have long since been put forward by Nordic and Germanic philologists and refuted by others. I cannot give appropriate credit to predecessors along the way without turning

---

[4] This paper does not deal with types of Danish stød other than the mainstream one, i.e., there is no reference to 'vestjysk stød' or to 'kortvokalstød'. Ejskjær (1990) gives a lucid presentation of the Danish stød/tone scenario.

[5] Editors' note: the original publication contained a fairly comprehensive selected bibliography which has been interspersed into the list of references at the end of the book.

this into a very bulky presentation of the research history thus compromising transparency.

My point in putting this paper forward is not to express compliance with views that are familiar to any Nordic philologist, but to argue that it may be illuminating to see the relationship between different, in themselves extremely well-studied, phenomena in a new light.

It would seem a must to throw sideways glances at the workings of umlaut in West Germanic when proposing such a theory, but I have to put that completely aside. My model works within the bounds of North Germanic (for simplicity I pretend that there is a clear branching of Germanic into East, West, and North Germanic); and I consider it a separate, and very difficult, question how plausible the model is from a common Germanic perspective. Although umlaut certainly occurs within West Germanic as well, there is a vexing difference between the way it is attested in Scandinavian, Anglo-Saxon, and Old High German.

In the following sections,[6] I first present the bulk of challenges that face any theory about the early developments in Nordic, the subsequent presentation of the theory being an attempt to deal with a number of these challenges. I realize that the condensed section on Challenges is very heavy reading. In fact, it is not a prerequisite to a scrutiny of the theory itself, but may be consulted if the reasons for specific features of it remain unclear otherwise.

15.2. SOME EXPLANATORY CHALLENGES

15.2.1. Umlaut

(i) Looking at the mass of variegated data it seems virtually impossible to account exhaustively for the instances in which umlaut has occurred as against the instances in which it did not occur, especially since there are often variant forms across Nordic, and sometimes even within the same language norm. In many cases the last resort is to speak of *analogy* or *levelling* or of *reverse umlaut* as the reason for the unexpected

---

[6] In the transcription of reconstructed or attested wordforms I render long vowels as sequences of two identical vowels rather than using the acute accent or the macron (the superscript bar) as a length mark. For transparency, this convention is extended even to Old Norse forms. Morae—other than those of stress syllables—which are postulated to be prominent at a particular point in a historical sequence of events are underlined.

occurrence, or unexpected non-occurrence, of umlaut. The challenge, then, is to constrain these concepts in order to retain their explanatory value.

Late neogrammarians (notably Brøndum-Nielsen) used the concept of morphologically motivated *analogy* very liberally in explaining counter-instances to Kock's umlaut theory, for example. As will be apparent throughout the paper, I restrict its application to the early history of Nordic in principled ways. More specifically, I argue that paradigmatic simplification was hardly operative during the transition from Ancient Nordic to Old Nordic, but only later. To the extent that early analogy was at work, it was a matter of generalizing across morphological categories *not* across each inflectional paradigm. Since this is an important component of the theory I shall briefly outline how, in my view, paradigms behaved in the transitional period.

The structural changes that happened then removed many occurrences of stem-forming, post-tonic vowels (occurrences of *-i- in i-stems, etc.) and at the same time dramatically increased the number of stem-vowel alternations in inflectional paradigms. The overall effect was to make forms within a paradigm *less similar to each other*. Certain forms became highly marked, by umlaut or by their syllable number, or both, and such marked forms might eventually be generalized morphologically (e.g. *i*-umlaut becoming a marker of singular rather than 2./3. singular in strong verbs). Otherwise, the high paradigmatic complexity was essentially preserved all through Old Nordic and made it even to present-day Insular West Nordic, particularly Icelandic but in part also Faroese (ON *u*-stems such as *örn* and consonant stems such as *tönn* with $a \sim \ddot{o} \sim e$ alternation in their inflections are good cases in point).

The opposite tendency, which became operative only later, was to generalize less marked features of inflection across a particular paradigm. Paradigmatic uniformation is morphological simplification but at the same time it *decreases* the mutual distinctiveness of inflectional forms in their overall shape. Generalization of one particular alternant of the stem vowel contributes to that since forms are distinguished by their overall shape, not just by their endings (in fact, the segmentation of forms into stems and endings is essentially a descriptive linguistic tool). Forms may of course coalesce more or less haphazardly, because of sound changes, but the coalescences may also be part of a larger scheme.

There were two main routes to paradigmatic uniformation through-out the history of the Nordic languages. One was grammatically moti-vated coalescence of form-classes, e.g. simplification of the grammat-ical case or number system. Across much of Nordic, this happened massively in medieval times, although more or less locally. The other has to do with the heavily inflectional type that arose at the transi-tion from Ancient Nordic to Old Nordic. In later Nordic languages (excepting Icelandic) there has been a tendency to move back towards a more agglutinative type, as in Early Ancient Nordic. The exploita-tion of these routes to paradigmatic uniformation makes much of the Nordic material from early medieval times onwards less transparent in terms of application or non-application of umlaut or syncope than the conservative Icelandic data.

(ii) A key problem for any theory of umlaut is that masculine *i*-stem nouns show *i*-umlaut throughout the inflection if the stem is long but are devoid of such umlauting if the stem is short, whereas both long and short feminine *i*-stem nouns are mostly devoid of *i*-umlaut. The most vexing observation is that we encounter just as much, or just as little, umlaut in the singular as in the plural, even though Ancient Nordic must have had a long *i*-vowel in the plural which is still preserved as a short *i*-vowel in Old Nordic i.e. the plural forms provide a seemingly prototypical input to umlaut, in nouns with both long and short stems. For analogy (plus capricious variation patterns) to be a valid explanation of the forms we actually encounter, one must appeal to the fact that *i*-umlaut never became a general marker of plurality in Nordic (contrary to German). In the numerically-prevalent noun classes (*a*-stems and *n*-stems) there is no such umlaut in the plural at all, and in minor noun classes (*u*-stems, 'root stems') it occurs only in certain case forms. Otherwise, the singular and plural forms agree in vowel quality (except for *u*-umlaut as a diacritic marker of dative plural). Thus it is a possible way out to claim that analogy has been at work, making *i*-stems agree with that scheme. Still, it is disturbing to have a massive bulk of exceptions to the phonological processes that are otherwise at work. If one can come up with a theory that accounts for the umlaut difference between short and long masculine *i*-stems in terms of independently motivated umlaut-rules, it obviously has a much stronger explanatory force.

(iii) Another crux is the relationship between umlaut and the occur-rence of an apical or coronal fricative after the *i*-vowel in Ancient

Nordic. If one looks at Ancient Nordic word templates with a *VCVC-sequence of which the first short vowel was stressed and the second an unstressed *i*-vowel, Old Nordic exhibits more umlauting of the stressed vowel if the consonant following the second vowel was an apical or coronal (sibilant) fricative in Ancient Nordic. The concept of '*R*-umlaut' was introduced long ago into historical Nordic philology in order to explain the umlaut in forms such as ON *ker* versus Danish *kar*, and that makes perfect sense assuming that Late Ancient Nordic *R* had a palatal feature, although it originated from a voiced dental sibilant *z* and ended up as a trill coalescing with *r*. It is more tricky to account for the behaviour of forms containing *-iR-. In the neogrammarian era an attempt was made to solve the problem by introducing a more complex '*iR*-umlaut'. That was not embraced generally by the Nordic philologists, however. The umlauted forms that spell trouble in particular are present tense singular forms of short-stem strong verbs and *ja*-verbs, comparative and superlative forms formed with *-i-* after a short stem, and nominalizations from short-stem verbs.

(iv) Next there is the paradoxical relationship between syncope and *i*-umlaut. Syncope of a palatal vowel has happened in many instances without umlauting (or at least, without a lasting umlaut) of the stressed vowel; in other instances the palatal vowel has undergone syncope but the stressed vowel is umlauted; in the remaining instances a palatal vowel is preserved after an umlauted stressed vowel.

Axel Kock's famous umlaut theory attempted to solve the paradox by positing three chronologically successive events (periods), which I like to paraphrase as follows: (a) syncope with umlaut, (b) syncope without umlaut, and (c) umlaut without syncope. Although many philologists have expressed strong reservations about Kock's chronology, or complete rejection of it, his theory still seems to enjoy the status of being the implicit frame of reference. It is, however, typologically quite implausible and also counter-intuitive. Positing a final period in which *i*-umlaut happened *without* syncope makes it a void claim that the first round of umlaut was dependent on syncope.

The first two periods in Kock's theory are supposed to account for monosyllabic wordforms such as ON *gestr* and *halr* (< *gastiR*, *haliR*). In dealing with those it is definitely relevant to distinguish between long and short stems because there is much more umlaut in the former than in the latter, but that in itself does not warrant a chronological succession either in the realm of umlaut or in the realm of syncope. The only empirical argument in favour of any chronology is that there is some evidence suggesting that syncope happened somewhat earlier after long rather than after short stems. To tie that up with the occurrence versus non-occurrence of umlaut is, however, a mere construction. The obvious alternative is to assume that umlaut happened before syncope but was somehow sensitive to word structure.[7]

Kock's periodization of *i*-umlaut, with its unlikely umlaut-free interval, becomes even more bizarre if one compares it with the corresponding periodization of forms with *u*-umlaut: in order for Kock's syncope chronology to make sense, it must likewise posit two rounds of syncope (after long and short stems) in forms with post-tonic **u*; but the data do not invite a distinction between syncope with and without *u*-umlaut. One may suggest that *u*-umlaut was not sensitive to the length of the stress-syllable, unlike *i*-umlaut, or that *u*-umlaut spread more by analogy than *i*-umlaut, but either contention can be stated without making appeals to chronology.

(v) In explaining the umlaut mechanism one faces the question as to at what point the umlauted vowels became separate phonemes. The structuralist theory made it precise that umlaut vowel qualities may have been present prior to syncope but were 'phonologized' by syncope, umlauted vowels becoming distinctive once the conditioning factor was removed, as in **gastiR* > **gæstiR* > *gæstr* (e.g. Diderichsen 1938: 5, 1946: 75).

Andersen (1956) reacted against that view. The attested Ancient Nordic form -*gestumR* that he used as counter-evidence has since been given a different interpretation (Santesson 1989), which invalidates it as evidence in support of his claim. Still, Andersen had a point in that there has been too much emphasis on the connection between umlaut and syncope. That easily leads to the wrong conclusion that the new vowels became functional only in wordforms in which the umlauting vowel was lost, but in fact 'phonologization' of umlauted vowels occurred also before non-syncopated -*i*- the moment the post-tonic

---

[7] In my theory (below) the distinction between long and short stems is only indirectly interesting for umlaut and syncope. My claim is that the mora number of the stress-syllable determines the rhythmicization of post-tonic syllables, the prominence pattern of the latter being crucial for both umlaut and syncope.

vowel system was simplified from the five or six Ancient Nordic vowels *i e (æ) a o u* to the three Old Nordic vowels *a i u*. When, for example, the vowel *-i(-)* in *ia*-stem nouns coalesced with Late Ancient Nordic *-e(-)* > *-i(-)* in the dative singular ending of *a*-stem nouns, the distinctive difference jumped from the post-tonic syllables to the main syllables, as in *gærði* (ON *gerði*) versus *garði*. The interesting question is to what extent this qualitative change in the post-tonic vowel system can be dated relative to the post-tonic vowel shortenings and losses which I here subsume under the term *syncope*.

If one insists on positing chronological layers of *i*-umlaut one should thus keep in mind that not only syncope but also the loss of post-tonic vowel contrasts must be aligned chronologically with what happened in the main syllables of different word types.

15.2.2. Syncope

(i) The most important question was already raised above: did the shortening of long vowels (or diphthongs) occur as a separate event after the deletion of short vowels, or are both phenomena reflexes of a more general process of vowel mora dropping?

The latter interpretation invites a mora-counting principle according to which vowel morae outside the stressed syllable were alternately deleted (syncopated) or retained, short vowels being monomoraic and long vowels or diphthongs bimoraic (terminological differences aside, the basic insight goes back to the late nineteenth century).

(ii) What then about the stress-syllables? Long vowels and diphthongs are of course bimoraic. Now, it is well known that words whose stressed syllables were heavy according to the Old Nordic metric principle (i.e. syllables with V: or VV, or with VC followed by another C) all behaved in the same manner with respect to syncopation pattern, but differently from words whose stressed syllable was light (i.e. syllables of the structure VC *not* followed by another, homosyllabic C). It follows that in Old Nordic a consonant, even a voiceless one, formed a bimoraic complex (nucleus) with a preceding short vowel if the syllable was closed by an additional consonant. That includes cases in which the postvocalic consonant was long and thus somehow equivalent to a CC sequence consisting of a moraic C plus an identical but non-moraic C. (Needless to say, the above is a simplistic exposition compared to the highly sophisticated analyses of Nordic metrical structures that have been made in recent years; for moraic and non-moraic, readers may choose to substitute 'metric' and 'extra-metric'.)

(iii) Under the assumption of alternately syncopated and retained vowels, how can we determine the starting-point, polarity and direction of the iterative process that accounts for deletion of every other mora? If counting from the beginning of the word, it is clear from the data that stressed syllables count as stressed in their (monomoraic or bimoraic) entirety i.e. the principle of alternating deletion and retention applies only to the string *after* the first syllable. That, however, raises a set of questions about how the moraic weight of the first syllable (i.e. a long stem versus a short stem) influenced the deletion pattern within the unstressed part of the word. The moraic weight of the first syllable might conceivably determine (a) whether the wordform was prone to undergo syncope at all; (b) whether syncope happened at one or another chronological period; (c) whether it was the odd-numbered or the even-numbered morae that underwent syncope.

(iv) Syncope could apply in different places in a wordform but does not normally seem to have reapplied to a string (otherwise, forms of several morae or even of several syllables would eventually all end up monosyllabic). This suggests that within each wordform a set of morae was syncopated in one run according to some principle of selection. How, then, does one account for the forms where two immediately successive syllables both underwent syncope? The relevant forms include supine and perfect participle forms of *ia*- and *ja*-verbs (e.g. *hengdr*), certain superlative forms (the type *yngstr*), and nominal derivations with a suffix containing a dental fricative (the type *þyngd*, also cf. Section 15.2.1.(iii) above).

(v) A corollary to (iv): How does one define the strings relevant to the deletion of a particular mora, and how does one explain why such a string is immune to syncope once it has happened? Did syncope of one mora in such instances leave a prosodic or segmental trace, which prevented the process from re-applying and deleting another mora as well?

(vi) Was the syncope pattern determined entirely by a principle operating across the word from left to right, or did the closeness of a vowel to the end of the word influence its proneness to be syncopated?

15.2.3. **Stød-genesis and tonogenesis**

(i) From a modern Nordic perspective the stød shares important, non-trivial features of distribution with the tonal accent 1 (the 'acute accent') of Swedish and Norwegian. Notably, these word accents, stød and (to a varying extent) accent 1, occur not only on monosyllables but under well-defined circumstances also on *dissyllabic* wordforms. There are five different scenarios in which monosyllabic accentuation has emerged on dissyllabic wordforms.

The first three involve inherited simplex wordforms:

1 Monosyllabic but grammatically complex forms (types such as *hendr* 'hands,' *breidd* 'width') have widely retained their accentuation irrespective of later conversion to bisyllabicity in some or all of the Nordic languages.
2 Monosyllabic but grammatically complex forms (types such as *breidd* 'width', *lengst* 'longest', *hengd* 'hanged, pp.', *lands* 'country, gen.sg.') have retained their accentuation irrespective of elaboration by inflection or compounding.
3 Monosyllabic words have retained their accentuation form irrespective of the addition of enclitic material; the spectacular case being the definite article (e.g. *land* + *it* > *land-it* 'the country', *lands* + *ins* 'of the country').[8]

In all three scenarios there arose accentual contrasts with simplex forms that were dissyllabic in Old Nordic (e.g. *hendir* 'happens', *breiddi* 'laid out, pret.', *hengdi* 'hanged, pret.', *bundit* 'tied, pp.'), the latter being characterized in Danish by the absence of stød, in Swedish and Norwegian by tonal accent 2 ('gravis accent').

The two remaining word types were dissyllabic from the start.

4 Compound verbs with an adverbial (prepositional) first part (e.g. *aftale* 'make an agreement') were accentuated like monosyllables, i.e. stød on the second part in Danish, tonal accent 1 on the composite wordform as a whole in Norwegian. Similar compounds with a noun stem as the second part (e.g. *aftale* 'agreement'), on the contrary, behaved as truly dissyllabic forms and thus they remained stød-less in Danish and eventually acquired tonal accent 2 in Norwegian.[9]

---

[8] It deserves to be mentioned that genitive -*s* itself behaved as enclitic material, in accordance with its postposition-like behaviour. This is evidenced by the distribution of the stød in Danish: short stød-less stems such as *tal* 'number' did not acquire stød in the genitive: *tals* (as against the stød in East Danish in heavy-syllable words such as *hals* 'neck').

[9] Cf. Rischel (1963: 155). Standard Swedish, on the contrary, has accent 2 on both verb and noun in such cases as *avträda, avträde*.

5 Dissyllabic word stems with an iambic stress pattern (such as Danish *betale*, mostly borrowings from Low German) acquired stød in Danish and tonal accent 1 in Swedish and Norwegian, irrespective of inflection.

Because of these and some additional parallels between the distribution of stød and of tonal accent 1 it has been customary to see the stød and accent 1 as manifestations of the same development of a word accent. Under that assumption, the next challenge is to explain how one developed into the other, or how they diverged from a common source.

(ii) In spite of the above parallels between stød and tonal accent 1, however, one cannot just account for the stød as a historical variety of the Swedish or Norwegian tonal accent 1. Explanations along that line fail completely when it comes to the combinability of accents within the same word form. The Swedish and Norwegian tonal accents are true word accents in the sense that a word form, simplex or composite, contains at most one tonal accent, be it accent 1 or 2. The stød, on the contrary, is distinctive at the syllable level. It can occur several times within the same word and even on two or more adjacent syllables if they are all heavy (conversely, many Danish compounds do not contain a single stød, even though several of the syllables are heavy). Thus, there is a deep-rooted typological difference between the accentual systems of Danish, Swedish, and Norwegian. That may spell trouble for theories such as that of Riad (2000 and elsewhere) that attempt to explain the stød as a reflex of a scenario similar to that of Swedish.

(iii) There is another major area of discrepancy between stød and tonal accent 1. The tonal accents of Swedish and Norwegian require a stretch of two syllables in order to be mutually distinctive; on the other hand, they are insensitive to the internal composition of the syllables within the stretch that carries the tonal accent. It is the other way round with the stød. It is distinctive even in monosyllabic words but it can occur only if the stressed syllable is of a certain structure, which Basbøll (2005) defines as bimoraic according to Danish metrical rules. Unlike the concept of heavy syllable in Old Nordic, a sequence of vowel plus consonant cannot qualify as bimoraic and thus be a potential carrier of the stød, unless the consonant is high on the scale of sonority.

(iv) A historical stød-theory must be able to account satisfactorily for the striking similarities as well as the striking typological differences between the accentual systems of Danish, Swedish, and Norwegian. If these different systems are to be traced to the same origin, it has most explanatory potential to assume that the reshuffling of word structures during the syncope stage led to the development of pitch contours on stressed and/or heavy syllables, with combinatory possibilities in complex word forms much like stød and non-stød in later Danish.

(v) The final task is to account for what happened to Nordic accentuation when Danish, Swedish, and Norwegian split company. For Swedish and Norwegian one must explain how a pattern of syllable pitches was simplified into a binary set of prosodic long components, which remained distinctive only in words of more than one syllable. For Danish one must explain how certain pitch contours ended up as contrastive phonation types, and why that happened only with syllables that were heavy and sonorous, the pitches being otherwise absorbed into the general intonation contours.

15.3. ASSUMPTIONS BEHIND THE PRESENT THEORY

15.3.1. The general pattern

(i) In Ancient Nordic the rhythmicization of wordforms was based on a mora-counting principle giving *prominence to every odd-numbered mora*, counting from the beginning of the stress-syllable and up to the end of the final syllable, with the important exception that a syllable could not have rising prominence (i.e. a long vowel could not receive prominence on its *second* mora). In some wordforms a non-initial long syllable (e.g. the syllable *-and-* in nominalized present participles) counted as a new prosodic line-up point so that the odd-numbered morae counting from the beginning of that syllable were prominent. It is likely that prominence was realized primarily in terms of higher pitch.

(ii) *Umlaut* (here only *i*-umlaut of back vowels is considered) is taken to have been regressive vowel harmony spreading from a vowel that was (at that moment) prominent. A once-umlauted vowel normally remained umlauted even if some other structural change removed the conditioning factor. The vowel harmony rule was in force through most of Late Ancient Nordic, i.e. over a certain stretch of time *i*-umlaut applied whenever the structure of a wordform permitted it (e.g. after other structural changes to the word-form).[10] It ceased to operate, however, before a separate event, *syncope* (see (iv) below), happened at the transition to Old Nordic.

(iii) At some point in time a *new word contour* replaced the old one, its overall effect being to make the pitch contours on wordforms fall at the end. Four distinct versions of the new contour principle conspired to maximize the occurrence of that pattern, two of them (1–2) being Common Nordic, whereas the remaining two (3–4) established a dialect distinction (an isogloss) between Danish and Swedish:

1 The default version of the principle was for a wordform to have prominence on its stress-syllable and low pitch on its last mora, with a high-pitch mora preceding the low-pitch mora and occurring as close to the end as possible.
2 A long final vowel *without* previous prominence (cf. the blocking of rising pitch/prominence on long vowels mentioned in (i) above) behaved prosodically like a short vowel: it retained its final low pitch, the pre-final high-pitch receding to an earlier mora (if necessary to the already stressed first vowel).
3 Long monosyllables inherited from Early Ancient Nordic, having two morae, subsumed the high and low pitches within their bimoraic stretch. That applied generally to Swedish and Norwegian. Danish, however, thoroughly changed its mora structure (its 'definition' of mora) in stress-syllables, only a voiced (sonorous) second mora being from now on relevant to word-contour prosody. Monosyllables that ceased to count as bimoraic underwent a truncation in Danish of the expected high–low pitch pattern into high-pitch (on the first and only mora, according to the new definition).
4 Short monosyllables, having only one mora, likewise behaved differently in Swedish-Norwegian and in Danish. In Swedish and Norwegian they followed suit with other wordforms in getting a sharply falling pitch, thus concentrating the high–low pattern on one mora; the reason this pattern remained uniform across syllable-types may be that these languages fairly early on developed a uniform syllable length, all stressed monosyllables becoming long. Danish did not have a general change of the quantity pattern in monosyllables;[11] there was a continued contrast between long and short stress-syllables, and on monosyllables of the latter structure the

[10] Like other umlaut theories this theory must incorporate umlaut caused by glides: a process with the same result as *i*-umlaut but caused by a palatal glide ('j-umlaut'), rounding caused by a labiovelar glide ('w-umlaut'), and fronting of a back vowel in monosyllables with final *-*R*, particularly in West Nordic ('R-umlaut'). I do not go further into these processes here, but see Section 15.6.3 about *i*-umlaut and other related processes.
[11] But only sporadic lengthening of vowels, cf. note 12 below.

pitch contour was truncated so that only the high-pitch remained (i.e. on the first and only mora).

(iv) *Syncope* in Late Ancient Nordic deleted all non-prominent morae of a wordform except that the default rule of long vowels was to lose only the second mora (thus syncope in the broad sense subsumes both loss of short vowels and shortening of long vowels). Syncope was a time-bound process according to this theory and did not reapply to the affected wordforms once the round of syncope was over (thus my assumptions about syncope are quite unlike those about umlaut above).[12]

(v) Certain types of word stems (cf. Section 15.2.3) became *prosodic islands* that were accentuated like monosyllables.

(vi) A wordform to which *enclitic material* was added always behaved as a prosodic island retaining its accentuation irrespective of the material added by enclisis.

(vii) Both of the above 'island' principles (v) and (vi) led to an early *tonal contrast* between such wordforms which constituted a prosodic island, and wordforms that were plainly dissyllabic. This Old Nordic scenario was continued in South Jutland tonal dialects (with apocope) and in most of Swedish and Norwegian (with variegated phonetic realizations of the tonal accent contrast across dialects).[13]

(viii) With only sporadic occurrence across the Nordic area, the circumflex contour (high–low) led to *distinctive tone in monosyllables*, or in compounds containing a monosyllabic first part, e.g. the rising tone of forms such as *Fyn* in the East Funen dialect and the tonal contrast between compounds with heavy and light first syllables in the Danish Ærø dialect (*modvind* versus *medvind*).

---

[12] A variety of contractions of wordforms in Nordic dialects (West Danish apocope, etc.) must be considered as phenomena that occurred after and quite independently of the Late Ancient Nordic syncope.

[13] Thus I disagree with the suggestion that the development of contrastive tonal accents in Swedish arose in compounds. As for tonal Danish dialects it deserves to be mentioned that we owe our insights about the tonal pattern of the Ærø dialect to Kromann (1947), but that he has been found to be factually wrong in postulating a tonal accent distinction in the Zealand dialect as well. The latter conclusion was drawn decades ago at a session headed by the late dialectologist Poul Andersen, in which Kromann was unable to demonstrate the alleged accentual distinction, and in which I happened to participate myself (Riad, in some of his work, unfortunately took Kromann's presentation at face value).

(ix) In most dialects of Medieval Danish the tonal contrast developed into *a contrast between stød and non-stød*, the phonation type that we call stød appearing on bimoraic syllables with a circumflex (rising–falling) pitch contour.[14]

(x) Eventually, the falling pitch contour characterizing all stressed dissyllables in Danish (both with and without the stød) split into two *regional varieties: a West Danish falling contour and an East Danish rising(–falling) contour*.

15.3.2. Strings with intervocalic voiced dental fricatives

Viewed from the perspective of my general theory, there is something altogether deviant about the diachronic development of words that contained *-VðV-* and *-VRV-*-sequences in Ancient Nordic, both with respect to the way syncope works and with respect to the genesis of stød. Since these phenomena are supposed to be widely separated in time, it is significant that we are *in both cases* in need of a special explanation of what happens in words containing the above-mentioned strings.

As for syncope, there are a host of instances in which two or three consecutive vowel morae are dropped around a dental fricative. This occurs in the past participle of all verbs whose stem used to end in a short vowel, i.e. forms such as **doomiðaR > døømdr*, as well as adverbial comparatives such as **langiRa > lengr*, in which we encounter the same basic pattern as in **doomiðaR* but with intervocalic **-R-* not **-ð-*. According to my theory, the stem-formative vowel **-i-* in such a form must have been prominent in order to cause umlaut, but the

---

[14] Off-hand, stød-genesis would seem to be datable within medieval Danish since we encounter the stød on monosyllables which eventually underwent consonant shortening in Danish (e.g. *kall > kal'*, spelled *kald*, with a short consonant and stød), and on the other hand on monosyllables which did not qualify for stød assignment until vowel lengthening had taken place, (e.g. *skip > ski'b*, *akr > a'ger*, both with a long vowel and stød). As for consonant shortening, however, that may be a very late process (cf. Brøndum-Nielsen 1932: §421). As for lengthening of monosyllables, Brøndum-Nielsen (1950: §190) assumes that it happened (at least west of Øresund) in analogy with inflected forms with an open syllable. Even a plausible dating of that secondary lengthening would hardly help us with the dating of the stød genesis either since the stød on such forms may have arisen much later than elsewhere. My point is that the stød would be automatically assigned to new forms of appropriate structure once it had become the default accentuation of long, sonorous monosyllables (cf. Basbøll's stød theory for Modern Danish, e.g. Basbøll 2005: chs. 10–12 & 14–16; see Basbøll 2001: 4–8 for an easy overview, and Basbøll 2003).

dropping of it suggests that it had become non-prominent when the word contour was reshuffled.

There is a somewhat similar scenario with nouns that are *-iþoo-formations: the augmented stem started out having three post-stress vowel morae, of which the first caused umlaut, but it ended up with none, e.g. *þungiþoo > þyngd. Thus, originally trisyllabic forms shrank to monosyllables resembling old *-ti-formations (such as *skul-ti- > skyld, skuld).

As for stød, it is conspicuous that these very same wordforms perform as prosodic islands retaining the stød of their monosyllabic form even if the word form becomes dissyllabic. This is seen, for instance, in the Danish past participle plural dømte, with a conspicu-ous stød since other e-plurals in Danish are stød-less (as is the preterite form dømte), and the uninflected Danish form tyngde (< *þungiþoo), likewise with a conspicous stød considering that the stem has two syllables.

In my view, theories about syncope and stød-genesis are obliged to account for this convergence of two kinds of aberrant behaviour. My current guess is that some coarticulatory process happened in the just-mentioned sequences, making them behave essentially like weak long vowels in terms of susceptibility to pitch prominence (although long vowels were not always prosodically weak). That seems to me plausible if ð at that time was rather sonorous (cf. that there is much coarticulation of vowel plus [ð] in Modern Danish); as for ‘R’ < *z, the assumption is the more plausible since the voiced sibilant eventually ended up as a sonorant. Such coarticulation might transform these particular VCV-sequences into phonetically coherent strings that were particularly susceptible to shortening, and the fact that they ended up being monosyllabic may explain why they became accentual islands: the high–low word-contour was placed firmly on the stress syllable due to the exorbitant contractions.

As for forms that were originally trisyllabic, the treatment of these particular vowel–consonant–vowel sequences may have been subject to variation. Dissyllabic forms such as hennar, yngri are generated perfectly well by the general prosodic rules posited in Section 15.3.1. Plural forms of participles, such as døømdar (Danish dømte), however, ended up having the stød in Danish like the corresponding singular forms.

It remains to be explained why heavy contraction and stød genesis did not happen in weak preterite forms such as *døømði > Dan.

dømte (without stød). Unlike the transparent etymology of the past (passive) participles, the story of weak preterites is extremely controversial. Since it is difficult to posit Early Ancient Nordic wordforms underlying the extant preterite forms, it is rather futile to talk about their ancient prosodic pattern. What is beyond doubt is that the forms generally reconstructed for Early Ancient Nordic were in themselves due to heavy contractions across a word boundary. That may have blocked the possibility of coarticulation of $*\text{-}V\eth V$-sequences along the lines suggested above.[15]

15.4. A REPERTORY OF SYNCOPE AND UMLAUT CASES AS HANDLED BY THE THEORY

The following is a selection of crucial form types the history for which all theories about i-umlaut and syncope should be able to account for. It is shown how the proposed theory handles the diachronic derivation of these forms (the alpha-numerical codes accompanying each example refer to entries in the next section: 'Summary of principles and rules').[16]

booni- > *booni̠* > *bøøni̠* > *bøøni* > *bøøn* (b3,c1,d3,e1,e2)
mauiz > *mawiR* > *mawR* > *maaR, mæær* (a2,d3,e1,e2)[17]
mauiooz > *maujooR* > *maujo̠oR* > > *mæyjo̠oR* > ON *meyjar* (a2,b3,c2,d3,e1,e2)
handiz > *handi̠R* > *hændi̠R* > *hændiR* > *hændr/hendr* (b3,c1,d3,e1,e2)
gastiz > *gasti̠R* > *gæsti̠R* > *gæstiR* > *gæstr/gestr* (b3,c1,d3,e1,e2)
gastiiz > *gastii̠R* > *gæstii̠R* > *gæsti̠R* > *gæstir/gestir* (b3,c1,e1,e2)
haliz > *haliR* > *halr* (e1,e2)
haliiz > *halii̠R* > *halir* (d2,e1,e2)

---

[15] It has been repeatedly suggested that Germanic weak preterites contain the auxiliary verb *dee-* 'do', which suggests that they arose with transitive verbs or at least with action verbs. Rasmussen (1999) has, in my view, presented the most convincing solution. He sees them as haplologized phrases consisting of accusative forms of the passive participle plus inflected forms of *dee-*, e.g. *doomiða ðeðee* 'made sentenced' > *doomiðee* > *døømdi* 'sentenced, 3.sg.pret.'

[16] The alternative spellings with *æ* and *e* refer to different conventions when rendering the vowel in Old Danish and Old Norse. Note that I always render long vowels as double vowel symbols.

[17] The form *mæær* is West Nordic and can be explained as due to '*R*-umlaut'. If one posits a composite '*iR*-umlaut' (which is not done in this paper) the syncopated pre-stage to *mæær* comes out as **mæwr*.

*arniuz > *arniuR > *ærniuR > *ærniR > ON ernir (b3,c1,d3,e1,e2)
*suniuz > *suniuR > *suniuR > *syniuR > *syniR > synir (b3,d3,c1,e1,e2)
*doomia > *doomia > *døømia > *døømi > døømi (b3,c1,e1,e2)
*bandilaz > *bandilaR > *bændilaR > *bændilR > bændill/bendill
    (b3,c1,e1,e2)
*katilaz > *katilaR > *katilaR > *kætilaR > *kætilR > kætill/ketill
    (b3,d3,e1,e2)
*katilee > *katilee > *katle > *katle = katli (b3,e1,e2)
*taliðee > *taliðee > *talðe > talðe = talði (b3,e1,e2)
*talian > *taljan > *taljan > *tæljan > tæljã (> tælja) (a1,b1,c2,e2)
*doomian > *doomian > *doomian >*døømian > *døømian > døømã
    (> døøma) (b1,b3,c1,d3,e1,e2)
*haanizooz > *haaniRooR > *hææniRooR > *hææniRooR > *hæ(æ)nRaR
    (> hænnar) (b3,c1,d1,e1)
*ungizee > *ungiRee > *yngiRee > *yngiRee > *yngRe (> yngri)
    (b3,c1,d1,e1)
*doomiðooz > *doomiðooR > *døømiðooR > *døømiðooR > *døømðaR >
    døømdar (b3,c1,d1,e1)
*doomiðaz > *doomiðaR > *døømiðaR > *døømiðaR > *døømðR > døømdr
    (b3,c1,d1,e1,e2)
*taliðaz > *taliðaR > *taliðaR > *talðR > taldr (b3,c1,d1,e1,e2)
*geßandiz > *geßandiR > *geßandiR > *geßandiR > *geßendiR >
    *geßendiR > *geßendR > ON gefendr (b1,b3,c1,d3,e1,e2)

15.5. SUMMARY OF PRINCIPLES AND RULES APPLYING UP TO OLD NORDIC

(a) Early hiatus rules (mora loss and syllabification)

1 If a high vowel preceded by a short vowel + consonant is followed by a non-high vowel it changes into a glide (e.g. *VCia > VCja*); the glide is eventually lost if no longer followed by a vowel.
    *talian > *taljan [> *taljan > *tæljan > tæljã (> tælja)]
2 A high vowel changes into a glide between vowels, optimizing syllabification.
    *mauiz > *mawiR [> *mawR > maaR, mæær]
    *mauiooz > *maujooR [> *maujooR > > *mæyjooR > ON meyjar]
3 In connection with intervocalic glide formation, the preceding vowel may or may not be lengthened quite early, with different consequences for later processes.
4 A non-high vowel plus a high vowel (if not undergoing (a2)) combine to form a diphthong.

(b) *Early metric principles*

1 A vowel plus a word-final nasal form a prosodically-prominent complex with nasalization of the vowel; eventually, final *n* vanishes (under conditions to be specified).

doomian > *doomian* [> *doomian* >*døømian* > *døømian* > døømã (> *døøma*)]

[*talian* >] *taljan* > *taljan* [> *tæljan* > tæljã (> *tælja*)]

[*geβandiz* >] *geβandiR* > *geβandiR* > [*geβandiR* > *geβendiR* > *geβendiR* > *geβendR* > ON *gefendr*]

2 Heavy syllables are bimoraic.

3 Odd-numbered morae, counting from the beginning of the word, are prosodically prominent in terms of high pitch, except that a long vowel that starts on a low pitch remains low-pitched throughout (pitch flattening). The prominence pattern is readjusted if, e.g., early vowel lengthening takes place.

booni- > *booni* [> *bøøni* > *bøøni* > bøøn]

[*mauiooz* >] *maujooR* > *maujooR* [> *mæyjooR* > ON *meyjar*]

handiz > *handiR* [> *hændiR* > *hændiR* > hændr/hendr]

gastiz > *gastiR* [> *gæstiR* > *gæstiR* > gæstr/gestr]

gastiiz > *gastiiR* [> *gæstiiR* > *gæstiR* > gæstir/gestir]

arniuz > *arniuR* [> *ærniuR* > *ærniR* > ON *ernir*]

suniuz > *suniuR* [> *suniuR* > *syniuR* > *syniR* > synir]

doomia > *doomia*[> *døømia* > *døømi* > døømi]

bandilaz > *bandilaR* [> *bændilaR* > *bændilR* > bændill/bendill]

katilaz > *katilaR* [> *katilaR* > *kætilaR* > *kætilR* > kætill/ketill]

katilee > *katilee* [> *katle* > *katle* = katli]

taliðee > *taliðee*[> *talðe* > talðe = talði]

doomian > *doomian* [> *doomian* >*døømian* > *døømian* > døømã (> *døøma*)]

haanizooz > *haaniRooR* [> *hææniRooR* > *hææniRooR* > *hæ(æ)nRaR* (> *hænnar*)]

ungizee > *ungiRee* [> *yngiRee* > *yngiRee* > *yngRe* (> yngri)]

doomiðooz > *doomiðooR* [> *døømiðooR* > *døømiðooR* > *døømðaR* > døømdar]

doomiðaz > *doomiðaR* [> *døømiðaR* > *døømiðaR* > *døømðR* > døømdr] *taliðaz* > *taliðaR* [> *taliðaR* > *talðR* > taldr]

[*geβandiz* > *geβandiR* >] *geβandiR* > *geβandiR* > [*geβendiR* > *geβendiR* > *geβendR* > ON gefendr]

(c) *Umlaut and other processes with a similar output*

1 A prosodically prominent palatal vowel colours the vowel of a preceding syllable (*i*-umlaut working as vowel harmony). Umlaut is normally

non-reversible, an umlauted vowel retaining its quality even if the conditioning factor is no longer there.[18] In the period in which it is still operative,
umlaut reapplies if the word structure is modified so as to feed umlaut (see
(d3) below).

[*booni- >] *boon*i* > *bøøn*i* [> *bøøni > bøøn]

[*handiz >] *handi̱R > *hændi̱R [> *hændiR > hændr/hendr]

[*gastiz >] *gasti̱R > *gæsti̱R [> *gæstiR > gæstr/gestr]

[*gastiiz >] *gastii̱R > *gæstii̱R [> *gæsti̱R > gæstir/gestir]

[*arniuz >] *arniu̱R > *ærniu̱R [> *ærni̱R > ON ernir]

[*suniuz >] *suniu̱R > *suniu̱R [> *syniu̱R > *syni̱R > synir]

[*doomia >] *doomi̱a > *døømi̱a [> *døømi̱ > døømi]

[*bandilaz >] *bandi̱laR > *bændi̱laR [> *bændi̱lR > bændill/bendill]

[*doomian >] *doomi̱an > *doomi̱an >*døømi̱an [> *døømi̱an > døømã
    (> døøma)]

[*haanizooz >] *haani̱RooR > *hææni̱RooR [> *hææni̱RooR > *hæ(æ)nRaR
    (> hænnar)]

[*ungizee >] *ungi̱Ree > *yngi̱Ree [> *yngiRee > *yngRe (> yngri)]

[*doomiðooz >] *doomi̱ðooR > *døømi̱ðooR [> *døømiðooR > *døømðaR
    > døømdar]

[*doomiðaz >] *doomi̱ðaR > *døømi̱ðaR [> *døømiðaR > *døømðR >
    døømdr]

[*geβandiz > *geβandiR > *geβandi̱R >] *geβandi̱R > *geβendi̱R
    [> *geβendiR > *geβendR > ON gefendr]

2 A palatal glide preceding a prominent vowel colours the nearest preceding
   vowel (' *j*-umlaut').

[*mauiooz > *maujooR >] *maujooR > > *mæyjooR [> ON meyjar]

[*talian > *taljan >] *taljan > *tæljan [> tæljã (> tælja)]

(d) Secondary rhythmic principle (word-demarcating pitch-contour formation)

[Constraints:]

1 A post-stress sequence VCV in which the intervening consonant is a voiced
   dental fricative (ð, z) loses (is devoid of) pitch prominence. This constraint
   does *not* apply to already contracted forms such as weak preterites.

[*haanizooz > *haani̱RooR >] *hææni̱RooR > *hææni̱RooR [> *hæ(æ)nRaR
    (> hænnar)]

[*ungizee > *ungi̱Ree >] *yngi̱Ree > *yngi̱Ree [> *yngRe (> yngri)]

[*doomiðooz > *doomi̱ðooR >] *døømi̱ðooR > *døømi̱ðooR [> *døømðaR
    > døømdar]

---

[18] 'Phonologization' of the umlaut vowel.

[*doomiðaz > *doomiðaR >] *døømiðaR > *døømiðaR [> *døømðR >
døømdr]

[*taliðaz >] *taliðaR > *taliðaR [> *talðR > taldr]

2 If the last two vowel morae of a word form a long non-prominent vowel,
that bimoraic stretch cannot acquire new prominence.
*haliiz [> halir]

[Assignment rule:]

3 The last mora of a word becomes (or remains) low-pitched, and post-
stress pitch prominence falls on the nearest preceding mora that can receive
prominence. If a stressed wordform is already monosyllabic it gets a falling
tone (high + low pitch on one syllable). Corollary to (d3): the umlaut rule
(c1) reapplies.

[*booni- > *booni >] *bøøni > *bøøni [> bøøn]

[*handiz > *handiR >] *hændiR > *hændiR [> hændr/hendr]

[*gastiz > *gastiR >] *gæstiR > *gæstiR [> gæstr/gestr]

[*arniuz > *arniuR > *ærniuR >] *ærniR > ON ernir

[*suniuz > *suniuR > *suniuR > *syniuR >] *syniR > synir

[*katilaz > *katilaR > *katilaR > *kætilaR >] *kætilR > kætill/ketill

[*doomian > *doomian > *doomian >*døømian > *døømian >] *døømã >
døømã (> døøma)

[*geβandiz > *geβandiR > *geβandiR > *geβandiR >] *geβendiR >
*geβendiR [> *geβendR > ON gefendr]

(e) *Word-structure modifications following secondary rhythmicization*

1 Syncope proper: prosodically non-prominent morae (also non-prominent
morae flanking a voiced dental fricative) are dropped all across a wordform
with two scenarios: (i) short non-prominent vowels are dropped; (ii) the
second, non-prominent mora of a long vowel is dropped (i.e. the vowel
is shortened).[19] Syncope (understood as a process that was quite distinct from context-specific vowel shortenings and losses belonging to early
Ancient Nordic) happens once as a sweeping process, which afterwards
ceases to operate in the transition phase to Old Nordic.

[*booni- > *booni > *bøøni >] *bøøni > bøøn

[*mauiz >] *mawiR > *mawR [> maaR, mæær]

[*mauiooz > *maujooR > *maujooR > >] *mæyjooR > ON meyjar

[*handiz > *handiR > *hændiR >] *hændiR > hændr/hendr

[*gastiz > *gastiR > *gæstiR >] *gæstiR > gæstr/gestr

[*gastiiz > *gastiiR >] *gæstiiR > *gæstiR [> gæstir/gestir]

[*haliz >] haliR > halr

---

[19] This formulation does not capture monosyllabicity in feminine *-oo-stems, cf. *-iþoo-
formations.

[*haliiz >] haliiR > halir
[*arniuz > *arniuR >] *ærniuR > *ærniR [> ON ernir]
[*suniuz > *suniuR > *suniuR] > *syniuR > *syniR [> synir]
[*doomia > *doomia >] *døømia > *døømi [> døømi]
[*bandilaz > *bandilaR >] *bændilaR > *bændilR [> bændill/bendill]
[*katilaz > *katilaR > *katilaR >] *kætilaR > *kætilR [> kætill/ketill]
[*katilee >] *katilee > *katle [> *katle = katli]
[*taliðee >] *taliðee > *talðe [> talðe = talði]
[*doomian > *doomian > *doomian >*døømian >] *døømian > døømã
    (> døøma)
[*haanizooz > *haaniRooR > *hææniRooR >] *hææniRooR > *hæ(æ)nRaR
    (> hænnar)
[*ungizee > *ungiRee > *yngiRee >] *yngiRee > *yngRe (> yngri)
[*doomiðooz > *doomiðooR > *døømiðooR >] *døømiðooR > *døømðaR
    [> døømdar]
[*doomiðaz > *doomiðaR > *døømiðaR >] *døømiðaR > *døømðR
    [> døømdr]
[*taliðaz > *taliðaR >] *taliðaR > *talðR [> taldr]
[*geßandiz > *geßandiR > *geßandiR > *geßandiR > *geßendiR >]
    *geßendiR > *geßendR [> ON gefendr]

2 Readjustment: after syncope the prosodic pattern is readjusted in accordance with (d3) above. Certain qualitative coalescences happen in the system of unstressed vowels (at that point, i-umlaut has ceased to operate as a regular process).

(f) *Late prosodic processes (not specified in detail here, cf. Section 15.3.1, (v)–(x) above)*

1 Circumflex contour formation: if a dissyllabic word form ends up becoming monosyllabic, its high–low (HL) pitch pattern is concentrated on the stress-syllable, as in old monosyllables. The stød is the Danish reflex of the HL contour concentrated on one (stressed) syllable.
2 Various Nordic dialects develop either contrastive tone or contrastive stød out of the word-demarcating pitch contours emerging in Old Nordic.

15.6. DISCUSSION AND CONCLUSION

The theory proposed here is a speculative proposal. I must admit that some components of it have limited empirical support, although they are crucial in helping to account for the historical data. Altogether, I

have attempted to keep the number of basic assumptions to a minimum, but they all deviate from traditionally-held views. The most
important are:

1 umlaut as vowel harmony working over a long period and spreading backwards from a prosodically-prominent vowel;
2 establishment of a new, word-demarcating rhythm/pitch contour in Late
  Ancient Nordic;
3 syncope based on the resulting metric templates (not on earlier mora-
  counting templates);
4 stød-genesis and tonogenesis based on the falling tone contour that
  wordforms acquired according to the new metric templates.

In my view, the resulting scenario in its totality is not typologically
implausible if one compares it with the complicated rhythm and
tone mechanisms that have been described for languages across the
world (including sub-Saharan languages and Eskimo languages, for
example).

15.6.1. **Hiatus and prominence**

It is a relevant issue within the bonds of my theory how prominence
rules and hiatus rules at the earliest stage interacted. Above, I have
taken glide formation in hiatus to precede prominence rules since that
makes it easy to set up a flow of consecutive processes, but this may
be a descriptive rather than a historical order of events. It should be
noted that the reconstructed forms for Early Ancient Nordic which
I take as a point of departure, although otherwise entirely consistent
with traditional assumptions, are abstract in the sense that they sometimes contain strings of several consecutive vowel morae, which at any
time would be processed by some syllabification rule in order to be
pronounceable. In other words, the input representations are *phonemic*
not phonetic. Seen from that perspective both phenomena, hiatus rules
and prominence rules, were well-formedness constraints on output
forms at a given time, although they had phonemic consequences
eventually. With a proper formulation of the distribution (and redistribution) of syllabicity on consecutive morae, glide-formation, e.g. in
talian > *tælja*, can be explained as coinciding with non-prominence,
thus lending credibility to my claims about alternating prominence in
Ancient Nordic.

15.6.2. **Umlaut and syncope**

In this theory there is no such thing as separate syncope periods. Syncope in Late Early Nordic did not reapply in new waves over time; all vowel droppings and vowel shortenings across a word were part of the same shrinking process. That, of course, does *not* mean that everything happened at once, nor does it exclude that there may have been intermediate forms with variation. Some vowel morae were undoubtedly lost before others.

My model implies the claim that at one point, a weakly stressed vowel was more prominent after a long rather than after a short stem. At a later point, after the new rule of prominence on the penultimate mora, the last mora became non-prominent in both cases.[20]

The general assumption, on the contrary, is that there was less prominence on the vowel after a long than after a short stem. There is nothing in my theory that prevents such a scalar difference from having arisen even *later*, i.e. in Late Ancient Nordic,[21] when syllables and their relative weight had come to play a greater role in word rhythm than morae. So-called vowel balance ('jamvikt') in a Central Norwegian area might be a reflex of such a development. The scanty runic data suggesting earlier syncope after long than after short stems are not absolutely compelling (there might, for example, have been an inertia in the spelling of forms which did not undergo any rhythmical or qualitative changes in Late Ancient Nordic prior to syncope). The evidence is altogether weak.[22] If, however, there was a development of binary prominence patterns into scalar values, then that phenomenon is peripheral to my umlaut-and-syncope theory.

As for syncope as such, I find it attractive to avoid a model in which there may be any number of consecutive applications of syncope to the output from the preceding round of application. For one thing, such a model easily becomes over-generating; another thing is that one may

[20] Since the prominence shift to the penultimate mora posited in my theory happened before syncope, the theory has no affinity to Penzl's controversial proposal that syncope happened earlier after short than after long stems (Penzl 1951).

[21] Not Early Ancient Nordic, as suggested by the infelicitous formulation in Rischel (2001: 20).

[22] Bisyllabic participle forms such as *taliðr* and *talinn* (occurring beside the also occurring and more expected *taldr*) should not be taken as evidence for less proneness to syncope after short syllables since they must be due to influence from the participles of strong verbs, with which *ja*-verbs had some structural affinity.

be forced to posit implausible intervals of non-syncope between waves of syncope (cf. the succession of two periods of syncope in Kock's theory).

My rejection of a connection between *i*-umlaut and syncope does not at all entail the rejection of an umlaut chronology as such. One can certainly preserve the notions of *elder i-umlaut* and *younger i-umlaut* within the framework of my theory, the former being umlaut that applied already in the era of early Nordic rhythmicization (prominence on odd-numbered morae), the latter being the umlaut that applied after the retraction of prominence from the ultimate to the penultimate mora had created new structures it could apply to. Examination of my examples in Sections 15.4 and 15.5 above will show that, in spite of the different descriptive framework, the relative chronology posited here agrees well with the established one, which dates back to Axel Kock. Quite unlike Kock's theory, however, there is no difference in kind between elder and younger *i*-umlaut within the framework of my theory; it is a mere difference of chronology.

As I see it, the attractiveness of the theory presented here—in spite of its difficulties—is that it envisages an overall framework in which such major processes as umlaut, syncope, and stød-genesis all seem to fall in place. Most of the attested ON forms can be derived quite mechanically from reconstructed Ancient Nordic by applying the set of phonological rules I have sketched above. There is no instance in the selected but variegated data presented above in which I appeal to *analogy* in accounting for the presence or absence of umlaut; the umlaut pattern of masculine *i*-stems in particular is handled by the theory in terms of mechanical rules. I consider that to be one of the strong features of the theory.

Unfortunately, there remain some important form types that are unaccounted for, as they are in most or all other umlaut and syncope theories. Since those forms cannot be captured by the theory itself, they may require appeal to the notion of analogy, or at least to morphology. As of now I have to revert to explanations similar to those forwarded by the neogrammarian scholars (Kock, Brøndum-Nielsen, and others). I shall mention some issues in ascending order of severity for my theory.

The first issue is the frequent absence in Nordic of umlaut in long *feminine i*-stem nouns. Since there is a lot of variation over dialects and between compound and non-compound forms, one cannot expect to be able to formulate any mechanical rules. The feminine *i*-stems have only few characteristics defining them as such across the inflectional paradigm, so this is an instance in which both analogy and contamination between different noun-classes seem to have been at work, causing massive exceptions to the sound laws.

The second issue is umlaut in a few comparative forms with a short stem, e.g. *ytri, betri*. I have not attempted to adjust my theory so as to account for them. There are two traditional explanations: (i) an alleged combinatory umlaut, '*iR*-umlaut' affecting long and short stems alike; (ii) analogy from the greater number of dissyllabic comparative forms with long stems, such as *yngri*.

The third issue is umlaut in the present singular forms of short-stem strong verbs and *ja*-verbs. Again, the Nordic data show variation, suggesting that it was not just a matter of a mechanical process of umlauting in such forms. I do not see how any theory (including the assumption of a combinatory '*iR*-umlaut', see above) can account convincingly for umlaut in the verb form *telr* (< **taliR*) versus the expected absence of umlaut in the noun form *halr* (< **haliR*) except by resorting to grammatical and/or statistical criteria involving analogy, as has traditionally been done. Obviously, there were a lot of long-stem strong verbs whose *i*-umlaut became a diacritic feature of the present singular (even causing a late restructuring of the first person singular form in **-u* into an *i*-umlauted monosyllabic form so as to fit in with the second and third persons), and that feature was extended to all verbs with a monosyllabic present singular, i.e. strong verbs with a short stem and *ja*-verbs as well.

As for forms in which syncope has *not* occurred, there are two major exceptions to the *i*-umlaut rules: (1) two morphological categories in which expected umlaut fails to appear; (2) a morphological category in which an umlauted vowel is followed by a non-umlauting vowel.

1 Past participles in *-in-*, such as *haldin(n)*, fail to exhibit *i*-umlaut (the vowel shift in ON *tekin(n)* is not *i*-umlaut proper but due to early palatalization of the intervening dorsal consonant). On comparative evidence one might expect either **-an-* or **-in-* in these participles. The lack of umlaut may somehow reflect a variation over such forms, possibly resulting in an intermediate variant **-en-* which escaped syncope only to coalesce with **i* when the inventory of unstressed vowels shrank to three entities *a, i, u*. Similarly,

the nom. sg. of masculine *n*-stems ends in non-umlauting *-i* in Old Nordic, reflecting a former non-high vowel.

2 The dative plural of long *i*-stem nouns has *i*-umlaut in spite of *-u-* in the following syllable all across Nordic: *gæstum* (ON *gestum*). One expects *-im(i)z* rather than *-um(i)z* in early Germanic (cf. Gothic *-im*). Assuming that there was a morphological change *-imR* > *-umR* (> *-um*) after the umlaut era,[23] the occurrence of *i*-umlaut is straightforwardly explained within the bonds of my theory. The theory predicts that *i*-umlaut applied to *gastimR* > *gæstimR*. Some time after that, then, a morphological substitution *gæstimR* > *gæstumR* (> *gæstum*) happened. Short-stem nouns, on the contrary, did *not* undergo *i*-umlaut but just had morphological substitution: *halimR* > *halumR* (> ON *hölum* by late *u*-umlaut). This is also consistent with the theory since it was only later that *-mR* < *-m(i)z* was reduced to word-final *-m* (a word-final nasal already at the beginning of the Late Ancient Nordic period would have made the last vowel mora prominent according to principle (b1) in Section 15.5, thus conceivably triggering a spurious *i*-umlaut in the dative plural, as against all other forms).

An alternative explanation of (2) would be that the umlauted vowel in the dative plural is due to a Late Ancient Nordic generalization of the umlauted stem vowel throughout all inflected forms: *gastumR* > *gæstumR* so as to comply with *gæstiR*, *gæsti*, etc. I do not think there is any basis whatsoever for that assumption. It would run counter to the general tendency to *increase* stem-vowel alternations during the transition from Ancient Nordic to Old Nordic.

It is quite different with the assumption that *-im(R)* > *-um(R)* was due to a uniformation of the way in which nouns formed their dative plural, namely by means of the ending *-um(R)*. This is exactly how morphological uniformation worked in the transitional period from Ancient to Old Nordic: it operated within form-classes, i.e. *across paradigms*, so as to increase the one-to-one correspondence between form and grammatical meaning. That was illustrated already in the paragraph above about the present singular of short-stem strong verbs

[23] It should be kept in mind that Transitional Ancient Runic '*-gestumR*' is not a wordform but an artifact of faulty philological analysis, as shown brilliantly by Santesson (1989), and thus it does not bear witness to the age of the dative plural in *-um* in *i*-stems, as was previously assumed. I wish to add in passing that one can wonder why the form *-gestumR* was not met with more suspicion long ago since the alleged use of runic *e* to denote the *i*-umlauted reflex of *a* runs counter to the morphophonemic character of runic writing at the time when the shorter fuþark replaced the longer (cf. Rischel 1963).

(which could not undergo *i*-umlaut according to my theory): the form–meaning correspondence was increased by the generalization of alternations such as $a \sim æ$, $u \sim y$ to mark the present singular in these verb paradigms, as they did in the paradigmatically similar long-stem strong verbs.

By way of conclusion it should be pointed out that this kind of analogy applies to specific form-classes not to whole paradigms (except for words that are mutually related by derivation, e.g. verbs and nominalizations). Thus there was no way in which the *i*-umlaut in long *i*-stem nouns could be generalized to short *i*-stem nouns, for in this case *the whole paradigm* was umlauted, so the new vowel just formed part of the phonological shape of the word without conveying any information about form-class.

15.6.3. **i-umlaut and other related processes**

The transition from Ancient Nordic to Old Nordic was characterized above all by dramatic changes in the vowel pattern, involving qualitative changes in stressed vowels and loss or shortening of unstressed vowels. Stressed vowels underwent a whole array of modifications. Besides the kind of *i*-umlaut considered in this paper, there was *i*-umlaut of front vowels, *a*-umlaut, *u*-umlaut (here understood as umlaut caused by a syllabic *u*, unlike *w*-umlaut), breaking, and consonant-conditioned vowel colouring (so-called *R*-umlaut, *w*-umlaut, and *j*-umlaut). If one strives to view all these processes as parts of a complex scenario, it is a possible objection to my theory that it fails to qualify as 'unified' in that sense. In spite of the cover label 'umlaut' and the obvious connections between *u*-umlaut and breaking, however, the phenomena are very different. If viewed jointly, they involve changes in all the major distinctive features of vowels, and I would claim that different mechanisms are involved.

Let us look first at the various kinds of umlaut that are supposed to be caused by a vowel in a following syllable. Whereas *i*-umlaut of back vowels is place assimilation and *u*-umlaut is rounding assimilation, one observes that *i*-umlaut of front vowels, *a*-umlaut, and breaking all affect vowel height. There is a priori no reason why all these processes should have occurred within the same time period and under structurally comparable conditions. They may not even have been equally dependent on the presence of a following vowel (actually, that has been disputed both for *a*-umlaut and for breaking).

There was, however, a typological affinity between *i*-umlaut and *u*-umlaut. Both processes were triggered by high vowels, and both processes affected the 'tonality' of vowels as manifested auditorily by the vowel timbre ('hell' versus 'dunkel'), and acoustically by the distance between the first and second (plus third) vowel formants. In articulatory terms, *i*-umlaut changed the front–back position of the tongue body, and *u*-umlaut changed the articulation in terms of lip-rounding.

From a language-typological perspective most vowel systems across the world exhibit an interaction between front–back position of the tongue body and rounding, limiting the tonality steps to two (typically: front unrounded [i, e] vs. back rounded [u, o]) or even to one for the most open vowel (i.e. some kind of central or back, unrounded '[a]'). That is indeed the situation obtaining in Early Ancient Nordic. In Late Ancient Nordic, umlaut increased the tonality steps for non-low vowels to three (front unrounded, front rounded, back rounded), again with a different situation for the most open vowel articulation although the Old Nordic phonetics for that part of the vowel space is controversial. We know that *i*-umlaut of **a(a)* created a front vowel *æ*, and that *u*-umlaut of **a(a)* created a rounded vowel (rendered in this paper as *ö*), but historical and comparative evidence does not tell us whether these two new vowel qualities were, in the beginning, as open as, or less open than, *a*, or whether *ö* was, in the beginning, a central or a back vowel.

In any case, the two articulatory dimensions of rounding and front–back position interacted all across the vowel space rather than being mutually independent (orthogonal), exactly as one would expect on typological grounds. This interrelatedness between dimensions must be taken into consideration if one attempts to account for the phonetic processes of umlaut.

A strange thing about *u*-umlaut is that it applied *regularly* only to **a* (or its long counterpart), unlike *i*-umlaut and *j*-umlaut which applied to all back vowels, and *w*-umlaut which applied (more or less irregularly) to all front vowels. I see it as a challenge for future theories about umlaut to explain this lack of symmetry. Its very existence casts doubt on the parallelism between the processes of *i*-umlaut and *u*-umlaut.

Whether the above is a true statement about *u*-umlaut, however, depends on one's theory of breaking. When **e* surfaces in West Nordic as *jö* and in East Nordic as *jo* in a word such as Icelandic *jörð*, Danish and Swedish *jord*, there are a variety of possible explanations, all of which have been considered in the literature. Since the word has ended in -*u* in Late Ancient Nordic, it is self-evident that a vowel-harmony process akin to *u*-umlaut has been involved. If it had the same domain of application as in plainly umlauted forms, there must have been an intermediate step with breaking **e* > **ja* so as to feed *u*-umlaut **ja* > **jö*. The East Nordic reflexes of '*u*-breaking', however, seem more suggestive of an intermediate step with a higher vowel after *j*, either such that vowel harmony accompanied the breaking process itself or such that **e* first became **je* or **jæ* and then harmonized with the following vowel. Since this can still be considered an open issue, I leave breaking entirely out of consideration here.

Concentrating now on plain *u*-umlaut, as in **barnu* > West Nordic *börn*, Danish *børn*, it is clear that this phenomenon must somehow find a place in a more complete version of the theory presented in this paper. There are, however, very great differences between the Nordic *i*-umlaut and *u*-umlaut scenarios. These differences are so pervasive that I cannot handle *u*-umlaut within the bonds of this paper without losing track of the main issues. In return, a few scattered observations on the behaviour of *u*-umlaut are presented in an Appendix at the end of this paper.

Next there is vowel colouring by a following consonant or glide. One might argue that an adequate theory of *i*-umlaut should posit the same phonetic process underlying Old Nordic forms such as *døøma* and *tælja*, since these are originally similar formations (-*ia*-/-*ja*-verbs) whose different behaviour reflects the quantity of the stem syllable. In my theory the umlaut in these forms did *not* arise through the same type of process: the former is vowel harmony depending on a specific rhythm pattern (the first mora of **-ia-* being prominent after a long stem syllable although it later lost prominence and was eventually lost) whereas in the latter case there was co-articulation of the stem vowel with the palatal glide resulting from a hiatus rule (the first mora of **-ia-* being non-syllabic after a short stem syllable).

According to my theory, umlaut must have entered the language *after* the hiatus rules of Ancient Nordic had established fixed templates such as **-VVCia-*/**-VCCia-* versus **-VCja-*. That **-i-* ~ **-j-* alternation may have arisen quite early; it predated Late Ancient Nordic developments such as the change of vowel plus *h* into a long vowel (we can observe the post-consonantal glide in forms such as *hlahian* > *hlahjan* > *hlææja*). I would not place Nordic *i*-umlaut before the middle of the Ancient Nordic period, even though I claim that umlaut was, from then on, productive over a relatively long period (possibly up to the time frame in which syncope happened).

A separate path of vowel colouring before a glide is warranted in any case since similar vowel colourings happened before other non-syllabic sounds than *j*. Notably there were instances of fronting before *R* (e.g. *kaR* > ON *ker*) and extensive rounding before *w* (e.g. *sinkwan* > ON *søkkva*, Dan. *synke*). One can observe that i- and *j*-umlaut, *R*-umlaut, and u- and *w*-umlaut 'conspired' to a varying extent to produce a total of four new vowel phonemes (each short and long). The five processes thus converged significantly in their output but that does not make them into related or even identical processes.

As for the question whether umlaut in *tælja* was caused by a vowel or a glide, umlaut before *w* is interesting in that it affected a wider repertory of vowels than umlaut before *u* (which in essence affected short and long *a*). That suggests that rounding before a vowel and before a glide were distinct events. The syllabicity alternation *u* ~ *w* occurred under conditions comparable to those of *i* ~* j*, and this parallelism is weakly supportive of a similar claim about *i*- and *j*-umlaut being distinct events.

15.6.4. Stød genesis

In my account of stød- and tone-genesis[24] the central notion is the following: if a monosyllable had a sharply falling pitch distributed over a long sonorous stretch, its pitch drop developed into a phonation type with irregular vocal fold vibrations towards the end, namely the stød. This linking of the stød to falling tone is probably not very controversial (I share it with other scholars); the new contention on my part is that this pitch drop can be traced back to the rhythmic patterns generated by the umlaut-and-syncope model above.

---

[24] As presented also, in slightly different form but with additional details, in Rischel (2001).

It remains tricky to explain how the stød got its distribution in loanwords from Low German with an iambic stress pattern. Maybe the stød had simply become the default accentuation of new word structures already at that time. As for words with two layers of morphology added onto a monosyllabic stem, such as plurals of participles (*dømt-e*), the presence of the stød suggests that they had become prosodic islands. That might be due to their contracted stem, with double syncope, or to their morphological complexity, most likely to a combination of both.

I shall not go further into the stød-part of my theory here but just repeat that it requires word-structure adjustments in Ancient Nordic similar to those required by my account of syncope. Thus, the two can be seen as separate parts of a unified theory.

On the other hand, my stød theory (cf. the outline in Rischel 2001) is robust in the sense that it can be appraised without any reference whatsoever to my assumptions about umlaut; I suppose it may stand even in the case that my umlaut theory is refuted or becomes obsolete in the light of new and better theories about the complex relationship between syncope and umlaut.

15.7.   FINAL REMARKS

In this presentation I have deviated from some of the most basic tenets in the Nordic philological tradition and deliberately chosen an almost agnostic approach, thus avoiding being caught by masses of complex and mutually contradictory evidence from old sources, place-names and more recent dialects, with which I was brought up half a century ago like other traditional Nordic philologists. In this way, I feel, it has been possible to trace the main lines of development and still cope with the core repertory of word forms that have been discussed intensively in the literature over some 130 years. The ultimate test of any model, of course, is how it would handle a representative sample of *all* kinds of linguistic raw data that have been accumulated and presented by Nordic philologists and dialectologists over that period.

To my knowledge the theory presented in this paper differs from other competing theories about either umlaut or stød-genesis in that it presents a diachronic framework capturing both on the same explanatory basis, namely in terms of a few simple assumptions about Ancient

Nordic word prosody. As stated in the Introduction, I take that in itself to be a strong argument in favour of the theory, considering that umlaut and stød were two profoundly different types of phenomenon and moreover were mutually independent and separated in time.

It may seem less of a novelty that syncope is also explained on the same basis as umlaut since it has been customary to see a direct connection between these two phenomena. According to my theory, however, there was no such connection between umlaut and syncope. The two phenomena were totally distinct and separated in time, but both kinds of processes operated on strings with the same kinds of crucial properties.

Thus I think it is warranted to claim that this is a unified theory capturing three basically independent historical processes.

15.8. APPENDIX: *U*-UMLAUT

The attested Early Nordic data do not give clear evidence for a dependence of *u*-umlaut on the prominence pattern as defined by the quantity of the stress-syllable, i.e. it is not very obvious that umlaut caused by a syncopated *u* was regular in long syllables but exceptional or secondary in short syllables. It is, therefore, possible to argue in favour of another, seemingly simpler route of explanation, namely that *u*-umlaut applied independently of prosodic prominence, unlike *i*-umlaut.

That is not a compelling argument against extending the theory presented in this paper to *u*-umlaut, since there is a plausible explanation within the bonds of the theory, namely that the umlauted vowel (*ö* ~ *a*) acquired a diacritic function as part of certain inflections and was therefore generalized from long to short stems. It should be noted that *u*-umlaut affected only parts of inflectional paradigms or individual inflected forms, not whole paradigms (unlike *i*-umlaut in long versus short *i*-stem nouns, which simply made the words lexically different in their phonological representations). One can argue, therefore, that the morphological extension of *u*-umlaut to short stems was the same mechanism as the extension of *i*-umlaut to short stems in the present singular of strong verbs, or in the dative singular of *u*-stems.

Still, lacking further evidence, *u*-umlaut fails to yield independent support for the theory. All I can claim at this point is that it is possible to construe an *u*-umlaut scenario that is consistent with it.

Another difference between the umlaut scenarios is that *u*-umlaut has a strange geographical distribution in the extant Nordic languages, being in full force in westernmost Nordic and almost absent in easternmost Nordic. The skewed distribution is, however, no argument against generalizing my umlaut theory to apply to *u*-umlaut as well. Forms in early written sources and in various dialects (cf. Benediktsson 1963) suggest that *u*-umlaut used to occur all over Nordic, perhaps with the exception of some eastern fringes, but later receded in favour of non-umlauted *a*. That development led to the near-elimination of umlauted forms in East Nordic, and to a greater or lesser extent in regional varieties of Norwegian, whereas the umlauted forms are intact in Icelandic and in part in Faroese as well.

A third difference between the *u*-umlaut and *i*-umlaut scenarios is that the packages of processes involved do not line up entirely in terms of relative or absolute chronology. The crux is that a rounded high vowel triggered *u*-umlaut of **a* in the preceding syllable whatever the original vowel quality of the post-tonic vowel, be it **u* or **o* (long or short; in some instances the ultimate source was diphthongal **au*). In contrast, *i*-umlaut did not happen in front of *i* < **e* or *i* < **ee*, i.e. at the time the qualitative changes happened in the system of unstressed vowels, *i*-umlaut had already ceased to operate.

A priori it may seem tempting to assume that the seemingly parallel changes **o* > *u* and **e* > *i* were parts of one complex change in the system of unstressed vowels at the transition to Old Nordic. Under that assumption one would be forced to assume that *u*-umlaut before a preserved, umlaut-causing vowel happened later than *i*-umlaut, since the former happened also before secondary -*u*-.

That does not hold water, however. The coalescence of short **o* and **u* happened some time in Ancient Nordic, and it does not align with the qualitative changes in the palatal series. As for the qualitative *and* quantitative change **oo* > *u*, that was not a generalized process like **ee* > *i*; it happened only in specific phononological environments and must be dated back into Ancient Nordic. At the time of syncope (understood as regular losses of non-prominent vowel morae), post-tonic **-oo* was still widely preserved as a long vowel but it was now indisputably of more open quality (unsurprisingly, it continued to be written with the same ancient rune as stressed *o*). In the late round of vowel mergers, *-oo* therefore coalesced with *-a*, not with *-u*. A parade example of the dual reflexes of *-oo-* is the old first person singular ending *-oo*, with early shortening to -*u*- in the reflexive form *kalloo-mik* > ON *köllumk* versus late shortening to -*a* in the non-reflexive first singular *kalloo* > ON *kalla*.

Thus one can hardly make any inferences from vowel mergers to the relative chronology of *u*-umlaut and *i*-umlaut.

Fourthly, *u*-umlaut differs from *i*-umlaut in the proliferation, in ON and later Icelandic, of forms such as *kölluðu, spökustum* < Late Ancient Nordic *kallaðu, *spakastum(R)*. Such forms show that the regressive vowel harmony caused by *u* was extended so as to apply even to unstressed *a*. That an unstressed, umlauted vowel switched all the way to *u* is unsurprising since the unstressed vowel pattern consisted of just *a*, *i*, and *u*; what is really significant for the chronology of *u*-umlaut is that it triggered subsequent umlauting of the stressed vowel as well. This chain of changes is clearly a late phenomenon and difficult to reconcile with a limitation of *u*-umlaut to the time before syncope.[25] The sequence *ö..u..u* became canonical in Icelandic and was generalized even to inflected forms of modern loanwords, such as the dative plural of *banani*, which is *bönunum* (whereas Faroese, for example, has made the opposite choice, the modern form corresponding to ON *kölluðu* being *kadlavu*, spelled *kallaðu*).

At some point (well *after* the transitional period between Late Ancient Nordic and Old Nordic) language-specific simplifications happened across paradigms. Faroese, for example, generalized the (late) umlaut vowel *ö* beyond forms with final -*u*(-), as in *gata, götu* > *gøta, gøtu*.

There is a fifth difference between *u*-umlaut and *i*-umlaut as a corollary of the just-mentioned difference in timing. As argued by Benediktsson (1963), the stress-vowel *a* and its umlauted counterpart never came to be contrastive in front of preserved *u* (quite unlike the umlaut vowels caused by *i*-umlaut, which contrast with their non-umlauted counterparts). Benediktsson speaks of an Archiphoneme

---

[25] On the other hand, *u*-umlaut agrees with *i*-umlaut in applying in its canonical form, with the reflex *ö* < *a*, to the heavy second syllable in forms such as *geßandum(R)* > ON *geföndum*.

'*å*' in this position and explains a strange variation in early scribal practices as being due to the lack of contrast. Given that the quality of stressed **a* was in phonetic limbo in this position, it is no wonder that the *u*-umlaut scenario, viewed across the Nordic area, became complex. Since the prosodic prominence pattern changed substantially with the completion of syncope, it is possible that, at that time, the alternative assignment of **å* to either *a* or *ö* was no longer regulated by syllable prominence i.e. in its very latest phase of vowel-quality assignment, *u*-umlaut may have become an across-the-board type of vowel harmony, although the choice of *ö* over *a* (or vice versa) was geographically restricted. Such a late scenario would have no relevance for the workings of *i*-umlaut since, according to my theory, *i*-umlaut ceased to operate before syncope.

That *u*-umlaut before preserved *u* had its stronghold in West Nordic may conceivably have to do with vowel epenthesis, i.e. the insertion of a svarabhakti vowel *u* in word-final clusters of the structure C_*r*. That process is not expressed in writing in very early sources but only later (in the thirteenth century). Still, I would contend that, at a purely phonetic level, word-final, post-consonantal -*r* may have acquired syllabicity quite early in Old Norse although it did not yet count structurally and metrically as a syllable. (This is not typologically far-fetched: a Danish imperative form such as *hamr* is either avoided by speakers or pronounced as rhyming with *kammer*; it also deserves to be mentioned that pretonic syllables exhibit such quasi-syllabicity in many South East Asian languages.) In other words, the epenthetic vowel may have been a spoken option for some time before it was expressed in the basically conservative Old Icelandic spelling. In West Nordic we encounter this development of -*r* > -*ur* after the stem vowel *a*, both in inflected forms such as *sandr* > *sandur* and in stems with a final *r*-cluster such as *akr* > *akur*. Such epenthesis made the alternants *a* ~ *ö* phonologically unpredictable before -*ur*; note that one finds the stem vowel *ö* before -*ur* both in forms with epenthesis, e.g. the nominative singular of *u*-stems (*vörður*), and in forms with historical -*u*-, e.g. the nominative/accusative plural of feminine *n*-stems (*stjörnur*, nom. sg. *stjarna*). Thus *a* ~ *ö* turned into a diacritic marker even in this position (in Faroese it is even more tricky because there was a dialect-specific merger of -*u*(-) and -*i*(-) in certain phonological environments).

One should note that nothing similar to that could happen in East Nordic, the epenthetic vowel there being of schwa-type (expressed by *e* or *æ*) and thus not immediately coalescing with either *i* or *u* in post-tonic syllables.

Concluding remarks: Because of the many complications sketched above I have preferred to refrain from presenting a formalized account of *u*-umlaut in this paper.

16

Diphthongization in Faroese[1,2]

16.1. INTRODUCTION

The Faroese language[3] has among its most characteristic properties an abundance of diphthongs. Some of these are reflexes of Old West Scandinavian (abbreviated OWS) diphthongs, some are reflexes of vowel–consonant combinations, and finally a number of diphthongs have developed from OWS single vowels.

The diphthongs of Faroese are interesting from a general linguistic point of view, both because the inventory is typologically remarkable and because a comparison of the proto-language (OWS) and Modern Faroese (abbreviated MF) reveals some very puzzling developments of this system. The phonetic changes involved are in part very difficult to explain, at least if the case of each MF diphthong is considered in isolation. It is the aim of this paper to demonstrate that the various diphthongizations and other sound changes which can be observed are manifestations of a thorough reorganization of the whole vowel system that took place in the Faroese language of the Middle Ages (here termed 'Old Faroese': OF).

The difficulty with Faroese sound history (compared to the other Nordic languages) is that the sources covering the period from the early Middle Ages to the late eighteenth century[4] are scanty and for

---

[1] Reprinted from *Acta Linguistica Hafniensia* XI, 1 (1967/1968): 89–118.

[2] Some of the ideas expressed in this paper were summarized in Rischel (1966).

[3] West Scandinavian. The Faroe Islands are situated somewhat over 200 miles north of Scotland (northwest of the Shetland Islands).

[4] The works of J. Chr. Svabo from the late eighteenth and early nineteenth centuries, particularly his Faroese dictionary (*Dictionarium Færoense*, ed. Chr. Matras for the Societas Litterarum Færoensium Hafniensis, 1966), are inexhaustible sources of information about the language of that age, compiled with outstanding skill. His phonetic orthography reveals that the sound pattern of the eighteenth century was on most points quite similar to that of our time. The sources before Svabo are of incomparably lesser value, since a phonetic

the most part of very questionable value. A good deal of information extracted from these sources by the Norwegian scholars Marius Hægstad (1917) and Håkon Hamre (1944), also concerning the development of the vowel system; but it should not be overlooked that there is a danger of circularity in their approach, since the graphical forms adduced as evidence are in many cases phonetically equivocal, to say the least. Other valuable contributions have been made by Jón Helgason and Mikjel Sørlie, who have been particularly interested in deciding whether certain medieval manuscripts are of Faroese origin, cf. Helgason (1951, 1952) and Sørlie (1936, 1965).

Recently, the development of the Faroese vowel system has been scrutinized from a structuralist point of view by Chapman (1962) and later by Amundsen (1964). To take up the problems again would indeed seem rather superfluous if either one or the other had offered a convincing explanation of the whole structural change. However, in the opinion of the present author this is not the case. Chapman compares the vowel systems of OWS and of modern Icelandic and Norwegian dialects with a structurally elegant phonemic model of the Faroese vowel system, but the symmetry of the latter (and its superficial resemblance to the others) is deceptive as it has no phonetic justification, so that the model hampers, rather than facilitates, the understanding of the tendencies of development.[5] Amundsen follows the vowel system in its various shapes from OWS to MF arguing that early Faroese must have developed a system with too many vowel phonemes, and that for this reason some of the vowels were later diphthongized, thus reducing the number of distinct degrees of aperture and places of articulation. However, there is no conclusive evidence for the intermediate, overloaded system he posits,[6] though it certainly offers a possible alternative to the explanation suggested below.

Both authors narrow their scope of study substantially by considering only one dialect of Faroese, viz. the dialect of the area around the main city Tórshavn, which is generally used in textbooks

interpretation of them must frequently be based on hypotheses about the developments from OWS to MF, rather than the other way round.

[5] The diphthongs which are rendered as /ui, yu/ in the present paper are /oi, ou/ in Mr. Chapman's presentation, and he has /o, ɔ/ instead of /y, o/. As pointed out by O'Neil (1964a), the phonetic basis for his analysis is somewhat erroneous.

[6] Most surprising is that Mr. Amundsen assumes that the reflex of OWS /o/ used to be more open than those of OWS /e, ø/, although in MF all three vowels are on line and obviously structurally on a par (if there is any difference in their long reflexes, /øː/—the long counterpart of /ø/—is the most open).

and dictionaries and thus constitutes a kind of official norm at least in the minds of people abroad. Unfortunately, this dialect is in some respects clearly a transitional one: it represents a mixture of developments which stand out more clearly if more peripheral dialects are considered.

To be true, the dialect geography of the Faroes is an almost unexplored field, which explains that the possibility of making internal reconstructions by comparing MF dialects has not been made use of to any great extent. However, even the most conspicuous dialect differences (which are for the most part mentioned in the literature on Faroese[7]) reveal a number of interesting facts. Throughout the present paper this evidence has been made use of.[8]

This paper is confined to the formulation of a structural hypothesis. It draws heavily upon earlier work by other scholars but tries to incorporate their observations in a general framework. It goes without saying that the hypothesis may eventually be refuted by external evidence, particularly if we arrive at a better understanding of the phonetic and phonemic values of the Faroese word forms scattered in written (Norwegian or Danish) sources from the Middle Ages and later. Moreover, in continuation of Chapman's approach, a thorough comparison with other reflexes of OWS (Icelandic, Norwegian, Shetland Norn, etc.) might throw light on the still obscure problem whether some of the sound-shifts were spontaneous or due to borrowing.

16.1.1. Dialect areas of the Faroes

For the following survey of OWS and MF equivalents a rough partition of the Faroes into major dialect areas is required (Fig. 16.1).

The Faroes form a triangle with a northeastern angle: the Norðuroyar ('northern islands'); a western angle: the small island of Mykines; and a southern angle: the island of Suðuroy ('southern island'). Inside the Norðuroyar we find Eysturoy ('eastern island'), and west of that is Streymoy, whose southern part forms the geographical

---

[7] A good deal of general information can be extracted from the phonetic appendix by Jakob Jakobsen in Hammershaimb (1891). Specimens of three different dialects in narrow transcription using the IPA alphabet are found in Hagström (1967). See Hagström for further references. A survey of the dialects has been given by O'Neil (1963).

[8] In addition to my personal records of dialect material from the years 1954 and 1960, I have had access to a collection of tape recordings made by Napoleon Djurhuus and Chr. Lisse in 1955 and deposited at the Institute of Danish Dialectology.

Figure 16.1

and cultural centre of the Faroes with the main town Tórshavn.
Southern Streymoy is surrounded by some small islands: Hestur,
Koltur, Nólsoy. West of Streymoy (between that and Mykines) is the
island of Vágar. South of Streymoy is Sandoy, and between that and
Suðuroy to the extreme south are two minor islands: Skúvoy and
Stóra Dímun.

Probably the most obvious dialect border is between the southern
islands including Sandoy on the one hand and the more northerly (and
western) islands on the other.[9] A single feature will suffice to define this
border: OWS /a/ before /ng/ is reflected in the southern area as /a/ but
elsewhere as /e/ (in a word like *ganga* '(to) go'). But another obvious
border is between the central (and western) area including southern Streymoy on the one hand, and the northeastern area including

---

[9] Referred to as 'South of the fjord' and 'North of the fjord' (i.e. Skopunarfjörður
between Sandoy and Streymoy), respectively.

TABLE 16.1 *The vowel system of Old West Scandinavian*

	Front				Back			
	Unrounded		Rounded		Unrounded		Rounded	
Long:								
close	/iː/	(*i*)	/yː/	(*y*)	—		/uː/	(*ú*)
mid	/eː/	(*é*)	/øː/	(*ǿ, œ*)	—		/oː/	(*ó*)
open	/æː/	(*ę́*)	—		/aː/	(*á*)	/ɔː/	(*ǫ́*)
Short:								
close	/i/	(*i*)	/y/	(*y*)	—		/u/	(*u*)
mid	/e/	(*e*)	/ø/	(*ø*)	—		/o/	(*o*)
open	—		—		/a/	(*a*)	/ɔ/	(*ǫ*)

northern Streymoy on the other: OWS /ei/ is /ai/ in the former but /oi/ [ɔi] in the latter.[10] By these and other isoglosses three main areas are established, which may be termed 'southern' (abbreviated S), 'central' (C), and 'northern' (N). Within each area, however, there are minor differences in the reflexes of OWS vowels and diphthongs, so that it is expedient to further divide the northern area into (a) Norðuroyar (No) and (b) Eysturoy + northern Streymoy (NStr), the central area into (i) southern Streymoy + surrounding islands (SStr) and (ii) Vágar etc. (Vá), and the southern area into (i) Sandoy + smaller islands (Sa) and (ii) Suðuroy (Su). (Nólsoy has a less clear status, being transitional between central and southern dialects.)

16.1.2. Vowel system of Old West Scandinavian

The vowel system of OWS can probably be set up as shown in Table 16.1. (Old Icelandic orthographic correspondences are given in parentheses.)

For the purpose of the present paper the problem of a possible distinction between short /e/ and /æ/ in the oldest stage of the language is of no consequence. The later developments clearly point to /e/, i.e. a vowel corresponding in aperture to /ø, o/. /aː, a/ may belong below the other vowels, i.e. as constituting a separate category with

---

[10] There may be an old difference of settlement between SStr and NStr, cf. Rischel (1964*b*: 38–9; 48–9).

respect to tongue-height, but it can be claimed that this difference is 'nondistinctive'.[11]

The following diphthongs were found:

/ei/ *(ei)*   /øy/ *(ey)*   /au/ *(au)*

which had no distinction of long : short.[12]

The system tabulated here can be posited without modification for the proto-language from which Faroese developed. This language is here (somewhat loosely) termed 'Old West Scandinavian' (OWS) when referred to as the common ancestor of Icelandic, Norwegian, and Faroese, whereas the name 'Old Faroese' (OF) is used for a later stage exhibiting some features peculiar to or characteristic of Faroese.

The quality of the vowel here rendered as /ɔ/ is a controversial point (in Faroese the short vowel coalesced with /ø, øː/ in some positions and with /o/ in others; the long vowel coalesced with /aː/); but this particular problem is slightly outside the focus of the present paper. The quality of the diphthong /øy/ is more crucial. Icelandic evidence points to /ey/, Norwegian evidence points to /øy/ in OWS. OWS /øy/ is assumed below.

16.1.3. Vowel system of Modern Faroese

The vowel system of Modern Faroese has been the subject of several papers, and a great variety of phonemic solutions have been offered.[13] This is not because Faroese has become a favourite hunting ground of structuralists with a preference for restatements and rearrangements, but rather because the sound system of the language *is* difficult to describe adequately. This is probably true in particular if one wishes to set up an autonomous phonemic system (i.e. without a morpho-phonemic basis). A serious approach along this line reveals that there are numerous instances of non-uniqueness in the structural arrangement, i.e. the linguist is forced to make choices among competing solutions. This indeterminacy of the system is in itself an interesting characteristic of the Faroese language but rather discomforting if an

---

[11] Cf., however, the arrangement in Rischel (1967: 11–12).

[12] This feature sets off the true diphthongs of OWS from other phoneme combinations which have often been called diphthongs (in particular those resulting from 'breaking'), cf. Benediktsson (1968: 53).

[13] Most recently by Werner (1968) with references to earlier analyses (not including that of Hagström 1967 nor Skårup's brief 1959 paper).

expedient frame of reference is required for a study like the present one.

It may be argued that it is a fallacy to describe sound changes in terms of a phonemic model which is in some respects arbitrary. It may indeed be argued that the phonological doctrine of transformational grammar provides a more adequate description. This has been emphasized in a paper on MF vowel morphophonemics by O'Neil (1964*b*), who further claims that the ordered rules he sets up to account for the relations between morphophonemes and allophones reflect stages in the history of Faroese.

In spite of its theoretical interest O'Neil's account does not altogether convince the present writer that his description of 1964*b* is necessarily the most adequate account and the best basis for historical work. Both the segmentation (essentially the distinction between diphthongs and monophthongs in the underlying system of morphophonemes) and the ordering of rules provoke questions on the part of the reader; in particular, the rules set up to take care of the quantity system, which is the main source of complication in MF phonemics, seem somewhat artificial as they stand.

In MF vowel length can be considered a function of the length (or complexity) of the following consonant (group) *or* vice versa, since the sequence *vowel + consonant* in stressed syllables is either [V:C] or [VC:]. There are numerous alternations between short and long vowel (diphthong), most conspicuously in inflected forms with and without a consonantal suffix ([ci:k] 'live (fem.)' – [cɪkt] 'do. (neut.)', etc.). This relationship is taken care of in O'Neil's model by one rule making all vowels 'tense' (tenseness involving length), and a second rule making the vowels short again before long consonants or clusters. However, as the rules are formulated, they imply also the introduction of tenseness, i.e. lengthening, and a subsequent shortening in forms like [fɪt:] 'nice (fem. & neut.)', where no reality can be attached to them. It is a rather controversial statement that these rules reflect the historical development in a very direct way.—This, of course, by no means invalidates the claim that a higher degree of adequacy can be obtained in a generative phonology of Faroese than in an autonomous one. Some of the problems of Faroese phonology (including the handling of distributional as well as morphophonemic evidence) will be discussed in a forthcoming paper.[14]

---

[14] Editors' note: Chapter 5 in this volume.

The phenomena to be dealt with in the present paper are, in the terminology of transformational grammar, *low level rules* affecting the phonetic arrangement of the vowel pattern and operating on phonetic sequences only. This means that the MF reflexes of OWS vowels and diphthongs to be dealt with here can be defined in terms of phonetic environments not morphological ones (except that all phenomena are tacitly assumed to take place within word boundaries). Thus the reflexes of OWS /ei/ and /ɔː/ are given as /ai/ and /ɔː/, respectively, although in certain verb forms (past tense singular of verbs like *skína* '(to) shine') the former is frequently MF /ei/, and in certain other verb forms (past tense plural of verbs like *bera* '(to) carry') the latter is regularly MF /ou/. The presence of these morphologically-conditioned reflexes does not seem to influence the development of the phonetic pattern as such.

It is generally and traditionally assumed that the 'inverse correlation' of vowel length and consonant length in MF (as in most other modern Nordic languages) came about through two processes: (i) a lengthening of short vowels before a single short consonant; (ii) a shortening of long vowels (diphthongs) before long consonants or clusters (in some, not all cases), the second process taking place probably somewhat later than the first. I have found no evidence against this assumption, which also underlies the present work. This is important to state here, since it has motivated a division of the present paper into two sections: one dealing with the pattern of vowels in the position before a single short consonant, and another dealing with the pattern in the position before a long consonant or a cluster. From the point of view of MF the former deals with *long syllable nuclei*, and the latter deals with *short syllable nuclei*. From the point of view of phonetic patterning each of these subsystems can be considered as a self-contained whole, although there are of course morphophonemic interrelations between them which more or less directly reflect the historical process of shortening by which the latter was partially derived from the former.

In the following presentation long and short syllable nuclei are distinguished consistently (the former are given as diphthongs with two full vowel symbols or as vowels with length /ː/; the latter are given as diphthongs with the second vowel symbol raised to indicate shortness or as vowels without length). The two subsystems must obviously be consistently distinguished in the discussion no matter whether they are considered to be phonemically distinct (in one sense or another) or not. The problem of phonemic distinctness in itself is of marginal interest in the context of this paper, since it is a matter of interpretation of the difference [V:C] : [VC:], which is unquestionably phonemic in itself.

Within each subsystem, however, the entities listed are all mutually contrastive (commutable). Thus, in one sense they have a phonemic status, and I have preferred to give them as phonemic symbols, i.e. between slant lines, particularly because phonetic brackets might suggest that the symbols represent closely the phonetic values of the segments. Since little can be known about the exact phonetic qualities in the past, it seems preferable to use a rough notation throughout whose symbols are labels defined by only those features which we know with some certainty to have played a role in the development of the present pattern. Of course, this involves a postulate, but the more obvious points of uncertainty will be mentioned.

The present paper deals only with entities that are reflexes of OWS vowels or true diphthongs. Also combinations of the vowels /e, ø, o, a/ with /v/ are widely reflected as phonetic diphthongs (with second element [u]) in MF, but these have a very limited distribution, occurring mainly before /n/ in words like *navn* [naun] 'name' (in most other cases of vowel + /v/ + consonant the two consonants have been interchanged, cf. MF *alva* '(to) get' vs. OIcel. *afla*). These historically secondary diphthongs have been left out of the present study (although with some hesitation), the assumption being made that the development of the old vowels and diphthongs can be stated without reference to them.

TABLE 16.2 *Phonemic monophthongs*

	Front		Back	
	Unrounded	Rounded	Unrounded	Rounded
Long:				
close	/iː/	—	—	/uː/
mid	/eː/	/øː/	—	/oː/
open	/æː/	—	—	/ɔː/
Short:				
close	/i/	/y/	—	/u/
mid/open	/e/	/ø/	/a/	/o/

TABLE 16.3 *Phonemic diphthongs*

Long:
 2nd element front (palatal): /ei/, /ai/, /ui/, /oi/
 2nd element back (velar): /yu/, /ou/ (or /øu/, depending on the dialect)
Short:
 2nd element front: (Su /e^i/), /a^i/, /u^i/, /o^i/
 2nd element back: (Su formerly /y^u/, /o^u/)

The short vowels /i, y, u, e, ø, a, o/ are in IPA phonetic notation approximately [ɪ, ʏ, ʊ, ɛ, œ, a, ɔ], respectively (/a/ is not a particularly retracted vowel, though I have ventured to define it as more back than /e/ and /æː/). Long /iː, uː/ are [iː, uː], sometimes with a clearly discernible glide from a slightly more open quality toward narrow [i, u]. Long /eː, øː, oː/ are rather close to IPA [eː, øː, oː] in quality but frequently gliding from [e, ø, o] toward a more open articulation. With some speakers the difference in quality between long /eː, øː, oː/ and short /e, ø, o/ is not very great.[15]

The symbols /æː, ɔː/ stand for entities which differ rather much in phonetic manifestation from one dialect of Faroese to the other. In the extreme northeast (No) very open, unrounded monophthongs (better symbolized as /æː, aː/) occur, but in most other dialects they manifest themselves as phonetic diphthongs with [a] as the second element, approximately [ɛa, oa]. In those dialects it is possible to rewrite the two entities as phonemic diphthongs: /ea, oa/, but it is not self-evident that this restatement should be made (particularly because they are always monophthongal, or gliding in the opposite direction, before /a/ of a following syllable). Whenever there is a reason to point to the diphthongal character of these two items, they are rewritten [ɛa, oa]. The southernmost dialect (Su) lacks /æː/ completely.

[ɔ] is the short equivalent to both of the long entities [oː, oa]. The symbolization of [ɔ, ɔi, ɔu] as /o, oi, ou/ rather than /ɔ, ɔi, ɔu/ is in a sense arbitrary.

The phonetic values of the diphthongs can be assessed roughly from the allophonic description of the single vowel phonemes above: /ui/

---

[15] The results of some preliminary acoustic measurements on Faroese long and short vowels have been published in Rischel (1964*a*).

consists of [ʊ] plus a narrow palatal offglide, /ou/ is [ɔ] plus a narrow velar offglide, etc. The diphthongs are (slightly or obviously) closing. The palatal second element /i/ varies somewhat according to the character (rounded or unrounded) of the first element.

The entity that is here rendered as /yu/ has been set up by several scholars as a unit phoneme which is then considered the long counterpart of short /y/, and it has mostly been symbolized as a narrow central vowel. However, as will appear from the description below, it does not pattern like the monophthongs /iː/, /uː/ etc., and phonetically it is in no sense an equivalent to /øː/, but quite obviously rather an equivalent to /øu/ in the dialects (mainly northern and western) which have this diphthong instead of /ou/, i.e. gliding from a rather front place of articulation and backward.[16] It must be admitted that there is no /yː/ (except perhaps sporadically in loanwords), just as the system has been set up without any /aː/.[17]

The subsystem of vowels occurring in absolutely unstressed position is /i, a, u/ or reduced varieties of this set (cf. Hagström 1967).

16.2. MODERN FAROESE REFLEXES OF OWS VOWELS AND DIPHTHONGS

As mentioned above the distribution of long and short vocalic entities in MF is basically different from that of OWS, old long vowels and diphthongs having been shortened before long consonants or (certain) clusters, whereas short vowels were lengthened before short, single consonants or in open syllables, cf. the comprehensive study by Benediktsson (1968). Although the developments taking place in these two types of environment are of course closely related, it seems expedient to consider MF long and short reflexes of the OWS entities separately.

---

[16] Hagström (1967) has unit phonemes /ú, ó/ instead of diphthongs /yu, ou/, but note that both are treated alike. In other respects the presentation of this paper closely resembles that of Mr. Hagström. For a still closer model, see Werner (1968).

[17] Long /aː/ without diphthongization occurs sporadically in loanwords like *statur* 'state', and also alternating with /æː/ in *hari* 'hare' (undoubtedly a loanword as well).

16.2.1. **The development of MF long vowels and diphthongs**

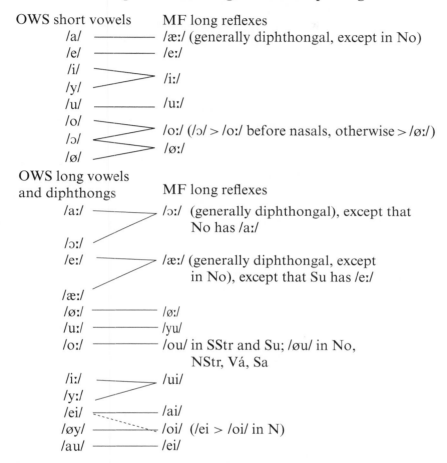

OWS short vowels   MF long reflexes
/a/ ——————— /æ:/ (generally diphthongal, except in No)
/e/ ——————— /e:/
/i/
/y/ ————— /i:/
/u/ ——————— /u:/
/o/
/ɔ/ ————— /o:/ (/ɔ/ > /o:/ before nasals, otherwise > /ø:/)
/ø/ ————— /ø:/

OWS long vowels
and diphthongs   MF long reflexes
/a:/ ————— /ɔ:/ (generally diphthongal), except that
                      No has /a:/
/ɔ:/
/e:/ ————— /æ:/ (generally diphthongal, except
                      in No), except that Su has /e:/
/æ:/
/ø:/ ——————— /ø:/
/u:/ ——————— /yu/
/o:/ ——————— /ou/ in SStr and Su; /øu/ in No,
                      NStr, Vá, Sa
/i:/
/y:/ ————— /ui/
/ei/ ————— /ai/
/øy/ ————— /oi/ (/ei/ > /oi/ in N)
/au/ ——————— /ei/

The symbolizations /ɔ:, a:/, and likewise /ou, øu/, indicate dialect varieties (the symbols for indicating these being readily at hand), but obviously not items that are (with the origin given here) mutually commutable within any one dialect. The symbolization /øu/ for the reflex of OWS /o:/ in the northern and western dialects is perhaps inadequate. The first element may have very little (or no) lip-rounding (→ [æu]) (the Sa reflex is /øu/ in the west, /ou/ in the east).

   The schemes are valid only for *vowel before consonant* (the particular developments before heterosyllabic vowel being disregarded entirely in this paper). Several coalescences are observed. All dialects have a coalescence of OWS /aː, ɔː/, of OWS /eː, æː/, of OWS /øː, (ø), ɔ/, of OWS /iː, yː/, and of OWS /i, y/. Moreover, most dialects have a coalescence of OWS /eː, æː/ and /a/, and some a coalescence of OWS /ei, øy/ (furthermore, the Sandoy dialect seems to have had a delabialization of the reflex of OWS /øː (ø), ɔ/, which however has not caused a coalescence with the reflex of OWS /e/ in the modern dialect).[18]

The MF long reflexes of OWS short vowels are listed as monophthongs. Some of them are glides whose beginning and end may be rather different, although it is essentially a matter of tongue-height. /æː/ is definitely phonetically diphthongal in many occurrences, although, as will be shown later, it does not share all the properties defining the 'true' diphthongs of MF.

The MF reflexes of OWS long vowels and diphthongs give a more confusing picture. However, two sharply different trends can be distinguished. (i) OWS /iː, yː, uː, oː/ have become diphthongs with a narrow (palatal or velar) second component. (ii) OWS /eː, æː, øː, aː, ɔː/ have developed into entities whose tendency for glide or diphthongization goes in the opposite direction: from more close toward more open. It will be shown below that the distinction between these two subsets is of fundamental importance. For the sake of brevity they will be referred to as the 'closing' system and the 'opening' system, respectively.

16.2.1.1. *The 'closing' system*

A comparison of Faroese and Icelandic shows a striking difference in the development of OWS /iː, yː, uː/ and /i, y, u/. Both languages share the coalescence of /iː/ and /yː/, and similarly of /i/ and /y/, but the relationship between the set of OWS *long* vowels and the set of OWS *short* vowels is entirely different. In Icelandic the OWS short vowels became less close, and /u/ was fronted, the reflexes being /ɪ, ʏː/. The old long vowels remained close: /iː, uː/; and there is no coalescence of the two sets in Modern Icelandic. In Faroese, on the other hand, the old short vowels are preserved as close vowels /iː, uː/, very much resembling the Icelandic reflexes of OWS long /iː, yː/ and /uː/; the old long vowels, on the other hand, are reflected as diphthongs. There is obviously a connection here: in both languages the old distinction between long and short was replaced by a qualitative difference, and thus a coalescence was avoided, but in Faroese the reflexes of OWS long vowels had to change (to speak metaphorically) because by the

---

[18] Jakobsen (1891: 460) cites this feature as peculiar to the Skúvoy dialect.

quantity shift the old short vowels would take up their place, whereas in Icelandic there was no such force acting on them. (The situation in Faroese is more closely related to that of certain Norwegian dialects, but the comparison with Icelandic may help to set off the conditions of development.)

This appeal to 'structural pressure' does not explain why the close long vowels of Faroese developed exactly the way they did, nor does it allow the linguist to determine whether the OWS long and short vowels became qualitatively different before or just at the time of the quantity shift,[19] although it may be argued that the qualitative difference became *phonemic* at that time.

The most interesting question is: how did OWS /iː/ develop into MF /ui/, a sound shift that is not found anywhere else at least in the Western branch of the Nordic languages? It goes without saying that this development cannot be 'explained' in simple phonetic terms (in strangeness it is matched only by the development of OWS /au/ into MF /ei/).

It has been suggested that the coalescence of OWS /iː, yː/ resulted in /yː/ in contradistinction to the coalescence of OWS /i, y/ which resulted in /i/ with later lengthening to /iː/ in certain positions. An adherent of this explanation is Amundsen (1964) who also contends that /uː/ became a central (?) vowel /ú/ and was thus kept distinct from the reflex of OWS /u/. Thus, according to Amundsen, the development of OWS /iː, yː, uː, i, y, u/ resulted in a series of four close vowels: /iː, yː, úː, uː/ (length marks mine), and he explains the development of the diphthong /ui/ as due to an overloading of the system with two intermediate vowels between /iː/ and /uː/ (whereas /úː/ remains a monophthong in his system). However, this scheme neither explains *why* the coalescences of long and short /i, y/ took opposite directions in Faroese (which is not the case in other descendants of OWS) nor *why* a distinction of four close vowels could not be sustained. On the other hand, a development /yː/ > /iː/ (like /y/ > /i/) would seem to provide a rather hopeless basis for the development of /ui/. It must be admitted that the genesis of MF /ui/ is a crux.

If we turn for a moment to the reflex of OWS /oː/ we find in MF a closing diphthong /ou/ or /øu/ (/eu/?). According to Amundsen /oː/

---

[19] It is probably near impossible to date the quantity shift in Faroese in absolute terms; in Icelandic it took place in the sixteenth and seventeenth centuries, but it was (considerably) earlier in Norwegian and probably also in Faroese.

first became more close and later diphthongized, but it is difficult to find a compelling reason for this contention.[20] It is obvious, however, that /oː/ acquired a special status in the vowel system of PF after /eː/ had coalesced with /æː/ (their common reflex being undoubtedly a more open vowel). A distinctive opposition of three degrees of aperture was now found *only* in the back vowels: /uː/ versus /oː/ versus /aː, ɔː/. This situation made /oː/ susceptible to change and to association with entities outside the subsystem to which it used to belong.

The diphthongs /ei/ and /øy/ constituted a subsystem of their own defined as 'mid' + 'close'. There was no back (velar) item in this subsystem, and it seems likely that /oː/ in Faroese (as well as in Icelandic and possibly more widely) became associated with these diphthongs and became phonemically /ou/. The new set /ei, øy, ou/ constituted a symmetric pattern with /iː, yː, uː/:

$$\text{/iː/ \quad /yː/ \quad /uː/}$$
$$\text{/ei/ \quad /ɔy/ \quad /ou/}$$

and it seems that a structural reconfiguration took place in PF by which these six entities came to form a subsystem (with the reflex of OWS /au/ as a 'leftover'). The possibility of this rearrangement may be more obvious if it is considered that the narrow long vowels may well have been pronounced as closing glides (as they still are in some Norwegian dialects); the crucial point is that at some point they acquired the status of two-segment units (which can be indicated by rewriting them, somewhat artificially, as /ii, yy, uu/).

That such a subsystem emerged, is not just an empty postulate. In MF we can observe a development which is common to the reflexes of OWS /iː, yː, uː, ei, øy, oː, au/ but shared by no other vowel: in open syllables occurring word-finally or before a heterosyllabic vowel the most common reflexes of these vowels and diphthongs are combinations of *short vowel* + *long consonant or consonant cluster*. The reflexes of /iː, yː, ei, øi, au/ contain a palatal stop or rather affricate (here symbolized /gj/), e.g. OWS *ný* 'new', *ey* 'island' = MF /nugj, ogj/. The reflexes of /uː, oː/ contain a velar stop plus a labial spirant, e.g.

---

[20] According to Amundsen's (1964) survey /oː/ became quite close and thus contributed to push the old /uː/ forward (cf. standard Norwegian and Swedish); but later moved back (?) to a position intermediate between the reflexes of OWS /u/ and /o/ before being diphthongized.

OWS *kú* 'cow', *tó* 'spinning material' = MF /kigv, tegv/ (the latter also /togv/).

In MF these particular sound combinations alternate with diphthongs (and are even in free variation with them in certain words). Notably the spirant *ð*, which has disappeared in Faroese, blocked the development of the consonantal manifestations, so that for instance OWS *búa* '(to) dwell' is MF /bigva/, but past tense *búði* is /byui/. If we start from diphthongal representations of all the items in question it is possible to set up fairly simple rules to account for the processes, a palatal second element being replaced by a palatal affricate, and a labio-velar second element being replaced by velar stop plus labial spirant (in recent distinctive feature terminology it is obviously the feature 'grave' that distinguishes the two subsets). Historically it is most likely that the consonantal variants did not come into existence before the entities had got roughly the diphthongal values they have in MF, the most obvious testimony being OWS /au/ with the MF reflex /egj/, cf. *taug* 'rope', MF /tegj/, which presupposes the development OWS /au/ > MF /ei/ (as the example shows, a dorsal spirant, i.e. OWS [ɣ] which has disappeared in MF, did *not* block the eventual introduction of a stop).

This important feature (to be further discussed later) confirms that at some point in the history of Faroese all the entities listed above came to behave as one category which will here be termed 'closing diphthongs'.

In the position immediately before weakly stressed /a/ (without or with an intervening lingual spirant, which is lost in MF) also some of the other OWS vowels have developed into closing diphthongs in certain dialects, particularly in Vá, cf., e.g., words like *dagar* 'days' (OWS *dagar*), *fáa* '(to) get' (OWS *fá*), *kvøða* '(to) chant' (OWS *kveðja*), whose pronunciation can probably be symbolized [dɛijar], [fɔuwa], [kvɣuwa]. More generally, there is a tendency for all vowels to have a more close (either monophthongal or closing) articulation in this position than elsewhere; in Su this occurs even before /i, u/. The developments in these particular types of environments have been left out of consideration in the present paper. As for the development in Vá of closing diphthongs particularly from OWS /eː, æː, a/ and /aː, ɔː/ it is worth mentioning that the consonantal expansions (vowel plus /gj, gv/) found with the 'true' closing diphthongs do not take place here.

If we return now to OWS /iː, yː, uː, ei, øu, oː/ there is an interesting symmetry in the development of these entities in the northern dialects. Assuming that /oː/ > /ou/, one can posit a later development

$$
\begin{array}{ll}
\text{/iː, yː/} \quad \text{/uː/} \\
\text{/ei, øy/} \quad \text{/ou/}
\end{array}
\quad > \quad
\begin{array}{ll}
\text{/ui/} \quad \text{/yu/} \\
\text{/oi/} \quad \text{/øu/}
\end{array}
$$

the front ones becoming back-front,[21] and the back ones becoming (more or less) front-back. It would be naive to postulate that these developments must be simultaneous, but the symmetry of the end result can hardly be a coincidence.

OWS /iː/ and /yː/ have fallen together in all dialects of MF (MF /luita/ is equivalent to OWS *líta* '(to) look' as well as OWS *lýta* '(to) disfigure'). In the North also /ei/ and /øy/ have fallen together (northern MF /oira/ is equivalent to both OWS *eira* '(to) spare' and OWS *eyra* 'ear'). It is important to note that /ui/ and /oi/ share with OWS /yː/ and /øy/ (/ey/) the feature of lip-rounding, whereas they differ from /iː/ and /ei/ both in place of articulation and lip-rounding (of the first part of each entity).

In the South (Su) OWS /ei/ and /oː/ developed differently from what is found in the North. The reflex of /ei/ is /ai/, and the reflex of /oː/ is /ou/ as postulated for PF, although with a rather open first element in MF (i.e. [ɔu]). This is true also of some of the central dialects (SStr), whereas Vá has /øu/ or perhaps /eu/, west Sa /øu/, and Nólsoy a diphthong with a very open first element, for OWS /oː/.

Thus it is only in the close series (OWS /iː, yː, uː/) that back-front and front-back diphthongs have developed everywhere. This leads to the assumption that the diphthongizations were conditioned in the first place by properties of the pattern of close vowels. The explanation is straightforward, since it is exactly in the close series that the quantity shift would entail a coalescence of old long and short entities unless they were differentiated qualitatively (the more open series being diphthongs in the PF pattern assumed here—/ei, øy, ou/—the lengthening of short vowels did not in itself necessitate any further changes). Consequently, it may be assumed that a qualitative difference was first established between /iː, yː/ on the one side and /i, y/ on the other, and similarly between /uː/ and /u/, and that PF /ei, øy, ou/ followed the pattern of development of /iː, yː, uː/ in the north but only partially in the central and southern dialects.

---

[21] Although, as Jakobsen (1891) states, /ui/ may be more front in the northernmost dialects than elsewhere.

The next step is to determine what the qualitative difference was between the reflexes of OWS /iː, yː/ and /i, y/, and between the reflexes of /uː/ and /u/, before they developed into the MF reflexes /ui/ and /yu/. As mentioned above, Amundsen (1964) suggests a development *via* four close vowels, which may be summarized like this (symbols mine):

/i, y/ /iː, yː/ /uː/ /u/ > /iː/ /yː/ /ʉː/ /uː/ > /iː/ /ui/ /yu/ /uː/

The difficulty with this hypothesis is that it is impossible to provide any substantial evidence in favour of the existence of four close monophthongs at some stage in Old Faroese. A development of OWS /uː/ into MF /yu/ via a central vowel /ʉː/ does not seem any more likely than a gradual diphthongization, i.e. a gradual fronting of the *initial part* of the long vowel, which would lead directly from /uː/ to /yu/. It is similarly impossible to argue convincingly that a development /iː/ > /ui/ *must* go via /yː/. Here, too, a gradual diphthongization may be assumed, and this may well have been prior to the loss of the distinction between the reflexes of OWS /iː/ and /yː/. It is likely that these first became closing glides (as in many West Norwegian dialects), and that the initial and final parts were then differentiated from each other. In /yː/ this ultimately resulted in a back-front diphthong, and /iː/ may well have developed in a similar direction. The two entities may have fallen together at any time during this process; it is worth noting that they would become decreasingly easy to distinguish orally the more the articulation moved backwards.

Both 'explanations' of the development of /iː, yː, uː/ given above are entirely speculative, but the latter has certain technical merits compared to the former. First it does not require the assumption that short /y/ had become unrounded /i/ before the lengthening (this assumption, which is obviously required by the other hypothesis, is not supported by any conclusive evidence). Secondly, it establishes a perfect parallelism between the reflexes of OWS /iː, yː, uː/ on the one hand and those of /ei, øy, oː/ on the other, so that the (northern and southern) developments of these entities can be explained entirely on the *same* basis:

1 All entities in question assumed a somewhat more open quality of their first element (this is not marked in the notation used here).
2 Entities possessing the same 'tonality' features (place of articulation, lip articulation) behaved wholly or partly alike: the front rounded /øy/ became back-front like /yː/, the front unrounded /ei/ became back-front (or perhaps rather central-front in the case of the reflex /ai/) and partly also rounded

like the ultimate outcome of /iː/; and finally the back rounded /ou/ (< /oː/)
became front-back (or central-back) like /uː/ in some dialects but remained
back in others.

An entirely different, and very interesting, hypothesis has been proposed by Chapman (1962: 147–58), who claims that if /y/ became
/i/ it is most likely that /yː/ also became /iː/. He suggests that the
MF diphthong (in my notation /ui/) has been borrowed from a West
Norwegian dialect (Agder), where something very similar is found as
the reflex of OWS /yː/, the point being that /ui/ came to represent OWS
/iː/ and /yː/ indiscriminately, since the two entities had fallen together
in Faroese.—Since OWS /øy/ is [ɔy] or [ɔi], i.e., it is similar to MF /oi/,
in the same Norwegian dialect the hypothesis would gain ground if
the case of the more open diphthongs could be taken care of as well.
In order to account for this a similar coalescence of /ei/ and /øy/ by
delabialization of the latter must be assumed for northern Faroese, this
being necessary in order to motivate the replacement of /ei/ by /oi/. It
should be noticed that Icelandic has just this coalescence of OWS /ei/
and /øy/ (or /ey/: the latter transcription is suggestive of the possibility
that the distinction was eventually carried by the second element only).
Northern Faroese may have had a situation similar to the Icelandic
one.

   It can hardly be disproved that Faroese had a delabialization of /y/
in all environments, i.e. also when long and in diphthongs. However,
this requires that /iː, yː/ must have been replaced by /oi/ *before* the
quantity shift (in order not to fall together with old /i, y/), unless
they had become a closing (front, unrounded) glide, which by its
gliding quality was distinguished from lengthened /i, y/. In the latter case it would seem strange that Faroese did not retain its own
reflex of /iː, yː/ which must then have been similar to the reflex of
/iː/ in the Agder dialect in question, rather than borrowing the other
diphthong.

   Chapman's hypothesis is attractive but not entirely convincing. It
postulates that Faroese first had a similar development of long and
short vowels (/y/ > /i/, /yː/ > /iː/) as in Icelandic, although the general appearance of the MF vowel pattern is not suggestive of any
association between old long and short entities in their development.
Afterwards, a strong influence from a particular Norwegian dialect
is assumed. It is entirely correct, as pointed out by Chapman, that
the Faroe Islands were closely connected (administratively) with the

southernmost (and eastern) parts of Norway, including Agder, and influence from this part of Norway is very likely indeed (although many of the similarities can probably be classed as 'drift' rather than borrowing in a very categorical sense). But, as Chapman also remarks, the particular dialect of interest here is geographically very isolated in the valley of Setesdal, and more evidence is necessary in order to make it very likely that there was a particularly close connection between the Setesdal and the Faroes, and that the dialect of the former had a sufficiently high prestige to condition borrowing from it to the latter.

The OWS diphthong /au/ is in all MF dialects an unrounded front diphthong /ei/. It is possible that fronting here is a manifestation of the general 'horizontal' diphthongization. The simplest assumption is that /au/ first became /eu/ or /ey/ (without falling together with the reflex of OWS /øy/)[22] and later changed to /ei/ (without falling together with the reflex of OWS /ei/, which was no longer /ei/),[23] possibly pushed by fronted reflexes of OWS /o:/ (/øu, eu/). The development /au/ > /ei/ is phonetically strange, but note that /eu/-like reflexes occur in Norwegian, and that Icelandic has a front diphthong, too: [œy].

16.2.1.2.   *The 'opening' system*

The subsystem constituted by OWS nonclose long vowels was changed drastically by the merging of /e:/ and /æ:/, the disappearance of /o:/ from this subsystem (cf. above), and the merging of /a:/ and /ɔ:/. Only /ø:/ was not affected by coalescences among OWS long vowels.—In the northernmost dialect (No) the reflexes of OWS /e:, æ:/ and /a:, ɔ:/ are monophthongal /æ:/, /a:/ (the latter a back vowel); most other dialects have /æ:/, /ɔ:/ with diphthongal manifestations in most environments (= [ɛa], [ɔa]), except that /e:, æ:/ became /e:/ in the southernmost dialect (Su). Nowhere did the difference of aperture (tongue-height) continue to have a minimally distinctive function among reflexes of these OWS long vowels:

	No			Su			Others	
	/ø:/		/e:/	/ø:/			/ø:/	
/æ:/		/a:/			/ɔ:/	/æ:/		/ɔ:/

[22] Spellings with *eu* and *ey* occur sporadically in old sources: see Hamre (1944: 31–2).

[23] Kolsrud (1951: 23) incorrectly states that 'Færøyane har samanfall av au (skr. *ey*), vel gjenom *øy*, med ei'. There is no overlapping anywhere between the two diphthongs.

However, the OWS short vowels /e, ø, o, a, ɔ/ were lengthened and partly filled out holes, partly merged with reflexes of OWS long vowels, the only substantial changes in these formerly short vowels being that /ɔ/ became /oː/ before nasals but /øː/ elsewhere, and that /a/ became /æː/ ([ɛa]) everywhere except in some very specific environments. Thus the full subsystem has assumed this shape:

	No			Others	
/eː/	/øː/	/oː/	/eː/	/øː/	/oː/
/æː/		/aː/	/æː/		/ɔː/

i.e. essentially the same everywhere, although the origin of the individual entities in the various dialects is not identical.

It is seen that a kind of symmetry was re-established by these rearrangements, the end result being very similar to the appearance of the earlier subsystem of OWS long vowels after the coalescence of /aː, ɔː/.—Eventually, lengthened /i, y/ and /u/, i.e. MF /iː/ and /uː/, together with the items tabulated above, came to constitute the entire system of long unit vowel phonemes (cf. Section 16.2.1.1 above).

The diphthongization of Faroese /æː, ɔː/ in dialects other than No, and their status as unrounded monophthongs in No, can hardly be 'explained', but it is worth noting that on this point, as with the reflexes of OWS /ei, oː/, No has a different pattern of development from the more southerly dialects. The reflexes of OWS /eː, æː/ as /eː/ in Su have hardly any connection with the monophthongal reflex in No, the position of the two reflexes in the pattern being quite different. The problem of /æː/ and /ɔː (aː)/ will be touched upon later in this paper.

The subsystem considered here differs strikingly in its whole development from the 'closing' subsystem. There is no hindrance to the merging of OWS long and short vowels; if there is any driving force in the development, it is rather a tendency to restore a symmetric vowel system.

16.2.2. MF short reflexes of OWS vowels and diphthongs

Probably somewhat later than the lengthening of short vowels in open syllables or before short consonants, a shortening of long vowels and diphthongs before long consonants and clusters took place. The most general MF short reflexes are shown below:

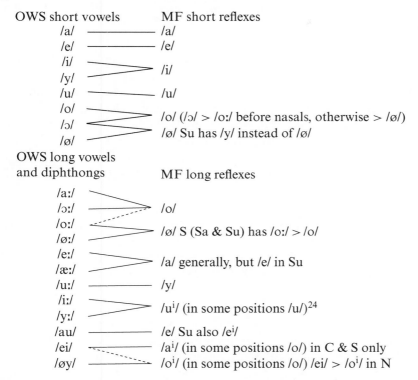

OWS short vowels   MF short reflexes
/a/ ——————— /a/
/e/ ——————— /e/
/i/
/y/ > /i/
/u/ ——————— /u/
/o/
/ɔ/ > /o/ (/ɔ/ > /oː/ before nasals, otherwise > /ø/)
/ø/   /ø/ Su has /y/ instead of /ø/

OWS long vowels
and diphthongs   MF long reflexes

/aː/
/ɔː/ ——————> /o/
/oː/
/øː/ > /ø/ S (Sa & Su) has /oː/ > /o/
/eː/
/æː/ > /a/ generally, but /e/ in Su
/uː/ ——————— /y/
/iː/
/yː/ > /uⁱ/ (in some positions /u/)²⁴
/au/ ——————— /e/ Su also /eⁱ/
/ei/ ———— /aⁱ/ (in some positions /o/) in C & S only
/øy/ ——————> /oⁱ/ (in some positions /o/) /ei/ > /oⁱ/ in N

The scheme does not take care of some specific developments of vowels before *ng*. In this position OWS /a/ (cf. OIcel. *ganga* '(to) go') is reflected as /e/ in the northern and central dialects, and OWS /e/ (and /æː/) is generally reflected as /o/ (except that Sa also has /a/ in more specific environments). It is generally assumed that these reflexes of OWS /a/ and /e/ (which are not without morphological 'exceptions', e.g. plural forms like OIcel. *stengr* 'sticks' occur with MF /e/) are the outcome of diphthongizations followed by a shortening and loss of the second element of the diphthongs. The development /a/ > /e/ is a highly controversial problem, and it cannot be handled in this paper. The development /e/ > /o/ is most reasonably explained as /e/ > /ei/ > /oi/

²⁴ It may be more correct to say only that there is no distinction monophthong : diphthong before palatal clusters and long consonants—the preceding vowel may sound more or less diphthongal.

> /o/ (possibly with more intervening stages), cf. the general north-
ern development of the *old* diphthong /ei/. The interesting fact is
that /e/ > /o/ has a much wider geographical distribution than OWS
/ei/ > /oi/.

In the general type of complex or long consonantal environment
the scheme above shows a number of coalescences among the short
reflexes of OWS vowels and diphthongs. Some of these directly correspond to coalescences among the long reflexes of the same entities, cf.
the scheme above in Section 16.2.1: all dialects have coalescences of
OWS /eː, æː/ OWS /aː, ɔː/, OWS /iː, yː/, OWS /i, y/, and OWS /øː, ø,
ɔ/ (except before nasals). Moreover, OWS /eː, æː/ have coalesced with
/e/ in Su but in all other dialects with /a/ (this latter development is
also found in the northernmost end of Su); and OWS /ei/ and /ey/ have
coalesced in the north.

Other coalescences are specific to the short reflexes. OWS /aː, ɔː/
have coalesced with /o/ everywhere. OWS /øː, ø/ and /ɔ/ (except before
nasals) have coalesced with /uː/ (reflected as [ʏ]) in Su but not elsewhere, and OWS /oː/ has (now) coalesced with /aː, ɔː, o/ in Su but
with /øː, ø, ɔ/ elsewhere. OWS /au/ has coalesced with /e/ (although
not generally in Su).

Hamre (1944: 21–7, 29–32) has pointed out that some of the
short reflexes of OWS short vowels and diphthongs can be explained
directly as shortened forms of the long reflexes. This entails that the
diphthongizations and other changes affecting the system of long
reflexes must for the most part have taken place before the shortening
of vowels before long consonants or clusters. For example, OWS /uː/
being MF /yu/ ~ /y/, the short /y/ should not be explained as due
to the fronting of shortened /uː/ but as due to a shortening of the
reflex /yu/, i.e. essentially as a dropping of the second element of the
diphthong.

16.2.2.1. *The 'closing' subsystem*

Diphthongs with a velar second element generally have monophthongal short counterparts, whereas diphthongs with a palatal second element mostly have diphthongal short counterparts. In the dialects in the
north and in the south the short reflexes generally correspond directly
to the first element of the long reflexes or—in the case of diphthongs—
are simply shortened versions of them:

No & NStr:

/ei/–/e/		/ui/–/uⁱ/	/yu/–/y/
		/oi/–/oⁱ/	/øu/–/ø/

Su:

/ei/–/eⁱ/	/ai/–/aⁱ/	/ui/–/uⁱ/	/yu/–/y⁽ᵘ⁾/	
		/oi/–/oⁱ/		/ou/–/o⁽ᵘ⁾/

Before velar consonants (and in certain other environments) the short counterparts of all diphthongs are normally monophthongal, /ui, oi/ being matched by /u, o/, and /ai/ similarly by /o/ (e.g. the MF forms corresponding to OIcel. *steikt* 'fried' and *lágt* 'low (neut.)' both have /o/, although the stems are otherwise found with /ai/ and /ɔː/, respectively). It is not surprising that the second element of these diphthongs is dropped in such environments, but the vowel /o/ as the counterpart of /ai/ demands a special explanation. Obviously it is somehow related to the shift /e/ > /o/ before the velar nasal reported above. The development /ei/ > /oi/, which is otherwise a northern feature, must have had a wider distribution notably before velars, possibly because in these environments the contrastive function of this particular development was essential to avoid a coalescence with /a/ in the process of shortening of the normal reflex /ai/. Again it is seen that there is a general tendency to avoid certain types of coalescences but not others.

The reflex of OWS /au/ is generally reduced to /e/ except in Su, where it is treated like other MF diphthongs with a palatal second element. Maybe this has to do with an old difference between dialects in which the MF value /ei/ was reached earlier, and others in which it was reached later (spellings in old sources suggest that such differences existed). If /au/ was still /eu/ rather than /ei/ at the time of shortening, it quite naturally behaved like other diphthongs with a velar second element, i.e. dropped the second element. However, another observation can be made, which is structurally more interesting. In the Su dialect, which has preserved short /eⁱ/, a short diphthong reflecting OWS /oː/ (/oᵘ/) existed until late in the nineteenth century.[25] It is possible that the genuine situation of Su (now changed by the advent

---

[25] J. H. Schrøter's collection of ballads from 1818 (cf. Matras 1951–53) has some instances of *ou* in positions where shortening had taken place: *stourt, outtast* (the last-mentioned form cannot be constructed by analogy), and similarly in his translation of the Gospel according to St. Matthew (published 1823): *Oudnina* etc. Hammershaimb (1891: LX) mentions southern forms like *stourt, douttir*.

of /o/ as the counterpart of /ou/) used to be one in which closing dipthongs (except before velars and palatals) altogether remained diphthongs when shortened.[26] If this holds true, it constitutes quite an essential difference between Su and other dialects in their past history.

In the more central dialects the picture varies as to the reflexes of OWS /oː/. Vá has /øu/–/ø/ or /eu/–/ø/ (obviously a further development of /øu/–/ø/), but SStr has /ou/–/ø/, and west Sa the opposite: /øu/–/o/. The only sensible explanation is that SStr used to go with the northern and western dialects (long /øu/), and that Sa used to go with the southernmost dialect (long /ou/), but that this picture was spoiled (after the development of the short reflexes /ø/ and /o/) by dialect mixture affecting the long reflexes.[27]

As mentioned in Section 16.2.1.1, the closing diphthongs have sometimes developed into combinations of vowel plus consonant (cluster). This can be explained *grosso modo* as a substitution of a stop (cluster) for the second, narrow element. However, in the series with velar second component there is mostly also a change in the first element: OWS /uː/ is /igv/ everywhere (alternating with the basic reflex /yu/ and short /y/), and /oː/ is /egv/ (alternating with /øu, eu/ or /ou/ and short /ø/) except in the extreme south where it is /ogv/ (alternating with long /ou/ and short /o/).

One would definitely expect the northern and central dialects to have /ygv, øgv/ from /yu, øu/ (possibly /egv/ from /eu/), and the southern ones to have /ygv, ogv/ from /yu, ou/, especially if it occurred at the time of (or not much later than) the quantity shift. As a matter of fact there is positive eighteenth- and nineteenth-century evidence on this point. Svabo (cf. note 4) who spoke the Vágar dialect consistently writes *ygv* and *ögv* toward the end of the eighteenth century, and in a letter to Rasmus Rask in 1829 the Faroese Jens Davidsen states that 'w should be pronounced after g in words like Bygw, mygwandi, which stem from Bú, múandi, and this ygw is an extension of ú (yw), which

---

[26] Schrøter renders the short reflex of OWS /uː/ as *u* (*djupt, frudna*) in accordance with his symbolization of the long reflex. This may be a southern feature pointing to /yu/- /yᵘ/ rather than /yu/-/y/ (Svabo 1966 in his Vágar dialect distinguishes the short reflex from the long one by writing *y*).

[27] See Hamre (1944: 26). An important feature in this context is that Nólsoy just east of South Streymoy goes with the southern areas with /ou/–/o/ (in Nólsoy the diphthong is very open and can perhaps be rendered as /au/). Thus SStr is not really separated from areas with old /ou/.

old people mostly pronounce ygw, like ow ogw'.[28] Although Davidsen is concerned with matters of normative spelling, there is no reason to believe that his information concerning current and elderly (southern) pronunciation is incorrect. On the other hand the modern reflexes are also attested from the same time. J. H. Schrøter's ballad manuscript from 1818[29] generally has *ig(g)v, egv* (occasionally *ögv, ogv* for the latter).

A replacement of /ygv, øgv/ by /igv, egv/ is—considered as a spontaneous phonetic process—a rather unlikely phenomenon. A more adequate description is obtained if the alternation between diphthongs and vowel–consonant complexes is considered as a morphophonemic process that also operates in the modern language. By this process the velar property of (the second element of) /yu, øu/ is taken over by the stop /g/, and the labial property of the diphthongs (lip-rounding) is taken over by the labial spirant /v/ (probably formerly [w]). The remaining vocalic element is manifested as an unrounded front vowel, frontness being the only feature unaccounted for. Thus the development of /igv, egv/ can be explained simply as a 'differentiation' between the first and second parts of the complexes, and it poses no chronological problem that these complexes may have existed along with /ygv, øgv/, gradually replacing these latter. It is possible that /igv, egv/ have developed first in dialects with extreme manifestations of the diphthongs as something like [iu, ɛu], but this is not a necessary condition.[30]

16.2.2.2. *The 'opening' subsystem*

The long reflexes of OWS /eː, æː, øː, aː, ɔː/ described in Section 16.2.1.2 were presented as part of a subsystem characterized by a rather open quality of the last part of each entity. It was found that there are several coalecences within this subsystem among reflexes of OWS long and short vowels, and similarly among their short counterparts.

---

[28] Skårup (1964: 60). Translation mine. Hammershaimb (1891) and Jakobsen (1891: LXI and 440), also refer to southern (Su) pronunciations of the vowel–consonant complex *úgv* as *ygv* or with a central rounded first element.

[29] See note 24.

[30] Hægstad (1917: 113) postulates that /uː/ > /igv/ has to do with the general 'itakism' of /y/ to /i/. This does not seem immediately likely, since the short reflex of /uː/ did not become /i/ elsewhere. Moreover, Hægstad suggests a development via short *u*, i.e. *kuggv > kyggv > kiggv*. This just poses another question: why did a back vowel become fronted before a velar stop (but not elsewhere)?

The correspondences /æː/–/a/ and /aː/–/o/ in No (as long and short reflexes of OWS /eː, æː, a/ and /aː, ɔː/, respectively) suggest that the general principle formulated for the 'closing' system above can hardly be generalized to the 'opening' system: there is no possibility of arriving at the short correspondences by cutting off the last part of the long ones. It seems more likely that all of these entities were essentially monophthongal throughout the epoch of the quantity shift (cf. Hamre 1967: 285).

For OWS /eː, æː/ and /a/ early long and short reflexes /æː/–/æ/, /aː/–/a/ (not to be confused with later No /aː/!) may be postulated. It is reasonable to assume that a coalescence might result in /æː/–/a/, except in Su where the former set coalesced with /eː/–/e/ from OWS /e/ instead. For OWS /aː, ɔː/ it is also reasonable to assume monophthongal long and short reflexes /ɔː/–/ɔ/, the short reflex later coalescing with /o/, phonetically [ɔ].

The diphthongal reflexes ([ɛa] and [ɔa]) may well be much later developments (not taking place in No). No /aː/ (back vowel) for /ɔː/ is probably a delabialization of /ɔː/ rather than a direct reflex of the original /aː/, since the short counterpart is /o/ (i.e. [ɔ]) not /a/; as a matter of fact there is probably no compelling reason to distinguish in the phonemic symbolization between No /aː/ and central and southern /ɔː/; the variation may be considered allophonic.

The short reflex of OWS /øː, ø, ɔ/ is /ø/ in most dialects and has widely coalesced with the short reflex of OWS /oː/. In Su, however, the short reflex of /øː, ø, ɔ/ is /y/, i.e. there is a coalescence with the short reflex of OWS /uː/ instead. It is interesting to note that the short reflex of /oː/ in this dialect is /o/ not /ø/, which means that there is no short /ø/ at all in the modern dialect. It looks as if there has been a tendency to avoid having too many phonemes in this part of the vowel system by utilizing all possibilities of merging, but it is hardly worthwhile going too deeply into this here.

16.3.   THE EVIDENCE OF PALATALIZATION

No coherent relative chronology has been offered for the various events postulated in this paper. The quantity shift has been used as an important point of reference, but it is a serious complication that neither the age nor the extension in time of the change is well known. However, another useful though still relative point of reference is constituted by the development of dorsal (velar) consonants into palatal ones before certain front vowels. This is clearly a further development of the palatalization known from Icelandic, for example; developments similar to the Faroese one are known from Norwegian dialects. The phenomenon will here be referred to as the 'palatal shift', abbreviated PS.

A consideration of MF evidence leads to the somewhat surprising conclusion that the PS seems to have been confined to consonants *before close or half-close unrounded front vowels*. There is thus no PS before the reflexes of OWS /æ:, ø:/ (in contradistinction to the case in Icelandic). There *is* PS before the reflex of OWS /y/, namely /i/, but this may be explained if we assume that /y/ became /i/ before the PS.

There is no PS before the back-front reflexes of OWS /i:, y:, ei, øy/ or before the /ai/ reflex of /ei/. This suggests that the change of these entities took place before the PS. As for the reflexes of OWS back vowels and diphthongs, there is PS before the reflex of /au/, i.e. /au/ probably became /eu/ (rather than /øy/, or the like) before the PS. There is, however, no PS before the front–back reflexes of OWS /u:, o:/ or their short front vowel counterparts. This agrees with the general observation that there seems to be no PS before rounded vowels, but it may also be interpreted as an indication that the fronting of these entities took place after the PS (there is no particular reason for the latter assumption). It is particularly interesting that there is no PS before the reflexes /igv, egv/ of /u:, o:/ (cf. OWS *kú* 'cow', *kóf* 'thick fog', MF /kigv, kegv/). This does not invalidate the general formulation above, since it is likely that /i, e/ in this context are of recent origin.

There is no PS before /æ:/ ([ɛa]) reflecting OWS /e:, æ:, a/, which agrees with the definition of Faroese PS given above. There is, however, no PS before Su /e:/ < /e:, æ:/ either (though there *is* before /e:/ from OWS /e/), which agrees well with the assumption made above that this is a comparatively late development.

Thus if it is assumed that the PS in Faroese took place only before /i, e/ (alone or in the diphthong /eu/ > /ei/) the relative chronology that can be established on the basis of the PS confirms the hypotheses made in this paper on several points, and it does not in any instance contradict them.

The problem is that this whole argumentation may be based on a misinterpretation of the evidence of the PS in Faroese. Zachariasen (1966) has made a fairly detailed study of this phenomenon. His material (to which the reader is referred for more detailed information about the distribution of the PS) agrees well with the statements made in this paper but he interprets it differently. According to Zachariasen the dorsal consonants of early Faroese were more or less palatalized depending on the more or less advanced place of articulation of the following vowel, and he supposes that the distribution of palatals and velars in MF developed in three phases: (i) a re-adaptation of the place of articulation of the consonant to that of the vowel when OWS /ei/ changed; (ii) a loss of palatalization before certain front vowels under the impact of the development of similar vowels *without* palatalization of preceding consonants (fronting of /ɔ, uː, a/); and (iii) a change of palatalized /k, g/ into palatals merging with the reflexes of OWS /kj, gj/, after which finally the merging of /e/ with /æː/ or of /e/ with the first component of [ɛa] took place.

There are here two competing hypotheses. It appears to the present author that the simplest account of the PS in Faroese is obtained if it is considered to be a change occurring at a definite time (probably by foreign influence, cf. Norwegian and Icelandic) and for some unknown reason confined to the position before /i, e/, but it must be admitted that this is not the only description possible.

As long as the history of the Faroese palatals is such a controversial matter, it may be wisest to avoid using the PS as a proof of alleged developments within the vowel system.

16.4. GENERAL CHARACTERISTICS OF FAROESE DIPHTHONGIZATION

As shown at the beginning of this paper there is no simple phonetic relationship between the vowel patterns of Old West Scandinavian and Faroese. Nevertheless some general tendencies of development have been pointed out:

1 The old difference between long and short vowels has largely been replaced by a qualitative difference. As stated by Benediktsson (1968) this is 'at least a widespread, if not a universal, characteristic of the Nordic languages', although it must be added that it manifests itself most clearly in the West (Danish, in particular, has had a number of changes which more or less obscure the tendency in question).

2 The differentiation of old and short vowels has been achieved in Faroese by a change of the old *long* vowels (the old short vowels became more open in positions where they remained short but not in positions where

they were lengthened). Faroese is similar in this respect to some West Norwegian dialects, but dissimilar to most other Nordic languages or dialects, differentiation by 'opening' of the old short vowels being more general.

3 The change of the old long vowels can be described as diphthongization. In this respect, too, Faroese resembles some West Norwegian dialects (cf. Christiansen 1948: 166), although there are essential differences. In connection with the diphthongization some of the old long vowels came to form a new subsystem together with the old diphthongs, which to some extent conditioned the later developments. This resembles the situation in Icelandic, although the 'closing' subsystem in that language includes OWS /æː, øː, aː, ɔː/, which are 'opening' in Faroese.

4 The shortening of old long vowels or diphthongs before long consonants (consonant clusters) resulted partly in short diphthongs, partly in loss of the second element of the diphthongs (old or newly developed). In this respect, too, Faroese agrees well with West Norwegian, although the pattern of Faroese is more complex.

The general features summarized here have, of course, been observed earlier by Scandinavian philologists.[31] However, this paper has postulated also that

5 internal pattern reorganizations may have played a greater role in guiding the development than generally acknowledged, and that
6 there is evidence that the northern and southern dialects followed somewhat different lines of development, and that the central dialects of the Faroe Islands exhibit a mixture of these.

In accordance with Hamre (1944) it has been argued in this paper that a relative chronology can be established between certain phenomena, in particular that the old long vowels and diphthongs had by and large obtained their MF qualities before the reductions before long consonants or consonant clusters. This implies the postulate that the developments discussed in this paper can be accounted for in terms of phonetic patterning, i.e. in terms of 'low level rules'. This approach may be challenged on the grounds that it neglects the fact that the long and short reflexes of OWS vowels and diphthongs are structurally (morphophonemically) associated also in MF. It would seem a valid assumption that because of this continuous association qualitative

---

[31] Chapman (1962: 131–7) is unfortunately almost silent about the relations between the history of long and short entities in Faroese.

changes in the long reflexes might have caused certain changes in the corresponding short reflexes, and vice versa.

The answer to this objection is that the gross features of development do not immediately support the assumption of such a phonetic attraction between long and short entities in MF,[32] cf. in particular the alternation of /ou/–/ø/–/egv/ in the central dialects. On the other hand it goes without saying that the history of the Faroese vowels cannot be stated in a few sound laws. It must be emphasized in particular that a penetrating study of the dialect geography of individual word-forms would reveal a number of apparent exceptions to the general sound laws (one conspicuous case is the reflection in the northernmost dialects of Su of OWS /eː, æː/ as short /e/ in some forms but as short /a/ in others);[33] some of these may be crucial to a deeper understanding of the whole development. It is hoped that future work along such lines will soon make the present study and those preceding it obsolete.

---

[32] Although there are, of course, particular instances which may be explained this way. In the 1880s Jakob Jakobsen recorded an a-sound (i.e. unrounded) as the short reflex of OWS /aː/ in a northern dialect. (Prof. Christian Matras in personal communication). It seems likely that this represents a sporadic attraction of the short vowel to the long reflex, which is now unrounded (there is no doubt that the dialect formerly had a rounded vowel in both cases). There may be numerous other cases of this kind.

[33] Notes from lectures by Professor Matras.

17

Devoicing or Strengthening of Long Obstruents in Greenlandic[1]

17.1. INTRODUCTION: THE OBSTRUENT PATTERN

It is a well-known characteristic of West Greenlandic Eskimo that this type of Eskimo (unlike North Alaskan Inupiaq, for example) has complementarity of *voiced and voiceless fricatives*, short fricatives being voiced and long ones voiceless (in the new Greenlandic orthography, which is used in this paper. *g* and *r* symbolize voiced velar and uvular continuants, and *gg* and *rr* their long voiceless counterparts, whereas the corresponding labial set is distinguished orthographically as *v* versus *ff*). In accordance with the principle of feature distribution just stated we find that voiced fricatives are automatically replaced by voiceless segments in environments where they are long by true gemination (or by assimilation), for example *iga-* 'to cook' – *iggavik* or *igaffik* 'kitchen', *neripput* 'they ate' – *nerripput* 'they shared a big meal'.

Morphophonemically, this apparently straightforward pattern is complicated in that long and short fricatives regularly participate in deviating alternation sets. Although the short (voiced) fricatives *v, g, r*, and the long (voiceless) fricatives *ff, gg, rr* all occur quite frequently in West Greenlandic, the source of a long geminate fricative does not necessarily appear synchronously as a short fricative, nor does a consonant which appears synchronously as a short fricative necessarily remain fricative under gemination. We rather find a preponderance of alternations between a 'weak grade' short alternant and a 'strong grade' long alternant. Diachronically, this has to do with a weakening

[1] Reprinted from *Riepmočála: essays in honor of Knut Bergsland, presented on the occasion of his seventieth birthday,* ed. B. Brendemoen, E. Hovdhaugen, and O. H. Magga, Oslo: Novus (1984): 122–35.

process, as appears inter alia from the pioneering comparative studies of Hammerich and Bergsland. As for old short fricatives, the normal situation for *g* and *r* was to be lost intervocalically, the result being that geminate *gg* and *rr* frequently alternate with zero (cf. *naggat* 'end' derived from *naa-* 'to end'; *unarrat* (old) pl. of *unaaq* 'harpoon shaft') rather than with *g* and *r*. On the other hand, a large number of new occurrences of voiced fricatives arose by lenition of old short *stop consonants* in intervocalic position, whereas stops were preserved when geminated or occurring in clusters. In this way we get a number of alternations between *v* and (*p*)*p*: compare *kujavarpoq* 'has moved further to the south' versus *avannarparpoq* 'has moved further to the north' (*-var-* vs. *-par-*), and particularly between *g* and (*k*)*k*, *r* and *qq* (cf. *aalisagaq* 'fish' – pl. *aalisakkat*; *ujarak* 'stone' – pl. *ujaqqat*). In a number of cases, finally, we encounter old short stop consonants which have been preserved, that is protected from lenition, in the position after the first (single) vowel of roots (cf. Bergsland 1955: 12), this position after the first mora being in general a 'strong' position. Such short stops, then, engage in alternation with long stops if they stand (or used to stand) in the just-mentioned strong position (consider *napavoq* 'is in upright position' – *napparpaa* 'puts it in upright position'; *nukik* 'strength' – *nukkiorpoq* 'forces himself, uses his strength'; *niaqoq* 'head' (as suggested by Bergsland probably from *nayquq) – pl. *niaqqut*).

In the dental or (with a more adequate labelling) coronal series of obstruents there is the complication that West Greenlandic exhibits two *sibilants*, which are voiceless even when short. One is a plain *s*, the other has a more retracted point of articulation. In the (new) orthography they are not distinguished, and they are actually kept distinct only in a geographically limited area (within which they are expected to merge eventually). Both *s*-phonemes occur phonemically long and short, but in cases of morphological alternation involving gemination the regular and frequently occurring patterns are: (i) short plain *s* alternating (like *j*) with the long affricate *ts* (cf. *nasaq* 'cap' – pl. *natsat*), and (ii) zero alternating with retracted *ss* (c.f. e.g. *iluliaq* 'iceberg' – pl. *ilulissat*).

The development of the sibilant subsystem is a very complex issue, which is much debated in current work. In the present context it may suffice to mention that in forms such as *nasaq* the plain *s* derives from a former affricate, in some other forms from a stop consonant *t, and that the retracted *s* derives from a voiced (post)alveolar or palatal fricative. All of this is supported by the retention of the older state of affairs in other Eskimo languages or dialects. What is suggested by authoritative linguistic reconstructions (based above all on Bergland's work), is that the proliferation of voiceless sibilants in West Greenlandic is a secondary phenomenon. It is noteworthy that we have within this subsystem a genuine instance of seemingly unconditioned, spontaneous devoicing of a fricative taking place also if the fricative is phonetically (and phonemically) *short*, viz. in numerous forms such as *isi* 'eye', *aasaq* 'summer', *puisi* 'seal' (all with the retracted *s*).

Finally, West Greenlandic has also a *lateral l*, which switches manner of articulation and crucially enters the obstruent pattern under gemination (see later), although the *nasal* sonorants geminate without any change in manner of articulation, e.g. *ameq* 'skin' – pl. *ammit* with a voiced nasal in both cases.

17.2. GEMINATION AND DEVOICING

Consonant gemination as a kind of syllable-strengthening process is a very old feature of Eskimo. It is shared by the other dialects of the Eastern (Inupiaq) branch of Eskimo, and, as pointed out by Bergsland, its previous existence also in the Western (Yupik) branch may be inferred even though the quantity pattern which still survives in Eastern Eskimo was eventually replaced by a very different quantity pattern in Yupik (with drastic changes such as shortening of old geminates and secondary processes of new gemination or lengthening affecting both consonants and vowels). On this point, then, the dialects of the Eastern branch are more archaic. On the other hand, the old pattern must obviously have involved straightforward alternations of single and geminate consonants with the same manner of articulation, unlike the situation in Modern West Greenlandic, where—as already stated—we have a complex situation with four types of manner alternation accompanying gemination, viz.

1 zero alternating with long voiceless fricative;
2 short voiced fricative alternating with long voiceless fricative;
3 short voiced fricative alternating with long voiceless stop;
4 short nasal or stop alternating with long nasal or stop (without change in voicing).

Whereas the fricatives in set (3) must be assumed to have acquired voicing as a corollary of lenition of old stops, comparative evidence is unanimously in favour of voicelessness being a secondary feature in sets (1) and (2). Voicelessness in these sets is, in a dialect-geographic perspective, a feature which is highly characteristic of Greenlandic.

In North Alaskan Inupiaq, for instance, there is alternation between short and long *voiced* continuants in cases corresponding to those above. Since the voiceless member of each pair is obviously secondary compared to the voiced one, there is overwhelming evidence, both from internal reconstruction and from dialect comparison, of a Greenlandic sound change replacing voiced by voiceless articulation under certain conditions involving length. It is very natural that Greenlandic Eskimo is often mentioned as evidence in support of the claim that there is a universal tendency for long fricatives to become voiceless by a spontaneous sound change.

There are some inherent difficulties with the assumption of spontaneous devoicing, however. It is true that one may well expect voicing to be hampered if there is a long interval of strong constriction, as in true fricatives (because most of the pressure drop then takes place across the oral constriction instead of taking place across the glottis, as is necessary for sustained vocal fold vibrations): but the voiced continuants in contemporary Greenlandic are not all that fricative. This, of course, does not prevent us from assuming that these sounds used to be strongly fricative obstruents, at least in their geminate versions (this is consistent with their articulation in North Alaskan Inupiaq). Still, one may ask why across-the-board devoicing—if it is such a natural process—should happen only in Greenlandic, considering that there is no direct evidence that the fricative articulation in old Greenlandic was particularly favourable to devoicing.

It is a much more serious challenge to the devoicing hypothesis that the voiced–voiceless alternation *occurs also with the lateral l*, as in *ukaleq* 'hare' – pl. *ukallit* (where *l* is a short voiced lateral or slightly flapped sound, and *ll* a long voiceless lateral fricative). All evidence suggests that this is 'from the start' a true lateral consonant, and it differs morphophonemically from the ordinary fricatives in that there is just one alternation set, viz. (voiced) *l* – (voiceless) *ll*, i.e. no alternation involving either zero or a geminate stop in (Central) West Greenlandic. (In cases such as *atserpaa* 'signs it' from *ateq* 'name' and *-(l)erpaa* 'provides it with sth.' the *l* enters the process by which *ts* arises, but compare analogous examples such as *imaq* 'content' – *immerpaa* 'fills it out').

If we wish to understand the diachronic developments underlying such voiced–voiceless alternations as *v–ff, g–gg, r–rr*, and indeed *l–ll*, in Greenlandic, there are three different sources of insight. The first is comparative evidence from other types of Eskimo outside Greenland, and above all around the Bering Strait, where more archaic phonologies are found. We have seen already how this is suggestive of spontaneous devoicing of long obstruents and even of the long lateral in Greenlandic. Let us consider now what the other types of evidence have to tell.

The *dialects of Greenlandic Eskimo* proper have until quite recently received little (if any) attention in comparative Eskimo studies. By and large the central dialect of West Greenlandic has been taken to be representative of Greenlandic Eskimo as a whole. Textbooks on Greenlandic have contributed to this notion of Greenlandic as being more or less one dialect by hardly mentioning the issue, but part of the reason is that there has been a lack of adequate and manageable descriptions of other dialects and a lack of concise dialect-geographic surveys. The pioneering work with regard to phonological dialect surveys was done by Petersen (1969/70, 1975) less than two decades ago (also cf. the useful survey in Fortescue 1983).

If we look at Petersen's chart of phoneme correspondences it is noteworthy that the voiceless fricatives *ff, gg, rr* of West Greenlandic are matched by stops in the northernmost (Upernavik) and southernmost (Cape Farewell) fringe areas of West Greenland and in the East Greenlandic dialect. Voiceless *ll* is matched by a stop in southernmost West Greenlandic and in East Greenlandic. —To be strictly correct, exception must be made for some instances in which the easternmost Inuit dialects had a voiceless lateral already before the specifically West Greenlandic devoicing; in these instances East Greenlandic has developed (*t*)*s* directly from the old voiceless lateral, for example: East Greenlandic *atsinaaq*, West Greenlandic *allunaaq* 'rope, string' from something like *akʟunaaq* with 'ʟ' symbolizing the voiceless lateral.

The stop consonant reflexes in these Greenlandic dialects far off Central West Greenlandic are straightforward for *gg* and *rr*, which are matched by *kk* and *qq*, respectively. As for *ff*, Upernavik and East Greenlandic have *pp*, but Cape Farewell has dorsal *kk* (*rf* is matched by *qq*). As for *ll*, East Greenlandic has *tt* (now often written '*dd*'), but Cape Farewell has a supradental affricated stop which is phonemically distinct from *tt*. These discrepancies (which can be explained) are not at issue here; the general observation to be made is that there are two main categories of reflexes of old long non-nasal sonorants in Greenlandic: (i) as long voiceless continuants and (ii) as long stops with or without affrication. As a sweeping statement, we may say that West Greenlandic exhibits the former, East Greenlandic the latter, although the fringes of West Greenlandic largely side with East Greenlandic.

How does this tie in with the explanation of voiceless *ff, ll,* etc. in West Greenlandic as being due to spontaneous devoicing? If one insists that we have such devoicing in the West Greenlandic examples, it is appropriate to search for an unrelated explanation for the development in East Greenlandic, for it does not seem particularly convincing that the newly-developed long voiceless continuants spontaneously went on and became stops (although such a further shift cannot be *excluded*). There is certainly no evidence that the development from old voiced geminate continuants to stops ever went through anything like the stage encountered in modern Central West Greenlandic. On the other hand, it would seem utterly strange for Greenland to have *two* basically different processes affecting the long voiced continuants considering how unaffected these consonants are in most of the remaining Eskimo area. Neither of the two alternative approaches being overwhelmingly attractive, the situation invites a diachronic hypothesis according to which the Greenlandic dialects as a whole share a strenghthening of some kind of the old voiced geminates into a series of reflexes which provide a natural starting point for *both* of the ultimate developments: into voiceless fricatives and into stops.

Here the third source of evidence comes in, viz. the *spellings in old Greenlandic sources*.

17.3.   OLD GREENLANDIC SPELLINGS

The first truly systematic *and* phonetically interpretable transcription of Greenlandic Eskimo (and of Eskimo in general) was the one developed by Samuel Kleinschmidt around the middle of the nineteenth century and used even today, although the new orthography of 1973 is gradually taking over. There is a considerable bulk of sources dating from before Kleinschmidt, but the (seventeenth- and) eighteenth-century sources have not been much utilized in diachronic phonology because of glaring inadequacies with regard to such features as length, the distinction between velar and uvular stops, and the rendering of vowel qualities. Nevertheless, there are very important insights to be gained from this early material, and this is very much true with respect to the question of what happened to the old voiced geminates in Greenlandic.

With regard to voicedness or voicelessness of fricatives the earliest useful sources from the second half of the seventeenth and the first half of the eighteenth century (i.e. sources which in part antedate, in part postdate Hans Egede's arrival in Greenland in 1721) are clearly suggestive of voicedness of *both* short and long fricatives. For example, in a 1654 word list preserved in a manuscript (of P. H. Resen's Danske Atlas) from the 1680s we find short intervocalic fricatives rendered as *v*, *g*, *r* in accordance with modern orthographical usage: *Ivirning* (now: *ivianngit* with plural *-t*) 'breasts', *Acago* (i.e. *aqagu*) 'tomorrow', *Kameresin* (i.e. *qimerissat*) 'eyelashes', though deviant spellings also occur. As for the long intervocalic fricatives, we find such spellings as *b*, *g(j)*, *gg* corresponding to *ff*, *gg* of the modern orthography—for example *Sibian* (*siffiaq*, or rather *siffiat* 'your-') 'hip', *Sigju* (i.e. *sigguk*) 'trunk', *Naggesung* (i.e. *nerrersooq*) 'inclined to eat a lot' (in the old source translated as *Essen*, i.e. 'to eat').

Although the earliest spellings are understandably inconsistent they definitely suggest that the long (geminate) consonants in such cases were *not* voiceless fricatives (the old evidence is very conflicting with regard to *rr*, however, which was sometimes spelled *ch* etc., probably to indicate the rasping quality of the uvular fricative which was more audible when it was a long segment). It is, on the other hand, impossible to see from spellings such as those illustrated above whether the long segments were fricatives or lax (voiced) stops. Offhand the (for a long time dominant) spelling *b* or *bb* for modern *ff* seems strongly suggestive of realization as a bilabial stop which, however, must have been different from the 'true' stop consonant /p/ (the latter is mostly rendered as *p* or *pp* in old sources). If that is true, the same might be expected for the long velar segment and possibly for the long uvular segment. This would be in agreement with the later reflexes in East Greenlandic (although not with the reflex /kk/ for */vv/ in the Cape Farewell dialect), but it would be hard to reconcile such an interpretation with the fact that these long segments started out as fricatives and have fricative reflexes in modern West Greenlandic. A development voiced fricative → stop → voiceless fricative seems too far-fetched to deserve serious consideration. It seems much more likely that the long labial fricative sounded too different from the labial fricatives occurring in Danish or German to warrant a symbolization such as *v* or *w*; in all probability this long fricative was articulated as a narrow *unrounded* (slit-articulated) bilabial fricative which to a Danish or German ear sounded more like a voiced *b* than a *v* or *w*.

The orthography of the manuscripts and published works following the colonization in 1721 is of course characterized by considerable improvements, but there are no dramatic changes in the rendering of the fricatives. It is noteworthy that as late as the beginning of the nineteenth century Otho Fabricius in his dictionary (Fabricius 1804) gives spellings such as 'Sabbiorbik v. Sagviortarbik' for what is now spelled *saffior(tar)fik* 'forge' (Fabricius also: 'anvil'). His vacillation here and elsewhere between *b(b)* and *gv* reflects a dialect difference in the pronunciation of the Greenlandic labial fricative, as pointed out by Petersen, the spelling *gv* representing a South Greenlandic labialized velar fricative (cf. the development of */vv/ into /kk/ in the Cape Farewell dialect mentioned above). What is interesting in the present context is that neither of the alternative spellings is suggestive of voicelessness (since the letter *f* would be the obvious way to indicate voicelessness according to its use in Danish). It is hard to know to what extent this seemingly very conservative transcription reflects stability in the phonology and to what extent it just reflects loyalty towards an orthographical tradition for which the early word lists of 1654 may have played a considerable role.

But in any case, the spelling *gv* was not customary before Fabricius entered the scene with his special knowledge of the southern Frederikshaab (Paamiut) dialect, so the odds seem in favour of the assumption that voicelessness of such long segments or clusters postdates the beginning of the nineteenth century.

For the long velar fricative the spelling is regularly *gg* (which also occurs along with *g* to represent the short voiced velar fricative); it is only with the uvular point of articulation that the spelling is suggestive of a specific (strident or voiceless?) manner of production of the fricative when long (cf. the remark on earlier spellings above). For the long uvular Fabricius has such spellings as *Noŕak* 'calf (specifically of caribou)' (now spelled *norraq*) with a diacritic mark on *r* to distinguish it from the short uvular of such forms as *torájuvok* (now: *toraajuvoq*) 'is certain of aim when shooting'. Similar spellings occur until Kleinschmidt's orthography settles on *rr* versus *r* by the middle of the nineteenth century.

If we turn now to the *lateral* continuant, the spellings of the eighteenth and nineteenth centuries are much more suggestive of a phonological development. The preferred spelling in early sources is *l* or *ll* (consonant doubling did not serve to indicate length in pre-Kleinschmidt orthography), no matter whether the lateral is long or short, but only in instances where the consonant or cluster was voiced. Clusters appearing at that time with a voiceless lateral were spelled differently, as seen from numerous, more or less consistently used spellings with *tl* or *kl* in Paul Egede's dictionary of 1750.

As for clusters with a preceding velar, those with a voiceless lateral were spelled with *kl* (sometimes *ktl*), for example *Aklunák* 'rope, string' (now *allunaaq*; with early voicelessness as evidenced both by dialects west of Greenland and by the East Greenlandic reflex *atsinaaq* mentioned earlier) as against *Segluvok* (now *salluvoq*) 'he lied'. With a preceding uvular the apparent voiceless–voiced distinction is mostly expressed by *rtl* or *rkl* vs. *rl*, as in *Tórtlorpok* (now *torlorpoq*) 'called out', *torkluluanga* (i.e. *torlulavaanga* in modern spelling) 'he was calling for me' versus *Korlórpok* (i.e. *qorlorpoq*) 'poured down (e.g. through a funnel)'. In cases where there is etymologically no labial, velar, or uvular preceding the lateral, the long lateral (or dental stop plus lateral?) is expressed in either of two ways, viz. *tl* contrasting with *l* (or *ll*), as in *Itlerbik* (now *illerfik*) 'chest', versus *Sillit* 'whetstone' (also occurring with the spelling *Silii* in seventeenth-century lists). The former spelling is particularly well attested with affixes such as *-tlar*... 'forcefully' or contemporative *-tlu-* (only sporadically *-(l)lu-*; *-tlu* being the regular post-consonantal alternant), both of which occur in numerous illustrative phrases in Paul Egede's dictionary (1750), as against other words with *-l-* or *-ll-*. Examples are, on the one hand: *Usitlarau* (now *usillaaraaq*) 'is generally heavily loaded', *torartlugo* (now *toraarlugu*) 'heading towards it', on the other hand: *-ngilet* (with indisputable gemination due to plural inflection) as attested in several forms such as *ajungilet* (i.e. *ajunngillat*) 'they are good (literally: not bad)', and perfective stems with gemination such as *Aúlarpok* or *aularpok* (now *aallarpoq*) 'he left' (derived from the stem *aula- 'to move'). There can be no doubt whatsoever that *tl* and *l(l)* reflect two formerly contrasting long items.

Although the spellings involving the expected *voiceless* lateral are not phonetically transparent they can be construed to indicate that there was either a fully developed stop segment in the beginning or a tendency toward such 'segmentalization'. This would off-hand explain the East Greenlandic reflex /ts/ as a modification of a cluster */tʟ/. As for the forms with an expected *voiced* lateral, the evidence is overwhelmingly in favour of a plain, long voiced segment in eighteenth-century Greenlandic.

Eventually, however, spellings with -*dl*- take over, though exhibiting some confusion with -*gl*- (eventually written -*gdl*-). Fabricius (1804) writes *sidlit* for 'whetstone', *Aùdlarpok* for 'he left', etc., a type of spelling which is virtually (totally?) nonexistent in Paul Egede's dictionary of half a century earlier. There is reason to believe that this signals a development of a stop segment at the beginning of the long lateral, i.e. 'segmentalization' in a straightforward sense.

It is hard to determine when exactly the voiceless clusters merged with the voiced ones since Greenlandic orthography through the ages is characterized by considerable loyalty towards earlier spellings of individual words. Variant spellings in Fabricius (1804) such as *tórdlorpok* = *tórklorpok* for Egede's *Tórtlorpok* are suggestive of ongoing merger around 1800. Taken together with forms such as *iklerbĭk* 'chest' for Egede's *Itlerbik* the above example suggests that '*kl*' tended to be generalized (due to spurious etymologizations, or because of sporadic development of a velar before the long lateral?) as the way to render the voiceless lateral. It is less likely that the variant spellings with '*rkl*', '*rdl*' indicate a development from voiceless long lateral to voiced lateral. Rather, they may be indicative of the opposite, viz. that clusters stemming from a long voiced lateral, or from a stop plus a voiced lateral, were being devoiced, thus obviating the need for distinct spellings of those clusters that already had a voiceless lateral.

By this merger '*dl*' came to symbolize a voiceless lateral, mostly with a preceding stop consonant symbol. This usage was generalized by Kleinschmidt, and in some cases he combined the tendency to use a velar symbol in front of the lateral with the use of '*dl*' to symbolize voicelessness, spellings such as *igdlerfik* resulting from this fusion of earlier usages. Kleinschmidt however distinguished between *vdl, tdl*, and *gdl* to indicate what is now a plain long voiceless lateral, although it is not clear to what extent this was based on phonetic reality. (The '*g*' in *igdlerfik* cannot be a priori excluded as a spontaneous development, a differentiation of some kind, but the '*v*' in Kleinschmidt's *avdla* 'other' must be totally erroneous. A check of labialization of consonant clusters in an archaic type of Upernavik dialect, which otherwise has preserved several instances of labialization, gave a negative result for this word as expected on comparative grounds, and Kleinschmidt's spelling is glaringly at variance with Fabricius' *Adla* half a century earlier.) One must fully subscribe to Bergsland's (1955: 2) characterization of Kleinschmidt's spellings of such complexes as being 'often without etymological foundation'.

17.4. CONCLUSION

The orthographical evidence strongly suggests that the voicelessness of the long lateral developed *not* as spontaneous devoicing but as 'segmentalization' (differentiation of the continuant into stop plus continuant). The next step was devoicing of all such clusters with an initial stop, and, finally, as quite a late process which has not yet been completed in all dialects, the clusters underwent regressive assimilation (irrespective of their origin as a cluster or as a geminate). The last step in this development is well attested on independent grounds since simply *all* constant clusters have undergone it (with the exception that *ts* has remained an affricate, and that the cluster-initial uvular of clusters such as *rl, rf*, etc. has left a trace affecting the preceding vowel). Thus, the only weak link in this explanation is the contention that clusters of stop plus voiced lateral became fully voiceless. Is such devoicing inherently more likely than spontaneous devoicing of a long intervocalic lateral? I think it is. The conditions for devoicing of the lateral would presumably be favourable after a (possibly voiceless) stop, particularly since one may expect a more fricative articulation immediately after a (homorganic) stop than elsewhere.

Taking a well-known word such as *illu* 'house' (the source of the term *igloo*), we may now follow the development of an old cluster. The contention is that the spelling forms occurring over time should be taken essentially at face value: we start with a cluster '*gl*' in the oldest sources, as etymologically expected (Paul Egede's *Iglo*), then in the nineteenth century comes the spelling with '*gdl*' indicating possibly both segmentalization and devoicing (this is the spelling found in Kleinschmidt, but actually not invented by him, cf. that Steenberg (1849) has *igdlo* although his spelling is otherwise completely pre-Kleinschmidtian); and today we have the new spelling '*ll*' reflecting complete assimilation and merger of voiced and voiceless clusters (so that the voiceless lateral can be taken as an allophone of /l/ in modern West Greenlandic). —Although the old spellings have been almost ridiculed, they may not have been far off the mark, and if the new orthography is scorned by some Greenlanders because of spellings such as '*ll*', which allegedly fail to indicate the special character of the long lateral, this controversy reflects the strange fact that the digraph '*dl*' had come to mean 'voiceless lateral' although it probably started out as a straightforward and indeed adequate marking of segmentalization (cf. the pronunciation of words such as *kalla* ('kadla') in various West Scandinavian languages and dialects).

With regard to such segmentalization and subsequent devoicing and assimilation, interesting support may be found in the observations of Holtved (1952) on the Polar Eskimo dialect, where he reports variant forms with regard to stop plus lateral (as in *illu* 'house')—exhibiting more or less exactly such a chain of development under way (and apparently compressed into a short time span, as would also have been the case with West Greenlandic some 100–200 years ago).

The old spelling evidence for West Greenlandic is sadly non-informative with respect to the various fricatives dealt with earlier, but it is tempting to generalize from the above explanation of how the lateral devoiced and suggest that such segmentalization into voiced and eventually devoiced affricate-like clusters occurred also in other instances (spellings such as *bb, gg* do not at all rule out the possibility that there was a change from long narrow fricative to stop plus homorganic fricative without change of orthography). The only cluster for which the spelling evidence is clearly in disfavour of this interpretation is /rr/. Spellings such as *kr*, which might be expected in the case of segmentalization, are conspicuously absent, so maybe we must reckon with spontaneous devoicing here (which is not very surprising, considering the natural tendency for uvular frication to involve much stridency).

It must probably remain an open question whether the long labial and velar fricatives were segmentalized into stop plus fricative or just developed very narrow allophones favouring spontaneous devoicing. The virtues of the former assumption are that it permits a generalized account for old clusters as well as old long continuants (involving fricatives and the lateral, although apparently with the uvular taking a separate course, as it does rather generally in Greenlandic phonology), and that it provides a basis for deriving the West and East Greenlandic forms fairly directly from a common denominator (the old long */ll/ of *aallarpoq* going via the common base /dl/ or /tl/ to East Greenlandic /tt/ by progressive assimilation only, and to West Greenlandic voiceless /ll/ by progressive devoicing assimilation followed by regressive articulation with regard to all other features).

Such 'generalizability' is certainly no proof that the *truth* about these developments has been disclosed; for one thing, the alleged common denominator accounting for the strange developments in East and West Greenlandic may be at best a matter of drift, meaning that the two dialects, before moving apart, have passed independently through related or even identical steps of change (which may not at all have been simultaneous in the two areas: cf. the related but much belated developments in twentieth-century Polar Eskimo or the now ongoing regressive cluster assimilation in Canadian Eskimo which, as it were, repeats the development of West Greenlandic a century ago).

Much is totally unknown about the earlier stages of the Greenlandic language, and—especially with regard to phonology—this is true even of the historical period. If progress is to be made it requires the combination of comparative expertise and painstaking philological analysis of the old sources so outstandingly reflected in Bergsland's work, going hand in hand with utilization of recent explorations in Greenlandic dialectology. The present paper just outlines one of the controversial topics in which Greenlandic diachronic phonology is so rich.

18

The Role of a 'Mixed' Language in Linguistic Reconstruction[1]

18.1.   INTRODUCTION

Long after Bloomfield's well-publicized success in applying the comparative method of Indo-European studies to mutually related North American languages, numerous oral (non-written) languages of the World still await rigorous genetic comparison, being at most classified tentatively (typically on a lexicostatistic and/or a typological basis). Several of these languages (particularly in Oceania) give comparativists a very hard time because the demographic and cultural situation of the language communities has invited confusing variation and change.

This paper deals with an oral language of this kind called Mlabri (Mla Bri 'forest people', an ethnonym of exactly the same kind as Orang Utan). It is spoken by small groups of hunter-gatherers who roam the mountain forests of Northern Thailand and Western Laos. As I shall attempt to show, there is an old stratum in the language which shares its origin with some local languages spoken by villagers on a quite different level of material culture. Once that relationship is established, one can begin to sort out what has happened to the language over time. Conversely, one can use this mixed hunter-gatherer language as an important factor in the reconstruction of the remote history of other, more well-known languages for the very reason that it has partly led its own life as the vehicle of a sharply different material and spiritual culture, with only very slack ties to the remainder of the cultural and linguistic area in which it originated. It is not just a matter

[1] From *Proceedings of the 17th International Congress of Linguistic Sciences 2003*, Prague: Matfyzpress (CD-ROM).

of looking for fossilized forms and remnants of old vocabulary; I shall demonstrate that, on the contrary, Mlabri has preserved essential structural features of the ancestral language better than its closest cognates.

Forty years ago the available data on Mlabri consisted of two short word lists (Bernatzik 1938; Nimmanhaeminda 1963) made by amateurs and so unlike each other that they seemed to represent different languages. More recent research has shown it to be one language and phonologically almost one dialect, although its speakers have split into at least three clan-like groups, each with its own territorial affiliation. Mlabri communities of each group tolerate idiosyncratic pronunciations without stigmatization of aberrant speakers, but at the same time each of the three extant ethnolects, viewed as a whole, is remarkably stable over the time span during which it has been observed, and they are all remarkably similar in their phonologies, except for characteristic differences in intonation. It is as if Mlabri phonology is something that remains essentially invariant over time and space. In return there is a very considerable lexical polarization among the clan-like groups.

Across Mlabri one can now observe a complex of different lexical usages, involving regional, gender-based and to some extent generation-based jargons. The differences in the vocabulary of domestic communication across the groups are very conspicuous and may almost hamper communication in spite of the familiar pronunciation of the many shared words. As for the tendency to split the lexicon into female and male lexical usage, it is sometimes so that the ethnolects agree on the gender assignment of lexical items (e.g. a male versus a female term for 'hair') but there is often no correlation of usage across the ethnolects, which may suggest that such splits are recent.

A further parameter in distinguishing lexical usages is the more or less indigenous status of lexical items: some are felt to be fully-fledged Mlabri words, others are felt by some or all speakers to be loanwords. Innovation through borrowing has been and still is a major source of lexical dynamism. Occasional interference or more extensive symbiosis with highland villagers has triggered fairly extensive borrowing from their languages in spite of the relative isolation of the Mlabri people.

All the above-mentioned relationships must be captured in their interlocking in order for us to be able to construe a historical scenario for Mlabri, since the sound changes that can be shown to have happened within Mlabri proper are few and in themselves offer fairly little by way of relative diachrony.

Except for an unpublished, short word list by Michel Ferlus, professional linguistic fieldwork on Mlabri started only two decades ago. For the most well-known variety a fairly extensive word list was worked out by S. Egerod and myself (1987*a*, 1987*b*). Another, practically extinct variety was the subject of a later monograph (Rischel 1995). There is a third variety with less than thirty speakers (in Laos), which has been investigated in detail only since 1999 (Rischel 2000). An overall dictionary in the form of a database is now in preparation.

18.2.   THE GENETIC PLACEMENT OF MLABRI

On the basis of lexical cognates Mlabri is widely assumed to belong to the so-called Khmuic branch of Mon-Khmer (Austroasiatic). The most well-attested language of this branch (or sub-branch) is Khmu' or Kammu (Premsrirat 1993; Svantesson *et al.* 2002). Among other, more or less closely related languages of Northern Thailand–Laos–Vietnam one can mention Tin (Filbeck 1978), Phong (Kingsada and Kosaka 1999), Ksing Mul (Solntsev *et al.* 1990), and Khabit (Thê' 2000).

There is no definitive Stammbaum for (Northern) Mon-Khmer, however, much of the classification into branches being based on lexicostatistics. In any case, the placement of Mlabri is ill-defined, both because there are mismatches between phonological, morphological, and syntactic alignments and because of a mixed lexicon.

Looking at the Mlabri lexicon, the etyma that catch the eyes of comparativists familiar with Northern Mon-Khmer may be deceptive. Mlabri has a rich and (for all of its internal variation) very conservative phonology, and it has a potential to incorporate loanwords in an unmodified form that is preserved faithfully for centuries, as living fossils (including Ancient Thai words). The Mlabri borrow to a large extent, both culturally and lexically, and it has been an initial obstacle to progress in genetic-comparative work that the most obvious affinities with neighbouring languages are secondary and contact-induced.

Observers familiar with Kammu can find look-alikes which show a baffling similarity or even identity between Kammu and Mlabri. Some, such as **mat** 'eye', are totally inconclusive because they are invariant over most or all of Mon-Khmer (their phonological structure is of a particularly stable kind). There are, however, nontrivial shared forms such as: **kampoŋ** 'skull', **kɯɯr** 'thunder', **kr.waːt** 'broom', **trlam pam** 'moth', **trlɔh** 'pot'. One may therefore expect a particularly direct genetic connection, but it belongs in the picture that there has been recent and considerable contact between speakers of the two languages (some Mlabri speakers still know Kammu), so borrowing has happened. One reason I believe in this explanation is that only a small minority of the lexical items are shared by the two languages in terms of highly similar forms.

Tin is another Mon-Khmer language spoken by highland villagers. They are supposed to be autochthons of the regions on both sides of the Thailand–Laos border where the Mlabri have been encountered in fairly recent time, i.e. the southwestern outskirts of the vast area over which Kammu is spoken. The language comprises two dialect clusters, which Filbeck (1978) refers to as Prai and Mal. It is my own impression that Prai covers a considerably larger area (stretching well into Laos) than Mal. These two dialect clusters are lexically so different that one may well speak of distinct languages, but they are phonologically rather close, and all Prai and Mal dialects share a very pervasive sound shift, which must have happened after Tin became differentiated into Prai and Mal: mutation of word-initial stop consonants (*voiceless > aspirated, *voiced > voiceless). By comparing a wide array of Prai and Mal dialects spoken in Thailand, Filbeck (1978) reconstructed Proto-Tin and, by further internal reconstruction, a pre-stage: Pre-Tin.

Thus, from a diachronic phonological perspective, Tin belongs to the well-researched languages. Lexically, however, it has been documented much less than Kammu (my own use of Tin data is based in part on field notes from a variety of dialects, in part on information from the two leading specialists: David Filbeck and David Jordan, who have been working for many years on Mal and Prai lexicons respectively). If one has access to sufficient lexical data, the affinity between Mlabri and Tin becomes obvious but also intriguing because it comprises different chronological layers including recent loans from Tin. I shall mention two diagnostic examples, both of which show the same etymon occurring in different chronological layers.

The first example is Mlabri **khɔt** 'spear'; the very same form occurs in Prai and in a Prai-influenced Mal dialect, whereas its cognate in Mal proper is **khɔjh** (now mostly replaced by the Thai word). The finals **-t** and **-jh** are Prai- and Mal-specific reflexes of a Mon-Khmer sibilant, which turns up in Mlabri as an aspirated lateral **-lh** (e.g. Mlabri **poːlh** 'barking deer' < Khmuic ***poːs**, cf. Kammu **pu as**, Tin **phɔːt/phɔjh**). The form **khɔt** in Mlabri can only be due to recent borrowing from Prai (after the mutation of voiceless stops). Offhand it seems strange that the Mlabri should borrow their basic term for a traditional implement like the spear from the Tin, and I have recently found that the word is in fact preserved (although apparently in only one Mlabri area) in its pre-mutational, genuine Mlabri form **koːlh**, viz. as a term referring to the wooden shaft of the traditional spear, although the same speakers cite **khɔt** as their standard word for 'spear' as such.

In the other example of chronological duality, the semantic split is stronger. Mlabri has borrowed the Tin word **kluɯʔ**, a noun classifier for pots, in recent time. In Tin, **kluɯʔ** (or **kuɯʔ**) is polysemic since it also means 'head', but in the latter meaning Mlabri has a markedly different form **glɤːʔ**. Genetic comparison shows **glɤːʔ** to be the true Mlabri cognate of the Tin form. The etymon must have existed all the time in both Mlabri and Tin in the meaning of 'head' (the cognate in Kammu means 'hair'!) but when it entered Mlabri once more, in a mutated Tin form, it was in a derived function: as noun classifier.

On closer inspection the linguistic connection between Mlabri and Tin is both more intimate and more complex than that between Mlabri and Kammu. My hypothesis is that Mlabri and Tin share a common layer of Mon-Khmer lexicon which postdates the genetic connection between Mlabri and Kammu. This old Mlabri–Tin connection is crucial for the understanding of the diachrony of both languages. Mlabri and Tin have a common heritage comprising several words which, when viewed jointly, seem to unite these two languages as a subgroup distinct from Kammu and other Khmuic languages (although most of the words may ultimately be retrievable outside Mlabri–Tin). The following cognate pairs (with Tin forms taken from Tin Prai) are chosen so as to show (i) the high degree of agreement in sonorant consonants versus (ii) frequent misfits in vocalism, (iii) regular offsets due to mutation of stop consonants in Tin, and (iv) different handling of initial clusters or presyllables. The three types of phonological offset (ii)–(iv), when found between cognates, provide a criterion for shared old vocabulary (as against recent loans from Tin into Mlabri). For example Mlabri **meːm** 'blood' – Tin **miam**; Mlabri **wɤːŋ** 'chin' – Tin **waŋ**; Mlabri **wɤːk** 'water, to drink' – Tin **ɔːk**; Mlabri **kwʌŋ** 'seed' – Tin **khwaŋ**, Mlabri **kəplah** 'classifier for cloth' – Tin **phlah**; Mlabri **ɟraː** 'thin, skinny' – Tin **siraː**.

Being forest-bound over many centuries, Mlabri has bypassed a number of major sound changes that happened in languages closer to the mainstream such as Kammu or Tin, changes which were either areal or more or less language-specific. The most pervasive, fairly early changes of which we can observe regular effects in modern Tin are consonant mutation and diphthongization. When David Filbeck (1978) worked on Tin historical phonology there was nothing to suggest a specific Mlabri–Tin connection, and quite naturally he did his reconstruction without any glance at Mlabri. I later pointed out that there is such a connection (Rischel 1989*b*) and that the oldest layer of shared words shows remarkable agreement between Mlabri and Filbeck's Pre-Tin. This is true on essential points; on other points it is possible to go further back and show that Mlabri has preserved an archaic phonology predating Filbeck's Pre-Tin. It makes the phonological history of Tin fall better into place within Northern Mon-Khmer if one posits a first stage common to Tin and the old Tin-like stratum in Mlabri: that is, a stage which marks the very first branching-off from other Khmuic. I have called this hypothetical stage 'Tinic'.

The next question is what to make of the presence of an early Khmuic layer shared with Tin. It suggests that Mlabri and Tin were straightforwardly sister languages forming a 'Tinic' sub-branch of their own within Khmuic. That is indeed a likely scenario, although it is enigmatic that the Tinic-speaking people would include hunter-gatherers unless one or more stray groups split off socially and became forest-bound, rather than being primordial hunter-gatherers. The origin of the largest Mlabri group has recently been subjected to ethnobiological investigation, and the resulting genetic evidence strongly suggests (Mark Stoneking, personal comm.) that this group was founded somewhere between five and eight hundred years ago. In terms of time frame that would be perfectly consistent with the Tinic hypothesis, although two questions must obviously be addressed: (i) Do the Mlabri subgroups seem to have a joint ethnic origin? (ii) How do the Tin villagers on both sides of the Thailand–Laos border fit into this pattern?

Linguistically as well, the Tinic hypothesis raises important questions. The evidence is ambiguous. Thus, many Mlabri–Tin cognates are dissimilar in ways that are suggestive of other Mon-Khmer layers in Mlabri, which may then antedate or postdate the Pre-Tin connection. In fact, the majority of Mon-Khmer etyma in Mlabri seem non-Tinic; some resemble distant Khmuic languages (e.g. Mlabri = Phong ɯɯm 'to bathe', Mlabri **micmec**, Phong **mec** 'ant'); others are not even Khmuic in their phonology. Still, that may not be a blow to my Tinic hypothesis: we may be facing a situation of the Albanian or Armenian type, with maybe most of the inherited vocabulary having been replaced over time.

It is conspicuous that whereas Mlabri phonology is remarkably homogeneous and apparently highly static, there has been much lexical change. There is a conspicuous heterogeneity in Mlabri syntax as well, some phenomena being Chinese or Burmic rather than Austroasiatic in kind. Thus one can make a case for Mlabri being a 'mixed language': possibly from the very beginning the result of intensive contact and local convergence within that ethnic group between Tinic and some other language or languages.

18.3.   COMPARING LEXICONS: MLABRI AND TIN

The case of Mlabri and Tin demonstrates, in my view, that cross-language comparisons of lexicons is a very difficult issue when it comes to oral languages spoken by small or scattered groups (it is certainly not favourable to lexicostatistics and glottochronology cf. argumentation in Rischel 1993). For one thing, we do not, by far, have access to the full vocabulary of either Mlabri or Tin. Secondly, both Mlabri and Tin exhibit much lexical variation across groups of speakers; in the case of Tin the two main dialect clusters (Prai, Mal) are so different lexically that it may be justified to speak of two different languages. In many cases such lexical differentiation suggests that the proto-language had synonym pairs of which one item was preserved in one variety of the language, and the other item in another variety; in other cases it may be a matter of borrowing or of neologisms replacing obsolescent words. In Mlabri even words for the most central concepts are often borrowed, unlike the expectations underlying Swadesh's word lists, for example.

When sorting out what was borrowed and why, it seems necessary to distinguish at least the following compartments of the lexicon, which differ in terms of spheres of usage and communicative function: (i) traditional vocabulary related to the survival or subsistence culture; (ii) non-traditional vocabulary (neologisms, borrowings) accompanying non-indigenous technology; (iii) daily vocabulary used in the domestic sphere; (iv) basic vocabulary used when communicating with outsiders, e.g. for the purpose of barter trade. Loanwords will of course appear primarily under (ii) and (iv) above but intrude into the domestic sphere (iii). Thus even the seemingly most 'basic' vocabulary is frequently replaced by material from peer-languages, material which constitutes 'noise' from the point of view of genetic language comparison (as when Mlabri has loanwords in such areas as personal pronouns and names for body-parts).

With such a low-status language as Mlabri, then, the core vocabulary that has been in the language for a long time is not necessarily found by using standard questionnaires but rather by retrieving forest-bound traditional vocabulary as defined under (i) above: names of animals and plants and terminology related to hunting, gathering, traditional medicine, traditional cooking, etc., as well as terminology related to mythology and religion. This is the very part of the lexicon that may remain fairly invariant until it is lost along with the traditional knowledge for which it used to be the carrier; in Mlabri this is confirmed by the finding that traditional terminology is shared to a high degree among the three clans. The shared terminology relating to traditionally important concepts may involve synonymy, as when all ethnolects share a word pair for 'elephant': the ordinary Mon-Khmer word **cha:ŋ** and an onomatopoeic form **pompo:** which, as far as I am aware is specific to Mlabri.

Zoological terminology provides an interesting window on to language-internal lexical innovation. Some such cases may reflect fairly recent contact with village life. An example is a metaphorical use of the word for 'wing': **chrkɛŋ** in the meaning of '(domesticated) hen, chicken' (the alternative being extension of the denotation of **ʔjoc** 'fowl'). Creative word formation also occurs, as when one ethnolect has a strange word for 'dog': **braɲ** instead of the traditional word: **chɔ:ʔ** (itself possibly a borrowing). The form **braɲ** can be construed to mean something like 'small horse' since it is related by sound symbolism to the word for 'horse': **braŋ**. Ideally, the analysis of such relationships is a prerequisite to serious lexical comparison of Mlabri with related languages.

From the perspective of the Tinic hypothesis, it is thought-provoking that superficial comparisons between Mlabri and Tin vocabularies have not so far shown any high degree of sharing of traditional vocabulary as defined above. Offhand this may be interpreted in several ways. The Mlabri language may have a component of forest-life terminology which it received from a source other than Tin (a speculative but meaningful scenario is that the Mlabri were 'originally' of mixed lineage, with male members experienced in hunting coming from ethnic groups other than the Tin). It may also be that the Mlabri developed such terminology language-internally after their first separation from the Tin. Or maybe much of this terminology existed at the Tinic level but was since lost in Tin, which was more closely associated with village life. To address this issue is difficult because of limited access to the entire lexicon of Tin in its various dialects. One cannot rule out that Mlabri and Tin will turn out to share more terminology if one digs more deeply into Tin as well.

18.4.   THE KEY ROLE OF MLABRI IN GENETIC-COMPARATIVE WORK ON KHMUIC

As will be apparent from the above, Mlabri is very close to being what some linguists have called a 'mixed language'. Such languages are not the first on the list when one looks for languages to compare for the purpose of establishing a language genealogy. The point of the present paper is to claim that if the scenario is understood and the data are sufficiently under control, such a language can nevertheless be assigned a key role in genetic-comparative work if it has properties that counterbalance a messy lexicon—*in casu* the conservatism of Mlabri phonology and to a lesser extent of Mlabri morphology.

I have already mentioned that if we look at phonology only we are almost deprived of chronological depth within Mlabri proper, but it is by virtue of that very constancy *vis-à-vis* other Khmuic languages that Mlabri may well become a key element in comparative work on Northern Mon-Khmer. It is crucial for the historical study of Tin in particular because of the old, direct ties between the two languages.

It may arouse more attention if linguists realize that like Kammu (Svantesson 1983: 36–8) Mlabri provides a window on to the fairly remote history of Thai. In addition to inherited or borrowed Mon-Khmer words both Mlabri, Kammu, and Tin have an old layer of culture words borrowed from Southwestern Tai, a cluster of former dialects developing into languages such as Ancient and Modern Central Thai, Northern Thai, and Lao (Laotian). These old loans from Tai can most often be distinguished from later loans by their phonology, and, because the languages of the area have undergone partly different sets of sound changes, it is sometimes possible to determine whether Mlabri got a certain lexical item through one or another lending language, either at an early time or in recent times.

It is noteworthy that the earliest Thai or Lao loanwords in Mlabri have in most respects preserved the form they are supposed to have had in Ancient Thai, the language of the earliest Tai inscriptions, as a testimony of the conservatism of Mlabri phonology. Occasionally, the Mlabri form of an old loan suggests that the present Thai spelling, for all of its long tradition, is etymologically in error. An example is **hmiʌŋ** 'fermented tea': Thai spelling suggests a plain nasal *m- (and Prosody 1) in Ancient Thai but reflexes in Lao, Northern Thai, and Kammu corroborate the Mlabri evidence for *hm- (and Prosody 2).

Other examples of old Tai wordforms surviving in Mlabri are: **bɛ:** 'raft', **ʔba:** 'dumb', **guɯt** 'think', **hlek** 'iron', **hmu:/hmu:ʔ** 'group'. The onsets of all these forms underwent consonant mutation in Thai/Lao several centuries ago, so the source from which these words ended up in Mlabri must have had them as part of its lexicon quite early. It is quite possible that some of the loans even predate the splitting-off of Mlabri from other Khmuic. If one or another of these words entered Mlabri from an intermediate source such as Kammu or Tin, it must have happened before the intermediate language underwent any phonological change that could affect that particular word.

Although this potential for loanwords to throw light on the lending language awaits exploitation in the historical study of Thai and Lao, I shall here focus on Mon-Khmer with a view to the relationship of Mlabri to Kammu and to Tin in particular.

Painstaking comparative analysis involving all Mon-Khmer languages is still a matter for the future. The reason Mon-Khmer specialists have long been speaking of Khmuic as a branch is that there are lexical affinities among these languages, which are spoken in roughly the same part of Southeast Asia. Typologically, it is a heterogeneous language cluster, which probably split up into sub-branches very long ago (if it were ever a well-defined branch). Tin and Northern Kammu occupy a somewhat special position by having undergone consonant mutations resembling those of Tai languages (such as Lao and Central Thai): as said earlier, Tin voiceless obstruents became aspirated, and voiced obstruents became voiceless; in Northern Kammu voiced and voiceless consonants merged with resulting (register or) tonogenesis.

Otherwise, these two languages are in no sense close, lexically or otherwise. Kammu is of prototypical Mon-Khmer structure, with a rich affixal pattern and with a proliferation of so-called sesquisyllabic wordforms consisting of a presyllable plus a full stress syllable. Tin, at the other extreme, has not much transparent derivational morphology and tends towards monosyllabicity (except for the development of a Prai word template **si-CV(C)** from certain complex mono- or sesquisyllabic structures).

By confronting Tin with Mlabri I think one can establish that Tin has undergone drastic simplifications of word structure at an early time, more precisely: after the Tinic stage but before the Pre-Tin stage. From a comparative Mon-Khmer perspective the onset structure of Tin words is atypical. Comparison with Mlabri often makes it possible to identify Tinic presyllables and initial consonant clusters that had arisen by various kinds of affixation, but which underwent reduction in Tin or were irretrievably lost.

A typical example of Mon-Khmer word formation is causative formation by means of various affixes, of which the most widespread is a prefixed labial stop. In Tin (the cited forms below are mostly Prai) there are vestiges of a now unproductive causative formation but little evidence of its original phonology. In some instances, prenasalization of the onset, as in **mpoh** [ᵐboh] 'to boil', **nthec** [ⁿthec] 'to tear', etc., suggests that the prefix in Tin was a nasal. With unaspirated stops the nasal component is not always phonetically prominent, whereas these stops are voiced (and non-glottalized) and thereby exceptional within the sound pattern of Tin; in a minimal pair with causative derivation such as **mpɤl** [ᵐbɤl] 'to kill' – **pɤl** [pɤl] 'to die' I hear a salient difference of voiced versus voiceless.

Now Mlabri enters the scene. Mlabri has preserved the labial causative prefix throughout its lexicon as a pretonic syllable **pa-** or **ba-**. There are two forms because of an allomorphy which has developed specifically in Mlabri and which is dissimilatory, as seen in **pagoh** 'break something' (from **goh** 'break apart') vs. **bakot** 'bend something' (from **kot** 'be bended'). With that knowledge in mind we may return to the causative verbs 'to boil', 'to kill', and 'to tear'. The Mlabri cognates of the Tin causative forms **mpoh, mpɤl, nthec** are **paboh, pabɯl, batac**, which in Mlabri are transparent derivations from the intransitive verbs **boh** 'to be boiling', **bɯl** 'to die, dead', and **tac** 'to be worn'.

The story, then, seems to be that in early Tinic the generalized causative marker was a prefixal syllable or presyllable consisting of a labial plus a more or less articulated vowel. Although onset stops underwent mutation in Tin, the original voiced stops retained voiced allophones when covered by the prefix. Eventually the prefix reduced to a more or less audible prearticulation, which retained two features of the old syllabic prefix by virtue of being a nasal, namely (i) the oral closure of the old affix-initial stop and (ii) the sonority associated with former syllabicity, whereas it assimilated in terms of place features.

With all the 'Tinic' data from Mlabri in place, it becomes compelling to assume that Tinic used to exhibit a much more prototypical Mon-Khmer type, both in terms of phonology and productive morphology. Mlabri has remained at a conservative stage in many ways, although its morphology is now much restricted compared to Kammu, for example. We can now conclude that also Tin must have been much like Kammu in structure, although it has drifted away from that type because of the wearing down or mutation of material occurring initially in wordforms. Some presyllables were lost, others coalesced into rudimentary material. (Drastic changes over time in the onset structure of Mon-Khmer words are not found only in Tin; they are widespread across Mon-Khmer.)

A fairly simple but illustrative case, where Mlabri throws light on the etymological relationship between Tin and Kammu, is a word for 'tooth', which occurs all over Khmuic in more or less similar shapes. It has the onset **s-** in Tin but **r-** in Northern Kammu; historically, the latter is a reflex of **hr-** (attested elsewhere), which does not make the relationship to Tin more transparent. Now, in Mlabri we find a cluster **thr-** in this etymon. The Mlabri aspirate **th** is a regular continuation of Mon-Khmer *s (this is one of the very few sound changes attested for Mlabri), and there is also plenty of independent evidence for Kammu **h** as a continuation of Mon-Khmer *s. Thus the evidence of Mlabri enables us to reconstruct *sr- for a pre-stage of Kammu and Tin. The end result is that Kammu, Tin, and Mlabri forms such as (**hraːŋ>**) **raːŋ, siaŋ, threːŋ** line up perfectly as *sraːŋ at a Proto-Khmuic level, Tin having simplified the cluster—as is typical of Tin—after having split company from Mlabri. (Since this reconstruction was first suggested, its validity has been corroborated by the hitherto little-known language Khabit, spoken in Northeastern Laos, close to Vietnam, which has the etymon in the form **s(ə)ruəŋ**. (Source: the word list of Kingsada and Kosaka 1999.)

The case-studies above suggest that the extensive lexical data that Mlabri is now yielding can be used with some confidence in comparative work, although Mlabri is itself a strange bird, with feathers of sometimes obscure origins.

19

Typology and Reconstruction of Numeral Systems: The Case of Austroasiatic[1,2]

19.1. AUSTROASIATIC AND OTHER NUMERAL SYSTEMS AS OBJECTS OF TYPOLOGICAL STUDY

When speaking about reconstruction and typology one most often refers to the greater or lesser relevance of phonological typology for reflections about the sound pattern of a proto-language, or (less often) to similar considerations in the realms of morphology and syntax. The present paper is rather marginal in the sense that it deals with the lexicon, and more specifically with a closed set of morphemes which exhibits somewhat particular morphosyntactical and phonological behaviour.

In this realm, as well, it is entirely possible and often necessary to adduce typological considerations in genetic comparisons and reconstructions. However, typology here assumes a somewhat different character since it involves considerations of inherent properties and uses (functions) of number systems, and the possible effect of system and function on the expression of individual numbers as numerals in the

[1] Reprinted from *Linguistic Reconstruction and Typology*, ed. J. Fisiak, Berlin: Walter de Gruyter (1997): 273–312.

[2] The present paper is a revised and slightly expanded version of my presentation at the Rydzyna Symposium; I am grateful to the Indo-Europeanists and other participants in this symposium for their comments. Some of the topics dealt with here have also been presented at a Mon–Khmer workshop headed by Professor Gérard DifDoth as part of the Sino-Tibetan Conference in Berkeley in 1992, and also in Lund at a recent graduate symposium on East Asian languages headed by Dr. Jan-Olof Svantesson; on both occasions I received stimulating criticism. Julia Eliott helped me to do fieldwork with Tin speakers in California. Finally, I wish to thank Professor Eric P. Hamp, my colleague Dr Jens Elmegård Rasmussen, and Professor Norman H. Zide for important bibliographical references.

languages of the world.[3] Such considerations are particularly necessary in the case of numerals, as these have a very specific semiotic
status.

Numeral systems occupy a special status in languages because the
underlying mathematics works, or at least may work, in terms of an
unbounded set of equally spaced parameter values (the whole numbers): '2' is more than '1', '3' is more than '2', and so on more or
less infinitely, and the increment for each such step is exactly the same
as for all others. This is unlike the conceptual organization of other
semantic fields. Nevertheless, the inventory of primitive numerals in
any language is limited, and mostly very limited, higher numbers being
for the most part expressed in complex ways if they are at all expressed.
Thus, in spite of the open-ended nature of counting, the numerals of a
given language do in a significant way form a closed set, and the items
of such a set form a system, not just a parameter. In this sense the
functional and semantic study of low numerals is comparable to the
study of semantic fields such as those coded in terms of pronouns or
kinship terms, or even colour terms. Studying a numeral system means
studying a part of language design; one may speak of the underlying
number system with its rules as 'native mathematics', but the study of
numerals should not be confused with the study of mathematics in the
abstract, logical sense.

Some of the issues that are relevant to the issue of a typological
versus a historical–comparative study will now be mentioned by way
of introduction. We shall first briefly consider some inherent properties
of numeral systems, and afterwards, the functions of numerals will be
considered.

19.1.1. **Inherent properties of numeral systems**

Obviously, these are in part universal, in part language- and culture-
specific, and they include such features as (1) to (4) below.

---

[3] Strictly speaking the present paper cannot be said to make valid typological claims
since that would require exhaustive handling of a large and representative sample of the
world's 4,000–6,000 languages; I have attempted to focus just on important and characteristic features of numeral systems on the basis of a fairly wide range of data. When
typological considerations appear explicitly in the literature on numerals, it is often on the
basis of broad documentary surveys from around the beginning of this century, the most
cited source being Eells (1913). In this field, as in other fields of linguistics, it holds true
that there are numerous language communities for which reliable linguistic information has
become available only much more recently, or is still emerging. This is very much true also
of the tribal Mon-Khmer languages which are the main topic of the paper.

(1)   The meaning and syntax of quantifying words of various kinds in a
      language and their interplay with numerals.

Etymologies for numerals must always take into account the possibility of such material being originally not numerals but perhaps
pronouns or words from other classes.

In the case of Austroasiatic numerals this is an important issue in
the explanation of numerals above '10', which are not at issue in the
present paper. One of the major questions is to what extent numerals
originated as collective nouns, and to what extent they were originally
verbs (there is some discussion of this in Zide 1976). As for the old
numerals between '1' and '10', which for the most part have resisted
convincing etymological explanation, the question of a former word
class is immediately relevant with regard to numerals which may have
originated as words for 'hand'; this issue is taken up repeatedly below.

(2)   Base number: the use in 'native mathematics' of one particular base
      number (or the use of several such base numbers)[4] to generate a large
      inventory of numbers from a finite inventory of simplex numerals.

---

⁴ The concept of base number plays a rather marginal role in the present paper. However,
to make the terminology precise it may be useful to make a few comments about linguistic
aspects of the mathematical concept of base number. The universal linguistic property of
such systems, I think, is that there is cyclicity in the numeral expressions: numbers higher
than a base number are expressed by concatenations of numerals below the base numeral
with the base numeral itself. This principle of simple cyclicity in linguistic expressions of
number (which is in fact not all that simple, since it may involve both additive expressions,
multiples of a base number, and powers of a base number) is often overruled by other
means of expression, particularly: (i) specific expressions for small deviations in terms of
'undershoot' (cf. Greenlandic Eskimo qulaaluat or quliŋiluat '9', literally 'inside 10') or
'overshoot' (cf. the Germanic words for '11' and '12'); (ii) specific or morphologically
irregular expressions for very salient numbers (often including multiples or powers of
the base, cf. hundred, thousand, million); (iii) the use of such lexicalizations as higher
base numerals in power expressions (cf. thousand, ten thousand, a hundred thousand as
against simplex lexemes in Thai); (iv) the use of such lexicalizations as competing bases
in multiplicative expressions (cf. '20' versus '10' in Danish and to some extent in French, cf.
Danish firs(indstyve), French quatre-vingts '80'); (v) what I call 'pseudo-bases' in additive
expressions (cf. Eskimo '7' to '8' as discussed later in the text).
   It seems to me quite necessary to make some kind of distinction between the linguistic
design of a numeral system and a mathematical though culture-specific (i.e. 'native mathematical') concept of base in a number system, although this distinction is not always made
explicit in the literature. It has much affinity, but is certainly not identical, with a distinction
between, on the one hand, the numerals appearing in spoken language and to a greater or
lesser extent in writing as a reflex of spoken language, and on the other hand, graphic
number symbols such as Roman or Arabic numbers, which constitute a linguistic code
of their own with its separate inner and outer syntax. The latter type of code is outside
the kind of data treated in this paper but that does not mean that the underlying 'native
mathematics' is outside its scope.

As Stampe (1976: 601) puts it: 'The base number of a number system... must be defined as that number from which counting starts over' (which does not necessarily mean that numbers above the base number are all expressed by synchronically transparent complex forms). That is, the concept of base number is associated with cyclicity. Linguistic expressions of number may display such cyclicity in various ways.

Numeral systems associated with counting on fingers mostly exhibit the base ten, so that there is no cyclicity below '10'. This generally implies that each of the nine lowest numerals has a lexically unique and seemingly arbitrary expression, which then most often defies etymological explanation. The numeral '10' may either be a similarly 'arbitrary' (synchronically 'unmotivated') label, or it may be a collective expression of some kind. The former of these two situations is what we mostly find in Mon-Khmer languages.

However, base five is also sometimes found. Within mainland Southeast Asia there may be only one case of this, but this is in fact a very interesting one, since it is a matter of one of the culturally most prominent languages of the area from ancient times, viz. Khmer. Khmer has straightforward Mon-Khmer etyma for '1' to '5' ('5' being a reflex of a well-known etymon *pram*), but the numerals between '5' and '10' are different: they start a new cycle involving use of the base five in a prototypical way: '6' is expressed by a concatenation of expressions for '5' and '1', '7' is made up of '5' and '2', and so on (for details, see Jacob 1965; Jenner 1976).

Counting low numbers to the base five occurs at least in one other place within Austroasiatic, viz. in the Munda language Turi (Onde, Orea). In that language the word *ti* 'hand' crucially enters the counting system, '5' being expressed as a unit: *miad' ti*, literally 'one hand'. The following numerals are then straightforward: '6' is *miad' ti miad'* 'one hand one', '7' is *miad' ti baria* 'one hand two', etc. This goes on up to '10', which is *baran ti*, literally 'two hands', and then the addition of numerals starts over again on the next cycle: '11' is *baran ti miad'* 'two hands one', etc. (data from P. Ponette 1972, cited by Zide 1978: 40).

Such counting to the base five is, to my knowledge, not found elsewhere within Austroasiatic. However, it occurs in the Ilongot language of Luzon (Vanoverbergh 1937: 194–6) and is well known from other language families around the world. This can be quickly corroborated, e.g. by consulting the linguistic survey classic *Les*

Langues du Monde (Meillet and Cohen 1952), according to which it is documented for Hyperborean ('Paleosiberian') languages (Jakobson 1952: 422–3), for Melanesian (Leenhardt 1952: 686, on Sesake), and for Bantu languages (the latter displaying a wide variety of counting systems—partly as linguistic contact phenomena—including expressions such as '5 + 1', '5 + 2', '5 + 3', and '5 + 4' (van Bulck 1952: 870). As for American Indian languages, a covert type of base five counting is found, e.g. in Aztec and Shuar (see discussion later); moreover, Picard (1986) makes a strong case for the reconstruction of a straightforward base five system for low numbers in Proto-Algonquian (viz. a system in which 'the forms for 6–8 contain the roots of 1–3 plus the form for 5', cf. Picard 1986: 76). The notion of counting '6' and upwards by adding low numerals to '5' being so basic because of its obvious association with finger counting, it is no wonder that linguistic expressions reflecting such counting have developed spontaneously over and over again in different quarters of the world. It is more remarkable that such base five numerals are so comparatively rare.

(3) Psychologically salient quantities and units (such as the dyad or pair and the triad) and culture-specific prominent quantities and units (such as the number seven or the dozen).

These sometimes interfere in complex ways with the basic numeral system in expressions of number. In the case of Austroasiatic numerals up to '10' there are two relevant considerations.

One consideration has to do with the lowest three or four numerals, i.e. those that have a special psychological salience in a universal sense. As stated by Hallpike (1979) and others, very small sets of items are quickly visualized or perceived ('subitized') as composed of discrete items. In Proto-Indo-European the four lowest numerals stand out by being inflected; in Slavonic languages there is another widespread grammatical property of '2', '3', '4', viz. that they take a special case/number form of the quantified noun. All of this is suggestive of a difference in conceptualization between numbers under five (viewed as specifying co-occurrent but discrete items), and numbers from five on (viewed as specifying collections of items). It is exactly the three or four lowest numerals that are preserved in most Austroasiatic languages, including several languages in which there are no traces left of the higher numerals (Thai numerals being used instead).

The other consideration has to do with the significance of the unity of fingers on one hand; this is a complex, culture-specific issue since the size of the relevant set varies between four and five.

(4)   Choice of points of reference to be used in counting, e.g. counting on fingers, on joints, or on other parts of the body.

This is obviously a major issue when discussing etymologies of 'primitive' numerals. Native counting systems do not always use ten fingers (and toes) as fixed points in counting, although this is widely done, and they do not always refer to hands and fingers the way we would expect them to do.

It was mentioned above that Khmer, unique among Mon-Khmer languages, has a prototypical base five system. However, within another branch of Mon-Khmer, viz. in Waic languages, there is a quite sporadic occurrence of another type of numeration which in a more abstract sense also involves counting to the base five. For Waic languages Diffloth (1980: 156) reconstructs '6' as *lɛs and 'seven' as *'ar-lɛs (these are preserved in many Waic languages, e.g. Wa lìah, 'alìah). The first component of the latter clearly means '2'; in fact, the numeral '2' is reconstructed (Diffloth 1980: 149) as *l'ar of which the initial lateral must be a secondary augmentation according to comparative evidence (most Mon-Khmer languages have a labial initial: baar, or the like). That the numeral '7' involves '2' makes sense only if it is conceived as a base five system, but offhand the expression seems to make '7' the 'second six'. Is this something which one finds elsewhere?

It is, in fact. In Eskimo, which exhibits a prototypical instance of a counting system associated with fingers and toes, the term for '5' refers to the completion of one hand (Greenlandic tallimat, Yup'ik talliman '5' is related to Greenlandic taleq 'arm'), and '10' to the completion of the upper extremities (Greenlandic qulit, Yup'ik qulen is etymologically and even synchronically transparent as a plural formation of a word stem meaning 'area above'). Greenlandic and other Eskimo languages have numeral systems involving both base five and base ten (and even base twenty), but this is only fully true in an abstract, arithmetical sense. The term for '6' is not composed of '5' and '1' but is a simplex word arfineq or—if spoken as a single numeral—arfinillit, which etymologically has to do with the term for 'edge of hand'. Clearly, '6' is the numeral on which counting has switched to the pinkie on the second hand (in traditional Eskimo counting, as in the

Mlabri counting method of northern Indochina, the fingers on each hand are normally used, starting with the little finger). The terms for '7', in turn, are based on that for '6', but this is only true linguistically not mathematically, for '7' is not composed of '6' and '1' but of '6' and '2': *arfineq marluk* (*marluk* is '2'), and similarly '8' is *arfineq pingasut* (containing *pingasut* '3').

Thus, in Eskimo, '7' and '8' are expressed as the second and the third member of the series starting with '6'. Mathematically, the numeral '6' (and similarly '11' and '16') assumes the role of quasi-base for the following two or three numerals within the group. Such deviations from 'ideal' numerical expressions in a base five system are, I think, good illustrations of the deep-rooted difference between linguistic and purely arithmetical systems.

Cases like Greenlandic '6' – '7' – '8' may occur much more widely. Somewhat similar data are attested for Shuar of Eastern Ecuador (an Amazon Indian language of the Jivaroan ethnolinguistic family). The Shuar express '5' in terms of completion of the hand ('hand' being *ewéh*), and one might thus expect the terms for '6' and '7' (etc.) to contain this etymon for 'hand' plus the numerals '1', '2', etc. However, according to different sources, '6' may be expressed either by a phrase literally meaning 'here I have a hand', i.e. presumably, the second hand, or by a phrase meaning 'one added'; '7' may be either 'two fingers' or 'two added', etc. (this account is based on data cited in Gnerre 1986: 77, 86).

Another instance of base five counting, but with different base morphemes in the expressions for '5' and for '6' – '7' – '8' – '9', is found in Aztec. I here refer to data on the numerals as they are set up and explained in Payne and Closs (1986: 214–16, based on Classical Nahuatl data from Thelma D. Sullivan).

Aztec clearly has groups of five, corresponding to the four sets of five digits. The first group of numerals comprises four lexically primitive terms for '1' to '4', *ce, ome, (y)ei, nahui*, and a word for '5', *macuilli*, which seems to mean 'a taken hand'. In the next group of five, the numerals '6' to '9' clearly all share the morphological material *chicu(a)-*, [čik^w(a)-] followed by a numeral of the series '1' to '4': *chicuace, chicome*, etc. Although Payne and Closs do not make any statement about morphology here, they paraphrase these numerals as 'five plus one', 'five plus two', etc., thus suggesting that *chicua* and *macuilli* are suppletive expressions for '5'. This may be right, but apparently there is no obvious etymology for *chicu(a)* as an Aztec word outside the numerals in question.[5] A priori it would seem natural to expect this lexeme to have originally meant something different from *macuilli*. This raises the question whether paraphrases such as 'five plus one' for *chicuace* really do justice to the underlying semantics from a diachronic point of view, no matter how adequate they may be in terms of 'native mathematics'.

What we learn from Shuar and Aztec is, then, that systems in which '6' – '7' – '8' – '9' are counted to the mathematical base five do not necessarily use the word for '5' in forming the following numerals. It would make sense to assume that there is a system-inherent reason for this, and such a reason might be sought in the type of semantics underlying the Eskimo system, although this is not explicitly supported by the other languages mentioned here.

This line of reasoning may be extended to the case of Waic. The problem is that the etymological relationships are not very transparent in Waic either. The shared component *les* of the numerals '6' and '7' (see above) is not the etymon for '6' found in other Mon-Khmer languages. One might just give up on it, but the apparent typological parallel with Eskimo suggests that one should perhaps look for an old Mon-Khmer noun signifying something similar to Greenlandic *arfineq*. Whatever signification *les* had before it came to function as a numeral, the pattern of '6' and '7' in Waic seems entirely parallel to the pattern displayed by the Greenlandic expressions for these two numerals.

A question of a different kind is whether counting on fingers necessarily leads to the use of a mathematics with base five or ten, although this might seem archetypal. There is some evidence that another, competing mode of counting involves only four fingers on each hand. This issue will be taken up later.

19.1.2. **Functional aspects of numeral systems**

If the internal structure of a numeral system is interesting in a historical context, this is no less true of the functional aspects of numeral systems.

It is important to take into consideration uses of numerals that one might expect even in 'primitive' society, and to acknowledge that the inventory of numerals may not have been invariant over such different

---

[5] Dr Una Canger, personal communication.

uses in a particular culture. From the remote past, most of the following basic activities must have been quite widespread:

1 Reciting a series of numerals as an end in itself, e.g., to measure time, or as a ritual or game (mostly using just a few of the lowest numerals).
2 Counting items audibly (by speaking an incremental series of numerals each tagged to an individual item until all items have been labelled, an activity normally starting from '1' and thus strongly favouring the use of the lowest numerals).
3 Stating the exact, total number of items in a set (without necessarily counting, since it may be a prescriptive statement) using a numerical expression.
4 Giving an estimate of the size of a set of items by using a complex, approximative expression such as *four to five*, or a single numerical or collective expression (estimates often involve 'round numbers', which are typically fractions or multiples of base numbers, cf. Sigurd 1988; in administratively developed cultures estimates may involve extremely high numerical values).
5 Specifying the serial number of a particular item within a limited, ordered set, e.g., referring to time or date with cyclic expressions (uses which typically involve rather low numbers).
6 Using a numerical expression to refer to a particular item in an open-ended series (cf. chronology in developed cultures, which may involve exact specification of very high numbers).
7 Using—in a developed culture—more or less arbitrary number tags, as when assigning personal numbers to soldiers (since the uniqueness of each individual tag and possibly also its placement within a hierarchy is crucial, this use of number may involve particularly complex expressions).

Many languages have a morphological distinction between cardinal numerals used in some functions (such as 1–4 above), and ordinal numerals used in others (such as 5–6); some languages also have morphologized distributive and/or multiplicative numerals (i.e. expressions with meanings such as 'three each' or 'three times'). I shall not go into these matters since they are not relevant to my discussion of Austroasiatic (see Gvozdanović 1985: 141 ff. for an extensive discussion of the relationship between cardinal and ordinal numerals within the grammatical framework of languages).

In the above (very sketchy) enumeration of uses of numerals I have totally disregarded more or less sophisticated applications of algebra (in cultures that have developed such abstract activities as explicit addition of sums to each other, or subtraction or multiplication) and also disregarded the crucial differences between the use of number in cultures with writing and cultures without writing. Still, the list above may suffice to highlight the inherent functional complexity of numerals.

The greater or lesser frequency of one or another application of numerals in daily life in the remote past may be relevant to the early history of the numerals of a language. This is true, e.g. if one argues that 'adjacent' numerals in a series have influenced each other phonologically (in terms of alliteration or in other ways) or morphologically. It is true if cardinal versus ordinal numbers are at issue. And it is true if the question is whether it is likely that words from 'major' word classes may have invaded a numeral system.

Since we normally have little or no access to reliable historical information on such matters it is important to avoid being 'one-eyed' when giving functional reasons for historical developments, and it may be useful to look—with some caution—at typical and hence perhaps archetypal uses of numerals in present-day 'primitive' societies.

The importance of function and use for the identity of numerals may be illustrated with data from the northern branch (or perhaps rather cluster) of Mon-Khmer languages that is called Khmuic (cf. Thomas and Headley 1970). The impression one gets from word lists and other literature about Khmuic languages is that only a few of the lowest Mon-Khmer numerals exist in these languages, viz. at most '1' to '4', otherwise '1' to '3', or, as the minimum, '1'. According to some accounts, even these numerals are used only in quantifying expressions such as 'one day', 'two days'; in other functions (cf. the enumeration of possible functions of numerals above) one uses a full set of numerals borrowed from Laotian/Thai (henceforth referred to as 'Thai' numerals). David Thomas has aired the assumption that Khmuic languages, unlike other Mon-Khmer, had lost much of their inventory of numerals before acquiring the present system: they 'apparently didn't switch to a decimal system at the same time as the others, so that when the Tai peoples conquered the Khmuic area there was no local decimal system to compete with the Tai system; so the adoption of the higher numerals has led to total abandonment of Mon-Khmer numerals in Mal, tenuous retention of only 1, 2, 3 in Khmu' alongside the full Tai set, and retention of 1, 2, 3 in Puôc and Tayhat' (David Thomas 1976: 72).

By working personally with some of these languages, I have had this scenario confirmed as regards daily usage. However, if one asks specifically for traditional number names, as they used to be spoken, e.g. as a ritual or nursery rhyme, or just to show one's competence in counting from '1' to '10', it turns out that some people know this whole list in its typical Mon-Khmer shape. This is true, for example, of Mlabri and Tin and Khmu', all of which are found in the northern Thailand–Laos border region. The numerals thus surviving are strictly limited to a series without cyclicity, i.e. there is no evidence in this material of a base number (whereas the use of Thai or Laotian numerals by the same peoples involves the base ten). This probably reflects a limitation of the use of these indigenous numbers to domestic hill-tribe life, as against the use of a more complex system of Thai/Laotian numerals for external purposes. If we speak about spheres of usage rather than wholesale cultures, this is not inconsistent with Greenberg's contention that 'The typological division between systems without bases and those with at least one base has at least a gross correlation with technological level' (Greenberg 1978: 291).

It is not all that surprising that all of the ten lowest numerals of Mon-Khmer origin can be retrieved in Khmuic today, since they are attested already from the 1860s and for Mlabri from 1962 (which blatantly contradicts David Thomas's assumption as referred to above). Much better data are available now both for Mlabri (Egerod and Rischel 1987*a*, 1987*b*) and Khmu' (Rischel, unpublished field data from Ban Nam Puk, Thailand, 1993).[6] As for Tin, there was no evidence of a full list of Mon-Khmer numerals up to '10' until I recorded the list in 1992 from two Tin refugees from Laos who had resettled in the USA. (Among Tin speakers in Thailand I have been totally unable to retrieve the list.) I shall, therefore, cite Tin below as a reference set, although it has one flaw: '10', although not a Thai loan, is not the old Mon-Khmer numeral either, but a collective expression (of which *ma-* is a pretonic version of the numeral 'one'):

(5)   *muʌj* '1'   *thuʌl* '6'
       pia(r) '2'   *gul* '7'
       phɛ' '3'   *thi'* '8'
       phon '4'   *gat* '9'
       sɔɔŋ '5'   *(ma) tuk* '10'

(The numeral '2' ends in **r*, but in many Tin dialects syllable final **r* has undergone phonological change so that its reflex is either a glide or sometimes zero.)

---

[6] Dr Frank Proschan kindly made me aware of the strong preservation of Mon-Khmer numerals above '3' in a Khmu' village in northern Thailand, where virtually everybody seems to know them. This is particularly noteworthy since these numerals were supposed not to exist today (cf. Svantesson 1983: 74–5).

I was told that the list of numerals above is no longer generally known among Laotian Tin people, and I assume that it emerges only under particular circumstances, being, as it were, part of their folklore. In quantifying expressions they apparently use only the very lowest numerals, like the Tin of Thailand.

A somewhat different separation of functions is found in Mlabri. This tribe of hunter-gatherers know a Mlabri list of numerals up to '10', which is genuinely Mon-Khmer (and specifically Khmuic, as is evident from comparison with other languages). They recite these numerals while counting on fingers in the same fashion as traditionally used, e.g. by East Greenland Eskimos. The Mlabri numerals, as they have been recorded by Egerod and Rischel (cf. our published vocabulary, Egerod and Rischel 1987*a*, 1987*b*), and later by myself, are as follows (with indications of vowel length added, unlike earlier records):

(6) *mɔɔj* '1'   *taal* '6'
     bɛɛr '2'   *gul* '7'
     pɛ' '3'   *tii'* '8'
     pon '4'   *gajh* '9'
     thəəŋ '5'   *gal* '10'

All these numerals have a weak status outside the recited numeral series. This is true even of '1'. As a quantifier or article meaning 'one (single)' they use a derivative (e.g. *dəmɔmlaa'* 'one person'). The only numerals that are very frequently used in quantifying expressions, are '2' and '4'. Even the Mlabri numeral *bɛɛr* is often replaced by a Thai loan: for *bɛɛr mlaa'* 'two persons' one tends to say *sɔɔŋ mlaa'* with the Thai word for '2' (which is confusingly similar to the general Khmuic etymon for '5', cf. later). The case for *pon* '4' is weaker, but for a different reason: the meaning of *pon mlaa'* should be 'four persons' but most often it more vaguely means 'several persons, the whole group'.

On a few occasions I have heard expressions involving two consecutive Mlabri numerals in estimates of numbers, e.g. *gajh-gal tawm* 'nine or ten days'. I strongly suspect that this is a calque from Thai. It is my impression that the Mlabri always switch to expressions consisting entirely of Thai lexical material (numeral plus classifier) if they have to specify exact numbers above '5'. The concept of exact numbers above '5' probably has little function in their own culture but may become relevant if, for example, an appointment or a bargain is made with somebody from the outside (even so, many Mlabri have little command of number). To specify a time span or a time in the future, e.g. 'for five days' or 'in five days', the Mlabri may use audiovisual means: a gesture indicating, e.g. the movement of the sun may be repeated the appropriate number of times, each time accompanied by exactly the same oral explanation of the meaning of the gesture. In this way the abstract concept of number may apply without any need for linguistic coding in terms of exact numerical expressions.

As stated already, the total set of Mlabri numerals occurs as a kind of recital, which may have (had) a magic purpose but which also seems just to serve the purpose of demonstrating a competence expected of a genuine Mlabri male; there is certainly nothing secret about it. It is also possible to use the whole series as a summing-up quantifier expressing a large number, as when a Mlabri explained to me about a group of several people who were once encountered in the forest: *mɔɔj bɛɛr pɛ' pon thəəŋ thaal gul ti' gajh gal mlaa'* 'they were one, two ... ten persons!' On the other hand I have never come across a Mlabri who had an immediate grasp of the numerical values of Mlabri numerals above '4'; a task in which a randomly picked Mlabri numeral is to be given a quantitative meaning seems to require starting from '1' and counting all the way up to the numeral in question.

All of this seems to suggest that beyond the very lowest numbers (those which can be 'subitized', cf. above), Mlabri numerals are at most used as an accompaniment to the counting of items. They are hardly individualized at a higher abstraction level, as they are in languages in which each numeral by itself can be used to represent the size of a collection of items (the 'Cardinality Principle', cf. Hurford 1987: 305; Gvozdanović 1992: 3).

There is a quite different peculiarity of the Mlabri numeral system which is interesting from a typological point of view. To exactly specify the odd numerals '3' and '5' the Mlabri often use phrasal expressions such as *sɔɔn gɛɛŋ hlooj* 'three houses', *hlooj* apparently meaning something like 'and an extra one'. Thus we have here a rather unusual instance of counting in pairs; it should be noted that this is not linked to the use of either Mon-Khmer or Thai numerals in Mlabri speech, but is part of the numeral grammar of the language.

To make things more complicated, in the area where Mlabri is spoken, some dialects of Tin exhibit a quite separate (and hitherto largely neglected) system of expressing numbers up to '10'. It was published by Kraisri Nimmanhaeminda (1963) in a rather distorted version, which he refers to as 'Tin Sagad' numerals. Since I have subsequently recorded much more extensive material both from Tins in Thailand and from Laotian Tins, a discussion of Nimmanhaeminda's list in particular is of minor consequence here. I shall just reproduce what I would reconstruct (on the basis of many different sets of data, including those of Nimmanhaeminda) as the least distorted and most complete version. It should be noted that *thii* means 'hand', and that *phia* means 'one of a pair, alter'; *phia* may be augmented with *m-* reflecting the numeral 'one'. The syntax and semantics should be transparent enough in spite of the inexact paraphrases:

(7) '5':   *(m)phia thii* 'one of the hands'
    '6':   *piar phɛ'* 'two threes'
    '7':   *(m)phia phɛ' (m)phia phon* 'one of them three, the other four'
    '8':   *piar phon* 'two fours'
    '9':   *(m)phia phon (m)phia thii* 'one of them four, and the other hand'
    '10': *piar phia thii* 'both of the hands'

This, then, is a sophisticated system of numeral expressions each referring to the addition of a number of fingers on one hand to a number of fingers on the other hand (except for '5' which is counted on one hand). The various recordings I have of it are often more or less corrupt (though mostly less than Nimmanhaeminda's version) in that they mix up the two lexemes *pia(r)* '2' and *phia* 'one of a pair' in the complex numerals, which is no wonder considering how confusingly these components are distributed. Some dialects have preserved only one or two of the forms above (the expression for '5' seems particularly robust); some have lost them completely. However, the complex numerals above are without exception forms that I have got from good informants speaking conservative dialects, and they certainly constitute a system with a perfect inner logic.

Counting in this manner involves the hand with its five fingers without involving the notion of a base five. The system has no parallels that I know of elsewhere in Austroasiatic (there is a slight similarity with the Munda language Turi in the use of unit expressions referring to hands for '5' and '10', but that is all). However, the notion that the even numerals above five are the doubles of numerals below five is found in widely different languages, so that '6' and '8', for example, are expressed either 'multiplicatively' in terms of '2' and '3', '2' and '4' (cf. Jakobson 1952: 422 on Gilyak) or 'additively' in terms of '3' and '3', '4' and '4', as in Tin. Salzmann (1950: 78) cites Chipewyan

'6' as being expressed by a form meaning 'each side three', exactly as in Tin.

One may also encounter numeral systems exploiting the same mathematical idea but in a less similar fashion. There seem to be traces of some such pattern in Atayal (Formosan Malayo-Polynesian). As it appears from Søren Egerod's elicited and reconstructed forms of Atayal numerals (Egerod, personal communication), '6' to '10' are set off from '1' to '5' in that the former all begin in *m*-, which is consistent with the assumption that 'being beyond the five fingers of one hand' is a salient notion in counting. However, it is not a base five system: '6' to '10' do not represent a new cycle of '1' to '5' as in Khmer; rather, Atayal '6' and '8' seem to contain the stems of '3' and '4', respectively, whereas '10' contains a stem meaning 'to count'. Thus, although the prefixal material on '6' to '10' may somehow mark these numbers as being beyond five, it makes perfect sense to speculate that they are in fact reflexes of expressions referring to equal numbers of fingers on both hands, as in Tin.

Returning to the more transparent two-hand system in Tin, one may wonder why a Mon-Khmer language would ever develop such an awkward numeral system given the options that were already available: the old simplex numerals of Mon-Khmer origin and the Thai numbers. The explanation may be that the two-hand system of numerals was developed for a specific purpose. Some of my informants explained to me that these expressions formerly were, or still are, used when expressing quantities, e.g. in selling things (one informant even claimed that these were a kind of secret language used among kinsmen not wanting another party to understand the bargaining that was going on). In other functions the same persons would use either the traditional Mon-Khmer numerals or the Thai (Laotian) numerals.

Association of the numerals above with small trade may thus explain the specific way in which they involve finger and hand counting. This kind of reference to the role of manual counting modes in trade language has been used more spectacularly by Eric Hamp in his novel explanation of the strange, seemingly subtractive Ainu numerals above '5': according to Hamp (1969) these may be due to a very specific Far Eastern mode of finger counting proceeding forth and back on one hand.

The conclusion with regard to Tin, which is generally considered to have only vestiges of Mon-Khmer numerals, is that it actually possesses four functionally distinct sets of numerals up to '10', which have probably been used in largely complementary functions. One (the standard set of numerals for expressing numbers and for counting) is shared in its totality with the dominant Thai language of the area (Northern Thai or Laotian). A second set (used in quantifying noun phrases) is partly Mon-Khmer, partly Thai. A third set (known by a few as folklore) is the more or less complete series of traditional Mon-Khmer numerals. Finally, the fourth set (possibly still used for some local purposes) is composed of the traditional Mon-Khmer numerals up to '5' plus more or less complex expressions involving the notions of 'one of a pair' and 'hand' for the numbers up to '10'.

To be exhaustive I wish to mention that some Laotian Tin speakers know still other sets of low numerals used in their original, multilingual habitat, although these are considered extraneous to the Tin language itself. One type of numerals from '1' to '10' is particularly interesting: it is a nursery rhyme (formerly taught to the Tin speakers when they were very young) in which the Laotian name of each numeral is distorted in some fashion but is in some cases still recognizable.

In one variant of the nursery rhyme the numerals are replaced by more or less meaningful words or word combinations of which each rhymes either with the appropriate Laotian numeral or with an immediately adjacent numeral within the nursery rhyme itself. The rhyming principles involve both end rhymes and (to a lesser extent) assonances. Disregarding tones, the numerals '1' to '10' may run as follows if rhyming entirely with the official numerals: *liŋ khiŋ, lɔɔŋ khɔɔŋ, ma kham, caw pii, mak waa, cap cok, mɔk het, 'ɔt 'ɛt, mak paw, mak/maj ñip*. In another variant the two rhyming principles are mixed: *'an niŋ, 'an nɔɔŋ, 'an kɔɔŋ, kacaaw, 'an naaw, 'an nok, 'an hok, 'an hɔɔk, makɔɔk, kacik*. Such nursery rhyme numerals are probably known in many cultures. The design is similar to that of the 'North Country Score' of England, a set of numerals (*yan, tan, tethera, pethera, pimp, sethera, lethera, hovera, covera, dik*, etc.) which, quoting Greene (1992: 551), 'are said to have been used for counting sheep, stitches in knitting, etc., as well as in children's games', and which he sees as 'deriving from contacts between Welsh and English speakers within the last few hundred years' (1992: 552). The reason for mentioning such nursery rhymes at all in connection with the Tin (although they are not even Tin numerals) is that their presence as part of a (more or less forgotten) cultural heritage from childhood adds interestingly to the complexity in the realm of counting.

A study of 'the numerals of Tin' would never be adequate without a consideration of the several coexisting sets which together make up the total knowledge of numerals within that small ethnic group. This probably holds true much more widely.[7] There are many, more or less strange, environments in which numerals may occur; unless this is taken into consideration when searching for old or current material one may never dig up all that is to be found within this particular subsection of the lexicon.

The functional aspect leads on to a third, language-external consideration: the possibility of a numeral system having been shaped by influence from another language and/or culture. Numerals constitute an extremely confusing field with regard to linguistic borrowing. On the one hand numerals may belong to the most stable and most fossilized linguistic material in a language family. On the other hand numerals seem extremely susceptible to replacement if the cultural situation favours it. At least, this has been the case widely in Southeast Asia. The Thai numerals are largely borrowings. At a later stage, some Mon-Khmer languages have borrowed most or all of their numerals from Thai (or Laotian), maybe retaining their indigenous numerals up to '3' or '4' for use in quantifying expressions only (cf. the discussion of Tin above).

Moreover, language contact may well lead to pervasive structural changes as well, e.g. change of base number. One of the controversial issues in the study of Austroasiatic numerals is what the source of the present preponderance of decimal counting is. It is no less of a question than why Khmer, alone among all Mon-Khmer languages, exhibits an (old) system of counting to the base 5.

Numeral systems constitute a field which has attracted mathematicians, anthropologists, psychologists, and linguists alike, and the theoretical literature that is directly relevant to the linguistic aspects of numerals is fairly extensive but in my view not always all that revealing.[8]

[7] A similar differentiation of usage for numerals may be what underlies the apparent coexistence of two sets of numerals above '5' for Khmer until early in this century, one (the well-known one) being an old, but secondary, system to the base of five, the other (known from only one source) being the expected old Mon-Khmer series and perhaps dating back to Proto-Khmer (cf. Jenner 1976: 48 and note 10 below).

[8] I wish to mention a few monographs and collections of papers on numbers and numeral systems from the latter half of this century (there are useful references to important earlier studies both in these and in Salzmann's small paper of 1950). Menninger (1958) is maybe the classic in number studies from the point of view of philology; its emphasis is

Within Indo-European studies, the numerals have always been a realm in which etymological work met with frustrations. The recent, monumental volume edited by Gvozdanović (1992) shows the state of the art in the comparative study of Indo-European numerals.[9] One might perhaps expect that such a result of the joint efforts of several leading scholars in the field would have more or less solved the mysteries surrounding these etyma and at the same time given a definitive characterization of Proto-Indo-European counting both in relation to the general typology of numeral systems and in relation to cultural history. That, however, is not what we learn from the impressive volume, for all of its merits. Rather, except for the introduction by the editor, it is oriented remarkably little towards typological considerations of a general kind, even when issues such as the ones I have enumerated above might seem most relevant. Apparently it has not been considered fruitful to engage in speculations on a typological basis or desirable to go much beyond a careful collection of the comparative evidence available within the various major branches of Indo-European.

The truth about numerals in Indo-European is, of course, that attempts to explain the origin of individual low numerals (up to '10') are still remarkably unsuccessful (many scholars would probably just say that hunting for etymologies in this field is not a particularly useful endeavour at all). The safest one can say is that there is strong evidence of a decimal system from early time, although this clashes with the peculiar structure of the old numerals '4' and '8' (see below).

There are other language families in which even the lowest numerals are etymologically much more transparent, although the data for comparison are mostly extremely meagre. It is then typically the case

on the early and medieval cultural history of Arabic and European numerals. From the point of view of linguistic theory, however, it is not very sophisticated. Hallpike (1979) views numerals from a quite different angle: his monograph gives interesting information on the psychological aspects of the basic concept of number. As for more specifically linguistic aspects, the papers in Corstius (1968) are for the most part (with exceptions such as Merrifield's paper) of marginal interest to the present issue. The same is true of Hurford (1975), which is an ambitious attempt to handle numerals within a formal linguistic theory. Hurford (1987) has a very different approach and is in my view more revealing to the student of the comparative and typological aspects of numerals. The universals aspect (or, as Greenberg puts it more carefully, that of generalizations about numeral systems) is treated by Greenberg (1978). As for information on individual languages, I wish to mention in particular the papers in Closs (1986), which give excellent data and discussions of several types of 'primitive' numeral systems.

[9] Although the volume was published only quite recently (after a new editor had stepped in) most of the papers had been completed well ahead of the year of publication (1992).

that the number names are very directly related to fingers or other parts of the body used for counting. Eskimo is a particularly well-known example of this (for Eskimo counting cf. Thalbitzer 1923). Altogether, there are languages enough all over the world which exhibit transparent reflexes of 'primitive counting' of various kinds to make consideration of counting typology a useful instrument in the genetic-comparative study of numerals. Such considerations may not solve any problems but they at least support assumptions about more or less specific modes of counting underlying present-day number systems.

The present paper deals with such aspects of the numerals in a language family for which comparative work is in its infancy, viz. Mon-Khmer languages, and more extensively: Austroasiatic languages (including both Mon-Khmer and Munda languages).

19.2.   HOW MANY FINGERS MAKE A HAND? FOUR-PLUS-FOUR OR FIVE-PLUS-FIVE COUNTING?

From a comparative perspective, the Austroasiatic numerals are characterized by a lot of more or less unpredictable variation. Since pure numerals have no denotation except for their numerical meaning, which may be secondary, etymological explanation is difficult and often impossible in this section of the lexicon. That is, since the time depth and hence the phonological variation across these languages is quite large, it becomes a very difficult issue to determine whether vaguely similar forms referring to the same number are etymologically related or not (cf. Section 19.3 below). This, in turn, makes it a problematic venture to reconstruct an underlying counting pattern for all of the Austroasiatic languages.

There are conspicuous etyma, however. An interesting numeral is '8', which in several languages either contains or just consists of a syllable made up of a voiceless dental stop plus an unrounded vowel or diphthong, e.g. in Khmuic: Mlabri *tii'*, Tin *thi'*, Khmu' *krti'*, Tayhat *kântây*, etc.; in Waic: Proto-Waic **te'* (Diffloth 1980: 100); and in a numeral series claimed to have been recorded for Khmer in 1914: '*kati*' (here cited from Jenner 1976: 48).[10] This numeral (or its main

---

[10]   Khmer otherwise has an expression meaning 'five-three'; as stated elsewhere in this paper, Khmer already in Pre-Angkorian time shows a secondary system of expressing number to the base of five (also cf. note 7 above).

syllable) must reflect a widely attested Mon-Khmer word for 'hand'. In most of the languages that share these two etyma for '8' and 'hand' their phonological expressions (disregarding prefixal material in '8') are simply homophonous.[11]

The wide distribution of the etymon for 'hand', $*tV(y)$ in its use as a numeral implies that that must be quite an old feature within a wide range of northern Mon-Khmer languages. Such an association would not make any sense unless it reflected an old mode of counting. The underlying idea must be that the number '8' marks the completion of either one total hand (if counting that high up was made with the fingers on one hand) or more plausibly of both hands. This does not make sense according to any mode of finger counting that I know of in present-day Mon-Khmer, but suggests that there once was a way of counting such that only four fingers on each hand, i.e. the four smaller fingers, were used.

The assumption, then, is that '8' was counted on four-plus-four fingers and represented the completion of counting on 'hands', i.e. a major station in counting,[12] corresponding to the role of '10' in most systems based on finger counting (including all of present-day Mon-Khmer).

This raises two questions. One is how good the evidence is for the plausibility of the old four-plus-four counting; in the apparent absence of genetic-comparative evidence one must look for typological support. This is what will be done below. The other question is what $*tV(y)$ originally meant: maybe it did not originally refer to the whole hand with its five fingers but only to the part with the four shorter

---

[11]   To be true, there is sometimes phonetic aberration between the two glosses 'hand' and '8', sometimes in the final (my list for Tin has *thi'* for '8', whereas 'hand' is *thii*), sometimes in the vocalic part (in the Angkuic language U of Yunnan, the word for 'hand' is *thi* but '8' is *thá*, according to the word list in Svantesson 1988). That may perhaps be due in some cases to numerals having been borrowed between Mon-Khmer languages; in other cases it may perhaps be due to the different stress patterns of numerals and substantives. Altogether, it does not invalidate the etymological identification of the two words, considering the mass of comparative evidence in favour of it. Neither does the pretonic syllable or presyllable often occurring on the numeral '8', since this is in many languages shared by other numerals between '5' and '10' and apparently marks the numeral as belonging to a set higher than '1' to '4'.

[12]   Note that this evidence for '8' meaning 'hand(s)' does not imply an assumption to the effect that Mon-Khmer used to have a number system to the base of eight, i.e., a truly octal system (with '9' expressed by a concatenation of '8' and '1', etc.). The only contention made is that the totality of eight fingers was crucial in the mode of counting underlying the lexicalization of number names.

fingers, or to that particular set of fingers in itself? I am not aware
of evidence for or against such an assumption within Mon-Khmer,
except that the existence of a semantic notion covering just the part of
the hand with the four shorter fingers in early Mon-Khmer is plausible
enough.[13]

As pointed out several times throughout this paper (also see
Section 19.3 below), it is conspicuous that the numerals up to '4' are
better preserved than any other numerals in Austroasiatic. There are
also often higher numerals of purely Mon-Khmer origin. These may
then be preserved in their (more or less) original Austroasiatic form,
but it is interesting that they may also be formed as composite expressions in which the first four numerals are used over again, and '5' is
referred to as a hand. This is done in a strange and elaborate way in
the complex Tin numerals presented above, and it is done in terms of
much simpler additive expressions to the base '5' in Khmer.

What is particularly noteworthy is that both Tin and Khmer exhibit
evidence for a coexistence of two such systems: one comprising a
full set of simplex Mon-Khmer numerals, the other exploiting only
the lowest four or five numerals to form all ten of them. As said
earlier (Section 19.1 above), I think this has an intimate connection
with the coexistence of different spheres of usage for numerals. It
may be true of several northern Mon-Khmer languages that the total
set of old Mon-Khmer numerals is preserved (or was preserved until
recently) as a ritual series, although some of the numerals have long
since been abandoned as numerals for use in quantifying expressions. That would explain why the 'original' Mon-Khmer numerals in
Tin, which I have retrieved up to '9', have not been noticed before
by Mon-Khmer scholars, and it would explain the strange case of
Khmer.

In Khmer, additive expressions to the base of five are totally dominant for '6' to '10' throughout the known history of the language,
being well documented in inscriptions. However, Jenner (1976) refers
to an anonymous French account of 'La numération chez les Khmêrs
ou Cambodgiens' (1914) with a quite different list of numerals which
are not formed on the base of five. These very decidedly belong to the
old Mon-Khmer stock; with the exception of '10' they are very similar

---

[13]   In Mlabri there is a specific collective designation for the four shorter fingers, which—
although it is not etymologically related to $*tV(y)$—shows the relevance of this semantic
notion in itself.

to forms found in some Mon-Khmer languages of eastern Indochina. Jenner (1976: 44, 48) takes the 1914 set seriously enough to posit it as that of the original Khmer numerals '6' to '10',[14] although he makes a number of amendments by comparing it with related Mon-Khmer languages (amendments for which I do not quite see the foundation) before reconstructing a set of Proto-Khmer forms on this basis. The list above '5' looks as follows in its original version (here cited from Jenner):

(8)   *kron*   '6'
    grul, grouil   '7'
    kati   '8'
    kansar   '9'
    ka(n)san   '10'

As for the etymological unity of Mon-Khmer, it was pointed out by David Thomas (1976: 71–2) that the evidence concerning counting systems is very complex. The terms for '1' to '4' are 'shared nearly universally', those for '6' to '9' on the contrary 'splinter the family into several groups', whereas the terms for '5' and '10' show larger groupings. On this basis he assumes that 'Proto-Mon-Khmer used a counting system based on 4, or more probably on 5' and that it was only under external influence that these languages converted to a decimal system: the prestige languages of the areas in which Mon-Khmer languages were spoken had decimal systems.[15]

Zide (1976), considering the whole scenario of Austroasiatic, proceeds along much the same lines, although he takes issue, in footnote 27 (1976: 18), with one aspect of Thomas' presentation, viz. the implication that there was no established set for 6 – 7 – 8 – 9 – 10 in Proto-Austroasiatic. Zide argues in favour of the early existence of a counting system based on sets of four: '1' to '4' and '6' to '9', in which '5' was separated off (1976: 8). As for higher counting, he emphasizes the importance of the unit '20', and he notes that a system with 'sets of four "in" sets of five' fits in with a vigesimal not a decimal system: 'Counting with twenties is presumably compatible with a lower counting unit of either four or five (and there is some evidence of these in a single system); decimality is not' (Zide 1976: 13). He also

---

[14] The relevance of the list certainly hinges on the conviction that the list of numerals really is from general Khmer, i.e. that it does not stem from one of the minor ethnic groups of the region speaking more or less similar Mon-Khmer languages.

[15] Cf. the reference to David Thomas's contention about Khmuic languages above.

points out that South Munda shows traces of a system of counting in twelves, which fits in less well with sets of fives than with fours. Unlike Thomas, Zide is otherwise rather noncommittal as to the age of decimal counting in Austroasiatic (he lists several arguments for and against its being an old feature of these languages).

It is high time now to see if there are good parallels to counting in 'sets of four', and to '8' marking the completion of hands, in numeral systems outside Austroasiatic.

The now extinct Chumash languages of California used to have extremely variegated systems of numeration, as described by Beeler (1986: 115–17), but with basically just four root words, viz. the terms for '1' to '4'. Beeler makes the point that the Chumash numeral system is 'obviously quaternary; the only other root words employed are the words for multiples of four' (Beeler 1986: 116). The other root words in question are those for '8' and '16', whereas '12' is expressed in terms of its factorization into three times four.

This cyclicity in terms of four is the old pattern. However, there is evidence for 'an invasion of the Chumash system by a quinary or decimal based sequence' (Beeler 1986: 125); not surprisingly, loanwords are found for the new basic numerals '5' and '10'.

It would lead too far to summarize the fascinating account of these numeral systems given by Beeler; what is crucial in the present context is the evidence for old quaternary counting as seen in the numerals '5' to '7'. Beeler (1986: 116) states by way of an introduction to his analysis that 'The expressions meaning 5, 6, and 7 will be seen to contain the words for 1, 2, and 3, prefixed by an element *yiti-*, which from the exigencies of the system seems to mean "four"; "five" would be "four plus one", six "four plus two", and seven "four plus three".' The root *yiti-*, however, is not the word for '4'; Beeler tends to relate it to a verbal root signifying 'to come, come back, return'. Thus, apparently, it is the cyclicity of the quaternary number series rather than the base number four itself that is the salient notion.

Let us now look at the possible evidence for old modes of counting in Indo-European. Unfortunately, etymologies in this area of Indo-European studies are extremely tentative and speculative and for the most part highly controversial, and several of the numerals may well be loanwords with no Indo-European etymology. Thus, a survey of the suggested etymologies does not carry much typological weight. (On the contrary, it might be useful to view these etymologies themselves in a wider typological context.)

Still, the ancient numerals of the Indo-European family are highly interesting for the study of Austroasiatic, both because of apparent typological affinities and because some such affinities may have a historical explanation in terms of the well-known influence of Indian culture on languages and cultures of Indochina. The numerals that are most relevant to the present issue are '4', '5', '8', and '10'. Before going into the status of these numerals it should be mentioned, perhaps, that '6' has also played a special role: there seems to have been 'a culturally conditioned preference for counting in groups of sixes in Western Europe' (Hamp 1982: 179), as evidenced, e.g., by the concept of 'a dozen', the concept of 'a great hundred', i.e. 120, and most significantly by Old Irish *mórfesser* 'seven men', literally 'big six'. This somewhat muddles the issue as regards circumstantial evidence for four-plus-four versus five-plus-five modes of counting in ancient time.

Since Indo-European numerals above '10' show a very strong component of decimal counting, it is natural to see first if there is good evidence of this being an inheritance from Proto-Indo-European finger counting. We shall, therefore, look first at the etyma for '5' and '10' and their possible association with the completion of hands in a hand-based decimal counting mode.

It has been suggested that the Indo-European numeral '10': *dek'm̥t* (reconstructed with a final stop although there are reflexes of a secondary form *dek'm̥*, cf. Emmerick 1992: 325) is somehow composed of words meaning '2' and 'hand'. In spite of Menninger's optimistic note that 'Für diese Vermutung lassen sich einige nicht ungewichtige Gründe beibringen' (1958: 142), it has been pointed out that there are some technical problems with this otherwise extremely plausible etymology (see the discussion in Winter 1992: 17). Provided that it is correct, one expects the numeral '5' to exhibit a connection with 'hand' as well. Indeed, an etymology to that effect has been suggested, although '5' and '10' clearly cannot contain the same Indo-European etymon. The term that seems to occur in '10' is the 'general' word for 'hand' (etymologically the same as English hand), whereas the term occurring in '5': *penk^w(e)*, is something quite different. The possible relationship of the latter to finger counting is a matter of controversy, which will be taken up later.

Now to the numerals '4' and '8'. It seems that the Indo-European term for '8' and possibly that for '4' can be construed to reflect a four-plus-four mode of counting using only the shorter fingers (leaving out the thumb). The etymological evidence may be summarized as follows.

Indo-European '8' is apparently a dual form: *ok'to-ow (ending: *-ow 'dual'), which in itself suggests that the stem used to mean either 'four (fingers)' or 'hand'. This has made Indo-Europeanists suspect that Indo-European used to have a quaternary system of reckoning. Indeed, there is attestation in Indo-Aryan of a stem meaning 'four fingers' breadth' which is phonologically quite similar to the stem of '8' and might be the same etymon (cf. the more or less whole-hearted acceptance of this hypothesis in such reference works as Mayrhofer 1987: 142; Winter 1992: 13; Emmerick 1992: 300). Accordingly, it has been suggested that the Indo-European numeral '8' is the dual form of a term meaning 'tip of hand', that is the four fingers minus the thumb.

The notion of 'four' (and not just 'tip of hand') has probably been quite salient for the stem of *ok'to-ow since Proto-Kartvelian (Georgian) is reported to have borrowed *oxto- in the meaning of 'four' (this piece of evidence is the more remarkable since there are only two quite certain loans from Proto-Indo-European into Proto-Kartvelian, of which this is one, according to Shevoroshkin 1987: 237).

It is enigmatic that there is no corresponding simplex word surviving as '4' in Indo-European. The attested word for '4' is the totally unrelated *kʷetwores. By its particular phonological structure which obviously reflects its morphological complexity, this form stands out from all the other low numerals. That might suggest that the word used to refer to a plurality of a specific kind. However, *kʷetwores must be very old as a member of the low numerals since, like the others, it is faithfully preserved as the standard numeral across a vast array of Indo-European languages (Hamp 1992: 907 demonstrates that even the Albanian form is a continuation of Indo-European, not a loan from Latin). However, the word defies all attempts at a convincing etymology.

Anatolian shows evidence of a third root unrelated to both *ok'to- and *kʷetwores, viz. mi(e)u-; this word, which means something to do with '4' (but may be a collective rather than a cardinal numeral, cf. Eichner 1992: 76), is explained as based on an Indo-European adjective *meyu- meaning 'small' and thus may refer to the four smaller fingers (this etymology is accepted explicitly by Eichner 1992: 77).

In any case it seems that '8' has been a very salient unit: the totality of four plus four fingers (minus the thumbs). This assumption is clearly

corroborated if the term for '9' can be shown to refer to the start of a
new series (of eight). The Ossetic word *farast* 'nine' is very significant
since it literally means 'beyond eight' and thus suggests that, 'at least
from an Ossetian point of view' (Winter 1992: 14, quoting Abaev),
'eight' used to represent one completed set.

It might throw light on the question if the common Indo-European
word for '9' could be given a plausible analysis, either in an octal
framework or a decimal framework. It has been reconstructed as
newm̥ (cf. suggestions in Szemerényi 1960: 173), but the evidence
has been shown to be rather in favour of *newn̥* (disregarding for
the moment a further issue as to whether the numeral should be
reconstructed with an initial laryngeal, cf., e.g., Hamp 1975: 222 with
references). The old idea is that the numeral is somehow related to
new, although both the morphological status of the final -*n* and of the
initial occurring in Greek and Armenian (cf. Greek *ennéa*, Armenian
inn) must then be accounted for. The immediately most tempting solution to the deviant behaviour of Greek and Armenian is to assume
an innovation with a well-known morpheme (Greek *en*) prefixed to
convey a locative meaning. Accordingly it has been suggested that the
Indo-European numeral used to mean something like '(in the) new'
(an interpretation mentioned, though with much reserve, in Winter
1992: 12).

Offhand this may sound plausible in the context of an assumed octal
mode of counting. However, I find it hard to see how to perform finger
counting in such a way as to make '9' the start of a 'new' series if
we assume that '8' was counted as four plus four smaller fingers but
that the association of '10' with all fingers was nevertheless salient
(as it must have been, considering the overall decimal character of
the Indo-European numeral system). By sheer speculation one may
suggest two alternative ways to accommodate '9' within such a dual
finger counting system. One possibility is that Indo-European had two
complete counting modes which could be used alternatively: counting
on four plus four fingers up to '8' or on five plus five fingers up
to '10' (cf. David Thomas' reflections about Mon-Khmer). In that
case '9' would belong within the second half of the five plus five set.
Another theoretical possibility is that the four plus four series could be
extended up to '10' by adding the two thumbs after the smaller fingers.
That would account beautifully for Ossetic *farast*. However, in neither
case would '9' mean the commencement of a new series of four plus
four.

In fact, the explanation of *newn̥ as having to do with 'new' is not entirely convincing from a purely etymological point of view either. First the assumption of secondary prefixal material, in the case of Greek for example, does not work equally well for all forms. Secondly, and more importantly, it is at variance with a more recent reconstruction of the numeral '9' as having an initial laryngeal in Pre-Indo-European (cf., e.g., Hamp 1975: 222 with references). I suppose it is safest to regard the original meaning of Indo-European '9' as totally unexplained so far.

All of this leaves us with a crux in the case of '5'. As for '5' in Indo-European it looks like the etymon surviving, e.g. as German *Faust*, and it has been suggested that '5' may have 'referred to the hand clenched to form a fist' (here citing the discussion in Winter 1992). However, this may be a secondary association. The form of '5' stands out by having two full vowels, and it makes perfect sense to explain it as consisting of a word *pen plus *-kʷe 'and'. The first part of the numeral thus looks just like the first part of the word *finger*, and it makes perfect sense to assume that there is a primary association here; maybe it is the term for 'fist' that derives from the numeral, not vice versa. (I am indebted to Eric Hamp for crucial suggestions on this point.)

A transfer from '5' to 'fist' obviously presupposes that there was at some point in time a well-established mode of counting in fives. However, the first step of the assumed development is ambiguous. It might be that counting to '5' was from the very beginning completed on one hand so that it was the last finger of the first hand that was involved in the term for '5'. It might also be that '5' was originally counted as the first small finger on the second hand (the thumb of the first hand being skipped after the completion of '4' and perhaps reserved for later use, viz. in connection with '9'). In the absence of crucial evidence for choosing between these options I do not see that we can use the etymon for '5' to throw light on the question whether four plus four or five plus five counting came first. The only thing the etymological association between '5' and 'fist' may show is that a mode of five-plus-five counting was eventually established.

In any case, there may have been at some point a conflict between competing modes of counting in Indo-European, which constitutes an interesting parallel to Austroasiatic. The few pieces of unambiguous evidence furnished by low numbers under '10' are in favour of an original four-plus-four mode, but the formation of the numeral '10' (if indeed it meant 'two hands') and the decimal principle, which is clearly very old, are perhaps more easily understood if anchored in a five-plus-five counting mode.[16]

Let us finally look at the semantics of Indo-European '8' versus '10'. If the former used to refer to two sets of tips and the latter used to refer to two hands, the crucial difference between the two expressions is that one excludes and the other includes the thumbs. Unlike the second part of the numeral '10', which probably referred neutrally to the hand, the first part of the numeral '8' may have 'designated four fingers outstretched, with the thumb turned in' (Winter 1992: 17).

It is thus at least possible that the numerals '4', '5', '8', and '10' in the Indo-European numeral system all came from different gestures used in connection with counting or enumeration. If so they must reflect at least two different modes of counting: in sets of four and in sets of five. It is entirely understandable if the words for '(part of) hand' are different etyma in two such modes.

As mentioned several times in the present paper, Khmer has throughout its known history had a system which explicitly has '5' as its base ('6' is '5 + 1', etc.). I know of no evidence for that in Indo-European.[17]

Altogether, the Indo-European numeral system leaves room for much speculation, but I find it thought-provoking that there are conspicuous similarities between the basic issues in the reconstruction of Indo-European and Austroasiatic numeral systems.

---

[16] There is no numeral for '5' attested for the Anatolian branch of Indo-European, but there is a superficially similar word in Hittite: *panku*, which signifies a totality. A possibly spurious etymology has been suggested according to which *panku* is related to $*penk^w(e)$; this could be construed as evidence for early five-plus-five counting. However, as stated by Eichner (1992: 83), the Hittite word would, even according to this etymology, 'not be the reflex of a Proto-Indo-European numeral but merely that of a root from which, in Proto-Indo-European, a numeral had been derived'. (The Hittite evidence is actually likely to be entirely irrelevant, the word being a quite different etymon.)

[17] It has been suggested that the Indo-European etymon *six* may be associated with a root meaning 'grow', the idea being that '6' denoted an increment relative to '5'. This would be corroborative evidence for the assumption that already at an early time '5' was a significant unit of counting because of its association with the hand; it certainly does not provide any evidence that early Indo-European had a real base five system. There is, on the other hand, compelling evidence for the base ten system as an old feature of Indo-European (which does not exclude an even older four-plus-four system) since the Indo-European numerals following '10' are formed as complex expressions containing that very word.

19.3. UNITY AND VARIATION IN NUMERALS ACROSS AUSTROASIATIC

The number systems of Austroasiatic languages, i.e. mostly Mon-Khmer languages, were the subject of a special issue of *Linguistics* in 1976 to which a number of scholars in the field contributed (Diffloth and Zide 1976). One of the striking features of this selection of papers is how well it illustrates the scholarly involvement and at the same time the provisional character of much comparative work on Austroasiatic.

Another characteristic of the 1976 collection of papers is the paucity of material from Khmuic languages. As said earlier in this paper, the general assumption has been that the Mon-Khmer numerals above '4' were more or less absent in Khmuic.

To take the papers from the 1976 selection which represent the most ambitious and also the most useful surveys of Mon-Khmer numerals to date, viz. those of Jenner and of David Thomas, their most essential contribution to comparative Mon-Khmer is the arrangements of comparative lists of forms grouped by their similarities across languages. The impression one gets from these comparisons is somewhat contradictory.

On the one hand, there is obviously very considerable lexical variation in numerals across Austroasiatic, and also across otherwise closely related Mon-Khmer languages of inner Indochina. Referring back to some of the reflections in earlier sections of this paper, we may enumerate a number of potential sources of variation. Among these are processes such as: (i) the development of numerals from old collective nouns or verbs, (ii) the development of numerals from terms for body-parts, and (iii) the creation of new lexemes by prefixation or infixation to stems that occur in other languages as numerals or as collective nouns. Another, no less important, type of factor is (iv) the use of numerals for different purposes (which may lead to different coexisting numeral systems: consider the case of Tin). The final potential source of lexical variation to be mentioned here is language contact. The outcome may look like a historical 'accident', as with (v) the presence of a sub- or superstratum of etymologically aberrant material, or it may be more obvious that the phenomenon reflects communicative and/or political factors, as with (vi) the wholesale borrowing of partial or complete numeral systems between languages, in casu borrowing from Sino-Tibetan or Tai into Mon-Khmer, or borrowings between Mon-Khmer languages. Obviously, the factors enumerated here are not mutually independent: (vi) may be the effect of (iv).

In the literature on Austroasiatic numerals, there seems to be a widespread (explicit or implicit) assumption that lexical variation in this area may be due to words from different sources turning into numerals, the resulting occurrence of potentially competing synonymous expressions having been resolved differently in different languages (this assumption is aired by e.g. Zide 1976).

It is an interesting question what is likely to happen lexically to numerals which have an important status as cognitively salient units. The candidates par excellence are the numerals '5' and '10', with their natural associations with hands (cf. the discussions of these numerals, in Indo-European and elsewhere, in various sections above).

As for '5', which will be considered in some detail below, one might argue in two opposite ways. On the one hand, it is possible to argue that '5' should be a numeral of high stability as it is both the tail of the lowest, highly individualized numerals '1' to '4' and at the same time an important conceptual unit in itself (cf. '5' in Indo-European). On the other hand, one might argue that different modes of counting and different ways of conceptualizing the number '5' might lead to a convergence in meaning and function of terms which originally meant different things (in five-plus-five counting one might think of such concepts as 'unity', 'the first', 'completion', 'hand', 'cluster of fingers', etc.; in four-plus-four counting one might think of such concepts as 'new hand', '4 and 1', etc.).

At first sight, the latter expectation is nourished by Mon-Khmer evidence, since there seem to be several well-established forms meaning '5' (that is, not just one dominant term plus some rarely occurring relics) across the linguistic area. The variation observed is very much greater for the numeral '5' than for numerals below '5'. The Austroasiatic numerals '1' to '4' are found all over the area with remarkably little variation in spite of the considerable time span dividing the Munda languages from languages of eastern or southern Indochina. The forms one encounters may look something like *moi* or *moc* '1', *baar* '2', *pε* '3', *pon* '4', although with phonological variation, of course (many Austroasiatic languages have diphthongs especially in '2' and '4'; moreover, initial consonants may have undergone mutation, e.g. *b* > *p* in '2', and *p* > *ph* or development of high tone in '3' or '4'). More deviant forms are also found (e.g. forms of '2' without the labial in Waic and in some languages of the Malaccan peninsula), but by and large there is a surprising uniformity, as we see if we compare Santali *mit', bar, pɛ, pon* with Pre-Angkorian Khmer *moy, ver, pi, pon(n)*, or with Semoq Beni (South Aslan of the Malaccan peninsula) *muy, hma-hmar, hmpɛ'-hmpɛt, hmpon* (Semoq Beni data from Diffloth 1976), to take languages from three branches that are both linguistically and geographically extremely far from each other.

Also, some of the other numerals occur in conspicuously similar forms across several languages which do not otherwise seem particularly closely related. This is especially obvious if we look at languages which are altogether very conservative in their phonology, such as Mlabri of North Thailand and western Laos (Egerod and Rischel 1987*a*, 1987*b*; Rischel 1992). Mlabri has *gul* for '7' (I have recorded the same form in Tin as spoken in Laos), and *gal* for '10', two forms which I regard almost as living fossils. They are virtually identical with forms occurring in the Munda languages of India, for example Sora *gul* '7', *gəl* '10', or, with a suffix, Gorum *gul-gi* '7', *gal-gi* '10' (data from Zide 1978). This is certainly not a matter of recent borrowing; on the contrary, in many Munda languages such old Austroasiatic material is yielding to more recent loanwords mainly from Indo-Aryan, and there has been a lot of borrowing particularly of Thai numerals into Mon-Khmer languages. Numerals such as '7' and '10' above represent the old common heritage.

On the whole, in spite of very considerable variation in the numerals above '4' across the Mon-Khmer area, and of course particularly across all of the Austroasiatic languages, most of the numerals exhibit conspicuous partial similarities across different branches of languages. Thus, leaving aside obviously unrelated forms (which fall totally outside the general geographical pattern), one can often classify several variant forms of a numeral as 'look-alikes' that are suggestive of some kind of relatedness, and one might even label such a class of look-alikes an 'allofam'. It may be anything but obvious how to set up a proto-form accounting for the variety of present-day reflexes; however, the most conspicuous variation often pertains to the onset (the initial), which is known to be the least stable part of an Austroasiatic etymon, so that irregularities in that part of the numeral are often the least obstacle to etymological explanation.[18]

---

[18] There are various more or less plausible explanations for such onset variation available. It may have a morphological explanation: we may be observing the effect of prefixation or infixation. It may also be a matter of sporadic change, e.g. the initial of a numeral may

Now, what about the various forms of '5'? To what extent are they likely to be related? I shall attempt to demonstrate below that there is evidence in favour of a kind of relatedness across a wide gamut of forms since one may set up various crucial features which define a canonical base form for the numeral '5', as against other numerals. Thus one may actually relate a great number of different forms to each other phonologically, provided that cases of affixation and other morphological differences are properly identified.

In the following I shall first display the general structural types observed for the numeral '5' across Austroasiatic languages, basing my exposition on language material found in standard surveys such as that by David Thomas (1976) and in other standard sources (comparative monographs and dictionaries), and in the case of the northern Mon-Khmer branch called Khmuic (or Kammuic) also on data from my own field notes (viz. Mlabri /thəəŋ/, Khmu' *phiaŋ*, and Tin *sɔɔŋ* or *chɔɔŋ*). Along with this exposition I shall demonstrate that the forms for '5' in the different languages all share important phonological properties.

In the display of form types below, vowel quality (including monophthong versus diphthong) is disregarded, and aspirated stops are treated as unit phonemes. The sequential order of the types is organized first according to the final, then according to the consonant before the main vowel, and then according to increasing complexity of the initial part.

I /-m/:)   1. *prVm*; 2. *pV(')dVm*;
II /-n/:)   3. *phVn*; 4. *thVn*; 5. *sVn*; 6. *hVn*; 7. *pVTVn, pVsVn*;
III /-ŋ/:)   8. *phVŋ*; 9. *thVŋ*; 10. *sVŋ*; 11. *msVŋ*; 12. *CVsVŋ*

When looking at these structural types (each of which reflects several languages with different, though phonologically closely related, forms), one should be aware of the situation of comparative Mon-Khmer studies. This is a very exciting but also, in a sense, a very new field, since there has been a deplorable lack of reliable data on most Mon-Khmer languages until very recently. In spite of important early contributions by Maspero, Pinnow, and others, such fundamental issues as the question of whether Vietnamese is Austroasiatic were still unsettled not many decades ago. It is not until the last twenty years that systematic etymological work involving painstaking phonological

have approached that of another numeral due to the tendency to alliterate numerals which are adjacent in counting.

comparison within Mon-Khmer has seriously got under way (first and foremost as represented by the—largely unpublished—work of Gérard Diffloth). Moreover, etymological analyses or speculations to date have been largely confined to single branches or sub-branches of Mon-Khmer or even to comparative work on dialects of a single language, and the resulting etymological claims sometimes seem untenable in the light of evidence from other languages or subgroups. The discussion of numerals in this paper may, as a result, seem extremely provisional if viewed from more solidly-established fields of comparative linguistics.

Now to the etymological aspects of the numeral '5': David Thomas (1976) organizes his data for this numeral into two main groups, one comprising my types 1 and 2 above, and another comprising the rest. He calls these respectively the *pram*-group (after type 1) and the *pasong*-group (uniting features of my types 8 and 11).

The *pram*-group is represented by a number of South and North Bahnaric, Viet-Muong, Khmeric, and Pearic languages, that is languages in the eastern part of the Mon-Khmer area. In several of these languages the numeral is indeed *pram*, but in North Bahnaric bisyllabic forms occur, mostly something like *padam* (or *badam*) although Bahnar and Cua have *pa'-* as the first syllable (see data in Smith 1976: 62–3).

The North Bahnaric evidence seems to suggest a common formula for types 1 and 2: $p(V[')$-dVm, which one might tentatively postulate as the generalized proto-form for '5' in all languages exhibiting types 1 and 2 (Smith and Thomas reconstruct *$ba'dâm$ but for Proto-North-Bahnaric only). What then about *pram*? It could be derived from the above assuming that d has lenited to r if it came to form a cluster with the initial labial, as is the case in Khmer. The main difficulty with this solution is that the form *$pram$ can be assumed to go back to Proto-Khmer (Jenner 1976: 43), since it is attested already in Pre-Angkorian inscriptions, that is in the very oldest material available from the whole group of languages in question.

Thomas's *pasong*-group I would like to separate into two according to the final nasal, i.e. types 3 to 7 versus 8 to 12 in the list above.

The types in -*n* are found in Palaungic and Monic and in the distant Khasi language, i.e. in languages of the western part of the Mon-Khmer area. Let us start with forms without an initial labial. Thomas cites Mang (Palaungic[?]) *hân* and Khasi *san*; Thongkum (1984: 157) gives *chúun* for Nyah Kur (Monic) (Diffloth, 1984: 16, has the transcription *suun*). Since *$s > h$ is reported to occur as a regular sound shift in much of Palaungic, the Mang form conforms neatly to the others, i.e. we can posit a common formula *sVn*.

Forms with an initial labial include some with the aspirated *ph*. It occurs in some Palaungic, e.g. Lawa *phoan* or *phɔn* (Diffloth 1980: 142 reconstructs Proto-Waic **phən*); there are comparable forms in Lamet and Palaung. However, forms with *pVs-* or the like occur both in Palaungic and in Monic. For Palaungic there is the language Hu (of the Angkuic group within Palaungic) which has *paTán* (Svantesson 1991: 72); for Monic there is Mon itself: *pasɔn*.

Comparison of such forms as those of Khasi and Nyah Kur with such forms as those of Hu and Mon provide overwhelming evidence for a structure type *(pV)sVn*, which accounts also for the forms with *ph-* by the force of the Palaungic shift **s > h* referred to above. (The insight that *h* in Palaung forms of '5' reflects **-s* was put forward by David Thomas 1976: 69.) The occurrence of *T* in Hu requires an explanation. As Svantesson (1991) points out, it suggests a two-step development **s > T > h*, with Hu sharing only the first step (Svantesson's argumentation need not be given here). Thus everything falls into place.

Diffloth (1984: 142) reconstructs **pəsun* for Proto-Mon but derives the initial **pə-* from Proto-Monic **mə-* which, he says, may be 'a reduction of **muəy* one'. The same prefix is also found in Khmer.

What remains are forms in -*ŋ*, that is types 8 to 12 above. The types *phVŋ* and *thVŋ* are those represented by Khmu' and Mlabri, respectively.

The type *sVŋ* is found in West Bahnaric (which thus does not side with other Bahnaric), in much of Katuic, and in some Khmuic: Thaen and Tayhat (cf. Section 19.2 above). Examples are *sʌɲ* in Nyaheun, *siŋ* in Oi and Laveh (all classified as West Bahnaric, here cited from David Thomas 1976 but with modification to IPA notation).

Kuy (Kui, Suai, a Katuic language) is the source of type 12 with David Thomas's '*qasəəng*', a form which obviously contains unusual prefixal material which will be disregarded here. Sriwises (1978) only gives the monosyllabic form *sʌʌŋ*, which agrees with East Katuic on structure type 10 (cf. data from the East Katuic languages Brôu, Pacôh, and Katu in Dorothy Thomas 1976).

In David Thomas's survey there is one remaining type—*msəŋ* of Smaq Bri (Semelaic)—which invites the same explanation of the initial labial as the Proto-Monic prefix discussed above, i.e. that its initial labial nasal is originally the numeral '1'.

We now see that *ph-* in Khmu' *phiaŋ* invites the same analysis as *ph-* in the group with final *-n*, i.e. that the initial labial in Khmu' is due to prefixal material before the root *sVŋ*, and that aspirated *ph-* is the result of **p* and **s* becoming adjacent in a cluster. What then about the aspirate in Mlabri *thɔəŋ*?

The whole framework makes sense if the Mlabri form can be construed to be a parallel to the Monic form, i.e. a direct reflex of the main syllable of **(p[V])-sVŋ*. And indeed it can: Mlabri has independent evidence for *th-* as the reflex of a Mon-Khmer sibilant. To mention two rather safe etyma (in addition to those given in Rischel 1995: 45), Mlabri *thʌc* 'meat' and *thrɛɛŋ* 'tooth' have Khmuic correspondences with initial **s-* and **sr-*.[19]

We can now take stock of the forms in *-ŋ*: it seems that the underlying formula *(p)sVŋ, (m)sVŋ* can take care of all forms in *-ŋ* (except for the bisyllabic Kuy form above).

The overall result, then, is that all three sets—those in *-m*, those in *-n*, and those in *-ŋ*—are not only basically analogous in structure but behave in a surprisingly similar manner with regard to the existence of reflexes with and without labial prefixation.

Now, what happens if we go beyond Mon-Khmer and look at the distantly related Munda languages? In Munda languages we encounter forms such as *mon, mɔn* or *monloi, mɔlɔe* (see Zide 1978 with references to various sources); Zide reconstructs Proto-Munda **mV(X)nlaX(i)* or **mV(X)nlaX(y)* as a common denominator. At first glance this looks very different from Mon-Khmer. However, Zide (1976: 7–8) considers the possibility of deriving the first syllable, i.e. **ma(X)n-* or **mo(X)n-*, from **mV(C)-soŋ*, which puts it structurally in line with the repertory of Mon-Khmer forms listed above.

Zide (1976) cites Old Mon *msun*, Modern Mon *pəsɔn* as forms which are interestingly related to Munda '5'. He posits a Proto-Austroasiatic prefix *mV(C)*, which occurs as *mV-* in Munda and which may be a noun prefix with collective meaning. In Zide's opinion, forms without a prefix (if prefixless forms can be reconstructed for the proto-language) must be 'pre-quinary', whereas forms with a prefix 'represent a somewhat late stage, where sets of five were used in counting'.

---

[19] The former word is found only in one clan sociolect of Mlabri, and hence is missing in Egerod and Rischel (1987*a*, 1987*b*).

It is an interesting question how this prefix relates to the likewise very old numeral '1'. The relationship between Old Mon *m-* and Modern Mon *p-* in the numeral '5' further raises the question to what extent the prefix *$p(V)$-*, occurring in several other Mon-Khmer languages, has its origin in such a prefix *$m(V)(C)$-*, or whether perhaps the *m-* of the numeral '1' derives its nasality from an old nasal prefix denoting unity. Unfortunately, with the present knowledge of comparative Austroasiatic, we end up with futile speculations.[20]

To sum up: the end result of this extensive treatment of '5' in Austroasiatic is that, notwithstanding the size of the lexical variation, it has its strict and nontrivial limits:

1 Across Austroasiatic, the numeral '5' either has, or can be reconstructed to have had, a monosyllabic root. The forms mostly reflect an etymon of canonical *CVC* structure beginning in a dental (coronal) obstruent followed by a back vowel and ending in a nasal consonant.
2 In several languages all across Austroasiatic this monosyllabic root morpheme has been augmented by a *C(V)* prefix containing a labial stop or nasal and probably denoting 'unity', i.e. marking '5' as the completion of the first set of numerals.

The just-mentioned similarities across expressions for '5' in Austroasiatic may not seem particularly suggestive of etymological unity, and in fact in has not been generally recognized that they may be etymologically related to each other. However, the constant features of the initial and final of most occurrences of '5' actually set off this numeral

---

[20] Such speculation can be carried on: the shared initial consonantism (labiality plus oral closure) of the four lowest numerals in Austroasiatic might conceivably be a reflex of very old prefixation serving to mark '1' to '4' as a separate set. There is sporadic evidence suggesting a reconstruction of Austroasiatic '2' without initial labial since it occurs as such in such distant branches as Palaungic (northern Indochina) and Aslian (Malaccan Peninsula, here also with an initial suggesting an *n-prefix). This would open the possibility that the initial labial found in most languages is prefixal. However, there is conflicting comparative evidence which suggests, rather, stem initial *b in Proto-Austroasiatic '2' (cf. Diffloth 1976: 35, who ventures the suggestion that it should be reconstructed as *$bi'a:r$).

In numerals above '4', many languages show instances of prefixation or pseudo-prefixation of material of more or less obscure etymological origin, mostly so that a cluster of three or more numerals share the prefixal material. This may well have served to mark these as forming a higher set as against '1' to '4', or '1' to '5', although sub-branches of Mon-Khmer vary as to what particular higher set (if any) is marked off in this way.

from all other numerals of Austroasiatic origin.[21] For this very reason, the structural similarities one can observe across the variant forms of '5' are in fact so significant that they may well be due to common etymological origin, although there is so far no explanation that I know of for the occurrence of different places of articulation of the final nasal in different languages.

In some instances a form somehow belongs within the 'allofam' concept but does not quite fit; these instances are, however, surprisingly few. The final part of Munda '5' (with initial /l/) does not fit in with the canonical formula for Mon-Khmer '5' given above, but is reminiscent of the strange Waic word for '6' (which has no etymology; is there a connection?). This does not invalidate the generalization above, if Zide is right in seeing the pan-Austroasiatic etymon for '5' as hidden in the preceding part of the word. It is more problematic that *pram* for '5', found, e.g. in Khmer, does not fit too well into the scheme, since it has *r in the earliest records; it is very possibly a totally independent etymon (although its combination dental–vowel–nasal is in accordance with the general picture for '5' in Mon-Khmer).

The point of the above review was to attempt to account for phonological variation for the numeral '5' without recourse to explanations in terms of external factors. The definition of a 'canonical form' above is probably as far as we can get at present in attempting to trace the variation back to a unitary underlying representation. The observed basic homogeneity, both of the stem and of the optional prefix, is of 'allofam' nature; until more is known about systematic phonological correspondences within Austroasiatic it is difficult to get further and to set up rigid phonological reconstructions. However, that certainly does not deprive the conspicuous structural similarities of interest.

The relative success of an 'allofam' account for the numeral '5' does not, of course, mean that only one etymon for this numeral exists in Mon-Khmer, let alone in Austroasiatic. But Austroasiatic '5' seems to display much of the same surprising lexical uniformity that we find for all the low numerals in most branches of Indo-European. It is quite different with '10', however: in contradistinction to Indo-European, but like Finno-Ugric, the Austroasiatic languages display a host of

---

[21] Whereas this is the very formula which one would set up for '2' and '3' in modern Thai/Laotian, for example.

mutually entirely unrelated forms in the case of '10'. This finding (i.e. that '5' and '10' differ dramatically with regard to lexical stability in some language families but not in others), is worth looking into since it might possibly tell us something about constancy and variability in the old modes of counting.

19.4.   CONCLUDING REMARKS

In this paper I have attempted to stress the importance and usefulness of a typological approach to the study of numerals, also when the purpose is to trace the history of numerals or to reconstruct the numerals of a proto-language. Typology, in this case, must involve consideration of both the structural properties and the functional status of a numeral system.

In discussing structural features of the numeral systems in certain Austroasiatic languages, I found it useful to adduce typological parallels not only from other Austroasiatic languages, but also from unrelated languages. Such parallels, however, are of extremely limited interest unless one goes deeper into the overall structure of the numeral system of each language, and moreover considers the ways in which each numeral system is put to use. Unfortunately, grammatical and typological literature on numerals is often strangely silent about the latter, functional aspect.

Above, I have described a situation for one language, Mlabri, which has a full set of low numerals but hardly uses them, and a neighbouring language, Tin, which has four distinct (though overlapping) sets of low numerals. It makes little sense to study such numeral systems without taking an anthropological-linguistic approach in addition to the historical-comparative approach.

As to the relationship between finger counting, numerals, and base numbers, it was tempting to throw a sideways glance at the controversial evidence found in the realm of Indo-European numerals. The real or apparent parallels are thought-provoking. I have certainly had no substance to add to the wealth of etymological learning accumulated by Indo-Europeanists, but I wish to make the point that typological confrontations may be useful both ways, not only in the study of young fields such as Austroasiatic but even in a tradition-laden and awe-inspiring field such as Indo-European comparative philology.

On the other hand, the story of Austroasiatic '5' is in my view an illustration of the fact that typological considerations, for all their importance in historical study, cannot replace painstaking etymological comparison and reconstruction. The two approaches must be applied in unison if we are to ever sort out the intriguing isoglosses within Austroasiatic and find out which of them are due to phonological change, and which of them are due to the semantic convergence of different etyma.

20

The Mlabri Enigma: Is Mlabri a Primary Hunter-Gatherer Language or the Result of an Ethnically and Socially Complex Founder Event?[1]

20.1. INTRODUCTION: THE POSITION OF THE MLABRI AS AN ETHNIC GROUP

The ethnic group that call themselves 'forest-people', Mlabri, have recently attracted considerable attention because of a paper in *Public Library of Science* ('*PLoS*', Oota *et al.* 2005). It suggests, on the basis of biological evidence, that this particular hunter-gatherer group came into existence by a founder event probably no more than 800 years ago and has an old agricultural background. If that is true, we have here a case of cultural reversion.

I published a paper seventeen years ago (Rischel 1989*b*), in which I showed that the Mlabri language has a significant lexical layer reflecting an early connection with so-called Tin people speaking a cluster of Northern Mon-Khmer languages. Referring to that finding, as well as evidence from folklore, the *PLoS*-paper suggested that the Mlabri have ancestors that were ethnic Tin.

The Tin (or Lua') language cluster comprises two closely-related languages, Mal and Prai, which are spoken by mountain villagers in

---

[1] Paper read at the Hunter-Gatherer Workshop in Leipzig at the Max Planck Institute, August 2006. A shorter version, 'Hunter-gatherers in South and Southeast Asia with special reference to the Mlà Bri', will appear in Tom Güldemann, Patrick McConvell, Richard A. Rhodes (eds), *The Languages of Hunter-gatherers: Global and Historical Perspectives* (in preparation).

roughly the same area where the Mlabri still live. I have kept the options open as to whether Mlabri just borrowed intensely from Tin at that early time or whether Mlabri and Tin are sister languages. My claim about a Mlabri–Tin connection was based solely on linguistic evidence; there was no cultural or biological evidence suggesting any particular bond between the speakers of Mlabri and Tin. Even today, my point of departure in comparing the languages is strictly linguistic although it is now possible and interesting to view the Tin connection also from a cultural perspective.

20.2. MLABRI SUBGROUPS

Mlabri [mlaː? briː?] is spoken by three small groups that live in the mountain forests along the northernmost border between Thailand and Laos. A key element in traditional Mlabri culture is to live as foragers, who stay in the forest and thus remain invisible and unknown to the mainstream society. The traditional belief is that the spirits do not allow them to settle and to raise crops and livestock.

The largest Mlabri group, in my terminology the A-Mlabri (Egerod and Rischel 1987), comprises some 300 persons, all in Thailand, who have now largely given up their hunter-gatherer lifestyle and have acquired huts in, or adjacent to, peasant villages in the high mountains. The other group in Thailand (the B-Mlabri or 'Minor Mlabri', Rischel 1995) is almost extinct now. The third group (the C-Mlabri, Rischel 2000) number less than 25 persons who still live as hunter-gatherers in Laos. These three Mlabri subgroups speak varieties of the same dialect, with little difference in grammar and phonology except for sentence intonation. On the other hand, they speak quite distinct sociolects in the sense that there are large differences in vocabulary. That ties up with the fact that they form distinct clans, as it were: they have a tradition of avoiding each other and do not intermarry.

The differences in vocabulary across the Mlabri subgroups have apparently been fairly stable over recent time: they can be observed in the earliest, non-scientific word lists recorded forty to sixty years ago. I have nevertheless found that the lexical differences are often a matter of active versus passive usage or of speaking-style. It may turn out that both synonyms are known across the groups though each group of speakers strongly prefers one of the two options and consider the word used by the other group to be obsolete or somehow undesirable. Occasionally, a lexical item is female usage in one group whereas it is used by men and women alike in the other group. The moribund B-variety of Mlabri especially exhibits massive differences in male and female vocabulary. Moreover, lexical items shared by two or more groups are used in different or even opposite meanings; thus **rphɛp** means 'butterfly' in the A-group but 'cockroach' in the B-group.

I have gone into such detail with clan-bound vocabulary differences because they complicate the lexical comparison of Mlabri with other languages of the area. When scholars talk about Mlabri they invariably refer to A-Mlabri as it is known from short lists of basic vocabulary. Thus one easily gets the impression that this is a language with a very limited lexicon. In order to make fair comparisons one must not only have access to a larger sample of A-Mlabri but also include the other sociolects, which often exhibit important etyma that have not been retrieved in A-Mlabri. For simplicity I here speak of the sociolects as three independent branches of modern Mlabri although they are not lexically equidistant. If one disregards recent loanwords, the C-variety is intermediate between the A- and B-varieties, perhaps somewhat closer to the A-variety, but on the other hand the C-variety contains numerous Lao words in daily usage which make it stand apart from the Mlabri varieties spoken in Thailand.

20.3.   THE ORIGIN OF THE MLABRI

The origin of the Mlabri hunter-gatherers is an enigma. To judge from the biological evidence presented in the *PLoS* paper, there was a time less than a thousand years ago when the group consisted of only a couple of persons, very likely including just one woman. That might be due to near eradication, i.e. a bottleneck situation, or it might mean that the group came into existence through a founder event, as argued in the *PLoS* paper. The hypothesis that the Mlabri are descendants of village people switching to a hunter-gatherer lifestyle was in fact aired already in the 1960s, and similar assumptions have been made about other hunter-gatherer groups in mainland Southeast Asia (henceforth also SEA). The crux is that although these hunter-gatherers form small and mutually isolated groups, their languages are not linguistic isolates. On the contrary, they are related to the languages of much larger ethnic groups who live at a technologically more advanced stage involving rice cultivation. Thus, assuming that these hunter-gatherers are remnants of very old forager groups, they seem to have given up their former languages and adopted the languages of neighbouring food-producers (like the Pygmy in Africa did). That may be the case with some of the groups. In other instances, however, the hunter-gatherer culture may be secondary, i.e. there may have been a reversion from a food-producing lifestyle at some point in time.

One thousand years ago, mainland Southeast Asia was for the most part populated by peoples speaking Mon-Khmer, i.e. languages of the Austroasiatic language family. The demographic situation then changed dramatically because Tai peoples migrated down from southeast China.

> There is no known family relationship between Tai languages and Mon-Khmer languages. The so-called South-Western branch of Tai comprises present-day languages such as Central Thai, Northern Thai, and Lao. [Note that the Tai language family is always referred to with initial T-, the two present-day Thai languages with initial Th-.]

Some of the Mon-Khmer groups had large populations with advanced cultures, and they survived or merged with the Tai peoples, but the smaller peasant groups had much less access to arable land. Although we are accustomed to thinking of the hunter-gatherer lifestyle as a pre-stage to food-producing lifestyles such as agriculture, it seems plausible enough that some peripheral groups might switch to a forest-bound lifestyle because that improved their chances of survival after the area became more crowded. In fact, the situation with many ethnic groups in SEA is that they mix agriculture (at a low technological level) with some regular foraging and use of temporary shelters in the forest. Thus a switch to full-time foraging would hardly require the development of much new know-how in order to make a sustained life in the forest possible, provided that there was food enough.

Scholars have long considered the possibility of cultural reversion in the case of the Mlabri (e.g. Flatz 1963). Similar assumptions have been made about other hunter-gatherers speaking Austroasiatic languages. Arlene and Norman Zide thirty years ago looked at the culture words of hunter-gatherers speaking Mundaic and found that the vocabulary suggests early agriculture. They explicitly argued in favour of a 'reversion from a more complex culture to a simpler one' (Zide and Zide 1976: 1296).

In the case of the Mlabri, the *PLoS* paper suggests a scenario other than a deliberate switch to full-time foraging that would likewise lead to a hunter-gatherer culture. It involves just a few persons who broke out or were expelled from a village and fled into the forest, possibly merging with other forest-dwellers.

In my view, Mlabri material culture is consistent with either of these two scenarios. It strikes me as a typical survival culture, with an absolute minimum of tools and with a glaring absence of such a basic technology as pottery. What little handicraft and manufacturing of tools they do have is apparently shared with mountain villagers of the area. I think all of that is consistent with the assumption of a cultural reversion, as suggested by the *PLoS* paper.

The question, then, is: what villager group may have been involved? The *PLoS* paper points to the Tin or Lua' group as possible ancestors of the Mlabri. The Tins are peasants living in the high mountains of the region on both sides of the northern border between Thailand and Laos, just like the Mlabri. The Tins, like nearly all Austroasiatic groups of mainland Southeast Asia, were probably villagers eating rice as their staple food since time immemorial. There are faint traces of a dual lifestyle, as villagers and as hunter-gatherers, in the Mlabri language. For example, the standard expression for 'eating' is either 'to eat rice' (as it is in most Southeast Asian languages) or 'to eat tubers' (which is a forest phenomenon).

The biological data available for comparison did not, to my knowledge, involve sampling of the Tin people. It strikes me that the genetic samples from Southeast Asia with which the Mlabri data have been compared so far, according to the *PLoS* paper, are all from ethnic groups belonging to language families other than Mon-Khmer. Therefore, I take it that the assumption of a Tin connection, i.e. a Mon-Khmer connection, is based solely on regional and cultural and linguistic evidence, of which the *PLoS* paper cites me as main provider.

I see it as my task now to take a critical view of the comparative linguistic data, or perhaps rather of the *possibility* of doing comparative linguistic work in this field. Considering that fairly little comparative work has been done on Austroasiatic, and that very few proto-languages have been reconstructed within this family, it is not a priori self-evident that the Mlabri data are applicable to such endeavours at all. The historical comparison with neighbouring languages is made more difficult by the complete absence of historical records of older stages of these languages, the absence of inflectional morphology (which might otherwise have betrayed old structural features), and the abundance of areal linguistic features (which often make it difficult to spot old relatedness). If one looks at syntax, the use of grammatical particles might have given a cue, but these particles seem highly language-specific. Thus, one is left with the traditional philological method of establishing regular phonological correspondences, but that meets with the obstacle that the lexical differences across even the most similar languages are very great, and that many apparent cognates are loanwords. I hope to show, nevertheless, that one *can* establish linguistic relationships with some degree of precision.

By way of introduction to that topic I shall mention what culturally relevant information the humanities or cultural sciences can provide. In doing so I wish to express a *caveat:* when we face a cross-disciplinary challenge like the Mlabri scenario sketched by the biologists, it is crucial that the cultural and linguistic evidence meets rigid standards so that it can be taken seriously by all scholars. In cultural anthropology and archaeology, for example, it is bad to land in a skewed situation in which 'hard' evidence provided by the natural sciences is paired with 'soft' cultural data, which are then given a factual status that does not match their real, interpretive nature. Linguists know that linguistics can indeed provide hard data when it comes to language comparison but we do face poor and irresponsible scholarship in that field as well. I say this now because I may seem to be too reluctant to draw sweeping conclusions concerning the relationship between Mlabri and Tin.

20.4. MLABRI HISTORY AND CULTURE

First, I must emphasize that the historical records of the Thais do not say anything explicit about the small groups speaking northern Mon-Khmer languages. As for the Tins and Mlabri themselves their languages are purely oral languages, for which literacy is only being developed at this present time. Thus, the knowledge within these ethnic groups of their own remote past is based purely on oral transmission across generations. Unfortunately, there is precious little evidence of that kind.

If we leave cataclysmic stuff like the Great Flood myth aside, the most thought-provoking Mlabri story I know of tells us that the Mlabri used to be extremely numerous until they were almost eradicated by Thais using witchcraft. That might, of course, be construed as reflecting the tribe's recollection of a bottleneck situation. As for a possible genetic bond between the Mlabri and the Tins, it is interesting that the Tins are the only ethnic group with which the Mlabri themselves feel some bond. Still, the Mlabri consider them a quite distinct ethnic group. One elderly Mlabri recently explained to me that from the start there were two forest peoples: the Mlabri and the Tins. The former stayed on in the forest; the latter eventually became villagers. That runs counter to the scientific hypothesis about a villager origin for the Mlabri, but I see no reason to assume any factual background for the Mlabri myth about the origin of the Tins.

The *PLoS* paper refers to a Tin story according to which a boy and a girl were expelled from a Tin village but survived in the forest and had offspring, thus creating the Mlabri tribe by a founder event. I have heard the contents of that story in slightly different versions, and I have heard it in two different Tin villages, speaking Prai and Mal respectively. That suggests that the story may antedate the bifurcation of Tin into two languages and thus be several centuries old, although I have not had occasion so far to study the distribution of the story over the Tin area.

We can hardly draw any historical conclusions from such oral traditions. In my view, the most significant aspect of the story about the boy and the girl is the attitude it conveys. By telling it the Tin people explicitly recognize the Mlabri as their remote relatives. Since the Mlabri are at the absolute bottom of the social scale, and the Tins are just above them (with sporadic attempts to climb the social ladder), there would be no reason for the Tins to point to such a low-prestige connection unless it had some factual background.

That is probably as far as one can stretch the evidence furnished by oral traditions. If the Mlabri are descendants of Tin villagers, as suggested by the Tin story, one might perhaps expect these ethnic groups to share vestiges of myths and fairytales. I have not found positive evidence of that so far. On the contrary, Mlabri folklore differs from anything else that I know of in the area. That suggests that Mlabri spiritual culture has sprung from a different source than that of the Tins.

20.5. MLABRI IN THE CONTEXT OF
KHMUIC LANGUAGES

The cultural evidence leads us on to the main question: what does the *linguistic* evidence tell us about affinities between the Mlabri and Tin? There are a priori three hypotheses that deserve scrutiny based on linguistic comparison (I formulated this issue somewhat differently in Rischel 1993: 1456):

1 Mlabri is a separate Khmuic language on a par with Kammu and Tin; the specific affinities with Tin are due to old contact.
2 The essentials of Mlabri phonology and grammar and a significant part of its lexicon can be derived from a pre-stage of Tin.
3 Mlabri has a complex origin involving elements of Tin plus elements of at least one other language.

The most basic problem one must tackle when undertaking comparative work on languages of the area in which the Mlabri live is that there has been extensive borrowing both from Thai and Lao into those languages and also from prestigious mountain languages into less prestigious ones. This is tricky when it comes to the northern Mon-Khmer branch called Khmuic, in which scholars generally place Kammu and Tin as well as Mlabri plus some less-known languages in Laos and Vietnam. The branch is called Khmuic because it includes Kammu as the demographically most important language, but Kammu is rather deviant from the others when it comes to the lexicon.

The grouping of Mon-Khmer languages into the Khmuic branch is so far based primarily on degree of lexical similarity but lexico-statistics is poorly geared to such languages both because the core vocabulary is highly culture-specific (cf. Huffmann 1976b) and because of extensive borrowing and innovations. In the case of Mlabri it is noteworthy that one outstanding researcher (Smalley 1963) applied the method to two old word lists of languages called 'Mrabri' and 'Yumbri' and found that they were probably different languages. We know today that 'Mrabri' and 'Yumbri' are misnomers for two sociolects of Mlabri (Rischel 2000). As a consequence of such experiences I totally avoid any use of the method that is generally referred to as lexico-statistics. If I use counts and percentages later in this paper it is a matter of estimates based on random samples *not* on alleged core vocabulary (as defined by Swadesh).

We are now in a better position to speak about Khmuic as a separate branch of Mon-Khmer. As pointed out by Gérard Diffloth (personal communication) the so-called Khmuic languages share a very specific sound shift, namely the loss of *h between vowels. That feature is also shared by Mlabri and Tin, as exemplified by the word for 'blood': Mlabri **mɛːm**, Tin **miam**, both from *maham.

Another kind of evidence for a Khmuic connection is the retention of an ancient set of Austroasiatic numerals from 1 to 10, which in its entirety occurs only in Khmuic. They all occur in Mlabri, and I have retrieved them in Tin as well (except that the old numeral **gal** '10' has been replaced by a term **ma tuk** meaning 'a totality'). The Khmuic numerals are not functional in enumeration or counting any longer, but mastering the Mlabri set as a formula is proof of one's ethnicity as a Mlabri (their cognates elsewhere in Khmuic serve magical purposes).

Tin Mal and Prai are often lumped together as one language but in fact they differ so much in their everyday lexicons that they are said to be mutually unintelligible in practice, although the Tin groups consider themselves related to each other. I have found that the lexical differences are great and pervade widely different sections of the lexicon (Rischel 1993: 1452).

> I once made an informal and very rough estimate of the degree to which Mal and Prai have a shared lexicon by quasi-randomly picking 200 words from a Mal word list and looking for Prai words with the same glosses. That gave 78 more or less obvious cognates (of which at least 8 were shared loanwords), i.e. *38 per cent shared lexical items* in the random sample (a slightly different type of count gave 35.5 per cent shared items).
>
> (Rischel 1993: 1460)

The only conclusion I wish to draw from that now is that one does not get an adequate coverage of Tin for etymological comparison by looking at just one word list, however elaborate it may be. At least one dialect for each of the two Tin languages must be included. Whenever I speak of Tin cognates to Mlabri words it means that I have retrieved a cognate in a dialect of Mal or of Prai, or both (with better coverage of the lexicon of all dialects of Tin Mal and Prai the number of cognates would probably rise considerably).

The lexical discrepancies across both Tin and Mlabri are suggestive of a high degree of innovation in these languages. That is not necessarily true of Mon-Khmer in general. The lexicon of Kammu is surprisingly homogeneous across a vast area with a population approaching half a million. In this case, population density in itself seems to have played a major role in reducing variability. In contrast, the fairly small Tin population and the tiny Mlabri population have both split up into lexically divergent speech communities. That is conspicuous in the case of the two Tin languages, which for lexical reasons exhibit little mutual intelligibility although the separation between them may date back only a few centuries, and the same happened maybe a century ago with lexical polarization among the three varieties of Mlabri.

There is no language-external evidence that I know of which directly shows that the trifurcation of Mlabri is much more recent than the bifurcation of Proto-Tin into Mal and Prai. Since innovations and borrowing may happen at very different speeds in different languages it is not sufficient evidence that the two Tin languages are lexically more divergent than the three varieties of Mlabri. My reason for feeling convinced that the Tin split is much older is what I would call the *dialect profile* of Tin versus Mlabri. By that I mean the balance between lexical diversity and phonological diversity. My experience is that almost all words shared between varieties of Mlabri are shared *in identical shape* (though not necessarily with identical meaning). On the contrary, less than half of the words shared between Mal and Prai are identical, the rest are related but differ in shape because of sound-shifts or loss of structure.

> Looking at a sample of words in one of the Mlabri varieties and searching for matching words in the other (this was before the third variety of Mlabri, the Laos variety, was known) I found that 64.8% of the words occurred also in the other variety, and almost all of them (61.0% of the words in the sample) occurred in *phonologically identical shape*. When I made the same exercise with Mal and Prai, I found 35.5% matching words but that number shrank to less than half (15.0% of the words in the sample) if I required the words to occur in *phonologically identical shape* in Mal and Prai.   (Rischel 1993: 1460–1)

I would suggest this kind of measure as a useful rule-of-thumb when guessing about the chronological depth of recent branchings in oral languages. In any case, it suggests that the branching in Mlabri is very recent. If so, the available data on Mlabri show that it must have been implemented rather quickly, and that is understandable if it was a deliberate polarization that happened in connection with the establishment of clan-like subgroups.

If one looks at the oldest records of Mlabri word lists, which are forty to seventy years old (Bernatzik 1938, Kraisri Nimmanhaeminda 1963), as well as a short, unpublished word list compiled by Michel Ferlus in 1964 (cf. Ferlus 1974) they exhibit the very same discrepancies in lexicon and phonology between the three varieties of Mlabri that one can observe today.   (Rischel 1989*a*, 2000)

The case history of the three rapidly emerging sociolects of Mlabri suggests that innovation had been, to some extent, influencing the overall lexicon also before that time. For that reason alone we cannot expect to ever identify the Mon-Khmer or Tai source of *every* word in Mlabri, not even of those within the common core of all three sociolects.

20.6.   PREREQUISITES TO THE LINGUISTIC COMPARISON OF MLABRI AND TIN

When working with the lexicon of a so-called 'primitive' language one should be aware of the semantic shortcomings of comparative-linguistic studies. Some words have a referential meaning, others a predicative meaning, which enters word lists and is used when comparing it with other languages. If there is an additional meaning within a quite different sphere, it may be overlooked or at least disregarded in comparative-linguistic work. For the native speaker, however, word meanings which outsiders consider to be connotative or secondary may be just as tangible as the allegedly primary meanings, and the two meanings may be integrated from the perspective of the speaker because words reflect a holistic world-view with its supernatural and magical components. That semantic complication may be relevant if, for example, one is trying to establish the age and provenance of a word.

> An example is the Mlabri word **baʔaːʔ**, which refers to a bird-like monster that lives in the high forest and is deadly for humans if it enters their stomachs. The same word is also used predicatively to characterize things like snails, leeches, and polluted water as being repulsive and unfit for consumption. The Mlabri see the two meanings as aspects of one and the same word (to me the only common reference point is the potential of hurting one's stomach).

Like other researchers I disregard this potential complication in comparisons of lexical items for the simple reason that I know too little about the spiritual world of the various Khmuic peoples. I just wanted to make the point before embarking on the comparative enterprise.

When I began looking at the relationship between Mlabri and Tin and Kammu it was a necessary assumption that there would be phonological regularities connecting these languages to each other, but I found that the regularities still needed to be established more or less from scratch.

Before one can make serious claims about old connections one must at least be able to distinguish recent loanwords from old vocabulary. Like several other languages of the area, Mlabri has been somewhat influenced by Kammu. A striking example is the first person singular pronoun **oh** 'I,' which sides with Kammu **oʔ** as against ɤɲ or the like in virtually all other Khmuic languages.

> The meagre inventory of personal pronouns in Mlabri is otherwise of Pan-Khmuic provenance, as seen if we compare it with the distant Ksiing Mul language spoken in Vietnam:
>
> | | Mlabri | Ksiing Mul |
> |---|---|---|
> | 'you' | **mɛh** | **mih** |
> | 'we two' | **ah** | **aː** |
> | 'you two' | **bah** | **baː** |
>
> The pronoun **oh** 'I' is presumably a borrowing from Kammu; Mlabri has adapted it to the inherited pronominal system by generalizing final **-h**.

In terms of phonology, Kammu is mostly conservative, although it does have sound shifts on some points where both Mlabri and Tin are more conservative. A significant innovation in Kammu and some other Khmuic is the diphthongization of old Mon-Khmer **oː** to **ua** where Tin and Mlabri preserve a long rounded back vowel.

> An example is *poːs 'barking deer', Mlabri **poːl**, Tin Prai **pʰɔːt** as against Kammu **puas** (in Phong the latter form undergoes a further sound-shift **ua** > **wa** and becomes **pwas**).

On most points, however, *Mlabri and Kammu share the retention of a conservative, Old Khmuic sound system.*

Several Mlabri wordforms are shared with Kammu, for example **trlɔh** 'pot' and **chnʔdeh** 'pottery' (Kammu: **sndeh**). It is impossible on strictly formal grounds to decide whether such words were borrowed into Mlabri recently or long ago, or whether they are of equal age in both languages. In the case of words denoting pottery, language-external considerations are of help. Anthropologically, it has been documented that the indigenous culture of the Mlabri is based on the use of bamboo containers when preparing and storing food; if somebody uses jars and pots made of clay or iron they are acquisitions from the outside. That strongly supports the assumption that words such as **trlɔh** and **chnʔdeh** have entered the language along with barter trade with villagers. But it is often quite tricky to spot loanwords. Although modern language surveys list Mlabri as Khmuic together with Kammu and Tin, there is reason to suspect that the evidence for that classification is somewhat skewed by the presence of loanwords in Mlabri.

As is the case worldwide, real lexical cognates typically look much less alike than borrowings and may even be difficult to identify.

> For example, if Mlabri words have **kw-** it is tricky to spot the presence of cognates in Tin because there is often variation between a cluster of stop+sonorant and a single initial sonorant (such variation occurs more widely in Mon-Khmer, e.g. in Katuic). Thus, the Mlabri words **kwɛk** ('short-handled axe or similar implement') and **kwɛl** ('rotate') have the Tin Prai cognates **wɛk** and **wɛːl**.

It is an established fact that in Mon-Khmer languages the most stable and invariant part of words is the final consonant. Vowel correspondences are often tricky. Shorto (1976: 1041–2) demonstrated that there was variation over vowels already in Proto-Mon-Khmer and that that has produced 'irregular' cognates between related languages.

As for initial consonants, I often observe strange differences, e.g. in point of articulation, when looking for cognate sets across languages. As a consequence, it is sometimes difficult to distinguish between true cognacy and similarity by chance.

> For example, the Mlabri word **briːt**, meaning 'to tie around something and make a knot', has a counterpart **rit** with exactly the same meaning in the Sedang language. Whether these particular wordforms are true cognates (as I suppose they are) must ultimately be determined by painstaking historical-comparative work involving many Mon-Khmer languages also outside the Khmuic branch.

20.7.   TINIC

Back in 1989, when I first wrote about the Mlabri–Tin connection, I found that the Khmuic stratum in Mlabri must reflect a pre-stage of Tin, possibly a common ancestor language, which I called (and still call) 'Tinic'. David Filbeck (1978) had already worked out the historical phonology of Tin more than ten years earlier, understandably without including any comparison with Mlabri, but the earliest stage that Filbeck arrived at by internal reconstruction, starting from contemporary Tin dialects, is on several points fairly similar to the Tinic level I posited as a common denominator of Mlabri and Tin. I have since found Mlabri to be crucial for the adequate reconstruction of the earliest history of Tin. That does not mean that most of the words in Mlabri are Tinic; on the contrary the Tinic words make up only a minor fraction of the total vocabulary, but a significant one.

Testing the Tinic hypothesis by means of the lexicon easily becomes circular if the hypothesis is solely founded on a conspicuous set of cognates. Why not posit a competing hypothesis according to which Mlabri is genetically closer to Kammu, which it superficially resembles more in many cases? The old affinities to Tin would then be due to borrowing. My answer to that is that Mlabri and Tin share a phonological oddity which sets them off from most other Northern Mon-Khmer and which cannot reflect borrowing. It concernes the final Mon-Khmer sibilant *s, which underwent change both in Tin and Mlabri although it is preserved across most Mon-Khmer languages. For ancient *s Mlabri now has an aspirated final lateral in most instances, otherwise an aspirated palatal glide. Tin has an aspirated palatal glide or a dental stop. My assumption is that the final sibilant was apical and that it underwent a Tinic sound-shift into an aspirated *r*-sound *r^h*, followed by further changes that are typical of *r*-sounds all over the area, namely changes of a trill or tap into a lateral or a palatal glide, with the dental stop in Tin Prai as a further end-product.

We see that in a word I quoted earlier: Old Mon-Khmer *po:s 'barking-deer,' which is po:l^h in Mlabri, p^{h}ɔ(:)j^h in Tin Mal, and p^{h}ɔ:t in Tin Prai, whereas the sibilant is preserved in, for example, Kammu **puas** and Phong **pwas**.

I suggest considering this *elimination of the final apical sibilant* in Tin and Mlabri to be a defining criterion for a Tinic branch of (West) Khmuic.

Mlabri and Tin look deceptively different in morphology and phonology although they are likely to be historically closer to each other than either of them is to any other language. As for morphology, Tin has only lexicalized traces of affixation whereas there is an abundance of causative prefixation and nominalizing infixation in Mlabri. These are typical Mon-Khmer features and contribute to the overall appearance of Mlabri as a Mon-Khmer language. Kammu, on the other hand, has a much more complex affixation pattern than Mlabri. The relationship between Mlabri and Tin morphology is an open question so far. As for phonology, my assumption is that shortly after Mlabri branched off, Tin underwent drastic sound changes.

The most tricky problem is syllable number. In addition to monosyllables Mlabri has a proliferation of so-called sesquisyllabic word forms consisting of a presyllable plus a main syllable. In Tin, on the contrary, the great majority of words are monosyllabic. It is often apparent that this is due to loss of structure and structure simplification.

> The only frequent presyllable **si-** is specific to Prai (in a few instances, the cognate in Mal often has initial **h-**); it is clearly a repair phenomenon since it occurs even in loanwords, e.g. in **siɲuʔ** 'radio', in which it replaces a Thai syllable -**tʰa-** that is adequately represented in Mlabri **tʰaɲuʔ** (the full Central Thai word is **wíttʰajú ʔ**). In inherited words the joker presyllable replaces awkward clusters and/or presyllables, as when the Prai correspondences to Mlabri **jraː** 'skinny', **ço?uːm** 'smell' (verb) and **kinʔdeːp** 'large centipede' are **siraː**, **sijum** and **siʔep**.

Still, it is necessary to address a typological question: is it Tin or Mlabri that is of mainstream Khmuic type with respect to the exploitation of the two canonical Mon-Khmer word structures, i.e. monosyllables and sesquisyllables?

Among the Khmuic languages I have examined (which unfortunately do not include all of them for lack of sufficient data) there was only one that resembled Tin by greatly favouring monosyllables, namely the little-known language Phong. Mlabri and the remaining three test languages, Kammu, Khabit, and Ksiing Mul, all agree in having comparable inventories of monosyllabic and sesquisyllabic words, though sesquisyllabic words tend to take the lead over monosyllables.

> By taking available word lists and looking at the lexical entries beginning in unaspirated **k** (which is generally the most frequent initial) I got the following percentage of monosyllables:

Kammu:	47% (390 out of 833 words)
Khabit:	43% (18 out of 42 words)
Ksiing Mul:	roughly half of the words
Mlabri:	46% (192 out of 413 words)

The word lists were of very different size, and difficult to compare. For instance, some were given in a phonetic, others in a structural notation. In some lists, words in fixed expressions occurred as separate entries, in others not. Thus I could not use the same criteria in spotting monosyllabic versus sesquisyllabic entries. Even so, the observed ratio of monosyllables to words of more than one syllable is strikingly uniform across all these languages.

In brief, most of the Khmuic languages I have been looking at agree on having at least as many sesquisyllables as monosyllables. Those languages are not otherwise particularly close. On the contrary, they are lexically very divergent and are spread all over the Khmuic area. Therefore, I would claim that their proliferation of both sesquisyllables and monosyllables is an ancient Khmuic state of affairs. The remaining two languages, Tin and Phong, which are situated fairly close to each other inside the Khmuic area, are exceptional in that they agree in having almost eliminated the sesquisyllabic word structure in favour of monosyllabicity.

The wordforms in more than one syllable that we find in Mlabri may in many instances date back to the Tinic level. If the corresponding words in present-day Tin are monosyllables it is because the sesquisyllabic pattern had already collapsed in Proto-Tin.

If the presyllable occurred before a sonorant the sesquisyllabicity was preserved in Prai by the use of the joker presyllable referred to earlier (the *centipede*-example). If, on the other hand, the presyllable occurred before a stop, Tin has at most a trace of it in the form of prenasalization of the stop. An example is the Mlabri word t^hapu:l 'stomach' whose correspondence in Tin is $^mp^h$u:l (the aspiration on p^h is due to a predictable consonant shift: mutation). In Phong there is not even a trace of the presyllable in that word, the Phong form being **puɪl**. In Khabit, on the contrary, we find **smpu:l** with a fully preserved presyllable like in Mlabri, but *smpu:l would give *t^hmpu:l in Mlabri so there is the open presyllable in Mlabri t^hapu:l to be accounted for. Still, the close etymological connection between the forms in the four languages is obvious.

At this point it might be questioned how much insight is gained by tying the development of Mlabri up with the development of Tin. At first glance it just complicates the historical reconstruction of Tin. It should be considered, however, that even if one ignores Mlabri altogether, one still has to account for the large structural gap between Kammu and Tin. The only plausible explanation of that is that dramatic things happened in the very early history of Tin. Mlabri somehow fits into that scenario assuming that Mlabri split company with Tin at a rather early time.

Many of the presyllables I would like to posit for Tinic appear to have been lost without any trace whatsoever in Tin (as in Phong), along with loss of morphology. All of this makes it more complicated to do comparative etymological work on Mlabri and Tin, and some of the resulting lexical comparisons look less convincing at first glance. Thus, from the perspective of a historical reconstruction of Mlabri, one is in the strange situation that the best language for etymological comparison seems to have had a very dramatic history, the details of which are not well understood at all.

In contrast, the most convincing regularities are found in monosyllables with initial stop consonants. They involve *consonant mutation*, and that constitutes one of the important criteria for time-depth when one makes lexical comparisons between Mlabri and Tin or Kammu.

20.8. CONSONANT MUTATION IN TIN AND OTHER KHMUIC

I shall briefly review the scenario:

1 *Mlabri.* Mlabri exhibits no consonant mutation. The old distinction between voiceless and voiced stops is also preserved in three other Khmuic languages from which I have data: Khabit, Ksiing Mul, and Phong.
2 *Kammu.* Conservative Kammu dialects preserve old voiced and voiceless stops intact in syllable-initial position whereas other dialects have a scenario of tonogenesis accompanying devoicing of old voiced stops. That is probably a fairly recent phenomenon.

> *The devoicing scenario in Kammu:* across the dialects we find (i) the old state of affairs, (ii) an intermediate stage with breathy phonation of vowels after old voiced stops, (iii) complete coalescence of voiced and voiceless stops along with the development of tone. One of the dialects in Laos ('Khmu Rook', cf. Premsrirat 2002: xxxi & xlv) took a different course and aspirated old voiced stops probably due to influence from Lao, in which that very process happened several centuries ago.

The existence of different reflexes of the old voicing distinction in Kammu complicates the comparative work on Mlabri. That is because there are loanwords from Kammu in Mlabri, and it is not known in advance which dialect or dialects Mlabri borrowed from (Mlabri always borrows words *without* tone).

3. *Tin*. Tin has undergone a complex mutation, which typologically resembles the Germanic sound shift (Grimm's law). Its mechanism is quite different from devoicing in Kammu, both historically and typologically. In Tin one can observe that:

   I. old voiceless stops became aspirated;
  IIa. plain voiced stops were devoiced in absolutely initial position;
  IIb. plain voiced stops remained voiced elsewhere;
  III. glottalized voiced stops became (prenasalized) voiced stops.

The resulting pattern and its phonetic realizations are discussed in Huffmann (1976*a*: 582–3). In this paper I disregard the old glottalized series, since the words are mostly loanwords from Tai.

Mutation of the type we find in Tin can also be observed in distant branches of Mon-Khmer. That might seem to invite a scenario in which consonant mutation spread across a large area and also swept across Tin, possibly even after the separation of Mal and Prai, but that does not work since the areas exhibiting this type of mutation are geographically unconnected, and Tin is quite unique within Khmuic. It is more likely a spontaneous complex of sound changes, which happened in Tin proper, some time in the interval between the termination of the Tinic period and the later bifurcation of Proto-Tin into Mal and Prai.

It is, in my view, an open question how early or late the consonant mutations in Tin took place. They may have been separated by shorter or longer time spans, namely such that voiceless consonants acquired aspiration early, then the plain voiced consonants were devoiced, and finally—perhaps quite recently—the glottalized consonants lost their glottalization.

Loanwords from Tai in Tin are diagnostic but do not yield a simple answer when it comes to absolute datings (cf. the discussion in Rischel 1989*b*: 110–11 with reference to Filbeck's reconstruction of the scenario).

In the Mlabri context the possibility of dating the sound shifts is interesting because Mlabri has borrowed from Tin long after the Tinic period, but further study is needed to clarify the extent of that. All I need to add to earlier argumentation (Filbeck 1978; Rischel 1989*b*) is that mutation of old voiceless stops in Tin must necessarily postdate the first strong presence of Tai lowlanders in the twelfth or thirteenth century AD, since loanwords from Tai could enter Tin early enough to undergo mutation. This is true of an early borrowing of the Tai word for 'cultivated banana', which I have recorded in the Mal dialect of Ban Kwet with mutation of its initial consonant. The *banana*-word exists as a loanword in Mlabri as well, but there it has a form that suggests much more recent borrowing.

> Tin **kʰloj** or **kʰlwaj** 'cultivated banana' (Mal of Ban Kwet) is from Tai and originally has an unaspirated **k**, which mutated in Tin. The old consonant quality is preserved in Mlabri, which has **kuɤj** or **kwɤj** for the cultivated banana (Mlabri has **ʔjaːk** for 'wild banana'), but the loss of the lateral after **k** in the Mlabri form is diagnostic. In old loanwords from Tai, Mlabri preserves clusters, as in **kleːt** 'scales (on a fish)', so Mlabri has borrowed the *banana*-word recently from Northern Thai, which at some point in time dropped the lateral after stops.

There is ample evidence for the regularity of the consonant mutation in Tin, with such changes as **b** > **p**, **g** > **k**, **p** > **pʰ**, and **k** > **kʰ**.

> We can illustrate what happened in the old voiced series by taking the word for 'house', which is **gaːŋ** in conservative Kammu and **geːŋ** in Mlabri but **kiaŋ** in Tin Mal and thus shows mutation of *g to **k** in Tin. As for the old voiceless series, there is a tricky example of the correspondence between Mlabri **k** and the mutated Tin aspirate **kʰ**, namely the word for 'spear'. One variety of Mlabri has an old word for 'spear shaft', which is **koːlʰ** and whose direct cognate in Tin Mal is the general Tin word for 'spear': **kʰɔjʰ**. In Tin Prai the expected *and* attested correspondence of that is **kʰɔt**. To complicate matters, Mlabri has more recently borrowed that wordform from Prai as **kʰɔ(ː)t**, with a meaning now referring to the whole spear rather than just the shaft (i.e. a *pars pro toto* metaphor, which often occurs in Mlabri).

20.9. THE PHONOLOGICAL GAP BETWEEN MLABRI AND TIN

Mlabri and Tin have drifted apart to a surprising extent. The internal reconstruction of Proto-Tin and Pre-Tin that Filbeck performed (Filbeck 1978) had already revealed that there must have occurred a number of dramatic and rapid changes in the overall appearance of Tin several hundred years ago, but the full extent of these changes can be appreciated only by meticulous comparison with more conservative Mon-Khmer languages.

The specific sound-laws that connect Mlabri and Tin wordforms must ideally all be in place before quite definitive conclusions can be drawn about the provenance of specific lexical items in Mlabri. I made some observations already eighteen years ago (Rischel 1989*b*) and I have been addressing the issue recently, but I doubt that we shall ever know the full story. The development of vowels is particularly tricky. More often than not, one observes that vowel qualities differ moderately but often quite unpredictably between Mlabri and Tin, either in terms of aperture or in terms of front–back tongue position. The same is sometimes true of vowel length, which is unstable in Mlabri.

> We had both kinds of fluctuation in the 'spear'-word which I have already cited; another example is a word that occurs as **klɯʔ** in Tin (with mutation **g > k**) but as **glɤʔ** in Kammu and as **glɤːʔ** in Mlabri. Basically that word means 'hair on the head' but in Mlabri it now means 'head' by metaphorical extension.

As for vowel quality, there are also such offsets within Tin proper, sometimes so that one variety of Tin agrees more closely with Mlabri than the other.

> Mlabri **ɟɤːŋ** 'foot' has the direct match **cɤŋ** in Mal but 'foot' is **ceŋ** in Prai. Mlabri **mɔh** 'nose' corresponds to **moh** in Mal but **muh** in Prai.

Obviously, some mismatches between Mlabri and Tin can be cleared up within Tin proper, with Mlabri as the *tertium comparationis*. It is a task for the future to revisit Filbeck's (1978) comparative study of Mal and Prai in this new light.

> Some vowel discrepancies are due to vowel fronting before palatals in Tin, as when Tin has **sec** corresponding to a Mlabri form **tʰʌc** (an old Mon-Khmer word *sac meaning 'flesh' or 'pulp' that is not used in Kammu). If we add another process: loss of a glide after a front vowel, we see how Tin could get **kʰweː** for 'taro', which is preserved as **kwaːj** in Mlabri. Since conservative Kammu sides with Mlabri in having **kwaːj** one might consider categorizing that Mlabri word as a late loan but the greater surface similarity with Kammu is deceptive. Its Tin form has undergone consonant mutation **k > kʰ**, which testifies to the considerable age of the word in Tin as well. Mlabri is just more conservative. The Mlabri and Kammu form is in fact Proto-Mon-Khmer; exactly the same form is reconstructed for Monic, a distant branch of Mon-Khmer.   (Diffloth 1984)

An additional source of complication is that Mlabri often has an open syllable when the syllable in Tin is terminated by glottalization, and vice versa. That is a general Khmuic crux: also Kammu and Tin often disagree on that. At present, I simply have to accept fluctuations in vowel quality and length *and* syllable-final phonation when searching for look-alikes between Mlabri and Tin. Most often, the causes of such fluctuations are not yet known, also because many of the cognates are recorded in only one or the other of the two Tin languages.

The phonology of Mlabri has not been totally invariant over the centuries either. There are a few major changes, which make Mlabri look different from general Northern Mon-Khmer; none of them invalidates the Tinic hypothesis since they can all be fairly recent.

1 First, there is the change of syllable-final Mon-Khmer *-s into a voiceless lateral or glide, which I referred to earlier as a Tinic criterion although the consonant took different courses in Mlabri and Tin.
2 Secondly, Tin has preserved one of the syllable-initial Mon-Khmer sibilants (which I assume to have been apical) as s-, but in Mlabri that sibilant regularly changed into an aspirated stop t^h-.

> An example is the already cited word for 'flesh': Mlabri t^hʌc = Tin sec. The aspirated dental stop t^h- also occurs in loanwords. If it occurs in Mlabri its presence is always secondary; there is no basis for positing aspirated stops in Tinic.

3 There is monophthongization of *ia to ɛː in Mlabri.

> An important Mon-Khmer etymon, the word for 'root', appears with a diphthong in Khmuic: it is riəs both in Kammu and Phong, for example. Mlabri has monophthongization to reːlʰ, with the same vowel quality as in words with old *aː (the final consonant in the Mlabri word for 'root' is a regular reflex of *s, as explained elsewhere in this paper). Thus we encounter a coalescence in Mlabri between two syllable nuclei, which are kept distinct both in Kammu and in Phong.

Several wordforms, such as the numeral '2', beːr, have ɛː in Mlabri as against aː in Kammu. At first sight this seems suggestive of irregular vowel raising *aː > ɛː in Mlabri, but since the very same words have a diphthong ia in Tin, the behaviour of the vowel should be seen from a Tinic perspective. That makes perfect sense since we already know of a process of monophthongization ia > ɛː that affects Mon-Khmer words in *ia in Mlabri. My suggestion, then, is that Mlabri ɛː from Mon-Khmer aː is the result of a two-step process: the old Mon-Khmer vowel *aː had become ia in Tinic, and thus it could undergo monophthongization into ɛː in Mlabri. The question why the old vowel aː sometimes diphthongized in Tinic is tricky; it must be addressed at the Khmuic level.

> This diphthongization is reminiscent of so-called 'register' in several other Mon-Khmer languages, i.e. vowel changes conditioned by voicing in the

syllable onset. The occurrence of the phenomenon in Khmuic is strangely irregular, however.

As for the qualities of the vowels and diphthongs that have developed from *aː the scenario is like this:

(i) Kammu has preserved the long monophthong *aː everywhere, e.g. in baːr 'two'.

(ii) Khabit has diphthongization *aː > *ua > uə.

(iii) The other Khmuic languages I have data from all seem to have reflexes of a diphthongization *aː > *ia, as in Tin. The diphthongal reflex is preserved in Tin and Ksiing Mul; there is monophthongization into a long, low-mid vowel ɛː in Mlabri, and monophthongization linto a short high vowel i in Phong.

Examples:

(i) 'house' is gaːŋ in conservative Kammu, kiaŋ in Tin Mal, žəŋ in Ksiing Mul, geːŋ in Mlabri, jiŋ in Phong.

(ii) 'tooth' is hraːŋ in conservative Kammu, siaŋ in Tin Mal, tʰrɛːŋ in Mlabri, and hriŋ in Phong, but sruəŋ in Khabit.

(iii) 'rain' is kmaː in conservative Kammu, miaʔ in Tin Mal, mɛːʔ in Mlabri, and kmi in Phong.

(iv) 'blood' is maːm in conservative Kammu, miam in Tin Mal, miəm in Ksiing Mul, mɛːm in Mlabri, and mim in Phong.

What is important in the context of this paper is that the vowel reflexes in Mlabri and Phong can be seen as further developments of the diphthong we find in Tin. This is an exceptional case in which Tin is more phonologically conservative than much other Khmu. In any case, the conclusion is that *Mlabri actually sides with Tin* by having ɛː in words that have aː in Kammu but ia in Tin.

4 The Mlabri reflexes of the diphthongs *ia, *ua in loanwords from Tai are iɤː/jɤː and uɤː/wɤː with a long second vowel.

Thus, loanwords in *ia have *not* participated in the process *ia > ɛː stated in (3) above. Examples of loanwords with iɤː/jɤː, uɤː/wɤː from Tai *ia, *ua are: miɤː/mjɤː 'wife', gruɤː 'things', hwɤː 'head'.

20.10. PHONOLOGICAL CRITERIA FOR DELIMITING AN ETYMOLOGICAL SAMPLE

We can now approach the question of how to do convincing lexical comparisons between Mlabri and Tin, using a fairly traditional comparative method. Since words with presyllables degenerated in Tin, the basic regularities in Tinic comparative phonology are easiest to demonstrate if the words under study are monosyllabic. As I have mentioned already, close to half of the lexical entries in Mlabri are monosyllabic (to judge from the distribution of word types within all lexical entries beginning with **k-**), and I have made similar observations for other Khmuic languages. It is entirely possible to demonstrate the relatedness among these languages without going beyond monosyllables.

The other main category, the 'sesquisyllabic' wordforms with a presyllable before the stressed syllable, makes up roughly one half of the Mlabri vocabulary. Most sesquisyllables are completely lexicalized as monomorphemic items but several are transparent, as reduplicatives, as old compounds, or as words with affixation. From a Mon-Khmer perspective the derivational processes that produce transparent sesquisyllabicity in Mlabri words are trivial or even prototypical. Thus, if monosyllables in Mlabri show a definite Mon-Khmer association there is every reason to assume that that conclusion can be extended to words of more than one syllable although their form has crumbled in Tin.

The narrowing of the perspective to monosyllables still leaves us with a host of Mlabri-Tin look-alikes whose age in Mlabri we cannot determine. Fortunately, since Mlabri has escaped the consonant mutation that happened in Tin, the criterion of consonant mutation is diagnostic when making comparisons. Thus, in order not to mistake recent borrowings for old cognates the safest strategy is to look at words beginning in stops. I can illustrate the scenario by reference to the relationship between initial stops in English and German. If, for example, two obviously related wordforms agree on initial *t* in English and German, as in *table* and *Tafel*, or *tone* and *Ton*, then the similarity is genetically deceptive: it is a loan relationship. In order for both English and German to continue Proto-Germanic, they must *differ* crucially on the initial stop: if English has *t* then German must have *z*, as in *tooth* and *Zahn*; if, on the other hand, German has *t*, then English must have *d*, as in *Tag* and *day*. High German, like Tin, has had a language-specific consonant mutation; English has better preserved the Proto-Germanic state of affairs.

That is the way it is with Tin and Mlabri. If they agree on the quality of the initial stop as voiceless unaspirated *or* as aspirated, then that is hard evidence for some scenario of borrowing. The word may be a shared, recent borrowing from a Tai language, or it may be a borrowing from Tin into Mlabri which happened *after* the consonant mutation in Tin. In either case, the word is invalid in genetic comparison. If, on the contrary, Tin and Mlabri differ on an otherwise similar wordform in that only Tin shows mutation, then that is hard evidence for an old lexical affinity at the level which I call Tinic, or even before that.

As a consequence of the diagnostic value of consonant mutation I decided to restrict my sample of Mlabri monosyllables so as to include *only words in plain initial stops that mutate in Tin.*

After searching for etymologies across all these words I decided to limit the sample even further, namely to Mlabri monosyllables in labial and velar stops, i.e. **b/p/g/k**, because of specific complications with dentals and palatals. I also excluded some words which seem to have an imitative phonology, namely three words in **pr-** and **pl-** meaning 'to hiccup', 'to bark', and 'to flick away', the cognates of which vary unpredictably across the languages I have studied.

For example 'to hiccup' is **plʌk** in Mlabri but **clɤk** in Kammu; 'to bark' is **proh** in Mlabri but **kroh** or **truh** elsewhere.

All of these operations reduced the number of words but made the totality of remaining words more diagnostic.

The definitive sample includes not only words in single initial stops but also words in initial clusters of *stop+sonorant*. From a Mon-Khmer perspective one might therefore expect there to be some examples of *stop+nasal*, since that type of Mon-Khmer cluster is preserved, e.g. in Kammu but Mlabri sides with Tin in weakening all such clusters to aspirated nasals (this elimination of all old clusters in *stop+nasal* is yet another feature setting Tinic off from Kammu).

Examples are **pnɯr** 'wing' and **kneʔ** 'rat', where Mlabri has **hnʌr** 'wing' and **hnɛl** 'rat' (the discrepancy in the final part of the word for 'rat' is so far unexplained; Tin Prai has **sinɛ:** with a long open syllable and with the joker prefix **si-**).

When looking for cognates between Mlabri and Tin there are minor complications with voiced stops. Although Tin devoiced old voiced stops it happens that a Mlabri word has a Tin counterpart with voiced initial or prenasalized voiced initial.

There are a priori two scenarios leading to that situation. Some such words are recent borrowings into both languages, in which case prenasalization seems to be a Tin strategy to make the voicedness salient. In other such words the voiced consonant is old, and the expected devoicing in Tin was blocked by prefixal material. An example of the latter is the causative prefix, which is **pa-** or **ba-** in Mlabri whereas in Tin it predictably merges with a following voiced stop into ^{m}**b-**, ^{n}**d-**, etc. Thus, the Mlabri causative verb **pabuɩl** 'kill' has a Tin counterpart ^{m}**bɤl** or **bɤl** with preservation of voicing, whereas the underived Mlabri verb **buɩl** 'die' has the mutated counterpart **pɤl** in Tin.

Tin may even have prenasalized the voiced stop as the reflex of prefixal material plus a nasal in Mlabri. Thus, Prai ^{m}**brɛːŋ** 'bamboo flooring' corresponds to **diŋ^{m}rɛːŋ** or **dimrɛːŋ** (same meaning) in Mlabri.

20.11. SOCIOLINGUISTIC AND LEXICOGRAPHIC CRITERIA RELATING TO THE SAMPLE

It is an interesting issue how to define a Mlabri vocabulary that is representative of the inherited vocabulary. I first pooled my lexical data for all three Mlabri sociolects in order to capture as many etyma as possible, the rationale being that the three Mlabri sociolects might have split lexically by making different choices among available lexical alternatives (i.e. among existing synonyms or near-synonyms). But there is an alternative scenario: sociolects may split lexically by each creating or borrowing new words. If that is the main cause of lexical split, the inclusive approach inevitably dilutes the inherited core vocabulary. Moreover, when it comes to the semantics of lexical entries, my Mlabri data are of varying degrees of reliability. I spent much less time with the Mlabri in Laos than with the other groups, and it will require additional fieldwork to document their linguistic usage in sufficient detail.

In order to account for all that I made an even narrower sample, including only *words that I have recorded in more than one sociolect of Mlabri*. I then looked at the number of words whose origin was unknown to me and compared its ratio to the total set of words in the original sample and the narrow sample, looking just at words in **b** and **g**. The proportion of such words shrank from almost half to about one-third of the words. That suggests that lexical differences among the sociolects are often due to innovations happening after the three groups split up, and less often due to sociolect-specific retention of old vocabulary. Thus, although the narrow sample ended up being quite small, it seemed better geared than the original sample to throwing light on the relationship between Mlabri and Tin.

I decided to shrink the sample also from a lexicological perspective in order to facilitate comparisons. One must take into consideration that word lists for lesser-known languages tend to be made up of basic nouns and verbs; that is to a varying extent true of the rather limited vocabularies available for most Khmuic languages. As for Tin, there is no full dictionary of any variety of Tin available but only some unpublished word lists, which missionaries have kindly put at my disposal, plus my own, fairly short word lists from a couple of Tin dialects.

One of my urgent tasks, therefore, has been to collect more extensive lexical data on Tin myself, thus also rechecking the data in my sources. I have not got very far with that task so far, so my comparison of Mlabri with Tin inevitably gives a lower score than it may do eventually with a better command of the Tin lexicon. With the Mlabri lexicon I feel on safer ground after working with the language since 1982.

I therefore decided to stick to core vocabulary with tangible and well-defined meanings and with non-expressive phonological form (to the very limited extent that the last-mentioned criterion could be applied), so I stripped the provisional sample of four categories of words, namely

1 function words;
2 proper names;
3 words attested only in fixed expressions;
4 non-domestic terminology.

(By 'non-domestic' terminology I mean vocabulary that is peripheral or alien to the domestic environment, such as names of bird species in the wild forest.) I left words of all four categories out even in cases where I had good Mlabri–Tin correspondences because the main consideration was not to skew the quantitative analysis.

Comment: I realize that it may seem absurd to cut down on forest-bound vocabulary when talking about a hunter-gatherer language but there are two reasons for making that decision in the context of this particular study. For one thing, there is understandably little focus on such vocabulary in the Tin data as I could compare it with since they have been retrieved in a villager setting; to the extent that I identified lexical look-alikes to do with zoological and botanical nomenclature the question was whether they actually referred to the same species. Furthermore, hunting terminology which I failed to find in villager languages might either be ancient hunter-gatherer language or be innovations, e.g. code terms invented in order to ensure successful hunting. Thus the full inclusion of hunting terminology would add to the indeterminacy or 'noise' in the study, i.e. lexical items for which I have no safe etymology and whose age in the language I cannot even guess about so far.

20.12.   OPERATIONAL CRITERIA FOR COGNACY

What does it take for Mlabri wordforms to be safely regarded as Tinic? Systematic agreement with Tin is not a sufficient criterion for Tinic provenance. One must always consider the possibility that such wordforms are not *specifically* affiliated with Tin but are shared more widely among Northern Mon-Khmer languages. The only practical way I could test that was to check, for each word, whether I could retrieve it in Kammu as well (the short word lists of other Khmuic languages were rarely of much help). If many of the Mlabri words occurred also in Kammu that might suggest extensive borrowing, considering that Kammu is spoken very widely across Northern Laos and adjacent regions (its speakers form the largest ethnic group there with a thousand times as many speakers as Mlabri).

There are some old, fossilized Tai words in Mlabri that suggest that already many centuries ago the Mlabri engaged in barter trade with highlander villagers, using Lao or some other local language of the Tai family as a lingua franca. One wonders whether the high degree of isolation of the Mlabri group happened at a more recent time. If so, we have a succession of three stages: (i) early influence from the languages of neighbouring food-producers, (ii) little influence due to isolation, (iii) very recent influence due to new contact with neighbouring groups.

It is clear that some loanwords are evidence of a recent phase of barter trade in which the Mlabri visited both Kammu and Tin villages. I have looked closely at Mlabri words with aspirated initial p^h or k^h because I expected several of them to be loanwords from Tin with mutated Mon-Khmer $^*p$ and $^*k$. What I actually found was that almost all of them are loanwords from Lao or some other Tai language. That does not mean that borrowing from Kammu and Tin did *not* occur (the Tin word for 'spear', Prai k^hɔːt, is an example of a recent borrowing from Tin) but it was apparently the exception rather than the rule.

Across centuries it has been the lingua franca, not the local villager languages, that supplied most of the loanwords in Mlabri.

Altogether, my lexicographic findings do *not* support the assumption of much early lexical borrowing from Kammu into Mlabri since such borrowings tend to be recent. Rather, the basic affinities between the two languages are evidence of old relatedness and may go back more than a thousand years.

The complex Mlabri–Kammu connection is the main problem of the whole comparison. Wordforms shared with both Tin and Kammu are not unambiguous evidence for a Tinic association unless they are closer in form to reconstructed pre-mutational Tin than to Kammu. Unfortunately, that criterion will often fail to be met in words that are nevertheless likely to be Tinic. That is because Mlabri and Kammu have specific similarities in that they have conservative phonologies and morphologies and thus are much closer to a Khmuic pre-stage than the oldest form of Tin that one can reconstruct on the basis of Tin alone. Thus one is likely to underrate the closeness of Mlabri to Tin by applying this stringent criterion. Therefore, I established a supplementary set of words which I call 'ambiguously Tinic', namely words that are superficially more similar to Kammu but still fall into the Tinic picture if we allow for the kinds of phonological vacillations I observe in the unambigous Tinic words, namely minor differences in vowel quality, presence or absence of vowel length, and presence or absence of final glottalization.

If one looks across Mlabri lexicon there are also words which are indisputably Mon-Khmer but fail to show up in the Kammu and Tin sources. In most such cases they can be retrieved in other Khmuic languages.

> That is true, for example, of the Mlabri word for 'moon' or 'month', **ki:ʔ**, which occurs also in the Khmuic language Phong, so that it is well-established as Khmuic although Kammu and Tin have quite different words (one also meets a variety of terms for 'moon' in more distant Mon-Khmer, including forms corresponding to **ki:ʔ**). Then there are cases of the opposite kind, as when Mlabri has the word pair çəmɔɲ ~ çəmeɲ with a vowel variation which iconically refers to stars of different visibility ('big' versus 'small' stars); of these two variants one occurs as the general word for 'star' in Tin whereas the other occurs in Kammu. In this case I would claim that Mlabri preserves an ancient state of affairs which I do not know of in other Khmuic: the semantic field has undergone a lexical simplification elsewhere.

My observation is that there are few Mon-Khmer words in Mlabri which do not have cognates in the closest Khmuic languages. Admittedly, part of the reason may be that my search for cognates in other Mon-Khmer languages has been insufficient, but each examination of word lists of more distant Mon-Khmer languages has confirmed that picture.

20.13.   THE PROVENANCE OF WORDS IN THE SAMPLE

I shall now briefly summarize the results of my observations based on the sample of words in initial stops. It should be kept in mind that although I present some results in a quantitative form the essential thing is that my comparative approach is quite traditional. It is based on two assumptions:

1 If look-alikes agree in a systematic way, they are likely to be shared etyma rather than being similar by chance.
2 The meanings of related words often differ in typical ways such as extension or narrowing of their semantic range or transfer of meaning (metaphorical usage); such semantic offsets do not invalidate the claim that one has spotted true cognates if that assumption is supported by systematic phonological relationships.

> An example of change of usage affecting Tinic as a whole is the origin of the word for 'to eat', which occurs as **boŋ** in Mlabri and as **pɔŋ** in Tin. There is a word **bɔŋ** in Kammu, which fits perfectly, but that is an intensifier used after the ordinary word for 'to eat' so as to convey the meaning of 'to eat a lot'. I take that to be the same etymon, the Tinic use of it as an ordinary verb being probably secondary (such shared idionsyncracies are strong evidence for the assumption of a Tinic ancestor of Mlabri and Tin, of course). Altogether, I assume that several verbs in Tinic and more specifically in Mlabri may have arisen by the redefinition of intensifiers or expressive words as verbs.

Thus, my approach is in no sense similar to lexico-statistics, which in my view hinges on the assumption of semantic invariance in a core section of the lexicon.

The Mlabri words meeting the criteria for inclusion in my narrow sample amount to 178 words. A couple of words, such as **klip** versus **klap**, exhibit an ablaut relationship but on the whole the entries in the sample are mutually unrelated etyma. That is because my insistence

on monosyllabicity in the sample had the consequence that morphological derivations such as causative verbs and nominalizations were
weeded out.

Roughly 30% of the words in the sample have no etymology that
I know of so far. Those that are attested in Mon-Khmer (outside
Mlabri) amount to 54%, and the remaining 16% are of Tai origin. If we
then take the 96 words that I have identified as being of Mon-Khmer
provenance, the vast majority (92%) of those are attested in Khmuic.
I tried to make separate calculations for words in voiceless and voiced
initials and got similar percentages, so the pattern of distribution is
very clear.

The next step is to look at the Khmuic words in the sample and
divide them into subsets according to their provenance as Tinic, as
possibly Tinic, or as something else. The ratios then turn out to be
highly sensitive to the quality of the initial stop.

> Mlabri has absorbed loanwords with voiceless initial stops from a variety
> of languages over time whereas the possibility of borrowing words with
> voiced initial stops was more restricted. Therefore, it was to be expected
> that both the proportion of words of unknown origin and the propor-
> tion of identifiable loanwords would be larger in the voiceless set, so that
> the Tinic affiliation would come out more clearly in the voiced set. That
> expectation was borne out for words in **b-** and **g-** versus words in **p-** and
> **k-**. On the other hand, the point of articulation makes no difference with
> respect to the potential of borrowing. This was confirmed by the ratios:
> there is little difference between words in **b-** and **g-**, and likewise little
> difference between words in **p-** and **k-**. I therefore pool the words in two
> sets: with voiced and voiceless initial, and keep these two sets apart in the
> calculations but I do not go into the subsets of words in **b-**, **d-**, **g-**, **p-**, **t-**,
> and **k-**.

Of the Khmuic words in **b-** and **g-**, 62% satisfy my criteria for claiming
that they were shared with Tin at a Tinic level, and that percentage
rises to 83% if we include words that are formally ambiguous over
two kinds of etymology: they may be old Tinic words or loans from
Kammu. If we look at Khmuic words in **p-** and **k-** the percentages are
halved: they are only 35% and 41%, respectively.

The residue of identifiable Mon-Khmer cognates that are *not*
accounted for by the Tinic hypothesis is thus strikingly different for
words in **b/g** and for words in **p/k**; in fact, there are roughly three
times as many phonological misfits in the **p/k** set. I have no explanation for that. It may have to do with the pattern of borrowing from

neighbouring languages, but it seems far-fetched to assume a scenario in which Mlabri was borrowing words from some Khmuic language and preferred initial voiceless stops over initial voiced stops. Maybe some undetected factor in the past history of Tin phonology upsets the comparison of voiceless stops in Mlabri with aspirated stops in Tin.

> It may be too simplistic an assumption that true Tin cognates *always* have **ph-** if Mlabri has **p-**, and *always* have **kh-** if Mlabri has **k-**. The residue of ill-behaved Khmuic words suggests that the mutation pattern was perhaps more complex. Intriguingly, Tin sometimes sides with Kammu on having a voiceless initial; that suggests borrowing from Kammu at a post-mutational time but one would then expect those Tin words to be more similar to Kammu in overall shape than they are. Another possibility is that the mutation of *voiceless* stops into aspirates in Tin was subject to some phonological restriction although *voiced* stops mutated across the board. Thus the number of true cognates shared by Mlabri and Tin at the Tinic level may perhaps rise once the historical phonology of Tinic is better understood.

20.14.   CONCLUSION BASED ON THE SAMPLE

The percentages I have quoted are just meant to illustrate that there is a certain incidence of a shared lexicon in Mlabri and Tin. What is more important is that words in initial stops are diagnostic of a specific family relationship between Mlabri and Tin, and that the phonological correspondences are fairly straightforward if one compares Mlabri with reconstructed Proto-Tin. A corollary of this Tinic bond is that the Mon-Khmer appearance of Mlabri is hardly due to very extensive lexical borrowing from Kammu. A working hypothesis at this point, then, is that Mlabri and Tin are sister languages that have drifted apart very rapidly so that they now have only a modest amount of their lexicons in common.

20.15.   ABERRANT FEATURES IN MLABRI
LEXICON AND SYNTAX

The assumption about a close relatedness to Tin collides with another observation, namely that Mlabri is *not* fully fledged Khmuic. Some words that do occur in Tin show irregularities in their correspondences. Other Mlabri words are indisputably Mon-Khmer but do not, to my knowledge, occur in Tin. Finally, several Mlabri words are of quite unknown origin. Much of that can be explained as due to rapid changes in the lexicon over time, but the identified Tinic vocabulary in Mlabri is strikingly small (of the order of one to ten) compared to the known Mlabri lexicon in its totality. One must consider the possibility of an unknown substratum in Mlabri, or an early afflux of lexical material from an unknown source besides Tin and Kammu.

The existence of a mixed lexicon in Mlabri would be supported if some of the unidentified words in Mlabri had strongly deviant phonology. I have not observed that within the sample I have been talking about, but it is different if we go outside the sample. Mlabri has two glottalized stops **ʔb** and **ʔd**, which contrast with plain **b** and **d**. I examined a set of words beginning in **ʔb** and **ʔd** (45 in total) and found that their provenance is quite different from that of words with plain voiced initials: half of them are borrowings with conservative Tai phonology; the other half are either Mon-Khmer words with strange phonology or words of obscure origin. If we look at those, it is an open question where they come from and what is their age in the language; glottalized stops do not occur as separate phonemes in either Kammu or Tin. It makes sense to speculate that the glottalization is sometimes a historical reflex of a more complex onset. That area of etymological study deserves to be pursued.

Word-formation morphology is another area that should be studied further in order to determine the exact nature of the Mlabri–Tin connection. The data dealt with in this paper do not throw sufficient light on that topic, however.

Finally, the possibility of input from one or more languages *outside* Mon-Khmer should be scrutinized against other evidence than the major word categories I have concentrated on in this paper. *Grammar* is particularly important. Some syntactically important particles in Mlabri exhibit differences from Mon-Khmer in general. This is true of the existence (and extensive use) of three function words: a definite article **ʔat/ʔak** (Rischel 2006), a preverbal perfective particle **ʔa**, and a particle **di** which occurs in nominal as well as verbal constructions—the last-mentioned particle has a striking counterpart in Chinese. Again, a more detailed consideration of the topic would go beyond the scope of this paper.

20.16.   DISCUSSION

I see two possible explanations for the presence of Khmuic as well as non-Khmuic features in Mlabri.

1   One can stick to the Tinic hypothesis in its rigid form and assume that the founders of a new ethnic group, the Mlabri, spoke Tinic at an early point but that their grammar and lexicon underwent a pervasive influence from an unknown language at some point *after* the Tinic period. That might possibly happen if the Mlabri people migrated so much that their language could absorb components from a quite different language type, but then they must have migrated in a large loop over time, starting and ending in Khmuic territory. I have severe difficulties with that assumption.
2   The other possibility is that among the founders of the Mlabri group already there were speakers of a non-Khmuic language. That other language had non-Mon-Khmer features in its grammar, but it might still be a Mon-Khmer language. There is no solid evidence for Mlabri being a relic of a language from a quite different language family, let alone an isolate like the language of the Andamanese negritos.

The speakers of the unknown language may have been male food providers socializing with one or more village girls; I mentioned in the introduction to this paper that Mlabri still exhibits a sociolinguistic contrast between male and female vocabulary. Children growing up in the group would eventually integrate both languages into one. They would preserve the conservative phonology of the Tinic vocabulary but streamline word-formation, and their syntax was dominated by features from the other language.

If indeed the mysterious strangers were of the male gender, such a mixed origin would not spell trouble for the biological hypothesis either. Culturally, however, the scenario now becomes hazy: one cannot rule out the possibility that those hypothetical males speaking a non-Khmuic language were carriers of some kind of hunter-gatherer culture prior to the founder event posited by the biologists.

JØRGEN RISCHEL'S BIBLIOGRAPHY [1]

1957   *Morfonologi og morfofonemik.* [Besvarelse af universitetets prisspørgsmål i sammenlignende sprogvidenskab]. [S.l.], 1957, 103 pp.

1960   Über die phonematische und morphophonematische Funktion der sogenannten Worttöne im Norwegischen.
in: *Zeitschrift für Phonetik und allgemeine Sprachwissenschaft,* Bd. 13, Hft. 2, 1960, pp. 177–85. (Translated in 1983 into Norwegian.)

1961   *Componential Analysis of Phonemic Patterns.*
Bergen: Institutt for Nordisk Filologi, 1961, 44, 8 pp.

Om retskrivningen og udtalen i moderne færøsk.
in: *Jacobsen, M. A., Chr. Matras: Føroysk-Donsk orðabók.*—2. ed. Tórshavn: Føroya Fróðskaparfelag, 1961, pp. XIII–XXXVI.

1962   On functional load in phonemics.
in: *SMIL: Statistical Methods in Linguistics,* 1, 1962, pp. 13–23. (Stockholm: Språkforlaget Skriptor). [This volume Chapter 3.]

Review of: Aasen, Ivar: Brev og dagbøker I–III, ved Reidar Djupedal. Oslo: Det norske samlaget, 1957–60, 509 + 439 + 537 pp.
in: *Danske Studier,* 1962, pp. 134–9.

1963   *Debes, Lucas: Færøernes beskrivelse,* udg. for Selskabet til udgivelse af Færøske Kildeskrifter og Studier af Jørgen Rischel. Kbh.: Munksgaard, 1963, 2 vols. Year of original: 1673.

Morphemic tone and word tone in Eastern Norwegian.
in: *Phonetica,* Vol. 10, 1963, pp. 154–64. [This volume Chapter 10.]

1964   Nogle udtryk for geografisk beliggenhed i færøsk.
in: *Maal og Minne,* 1964, pp. 38–49.

Stress, juncture, and syllabification in phonemic description.
in: *Proceedings of the Ninth International Congress of Linguistics, Cambridge, Mass., 27–31 August 1962,* ed.: Horace G. Lunt. The Hague: Mouton, 1964, pp. 85–93. [This volume Chapter 6.]

Toward the phonetic description of Faroese vowels.
in: *Fróðskaparrit: Annales Societatis Scientiarum Faeroensis,* Bók 13, 1964, pp. 99–113.

---

[1] This list—until 1993—was compiled by the librarian at the Linguistics Library, at the (then) Department of General and Applied Linguistics, Lisbet Larsen. The remainder was compiled by Jørgen Rischel himself.

1965   Recording of synthetic vowels and their spectra.
in: *Quarterly Progress and Status Report / Speech Transmission Laboratory*, 3, 1965, pp. 25–6.

Review of: Allén, Sture: Grafematisk analys som grundval för textedering. Cph.: Nordisk Sprog- og Kulturforlag, 1965, 184 pp.
in: *Acta Linguistica Hafniensia: International Journal of General Linguistics*, Vol. IX, No. 1, 1965, pp. 114–17.

Studiet af nordisk sprog i U.S.A.—indtryk fra en rejse.
in: *Årsberetning / Selskab for Nordisk Filologi*, 1963/64, 1965, pp. 3–5.

1966   [Detailed English summaries].
in: *Diderichsen, Paul: Helhed og struktur: udvalgte sprogvidenskabelige afhandlinger. Selected Linguistic Papers with Detailed English Summaries.* Kbh.: Gads Forlag, 1966.

Phoneme, grapheme, and the 'importance' of distinctions: functional aspects of the Scandinavian runic reform.
in: *Interim Report No. 1, Research Group for Quantitative Linguistics, Stockholm*, 1966: 1–21. [This volume Chapter 14.]

Review of: Pilch, H.: Phonemtheorie. Teil I. Basel: Karger, 1964, XIV, 153 pp. (Bibliotheca Phonetica; 1).
in: *Acta Linguistica Hafniensia: International Journal of General Linguistics*, Vol. IX, No. 2, 1966, pp. 204–14.

1967   Experiments with sharp filtering of Danish and German vowels, [with] Eli Fischer-Jørgensen.
in: *ARIPUC: Annual Report of the Institute of Phonetics, University of Copenhagen*, No. 1/1966, 1967, pp. 89–90.

Heterodyne filter.
in: *ARIPUC: Annual Report of the Institute of Phonetics, University of Copenhagen*, No. 1/1966, 1967, pp. 13–14.

Instrumentation for vowel synthesis.
in: *ARIPUC: Annual Report of the Institute of Phonetics, University of Copenhagen*, No. 1/1966, 1967, pp. 15–21.

Phonetic transcriptions of Lepcha ritual texts with introduction.
in: *Siiger, Halfdan and Jørgen Rischel: The Lepchas: Culture and Religion of a Himalayan People*, Part 2. Cph.: The National Museum of Denmark, 1967, 153 pp.
(=Nationalmuseets skrifter. Etnografisk række; 11)

Preliminary experiments with the Fabre glottograph.
in: *ARIPUC: Annual Report of the Institute of Phonetics, University of Copenhagen*, No. 1/1966, 1967, pp. 22–30.

Siiger, Halfdan and Jørgen Rischel: The Lepchas: Culture and Religion of a Himalayan People, Part 2. Cph.: The National Museum of Denmark, 1967, 153 pp.
(=Nationalmuseets skrifter. Etnografisk række; 11)

Studies of diphthongs in Faroese.
in: *ARIPUC: Annual Report of the Institute of Phonetics, University of Copenhagen*, No.1/1966, 1967, pp. 56–7.

Studies of the prosodic properties of Danish words.
in: *ARIPUC: Annual Report of the Institute of Phonetics, University of Copenhagen*, No. 1/1966, 1967, p. 55.

1967/68   *Noter til dansk fonetik.* Odense: Odense Universitet, 1967–8, 30 pp.

1968   Diphthongization in Faroese.
in: *Acta Linguistica Hafniensia: International Journal of General Linguistics*, Vol. XI, No. 1, 1968, pp. 89–118. [This volume Chapter 16.]

Om strukturelle begrundelser for udviklingen af det yngre runealfabet. [On structural reasons for the development of the younger runic alphabet].
in: *Årsberetning / Selskab for Nordisk Filologi*, 1965–6, 1968, p. 14.

Speech synthesizer, [with] Svend Erik Lystlund.
in: *ARIPUC: Annual Report of the Institute of Phonetics, University of Copenhagen*, No. 2/1967, 1968, p. 34.

The Heterodyne filter of the Institute of Phonetics, [with] Svend Erik Lystlund.
in: *ARIPUC: Annual Report of the Institute of Phonetics, University of Copenhagen*, No. 2/1967, 1968, pp. 20–34.

1969   Constructional work on a function generator for speech synthesis.
in: *ARIPUC: Annual Report of the Institute of Phonetics, University of Copenhagen*, Vol. 3/1968, 1969, pp. 17–32.

Fourier analysis of photo-electric glottograms, [with] Børge Frøkjær-Jensen.
in: *ARIPUC: Annual Report of the Institute of Phonetics, University of Copenhagen*, Vol. 3/1968, 1969, pp. 128–34.

Notes on the Danish vowel pattern.
in: *ARIPUC: Annual Report of the Institute of Phonetics, University of Copenhagen*, Vol. 3/1968, 1969, pp. 177–205.

1970   Acoustic features of syllabicity in Danish.
in: *Proceedings of the Sixth International Congress of Phonetic Sciences held at Prague, 7–13 September 1967*, eds.: B. Hála, M. Romportl and P. Janota. Prague: Academia Publishing House of the Czechoslovak Academy of Sciences, 1970, pp. 767–70.

Consonant gradation: a problem in Danish phonology and morphology.
in: *The Nordic Languages and Modern Linguistics: Proceedings of the International Conference of Nordic and General Linguistics, University of Iceland, Reykjavik, 6–11 July 1969*, ed.: Hreinn Benediktsson. Reykjavik: Vísindafélag Íslendinga, 1970, pp. 460–80. [This volume Chapter 2.]

Morpheme stress in Danish.
in: *ARIPUC: Annual Report of the Institute of Phonetics, University of Copenhagen*, Vol. 4/1969, 1970, pp. 111–44.

Notes on the recent controversy about the phoneme in U.S.A.
in: *Bulletin du Cercle Linguistique de Copenhague 1941–65*, Bulletin VIII–XXXI, 1970, pp. 200–2.

1971   A comment on lexical insertion.
in: *ARIPUC: Annual Report of the Institute of Phonetics, University of Copenhagen*, Vol. 5, 1971, pp. 73–90.

A glottographic study of some Danish consonants, [with] Carl Ludvigsen and Børge Frøkjær-Jensen.
in: *Form & Substance: Phonetic and Linguistic Papers Presented to Eli Fischer-Jørgensen, 11th February 1971*, ed.: L. L. Hammerich, R. Jakobson and E. Zwirner. Cph.: Akademisk Forlag, 1971, pp. 123–40.

A study of consonant quantity in West Greenlandic, [with] Hideo Mase.
in: *ARIPUC: Annual Report of the Institute of Phonetics, University of Copenhagen*, Vol. 5, 1971, pp. 175–247.

Some characteristics of noun phrases in West Greenlandic.
in: *Acta Linguistica Hafniensia: International Journal of General Linguistics*, Vol. XIII, 1971, pp. 213–45.

1971/73 *Fonologiske grundbegreber.* [S.l.], 1971–3, 102 pp.

1972   A comment on lexical insertion.
in: *International Journal of Dravidian Linguistics,* Vol. 1, No. 2, 1972, pp. 84–99.

A formant-coded speech synthesizer, [with] Svend-Erik Lystlund.
in: *ARIPUC: Annual Report of the Institute of Phonetics, University of Copenhagen*, Vol. 6, 1972, pp. IX–XXX.

A study of consonant quantity in West Greenlandic, [with] Hideo Mase.
in: *International Journal of Dravidian Linguistics*, Vol. 1, No. 2, 1972, pp. 138–95.

Bemærkninger til det af Landsrådets sprog- og retskrivningsudvalg udarbejdede forslag til en ny grønlandsk retskrivning. [S.l.], 1972, 32 pp.

Compound stress in Danish without a cycle.
in: *ARIPUC: Annual Report of the Institute of Phonetics, University of Copenhagen*, Vol. 6, 1972, pp. 211–28. [This volume chapter 8.]

Consonant reduction in Faroese noncompound wordforms.
in: *Studies for Einar Haugen, Presented by Friends and Colleagues*, eds.: Evelyn S. Firchow *et al.* The Hague: Mouton, 1972, pp. 482–97. (=Janua linguarum, Series maior; 59) [This volume Chapter 5.]

Derivation as a syntactic process in Greenlandic.
in: *Derivational Processes: Proceedings of the KVAL Sea-borne Spring Seminar, held on board M/S Bore, April 9–10, 1972, Stockholm—Turku*, ed.:

F. Kiefer. Stockholm: Research Group for Quantitative Linguistics, 1972, pp. 60–73. [This volume Chapter 4.]

Resen, Peder Hansen: Atlas Danicus: Færøerne, eds.: Jørgen Rischel and Povl Skårup. Kbh.: Munksgaard, 1972, XLIX, 151 pp. (=Færoensia; 9)

1973   A glottographic study of some Danish consonants, [with] Børge Frøkjær-Jensen and Carl Ludvigsen.
in: *ARIPUC: Annual Report of the Institute of Phonetics, University of Copenhagen,* Vol. 7, 1973, pp. 269–95.

Indføring i fonologiske grundbegreber.
Kbh.: Københavns Universitet, Institut for Fonetik, 1973, 185 pp.

1974   *Topics in West Greenlandic phonology.*
Kbh.: Akademisk forlag, 1974, VIII, 478 pp. Dissertation.

1975   Asymmetric vowel harmony in Greenlandic fringe dialects.
in: *ARIPUC: Annual Report of the Institute of Phonetics, University of Copenhagen,* Vol. 9, 1975, pp. 1–48. [This volume Chapter 11.]

Ewens, Johs.: Jordfællesskab og Udskiftning på Færøerne, ed.: Jørgen Rischel.

Kbh.: Reitzel, 1975, 423 pp. 3 kort og 3 skemabilag. (=Færoensia; 10)

i-dialektip 'nalorssitsârūtai' pivdlugit.
in: *A/G: Atuagagdliutit / Grønlandsposten,* Nr. 40, 1975, p. 28.

Problemer og perspektiver i Hjelmslevs udtrykslære.
in: *PAPIR* 1, 3, 1975, pp. 86–101.

Problemer ved en generativ beskrivelse af dansk tryk.
in: *Årsberetning / Selskab for Nordisk Filologi,* 1971–73, 1975, pp. 22–32.

Topics in West Greenlandic phonology. (This is a brief presentation of the contents of the author's monograph. (Rischel 1974)).
in: *ARIPUC: Annual Report of the Institute of Phonetics, University of Copenhagen,* Vol. 9, 1975, pp. 253–61.

1976   *Norsk-engelsk ordbok: med oppslagsord på bokmål og nynorsk over-satt til amerikansk engelsk,* eds.: Einar Haugen, Jørgen Rischel *et al.*
Oslo-Madison: Universitetsforlaget–University of Wisconsin Press, 1976, 460 pp.

1977   Can phonological descriptions be made more realistic?
in: *ARIPUC: Annual Report of the Institute of Phonetics, University of Copenhagen,* Vol. 11, 1977, pp. 157–70.

Ordbogi: kalaallisuumit-qallunaatuumut: grønlandsk-dansk, eds.: Chr. Berthelsen, Jørgen Rischel *et al.* Kbh.: Ministeriet for Grønland, 1977, 240 pp.

Sproglige undersøgelser i Grønland.
in: *HUMANIORA: Beretning fra Statens Humanistiske Forskningsråd* 1974–6, 1977, pp. 76–8.

The IPUC speech synthesizer, [with] Svend Erik Lystlund.
in: *Miszellen IV*, Hrsg.: R. E. Ahrens. Hamburg: Buske, 1977, pp. 143–60.
(=Hamburger phonetische Beiträge; 22)

1978   Some general remarks on realism in current phonological work.
in: *Papers from the Fourth Scandinavian Conference of Linguistics, Hinds-gavl, January 6–8, 1978*, ed.: Kirsten Gregersen. Odense: Odense University Press, 1978, pp. 419–31. (=Odense University Studies in Linguistics; 3)

The contribution of Louis Hjelmslev.
in: *The Nordic Languages and Modern Linguistics, 3: Proceedings of the Third International Conference of Nordic and General Linguistics, The University of Texas at Austin, April 5–9, 1976*, ed.: John Weinstock. Austin, Texas: The University of Texas at Austin, 1978, pp. 70–80.

1979   Om tilpasningen af danske døbenavne til grønlandsk udtale.
in: *Eskimoernes vilkår i dag: 'majoritetssprogs indvirkning på eskimoiske minoritetssprog'*, eds.: B. Basse and K. Jensen. Århus: Arkona, 1979, pp. 163–71.

Parallel English edition: On the adaptation of Danish Christian names to the pronunciation habits of the Greenlandic language.
in: *Eskimo Languages: Their Present-day Conditions: 'Majority Language Influence on Eskimo Minority Languages'*, eds.: B. Basse and K. Jensen. Århus: Arkona, 1979, pp. 167–74.

1979/80   *Proceedings of the Ninth International Congress of Phonetic Sciences, held in Copenhagen, 6–11 August 1979*, eds.: Jørgen Rischel, Eli Fischer-Jørgensen, and Nina Thorsen. Cph.: University of Copenhagen, Institute of Phonetics, 1979–80, 3 vols.

1980   Filtering of EMG signals, [with] Birgit Hutters.
in: *ARIPUC: Annual Report of the Institute of Phonetics, University of Copenhagen,* 14, 1980, pp. 285–316.

Fischer-Jørgensen, Eli.
in: *Dansk biografisk leksikon*, Bd. 4, ed.: Sv. Cedergreen Bech. Kbh.: 1980, pp. 427–8.

Fonetik og sprogvidenskab: foredrag holdt i Lingvistkredsen 9.10. 1979.
in: *Institutavisen / Institut for Lingvistik*, No. 11, 1980, 15 pp.

Hjelmslev, Louis Trolle.
in: *Dansk biografisk leksikon*, Bd. 6, ed.: Sv. Cedergreen Bech. Kbh.: Gyldendal, 1980, pp. 379–81.

Holt, Jens Adolf.
in: *Dansk biografisk leksikon,* Bd. 6, ed.: Sv. Cedergreen Bech. Kbh.: Gyldendal, 1980, pp. 540–1.

Louis Hjelmslev's position in genetic and typological linguistics. F. J. Whitfield: Introduction, pp. 39–48; discussion by S. M. Lamb and Jørgen Rischel pp. 65–72.

in: *Typology and Genetics of Language: Proceedings of the Rask–Hjelmslev Symposium, held at the University of Copenhagen 3rd–5th Sept., 1979*, eds.: T. Thrane *et al.* Cph.: The Linguistic Circle of Copenhagen, 1980, pp. 65–72. (=TCLC: Travaux du Cercle Linguistique de Copenhague; 20).

Om det fonemiske princip i den grønlandske retskrivning af 1973.
in: *SAML: Skrifter om Anvendt og Matematisk Lingvistik,* 6, 1980, pp. 163–72.

Phrasenakzent als Signal des Objekts ohne 'Determiner' im Dänischen.
in: *Festschrift für Gunnar Bech*, Hrsg.: Mogens Dyhr *et al.* Kph.: Institut für germanische Philologie der Universität Kopenhagen, 1980, pp. 262–79. (=Kopenhagener Beiträge zur germanistischen Linguistik; Sonderbd. 1)

1981   A note on diachronic data, universals and research strategies.
in: *Phonologica 1980: Akten der Vierten Internationalen Phonologie-Tagung Wien, 29. Juni–2. Juli 1980*, Hrsg.: W. U. Dressler, O. E. Pfeiffer, J. R. Rennison. Innsbruck: Institut für Sprachwissenschaft der Universität Innsbruck, 1981, pp. 365–71. (=Innsbrucker Beiträge zur Sprachwissenschaft; 36) [This volume Chapter 13.]

Nogle komplicerende faktorer vedrørende verbers betoning i dansk.
in: *APILKU: Arbejdspapirer udsendt af Institut for Lingvistik, Københavns Universitet,* 2, 1981, pp. JR1–16.

Prof. Halfdan Siiger og mit arbejde med hans indsamlede sproglige kildemateriale.
in: *Halfdan Siiger og religionshistorien i Århus 1960–79.* Århus: Institut for Religionshistorie, 1981, pp. 24–7.

1982   *Acta Linguistica Hafniensia: International Journal of Linguistics,* Vol. XVII–XXVIII, eds.: Jørgen Rischel *et al.* Cph.: The Linguistic Circle of Copenhagen, 1982–96.

Fieldwork on the Mlabri language: a preliminary sketch of its phonetics.
in: *ARIPUC: Annual report of the Institute of Phonetics, University of Copenhagen*, Vol. 16, 1982, pp. 247–55.

Greenlandic as a three-vowel language.
in: *The Language of the Inuit: Historical, Phonological and Grammatical Issues*, ed.: Louis-Jacques Dorais. Quebec, 1982, pp. 71–80. (=Études Inuit Studies; 5, suppl. issue)

IJAL: International Journal of American Lingustics, Vol. 48–, eds.: Jørgen Rischel *et al.* Chicago, Ill.: The University of Chicago Press, 1982–.

On unit accentuation in Danish—the distinction between deep and surface phonology.
in: *ARIPUC: Annual Report of the Institute of Phonetics, University of Copenhagen*, Vol. 16, 1982, pp. 191–239. (Preprint for the 1983 edition in *Folia Linguistica.*) [This volume Chapter 9.]

Review of: Árnason, Kristján: Quantity in historical phonology. Cambridge: Cambridge University Press, 1980, 234 pp. in: *Nordic Journal of Linguistics*, Vol. 5, no. 2, 1982, pp. 163–71.

1983   *Indføring i fonologiske grundbegreber.* [Kbh.], 1983, 2, 185 pp.

Language policy and language survival in the North-Atlantic parts of Denmark. in: *Gegenwärtige Tendenzen der Kontaktlinguistik*, ed.: P. H. Nelde. Bonn: Dümmler, 1983, pp. 203–12. (=Plurilingua; 1)

Linguistics, phonetics, and field-work. in: *ARIPUC: Annual Report of the Institute of Phonetics, University of Copenhagen*, Vol. 17, 1983, pp. 125–44.

Morphemic tone and word tone in Eastern Norwegian. in: *Prosodi/Prosody*, eds.: Ernst Håkon Jahr and Ove Lorentz. Oslo: Novus forlag, 1983, pp. 266–76. (=Studier i norsk språkvitenskap; 2)

Om den fonematiske og morfofonematiske funksjonen til dei såkalla ord-tonane i norsk. in: *Prosodi/Prosody*, eds.: Ernst Håkon Jahr and Ove Lorentz. Oslo: Novus forlag, 1983, pp. 256–65. (=Studier i norsk språkvitenskap; 2) (Norwegian translation of the 1960 paper in *Zeitschrift für Phonetik und allgemeine Sprachwissenschaft.*)

On unit accentuation in Danish—and the distinction between deep and surface phonology. in: *Folia Linguistica: Acta Societatis Linguisticae Europaeae*, Tom. XVII, No. 1–2, 1983, pp. 51–97. [This volume Chapter 9.]

Spang-Hanssen, Henning. in: *Dansk biografisk leksikon,* Bd. 13, ed.: Sv. Cedergreen Bech. Kbh.: Gyldendal, 1983, pp. 581–2.

The abstractness paradox in Hjelmslevian linguistics. in: *Proceedings of the XIIIth International Congress of Linguists, August 29–September 4, 1982, Tokyo*, eds.: S. Hattori, K. Inoue. Tokyo: Proceedings Publishing Committee, 1983, pp. 884–7.

1984   A note on work in progress: secondary articulation in Thai stops, [with] Amon Thavisak. in: *ARIPUC: Annual Report of the Institute of Phonetics, University of Copenhagen*, Vol. 18, 1984, pp. 243–54.

Achievements and challenges in Thai phonetics. in: *International Conference on Thai Studies, August 22–24, 1984, Bangkok.* Bangkok: Chulalongkorn University, Thai Studies Program, 1984, pp. 1–35.

Devoicing or strengthening of long obstruents in Greenlandic. in: *Riepmočála: essays in honor of Knut Bergsland, presented on the occasion of his seventieth birthday*, eds.: B. Brendemoen, E. Hovdhaugen, and O. H. Magga. Oslo: Novus, 1984, pp. 122–35. [This volume Chapter 17.]

Grønlandsforskningen vender hjem.
in: *Berlingske Tidende,* 1984–03–13, sektion 1, p. 9.

Mlabri: skovmenneskene i Nordthailand og deres sprog.
in: *Årsskrift / Carlsbergfondet, Frederiksborgmuseet, Ny Carlsbergfondet,* 1984, pp. 19–23.

1985   An appraisal of research in the phonetics and phonology of Thai.
in: *ARIPUC: Annual Report of the Institute of Phonetics, University of Copenhagen,* Vol. 19, 1985, pp. 43–93.

Fieldwork data as input to instrumental analysis—a dilemma.
in: *Studia linguistica diachronica et synchronica: Werner Winter sexagenario anno MCMLXXXIII gratis animis ab eius collegis, amicis discipulisque oblata* quae redigenda curaverunt atque ediderunt V. Pieper, G. Stickel. Berlin: Mouton de Gruyter, 1985, pp. 709–22.

Indføring i fonologiske grundbegreber. Kbh., 1985, 185 pp.

Sproglig indledning og kommentar til Resens tysk-grønlandske ordliste.
in: *Grønland,* Årg. 33, No. 5-6-7, 1985, pp. 156–92.

Was there a fourth vowel in Old Greenlandic?
in: *IJAL: International Journal of American Linguistics,* Vol. 51, No. 4, 1985, pp. 553–5.

1986   Can 'the great tone split' in Thai be phonetically explained?
in: *ARIPUC: Annual Report of the Institute of Phonetics, University of Copenhagen,* Vol. 20, 1986, pp. 79–98.

Devoicing or strengthening of long obstruents in Greenlandic.
in: *ARIPUC: Annual Report of the Institute of Phonetics, University of Copenhagen,* Vol. 20, 1986, pp. 67–78. (Parallel publication of the contribution in 1984 to the festschrift for Knut Bergsland.)

Geografisk dialektfordeling og lydforandringer i grønlandsk.
in: *Vort sprog—vor kultur: foredrag fra symposium afholdt i Nuuk oktober 1981,* arrangeret af Ilisimatusarfik og Kalaallit Nunaata Katersugaasivia. Nuuk: Pilersuiffik, 1986, pp. 123–41.

Parallel edition in Greenlandic: Kalaallisut sumiorpaluutit agguataarnerat nipillu allanngorarnerat.
in: *Oqaatsivut kulturerpullu: Nuummi oktoberimi 1981-imi ataatsimeersuarnermi Ilisimatusarfimmit Kalaallit Nunaatalu katersugaasivianit aaqqissuutami oqalugiaatit.* Nuuk: Pilersuiffik, 1986, pp. 127–43.

Pioneers of Eskimo Grammar: Hans Egede's and Albert Top's Early Manuscripts on Greenlandic, eds.: Knut Bergsland and Jørgen Rischel, on the basis of preparatory work by Marie Krekling Johannessen and Ole Solberg. Cph.: The Linguistic Circle of Copenhagen, 1986, 188 pp. (=TCLC: Travaux du Cercle Linguistique de Copenhague; 21)

1987   A Mlabri–English vocabulary, [with] Søren Egerod.
in: *Acta Orientalia,* 48, 1987, pp. 35–88.

Is there just one hierarchy of prosodic categories?
in: *Phonologica 1984: Proceedings of the Fifth International Phonology Meeting, Eisenstadt, 25–8 June 1984*, ed.: W. U. Dressler. London: Cambridge University Press, 1987, pp. 253–59. (=Innsbrucker Beiträge zur Sprachwissenschaft; 36) [This volume Chapter 7.]

Phonetic transcription in fieldwork.
in: *Probleme der phonetischen Transkription*, Hrsg.: A. Almeida und A. Braun. Stuttgart: F. Steiner, 1987, pp. 57–77. (=Zeitschrift für Dialektologie und Linguistik; Beihft. 54)

Rasmus Rask 200 år: fem artikler i anledning af Rasmus Rasks 200-årsdag den 22. november 1987, ed.: Jørgen Rischel. Kbh., 1987, 16 pp. (=Humanist; 6, 14, Tillæg)

Some reflexions on levels of prosodic representation and prosodic categories.
in: *Nordic Prosody IV: Papers from a Symposium*, eds.: Kirsten Gregersen and Hans Basbøll. Odense: Odense University Press, 1987, pp. 3–30. (=Odense University Studies in Linguistics; 7)

Sprogforskeren Rasmus Rask 200 år.
in: *Humanist*, Årg. 6, No. 14, Tillæg, 1987, pp. 3–4.

Sproggranskeren Rasmus Kristian Rask: forskerbedrifter og bristede forhåbninger. Odense: Odense Universitetsforlag, 1987, 45 pp. (=C. C. Rafn-Forelæsning; 7)

'Yumbri' (Phi Tong Luang) and Mlabri, [with] Søren Egerod.
in: *Acta Orientalia*, 48, 1987, pp. 19–33.

1988   Dansk prosodi i genuint talesprog.
in: *SNAK: Nyhedsbrev om dansk talesprog i dets variationer*, Årg. 3, No. 2, 1988, pp. 18–19.

1989   Can the Khmuic component in Mlabri ('Phi Tong Luang') be identified as Old T'in?
in: *Acta Orientalia*, 50, 1989, pp. 79–115.

Fieldwork among spirits.
in: *Journal of Pragmatics*, Vol. 13, No. 6, 1989, pp. 861–9.

Fifty years of research on the Mlabri language: a re-appraisal of old and recent fieldwork data.
in: *Acta Orientalia*, 50, 1989, pp. 49–78.

Leksikon i field work: om sproget hos 'De gule blades ånder.'
in: *SPS: Skriften På Skærmen*, No. 3, 1989, pp. 109–12.

Om den grønlandske skoleordbog.
in: *SPS: Skriften På Skærmen*, No. 3, 1989, pp. 105–08.

Otto Jespersen's contribution to Danish and general phonetics.
in: *Otto Jespersen: Facets of his Life and Work*, eds.: Arne Juul and Hans F. Nielsen. Amsterdam: Benjamins, 1989, pp. 43–60. (=Amsterdam studies in

the theory and history of linguistic science. Series 3. Studies in the history of the language sciences; 52)

What language do 'the spirits of the yellow leaves' speak?: a case of conflicting lexical and phonological evidence.
in: *ARIPUC: Annual Report of the Institute of Phonetics, University of Copenhagen*, Vol. 23, 1989, pp. 87–118.

1990   A text-to-speech system for Danish, [with] B. Bagger-Sørensen *et al.*
in: *Signal Processing V: Theories and Applications: Proceedings of EUSIPCO-90: Fifth European Signal Processing Conference, Barcelona, Spain, September 18–21, 1990*, eds.: L. Torres, E. Masgran, M. A. Laguna. Amsterdam: Elsevier, 1990, pp. 1119–22.

Oqaatsit kalaallisuumiit qallunaatuumut = Grønlandsk-dansk ordbog, eds.: Chr. Berthelsen, Jørgen Rischel *et al.* Nuuk: Attuakkiorfik, 1990, 472 pp.

What is phonetic representation?
in: *Journal of Phonetics*, Vol. 18, No. 3, 1990, pp. 395–410.

1990/91   A survey of the speech synthesis project, [with] Peter Holtse and Henrik Nielsen.
in: *COWPAL: Copenhagen Working Papers in Linguistics*, Vol. 1, 1990/91, pp. 145–52.

COWPAL: Copenhagen Working Papers in Linguistics, Vol. 1–., eds.: Jørgen Rischel *et al.* Cph.: University of Copenhagen, Department of Linguistics, 1990/91–.

1991   Comments on the symposium.
in: *Music, Language, Speech and Brain: Proceedings of an International Symposium at the Wenner-Gren Center, Stockholm, 5–8 September 1990*, eds.: J. Sundberg, L. Nord, and R. Carlson. Houndmills: Macmillan Press, 1991, pp. 434–40.

Higher-level linguistic information in a text-to-speech system for Danish, [with] Peter Molbæk-Hansen.
in: *EUROSPEECH 91: Proceedings of the 2nd European Conference on Speech Communication and Technology, Genova, Italy, 24–26 September 1991*, Vol. 3. Genova, 1991, pp. 1243–46.

Invariance in the linguistic expression, with digressions into music.
in: *Music, Language, Speech and Brain: Proceedings of an International Symposium at the Wenner-Gren Center, Stockholm, 5–8 September 1990*, eds.: J. Sundberg, L. Nord, and R. Carlson. Houndmills: Macmillan Press, 1991, pp. 68–77.

Summary and discussion of speech and music combined.
in: *Music, Language, Speech and Brain: Proceedings of an International Symposium at the Wenner-Gren Center, Stockholm, 5–8 September 1990*, eds.: J. Sundberg, L. Nord, and R. Carlson. Houndmills: Macmillan Press, 1991, pp. 429–33.

The relevance of phonetics for phonology: a commentary.
in: *Phonetica*, Vol. 48, No. 2–4, 1991, pp. 233–62.

1991/92 *Sprogvidenskabelige Arbejdspapirer fra Københavns Universitet*, Årg. 1–., eds.: Jørgen Rischel *et al.* Kbh.: Københavns Universitet, Institut for Almen og Anvendt Sprogvidenskab, 1991/92–.

1992 A diachronic-typological view of the Faroese language.
in: *The Nordic Languages and Modern Linguistics 7: Proceedings of the Seventh International Conference of Nordic and General Linguistics in Tórshavn, 7–11 August 1989*, eds.: J. Louis-Jensen and J. H. W. Poulsen. Tórshavn, 1992, pp. 93–118.

Acharn Kraisri and phonetic notation.
in: *Thai-Yunnan Project Newsletter*, No. 18, 1992, pp. 16–18.

Dansk lingvistik i fortid, nutid og fremtid.
in: *Lingvistisk Festival: Lingvistkredsens 60 års fødselsdag 24. september 1991*, ed.: Frans Gregersen. Kbh.: Københavns Universitet, Institut for Almen og Anvendt Sprogvidenskab, 1992, pp. 13–35. (=Sprogvidenskabelige Arbejdspapirer fra Københavns Universitet; 2)

Formal linguistics and real speech.
in: *Speech Communication*, Vol. 11, No. 4–5, 1992, pp. 379–92. [This volume Chapter 1.]

Initiativområdet Dansk Talesprog i dets variationer: afslutning.
in: *SNAK: Nyhedsbrev om dansk talesprog i dets variationer*, Årg. 5, 1992, pp. 56–66.

Isolation, contact, and lexical variation in a tribal setting.
in: *Language Contact: Theoretical and Empirical Studies*, ed.: Ernst Håkon Jahr. Berlin: Mouton de Gruyter, 1992, pp. 149–77. (=Trends in Linguistics. Studies and Monographs; 60)

Kompendium i elementær lingvistik. Kbh.: Københavns Universitet, Institut for Almen og Anvendt Sprogvidenskab, 1992, 246 pp.

Contribution to *Language Sciences: A World Journal of the Sciences of Language.* Vol. 14–. Oxford: Oxford University Press, 1992–.

1993 Lexical variation in two 'Kammuic' languages.
in: *Proceedings of the Pan-Asiatic Conference on Languages and Linguistcs*, Vol. 3. Bangkok: Chulalongkorn University, pp. 1451–62.

1994 Nakrar málberingar um landafrøðiliga legu í føroyskum [translation into Faroese of a paper first published in *Maal og Minne 1964*, pp. 38–49]. in: *Málting, Tíðarrit um Føroyskt Mál og Málvísindi*, Nr. 1, 4. árg., pp. 2–11.

1995 *Minor Mlabri.* 367 pp. Copenhagen: Museum Tusculanum.

Sprog og begrebsdannelse.
in: *Sprog og tanke, Fire essays*, ed.: Poul Lindegård Hjorth. Copenhagen: Det Kongelige Danske Videnskabernes Selskab & Munksgaard, 1995, pp. 17–62.

Synspunkter på forskeruddannelsen. J. Rischel *et al.* Det Kongelige Danske Videnskabernes Selskab. 28 pp. + appendices.

Aspects of Danish Prosody, eds.: J. Rischel and H. Basbøll. Odense University Press.

Introduction [with H. Basbøll].
in: *Aspects of Danish Prosody*, eds.: J. Rischel and H. Basbøll. Odense University Press, 1995, pp. 3–20.

1996   Har forskningen i dansk sproghistorie en fremtid?
in: *Danske Studier*, 1996: pp. 5–21.

1997   Roman Jakobson and the phonetics-phonology dichotomy.
in: *Acta Linguistica Hafniensia*, 1997, vol. XXIX: pp. 121–47.

Typology and reconstruction of numeral systems: The case of Austroasiatic.
in: *Linguistic Reconstruction and Typology*, ed.: J. Fisiak. Berlin, New York: Mouton de Gruyter, 1997, pp. 273–312. [This volume Chapter 19.]

Det færøske sprogs mærkelige overlevelse.
in: *Fra Egtvedpigen til Folketinget, Et festskrift til Hendes Majestæt Dronning Margrethe II ved regeringsjubilæet*, eds.: P. Lindegård Hjort, E. Dal and D. Favrholdt, 1997, pp. 189–212.

Language Contact and Language Maintenance in Two Low-Prestige Minority Groups of Northern Thailand. 92 pp. + Appendices. Report available at the library of the Danish Center for International Studies.

Oqaatsit Kalaallisuumiit Qallunaatuumut—Grønlandsk Dansk Ordbog, 3rd ed. (reprinted 2002 and 2006), Chr. Berthelsen, Birgitte Jacobsen, Inge Kleivan, Robert Petersen, and Jørgen Rischel. Nuuk: Ilinniusiorfik, Undervisning smiddelforlag.

1998   Review of The Sounds of the World's Languages by P. Ladefoged and I. Maddieson.
in: *Journal of Phonetics*, 1998, 26: pp. 411–21.

Structural and functional aspects of tone split in Thai.
in: *Acta Linguistica Hafniensia*, 1998, vol. XXX: pp. 7–37. [This volume Chapter 12.]

Content, expression and structure: Studies in Danish Functional Grammar review paper.
in: *Acta Linguistica Hafniensia*, 1998, vol. XXX: pp. 220–4.

1999   Small languages and their speakers.
in: *European Review*, 1999, vol. 7, No. 2: pp. 191–218.

Talesprogets sære strategier.
in: *Mål og Mæle* 22. årgang, 1999, 2: pp. 22–26.

Fáment mál í fjareystri og hjá okkum [keynote speech about minority languages at a celebration in Tórshavn].

in: *Málting, Tíðarrit um føroyskt mál og málvísindi* 25 (= Nr. 1, 9. árg.), 1999, pp. 2–12.

2000   The dialect of Bernatzik's (1938) Yumbri refound?
in: *Mon-Khmer Studies*, 2000, 30: pp. 115–22.

Oqaatsinut Tapiliussaq—Oqaatsit Supplementsbind (Om det grønlandske sprog set i relation til det danske sprog), Chr. Berthelsen, Birgitte Jacobsen, Inge Kleivan, Robert Petersen, and Jørgen Rischel. Nuuk: Atuakkiorfik—Ilinniusiorfik. 184 pp.

Review of *Fonetik og fonologi, Almen og dansk* by Nina Grønnum.
in: *Acta Linguistica Hafniensia*, 2000, vol. XXXII: pp. 161–85.

2001   The Cercle linguistique de Copenhague and glossematics.
in: *History of the Language Sciences*, eds.: S. Auroux *et al.*, 2001, vol. 2.2: pp. 1790–806. Berlin, New York: Walter de Gruyter.

Fonetiske analysemetoder og fonetiske problemstillinger i færøsk.
in: *Moderne lingvistiske teorier og færøsk*, eds.: K. Braunmüller and J. L. Jacobsen, 2001, pp. 11–36. Oslo: Novus Forlag.

Lidt om postverbale verbaler.
in: *Sproglige åbninger. Festskrift til Erik Hansen*, eds.: Pia Jarvad *et al.*, 2001, pp. 183–93.

Shan—a Language in between Burmese and Thai. 68 pp. Report available at the library of the Danish Center for International Studies.

Den mærkelige danske udtale.
in: *Nye Traditioner. Festskrift til Sprogcenter IA*, ed.: O. S. Andersen, 2001, pp. 146–59. København.

To Honour Eli Fischer-Jørgensen. Festschrift on the Occasion of her 90th Birthday February 11th, 2001. Special issue of *Travaux du Cercle Linguistique de Copenhague* [edited with Nina Grønnum], Copenhagen, C.A. Reitzel.

2002   Notes on the pronunciation of an Eastern variety of Burmese.
in: *Linguistics of the Tibeto-Burman Area*, 2002, vol. 25.1: pp. 67–93.

Dilemmas and paradoxes in linguistic fieldwork.
in: *Proceedings of the Twenty-eighth Annual Meeting of the Berkeley Linguistics Society, General Session and Parasession on Field Linguistics*, eds.: J. Larson and M. Paster, 2002, 463–74.

Tröllini í Hornalondum.
in: *Eivindarmál, Heiðursrit til Eivind Weyhe á sexti ára degi hansara 25. apríl 2002*, pp. 299–311 (Tórshavn: Føroyar Fróðskaparfelag).

Nordic contributions to historical linguistics before 1800.
in: *The Nordic Languages, An International Handbook of the History of the North Germanic Languages*, eds.: O. Bandle *et al.*, 2002, vol. 1: pp. 108–15.

The contribution of the Nordic countries to historical-comparative linguistics: Rasmus Rask and his followers.
in: *The Nordic Languages, An International Handbook of the History of the North Germanic Languages*, eds.: O. Bandle *et al.*, 2002, vol. 1: pp. 124–33.

The contribution of Scandinavian neogrammarians.
in: *The Nordic Languages, An International Handbook of the History of the North Germanic Languages*, eds.: O. Bandle *et al.*, 2002, vol. 1: pp. 133–48.

2003   The Danish syllable as a national heritage.
in: *Take Danish—for Instance, Linguistic Studies in Honour of Hans Basbøll*, eds.: H. G. Jacobsen *et al.*, 2002, pp. 273–81.

The role of a "mixed" language in linguistic reconstruction.
in: *Proceedings of the 17th International Congress of Linguists, Prague* (CD-ROM, ISBN 80–86732–21–5). Prague: Matfyzpress. [This volume Chapter 18.]

Culture and language in a three-dimensional area.
in: *Language and Culture = Copenhagen Studies in Language*, 2003, 29: pp. 11–27.

2004   Some thoughts on sound change.
in: *Per Aspera ad Astericos, Studia Indogermanica in honorem Jens Elmegård Rasmussen*, eds.: A. Hyllested *et al.*, 2004, pp. 475–86. Innsbruck: Innsbrucker Beiträge zur Sprachwissenschaft.

Pan-dialectal databases: Mlabri, an oral Mon-Khmer language.
Paper given at the Lexicography Conference 24–6 May, 1984 at Payap University, Chiangmai (Thailand); to be downloaded from http://crcl.th.net/index.html?main=http%3A//crcl.th.net/sealex/.

In what sense is Mlabri a West Khmuic language?
Paper given at the 37th ICSTLL Mon-Khmer workshop on 29 September 2004, organized by Dept. of East Asian Languages, Lund University. The abstract may be found at http://www.ostas.lu.se/ICSTLL/MK_program.html.

2005   Preface (p. xi), Introduction (pp. xiii–xxxviii), Appendix (pp. 135–72: A detailed analysis of Bernatzik's Mlabri word list of 1938), and Selected Bibliography (pp. 173–5) to a new edition of Hugo A. Bernatzik: *The Spirits of the Yellow Leaves—The Enigmatic Hunter-Gatherers of Northern Thailand*. Bangkok: White Lotus.

Salient features of research activities within the humanities: How can the humanities be supported at a European level? [presented at a meeting of the Initiative for Science in Europe, Paris, November 2004].
in: *The Tree—Academia Europaea's Newsletter*, 2005, 20: pp. 22–4.

Articles in K. Brown *et al.* (eds.), *Encyclopedia of Languages and Linguistics* (2nd edn.) on The Copenhagen School (p. 196), Bohumil Trnka (p. 117–18) and W. F. Twaddell (pp. 179–80). Amsterdam: Elsevier.

Tilbage til junglen [about the origin of a hunter-gatherer tribe].
in: *Weekendavisen* Nr. 43, 28. oktober–3. november 2005, *Ideer*,
pp. 1–2.

2006   Replik til GeoArk [about pre-historic migrations in Greenland].
in: *Weekendavisen* 6.–12. januar 2006, *Ideer*, p. 8.

The 'definite article' in Mlabri.
in: *Mon-Khmer Studies*, 2006, 36, pp. 61–102.

Simulating speech the hard way: recollections from a bygone era in
instrumental phonetics.
in: *Phonetik und Nordistik, Festschrift für Magnús Pétursson zum 65.*
Geburtstag, eds.: K. Himstedt and C. Mogharbel, *Forum Phoneticum*, 2006,
73, pp. 185–213.

The Mlabri Enigma: is Mlabri a Primary Hunter-Gatherer Language or the
Result of an Ethnically and Socially Complex Founder Event?
Paper given at the workshop Historical Linguistics and Hunter-gatherer
Populations in Global Perspective, 10–12 August 2006, at the Max Planck
Institute for Evolutionary Anthropology, Leipzig, Germany. [This volume
Chapter 20.]

2007   *Mlabri and Tin Tracing the History of a Hunter-gatherer Language*,
Historisk-Filosofiske Meddelelser 99. Copenhagen: The Royal Danish
Academy of Sciences and Letters.

Malabri og Mon-Khmer: på sporet af oprindelsen til et samler-jæger folk
og dets sprog og kultur.
in: *Carsbergfondet. Årsskrift* 2007: 18–23.

2008   Danish.
in: *The Official Languages of the European Union*, eds.: C. Delcourt and
P. v. Sterkenburg. Amsterdam: John Benjamins.

A unified theory of Nordic i-umlaut, syncope and stød.
in: *NOWELE* 54/55, 2008, pp. 191–235. [This volume Chapter 15.]

Further: 1   a few biographies in the most recent edition of *Dansk biografisk Leksikon*
           2   numerous articles throughout *Den danske Nationalencyklopædi*, includ-
               ing the two supplements.

To appear

Hunter-gatherers in South and Southeast Asia—with special reference to
the Mla Bri.
in: *The Languages of Hunter-gatherers: Global and Historical Perspectives*,
eds.: T. Güldemann, P. McConvell, and R. A. Rhodes. Cambridge: Cambridge University Press (in preparation).

REFERENCES

ABBS, J. J. (1986). 'Invariance and variability in speech production: A distinction between linguistic intent and its neuromotor implementation', in J. S. Perkell and D. H. Klatt, *Invariance and Variability in Speech Processes* (Hillsdale, NJ: Lawrence Erlbaum), 202–19.

ABRAMSON, A. and ERICKSON, D. M. (1991). 'Tone shifts and voicing shifts in Thai: phonetic plausibility', *Pan-Asiatic Linguistics, Proceedings of the Third International Symposium of Language and Linguistics*, vol. I (Bangkok: Chulalongkorn University), 1–15.

ALNÆS, I. (1910). *Norsk uttaleordbok* (Kristiania: Bymaalslaget).

AMUNDSEN, S. (1964). 'Le vocalisme féroïen: Essai de phonologie diachronique', *Fróðskaparrit* 13: 54–61.

ANDERSEN, H. (1943). 'Til *u*-Omlyden i Dansk', *Acta Philologica Scandinavica* 1943 16: 258–86.

—— (1947). 'Det yngre Runealfabets Oprindelse', *Arkiv för nordisk filologi* 62: 203–27.

—— (1956). 'Urnordisk gestumR og dens betydning for i-omlyden', in *Festskrift til Peter Skautrup 21. januar 1956* (Aarhus: Universitetsforlaget i Aarhus), 9–15. Also in *Harry Andersen 1971. Runologica: Harry Andersens udvalgte runologiske afhandlinger: udgivne på hans 70 års dag 21.2.1971* (Copenhagen: Selskab for nordisk filologi), 68–74.

ANDERSEN, P. (1954). 'Dansk fonetik', in *Lærebog for talepædagoger* (Copenhagen: Rosenkilde og Bagger), 308–54.

ANDERSON, S. R. (1968). 'The vowel system of Faroese and the Faroese Verschär-fung', *M.I.T. Quarterly Progress Report* 90: 228–40.

—— (1972). 'Icelandic *u*-umlaut and breaking in a generative grammar'. In E. S. Firchow *et al.*, *Studies for Einar Haugen* (The Hague: Mouton), 13–30.

ANTONSEN, E. H. (1963). 'The Proto-Norse vowel system and the younger fuþark', *Scandinavian Studies* 35: 195–207.

ARGENTE, J. A. (1992). 'From speech to speaking styles', *Speech Communication* 11: 325–35.

BAADER, TH. (1938). 'Der Charakter des "Urallgermanischen" Konsonantensystems: eine Widerlegung der "landläufigen Lautverschiebungstheorie"', *Travaux du Cercle Linguistique de Prague* 8: 223–32.

BÆKSTED, A. (1943). *Runerne, deres historie og brug* (Copenhagen: Nyt Nordisk Forlag).

BASBØLL, H. (1969). 'The phoneme system of advanced standard Copenhagen', *Annual Report of the Institute of Phonetics. University of Copenhagen* 3: 33–54.

—— (1972). 'Some remarks concerning the stød in a generative grammar of Danish', in F. Kiefer, *Derivational Processes*, KVAL PM Ref. No. 729 (Stockholm), 5–30.

BASBØLL, H. (1978a). 'On the use of "domains" in phonology', in *Proceedings of the Twelfth International Congress of Linguists, Innsbrucker Beiträge zur Sprachwissenschaft* (Innsbruck), 763–6.

——(1978b). 'A note on boundaries and stress rules in Danish phonology', in E. Gårding, G. Bruce, and R. Bannert (eds.), *Nordic Prosody* (Lund: Department of Linguistics, Lund University), 65–71.

——(1982). 'Nordic i-umlaut once more: a variational view', *Folia Linguistica Historica* III(1): 59–86.

——(1993). 'The Nordic i-umlaut and natural principles of syllabification: a possible scenario?', *NOWELE* 21/22: 37–52.

——(2001). 'Om min nye stødanalyse', *Pluridicta* 38: 4–8 (Odense: Institute of Language and Communication, University of Southern Denmark).

——(2003). 'Prosody, productivity and word structure: the stød pattern of Modern Danish', *Nordic Journal of Linguistics* 26(1): 5–44.

——(2005). *The Phonology of Danish* (Oxford: Oxford University Press).

BEELER, M. S. (1986). 'Chumash numerals', in Closs (1986), 109–28.

BENEDIKTSSON, H. (1963). 'Some aspects of Nordic umlaut and breaking', *Language* 39: 409–31. Reprinted in Gúðrún Þórhallsdóttir et al., *Linguistic Studies, Historical and Comparative by Hreinn Benediktsson* (2002) (Reykjavík: Institute of Linguistics), 142–63.

——(1968). 'Indirect changes of phonological structure: Nordic vowel quantity', *Acta Linguistica Hafniensia* XI: 31–65.

——(1982). 'Nordic umlaut and breaking: thirty years of research (1951–1980)', *Nordic Journal of Linguistics* 5: 1–60.

BERGSLAND, K. (1955). *A Grammatical Outline of the Eskimo Language of West Greenland* (mimeographed, Oslo).

——(1959). 'The Eskimo-Uralic hypothesis', *Journal de la Societé Finno-Ougrienne* 61: 1–29.

——(1966). 'The Eskimo Shibboleth inuk / yuk', in *To Honor Roman Jakobson* (The Hague: Mouton), 203–21.

BERNATZIK, H. A. (1938). *Die Geister der gelben Blätter* (with word lists = : 167–8 and 237–40) (München: F. Bruckmann).

——(2005). *The Spirits of the Yellow Leaves. The Enigmatic Hunter-Gatherers of Northern Thailand.* (Originally 1938; new edition by J. Rischel; Bangkok: White Lotus Press).

BIERWISCH, M. (1966). 'Regeln für die Intonation deutscher Sätze', *Studia Grammatica* VII: 99–201.

BJERRUM, M. (1962). 'Forsøg til en analyse af det færøske udtrykssystem', *Acta Philologica Scandinavica* 25: 31–69.

BLOOMFIELD, L. (1914). *An Introduction to the Study of Language* (New York: Henry Holt).

——(1935). *Language* (London: Allen & Unwin Ltd.)

BOELES, J. J. (1963). 'Second expedition to the Mrabri of North Thailand', *Journal of the Siam Society, Bangkok* 51(2): 133–60.

BOLINGER, D. L. (1958). 'A theory of pitch accent in English', *Word* 14: 109–49.

——and GERSTMAN, L. J. (1957). 'Disjuncture as a cue to constructs', *Word* 13: 246–55.

BORGSTRØM, C. H. (1954). 'Språkanalyse som barnelek', *Norsk tidsskrift for sprog-videnskap* 17: 484–5.

BOURKE-BORROWES, D. (1926–7). 'Further notes on the Phi Tong Lu'ang', *Journal of the Siam Society, Bangkok* 20(2): 167–8.

BRAROE, E. E. (1979). 'Exceptions to Old Icelandic i-umlaut', *Studia Linguistica* XXXIII(1): 43–56.

BRESNAN, J. (1972). 'Stress and syntax: a reply', *Language* 48: 326–42.

BROCH, O. (1935). 'Rhythm in the spoken Norwegian language', *Transactions of the Philological Society* 1935: 80–112.

BRØNDUM-NIELSEN, J. (1932). *Gammeldansk Grammatik i sproghistorisk Fremstilling* II (Copenhagen: J.H. Schultz Forlag).

——— (1950). *Gammeldansk Grammatik i sproghistorisk Fremstilling* I, 2nd edn [1st edn 1928] (Copenhagen: J.H. Schultz Forlag).

BROWN, J. M. (1965). *From Ancient Thai to Modern Dialects* (Bangkok: Social Science Association Press of Thailand. Reprinted with the addition of other papers by White Lotus Co., Bangkok 1985).

——— (1975). 'The great tone split: Did it work in two opposite ways?', in J. G. Harris and J. R. Chamberlain, *Studies in Tai Linguistics in Honor of William J. Gedney* (Bangkok: Central Institute of English Language, Office of State Universities), 33–48.

——— (1985). 'The language of Sukhothai: Where did it come from? And where did it go?', in *From Ancient Thai to Modern Dialects and Other Works* (Bangkok: White Lotus Co.), 1–3.

BRUCE, G. (1977). *Swedish Word Accents in Sentence Perspective* (Lund: Gleerup).

——— and P. TOUATI (1992). 'On the analysis of prosody in spontaneous speech with exemplification from Swedish and French', *Speech Communication* 11(4–5): 453–8.

BULCK, G. VAN (1952). 'Les langues bantoues', in Meillet and Cohen (1952). 847–904.

CAPELL, A. (1967). 'The analysis of complex verbal forms', *Pacific Linguistics*, Series A, No. 11 (Papers in Australian Linguistics No. 2), 43–62.

CATHEY, J. E. (1972). 'Syncopation, i-mutation and short stem forms in Old Icelandic', *Arkiv för nordisk filologi* 87: 33–55.

CHAPMAN, K. G. (1962). *Icelandic–Norwegian Linguistic Relationships* (= Norsk Tidsskrift for Sprogvidenskap, suppl. to vol. VII) (Oslo).

CHOMSKY, N. (1970). 'Remarks on nominalization', in R. A. Jacobs and P. S. Rosenbaum (eds), *Readings in English Transformational Grammar* (Waltham, Mass.: Ginn), 184–221.

——— and HALLE, M. (1968). *The Sound Pattern of English* (New York: Harper and Row).

——— ———, and LUKOFF, F. (1956). 'On accent and juncture in English', in M. Halle, H. G. Lunt, H. McLean, and C. H. van Schooneveld (eds), *For Roman Jakobson: Essays on the Occasion of his Sixtieth Birthday* (The Hague: Mouton), 65–80.

CHRISTIANSEN, H. (1948). *Norske Dialekter 3: De viktigste målmerker og deres råderom* (Oslo: Johan Grundt Tanum).

CLOSS, M. P. (ed.) (1986). *Native American Mathematics* (Austin: University of Texas Press).

COLLIS, D. R. F. (1971). *Pour une sémiologie de l'esquimau*. Centre de linguistique quantitative de l'Université de Paris VI.

CORSTIUS, H. B. (ed.) (1968). *Grammars for Number Names* (Foundations of Language, Supplementary Series, 7.) (Dordrecht: Reidel).

DAVIDSON, J. H. C. S. (ed.) (1991). *Austroasiatic Languages: Essays in Honour of H. L. Shorto* (London: School of Oriental and African Studies).

DESSAINT, W. Y. (1981). 'The T'in or Mal', *Journal of the Siam Society, Bangkok* 69(1,2): 107–36.

DIDERICHSEN, P. (1938). 'Accent, Synkope, Omlyd', *Selskab for nordisk filologis årsberetning for 1937–38* (Copenhagen), 5–7. Reprinted with an English summary in Paul Diderichsen, *Helhed og Struktur* (1966) (Copenhagen: G.E.C. Gads Forlag), 27–30.

——(1945). 'Runer og runeforskning i nordisk belysning', *Nordisk Tidsskrift* 21: 319–34.

——(1946). *Elementær Dansk Grammatik* (Copenhagen, Gyldendal).

——(1947). 'Maal og Midler i Nutidens nordiske Filologi', in P. Andersen and J. Brøndum-Nielsen, *Det første Nordistmøde i København 24.–26. Jan. 1946* (= *Acta Philologica Scandinavica* XIX: 62–77). Reprinted with an English summary in Diderichsen (1957): 80–97.

——(1957). 'Udtalen af dansk rigssprog', *Danske studier* (Copenhagen: J.H. Schultz), 41–79.

——(1966). *Helhed og Struktur* (Copenhagen: G.E.C. Gads Forlag).

DIFFLOTH, G. (1976). 'Mon-Khmer numerals in Aslian languages', in: Diffloth and Zide (1976), 31–7.

——(1980). *The Wa Languages* Linguistics of the Tibeto-Burman Area, vol. 5, n. 2.

——(1984). *The Dvaravati Old Mon Language and Nyah Kur* Monic Language Studies 1. (Bangkok: Chulalongkorn University Printing House).

——and ZIDE, N. H. (eds) (1976). *Austroasiatic Number Systems, Linguistics* 174 (Special issue).

DORAIS, L.-J. (1972). 'Les parlers inuit du Nouveau-Québec: Eléments de phonologie' (ms).

DRESSLER, W. U. (1975). 'Methodisches zu Allegro-Regeln', in W. U. Dressler and F. V. Mareš (eds), *Phonologica* 1972 (München: Fink), 219–34.

——and MOOSMÜLLER, S. (1991). 'Phonetics and phonology: a sociopsycholinguistic framework', *Phonetica* 48: 233–62.

DYHR, N.-J. (1995). 'The fundamental frequency in Danish spontaneous speech with special reference to syllables boosted for emphasis', in J. Rischel and H. Basbøll (eds.), *Aspects of Danish Prosody* (Odense: Odense University Press), 49–67.

DYVIK, H. (1973). 'Forslag til forklaring av *i*-omlydens fravær i kortstavete synkoperte former', *Maal og Minne* 1973: 151–61.

EELLS, W. C. (1913). 'Number systems of the North American Indians', *The American Mathematical Monthly* 20: 263–99.

EGEDE, P. (1750). *Dictionarium Grönlandico-Danico-Latinum* (Copenhagen: Orphanotroph. Reg. Typogr. [Det Kongelige Waisenhuses Bogtrykkeri], IDC Micro-Edition H-178).

EGEROD, S. (1957). 'Essentials of Shan phonology and script', *The Bulletin of the Institute of History and Philology*, Academia Sinica, Vol. XXIX: 121–9.

——(1959). 'Essentials of Khün phonology and script', *Acta Orientalia* 24: 123–46.

——(1961). 'Studies in Thai dialectology', *Acta Orientalia* XXVI: 43–91.

——(1971). 'Phonation types in Chinese and South East Asian languages', *Acta Linguistica Hafniensia* XIII: 159–71.

——(1982). 'An English-Mlabri basic vocabulary', *Annual Newsletter of the Scandinavian Institute of Asian Studies* 16: 14–20.

——and RISCHEL, J. (1987*a*). 'A Mlabri–English vocabulary', *Acta Orientalia* 48: 19–33.

——and RISCHEL, J. (1987*b*). 'A Mlabri–English vocabulary', *Acta Orientalia* 48: 35–88.

EICHNER, H. (1992). 'Anatolian', in Gvozdanović (1992), 29–96.

EJSKJÆR, I. (1954). *Brøndum-målet. Lydsystemet i en Sallingdialekt* (København: J.H. Schultz).

——(1990). 'Stød and pitch accents in the Danish dialects', *Acta Linguistica Hafniensia* 22: 49–76.

ELIASSON, S. (1974). 'On the issue of directionality', in K.-H. Dahlstedt, *Proceedings of the Second International Conference of Nordic and General Linguistics (Umeå)*, 421–45.

EMMERICK, R. E. (1992). 'Iranian', in Gvozdanović (1992), 289–345.

FABRICIUS, O. (1804). *Den grønlandske Ordbog* (Copenhagen) (IDC Micro-Edition N-207).

FANT, G. and KRUCKENBERG, A. (1989). 'Preliminaries to the study of Swedish prose reading and reading style', *Speech Transmission Laboratory, Quarterly Progress and Status Report* 2 (79 pp.).

FERGUSON, C. A. (1978). 'Phonological processes', in Greenberg *et al.* (1978), 403–42.

FERLUS, M. (1974). 'Les langues du groupe austroasiatique-nord', *ASEMI* V(1): 39 ff.

FILBECK, D. (1976). 'On */r/ in T'in', *Austroasiatic Studies* I: 265–83 (The University Press of Hawaii).

——(1978). *T'in: A Historical Study* (= Pacific Linguistics Series B No. 49) (Canberra: Australian National University).

——(1987). 'New ethnic names for the Tin of Nan Province', *Journal of the Siam Society, Bangkok* 75: 129–38.

FIRTH, J. R. (1948). 'Sounds and prosodies', *Transactions of the Philological Society*: 107–52 (London).

FISCHER-JØRGENSEN, E. (1961). 'Some remarks on the function of stress with special reference to the Germanic languages', *Congrès international des sciences anthropologiques et ethnologiques*, Bruxelles-Tervuren 1948, Comptes–rendus, IIIe Section: 86–8 (printed in 1961).

——(1984). 'The acoustic manifestation of stress in Danish with particular reference to the reduction of stess in compounds', *Annual Report of the Institute of Phonetics, University of Copenhagen* 18: 285–93.

FLATZ, G. (1963). 'The Mrabri: anthropometric, genetic, and medical examinations', *Journal of the Siam Society, Bangkok* 51(2): 161–77 plus Appendices.

FOLEY, J. (1977). *Foundations of Theoretical Phonology* Cambridge Studies in Linguistics 20, (Cambridge: Cambridge University Press).

FORTESCUE, M. (1983). *A Comparative Manual of Affixes for the Inuit Dialects of Greenland, Canada, and Alaska*, in *Meddelelser om Grønland, Man & Society 4* (Copenhagen).

FOWLER, M. (1960). 'Stress-determined allophones in English', *Word* 16: 344–7.

FRETHEIM, T. (1991). 'The structural and pragmatic basis of an intonational reduction process in colloquial Norwegian', in Llisterri and Poch (1991), 25: 1–5.

FRIESEN, O. VON (1928). *Runorna i Sverige. En kortfattad översikt. Tredje omarbetade och utvidgade upplagan.* Föreningen Urds skrifter IV (Uppsala: J.A. Lindblads förlag).

FRØKJÆR-JENSEN, B., LUDVIGSEN, C., and RISCHEL, J. (1971). 'A glottographic study of some Danish consonants', in L. L. Hammerich, R. Jakobson, and E. Zwirner, *Form and Substance* (Festschrift for Eli Fischer-Jørgensen), (Copenhagen: Akademisk Forlag), 123–40.

GEDNEY, W. J. (1976). 'Notes on Tai Nuea', in T. W. Gething, J. G. Harris, and P. Kullavanijaya, *Tai Linguistics in Honor of Fang-Kuei Li* (Bangkok: Chulalongkorn University Press), 62–102.

GNERRE, M. C. (1986). 'Some notes on quantification and numerals in an Amazon Indian language', in M. P. Closs (1986), 71–91.

GREENBERG, J. H. (1978). 'Generalizations about numeral systems', in Greenberg, Ferguson, and Moravcsik (1978). 249–95.

—— FERGUSON, C. and MORAVCSIK, E. (eds) (1978). *Universals of Human Language.* Vol. 3 (Stanford: Stanford University Press).

GREENE, D. (1992). 'Celtic', in Gvozdanović (1992), 497–554.

GREGERSEN, F., ALBRIS, J. and PEDERSEN, I. L. (1991). 'Data and design of the Copenhagen study', in F. Gregersen and I. L. Pedersen, *The Copenhagen Study in Urban Sociolinguistics I* (Copenhagen: C.A. Reitzels), 5–39.

GRØNNUM, N. (1992). *The Groundworks of Danish Intonation. An Introduction* (Copenhagen: Museum Tusculanum Press).

GUIRAUD, P. (1960). *Problèmes et méthodes de la statistique linguistique* (Dordrecht: D. Reidel).

GVOZDANOVIČ, J. (1985). *Language System and its Change. On Theory and Testability.* (Trends in Linguistics, Studies and Monographs 30.) (Berlin, New York: Mouton de Gruyter).

—— (ed.) (1992). *Indo-European Numerals* (Trends in Linguistics, Studies and Monographs 57.) (Berlin, New York: Mouton de Gruyter).

HÆGSTAD, M. (1917). *Vestnorske maalføre fyre 1350*, vol. II, 2, second fasc. (Kristiania).

HAGSTRÖM, B. (1967). *Ändelsesvokalerna i färöiskan. En fonetisk-fonologisk studie* (= Acta Universitatis Stockholmiensis, New Series 6).

—— (1970). 'Supradentaler i färöiskan', *Fróðskaparrit* 18: 347–60.

HALLPIKE, C. R. (1979). *The Foundations of Primitive Thought.* (ch. 6: 'Number, measurement, analysis and conservation') (Oxford: Clarendon Press).

HAMMERSHAIMB, V. U. (1891). *Færøsk Anthologi* vol. I (reprinted 1947) (Copenhagen).

HAMP, E. P. (1967). 'Ever again on Danish Phonology', unpublished paper read before the Linguistic Circle of Copenhagen.

—— (1969). 'On Proto-Ainu numerals', in R. I. Binnick *et al.*, *Papers from the Fifth Regional Meeting of the Chicago Linguistic Society* (Chicago: Chicago Linguistic Society), 337–42.

—— (1975). 'Девяносто '90,' *Russian Linguistics* 2: 219–22.

—— (1982). 'Varia VII', *Ériu* 33: 178–83.

—— (1992). 'Albanian', in Gvozdanovič (1992), 835–921.

HAMRE, H. (1941). 'Om *u*-omlyd av *a* i færøysk', *Maal og Minne* 1941: 11–22.

—— (1944). *Færoymålet i tiden 1584–750* (Det norske Videnskaps-Akademi i Oslo).

—— (1967). 'Review of Mikjel Sørlie: En færøysk-norsk lovbok fra omkring 1310', *Scandinavian Studies* 39: 283–5.

HANSEN, Aa. (1956). *Udtalen i moderne dansk* (Copenhagen: Gyldendal).

—— (1967). *Moderne dansk. 1–3* (Copenhagen: Grafisk Forlag).

—— (1971). *Den lydlige udvikling i dansk II* (Copenhagen: G.E.C. Gad).

HANSEN, E. (1977). 'Infinitiv og bisætning som styrelse for præposition', *Danske Studier* 1977: 158–61.

—— (1980). 'Motorik und Lokalbestimmung einiger hochfrequenter verba ponendi im Dänischen', *Kopenhagener Beiträge zur Germanistischen Linguistik*, Sonderband 1: 189–98.

—— and LUND, J. (1983). *Sæt tryk på. Syntaktisk tryk i dansk* (Copenhagen: Lærerforeningens Materialeudvalg).

HARRIS, J. G. (1975). 'A comparative word list of three Tai Nüa dialects', in J. G. Harris and J. R. Chamberlain, *Studies in Tai Linguistics in Honor of William J. Gedney* (Bangkok: Central Institute of English Language, Office of State Universities), 202–30.

—— (1976). 'Notes on Khamti Shan', in T. W. Gething, J. G. Harris, and P. Kullavanijaya, *Tai Linguistics in Honor of Fang-Kuei Li* (Bangkok: Chulalongkorn University Press), 113–41.

HAUDRICOURT, A. G. (1965). 'Mutation consonantique en mon-khmer', *Bulletin de la Société Linguistique de Paris* 60: 160–72.

—— (1972). 'Two-way and three-way splitting of tonal systems in some Far-Eastern languages', in J. G. Harris and R. B. Noss, *Tai Phonetics and Phonology* (Bangkok: Central Institute of English Language, Mahidol University), 58–86. (First published in French in *Bulletin de la Société Linguistique de Paris* (1961) 56: 163–80).

HAUGEN, E. (1949). 'Phoneme or prosodeme?' *Language* 25: 278–82.

—— (1958). 'The phonemics of Modern Icelandic', *Language* 34: 55–88.

—— (1963). 'Pitch accent and tonemic juncture in Scandinavian', *Monatshefte* 55,4 (Heffner-Festschrift), 157–61.

—— (1969). 'Phonemic indeterminacy and Scandinavian umlaut', *Folia Linguistica* 3: 107–19.

—— (1976). *The Scandinavian Languages, An Introduction to their History* (Harvard and Cambridge University Press).

—— and JOOS, M. (1954). 'Tone and intonation in East Norwegian', *Acta Philologica Scandinavica* XXII: 41–64.

HELGASON, J. (1951). 'Kongsbókin úr Føroyum', *Utiseti* 6: 101–22.

—— (1952). 'Nøkur orð aftrat im Kongsbókina', *Utiseti* 7: 113–15.

HERDAN, G. (1956). *Language as Choice and Chance* (Groningen: P. Noordhoff).

—— (1958). 'The relation between the functional burdening of phonemes and their frequency of occurrence', *Language and Speech* 1: 8–13.

HESSELMAN, B. (1945). *Omljud och brytning i de nordiska språken. Förstudier till en nordisk språkhistoria* (Stockholm: Hugo Geber).

—— (1948–53). *Huvudlinjer i nordisk språkhistoria* = Nordisk Kultur vols. 3–4 (Uppsala: Schultz).

HILL, A. A. (1961). 'Suprasegmentals, prosodies, prosodemes', *Language* 37: 457–68.

HJELMSLEV, L. (1938). 'Essai d'une théorie des morphèmes', reprinted in
    Essais linguistiques (= Travaux du Cercle Linguistique de Copenhague XII,
    1959).
——(1939). 'The syllable as a structural unit', *Proceedings of the Third International
    Congress of Phonetic Sciences*: 266–72.
——(1951). 'Grundtræk af det danske udtrykssystem med særligt henblik på
    stødet', *Selskab for Nordisk filologi. Årsberetning for 1948–49–50*: 12–14. (English
    translation in 1973.)
——(1957). 'On unit accentuation', in *Bulletin du Cercle Linguistique de Copenhagen
    1941–65* (Copenhagen: Akademisk Forlag 1965), 202–5.
——(1973). 'Outline of the Danish expression system with special reference to the
    stød', *Travaux du Cercle Linguistique de Copenhague*, XIV (L. Hjelmslev: *Essais
    Linguistiques*, II), 248–66. (Danish original in 1951.)
HOCKETT, C. F. (1955). *A Manual of Phonology*. International Journal of American
    Linguistics 21, No. 4. (Baltimore: Waverley Press, Inc.).
——(1958). *A Course in Modern Linguistics* (New York: Macmillan, 3rd printing,
    1960).
HOLM, G. (1960). 'Om det nordiska *u*-omljudet', *Svenska Landsmål och Svenskt
    Folkliv* 1960: 79–136.
HOLTVED, E. (1951). *The Polar Eskimos I*, in *Meddelelser om Grønland*, vol. 152, I
    (Copenhagen: C.A. Reitzel).
——(1952). 'Remarks on the Polar Eskimo dialect', *International Journal of American
    Linguistics* XVIII: 20–4.
HUFFMANN, F. E. (1976*a*). 'The register problem in fifteen Mon-Khmer languages',
    Austroasiatic Studies I: 539–74.
——(1976*b*). 'The relevance of lexicostatistics to Mon-Khmer languages',
    Austroasiatic Studies I: 575–89.
HURFORD, J. R. (1975). *The Linguistic Theory of Numerals* (Cambridge Studies in
    Linguistics 16) (Cambridge: Cambridge University Press).
——(1987). *Language and Number* (Oxford: Basil Blackwell).
JACOB, J. M. (1965). 'Khmer numerals and numeral coefficients', in Milner and
    Henderson (1965). 143–62.
JACOBSEN, L. and MOLTKE, E. (1942). *Danmarks Runeindskrifter, Text.*
    (København: Einar Munksgaards Forlag).
JACOBSEN, M. A. and MATRAS, C. (1961). *Føroysk-donsk Orðabók*, 2nd edn.
    [1st edn. 1928] (Tórshavn: Føroya Fróðskaparfelag).
JAHR, E. H. (ed.) (1992). *Language Contact*. (Trends in Linguistics, Studies and
    Monographs 60) (Berlin, New York, Amsterdam: Mouton de Gruyter).
JAKOBSEN, J. (1891). Fonetisk Appendix i Hammershaimb (1891), 439–60.
JAKOBSON, R. (1952). 'Langues paléosibériennes', in Meillet and Cohen (1952),
    403–31.
——(1960). 'Closing statement: Linguistics and poetics', in Thomas A. Seebok, *Style
    in Language* (Cambridge, MA: MIT Press), 350–77.
—— and HALLE, M. (1956). *Fundamentals of Language* ('s-Gravenhage: Mouton).
—— FANT, G. M., and HALLE, M. (1961). *Preliminaries to Speech Analysis*.
    Fourth printing (Cambridge, Mass.: MIT Press). (First printing, 1952, Acoustic
    Laboratory, MIT.)

JENNER, P. N. (1976). 'Les noms de nombre en Mon-Khmer', in Diffloth and Zide (1976), 39–59.

JESPERSEN, O. (1913). 'Det danske stød og urnordisk synkope', *Arkiv för nordisk filologi* 29: 1–32.

—— (1934). *Modersmålets Fonetik* (Copenhagen: Gyldendal).

KARLGREN, H. (1962). 'Speech rate and information theory', in A. Sovijärvi and P. Aalto *Proceedings of the Fourth International Congress of Phonetic Sciences, Helsinki 1961* (The Hague: Mouton), 671–7.

KERR, A. F. G. (1924). 'The Khā Tawng Lûang', *Journal of the Siam Society, Bangkok* 28,2: 142–4.

KIEFER, F. (1972). Preprint for the conference on *Derivational Processes* in Stockholm–Åbo April 1972.

KING, R. D. (1971). 'Syncope and Old Icelandic i-umlaut', *Arkiv för nordisk filologi* 86: 1–18.

KINGSADA, T. and KOSAKA, R. (1999). 'Khabit' in T. Kingsada and T. Shintani, *Basic Vocabularies of the Languages Spoken in Phongxaly, Lao P. D. R.* (Tokyo: ILCAA), 22–42.

KIPARSKY, P. (1979). 'Metrical structure assignment is cyclic', *Linguistic Inquiry* 10: 421–41.

KISSEBERTH, C. W. (1970). 'On the functional unity of phonological rules', *Linguistic Inquiry* 1: 291–306.

KLOSTER JENSEN, M. (1958). 'Bokmålets tonelagspar ("Vippere")', *Årbok* (Universitetet i Bergen), Historisk-antikvarisk rekke nr. 2.

—— (1961). *Tonemicity* (Bergen: Norwegian Universities Press).

KOCK, A. (1888). 'i-omljudet och den samnordiska förlusten av ändelsesvokaler', *Arkiv för nordisk filologi* 4: 141–62.

—— (1896). 'Till frågan om *u*-omljudet i fornnorskan', *Arkiv för nordisk filologi* 12: 128–70.

—— (1901). *Die alt- und neuschwedische Akzentuierung* (Strassburg: Karl J. Trübner).

—— (1911–16). *Umlaut und Brechung* (Lund: Gleerup).

KOLSRUD, S. (1951). *Nynorsken i sine målføre* (Oslo: Jacob Dybvad).

KRATZ, H. (1960). 'The phonemic approach to umlaut in Old High German', *Journal of English and German Philology* 59: 463–79.

KRISTENSEN, M. (1898). 'Stødet i dansk. Småbidrag til dansk sproghistorie', *Arkiv för nordisk filologi* 15: 41–67.

KROMANN, E. (1947). *Musikalsk akcent i dansk* (Copenhagen: Ejnar Munksgaard).

KURYŁOWICZ, J. (1948). 'Contribution à la théorie de la syllabe', *Bulletin de la Société Polonaise de Linguistique* 8: 80–114.

LACHERET-DUJOUR, A. (1991). 'Phonological variations in read speech, reduction phenomena and speaker classes: do allophonic choices represent speaking style?', in Llisterri and Poch (1991). 38: 1–10.

LEENHARDT, M. (1952). 'Langues de l'Océanie', in Meillet and Cohen (1952), 675–90.

LEHISTE, I. (1960). 'An acoustic–phonetic study of internal open juncture', *Phonetica*, Suppl. ad Vol. 5.

LI, F.-K. (1977). *A Handbook of Comparative Tai* (University of Hawaii Press).

LIBERMAN, A. (1982). *Germanic Accentology I: The Nordic Languages* (Minneapolis: University of Minnesota Press).

LIBERMAN, M. and PRINCE, A. (1977). 'On stress and linguistic rhythm', *Linguistic Inquiry* 8: 249–336.

LINDBLOM, B., BROWNLEE, S., DAVIS, B., and MOON, S.-J. (1992). 'Speech transforms', *Speech Communication* 11, 4–5: 357–67.

LINELL, P. (1982). 'The concept of phonological form and the activities of speech production and speech perception', *Journal of Phonetics* 10: 37–72.

LLISTERRI, J. and POCH, D. (eds) (1991). *Proceedings of the Europoean Speech Communication Association Workshop on Phonetics and Phonology of Speaking Styles: Reduction and Elaboration in Speech Communication* (Barcelona).

LYNGE, H. (1955). *Inegpait* (= Meddelelser om Grønland 90,2).

MCCAWLEY, J. D. (1968). 'A note on Faroese vowels', *Glossa* 2: 11–16.

MARKSTRÖM, H. (1954). *Om utvecklingen av gammalt a framför u i nordiska språk* (Uppsala: Institutionen för Nordiska Språk vid Uppsala Universitet).

MARSTRANDER, C. J. S. (1952). 'De nordiske runeinnskrifter i eldre alfabet. Skrift og språk i folkevandringstiden', *Viking* 16: 1–277.

MARTINET, A. (1954). 'Accent et tons', *Miscellanea Phonetica* 2: 13–24.

MASE, H. and RISCHEL, J. (1971). 'A study of consonant quantity in West Greenlandic', *Annual Report of the Institute of Phonetics, University of Copenhagen* 5: 175–247.

MATRAS, C. (ed.) (1951–3). *Færoensia,* vol. III: *J. H. Schrøters Optegnelser of Sjúrðar Kvædi* (Hafniae: Ejnar Munksgaard).

——(ed.) (1966). *Dictionarium Færoense* (Societas Litterarum Færoensium Hafniensis).

MAYRHOFER, M. (1987). *Etymologisches Wörterbuch des Altindoarischen.* Vol. 1, n. 2 (Heidelberg: Carl Winter).

MEILLET, A. and COHEN, M. (eds) (1952–). *Les langues du monde par un groupe de linguistes sous la direction de A. Meillet et Marcel Cohen.* (Paris: Centre National de Recherche Scientifique).

MENNINGER, K. (1958). [1979] *Zahlwort und Ziffer* (Göttingen: Vandenhoeck und Ruprecht).

MERRIFIELD, W. R. (1968). 'Number names in four languages of Mexico', in Corstius (1968), 91–102.

MEY, J. L. (1969). 'Possessive and transitive in Eskimo', *Journal of Linguistics* 6: 47–56.

MILNER, G. B. and HENDERSON, E. J. A. (1965). *Indo-Pacific Linguistic Studies.* Part 2 (Amsterdam: North-Holland).

MOL, H. and UHLENBECK, E. M. (1959). 'Hearing and the concept of the phoneme', *Lingua* VIII: 161–85.

MOLBÆK HANSEN, P. (1991). 'The linguistic components of the Danish text-to-speech system', *Copenhagen Working Papers in Linguistics* 1: 153–62.

MOULTON, W. G. (1954). 'The stops and spirants of Early Germanic', *Language* 30: 1–44.

NGOURUNGSI PATAMADILOK, K. [thesis, s.a.]. *Outline of the Tai Ya Dialect,* University of Copenhagen (undated, from the 1980s [editors' note]).

NIELSEN, H. F. (2000). *The Early Runic Language of Scandinavia. Studies in Germanic Dialect Geography* (Heidelberg: Carl Winter Universitätsverlag).

—— (2002). 'Nordic–West Germanic relations', in O. Bandle *et al. The Nordic Languages I* (Berlin, New York: Walter de Gruyter), 558–68.

NIELSEN, K. M. (1960). 'Til runedanskens ortografi', *Arkiv för nordisk filologi* 75: 1–78.

NIMMANHAEMINDA, K. (1963). 'The Mrabri language', *Journal of the Siam Society* LI, Part 2: 179–83 + unpaginated word lists. ("Appendix I, Appendix II")

OHALA, J. J. (1974). 'Experimental historical phonology', in J. M. Anderson and C. Jones (eds.), *Historical Linguistics* II. *Theory and Description in Phonology.* Proceedings of the First International Conference on Historical Linguistics. Edinburgh, 2–7 Sept. 1973. (Amsterdam: North Holland), 353–89.

—— (1992). 'What is the input to the speech production mechanism?', *Speech Communication* 11, 4–5: 369–78.

O'NEIL, W. A. (1963). 'Domaine féroéen, The dialects of Modern Faroese: a preliminary report (1)', *Orbis* 12: 393–7.

—— (1964a), 'Review of: Chapman, Kenneth G.: *Icelandic-Norwegian Linguistic Relationships* = Norsk tidsskrift for Sprogvidenskab', supl. Bd. VII, 1962, 199 pp. *Scandinavian Studies* 36: 154–6.

—— (1964b), 'Faroese vowel morphophonemics', *Language* 40: 366–71.

OOTA, H., PAKENDORF, B., WEISS, G., VON HAESELER, A., POOKAJORN, S. *et al.* (2005). 'Recent origin and cultural reversion of a hunter-gatherer group', *Public Library of Science, Biology* 3(3): *e*71.

PAYNE, S. E. and CLOSS, M. P. (1986). 'A survey of Aztec numbers and their uses', in M. P. Closs, *Native American Mathematics* (Austin TX: University of Texas Press), 213–35.

PENZL, H. (1951). 'Zur Entstehung des *i*-umlauts im Nordgermanischen', *Arkiv för nordisk filologi* 66: 1–15.

PETERSEN, R. (1969/70). 'On phonological length in the Eastern Eskimo dialects', *Folk* 11–12: 329–44.

—— (1975). 'Sprog og dialekter', in P. Koch, *Grønland* (Copenhagen: Gyldendal), 194–204.

PHRA, W. W. (1926–7). 'Some information concerning the Phi Tong Luang obtained from a few residents in a village in the Nam Wa District East of Nan', *Journal of the Siam Society, Bangkok* 20, 2: 171–4.

PICARD, M. (1986). 'On the structure of the lower numbers in Pre-PA', *International Journal of American Linguistics* 52, 1: 72–7.

PIKE, K. L. (1967). *Language in Relation to a Unified Theory of the Structure of Human Behavior*, 2nd revised edn (The Hague, Paris: Mouton & Co.).

POLIBYENKO, T. G. and TXE, B. K. (1990). *Jazyk Ksingmul* (Moskva: Nauka).

POOKAJORN, S. and STAFF (eds) (1992). *The Phi Tong Luang (Mlabri): a Hunter-Gatherer Group in Thailand* (Bangkok: Odeon Store Publishers).

PREMSRIRAT, S. (1993). *Thai–Khmu–English Dictionary* (edited in Thai) (Mahidon University).

—— (2002). *Thesaurus of Khmu Dialects in Southeast Asia* (Salaya: Institute of Language and Culture for Rural Development, Mahidol University).

PRIETO, L. J. (1954). 'Traits oppositionnels et traits contrastifs', *Word* 10: 43–59.

PYLE, CH. (1972). 'On Eliminating BM's', mimeographed paper (Univ. of Michigan), in *Papers from the Eighth Regional Meeting Chicago Linguistic Society*, 14–16 April,

1972, eds P. M. Peranteau, J. N. Levi, and G. C. Phares. (Chicago, Ill.: Chicago Linguistic Society): 516–32.

RASMUSSEN, J. E. (1999). 'On the origin of the Germanic weak preterite', in *Selected Papers on Indo-European Linguistics* II (Copenhagen: Museum Tusculanum Press), 597–603.

RIAD, T. (1998). 'The origin of Scandinavian tone accents', *Diachronica* XV,1: 63–98.

——(2000). 'The origin of Danish *stød*', in A. Lahiri, *Analogy, Levelling, Markedness—Principles of Change in Phonology and Morphology* (Berlin, New York, Amsterdam: Mouton de Gruyter), 261–300.

RINGGAARD, K. (1980). 'The stød and the Scandinavian tonal accent', in E. Hovdhaugen, *The Nordic Languages and Modern Linguistics* (Oslo: Universitetsforlaget), 323–33.

RISCHEL, J. (1960). 'Über die phonematische and morphophononematische Funktion der sogenannten Worttöne im Norwegischen', *Zeitschrift für Phonetik und allgemeine Sprachwissenschaft* 13: 177–85. (Translated in 1983 into Norwegian.)

——(1961). 'Om retskrivningen og udtalen i moderne færøsk', in M. A. Jacobsen and C. Matras *Føroysk-Donsk orðabók*, 2nd edn (Tórshavn: Føroya Fróðskaparfelag), XIII–XXXVI.

——(1963). 'Morphemic tone and word tone in Eastern Norwegian', *Phonetica* 10: 154–61. Reprinted in E. H. Jahr and O. Lorentz (1983). *Prosodi/Prosody* 2: (Oslo: Novus), 266–73. [This volume chapter 10.]

——(1964a). 'Toward the phonetic description of Faroese vowels', *Fróðskaparrit* 13: 99–113.

——(1964b). 'Nogle udtryk for geografisk beliggenhed i færøsk', *Maal og Minne* 1964: 38–49.

——(1964c). 'Stress, juncture and syllabification in phonemic description', in H. G. Lunt, *Proceedings of the IXth Internatinal Congress of Linguists* 1962 (The Hague: Mouton & Co.), 85–93. [This volume chapter 6.]

——(1966). 'Studies of diphthongs in Faroese', *Annual Report of the Institute of Phonetics, University of Copenhagen* 1: 56–7.

——(1967). 'Phoneme, grapheme, and the "importance" of distinctions: functional aspects of the Scandinavian runic reform', *Research Group for Quantitative Linguistics (KVAL), Interim Report* No. 1 (Stockholm), 1–21. [This volume chapter 14.]

——(1969). 'Notes on the Danish vowel pattern', *Annual Report of the Institute of Phonetics, University of Copenhagen* 3: 177–205.

——(1970). 'Morpheme stress in Danish', *Annual Report of the Institute of Phonetics, University of Copenhagen* 4: 111–44.

——(1971a), 'A comment on lexical insertion', *Annual Report of the Institute of Phonetics, University of Copenhagen* 5: 73–90; also *International Journal of Dravidian Linguistics*, Vol. 1, No. 2, 1972: 84–99.

——(1971b), 'Some characteristics of noun phrases in West Greenlandic', *Acta Linguistica Hafniensia* XIII: 213–45.

——(1972). 'Compound stress in Danish without a cycle', *Annual Report of the Institute of Phonetics, University of Copenhagen* 6: 211–28. [This volume chapter 8.]

——(1974). *Topics in West Greenlandic Phonology* (Copenhagen: Akademisk Forlag).

——(1975). 'Problemer ved en generativ beskrivelse af dansk tryk', *Selskab for nordisk filologi, Årsberetning for 1971–73*, 22–32 (Copenhagen).

——(1980). 'Phrasenakzent als Signal des Objekts ohne "Determiner" im Dänischen', *Kopenhagener Beiträge zur Germanistischen Linguistik*, Sonderband 1: 262–79.

——(1981). 'Nogle komplicerende faktorer vedrørende verbers betoning i dansk', *Arbejdspapirer* II, JR1-16, Institut for Lingvistik (University of Copenhagen).

——(1982). 'Fieldwork on the Mlabri language: A preliminary sketch of its phonetics', *Annual Report of the Institute of Phonetics, University of Copenhagen* 16: 247–55.

——(1983*a*). 'On unit accentuation in Danish—and the distinction between deep and surface phonology', *Folia Linguistica* XVII: 51–97. [This volume chapter 9.]

——(1983*b*). 'Linguistics, phonetics, and fieldwork', *Annual Report of the Institute of Phonetics, University of Copenhagen* 17: 125–44.

——(1985). 'An appraisal of research on the phonetics and phonology of Thai', *Annual Report of the Institute of Phonetics, University of Copenhagen* 19: 43–93.

——(1986). 'Can the great tone split in Thai be phonetically explained?', *Annual Report of the Institute of Phonetics, University of Copenhagen* 20: 79–98.

——(1989*a*). 'Fifty years of research on the Mlabri Language: A re-appraisal of old and recent fieldwork data', *Acta Orientalia* 50: 49–78.

——(1989*b*). 'Can the Khmuic component in Mlabri ("Phi Tong Luang") be identified as Old T'in?', *Acta Orientalia* 50: 79–115.

——(1990). 'What is phonetic representation?' *Journal of Phonetics* 18: 395–410.

——(1991). 'The relevance of phonetics for phonology: a commentary', *Phonetica* 48: 233–62.

——(1992). 'Isolation, contact, and lexical variation in a tribal setting', in E. H. Jahr *Language Contact* (= Trends in Linguistics, Studies and Monographs 60) (Berlin, New York, Amsterdam: Mouton de Gruyter), 149–77.

——(1993). 'Lexical variation in two "Kammuic" languages', *Pan-Asiatic Linguistics, Proceedings of the Pan-Asiatic Conference on Languages and Linguistics* III: 1451–62 (Bangkok: Chulalongkorn University).

——(1995). *Minor Mlabri. A Hunter-Gatherer Language of Northern Indochina* (Copenhagen: Museum Tusculanum Press).

——(1997). 'Typology and reconstruction of numeral systems: the case of Austroasiatic', in J. Fisiak, *Linguistic Reconstruction and Typology* (Berlin, New York, Amsterdam: Mouton de Gruyter), 273–312. [This volume chapter 19.]

——(2000). 'The Dialect of Bernatzik's (1938) "Yumbri" Refound?' *Mon-Khmer Studies* 30: 115–22.

——(2001). 'Om stødets opkomst', *Pluridicta* 38: 16–25 (Odense: Institute of Language and Communication, University of Southern Denmark).

——(2002). 'The contribution of Scandinavian neogrammarians', in O. Bandle *et al. The Nordic Languages* I (Berlin, New York: Walter de Gruyter), 133–48.

——(2005). Preface (p. xi), Introduction (pp. xiii–xxxviii), Appendix (pp. 135–72), and Selected Bibliography (pp. 173–5) to Bernatzik (2005).

——(2006). 'The "definite article" in Mlabri', *Mon-Khmer Studies* 36: 61–102.

——and EGEROD, S. (1987). ' "Yumbri" (Phi Tong Luang) and Mlabri', *Acta Orientalia* 48: 19–33.

ROBERTS, A. R. (1961). Frequency of occurrence of segmental phonemes in American English (unpublished dissertation, Wisconsin).

ROMAINE, S. (1991). 'The status of variable rules in sociolinguistic theory', *Journal of Linguistics* 17: 93–119.

SALZMANN, Z. (1950). 'A method for analyzing numerical systems', *Word* 6: 78–83.

SANTESSON, L. (1989). 'En blekingsk blotinskrift', *Fornvännen* 84: 221–9.

SAUSSURE, F. DE (1916). *Cours de Linguistique Générale*, reprinted in 1968 (Paris: Payot); English translation *Course in General Linguistics* (1960).

SCHEUER, J. (1995). *Tryk på Danske Verber*, RASK Supplement Vol. 4 (Odense: Odense Universitetsforlag).

SCHOLES, R. J. (1971). *Acoustic Cues for Constituent Structure* (Janua Linguarum, Series Minor, 121).

SCHULTE, M. (1998). *Grundfragen der umlautphonemisierung* (Berlin: Walter de Gruyter).

SCHULTZ-LORENTZEN, C. W. (1927). *Dictionary of the West Greenland Eskimo Language* (= Meddelelser om Grønland LXIX).

——(1945). *A Grammar of the West Greenland Language* (re-issue 1967) (= Meddelelser om Grønland 129: 3).

SCHUMACHER, W. W. (1969). 'Zur Klassifizierung der Phi Tong Luang-Sprache.—Ein kommunikationsteoretischer Versuch', *Zeitschrift für Phonetik, Sprachwissenschaft und Kommunikationsforschung* 22,4: 360–3.

SEIDENFADEN, E. (1919). 'Further notes about Chaubun, etc.', *Journal of the Siam Society, Bangkok* 13,3: 47–53.

——(1927). 'The Kha Tong Lu'ang', *Journal of the Siam Society, Bangkok* 20,1: 41–8.

SEIP, D. A. (1954). *Palæografi. Norge og Island*, Nordisk Kultur XXVIII B. (Uppsala: Bonniers–Aschehoug–Schultz).

SELKIRK, E. O. (1978). *On Prosodic Structure and its Relation to Syntactic Structure.* Indiana University Linguistics Club. Also in T. Fretheim (ed.) *Nordic Prosody* II, 1980 (Trondheim: Tapir), 111–40.

——(1980). 'The role of prosodic categories in English word stress'. *Linguistic Inquiry* 11: 563–605.

SHEVOROSHKIN, V. (1987). 'Indo-European homeland and migrations', *Folia Linguistica Historica* 7: 227–50.

SHORTO, H. (1976). 'The vocalism of Proto-Mon-Khmer', *Austroasiatic Studies* II: 1041–67.

SIGURD, B. (1961). 'The code shift in Old Norse', *Studia Linguistica* XV: 10–21.

——(1988). 'Round numbers', *Language and Society* 17: 243–52.

SKÅRUP, P. (1959). 'Состав согласных Фарерского Языка' in *Вестник Ленинградского Университета* No 2, истории, Языка и литературы Выпуск: 160–5.

——(1964). *Rasmus Rask og færøsk*, Færoensia VI.

SKAUTRUP, P. (1944). *Det danske Sprogs Historie* I (Copenhagen: Gyldendal).

——(1947). *Det danske Sprogs Historie* II (Copenhagen: Gyldendal).

SKOMEDAL, T. (1980). 'Synkope, omlyd og bryting i nordisk', in E. Hovdhaugen *The Nordic Languages and Modern Linguistics* (Oslo: Universitetsforlaget), 120–39.

SMALLEY, W. A. (1961). *Outline of Khmu' Structure* (New Haven: American Oriental Society).

——(1963). 'Notes on Kraisri's and Bernatzik's Word Lists', *Journal of the Siam Society, Bangkok* 51,2: 189–201.

SMITH, K. D. (1976). 'North Bahnaric numeral systems', in Diffloth and Zide (1976), 61–3.

SØRLIE, M. (1936). *Færoysk tradisjon i norrønt mål.* (Oslo: Det Norske Videnskab-Akademi).

——(1965). *En færøysk-norsk lovbok fra omkring 1310: en studie i færøsk språkhistorie* (Tórshavn: Mentunargrunnur Føroya løgtings, Bergen-Oslo: Universitetsforlaget).

SOLÉ, M.-J. and OHALA, J. J. (1991). 'The phonological representation of reduced forms', in Llisterri and Poch (1991), 49: 1–5.

SOLNTSEV, V. M. *et al.* (1990). *Jazyk Ksingmul* (Moskva: Nauka).

SPORE, P. (1965). *La langue danoise* (Copenhagen: Akademisk Forlag).

SRIWISES, P. (1978). *Kui (Suai)–Thai–English dictionary* (Bangkok: Chulalongkorn University Language Institute).

STAMPE, D. (1976). 'Cardinal number systems', in S. S. Mufwene, C. A. Walker, and S. B. Steever (eds.), *Papers from the Twelfth Regional Meeting, Chicago Linguistic Society* (Chicago: Chicago Linguistic Society), 594–609.

STEBLIN-KAMENSKIJ, M. (1959). 'Concerning the three periods in the Scandinavian *i*-umlaut', *Arkiv för nordisk filologi* 74: 105–11.

STEENBERG, C. J. O. (1849). *Grønlandsk Grammatik* (Copenhagen: Salomon).

STRANGERT, E. (1987). 'Speech rhythm: data and preliminaries to a model', in K. Gregersen and H. Basbøll (eds.), *Nordic Prosody* IV (Odense: Odense University Press), 91–104.

SVABO, J. CHR. (1966, 1970). *Dictionarium Færoense*, ed. C. Matras (Copenhagen: Munksgaard).

SVANTESSON, J.-O. (1983). *Kammu Phonology and Morphology* (= Travaux de l'Institut de Linguistique de Lund XVIII) (Lund: CWK Gleerup).

——(1988). 'U', *Linguistics of the Tibeto-Burman Area* 11,1: 64–133.

——(1991). 'Hu—a language with unorthodox tonogenesis', in J. H. C. H. Davidson (1991), 67–79.

——TAYANIN, D., LINDELL, K., and LUNDSTRÖM, H. (2002). *Kammu–Yùan–English Dictionary.* Preliminary Edition (ms.)

SVERDRUP, J. (1924). 'Om idg. *bh *dh *gh i det eldste germansk', *Festskrift til Amund B. Larsen på hans 75-års fødselsdag 15. desember 1924.* (Kristiania: Forlagt av H. Aschehoug & Co).

SWADESH, M. (1946). 'South Greenlandic (Eskimo)', *Viking Fund Publ. in Anthropology* 6: 30–54.

SZEMERÉNYI, O. (1960). *Studies in the Indo-European System of Numerals* (Heidelberg: Carl Winter).

THALBITZER, W. (1923). 'The Ammassalik Eskimo. Contribution to the ethnology of the East Greenland natives (Part 2)', in *Meddelelser om Grønland* XL, 1921–1923 (Copenhagen: C.A. Reitzel).

THÊ', B. K. (2000). 'The Phong language of the Ethnic Phong which live near the Melhir Muong Pon Megalith in Laos', *Pan-Asiatic Linguistics, The Fifth International Symposium on Languages and Linguistics, Proceedings*, Vol. I (Hochiminh City: National University), 199–253.

THOMAS, D[AVID] (1976). 'South Bahnaric and other Mon-Khmer numeral systems', in Diffloth and Zide (1976), 65–80.
—— and HEADLEY, R. K. (1970). 'More on Mon-Khmer subgroupings', *Lingua* 15: 398–418.
THOMAS, D[OROTHY] (1976). *A Phonological Reconstruction of Proto-East-Katuic* (Work Papers Vol. XX, Suppl. 4.) Summer Institute of Linguistics North Dakota Session.
THONGKUM, T. L. (1984). *Nyah Kur (Choo Bon)–Thai–English dictionary*. (Monic Language Studies Vol. 2.) (Bangkok: Chulalongkorn University Printing House).
—— (1992). 'The language of the Mlabri (Phi Tong Luang)', in Pookajorn and Staff (1992): 43–65.
—— (1993). 'The raising and lowering of pitch caused by a voicing distinction in sonorants (nasals and approximants): an epidemic disease in SEA languages', *Pan-Asiatic Linguistics, Proceedings of the Third International Symposium of Language and Linguistics* Vol. III (Bangkok: Chulalongkorn University, Bangkok), 1079–87.
THORSEN, N. (1980). 'Word boundaries and F_0 patterns in advanced Standard Copenhagen Danish', *Phonetica* 37: 121–33.
—— (1983). 'Standard Danish sentence intonation—phonetic data and their representation', *Folia Linguistica* 17 (special issue on Prosody, edited by Hans Basbøll): 187–220.
TIENMEE, W. (1985). 'Classification by tone shapes and patterns of tonal splits and coalescences: Thai dialects of Thailand', paper for the *18th International Conference on Sino-Tibetan Languages and Linguistics*, 27–29 August 1985 (9pp.).
TINGSABADH, M. R. K. (1985). 'Some accents of Central Thai, a tonal study', paper for the *18th International Conference on Sino-Tibetan Languages and Linguistics*, 27–29 August 1985 (6pp.).
TRAGER, G. L. and SMITH, H. L. jr. (1951). *An Outline of English Structure*, SIL Occasional Papers 3.
TRIER, J. (1981). 'The Khon Pa of Northern Thailand, an Enigma', *Current Anthropology* 22,3: 291–3.
TRNKA, B. (1938). 'Phonological remarks concerning the Scandinavian Runic Writing', *Travaux du Cercle Linguistique de Prague* 8: 292–6.
TRUBETZKOY, N. S. (1939). 'Grundzüge der Phonologie', *Travaux du Cercle Linguistique de Prague* 7.
TWADDELL, W. F. (1938). 'A note on Old High German umlaut', *Monatshefte für deutschen Unterricht* 30: 177–81. Also in M. Joos (ed.) *Readings in Linguistics* I (Chicago and London: The University of Chicago Press), 85–7.
—— (1953). 'Stetson's Model and the "Suprasegmental Phonemes"', *Language* 29: 415–53.
VANOVERBERGH, M. (1937). *Some Undescribed Languages of Luzon* (Nijmegen: Dekker and van de Vegt N.V).
VOEGELIN, C. F. (1956). 'Linear phonemes and additive components', *Word* 12: 429–43.
WADSTEIN, E. (1894). *Der Umlaut von a bei nicht synkopiertem u im Altnorwegischen* (= *Skrifter utgifna af Humanistiska Vetenskapssamfundet i Uppsala* 3, 5) (Uppsala).
WANG, W. S.-Y. (1962). 'Stress in English', *Language Learning* 12: 69–77.

WEAVER, R. W. L. (1956). 'Through unknown Thailand', *Natural History,* 65: 289–95.

WEINREICH, U. (1954). 'Stress and word structure in Yiddish', *The Field of Yiddish,* published on the occasion of the bicentennial of Columbia University (U. Weinreich, ed.): 1–27.

WELLS, R. S. (1945). 'The pitch phonemes of English', *Language* 21: 27–39.

WERNER, O. (1963). 'Aspiration und stimmlose Nasale/Liquide im phonologischen System des Färingischen', *Phonetica* 9: 79–107.

——(1968). 'Welche Stufen phonematischer Reduktion sind für die Dialektgeographie sinnvoll? Das Vokalsystem des Färöischen', *Verhandlungen des zweiten internationalen Dialektologenkongresses*: 861–70 (Wiesbaden, Franz Steiner Verlag GMBH).

——(1970). 'Die Vokalisierung von *v* im Färöischen', in H. Benediktsson (ed.) *The Nordic Languages and Modern Linguistics* (Reykjavík, Vísindafélag Íslendinga), 599–616.

WESSÉN, E. (1968). *Die nordischen Sprachen* (= Grundriss der germanischen Philologie 4) (Berlin: Walter de Gruyter).

WIDMARK, G. (1959). *Det nordiska u-omljudet: En dialektgeografisk undersökning* (Uppsala: Institutionen för Nordiska Språk vid Uppsala Universitet).

WINTER, W. (1992). 'Some thoughts about Indo-European numerals', in Gvozdanović (1992), 11–28.

WULFF, K. (1934). *Chinesisch und Tai, Sprachvergleichende Untersuchungen*, Det Kgl. Danske Videnskabernes Selskab, Historisk-filologiske Meddelelser XX,3 (Copenhagen).

YOUNG, L. W. L. (1985). *Shan Chrestomathy* (Berkeley: Center for South and Southeast Asia Studies, University of California).

ZACHARIASEN, U. (1966). 'Skiftið millum framgóma- og afturgómaframburð av g og k í føroyskum', *Fróðskaparrit* 15: 74–90.

ZIDE, A. R. K. and N. H. ZIDE (1976). 'Proto-Munda cultural vocabulary: evidence for early agriculture', *Austroasiatic Studies* II (The University Press of Hawaii), 1295–334.

ZIDE, N. H. (1976). 'Introduction', in G. Diffloth and N. Zide (1976), 5–20.

——(1978). *Studies in the Munda numerals* (= Central Institute of Indian Languages Occasional Monograph Series 2.) (Mysore: Central Institute of Indian Languages).

AUTHOR INDEX

See the subject index for names of organizations. References to chapter notes are indicated as, e.g., 48n.

Abbs, James H. 5
Alnæs, Ivar 168n
Amundsen, Sigurd 313, 325, 328
Andersen, Henning 262n, 271n, 274n, 281
Andersen, Poul 30n, 288n
Anderson, Stephen R. 64, 66, 69n, 70–2
Antonsen, Elmer H. 263n, 265
Argente, Joan 19

Baader, Theodor 266
Bæksted, Anders 256n
Basbøll, Hans 104n, 126, 130, 276, 285, 289n
Beeler, Madison S. 391
Benediktsson, Hreinn 308, 309–10, 317n, 322, 340
Bergsland, Knut 344, 345, 353, 355
Bernatzik, Hugo Adolf 357, 418
Bierwisch, Manfred 109n
Bjerrum, Marie 65, 66, 69n
Bloomfield, Leonard 85, 173n, 356
Bolinger, Dwight L. 89, 93
Borgstrøm, Carl H. 94n
Braroe, Eva Ejerhed 276
Bresnan, Joan 153, 157
Broch, Tom 53n
Brøndum-Nielsen, Johannes 247, 273, 278, 289n
Brown, J. Marvin 213, 215–20, 221, 222, 225, 228, 229, 231, 232, 237, 238, 240–1
Bruce, Gösta 5
Bulck, Gaston van 373

Canger, Una 376n
Capell, Arthur 62n

Chapman, Kenneth G. 313, 330, 341n
Chomsky, Noam 36n, 41, 54, 67, 90, 103, 104, 113, 117, 119, 129
Christiansen, Hallfrid 341
Closs, Michael P. 375, 386n
Cohen, Marcel 373
Collis, Dermon Ronan F. 61n
Corstius, H. Brandt 386n

Davidsen, Jens 336
Diderichsen, Poul 28n, 257
Diffloth, Gérard 374, 387, 397, 399, 401, 402, 404n, 416
Dorais, Louis-Jacques 252
Dressler, Wolfgang U. 13, 22
Dyhr, Niels-Jørn 5

Egede, Hans 349
Egede, Paul 351, 352, 353
Egerod, Søren 213, 232, 358, 379, 380, 383, 399, 403n, 409
Eichner, Heiner 393, 396n
Ejskjær, Inger 36n, 276n
Eliasson, Stig 205n
Emmerick, Ronald E. 392
Engstand, Olle 4

Fabricius, Otho 251n, 350, 352, 353
Fant, Gunnar 11, 17
Ferguson, Charles A. 246
Ferlus, Michel 358, 418
Filbeck, David 358, 359, 361, 421, 425, 427
Firth, John Rupert 86
Fischer-Jørgensen, Eli 90, 103, 113n, 116, 118–19, 162, 190
Flatz, Gebhard 411

Foley, James 247
Fortescue, Michael 347
Friesen, Otto von 256
Frøkjær-Jensen, Børge 68n

Gerstman, Louis J. 93
Gnerre, Maurizio Covaz 375
Greenberg, Joseph 386n
Greene, David 384
Grønnum, Nina 5, 100, 136, 156, 165
Guiraud, Pierre 45n
Gvozdanovič, Jadranka 386

Hægstad, Marius 313, 337n
Hagström, Björn 64, 75n, 314n, 322n
Halle, Morris 36n, 41, 45–6, 67, 103,
    104n, 113, 117, 119, 129
Hallpike, Christopher R. 373, 386n
Hammershaimb, Vinceslaus
    Ulricus 335n
Hamp, Eric 27, 28, 383, 392, 393, 394,
    395
Hamre, Håkon 313, 331n, 334, 336n,
    338, 341
Hansen, Aage 28n, 248n
Hansen, Erik 137n, 139n, 141–2, 143n,
    145n
Hansen, Peter Molbæk see Molbæk
    Hansen, Peter
Haudricourt, André G. 218, 233
Haugen, Einar 67n, 87, 89, 168, 169,
    248n
Headley, Robert K. 378
Helgason, Jón 313
Herdan, Gustav 45n, 49
Hesselman, Bengt 274–5
Hill, Archibald 87
Hjelmslev, Louis 26, 41n, 87, 116,
    118
Hockett, Charles F. 48, 50, 90–1,
    94n
Hoff, Ingeborg 174n
Holtved, Erik 252, 354
Huffmann, Franklin E. 415, 425
Hurford, James R. 386n

Jacobsen, Birgitte 4
Jacobsen, Lis 270n

Jakobsen, Jakob 314n, 324n, 328n,
    337n, 342n
Jakobson, Roman 19, 28, 36, 45–6, 86,
    373, 382
Jenner, Philip N. 387, 390, 397
Jensen, Martin Kloster see Kloster
    Jensen, Martin
Jespersen, Otto 128, 148, 149, 151, 152
Jordan, David 359

Karlgren, Hans 12–13
Kiefer, Ferenc 54
Kingsada, Thongpheth 358
Kiparsky, Paul 131, 204
Kleinschmidt, Samuel 348, 350, 352–3
Kloster Jensen, Martin 48, 49–50, 173n
Kock, Axel 273, 274, 278, 280–1, 299
Kolsrud, Sigurd 331n
Kosaka, Ryunichi 358
Kristensen, Marius 275
Kromann, Erik 288n
Kruckenberg, Anita 11, 17
Kurylowicz, Jerzy 94n

Lacheret-Dujour, Anne 17
Leenhardt, Maurice 373
Lehiste, Ilse 92
Li, Fang-Kuei 218, 223n
Liberman, Anatoly 275
Liberman, Mark 100, 127, 128, 131,
    135, 275
Lindblom, Björn 5, 18, 19
Linell, Per 5
Lukoff, Fred 117
Lund, Jørn 137n, 139n, 145n
Lynge, Hans 185–6, 195

Marstrander, Carl J.S. 260n
Martinet, André 88n
Mase, Hideo 59n
McCawley, James D. 64
Meillet, André 373
Menninger, Karl 385n, 392
Mey, Jacob L. 55
Mol, Hendrik 51
Molbæk Hansen, Peter 4
Moltke, Erik 270n
Moulton, William G. 267

Nedergaard Thomsen, Ole *see* Thomsen, Ole Nedergaard
Ngourungsi Patamadilok, Kanchana 232–3
Nielsen, Hans Frede 271n, 273
Nimmanhaeminda, Kraisri 357, 381–2

Ohala, John J. 5, 25, 198n, 205
O'Neil, Wayne A. 64, 69n, 313n, 314n

Payne, Stanley E. 375
Penzl, Herbert 298n
Petersen, Robert 56n, 185, 187, 189, 192, 249n, 347, 350
Picard, Marc 373
Pike, Kenneth L. 87n, 92n
Ponette, Pierre 372
Premsrirat, Suwilai 358, 424
Prieto, Luis J. 88n
Prince, Allan 100, 127, 128, 131, 135
Proschan, Frank 379n
Pyle, Charles 115

Rasmussen, Jens Elmegård 291n
Resen, Peder Hansen 349
Riad, Tomas 275, 285, 288n
Roberts, A.R. 45n

Salzmann, Zdenee 382–3, 385n
Santesson, Lillemor 281, 301n
Saussure, Ferdinand de 94n
Scheuer, Jann 4
Schrøter, Jóhan Hendrik 336n, 337
Schulte, Michael 276
Schultz-Lorentzen, Christian Wilhelm 61n, 185
Seip, Didrik Arup 266n
Selkirk, Elisabeth 96, 99–100, 127, 128, 136
Shevoroshkin, Vitaliy 393
Shorto, Harry 420
Sigurd, Bengt 257, 377
Skårup, Povl 337n
Skautrup, Peter 247–8, 249
Smalley, William Allen 415
Smith, Henry Lee jr, 91
Smith, Kenneth D. 401
Solé, Maria-Josep 25

Solntsev, Vadim Mikhajlovič 358
Sørlie, Mikjel 313
Stampe, David 372
Steenberg, Carl Junius Optatus 353
Stoneking, Mark 361
Sullivan, Thelma D. 375
Svabo, Jens Christian 74n, 75n, 312n, 336n, 336
Svantesson, Jan-Olof 358, 364, 379n, 388n, 402
Swadesh, Morris 58, 415
Szemerényi, Oswald 394

Thalbitzer, William 185, 186, 192, 195, 387
Thê', Bui Khan 358
Thomas, David 378, 379, 390, 397, 400, 401–2
Thomas, Dorothy 402
Thomsen, Ole Nedergaard 4
Thongkum, Therapan L. 14
Thorsen, Nina *see* Grønnum, Nina
Tienmee, Wanna 229
Tingsabadh, M.R. Kalaya 238
Touati, Paul 5
Trager, George L. 91
Trnka, Bohumila 257
Trubetzkoy, Nikolai 89
Twaddell, W. Freeman 87

Uhlenbeck, Eugenius M. 51

Vanoverbergh, Morice 372
Verluyten, Paul 100

Wang, William S.-Y. 88n
Weinreich, Uriel 90
Wells, Rulan S 87n
Werner, Otto 64, 68, 73, 317n, 322n
Winter, Werner 392, 394, 395, 396
Wulff, Kurt 218

Young, Linda Wai Ling 232

Zachariasen, Ulf 339
Zide, Arlene R.K. 411
Zide, Norman H. 371, 390–1, 397, 399, 403, 405, 411

SUBJECT INDEX

References to notes are indicated as, e.g. 57n.

Languages are entered under the names used in the text, e.g. Prai and Mal are treated as dialects of Tin; most references for Inuktitut are entered under 'Greenlandic dialects' or 'West Greenlandic.'

ablaut 66
adverbial complements, unit
    accentuation 143–4
affixes
    Mon-Khmer languages 366–7
    Norwegian 171, 173–4
    West Greenlandic 54–63
affricates 71
age-related variation in language 17,
    192–3
agreement 61–2
Ainu 384
Albanian 393
Algonquian languages 373
allative case 62, 192
allomorphy 24–5
    Danish 30–5
allophones 26–43
allotones 218
Alluitsoq dialect 191
alternation
    Danish 30–43
    Faroese 69–71
    West Greenlandic 196–7, 198,
      343–8
    with zero *see* deletion
American Indian languages 373
Ammassalik dialect 185
Anatolian 393, 396n
Ancient Nordic 273, 274, 279–80,
    281–2, 286–7, 304–5, 306–7
Ancient Thai 216, 217, 218, 365
areal effects 217
Armenian 394

articles 138, 144, 145–7, 152
aspiration
    Danish 28
    Faroese 67, 68
assibilation 205n
assimilation
    Faroese 72, 74n, 75–7, 79, 80
    West Greenlandic 193–6, 353–5
asymmetric systems 180, 181–2,
    183–210
Atayal 383
Austroasiatic numerals 369–407
    base number 371–3
    functional aspects 376–87
    inherent properties 370–6
    Mon-Khmer languages 372, 378–82,
      383–5
auxiliary + main verb constructions
    142–3
Aztec 373, 375–6

baby talk 19
Bantu languages 373
base number 371–3
blocking
    Danish 144–5, 146–7
    West Greenlandic 61–2
borrowing *see* loan words
boundary markers 115
breaking 302, 304, 317n

Canadian Inuktitut dialects 251–2
Cape Farewell dialect 184–5, 187–97,
    347–8

case marking
  Nordic languages 301
  West Greenlandic 55, 62, 192
causative 366–7
Central Thai 211, 215, 220, 221,
  222, 229, 238–9, 239–40
Central West Greenlandic 184,
  346–7
checked syllables 213, 228
Chipewyan 382–3
Chumash languages 391
'closing' system 324–31
coalescence
  Ancient Nordic 308
  Old Nordic 278–9
  Old West Scandinavian 325–6,
    333–4
  and speech perception 50
  Thai 212, 216, 222, 223–4
collective nouns 371
commutation principle 86
comparative methodology 362–8,
  418–20, 429–38
compounds 103–15, 130–4, 159–60
consonant systems
  cluster simplification 66–81
  Danish 26–43, 46–7, 247–9
  diachronic universals 247–52
  English 49
  Faroese 64–81
  Greenlandic dialects 249–52
  Khmuic languages 424–6
  and language change 361, 424–6
  Mlabri 424, 425–6, 439
  Scandinavian runic writing 266–71
  strong vs. weak position 28–9,
    42–3
  Thai 212, 216, 223–5, 365
  Tin 425–6
contrast
  phonemes 48–51, 226–8
  tone 169, 220, 288
Copenhagen school 118
counting, points of reference 372–3,
  374–6, 382–4, 387–96
cross-linguistic differences 12–13
culminative contrasts 90–1

culture 378–9, 384, 410–12, 413–14
cyclic rules 103, 131–2

Danish
  age-related variation 17
  consonant system 26–43, 46–7, 247–9
  loan words 29–30, 121–2, 123–4, 248n
  Old Danish 123, 291n
  phonological rules 35–43, 103–15,
    116, 131–2, 135–7
  quasi-compounds 122
  semivowels 29, 32–4, 35, 42
  stød 126, 273, 275, 276n, 284–6,
    287–8, 289, 290–1, 305–6
  stress 4–5, 98, 100–2, 103–15, 116–66,
    285–6
  style variation 23
  syntax/semantics 137–52
  tonal dialects 288
  vowel system 37, 38, 39–40, 310
  writing system 247–9
'Danish' runes 255
data collection 3–4, 9–11
  audio recordings 187
  cross-language comparisons 418–20,
    429–38
  elicitation 8, 9
  questionnaires 187–8
  transcription methods 4–5, 23–4, 95,
    120, 320–2
dative plurals 301
deep structure, and stress placement
  155–66
deletion
  Danish 34–5
  Faroese 69–70, 75, 77, 78–9, 80
  West Greenlandic 344
depth of compounding 106, 108–12
derivation 54–63
determiners 146–7
devoicing 343–55
diachronic universals 245–53
diphthongs
  Faroese 312–42
  Kammu (Khmu') 419
  West Greenlandic 193, 194
directional affixes 57–8

directionality 205–10
discontinuous elements, stress
    patterns 152–5
Disko Bay dialect 184

Early Ancient Nordic 273, 287, 298, 303
East Greenlandic 184, 186, 191, 192,
    347
Eastern Canadian Inuktitut 251–2
Eastern Eskimo (Inupiaq) 345
Eastern Norwegian, tonal accents
    167–74
elicitation 8, 9
enclisis 58–62, 288
English
    consonant system 49
    stress 85, 90–1, 94, 113
    vowel system 225
entropy 48
epenthesis
    Nordic languages 310–11
    West Greenlandic 178–9
Eskimo see East Greenlandic;
    Greenlandic dialects; Inuktitut;
    Inupiaq; Polar Eskimo; West
    Greenlandic; Yupik; East
    Greenlandic

Faroese
    assimilation 72, 74n, 75–7, 79, 80
    consonant system 64–81
    deletion 69–70, 75, 77, 78–9, 80
    dialects 65, 314–16
    diphthongs 312–42
    influence of Norwegian 329–30
    neutralization 68, 80
    palatal shift 338–40
    vowel system 308, 309, 310, 317–42
    writing system 65, 66n, 80n
final consonants, Danish 29–30
foot structure, intonation 99, 100–2,
    136–7, 156, 161–5
formal linguistics see linguistics
fortis/lenis contrast 266–71
fricatives
    Ancient Nordic 289–91
    Danish 29, 30–43, 247–9

Greenlandic dialects 249–52, 349–53
Proto-Scandinavian 266–71
Thai 214
West Greenlandic 343–55
functional load 44–53, 86–7, 225

gemination, West Greenlandic 344,
    345–8
generalizability, phonological rules 22
generational differences in language
    17
generative phonology 116–19
genetic relationships, languages 358–62,
    415–40
Germanic languages, stress 90–3
gestures 381
glides 297, 305
    Faroese 69n
Greek 394, 395
Greenlandic dialects 183–210, 249–52,
    346–8, see also East Greenlandic;
    West Greenlandic
    numeral systems 61–2, 374–5, 376
    writing system 348–55

'Hälsinge' runes 255
hand, as counting unit 372–3, 374–5,
    376, 382–4, 387–96
hiatus 292–3, 297
hierarchical models 21–2, 47–8, 52–3
    prosody 96–102
    stress patterns 116, 119–66
Hittite 396n
Hyperborean languages 373

i-dialect, Greenlandic 183–210
i-umlaut 272, 274–5, 275–6, 277–82
iambic reversal 135–6
Icelandic 324, 338
    cluster simplification 80
    vowel system 181, 182, 225, 308,
    309
idioms 149–50
Ilongot 372
implicational hierarchies 21–2
Indo-Aryan 393
Indo-European numerals 386, 391–6

inherent stress 121–6
initial consonants, Danish 29–30
intergroupal variation 19
intonation
    Danish 100–2
    intonational foot structure 99, 100–2,
        136–7, 156, 161–5
    motherese 19
intra-word unit accentuation 128–30
Inuktitut 251–2, *see also* Greenlandic
    dialects
Inupiaq 345, 346, *see also* Greenlandic
    dialects
invariant forms 6–7

juncture 92–3, 115

Kammu (Khmu') 358–9, 364, 365–6,
    367, 379, 402, 403, 415, 419–20,
    421, 434–5, 437
    consonant system 424
    vowel system 428, 429
Kap Farvel dialect 184–5, 187–97,
    347–8
Khmer 372, 389–90, 396, 402
Khmuic languages 358–62, 378–82,
    383–5, 387–90, 400, 415–18,
    see also Mlabri
    and Tinic 420–4
Ksing Mul 358

labialization, West Greenlandic 190,
    194, 195–6
language change
    consonant systems 361, 424–6
    diachronic universals 245–53
    effect on writing systems 255–71
    and prosodic structure 272–311
    tone split 211–42
    vowel systems 322–38, 340–2, 361,
        427–9
Lao dialect 219, 220, 221, 222, 228,
    229, 236–8, 239–40, 365
Late Ancient Nordic 273, 288, 298, 303
left-branching structures 106, 133–4
lexical insertion 115

lexical variation 357, 397–9, 400–6,
    409–10, 416–17, 440
lexicalization hypothesis 199–200
lexicon
    cross-language comparisons 362–8
    traditional vocabulary 363–4
linguistics 3–25
    methodology 3, 4–7
    theoretical questions 14–25
loan words
    Chumash languages 391
    Danish 29–30, 121–2, 123–4, 248n
    Mlabri 357, 362–4, 364–5, 380–1,
        419–20, 434–5, 437
    Mon-Khmer languages 378, 384,
        425–6
    Munda languages 399
    West Greenlandic 177–9, 199–200,
        203–5
long vs. short languages 12–13
Low German, loan words in
    Danish 123–4, 248n, 306
Lua' 412

magic, and writing systems 256
Mal (Tin dialect) 359–60, 416, 425
Maniitsoq dialect 184
mass nouns 144–5
matching, consonants 29–30
Melanesian languages 373
metric rules 293
metrical grids 135–6
metrical phonology 96–7
minimal pairs 48–51
minus-juncture 92
mixed languages *see* Mlabri
Mlabri 356–68, 402, 403
    consonant system 424, 425–6, 439
    lexical variation 357, 362, 409–10,
        416, 417, 440
    loan words 357, 362–4, 364–5, 380–1,
        419–20, 425–6, 434–5, 437
    morphology 420–1
    numeral systems 379, 380–1, 399
    related languages 358–68, 415–40
    vowel system 427–8, 429

Mlabri people, origins and history 408–14, 440
Mon-Khmer languages 217, 358–62, *see also* Mlabri
  numeral systems 372, 378–82, 383–5, 387–90, 397–406, 407
  Thai loan words 364–5, 378
  word formation 366–7
Monic 401, 402, 403–4
mora-based models 272, 274, 282–3, 286–96
morphemes
  stress patterns 121–6, 158
  tonal accents 167–74
morphology
  Danish 26–43, 121–6
  Mlabri 420–1, 439
  Nordic languages 301–2
  Norwegian 167–74
  numeral systems 373
  Old Nordic 278
  Tin 367–8, 420–1
  West Greenlandic 54–63, 192, 196–7, 199–202
motherese 19
movement transformations, Danish 152–3, 154–7, 165–6
Munda languages 372, 382, 391, 399, 403–4, 405

naked objects 150–1
national languages 222
natural speech 3–5, 7–8
neutralization 46–7
  Faroese 68, 80
  Norwegian 171
Nordic languages 272–311
  phonological rules 292–6
  vowel systems 272–3, 274–5, 276–83, 307–11
North Alaskan Inupiaq 346, *see also* Greenlandic dialects
North Bahnaric 401
Northern Thai dialect 219, 221, 222, 228, 230–1, 239

Norwegian
  influence on Faroese 329–30
  tonal accents 167–74, 275, 284–6, 287, 288
  vowel system 308
noun phrases
  affixation processes 55–8
  Danish 139–42
  unit accentuation 139–42
  West Greenlandic 55–8
nuclear stress 129
numeral systems
  Aztec 373, 375–6
  base number 371–3
  Chumash languages 391
  functional aspects 376–87
  gestures 381
  Greenlandic dialects 61–2, 374–5, 376
  inherent properties 370–6
  lexical variation 397–9, 400–6
  loan words 378
  Mlabri 379, 380–1
  Mon-Khmer languages 372, 378–82, 383–5, 387–90, 397–406, 407, 416
  Munda languages 372, 382, 391, 399, 403–4, 405
  nursery rhymes 378–9, 384
  points of reference 372–3, 374–6, 382–4, 387–96
  psychological salience 373–4
  Shuar 373, 375, 376
  Tin 379–80, 381–5
  universals 373–4, 386n
  West Greenlandic 61–2
nursery rhymes 378–9, 384
Nuuk dialect 184

obstruents *see also* fricatives; stops
  Danish 28, 36n, 37
  Faroese 68, 69, 78
  Scandinavian runic writing 266–71
  Thai 214–15
  West Greenlandic 343–55
Old Danish 123, 291n
Old Icelandic 310

Old Mon 403–4
Old Nordic 273, 275, 278, 280, 287, 299, 309, 310
Old Norse 291n
Old Scandinavian 258–71
Old West Scandinavian 312, 316–17
    relationship with Modern Faroese 322–38, 340–2
open juncture 93
'opening' system 331–2
orthography *see* writing systems
Ossetic 394

Paamiut dialect 184
palatals, Faroese 71, 76–7, 338–40
Palaungic 401, 402
paradigmatic units 88–9
pasong-group 401–2
personal pronouns, Danish 139
phatic communication 19
phonemes 125, *see also* prosodemes; tonemes
    definition 89–90
    functional load 44–53, 86–7
    measurement of frequency 46
    and measurement of tempo 16–17
    and psychological reality 6
    segmentals 45–6, 50
    suprasegmentals 45–6, 126
    transition probabilities 44–5
phonetics, research methods 4–7, 9–11, 46–8
Phong 358, 422, 423
phonological phrase 99, 100
phonological rules 14–25
    constraints 205–10
    cyclic rules 103, 131–2
    Danish 35–43, 103–15, 116, 131–2, 135–7
    Faroese 66–81, 318–19, 322–38
    generalizability 22
    implicational hierarchies 21–2
    Nordic languages 292–6
    reduction 20–5
    vowel harmony 176–83
    West Greenlandic 58–9, 197–210

phonology *see also* consonant systems; names of individual languages and language groups; vowel systems
    deep vs. surface structure 155–66
    diachronic universals 245–53
    generative approach 116–19
    measurement of functional load 48–53
    research methods 4–7, 20, 24–5, 46–8
    theoretical questions 14–25
phrasal unit accentuation 4–5, 134–6, 155–66
pitch
    Danish 113, 114
    Thai 214–15, 218–19
place of articulation 71, 72, 80
Polar Eskimo 184, 185, 252, 354, *see also* Greenlandic dialects; West Greenlandic
polysynthetic languages 199–200
    West Greenlandic 54–63, 183–210
possessives, West Greenlandic 55–7
Prai (Tin dialect) 359–60, 366, 416, 425
pram-group 401
predicates, Danish 144–7
prepositional phrases, Danish 140–2
prominence 120
pronouns, Danish 139
prosodemes 85, 87–8, 89–92, 126, *see also* tonemes
    definition 89–90
prosodic islands 288
prosodic word 99, 272
prosody
    compounding rules 131–2
    description of 47–8, 85–95, 96–102
    and metrical phonology 96–7
    Nordic languages 272–311
    rules 170–4
    and segmental phonemes 86
    and syntax 99–102
    West Greenlandic 59
Proto-Algonquian 373
Proto-Austroasiatic 390–1
Proto-Fringe-Greenlandic 186
Proto-Germanic 266

Proto-Indo-European 373, 386, 392–3, 394, 396
Proto-Kartvelian (Georgian) 393
Proto-Khmer 401
Proto Monic 402
Proto-Scandinavian 258–71
Proto-Thai 211, 216, 239
proto-tone *A 230–9, 240
psychological reality 6, 197–8
psychological salience, numerals 373–4

quantifiers 371
    Danish 138
    Mon-Khmer languages 378, 380–1
quasi-compounds 122
questionnaires 187–8

real speech *see* natural speech
reduction
    Danish 104–12, 118–19
    effect on speech perception 15–16
    Faroese 64–81
    measurement 16–17
    rules 20–5
    stress patterns 104–12, 118–19
reliability 10–11, 24–5, 246–7, 252, 432
research methods 9
    cross-language comparisons 362–8, 418–20, 429–38
    data collection *see* data collection
    diachronic universals 245–53
    measurement of phenomena 16–17
    phonetics/phonology 4–7, 20, 24–5
    reliability 10–11, 24–5, 246–7, 252, 432
    transcription 4–5, 23–4, 46–8, 95, 120, 320–2
    validity 251
research questions 14–25
rhythm, and stress 91, 112, 272–3, 273–4, 282–3, 286, 294–6
right-branching structures 132–3
root morphemes, Norwegian 171, 172–3
rules *see* phonological rules
runic writing 254–71

sandhi processes 59
Santali 399
Scandinavian runic writing 254–71
    consonant system 266–71
    vowel system 260–6
Scoresbysund dialect 185
secondary stress, compound nouns 112, 114, 118–19
segmental phonemes 45–6, 50
    and prosody 86
segmentation
    effect of tempo 22–4
    and spellings 354
semantic unity 148–9
semantics
    Danish 137–52
    and prosodic structure 137–52
semivowels
    Danish 29, 32–4, 35, 42
    Faroese 71–2, 73
Semoq Beni (South Aslan) 399
sequential description, methodological problems 46–8
Shan dialect 219, 220, 221, 222, 228, 232–4, 239
short vs. long languages 12–13
Shuar 373, 375, 376
sibilants
    Faroese 78–9
    West Greenlandic 344–5
simplification
    consonant clusters 66–81
    morphology 278–9
    stress patterns 108–12
Sisimiut dialect 184
situational variation 19
sk-metathesis 74–5, 80
Slavonic languages 373
sociolinguistic variation 432–4, 440
sonorants
    Faroese 67–8, 71, 77–9
    Thai 214, 224
sound shifts 255–71, 416, 419, 420
South Jutland dialects 288
South Munda 391
Southern Thai dialect 221–2, 229, 234–6, 239

speech perception
  effect of coalescence 50
  effect of reduction 15–16
speech tempo 6, 9–25
  effect on phonological variants 14–25
  effect on stress patterns 98
spelling *see* writing systems
spirants 70
standardized languages 222
stød 126, 273, 275, 276n, 284–6, 287–8,
    289, 290–1, 305–6
stops
  Danish 28–9, 30–1, 35–8, 40–1, 247–9
  Faroese 67–70, 71, 72, 75, 76, 79–80
  Mlabri 437–8, 439
  Proto-Scandinavian 266–71
  Thai 214, 223
stratification 99–102
strengthening 248–9, 343–55
stress 45–6, 85–6, 87, 89–93
  compounds 103–15, 130–4
  culminative contrasts 90–2
  Danish 4–5, 98, 100–2, 103–15,
    116–66, 285–6
  deep vs. surface structure 155–66
  definition 120–1
  degrees of 112, 114, 117–19, 120–1
  Germanic languages 90–3, 94
  hierarchical rules 97–102, 104–15, 116
  juncture 92–3
  morphemes 121–6
  neutralization 171
  nuclear stress 129
  and rhythm 91, 112, 272–3, 273–4,
    282–3, 286, 294–6
  and stød 285–6
  syllabicity 93–4
  tree structures 129–30, 132–4, 135
  unit accentuation 100–2, 116–66
stridents 41
strong position 28–9, 42–3
styles 12, 17, 18–19
  age-related variation 18
  allomorphs 24–5
  effect on stress patterns 98, 100–2,
    109–10

suffixes
  Norwegian 171, 173–4
  West Greenlandic 196–7, 199–200
suprasegmentals 45–6, 85, 87–8, 89–92
  stød 126
  tonemes 167–74
surface structure
  and stress placement 124–5, 155–66
  and vowel harmony 193
'Swedish-Norwegian' runes 255
Swedish, tonal accents 275, 284–6, 287,
    288
syllabic function 259–60
syllabicity 93–4, 97
syllables
  borders 93, 216
  checked vs. unchecked 213, 221, 228
  definition 87
  structure 52–3, 422
syncope 272–3, 274–5, 276, 282–3, 288,
    289–92, 295–6, 298–305, 308–9
syntagmatic units 88, 89
syntax
  Danish 137–55
  and prosodic structure 99–102,
    137–55
  West Greenlandic 60–2

Tai languages 217
tempo *see* speech tempo
tenseness 36n, 318
terminology, definitions 120–1
Thai
  allotones 218
  consonant system 212, 216, 223–5,
    365
  dialects 212, 220–2, 230–41
  history of 214–20, 223–5, 228–9,
    364–5
  loan words in Mon-Khmer
    languages 364–5, 378, 380–1, 384,
    425–6, 434–5
  proto-tones 211, 212–13
  standardization 222
  tonal systems 211–42
  writing system 212–13, 222, 365

Tin
   consonant system 425–6
   lexical variation 416, 417
   morphology 420–1
   numeral system 379–80, 381–5, 388n,
      389, 399
   relationship with Mlabri 358, 359–64,
      365–8, 408–9, 412, 414, 415, 418–40
   vowel system 427–8
Tinic 420–4, 440
tone 45–6
   allotones 218
   contrast 169, 220
   Norwegian 167–74, 284–6, 287
   rules 170–4
   split 212–13, 214–20
   and stød 273, 275, 276n, 284–6
   Swedish 275, 284–6, 287
   Thai 211–42
tonemes 50, 85, 89, *see also* phonemes;
      prosodemes
Tórshavn dialect 313–14
trade languages 383
traditional vocabulary 363–4
transcription 4–5, 23–4, 95, 120, 320–2
transition probabilities 44–5
Turi 372, 382
Turkish, vowel harmony 176
typology
   Austroasiatic languages 369–407
   cross-language comparisons 362–8
   numeral systems 369–407
   sound change 246–7
   stress patterns 165
   Thai dialects 239–40
   tone split 228–30, 239–40
   vowel systems 303

U (Angkuic language) 388n
umlaut 66, 181, 182, 192, 272, 274–5,
   275–6, 277–82, 289–90, 291–2,
   293–4, 298–305, 307–11
unchecked syllables 213, 221
unilinearity principle 86
unit accentuation 100–2, 116–66, *see
   also* stress

universals 245–53, 373–4, 386n
Upernavik dialect 184, 185, 186, 187,
   191
Uummannaq dialect 184

validity 252
variation in language 6–7
   age factor 17, 192–3
   allomorphs 24–5
   lexical variation 440
   lexicon 357, 397–9, 400–6, 409–10,
      416–17
   sociolinguistic variation 432–4, 440
   speech tempo 9–25
   styles 12, 17
   transcription 9–10
velar consonants 269–71, 334–5, 339
verb phrases
   Danish 142–7
   unit accentuation 142–7
voicing
   Ancient Nordic 289–91
   Danish 28, 31–2, 38–40
   Faroese 67–9
   Greenlandic dialects 249–52
   Proto-Scandinavian 266–71
   Thai 214–15, 221, 224
   West Greenlandic 343–55
vowel harmony 88
   asymmetric systems 180, 181–2,
      183–210
   definition 175
   Nordic languages 275, 286–7, 309
   rules 176–83, 286–7
   Turkish 176
   West Greenlandic 177–210
vowel quantity
   Danish 39
   Faroese 318
vowel shifts 191, 194–6
vowel systems
   'closing' subsystem 324–31
   Danish 37, 38, 39–40
   diphthongs 312–42
   English 225
   Faroese 308, 309, 310, 317–42

vowel systems (*cont.*)
  Icelandic 181, 182, 225, 308, 309, 310
  and language change 322–38, 340–2,
    361, 427–9
  Mon-Khmer languages 427–8, 429
  Nordic languages 272–3, 274–5,
    276–83, 307–11
  Norwegian 308
  'opening' subsystem 331–2
  Scandinavian runic writing 260–6
  and stress accents 86
  umlaut 66, 181, 182, 192, 272, 274–5,
    275–6, 277–82, 289–90, 291–2,
    293–4, 298–305, 307–11
  West Greenlandic 177–8, 194–7

Waic 376, 399, 405
weak position 28–9, 42–3
West Greenlandic *see also* Inuktitut
  consonant system 249–52, 343–55
  i-dialect 183–210
  loan words 177–9, 199–200, 203–5
  morphology 54–63, 192, 199–202
  phonological rules 58–9, 197–210

vowel harmony 177–210
vowel system 177–8, 194–7
West Norwegian, influence on
    Faroese 329–30
Western Eskimo (Yupik) 345
word formation 363, 366–7, 439
word storage 199–202
words
  and measurement of functional
    load 48–51
  in West Greenlandic 59–61
writing systems
  Danish 247–9
  effect of sound shifts 255–71, 310
  Faroese 65, 66n, 80n
  Greenlandic dialects 250–1, 348–55
  and magic 256
  Old Danish 291n
  Old Norse 291n
  Scandinavian runic writing 254–71
  Thai 212–13, 222, 365

Yupik 345, 374, *see also* Greenlandic
    dialects; West Greenlandic

Printed and bound by CPI Group (UK) Ltd, Croydon, CR0 4YY